Advanced Information and Knowledge Processing

Series Editors
Professor Lakhmi Jain
Lakhmi.jain@unisa.edu.au
Professor Xindong Wu
xwu@cems.uvm.edu

T0205354

For other titles published in this series, go to
www.springer.com/series/4738

Youakim Badr · Richard Chbeir · Ajith Abraham ·
Aboul-Ella Hassanien
Editors

Emergent Web Intelligence: Advanced Semantic Technologies

Editors

Dr. Youakim Badr
INSA de Lyon
Université de Lyon
Département Informatique
7 avenue Jean Capelle
69621 Villeurbanne Cedex
France
youakim.badr@insa-lyon.fr

Dr. Ajith Abraham
Norwegian University
  of Science and Technology
Center for Quantifiable Quality
  of Service in Communication Systems
O.S. Bragstads plass 2E
7491 Trondheim
Norway
ajith.abraham@ieee.org

Dr. Richard Chbeir
Université de Bourgogne
LE21-UMR CNRS 5158
Faculté des Sciences Mirande
21078 Dijon Cedex
France
richard.chbeir@u-bourgogne.fr

Dr. Aboul-Ella Hassanien
Kuwait University
College of Business & Administration
Dept. Quantitative Methods
  & Information Systems
PO Box 5486
13055 Safat
Kuwait
abo@cba.edu.kw

ISSN 1610-3947
ISBN 978-1-4471-2561-7   ISBN 978-1-84996-077-9(eBook)
DOI 10.1007/978-1-84996-077-9
Springer London Dordrecht Heidelberg New York

British Library Cataloguing in Publication Data
A catalogue record for this book is available from the British Library

© Springer-Verlag London Limited 2010
Softcover reprint of the hardcover 1st edition 2010
Apart from any fair dealing for the purposes of research or private study, or criticism or review, as permitted under the Copyright, Designs and Patents Act 1988, this publication may only be reproduced, stored or transmitted, in any form or by any means, with the prior permission in writing of the publishers, or in the case of reprographic reproduction in accordance with the terms of licenses issued by the Copyright Licensing Agency. Enquiries concerning reproduction outside those terms should be sent to the publishers.
The use of registered names, trademarks, etc., in this publication does not imply, even in the absence of a specific statement, that such names are exempt from the relevant laws and regulations and therefore free for general use.
The publisher makes no representation, express or implied, with regard to the accuracy of the information contained in this book and cannot accept any legal responsibility or liability for any errors or omissions that may be made.

Printed on acid-free paper

Springer is part of Springer Science+Business Media (www.springer.com)

Preface

The success of the World Wide Web depends on the ability of users to store, process and retrieve digital information regardless of distance boundaries, languages and domains of knowledge. The universality and flexibility of the World Wide Web have also enabled the rapid growth of a variety of new services and applications based on human–machine interaction. The semantics of exchanged information and services should be useful not only for human to human communications, but also in that machines would be able to understand and automatically process web content. Semantics give well-defined meaning to web content and enable computers and people to work in cooperation. Today, the crucial challenge becomes the development of languages to express information in a machine processable format. Now more than ever, new advanced techniques and intelligent approaches are required to transform the Web into a universal reasoning and computing machine. Web intelligence attempts to deal with this challenge by exploiting information technologies and artificial intelligence approaches to design the next generation of web-empowered systems and services.

1 Introduction

The semantic Web plays a crucial role in the development of information technologies and services on the World Wide Web. It takes on new challenges in which the meaning of information enable computers to understand the Web content and imitate human intelligence in performing more of the tedious tasks involved in finding, sharing, and combining information on the web. Until now computers have not been able to fully accomplish these tasks without human intervention since web pages are designed to be understood by people, not machines. Tim Berners-Lee originally expressed his vision about the semantic Web. In his word, he wrote: "*[I] have a dream for the Web [in which computers] become capable of analyzing all the data on the Web—the content, links, and transactions between people and computers. A 'Semantic Web', which should make this possible, has yet to emerge, but when it does, the day-to-day mechanisms of trade, bureaucracy and our daily lives will be handled by machines talking to machines. The 'intelligent agents' people have touted for ages will finally materialize.*" Significant research efforts attempt to support this vision and propose a set of design principles, formal specifications, and languages specifically designed for a huge data space. Some of these include Resource Description Framework (RDF), Web Ontology languages (OWL), Semantic-based Query Languages and Logic Models to reason on the structure of knowledge embedded in Web-accessible databases and documents. Despite these initiatives, some of the challenges remain in a bottleneck due to the requirement for automating reasoning systems to deal with inconsistency, vastness, uncertainty, vagueness, and deceit in order to deliver on the promise of the Semantic Web. The discipline of Soft Computing has an evolving collection of methodologies, which aims to exploit tolerance for imprecision, uncertainty, and partial truth to study very complex phenomena: those for which more conventional methods have not yielded low cost and complete solutions. Today, Soft Computing provides an attractive opportunity for developing Web intelligence to represent the ambiguity in human thinking with real life uncertainty, reason on vagueness in ontologies, and makes possible the transition between the Web and its semantic successor. In this context, Semantic Web will enable the emergence of digital ecosystems of software and services delivered by the Internet. It will also extend the Internet with capabilities to reason on its resources and their relationships in order to develop the knowledge-based economy in the 21st century.

Why This Book is Interesting?   Industrial and technological demands to develop semantic-driven applications in business, commerce, marketing, finance and education have persuaded academia and scholarly communities across the world to include Web intelligence disciplines in their computer science curriculum. Moreover, many research centers are extensively working on this research field which demonstrates an important interest in building the next Semantic World Wide Web. The number of journals in this area has increased and the number of related conferences organized in the last ten years is overwhelming. However, there are relatively few books about web intelligence and semantic web taking into consideration knowledge discovery, semantic network, ontologies and artificial intelligence techniques such as neural network, fuzzy logic and mining algorithms as a new paradigm. Consequently, the need for a new book meets the increasing demands of academia and research communities and provides advanced techniques and methodologies to help undergraduates, graduates and researchers. The primary target audience for the book includes researchers, scholars, postgraduate students and developers who are interested in exploring various areas and disciplines about how semantic techniques and technologies can bridge the gap between users and applications on the web.

2 Book Organization

This book aims to gather the latest advances and innovative solutions in web intelligence and reporting how future services and web-based applications can gain competitive opportunities by applying different emergent semantic techniques to real-world problems. The main topics of this edited volume cover various advanced semantic technologies, use tools and software for collaboration and simulations of web intelligence, and finally provide case studies and applications in the field of semantic Web. It presents some of the latest advances of various topics in web intelligence and illustrates how organizations can gain competitive advantages by applying the different emergent techniques in the real-world scenarios. The book contains seventeen self-contained chapters which provide optimal reading flexibility. They are organized into four parts as follows:

- Web, Semantic and Intelligence
- Collaboration, Semantic and Intelligence
- Knowledge, Text, Semantic and Intelligence
- Applications and Case Studies

Part I deals with *Web, Semantic* and *Intelligence* and consists of four chapters.

In Chap. 1, *"The Dilated Triple"*, Rodriguez et al. present a simple model in which the meaning of a statement is defined in terms of other statements, much like the words of a dictionary are defined in terms of each other. This model serves to strengthen the association between concepts and the contexts in which they are to be understood. It provides a particularly simple means of contextualizing an RDF triple by associating it with related statements in the same graph. This approach, in combination with a notion of graph similarity, is sufficient to select only those statements from an RDF graph, which are subjectively most relevant to the context of the requesting process.

In Chap. 2, *"Semantic Web Technologies and Artificial Neural Networks for Intelligent Web Knowledge Source Discovery"*, Caliusco and Stegmayer present some basic concepts and foundations regarding the new Semantic Web and how it is populated with ontologies and why ontology-matching techniques are needed. The idea of software agents that travel the web carrying query request from users has also been addressed in this Chapter. The web knowledge source discovery task is been explained in detail and some motivating scenarios are introduced. To help users avoid irrelevant web search results and wrong decision making, efficient techniques and approaches for developing web intelligence with capabilities for discovering distributed knowledge source are presented.

Wang et al. in Chap. 3, titled *"Computing Similarity of Semantic Web Services in Semantic Nets with Multiple Concept Relations"* propose a novel approach based on application ontologies to improve the selection of semantic web services. After building application ontology by merging semantic service ontologies, the authors represent this application ontology as a fuzzy-weighted semantic net with multiple ontological concept relations, and calculate formal/compound concept similarity on it. The ontological concept similarity is finally used to calculate similarity of semantic services.

Chapter 4, *"General-Purpose Computing on a Semantic Network Substrate"* by Rodriguez presents a model of general-purpose computing on a semantic network substrate. The concepts presented are applicable to any semantic network representation. In the proposed model, the application programming interface, the run-time program, and the state of the computing virtual machine are all represented in the Resource Description Framework (RDF). The implementations of the concepts presented provide a computing paradigm that leverages the distributed and standardized representational-layer of the Semantic Web.

Part II consists of four chapters and deals with *Collaboration, Semantic* and *Intelligence*.

In Chap. 5, "*Agent Technology Meets the Semantic Web: Interoperability and Communication Issues*", Karanastasi and Matsatsini review the recent research on agent technologies and how this technology can serve the scopes of the Semantic Web project including web Agent and the Characteristics of Multi-Agent Systems, Agent Communication Languages, Knowledge and Query Manipulation Language, FIPA Agent Communication Language, and Ontologies.

In Chap. 6, "*Mining of Semantic Image Content Using Collective Web Intelligence*", Leung et al. describe an indexing method, whereby the aggregate intelligence of different Web users is continuously transferred to the Web. Such intelligence is codified, reinforced, distilled and shared among users so as to enable the systematic mining and discovery of semantic image contents. The described method allows the collaborative creation of image indexes, which is able to instill and propagate deep knowledge and collective wisdom into the Web concerning the advanced semantic characteristics of Web images.

In Chap. 7, "*Suited Support for Distributed Web Intelligence Cooperative Work*", Decouchant et al. present the PINAS platform, which provides means for supporting cooperative work on the Web. Using cooperative applications that are built employing the services of this infrastructure, several users can access and modify replicated shared entities in a consistent and controlled way. PINAS provides suited features, such as: user identification, multi-site user definition, user and entity naming, shared entity fragmentation and replication, storage, consistency, and automatic distributed updating. The authors propose seamless extensions to standard Web services that can be fully integrated within the Web environment.

In Chap. 8, "*Web services and Software Agents for Tailorable Groupware Design*", Cheaib et al. present a new groupware architecture model called UD3 that explicitly introduces the notion of tailor ability in designing collaborative applications. This model is based on the integration of web services and software agent technologies, thus using protocols of each while reinforcing their individual strengths in the context of tailorable groupware design. Web services are dynamically invoked by software agents in order to bring new behaviors, and hence, enhancing the collaboration process by dynamically adapting the services offered in the system to the users' preferences and not the other way around.

Part III consists of five chapters and focus on *Knowledge, Text, Semantic* and *Intelligence*.

In Chap. 9, "*Toward Distributed Knowledge Discovery on Grid Systems*", Khac et al. present a distributed data mining (DDM) system based on Grid environments to execute new distributed data mining techniques on very large and distributed heterogeneous datasets. The architecture and motivation for the design are presented. The authors developed prototypes for each layer of the system to evaluate the system features, test each layer as well as whole framework and building simulation and DDM test suites. Knowledge map layer, key layer of this system, is integrated in this framework.

In Chap. 10, *"Metamodel of Ontology Learning from Text"*, Wisniewski presents the metamodel of the ontology learning from text. The approach is based on the survey of the existing methods, while evaluation is provided in the form of a reference implementation of the introduced metamodel. The author has applied a qualitative evaluation by implementing some of the current state-of-the-art methods and illustrates how they can be described with a metamodel notation.

Ambiguity is a challenge faced by systems that handle natural language. To assuage the issue of linguistic ambiguities found in text classification, Chap. 11, *"An Analysis of Constructed Categories for Textual Classification Using Fuzzy Similarity and Agglomerative Hierarchical Methods"* by Guelpeli et al. proposes a text categorizer using the methodology of Fuzzy Similarity. The clustering algorithms Stars and Cliques are adopted in the Agglomerative Hierarchical method and they authors identify the groups of texts by specifying some type of relationship rule to create categories based on the similarity analysis of the textual terms.

In Chap. 12, *"Emergent XML Mining: Discovering an Efficient Mapping from XML Instances to Relational Schemas"*, Ishikawa proposes an adaptable approach to discovery of database schemas for well-formed XML data such as EDI, news, and digital libraries, which we interchange, filter, or download for future retrieval and analysis. The generated schemas usually consist of more than one table. Author's approach controls the number of tables to be divided by use of statistics of XML so that the total cost of processing queries is reduced. To achieve this, three functions namely NULL expectation, Large Leaf Fields, and Large Child Fields are introduced for controlling the number of tables to be divided. The author also describes the concept of short paths contained by generated database schemas and their effects on the performance of query processing.

In Chap. 13, *"XML Based Information Systems and Formal Semantics of Programming Languages"*, Despeyroux illustrates how techniques used to define the formal semantics of programming languages can be used in the context of the Web. The author also explores how techniques used in this context can be used to enforce the quality of information systems.

Part IV consists of four chapters and deals with *Applications* and *Case Studies*.

In Chap. 14, *"Modeling and Testing of Web Based Systems"*, Cavalli et al. present two methodologies to attain automatic test cases generation: The first uses extended finite state machines to model Web services composition described in BPEL, while the other uses UML to model Web applications. Together with the formal models of the web systems, this chapter presents methods for conformance and non-regression test generation.

As web applications are becoming ever larger, more complex and thus more demanding for their users, there is a growing need for customer support. Very often, it is provided by support centers via phone. However, the media break between browser and phone hampers the common understanding of user and consultant. As a result, support becomes ineffective and expensive, and users get frustrated. Screen sharing solutions are one possible solution for this problem, but they have major disadvantages like high bandwidth requirements, slow performance and, most importantly, the need for a client-side installation. These drawbacks are addressed by VCS, a concept and system for instant co-browsing, that runs directly within the users browser. It equally allows all participants of a support session to see and navigate the same web page on their screens, being aware of what the other person is currently doing on the page. People can directly interact with each other, jointly complete tasks and solve. The event-based nature of the synchronization approach to be presented further facilitates adaptation, so that users with heterogeneous end devices may collaborate. Niederhausen et al., in Chap. 15, *"Web-Based Support by Thin-Client Co-Browsing"*, present VCS and also discuss the special challenges that this approach entails.

In Chap. 16, *"NetPay Micro-Payment Protocols for Three Networks"*, Xiaoling and Grundy describe the NetPay micro-payment protocol that is actually extended from its original pay-per-click for web content to peer-to-peer networks and mobile device networks. The authors outline the key motivation for NetPay, the basic micro-payment protocol using e-coins and e-wallets, and the three variants of the protocol for different domains.

Chapter 17, *"Enforcing Honesty in Fair Exchange Protocols"* by Alaraj and Munro surveys the field of Fair Exchange Protocols and then presents a special type of protocol between a customer (C) and a merchant (M) that enforces one of them to be honest. It makes minimal use of a Trusted Third Party (TTP). The protocol has the features that it: (1) only comprises three messages to be exchanged between C and M; (2) guarantees strong fairness for both C and M; (3) allows both par-ties to be sure of the item that they will receive from the other party; and (4) resolves disputes automatically online.

3 Acknowledgments

We would like to thank the authors who provided excellent chapters and timely revisions. We are also grateful for their trust in us and patience during the review process. We would like to express our sincere thanks to the reviewers for their tremendous effort and challenging task of choosing high quality chapters, and their valuable criticism that greatly improved the quality of final chapter versions. The editors also would like to thank, Professor Lakhmi C. Jain, the editor-in-chief of the Advanced Information and Knowledge Processing (AI and KP) series of Springer for editorial assistance and excellent cooperative collaboration to produce this important scientific work. We hope this volume motivates its readers to take the next steps beyond building models to implementing, evaluating, comparing, and extending proposed approaches and applications. We finally hope that readers will share our excitement to present this volume on **Web Intelligence: Advanced Semantic Technologies** and find it useful.

4 About the Editors

Youakim Badr received his Ph.D. in Information Systems from the French National Institute for Applied Sciences in Lyon (INSA of Lyon). In 2004, he joined the faculty of the INSA of Lyon as Assistant Professor of Computer Science. Dr. Badr has worked extensively in the field of coupling XML documents and Object-Relational Databases. Through his research he has acquired skills in fields such as Interoperability, Modeling, System Architectures and Networking, and their application to various domains such as Business Processes, Supply Chains, Productions Systems and Virtual Enterprises. His current academic research interests include systems in both the service sector and ICT. In particular, he studies the ecosystem of services and the multidisciplinary modeling approach to design services through the integration of ICT, strategy and processes. He leads the Service-Oriented Enterprise research team which combines industrial and computer engineering approaches. Dr. Badr is vigorously involved in a series of international conferences. He served as General Co-Chair of ICDIM'07, CSTST'08, Programme Chair of INCOS'09, Track chair of IEEE DEST'10, AINA'10, ICETET'09, ICITST'08 and International Program Member of IAS'08, SITIS'07, JFO'07, WCNC'07 and ECWS'06. He is a professional member of ACM, IEEE Services Computing Community, MIL-RLabs/France coordinator, IEEE-SMC Technical Committee on Soft Computing, Digital Ecosystems Community, a member of OW2 and the Service Sciences working group of the Networked European Software and Services Initiative (NESSI).

Richard Chbeir received his Ph.D. in Computer Science from the INSA of Lyon, France in 2001. He is member of IEEE and ACM since 1999. He is currently an Associate Professor in the Computer Science Department of the Bourgogne University, Dijon, France. His research interests are in the areas of distributed multimedia database management, XML similarity and rewriting, spatio-temporal applications, indexing methods, and multimedia access control models. Dr. Chbeir has published (more than 40 peer-reviewed publications) in international journals and books (IEEE Transactions on SMC, Information Systems, Journal on Data Semantics, Journal of Systems Architecture, etc.), conferences (ER, WISE, SOFSEM, EDBT, ACM SAC, Visual, IEEE CIT, FLAIRS, PDCS, etc.), and has served on the program committees of several international conferences (SOFSEM, AINA, IEEE SITIS, ACM SAC, IEEE ISSPIT, EuroPar, SBBD, etc.). He has been organizing many international conferences and workshops (ACM SAC, ICDIM, CSTST, SITIS, etc.). He is currently the Vice-Chair of the ACM SIGAPP and the Chair of its French Chapter.

Ajith Abraham received his Ph.D. degree in Computer Science from Monash University, Melbourne, Australia. His research and development experience includes over 18 years in the Industry and Academia. He works in a multidisciplinary environment involving machine intelligence, network security, sensor networks, e-commerce, Web intelligence, Web services, computational grids, data mining, and applications to various real-world problems. He has given more than 30 plenary lectures and conference tutorials in these areas. He authored or coauthored more than 500 publications. He works with the Norwegian University of Science and Technology, Norway and also coordinate the activities of the Machine Intelligence Research

Labs (MIR Labs), which has representation in 47 countries. He is the Co-Chair of the IEEE Systems Man and Cybernetics Society Technical Committee on Soft Computing. He is the founder of several conference series, which are now sponsored by IEEE and also serves the editorial board of over 30 international Journals.

Aboul Ella Hassanien received his B.Sc. with honours in 1986 and M.Sc. degree in 1993, both from Ain Shams University, Faculty of Science, Ain Sham University, Egypt. On September 1998, he received his doctoral degree from the Department of Computer Science, Graduate School of Science and Engineering, Tokyo Institute of Technology, Japan. He is currently a Professor at Cairo University, Faculty of Computer and Information. He has authored/coauthored over 120 research publications in peer-reviewed reputed journals and conference proceedings. He serves on the editorial board and reviewer of number of journals and on the program committee of several international conferences and he has editing/written more than 18 books. He has received the excellence younger researcher award from Kuwait University.

5 List of Reviewers

Ahmed El Oualkadi (Universit Catholique de Louvain, Belgium)
Akira Asano (Hiroshima University, Japan)
Alfredo Cuzzocrea (University of Calabria, Italy)
Andries Engelbrecht (University of Pretoria, South Africa)
Bernard Grabot (LGP–ENIT, France)
Carlos Alberto Reyes-Garcia (Instituto Nacional de Astrofisica Optica Y Electronica, Mexico)
Chi Shen (University of Kentucky, USA)
Chrisa Tsinaraki (Technical University of Crete, Greece)
Christine Verdier (University of Grenoble, France)
Danielle Boulanger (University of Jean Moulin–MODEME, France)
Deborah Dahl (Conversational Technologies, USA)
Elizabeth Goldbarg (Federal University of Rio Grande do Norte, Brazil)
Estevam Hruschka Jr. (Federal University of Sao Carlos, Brazil)
Etienne Kerre (University of Gent, Belgium)
Gabriel Luque (University of Malaga, Spain)
Georgios Ch. Sirakoulis (Democritus University of Thrace, Greece)
Hiranmay Ghosh (Tata Consultancy Services, India)
Hiroshi Ishikawa (Shizuoka University, Japan)
Ignacio Ponzoni (Universidad Nacional del Sur, Argentina)
James Lu (Emory University, USA)
Jaroslaw Kozlak (University of Science and Technology Krakow, Poland)
Javier J. Sanchez-Medina (University of Las Palmas de Gran Canaria, Spain)
Kazushi Ohya (Tsurumi University, Japan)
Kubilay Ecerkale (Hava Harp Okulu, Turkey)
Mario Koeppen (Kyushu Institute of Technology, Japan)
Mario Ventresca (University of Waterloo, Canada)
Maytham Safar (Kuwait University, Kuwait)
Mei-Ling Shyu (University of Miami, USA)

Michael Blumenstein (Griffith University, Gold Coast, Australia)
Monica Chis (University of Cluj-Napoca, Romania)
Nadine Cullot (Bourgogne University, France)
Oscar Corcho (University of Manchester, UK)
Paolo Merialdo (Universita' degli Studi Roma Tre, Italy)
Patrick Siarry (Universit Paris 12, LiSSi, France)
Patrizia Grifoni (National Research Council of Italy, Italy)
Raquel Barco (Universidad de Malaga, Spain)
Sadok Ben Yahia (University of Tunis, Tunisia)
Saravanan Muthaiyah (George Mason University, USA)
Sebastin Lozano (University of Seville, Spain)
Selma Ayse Ozel (Cukurova University, Turkey)
Siti Mariyam Shamsuddin (University Technology of Malaysia, Malaysia)
Thanasis Daradoumis (Open University of Catalonia, Spain)
Thierry Badard (Universite Laval, Canada)
Thomas Hanne (Applied Sciences Northwestern Switzerland University, Switzerland)
Tianrui Li (Southwest Jiaotong University, China)
Tomasz Smolinski (Emory University, USA)
Urszula Markowska-Kaczmar (Wroclaw University of Technology, Poland)
Ying Ding (Indiana University, USA)
Yinghua Ma (Shanghai JiaoTong University, China)
Zhigang Zeng (Wuhan University of Technology, China)
Zhi-Hong Deng (Peking University, China)

Villeurbanne Cedex, France   Youakim Badr
Dijon Cedex, France   Richard Chbeir
Trondheim, Norway   Ajith Abraham
Safat, Kuwait   Aboul-Ella Hassanien

Contents

Contributors

Abdullah M. Alaraj Department of Information Technology, College of Computer, Qassim University, Qassim, Saudi Arabia, arj@qu.edu.sa

Lamine M. Aouad School of Computer Science and Informatics, University College Dublin, Belfield, Dublin 4, Ireland, lamine.aouad@ucd.ie

Flavia Cristina Bernardini Departamento de Ciência e Tecnologia—RCT, Pólo Universitário de Rio das Ostras—PURO, Universidade Federal Fluminense—UFF, Rua Recife, s/n, Jardim Bela Vista, Rio das Ostras, RJ CEP 28890-000, Brazil, fcbernardini@vm.uff.br

Ana Cristina Bicharra Garcia Departamento de Ciência da Computação, Instituto de Computação—IC, Universidade Federal Fluminense—UFF, Rua Passo da Pátria 156, Bloco E, 3° andar, São Domingos, Niterói, RJ CEP 24210-240, Brazil, bicharra@ic.uff.br

M.L. Caliusco CONICET, CIDISI-UTN-FRSF, Lavaise 610, Santa Fe, Argentina, mcaliusc@frsf.utn.edu.ar

Ana Cavalli SAMOVAR CNRS UMR 5157, Telecom & Management SudParis, 9 rue Charles Fourrier, 91011 Evry Cedex, France, Ana.Cavalli@it-sudparis.eu

W.S. Chan Department of Computer Science, Hong Kong Baptist University, Kowloon Tong, Hong Kong, wschan@comp.hkbu.edu.hk

Nader Cheaib IBISC CNRS FRE 3190, University of Evry, 91020 Evry Cedex, France, nader.cheaib@ibisc.fr

Xiaoling Dai The University of the South Pacific, Suva, Fiji Islands, dai_s@usp.ac.fj

Dominique Decouchant Laboratoire LIG de Grenoble, Grenoble, France; UAM-Cuajimalpa, México D.F., México, Dominique.Decouchant@imag.fr

Thierry Despeyroux INRIA Paris-Rocquencourt, Domaine de Voluceau, B.P. 105, F-78153 Le Chesnay Cedex, France, thierry.despeyroux@inria.fr

John Grundy The University of Auckland, Auckland, New Zealand,
john-g@cs.auckland.ac.nz

Marcus V.C. Guelpeli Departamento de Ciência da Computação, Instituto de
Computação—IC, Universidade Federal Fluminense—UFF, Rua Passo da Pátria
156, Bloco E, 3° andar, São Domingos, Niterói, RJ CEP 24210-240, Brazil,
mguelpeli@ic.uff.br

Wolfgang A. Halang Fernuniversität, 58084 Hagen, Germany,
wolfgang.halang@fernuni-hagen.de

Hiroshi Ishikawa Faculty of Informatics, Shizuoka University, 3-5-1 Johoku,
Naka-ku, Hamamatsu, Shizuoka, Japan, ishikawah@acm.org

Anastasia Karanastasi Decision Support Systems Laboratory, Technical
University of Crete, Chania, 73100, Greece, natasha@ergasya.tuc.gr

M-Tahar Kechadi School of Computer Science and Informatics, University
College Dublin, Belfield, Dublin 4, Ireland, tahar.kechadi@ucd.ie

Nhien An Khac School of Computer Science and Informatics, University College
Dublin, Belfield, Dublin 4, Ireland, an.lekhac@ucd.ie

Mounir Lallali SAMOVAR CNRS UMR 5157, Telecom & Management
SudParis, 9 rue Charles Fourrier, 91011 Evry Cedex, France,
Mounir.Lallali@it-sudparis.eu

C.H.C. Leung Department of Computer Science, Hong Kong Baptist University,
Kowloon Tong, Hong Kong, clement@comp.hkbu.edu.hk

J. Liu Department of Computer Science, Hong Kong Baptist University, Kowloon
Tong, Hong Kong, jiming@comp.hkbu.edu.hk

Stephane Maag SAMOVAR CNRS UMR 5157, Telecom & Management
SudParis, 9 rue Charles Fourrier, 91011 Evry Cedex, France,
Stephane.Maag@it-sudparis.eu

Malik Mallem IBISC CNRS FRE 3190, University of Evry, 91020 Evry Cedex,
France, malik.mallem@ibisc.fr

Nikolaos Matsatsinis Decision Support Systems Laboratory, Technical University
of Crete, Chania, 73100, Greece, nikos@ergasya.tuc.gr

Klaus Meißner Chair of Multimedia Technology, Technische Universität
Dresden, Dresden, Germany, kmeiss@inf.tu-dresden.de

Sonia Mendoza Departamento de Computación, CINVESTAV-IPN, México D.F.,
México, smendoza@cs.cinvestav.mx

A. Milani Department of Mathematics & Computer Science, University of
Perugia, Perugia, Italy, milani@unipg.it

Gerardo Morales SAMOVAR CNRS UMR 5157, Telecom & Management SudParis, 9 rue Charles Fourrier, 91011 Evry Cedex, France, Gerardo.Morales@it-sudparis.eu

Malcolm Munro Department of Computer Science, Durham University, Durham, UK, malcolm.munro@durham.ac.uk

Matthias Niederhausen Chair of Multimedia Technology, Technische Universität Dresden, Dresden, Germany, matthias.niederhausen@tu-dresden.de

Samir Otmane IBISC CNRS FRE 3190, University of Evry, 91020 Evry Cedex, France, samir.otmane@ibisc.fr

Alberto Pepe Center for Embedded Networked Sensing, University of California at Los Angeles, 3551 Boelter Hall, Los Angeles, CA 90095-1596, USA, apepe@ucla.edu

Stefan Pietschmann Chair of Multimedia Technology, Technische Universität Dresden, Dresden, Germany, stefan.pietschmann@tu-dresden.de

José Rodríguez Departamento de Computación, CINVESTAV-IPN, México D.F., México, rodriguez@cs.cinvestav.mx

Marko A. Rodriguez T-5, Center for Nonlinear Studies, Los Alamos National Laboratory, Los Alamos, NM 87545, USA, marko@lanl.gov

Tobias Ruch T-Systems Multimedia Solutions GmbH, Dresden, Germany, tobias.ruch@t-systems.com

Joshua Shinavier Semantic Network Research Group, Knowledge Reef Systems Inc., Santa Fe, NM 87501, USA, josh@fortytwo.net

G. Stegmayer CONICET, CIDISI-UTN-FRSF, Lavaise 610, Santa Fe, Argentina, gstegmayer@santafe-conicet.gov.ar

Xia Wang Fernuniversität, 58084 Hagen, Germany, xia.wang@fernuni-hagen.de

Marek Wisniewski Poznan University of Economics, Al. Niepodleglosci 10, Poznan, Poland

Fatiha Zaidi LRI, Université Paris-Sud 11, 91405 Orsay Cedex, France, Fatiha.Zaidi@lri.fr

Yi Zhao Fernuniversität, 58084 Hagen, Germany, yi.zhao@fernuni-hagen.de

Part I
Web, Semantic and Intelligence

Chapter 1
The Dilated Triple

Marko A. Rodriguez, Alberto Pepe,
and Joshua Shinavier

Abstract The basic unit of meaning on the Semantic Web is the RDF statement, or triple, which combines a distinct subject, predicate and object to make a definite assertion about the world. A set of triples constitutes a graph, to which they give a collective meaning. It is upon this simple foundation that the rich, complex knowledge structures of the Semantic Web are built. Yet the very expressiveness of RDF, by inviting comparison with real-world knowledge, highlights a fundamental shortcoming, in that RDF is limited to statements of absolute fact, independent of the context in which a statement is asserted. This is in stark contrast with the thoroughly context-sensitive nature of human thought. The model presented here provides a particularly simple means of contextualizing an RDF triple by associating it with related statements in the same graph. This approach, in combination with a notion of graph similarity, is sufficient to select only those statements from an RDF graph which are subjectively most relevant to the context of the requesting process.

1.1 Introduction

The World Wide Web introduced a set of standards and protocols that has led to the development of a collectively generated graph of web resources. Individuals participate in creating this graph by contributing digital resources (e.g. documents, images, etc.) and linking them together by means of dereferenceable Hypertext Transfer Protocol (HTTP) Uniform Resource Identifiers (URI) [5]. While the World Wide Web is primarily a technology that came to fruition in the early nineties, much of the inspiration that drove the development of the World Wide Web was developed earlier with such systems as Vannevar Bush's visionary Memex device [11] and Ted Nelson's Xanadu [32]. What the World Wide Web provided that made it excel as

M.A. Rodriguez (✉)
T-5, Center for Nonlinear Studies, Los Alamos National Laboratory, Los Alamos,
NM 87545, USA
e-mail: marko@lanl.gov

Y. Badr et al. (eds.) *Emergent Web Intelligence: Advanced Semantic Technologies,*
Advanced Information and Knowledge Processing,
DOI 10.1007/978-1-84996-077-9_1, © Springer-Verlag London Limited 2010

the *de facto* standard was a common, relatively simple, distributed platform for the exchange of digital information. The World Wide Web has had such a strong impact on the processes of communication and cognition that it can be regarded as a revolution in the history of human thought—following those of language, writing and print [20].

While the World Wide Web has provided an infrastructure that has revolutionized the way in which many people go about their daily lives, over the years, it has become apparent that there are shortcomings to its design. Many of the standards developed for the World Wide Web lack a mechanism for representing "meaning" in a form that can be easily interpreted and used by machines. For instance, the majority of the Web is made up of a vast collection of Hypertext Markup Language (HTML) documents. HTML documents are structured such that a computer can discern the intended layout of the information contained within a document, but the content itself is expressed in natural language and thus, understandable only to humans. Furthermore, all HTML documents link web resources according to a single type of relationship. The meaning of a hypertext relationship can be loosely interpreted as "cites" or "related to". The finer, specific meaning of this relationship is not made explicit in the link itself. In many cases, this finer meaning is made explicit within the HTML document. Unfortunately, without sophisticated text analysis algorithms, machines are not privy to the communication medium of humans. Yet, even within the single relationship model, machines have performed quite well in supporting humans as they use go about discovering and sharing information on the World Wide Web [10, 19, 21, 27].

> The Web was designed as an information space, with the goal that it should be useful not only for human-human communication, but also that machines would be able to participate and help. One of the major obstacles to this has been the fact that most information on the Web is designed for human consumption, and even if it was derived from a database with well defined meanings (in at least some terms) for its columns, that the structure of the data is not evident to a robot browsing the web. [4]

As a remedy to the aforementioned shortcoming of the World Wide Web, the Semantic Web initiative has introduced a standard data model which makes explicit the type of relationship that exists between two web resources [7, 8]. Furthermore, the Linked Data community has not only seen a need to link existing web resources in meaningful ways, but also a need to link the large amounts of non-typical web data (e.g. database information) [9].[1] The standard for relating web resources on the Semantic Web is the Resource Description Framework (RDF) [8, 28]. RDF is a data model[2] that is used to create graphs of the form

$$R \subseteq \underbrace{(U \cup B)}_{\text{subject}} \times \underbrace{U}_{\text{predicate}} \times \underbrace{(U \cup B \cup L)}_{\text{object}}, \tag{1}$$

---

[1] The necessity to expose large amounts of data on the Semantic Web has driven the development of triple-store technology. Advanced triple-store technology parallels relational database technologies by providing an efficient medium for the storage and querying of semantic graphs [1, 26, 29].

[2] RDF is a data model, not a serialization format. There exist various standard serialization formats such as RDF/XML, N3 [3], Turtle [2], Trix [13], etc.

where U is the infinite set of all URIs [6, 42], B is the infinite set of all blank nodes, and L is the infinite set of all literal values.[3] An element in R is known as a statement, or triple, and it is composed of a set of three elements: a subject, a predicate, and an object. A statement in RDF asserts a fact about the world.

> "The basic intuition of model-theoretic semantics is that asserting a sentence makes a claim about the world: it is another way of saying that the world is, in fact, so arranged as to be an interpretation which makes the sentence true. In other words, an assertion amounts to stating a constraint on the possible ways the world might be." [23]

An example RDF statement is (lanl:marko, foaf:knows, ucla:apepe).[4] This statement makes a claim about the world: namely that "Marko knows Alberto". The foaf:knows predicate defines the meaning of the link that connects the subject lanl:marko to the object ucla:apepe. On the World Wide Web, the only way that such semantics could be derived in a computationally efficient manner would be to note that in Marko's webpage there exists an href link to Alberto's webpage. While this web link does not necessarily mean that "Marko knows Alberto", it is the simplest means, without text analysis techniques, to recognize that there exists a relationship between Marko and Alberto. Thus, for machines, the World Wide Web is a homogeneous world of generic relationships. On the Semantic Web, the world is a rich, complicated network of meaningful relationships.

The evolution from the World Wide Web to the Semantic Web has brought greater meaning and expressiveness to our largest digital information repository [24]. This explicit meaning provides machines a richer landscape for supporting humans in their information discovery and sharing activities. However, while links are typed on the Semantic Web, the meaning of the type is still primarily based on human interpretation. Granted this meaning is identified by a URI, however, for the machine, there exists no meaning, just symbols that it has been "hardwired" to handle [41].

> "Machine usable content presumes that the machine knows what to do with information on the Web. One way for this to happen is for the machine to read and process a machine-sensible specification of the semantics of the information. This is a robust and very challenging approach, and largely beyond the current state of the art. A much simpler alternative is for the human Web application developers to hardwire the knowledge into the software so that when the machine runs the software, it does the correct thing with the information." [41]

Because relationships among resources are only denoted by a URI, many issues arise around the notion of *context*. Context-sensitive algorithms have been developed to deal with problems such as term disambiguation [30], naming conflicts [39], and ontology integration [40, 43]. The cause of such problems is the fact that statements, by themselves, ignore the situatedness that defines the semantics of such assertions [18]. Similar criticism directed towards the issue of semantics has appeared in other specialized literature [38, 47, 49]. Sheth et al. [37] have framed this issue well and

---

[3]Other formalisms exist for representing an RDF graph such as the directed labeled graph, bipartite graph [22], and directed hypergraph models [31].

[4]All resources in this article have been prefixed in order to shorten their lengthy namespaces. For example, foaf:knows, in its extended form, is http://xmlns.com/foaf/0.1/knows.

have provided a clear distinction between the various levels of meaning on the Semantic Web.[5]

- *Implicit* semantics reside within the minds of humans as a collective consensus and as such, are not explicitly recorded in some machine processable medium.
- *Formal* semantics are in a machine-readable format in the form of an ontology and are primarily used for human consumption and for machine hardwiring.
- *Soft* semantics are extracted from probabilistic and fuzzy reasoning mechanisms supporting degree of membership and certainty.

The model proposed in this article primarily falls within the domain of soft semantics. Simply put, the purpose of the model is to supplement a statement with other statements. These other statements, while being part of the RDF graph itself, serve to contextualize the original statement.

> "Contextualization is a word first used in sociolinguistics to refer to the use of language and discourse to signal relevant aspects of an interactional or communicative situation."[6]

The supplementary statements serve to expose the relevant aspects of the interaction between a subject and an object that are tied by a relationship defined by a predicate. With respect to the example of the statement (lanl:marko, foaf:knows, ucla:apepe), supplementary statements help to answer the question: "What do you mean by 'Marko knows Alberto'?". A notion from Ludwig Wittgenstein's theory of "language games" can be aptly borrowed: the meaning of a concept is not universal and set in stone, but shaped by "a complicated network of similarities, overlapping and criss-crossing" [46]. Following this line of thought, this article purposes a "dilated" model of an RDF triple. The dilated triple contextualizes the meaning and enhances the expressiveness of assertions on the Semantic Web.

1.2 The Dilated Triple Model

A single predicate URI does not provide the appropriate degrees of freedom required when modeling the nuances of an RDF relationship. The model proposed in this article enhances the expressiveness of a triple such that its meaning is considered within a larger context as defined by a graph structure. It thereby provides a machine with the ability to discern the more fine-grained context in which a statement relates its subject and object.

In the proposed model, every triple in an RDF graph is supplemented with other triples from the same RDF graph. The triple and its supplements form what is called a *dilated triple*.[7]

---

[5] A similar presentation is also presented in [41].

[6] Wikipedia (http://en.wikipedia.org/wiki/Contextualization).

[7] The Oxford English dictionary provides two definitions for the word "dilate": "to expand" and "to speak or write at length". It will become clear through the remainder of this article that both definitions suffice to succinctly summarize the presented model.

Fig. 1.1 The dilated triple T_τ

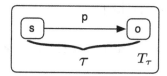

Definition 1.1 (A Dilated Triple) Given a set of triples R and a triple $\tau \in R$, a dilation of τ is a set of triples $T_\tau \subset R$ such that $\tau \in T_\tau$.

The dilated form of $\tau \in R$ is T_τ. Informally, T_τ servers to elaborate the meaning of τ. Formally, T_τ is a graph that at minimum contains only τ and at maximum contains all triples in R. The set of all non-τ triples in T_τ (i.e. $T_\tau \setminus \tau$) are called *supplementary triples* as they serve to contextualize, or supplement, the meaning of τ. Finally, it is worth noting that every supplemental triple in T_τ has an associated dilated form, so that T_τ can be considered a set of nested sets.[8] An instance of τ, its subject s, predicate p, object o, and its dilated form T_τ, are diagrammed in Fig. 1.1.

A dilated triple can be conveniently represented in RDF using a named graph [12]. Statements using the named graph construct are not triples, but instead, are quads with the fourth component being denoted by a URI or blank node. Formally, $\tau = (s, p, o, g)$ and $g \in U \cup B$. The fourth component is considered the "graph" in which the triple is contained. Thus, multiple quads with the same fourth element are considered different triples in the same graph. Named graphs were developed as a more compact (in terms of space) way to reify a triple. The reification of a triple was originally presented in the specification of RDF with the rdf:Statement construct [28]. RDF reification has historically been used to add specific metadata to a triple, such as provenance, pedigree, privacy, and copyright information. In this article, the purpose of reifying a triple is to supplement its meaning with those of additional triples. While it is possible to make additional statements about the dilated triple (i.e. the named graph component g), the motivation behind the dilated triple is to encapsulate many triples within a single graph, not to make statements about the graph *per se*.

The following sections will further explain the way in which a dilated triple contextualizes the meaning of a statement. Section 1.3 demonstrates, by means of an example, how supplementary triples augment the meaning of a relationship between two resources. Section 1.4 discusses how dilated triples can be compared and used by a machine to discern context.

1.3 Contextualizing a Relationship

The dilated form of $x \in R$, denoted T_x, provides a knowledge structure that is suited to contextualizing the meaning of an assertion made about the world. For example,

---

[8]The set of all dilated triples forms a *dilated graph* denoted $\mathcal{T} = \bigcup_{\tau \in R}\{T_\tau\}$.

consider the asserted triple

$$x = (\texttt{lanl:marko, foaf:knows, ucla:apepe}). \qquad (2)$$

What is the meaning of `foaf:knows` in this context? For the human, the meaning is made explicit in the specification document of the FOAF (Friend of a Friend) ontology (http://xmlns.com/foaf/spec/), which states:

> "We take a broad view of 'knows', but do require some form of reciprocated interaction (i.e. stalkers need not apply). Since social attitudes and conventions on this topic vary greatly between communities, counties and cultures, it is not appropriate for FOAF to be overly-specific here."

Unfortunately, the supplementary information that defines the meaning of `foaf:knows` is not encoded with the URI itself (nor in the greater RDF graph) and it is only through some external medium (the FOAF specification document) that the meaning of `foaf:knows` is made clear. Thus, such semantics are entirely informal [41]. However, even if the complexity of the meaning of `foaf:knows` could be conveyed by an RDF graph, the nuances of "knowing" are subtle, such that no two people know each other in quite the same way. In fact, only at the most abstract level of analysis is the relationship of "knowing" the same between any two people. In order for a human or machine to understand the way in which `lanl:marko` and `ucla:apepe` know each other, the complexities of this relationship must be stated. In other words, it is important to state "a constraint on the possible ways the world might be" [23] even if that constraint is a complex graph of relationships. For example, the meaning of `foaf:knows` when applied to `lanl:marko` and `ucla:apepe` can be more eloquently stated as:

> "Marko and Alberto first met at the European Organization for Nuclear Research (CERN) at the Open Archives Initiative Conference (OAI) in 2005. Six months later, Alberto began a summer internship at the Los Alamos National Laboratory (LANL) where he worked under Herbert Van de Sompel on the Digital Library Research and Prototyping Team. Marko, at the time, was also working under Herbert Van de Sompel. Unbeknownst to Herbert, Marko and Alberto analyzed a scholarly data set that Alberto had acquired at the Center for Embedded Networked Sensing (CENS) at the University of California at Los Angeles (UCLA). The results of their analysis ultimately led to the publication of an article [35] in Leo Egghe's Journal of Informetrics. Marko and Alberto were excited to publish in Leo Egghe's journal after meeting him at the Institute for Pure and Applied Mathematics (IPAM) at UCLA."

The facts above, when represented as an RDF graph with triples relating such concepts as `lanl:marko`, `ucla:apepe`, `lanl:herbertv`, `cern:cern`, `ucla:ipam`, `elsevier:joi`, `doi:10.1016/j.joi.2008.04.002`, etc., serve to form the dilated triple T_x. In this way, the meaning of the asserted triple (`lanl:marko`, `foaf:knows`, `ucla:apepe`) is presented in the broader context T_x. In other words, T_x helps to elucidate the way in which Marko knows Alberto. Figure 1.2 de-

Fig. 1.2 The dilated form of
(lanl:marko, foaf:knows,
ucla:apepe)

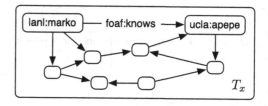

picts T_x, where the unlabeled resources and relationships represent the URIs from the previous representation.[9]

Even after all the aforementioned facts about Marko and Alberto's "knowing" relationship are encoded in T_x, still more information is required to fully understand what is meant by Marko "knowing" Alberto. What is the nature of the scholarly data set that they analyzed? Who did what for the analysis? Did they ever socialize outside of work when Alberto was visiting LANL? What was the conversation that they had with Leo Egghe like? Can their foaf:knows relationship ever be fully understood? Only an infinite recursion into their histories, experiences, and subjective worlds could reveal the "true" meaning of (lanl:marko, foaf:knows, ucla:apepe). Only when $T_\tau = R$,[10] that is, when their relationship is placed within the broader context of the world as a whole, does the complete picture emerge. However, with respect to those triples that provide the most context, a $|T_\tau| \ll |R|$ suffices to expose the more essential aspects of (lanl:marko, foaf:knows, ucla:apepe).[11,12]

Defining a triple in terms of a larger conceptual structure exposes more degrees of freedom when representing the uniqueness of a relationship. For example, suppose the two dilated triples T_x and T_y diagrammed in Fig. 1.3, where

$$x = (\text{lanl:marko}, \text{foaf:knows}, \text{ucla:apepe}) \tag{3}$$

and

$$y = (\text{lanl:marko}, \text{foaf:knows}, \text{cap:carole}). \tag{4}$$

---

[9]For the sake of diagram clarity, the supplemented triples are unlabeled in Fig. 1.2. However, please be aware that the unlabeled resources are in fact the URI encoding of the aforementioned natural language example explaining how Marko knows Alberto.

[10]For the purpose of this part of the argument, R is assumed to be a theoretical graph instance that includes all statements about the world.

[11]A fuzzy set is perhaps the best representation of a dilated triple [48]. In such cases, a membership function $\mu_{T_\tau} : R \to [0, 1]$ would define the degree to which every triple in R is in T_τ. However, for the sake of simplicity and to present the proposed model within the constructs of the popular named graph formalism, T_τ is considered a classical set. Moreover, a fuzzy logic representation requires an associated membership valued in [0, 1] which then requires further statement reification in order to add such metadata. With classic bivalent logic, {0, 1} is captured by the membership or non-membership of the statement in T_τ.

[12]The choices made in the creation of a dilated triple are determined at the knowledge-level [33]. The presentation here does not suppose the means of creation, only the underlying representation and utilization of such a representation.

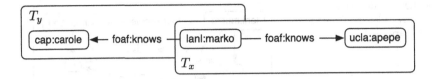

Fig. 1.3 The dilated triples T_x and T_y

Both T_x and T_y share the same predicate foaf:knows. However, what is meant by Marko knowing Alberto is much different than what is meant by Marko knowing his mother Carole (cap:carole). While, broadly speaking, it is true that Marko knows both Alberto and Carole, the context in which Marko knows Alberto is much different than the context in which Marko knows Carole. The supplementary triples that compose T_y may be the RDF expression of:

> "Marko was born in Fairfield, California on November 30th, 1979. Carole is Marko's mother. Marko's family lived in Riverside (California), Peachtree City (Georgia), Panama City (Panama), and Fairfax (Virginia). During his 10th grade high-school term, Marko moved with his family back to Fairfield, California."

It is obvious from these two examples that foaf:knows can not sufficiently express the subtleties that exist between two people. People know each other in many different ways. There are family relationships, business relationships, scholarly relationships, and so on. It is true that these subtleties can be exposed when performing a deeper analysis of the graph surrounding a foaf:knows relationship as other paths will emerge that exist between people (e.g. vacation paths, transaction paths, co-authorship paths, etc.). The purpose of a dilated triple is to contain these corroborating statements within the relationship itself. The purpose of T_x is to identify those aspects of Marko and Alberto's "knowing" relationship that make it unique (that provide it the most meaning). Similarly, the purpose of T_y is to provide a finer representation of the context in which Marko knows his mother. The supplementary triples of T_x and T_y augment the meaning of foaf:knows and frame each respective triple x and y in a broader context.[13]

1.4 Comparing Contexts

The "Marko knows" examples from the previous section are reused in this section to explain how dilated triples can assist a machine in discerning and comparing the broader meaning of a statement. In order to present this example, the notion of a contextualized process is introduced. A contextualized process, as defined here, is a human or machine that maintains a perspective or expectation of how the world must be.

---

[13]Examples of other predicates beyond foaf:knows also exist. For instance, suppose the predicates foaf:member and foaf:fundedBy. In what way is that individual a member of that group and how is that individual funded?

"Perspective in theory of cognition is the choice of a context or a reference (or the result of this choice) from which to sense, categorize, measure or codify experience, cohesively forming a coherent belief, typically for comparing with another."[14]

A perspective can be expressed in RDF by simply associating some process with a knowledge-base that defines what that process knows about the world. This knowledge-base can be derived, for example, from the process' history and thus defined as a subgraph of the full RDF graph. With respect to a perspective based on history, it makes sense that a process does not "experience" the whole RDF graph in a single moment, but instead, traverses through a graph by querying for future states and formalizing a model of past experiences [25]. The algorithm by which a process derives a new state is perhaps "hardwired" [41], but what is returned by that query is dependent upon the structure of the full graph and the process' historic subgraph. Furthermore, by capitalizing on the notion of a contextualization of both the perspective of the process and the meaning of a statement, that query can yield different results for different processes. In general, it is the interaction between the structure of the world and the context of the process that determines process' subjective realization of the world into the future.

Suppose a process were to take a path through an RDF graph that included such concepts as Marko's publications, the members of the Center for Nonlinear Studies, his collaborations with the Center for Embedded Networked Sensing, and the various conferences he has attended. Given this set of experiences, the process has built up a mental model of Marko that primarily includes those aspects of his life that are scholarly.[15] More generally, the process has been pigeonholed into a scholarly "frame of mind". Without any context, if that process were to inquire about the people that Marko knows (e.g. (lanl:marko, foaf:knows, ?o)), it would learn that Marko knows both Alberto and Carole. However, given the context of the process (i.e. the history as represented by its traversed subgraph), it will interpret "knowing" with respect to those people that Marko knows in a scholastic sense. Given Alberto and Carole, Marko knows Alberto in a scholarly manner, which is not true of Carole. There is little to nothing in Marko and Carole's T_y that makes reference to anything scholarly. However, in Marko and Alberto's T_x, the whole premise of their relationship is scholarly.

A simple way in which the process can make a distinction between the various interpretations of foaf:knows is to intersect its history with the context of the relationships. In other words, the process can compare its history subgraph with the subgraph that constitutes a dilated triple. If $H \subseteq R$ is a graph defining the history of the process which includes the process' traversal through the scholarly aspects of Marko, then it is the case that $|H \cap T_x| > |H \cap T_y|$ as the process' scholarly perspective is more related to Marko and Alberto than it is to Marko and Carole. That is, the process' history H has more triples in common with T_x than with T_y. Thus, what the process means by foaf:knows is a "scholarly"

---

[14]Wikipedia http://en.wikipedia.org/wiki/Perspective_(cognitive).

[15]It is noted that Marko is a complex concept and includes not only his academic life, but also his personal, business, hobby, etc. lives.

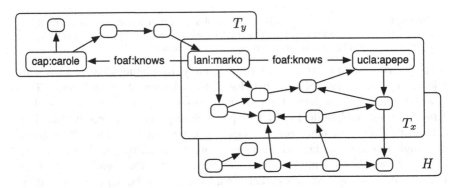

Fig. 1.4 The relationship between the context of a process and a dilated triple

`foaf:knows`. This idea is diagrammed in Fig. 1.4, where H has more in common with T_x than with T_y, thus an intersection of these sets would yield a solution to the query (`lanl:marko, foaf:knows, ?o`) that included Alberto and not Carole.[16] In other words, the history of the process "blinds" the process in favor of interpreting its place in the graph from the scholarly angle.[17]

The trivial intersection method of identifying the degree of similarity between two graph structures can be extended. Other algorithms, such as those based on a spreading activation within a semantic graph [14–16, 34] can be used as a more fuzzy and probabilistic means of determining the relative "semantic distance" between two graphs [17]. Spreading activation methods are more analogous to the connectionist paradigm of cognitive science than the symbolic methods of artificial intelligence research [36]. The purpose of a spreading activation algorithm is to determine which resources in a semantic graph are most related to some other set of resources. In general, a spreading activation algorithm diffuses an energy distribution over a graph starting from a set of resources and proceeding until a predetermined number of steps have been taken or the energy decays to some $\epsilon \approx 0$.[18] Those resources that received the most energy flow during the spreading activation process are considered the most similar to the set of source resources. With respect to the particular example at hand, the energy diffusion would start at the resources in H and the results would be compared with resources of T_x and T_y. If the set of

---

[16] H need not be a dynamic context that is generated as a process moves through an RDF graph. H can also be seen as a static, hardwired "expectation" of what the process should perceive. For instance, H could include ontological triples and known instance triples. In such cases, querying for such relationships as `foaf:knows`, `foaf:fundedBy`, `foaf:memberOf`, etc. would yield results related to H—biasing the results towards those relationships that are most representative of the process' expectations.

[17] This notion is sometimes regarded as a "reality tunnel" [44, 45].

[18] In many ways this is analogous to finding the primary eigenvector of the graph using the power method. However, the energy vector at time step 1 only has values for the source resources, the energy vector is decayed on each iteration, and finally, only so many iterations are executed as a steady state distribution is not desired.

resource in T_x received more energy than those in T_y, then the dilated triple T_x is considered more representative of the context of H.[19]

By taking advantage of the supplementary information contained within a dilated triple, a process has more information on which to base its interpretation of the meaning of a triple. To the process, a triple is not simply a string of three symbols, but instead is a larger knowledge structure which encapsulates the uniqueness of the relationship. The process can use this information to bias its traversal of the graph and thus, how it goes about discovering information in the graph.

1.5 Conclusion

While a single word may be used in any number of contexts, its precise meaning is never entirely the same [46]. This is not a difficult or unusual problem for human beings, as meaning is naturally contextualized by other facts about the world. Thus, humans can speak in broad terms without loss of meaning, as the finer details of the situation are understood in context. Humans possess an awareness of their current situation and a set of expectations about the world which allow them to discern the subtleties of its structure. In an effort to bridge the gap between the natural context sensitivity of human communication and the rigid context independence of the Semantic Web, this article has presented a simple model in which the meaning of a statement is defined in terms of other statements, much like the words of a dictionary are defined in terms of each other. This model serves to strengthen the association between concepts and the contexts in which they are to be understood.

References

1. Aasman, J.: Allegro graph. Technical Report 1, Franz Incorporated (2006). www.franz.com/products/allegrograph/allegrograph.datasheet.pdf
2. Beckett, D.: Turtle: Terse RDF triple language. Technical Report, University of Bristol (2006). http://www.dajobe.org/2004/01/turtle
3. Berners-Lee, T.: Notation 3. Technical Report, World Wide Web Consortium (1998). http://www.w3.org/DesignIssues/Notation3
4. Berners-Lee, T.: Semantic web road map. Technical Report, World Wide Web Consortium (1998)
5. Berners-Lee, T., Cailliau, R., Luotonen, A., Nielsen, H., Secret, A.: The World-Wide Web. Communications of the ACM **37**, 76–82 (1994)
6. Berners-Lee, T., Fielding, R., Masinter, L.: Uniform Resource Identifier (URI): Generic Syntax (2005). http://www.ietf.org/rfc/rfc2396.txt
7. Berners-Lee, T., Hendler, J.A.: Publishing on the Semantic Web. Nature **410**(6832), 1023–1024 (2001). DOI 10.1038/35074206

---

[19]Spreading activation on a semantic graph is complicated as edges have labels. A framework that makes use of this fact to perform arbitrary path traversals through a semantic graph is presented in [34].

8. Berners-Lee, T., Hendler, J.A., Lassila, O.: The Semantic Web. Scientific American **284**(5), 34–43 (2001)
9. Bizer, C., Heath, T., Idehen, K., Berners-Lee, T.: Linked data on the web. In: Proceedings of the International World Wide Web Conference, Linked Data Workshop. Beijing, China (2008)
10. Brin, S., Page, L.: The anatomy of a large-scale hypertextual web search engine. Computer Networks and ISDN Systems **30**(1–7), 107–117 (1998)
11. Bush, V.: As we may think. The Atlantic Monthly **176**(1), 101–108 (1945)
12. Carroll, J.J., Bizer, C., Hayes, P., Stickler, P.: Named graphs, provenance and trust. In: The Fourteenth International World Wide Web Conference, Chiba, Japan, pp. 613–622. ACM, New York (2005)
13. Carroll, J.J., Stickler, P.: RDF triples in XML. In: Extreme Markup Languages. IDEAlliance, Montréal, Québec (2004)
14. Cohen, P.R., Kjeldsen, R.: Information retrieval by constrained spreading activation in semantic networks. Information Processing and Management **23**(4), 255–268 (1987)
15. Collins, A., Loftus, E.: A spreading activation theory of semantic processing. Psychological Review **82**, 407–428 (1975)
16. Crestani, F., Lee, P.L.: Searching the web by constrained spreading activation. Information Processing and Management **36**(4), 585–605 (2000)
17. Delugach, H.S.: An exploration into semantic distance. In: Proceedings of the 7th Annual Workshop on Conceptual Structures: Theory and Implementation. Lecture Notes in Computer Science, vol. 754, pp. 119–124. Springer, London (1993). DOI 10.1007/3-540-57454-9_9
18. Floridi, L.: Web 2.0 and the semantic web: A philosophical view. In: North-American Computing and Philosophy Conference (2007)
19. Golder, S.A., Huberman, B.A.: Usage patterns of collaborative tagging systems. Journal of Information Science **32**(2), 198–208 (2006)
20. Harnad, S.: Post-Gutenberg galaxy: The fourth revolution in the means of production of knowledge. Public-Access Computer Systems Review **2**(1), 39–53 (1991)
21. Haveliwala, T.H.: Topic-sensitive pagerank. In: Proceedings of the 11th International World Wide Web Conference, pp. 517–526. ACM, New York (2002)
22. Hayes, J., Gutierrez, C.: Bipartite graphs as intermediate model for RDF. In: Proceedings of the International Semantic Web Conference, pp. 47–61 (2004)
23. Hayes, P., McBride, B.: RDF semantics. Technical Report, World Wide Web Consortium (2004). http://www.w3.org/TR/rdf-mt/
24. Hellman, R.: A semantic approach adds meaning to the web. Computer **32**(12), 13–16 (1999)
25. Heylighen, F.: Collective intelligence and its implementation on the web: Algorithms to develop a collective mental map. Computational and Mathematical Organization Theory **5**(3), 253–280 (1999)
26. Kiryakov, A., Ognyanov, D., Manov, D.: OWLIM—a pragmatic semantic repository for OWL. In: International Workshop on Scalable Semantic Web Knowledge Base Systems. Lecture Notes in Computer Science, vol. 3807, pp. 182–192. Springer, New York (2005)
27. Kleinberg, J.M.: Authoritative sources in a hyperlinked environment. Journal of the ACM **46**(5), 604–632 (1999)
28. Klyne, G., Carroll, J.J.: Resource description framework (RDF): Concepts and abstract syntax. Technical Report, World Wide Web Consortium (2004). http://www.w3.org/TR/rdf-concepts/
29. Lee, R.: Scalability report on triple store applications. Technical Report, Massachusetts Institute of Technology (2004)
30. Magnini, B., Serani, L., Speranza, M.: Making explicit the semantics hidden in schema models. In: Proceedings of the International Semantic Web Conference. Sanibel Island, Florida (2003)
31. Morale, A.A.M., Serodio, M.E.V.: A directed hypergraph model for RDF. In: Simperl, E., Diederich, J., Schreiber, G. (eds.) Proceedings of the Knowledge Web PhD Symposium. Innsbruck, Austria (2006)
32. Nelson, T.H.: Literary Machines. Mindful Press, Sausalito (1981)

33. Newell, A.: The knowledge level. Artificial Intelligence **18**(1), 87–127 (1982)
34. Rodriguez, M.A.: Grammar-based random walkers in semantic networks. Knowledge-Based Systems **21**(7), 727–739 (2008). DOI 10.1016/j.knosys.2008.03.030. arXiv:0803.4355
35. Rodriguez, M.A., Pepe, A.: On the relationship between the structural and socioacademic communities of an interdisciplinary co-authorship network. Journal of Informetrics **2**(3), 195–201 (2008). DOI 10.1016/j.joi.2008.04.002. arXiv:0801.2345
36. Rumelhart, D.E., McClelland, J.L.: Parallel Distributed Processing: Explorations in the Microstructure of Cognition. MIT Press, Cambridge (1993)
37. Sheth, A.P., Ramakrishnan, C., Thomas, C.: Semantics for the semantic web: The implicit, the formal, and the powerful. International Journal on Semantic Web and Information Systems **1**, 1–18 (2005)
38. Sowa, J.F.: Knowledge Representation: Logical, Philosophical, and Computational Foundations. Course Technology (1999)
39. Tierney, B., Jackson, M.: Contextual semantic integration for ontologies. In: Proceedings of the 21st Annual British National Conference on Databases. Edinburgh, UK (2005)
40. Udrea, O., Deng, Y., Ruckhaus, E., Subrahmanian, V.: A graph theoretical foundation for integrating RDF ontologies. In: Proceedings of the American Association for Artificial Intelligence (2005)
41. Uschold, M.: Where are the semantics in the semantic web? In: Proceedings of the Autonomous Agents Conference. Montréal, Québec (2001)
42. W3C/IETF: URIs, URLs, and URNs: Clarifications and recommendations 1.0 (2001). http://www.w3.org/TR/uri-clarification/
43. Wache, H., Vögele, T., Visser, U., Stuckenschmidt, H., Schuster, G., Neumann, H., Hübner, S.: Ontology-based integration of information—a survey of existing approaches. In: Stuckenschmidt, H. (ed.) IJCAI-01 Workshop: Ontologies and Information Sharing, pp. 108–117 (2001)
44. Wilson, R.A.: The evolution of neuro-sociological circuits: A contribution to the sociobiology of consciousness. Ph.D. thesis, Paideia University (1979)
45. Wilson, R.A.: Prometheus Rising. New Falcon, Reno (1983)
46. Wittgenstein, L.: Philosophical Investigations. Blackwell Sci., Oxford (1973)
47. Woods, W.A.: Meaning and links: A semantic odyssey. In: Principles of Knowledge Representation and Reasoning: Proceedings of the Ninth International Conference (KR2004), pp. 740–742 (2004)
48. Zadeh, L.A.: Fuzzy sets. Information and Control **8**, 338–353 (1965)
49. Zadeh, L.A.: Toward a perception-based theory of probabilistic reasoning with imprecise probabilities. Journal of Statistical Planning and Inference **105**, 233–264 (2002)

Chapter 2
Semantic Web Technologies and Artificial Neural Networks for Intelligent Web Knowledge Source Discovery

M.L. Caliusco and G. Stegmayer

Abstract This chapter is focused on presenting new and recent techniques, such as the combination of agent-based technologies and Artificial Neural Network (ANN) models that can be used for intelligent web knowledge source discovery in the new and emergent Semantic Web.

The purpose of the Semantic Web is to introduce semantic content in the huge amount of unstructured or semi-structured information sources available on the web by using ontologies. An ontology provides a vocabulary about concepts and their relationships within a domain, the activities taking place in that domain, and the theories and elementary principles governing that domain. The lack of an integrated view of all sources and the existence of heterogeneous domain ontologies, drives new challenges in the discovery of knowledge sources relevant to a user request. New efficient techniques and approaches for developing web intelligence are presented in this chapter, to help users avoid irrelevant web search results and wrong decision making.

In summary, the contributions of this chapter are twofold:

1. The benefits of combining Artificial Neural Networks with Semantic Web Technologies are discussed.
2. An Artificial Neural Network-based intelligent agent with capabilities for discovering distributed knowledge sources is presented.

2.1 Introduction

The web grows and evolves at a fast speed, imposing scalability and relevance problems to web search engines. Moreover, another ingredient is being recently added to it: data semantics. The new *Semantic Web* allows searching not only information but also knowledge. Its main purpose is introducing structure and semantic content in

M.L. Caliusco (✉)
CONICET, CIDISI-UTN-FRSF, Lavaise 610, Santa Fe, Argentina
e-mail: mcaliusc@frsf.utn.edu.ar

Y. Badr et al. (eds.) *Emergent Web Intelligence: Advanced Semantic Technologies,*
Advanced Information and Knowledge Processing,
DOI 10.1007/978-1-84996-077-9_2, © Springer-Verlag London Limited 2010

the huge amount of unstructured or semi-structured distributed knowledge available on the Web, being the central notion behind the Semantic Web that of ontologies, which describe concepts and their relations in a particular field of knowledge [1].

The knowledge source discovery task in such an open distributed system is a new challenge because of the lack of an integrated view of all the available knowledge sources. Therefore, if a part of the system wants to initiate, for example, a dynamic collaborative relationship with another one, it is difficult to know who to contact and where to go and look for the required knowledge. Besides that, the distributed development of domain-specific ontologies introduces another problem: in the Semantic Web many independently developed ontologies, describing the same or very similar fields of knowledge, co-exist. Those ontologies are not identical or present minor differences, such as different naming conventions, or higher level differences in their structure and in the way they represent knowledge. These problems can be caused, among other things, by the use of different natural languages, e.g. Paper vs. Artículo, different technical sublanguages, e.g. Paper vs. Memo, or use of synonyms, e.g. Paper vs. Article. Therefore, ontology-matching techniques are needed, that is to say, semantic affinity must be identified between concepts that, appearing in different ontologies, are related.

The web of the future will be composed by small highly contextualized ontologies, developed with different languages and different granularity levels. A simpler document in the Semantic Web will be composed by the website, the metadata that describe it and a domain ontology that represents the metadata semantics [16]. The websites will have, besides an ontology domain to describe the knowledge they can provide, an adequate structure to receive mobile software agents (i.e. an agent server) that will travel the net, for example looking for knowledge required by an end-user [2]. Considering that these agents will have their own ontology for communication, in this future context the main challenge will be how to go to the most relevant sites (avoiding waste of time) and how to communicate with them.

In addition, there must be a mechanism for defining ontology-matching, a key issue that agents have to deal with in the Semantic Web. Virtually any application that involves multiple ontologies must establish semantic mappings among them, to ensure interoperability. Examples of such applications arise in many domains, including e-commerce, knowledge management, e-learning, information extraction, bioinformatics, web services, and tourism, among others [9].

This chapter is focused on presenting new and recent techniques that can be used for improving web knowledge source discovery in the Semantic Web, such as the combination of agent-based technologies and Artificial Neural Network (ANN) models, which can be used for defining the matching operation between ontologies.

The structure of this chapter is the following: Sect. 2.2 introduces some basic concepts regarding the Semantic Web, Ontologies, Software Agents, and Artificial Neural Networks (ANNs). Section 2.3 discusses related work with knowledge discovery on the web. In Sect. 2.4, the web knowledge discovery task is explained in detail and some motivating scenarios are introduced. Section 2.5 presents a proposal for an ANN-based ontology-matching model inside a knowledge source discovery agent and a related performance evaluation. Finally, Sect. 2.6 presents the conclusions of this chapter.

2.2 Foundations

Semantic Web uses ontologies and a number of standard markup languages to formally model information represented in web resources so that it is accessible to humans and machines working co-operatively, perhaps with the assistance of intelligent services such as software agents, which use artificial intelligent (AI) techniques and models.

The purpose of this section is to provide an introduction to some concepts that are used along the chapter, regarding Ontologies, Ontology-matching, Software Agents and Artificial Neural Networks.

2.2.1 Ontologies and Ontology-Matching

Since ontologies have been used for different purposes in different disciplines, there are different definitions about what an ontology is, most of them contradictories [13].

In this chapter, an ontology is considered as an explicit representation of a shared understanding of the important concepts in some domain of interest. Ontologies usually are referred as a graph structure consisting of [8]:

1. a set of concepts (vertices in a graph),
2. a set of relationships connecting concepts (directed edges in a graph), and
3. a set of instances assigned to a particular concept (data records assigned to concepts or relations).

In order to define the semantics for digital content, it is necessary to formalize the ontologies by using specific languages as Resource Description Framework (RDF) and Web Ontology Language (OWL). On the one hand, RDF is a general-purpose language for representing information about resources in the Web. It is particularly intended for representing metadata about web resources, but it can also be used to represent information about objects that can be identified on the Web. On the other hand, OWL describes classes, properties, and relations among these conceptual objects in a way that facilitates machine interoperability of web content[3].

Ontologies provide a number of useful features for intelligent systems, as well as for knowledge representation in general and for the knowledge engineering process. However, in open or evolving systems, such as the Semantic Web, different parties could, in general, adopt different ontologies. Thus, merely using ontologies does not reduce heterogeneity: it raises heterogeneity problems at a higher level. Ontology-matching is a plausible solution to the semantic heterogeneity problem [8].

Ontology-matching aims at finding correspondences between semantically related entities of different ontologies. These correspondences may stand for equivalence as well as other relations, such as consequence, subsumption, or disjointness, between ontology entities.

Ontology-matching results, called alignments, can thus express the relations between the ontologies under consideration with various degrees of precision [12].

Alignments can be used for various tasks, such as ontology merging, query answering, data translation or Semantic Web browsing.

Technically, *ontology-matching*, can be defined as follows [12]:

The matching process can be seen as a function f which, from a pair of ontologies to match O_A and O_B, an input alignment A_1, a set of parameters p and a set of oracles and resources r, returns an alignment A_2 between these ontologies.

An alignment can be defined as:

Given two ontologies O_A and O_B, an alignment is made up of a set of correspondences between pairs of entities belonging to them.

Despite its pervasiveness, today ontology-matching is still largely conducted by hand, in a labor-intensive and error-prone process. The manual matching has now become a key bottleneck in building large-scale information systems. Hence, the development of tools to assist in the ontology matching process has become crucial for the success of a wide variety of applications [9].

There are different algorithms for implementing the matching process, which can be generally classified along two dimensions [8]. On the one hand, there is a distinction between schema-based and instance-based matching. A schema-based matcher takes different aspects of the concepts and relations in the ontologies and uses some similarity measure to determine correspondences. An instance-based matcher takes the instances which belong to the concepts in the ontologies and compares them to discover similarity between the concepts. On the other hand, there is a distinction between element-level and structure-level matching. An element-level matcher compares properties of the particular concept or relation, such as the name, and uses them to find similarities. A structure-level matcher compares the structure of the ontologies to find similarities. These matchers can also be combined.

In Sect. 2.5, a proposal for an ontology-matching model that combines several of these elements is presented. In this chapter, the *ontology-matching* model is defined formally as:

- *ontology-matching* : $c \rightarrow O_i$,
- *ontology-matching*$(c) = \{O_X, O_Y\}$, where c is a concept (it could be not only one concept, but more than one), O_X and O_Y are domain ontologies related to the same field than c.

2.2.2 Software Agents

Besides ontologies, software agents will play a fundamental role in building the Semantic Web of the future [16]. When data is marked up using ontologies, software agents can better understand the semantics and therefore more intelligently locate and integrate data for a wide variety of tasks.

Several authors propose different definitions for an agent [21, 31]. According to [27], an agent is everything that senses and acts on its environment, modifying it.

A software agent can therefore be considered as an autonomous software entity that can interact with its environment.

There are different types of agents such as [18]:

- Autonomous agent: it has the ability to decide when action is appropriate without the need of human intervention.
- Cooperative agent: it can interact with other agents or humans via a communication language.
- Mobile agent: it is able to migrate from one computer to another autonomously and continue its execution on the destination computer.
- Intelligent agent: it has the ability to learn the user preference and adapt to external environment.

A new emergent category, intelligent web (or personal) agents, rather than doing everything for a user, would find possible ways to meet user needs and offer the user choices for their achievement. A web agent could offer several possible ways to get what a user needs on the Web. A personal software agent on the Semantic Web must be capable of receiving some tasks and preferences from a user, seeking for information from web sources, communicating with other agents, comparing information about user requirements and preferences, selecting certain choices, and finally providing answers to the user [3].

An important distinction is that agents on the Semantic Web will not act in a completely autonomous way, but rather they will take care of the heavy load in the name of their users. They will be responsible for conducting the investigation, with the obligation to present the results to the user, so that he or she can make his or her decisions.

2.2.3 Artificial Neural Networks

There is no universally accepted definition of what Artificial Neural Networks (ANNs) are, or what they should be. They can be loosely defined as large sets of interconnected simple units which execute in parallel to perform a common global task. These units usually undergo a learning process which automatically updates network parameters in response to a possibly evolving input environment.

ANNs are information processing systems inspired by the ability of the human brain to learn from observations and to generalize by abstraction [14], according to the following characteristics:

- Knowledge is acquired by the network through a learning process.
- Connection strengths between neurons, known as synaptic weights, are used to store the knowledge.

Neural models have certain common characteristics. They are given a set of inputs $x = (x_1, \ldots, x_n) \in \Re^n$ and their corresponding set of target outputs $t = (t_1, \ldots, t_m) \in \Re^m$ for a certain process. The assumption of an ANN model is that the process that produces the output response is given by some unknown mathematical relationship $t = G(x)$ for some unknown, generally nonlinear, function G. Therefore, a candidate activation function AF (for G) is chosen and the approximation is performed using a given set of examples, named patterns; that is to say, a pattern consists of some inputs x and their associated target outputs t. The patterns are used to feed the ANN model, which contains a set of processing elements (called neurons) and connections between them (called synaptic weights). Each neuron has an activation function AF, which process the incoming information from other neurons.

Neural models may be considered as a particular choice of classes of functions $AF(x, w)$ where w are the parameters and specific procedures for training the network [25]. Training is similar to an optimization process where internal parameters of the neural model are adjusted, to fit the training data.

Training a neural network means adapting its connections so that the model exhibits the desired computational behavior for all input patterns. The process usually involves modifying the weights. Selection of training data plays a vital role in the performance of a supervised ANN. The number of training examples used to train an ANN is sometimes critical to the success of the training process.

If the number of training examples is not sufficient, then the network cannot correctly learn the actual input–output relation of the system. If the number of training examples is too large, then the network training time could be too long. For some applications, training time is a critical variable. For others, the training can be performed off-line and more training data are preferred over using insufficient training data to achieve greater network accuracy. Generally, rather than focusing on volume, it is better to concentrate on the quality and representational nature of the data set. A good training set should contain routine, unusual and boundary-condition cases [14].

2.3 ANNs and the Semantic Web: Literature Review

In this section, a review of current related work is presented, divided into two main research areas: searching and query answering on the Web, and proposals for ontology-matching using neural network models.

2.3.1 Searching and Query Answering on the Semantic Web

Considering the existence of webpage metadata, the problem of dynamic knowledge discovery in open distributed contexts has been addressed in the Helios Project [4]. Examples of open distributed contexts are Semantic Grids and Peer-based systems, where a set of independent peer nodes without prior reciprocal knowledge and no degree of relationship, dynamically need to cooperate by sharing their resources (such as data, documents or services). In the Helios Project, the authors assume that no centralized authority manages a comprehensive view of the resources shared by all the nodes in the system, due to the dynamics of the collaborations and variability of the requirements.

On the web, information is not described by a global schema and users used to query the web using their own terminology. Then, a semantic query answering system on the web has to rewrite the query with respect to available ontologies in order to use reasoning for providing answers. An example of this system is PowerAqua [20]. This system was developed to exploit the availability of distributed, ontology-based semantic markup on the web to answer questions posed in natural language. It does not assume that the user has any prior information about the semantic resources.

The problem of answering queries considering metadata has been studied also in Peer-based systems, mainly addressing the problem of routing queries over a network. For example, Edutella [23] provides an infrastructure for sharing metadata in RDF format. The network is segmented into thematic clusters. In each cluster, a mediator semantically integrates source data. The mediator handles a request either directly or indirectly: directly, by answering queries using its own integrated schema; indirectly, by querying other cluster mediators by means of a dialog-based query processing module.

2.3.2 Ontology-Matching and ANN Models

In response to the challenge of ontology-matching on the Semantic Web and in numerous other application contexts, several proposals have appeared lately, which apply machine learning techniques to create semantic mappings.

In a recent ontology matching state-of-the-art review [11], some tools based on ANNs are addressed that using information regarding ontology schemas and instances, produce rules for ontology integration in heterogeneous databases.

Several types of ANNs have been used for various tasks in ontology matching, such as discovering correspondences among attributes via categorization and classification, or learning matching parameters, such as matching weights, to tune matching systems with respect to a particular matching task [12].

Given schema-level and instance-level information, it is sometimes useful to cluster this input into categories in order to lower the computational complexity of further manipulations with data. The self-organizing map network can be used for this purpose where the neurons in the network are organizing themselves according to the characteristics of given input patterns. This kind of neural model is used in the X-SOM ontology mapper [7] which uses a neural network model to weight existing matching techniques, combined with reasoning and local heuristics aimed to both discover and solve semantic inconsistencies.

ANNs have been used to automatically recognize the connection between web pages with similar content and to improve semantic information retrieval together with synonyms thesaurus [33], or based on text documents [30]. SEMantic INTegrator (SEMINT) is a tool based on neural networks to assist in identifying attribute correspondences in heterogeneous databases [19]. It supports access to a variety of database systems and utilizes both schema-level and instance-level information to produce rules for matching corresponding attributes automatically.

During matching, different semantic aspects such as concept names, concept properties, and concept relationships, contribute in different degrees to the matching result. Therefore, a vector of weights has to be assigned to these aspects, which is not a trivial task and current research work depends on human heuristics. In [17], an ANN model learns and adjusts those weights, with the purpose of avoiding some of the disadvantages in both rule-based and learning-based ontology matching approaches, which ignore the information that instance data may provide. Similar to this idea, the work of [5] uses instances to learn similarity between ontology concepts to create then a newly combined ontology.

In the GLUE system [9], learning techniques are used to semi-automatically create semantic mappings between ontologies, finding correspondences among the taxonomies of two given ontologies: for each concept node in one taxonomy, the GLUE system uses a machine-learning classifier to find the most similar concept node in the other taxonomy.

Differently from the previous cited works, in [28] it is considered that labels at ontologies are human identifiers (names) for instances, normally shared by a community of humans speaking a common language inside a specific field of knowledge. It can be inferred that, if labels are the same, the instances associated to them are probably also the same or are semantically related [10]. A concept, on the other hand, can also be defined as representative of a set of instances. We can, therefore, infer that concepts that have the same instances are the same. And vice versa, instances that have the same mother concept (label) are similar. The assumption is that, to perform its tasks efficiently, an agent should be specialized in a specific domain context where it is assumed that different ontologies will manage similar concepts and content.

Those facts, combined with supervised learning by example (i.e. ANNs), can be better used by an agent to provide a more effective and more efficient response, compared to traditional retrieval mechanisms. This way, a mobile agent responsible for searching the web would not loose time and would only visit domains that could provide an answer and total response time would diminish because the knowledge would be available just-in-time for the system users. A proposal for the ontology-matching task using an ANN-based model is presented in detail in Sect. 2.5.

2.4 Web Knowledge Source Discovery

The simplest knowledge discovery mechanism is based on the traditional query/answer paradigm, where each part acts as both client and server, interacting with other nodes directly sending queries or requests, and waiting until receiving an answer. This is only possible if the domains are previously known to each other or if a collaboration relationship has already been established between them. When this is not the case, the discovery of knowledge is affected by the dynamism of the system. Some nodes join and some nodes leave the network, at any time. Besides, each domain is responsible for its own knowledge representation and management, because there are no a-priori agreements regarding ontology language nor granularity. A typical example of such a system is the Semantic Web [3].

In open distributed systems, several nodes (domains), probably distributed among different organizations, need resources and information (i.e. data, documents, services) provided by other domains in the net. Therefore, an open distributed system can be defined as networks of several independent nodes, having different roles and capacities. In this scenario, a key problem is the dynamic discovery of knowledge sources, understood as the capacity of finding knowledge sources in the system about resources and information that, in a given moment, better response the requirements of a node request [4].

When data is marked up using ontologies, software agents can better understand the semantics and therefore more intelligently locate and integrate knowledge for a wide variety of tasks. The following examples show two motivating scenarios for knowledge discovery on the Semantic Web:

- Scenario 1 (adapted from [9]):

  Suppose a researcher wants to find out more about someone met at a conference, whose last name is Cook and teaches Computer Science at a nearby (unknown) university. It is also known that he just moved to the US from Australia, where he had been an associate professor. On the web of today, it will be difficult finding this person, because the above information is not contained within a single webpage, thus making keyword search ineffective. On the Semantic Web, however, one should be able to quickly find the answers. A marked-up directory service makes it easy for a personal software agent to find nearby Computer Science departments. These departments have marked up data using some ontology, that includes courses, people, and professors. Professors have attributes such as name, degree, and institution. Such marked-up data makes it easy for the agent to find a professor with the last name Cook. Then by examining the attribute institution, the agent quickly finds the CS department in Australia. Here, the agent learns that the data has been marked up using an ontology specific to Australian universities and that there are many entities named Cook. However, knowing that associate professor is equivalent to senior lecturer, it can select the right subtree in the departmental taxonomy, and zoom in on the old homepage of the conference acquaintance.

- Scenario 2 (adapted from [28]):

  A researcher from an European university wants to identify potential partners in some American universities to collaborate on a project answering from the calling of the European Union Framework Program.[1] The main topic for the project is the Semantic Web, which is an unknown topic for the researcher and

---

[1] http://cordis.europa.eu/fp7.

therefore he knows no colleague who can help in the research. In addition, due to the project requirements, a senior researcher has to be contacted. Similarly to the previous scenario, this problem could be more easily solved in the Semantic Web by an agent capable of dynamically discovering the appropriate sources of knowledge, by dynamically matching ontologies belonging to different universities in Europe and America, looking for researchers in the Semantic Web topic.

Searching on the Semantic Web differs in several aspects from a traditional web search, specially because of the structure of an online collection of documents in the Semantic Web, which consists of much more than HTML pages. The semantics associated to the languages for the Semantic Web allows the generation of new facts from existing facts, while traditional databases just enumerate all available facts.

Traditional search machines do not try to understand the semantics of the indexed documents. Conventional retrieval models, in which the retrievals are based on the matching of terms between documents and the user queries, is often suffering from either missing relevant documents which are not indexed by the keywords used in a query, but by synonyms; or retrieving irrelevant documents which are indexed by unintended sense of the keywords in the query.

Instead, search agents for the Semantic Web should not only find the right information in a precise way, but also should be able to infer knowledge and to interact with the target domain to accomplish its duty [24]. In the next subsection, a proposal for a knowledge source discovery agent is presented.

2.4.1 A Knowledge Source Discovery Agent

In [28], an architecture for discovering knowledge sources on the Semantic Web was proposed. This architecture is shown in Fig. 2.1. The main components of the architecture are: the mobile agents, the Knowledge Source Discovery (KSD) agent, and the domains.

The mobile agents receive the request from the user and look for an answer visiting the domains according to a list of possible domains generated by the KDS. An example of a request for the previously described Scenario 2 could be: *Which researchers from Latin American universities work on the field of ontologies and neural networks?*

The KSD agent has the responsibility of knowing which domains can provide knowledge inside a specific thematic cluster [23] and to indicate a route to mobile agents on the web carrying a user request. The KSD agent just knows the location (i.e. the url) of domains that can provide knowledge, but it does not provide the knowledge, nor the analysis what the domain contains (i.e. files, pictures, documents, etc.).

The KSD agent is specialized in a determined field of knowledge. It has to be aware of all the domains related to this field. To do that, it periodically sends

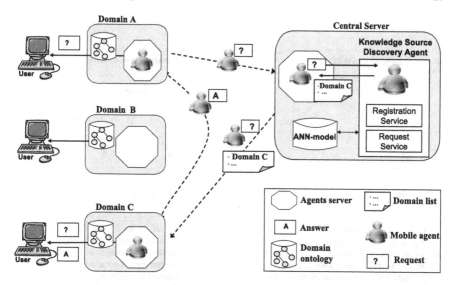

Fig. 2.1 A reference architecture for discovering knowledge sources [28]

crawlers to index websites (Google-search engine style), or the domains can register with the KSD agent when they want to be reachable (Yahoo-directory style). This task is carried out by the *Registration Service*.

Finally, the last components of the architecture are the domains. Each domain has its own ontology used to semantically markup the information published in its websites. An example of the domain content is shown in Fig. 2.2. Let us suppose that there are three domains (A, B, and C) which belong to the Research & Development (R + D) field of knowledge. The domain A uses the KA-ontology[2] provided by the free open source ontology editor Protege. The domain B uses the SWRC-ontology,[3] Semantic Web for Research Communities, which is an ontology for modeling entities of research communities and their relationships. Finally, the domain C uses an own-highly-specialized ontology model. All of these ontologies are implemented in Web Ontology Language (OWL).

In addition, RDF is used to define an ontology-based semantic markup for the domain website. Each RDF-triple assigns entities and relations in the text linked to their semantic descriptions in an ontology. For example, in the domain A, the following RDF-triples: (*O.C., interest, Semantic Grid*), (*O.C., interest, Semantic Web*) and (*O.C., interest, Ontological Engineering*) represent the research interests of O.C. described in the text (see the bottom area of Fig. 2.2). As can be seen in the figure, each domain may use a different ontology to semantically annotate the provided information even if they belong to the same field of knowledge.

The KSD agent is capable of identifying dynamically which domains could satisfy a request brought to it by a mobile agent. This dynamic knowledge discovery

---

[2]http://protege.cim3.net/file/pub/ontologies/ka/ka.owl.

[3]http://ontoware.org/projects/swrc/.

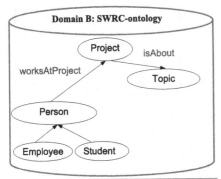

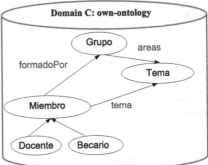

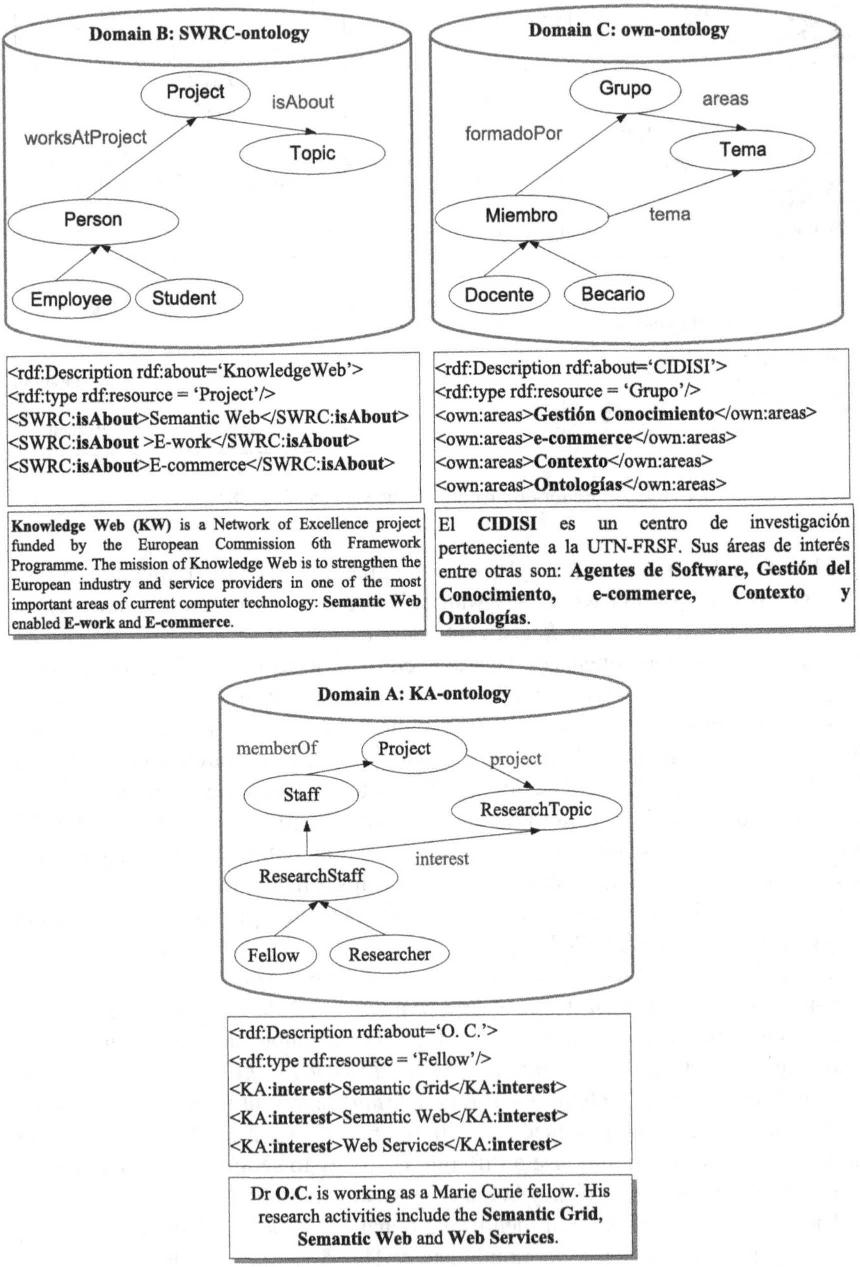

Domain B: SWRC-ontology
Project
isAbout
worksAtProject
Topic
Person
Employee
Student
<rdf:Description rdf:about='KnowledgeWeb'>
<rdf:type rdf:resource = 'Project'/>
<SWRC:isAbout>Semantic Web</SWRC:isAbout>
<SWRC:isAbout >E-work</SWRC:isAbout>
<SWRC:isAbout>E-commerce</SWRC:isAbout>
Knowledge Web (KW) is a Network of Excellence project funded by the European Commission 6th Framework Programme. The mission of Knowledge Web is to strengthen the European industry and service providers in one of the most important areas of current computer technology: Semantic Web enabled E-work and E-commerce.
Domain C: own-ontology
Grupo
areas
formadoPor
Tema
Miembro
tema
Docente
Becario
<rdf:Description rdf:about='CIDISI'>
<rdf:type rdf:resource = 'Grupo'/>
<own:areas>Gestión Conocimiento</own:areas>
<own:areas>e-commerce</own:areas>
<own:areas>Contexto</own:areas>
<own:areas>Ontologías</own:areas>
El CIDISI es un centro de investigación perteneciente a la UTN-FRSF. Sus áreas de interés entre otras son: Agentes de Software, Gestión del Conocimiento, e-commerce, Contexto y Ontologías.
Domain A: KA-ontology
memberOf
Project
project
Staff
ResearchTopic
interest
ResearchStaff
Fellow
Researcher
<rdf:Description rdf:about='O. C.'>
<rdf:type rdf:resource = 'Fellow'/>
<KA:interest>Semantic Grid</KA:interest>
<KA:interest>Semantic Web</KA:interest>
<KA:interest>Web Services</KA:interest>
Dr O.C. is working as a Marie Curie fellow. His research activities include the Semantic Grid, Semantic Web and Web Services.

Fig. 2.2 Domains belonging to the R + D field and their corresponding annotated ontologies

requires models and techniques that allow to find ontology concepts that have semantic affinity among them, even when they are different syntactically. In order to
do its responsibility efficiently, the KSD agent has to be able to match (probably different) domain ontologies. To face this ontology-matching problem, we propose the
use of a machine learning approach, in particular an ANN model with supervised
learning which is trained (and re-trained periodically) off-line with the data retrieved
as previously stated. The ANN-based matching model is stored in the KSD agent
Knowledge Base (KB) and it is explained in detail in the next section.

2.5 The ANN-Based Ontology-Matching Model Inside the KSD Agent

This section of the chapter presents an ANN-based model that can be used for ontology-matching purposes in the Semantic Web.

An ANN model can be classified according to the type of connections among
their neurons. A network is named feedforward if the flow of data is from inputs to
outputs, without feedback. Generally this topology has distinct layers such as input,
hidden and output, with no connections among neurons belonging to the same layer.
Inside the feedforward models, which are the most widely used, there is a model
named multi-layer perceptron (MLP).

The MLP model consists of a finite number of units called perceptrons (Fig. 2.3),
where each unit of each layer is connected to each unit of the subsequent/previous
layer. These connections are called links or synapses and they only exist between
layers. The signal flow is unidirectional, from the inputs to the outputs, from one

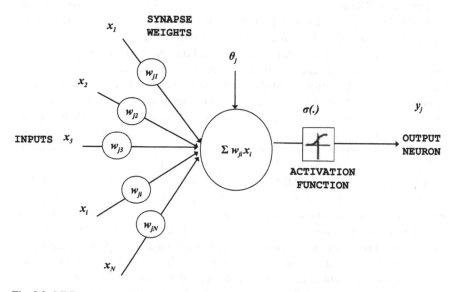

Fig. 2.3 MLP neuron model

layer to the next one, thus the term feedforward. The rules for the MLP model are the following:

- The jth neuron of the kth layer receives as input each x_i of the previous layer. Each value x_i is then multiplied by a corresponding constant, called weight w_{ji}, and then all the values are summed.
- A shift θ_j (called threshold or bias) is applied to the above sum, and over the results an activation function σ is applied, resulting in the output of the jth neuron of the kth layer. The MLP neuron model is the following:

$$y_j = \sigma \left(\sum_{i=1}^{N} w_{ji} x_i + \theta_j \right) \qquad (1)$$

where $i = 1, \ldots, N$, $j = 1, \ldots, M$, and some common choices for σ can be one of the following: the logistic sigmoid (equation (2)), the hyperbolic tangent (equation (3)) or the linear function (equation (4)).

$$\sigma(x) = \frac{1}{1 + e^{-x}}, \qquad (2)$$

$$\tanh(x) = \frac{e^x - e^{-x}}{e^x + e^{-x}}, \qquad (3)$$

$$y(x) = x. \qquad (4)$$

The number of layers and neurons in each layer are chosen a-priori, as well as the type of activation functions for the neurons. The number of neurons in the hidden layer is usually determined by trial-and-error in order to find the simplest network that gives acceptable performance. Then, the values of the weights w_{ji} and bias θ_j are initialized. These values are chosen so that the model behaves well on some set (named training set) of inputs and corresponding outputs. The process of determining the weights and thresholds is called learning or training.

In the MLP model, the learning is supervised and the basic learning algorithm used is called backpropagation [26, 29] which uses gradient descend to minimize the cost function (the error E) of the ANN model, generally defined as the mean square error (mse) between the desired output (targets) and the actual network output. During learning, the mse propagates backwards through the network, hence the term backpropagation, across the layers of the network model and the weights are changed accordingly to the error mismatch between the actual network outputs y and the target outputs t over all the training patterns [14].

A major result regarding MLP models is the so-called *universal approximation theorem* [6] which states that given enough neurons in the hidden layer, an MLP neural model can approximate any continuous bounded function to any specified accuracy; in other words, there always exists a three-layer MLP neural network which can approximate any arbitrary nonlinear continuous multidimensional function to any desired accuracy, provided that the model has enough neurons [15]. That is why this model has been more extensively studied and used during last years. It is worth noting, however, that the theorem does not say that a single-layer network is

Fig. 2.4 ANN-based ontology-matching model for a KSD agent

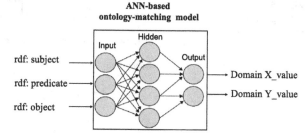

optimum in the sense of learning time or ease of implementation; moreover, the theorem does not give indications about the required number of hidden units necessary in order to achieve the desired degree of accuracy.

For neural networks, a matching problem can be viewed as a classification problem. The input to our problem includes RDF-triples instances belonging to the RDF annotations of the A KA-ontology domain, and similarly for domain B and C. We address this problem using machine learning techniques as follows: our ANN-based matcher uses schema-level information and instance-level information inside the A ontology to learn a classifier for A, and then it uses schema-level information and instance-level information inside the B ontology to learn a classifier for B. It then classifies instances of B according to the A classifier, and vice-versa. Hence, we have a method for identifying instances of $A \cap B$. The same idea is applied for more than two domains. Our approach just indicates which domains may be able to respond to a query, but it does not provide a similarity measurement for the analyzed ontology terms, differently from [10] where an ANN model is used for providing or combining similarity measures among heterogeneous ontology terms.

Applying machine learning to this context raises the question of which learning algorithm to use and which types of information to use in the learning process. Our model (a schematics representation of the general ANN-based ontology-matching model can be seen in Fig. 2.4) uses the standard backpropagation algorithm for supervised learning, which means that, for each input data point presented to the ANN model, there must be a corresponding matching output or target to be related with [32]. These {input/output} pairs are named training patterns.

Given a number of ontologies and their instances (belonging to the same field of knowledge), i.e. ontology X and ontology Y, training patterns are formed to train the proposed ANN-model by analyzing the RDF-triples belonging to the annotations of the ontology domains, as follows:

Input pattern: $\langle rdf{:}subject; rdf{:}predicate; rdf{:}object \rangle$,
Target pattern: $\langle DomainX_{value}; DomainY_{value} \rangle$

where the target pattern is a vector: the first position stands for ontology domain X and the second position stands for ontology domain Y. The value of each position in the vector indicates whether the input RDF-triple exists in the corresponding ontology domain (1) or not (0). This is better explained with a example in the next subsection.

Fig. 2.5 ANN-based
ontology-matching model:
training patterns example

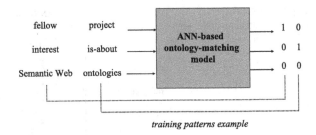

training patterns example

2.5.1 ANN-Based Ontology-Matching Model: Training Phase

Using the available data from all the domains (label names and associated instances from the RDF-triples used as semantic markup of the websites, as shown in Fig. 2.2), the ANN-based ontology matching model training patterns are formed.

Each output neuron is specialized in recognizing RDF-triples belonging to the domain ontology that the neuron represents. The label and instance strings are codified using the standard ASCII code and are then normalized into the activation function domain of the hidden neurons, before entering the model, because this significantly improves training time and model accuracy. A simple example of two training patterns is presented in Fig. 2.5.

For example, considering all three ontologies presented in Fig. 2.2, a training pattern indicating that the RDF-triple ⟨*fellow*; *interest*; *SemanticWeb*⟩ can be found on the Domain A ontology but not on B nor C would be:

Input pattern: ⟨*fellow*; *interest*; *SemanticWeb*⟩,
Target pattern: ⟨1; 0; 0⟩.

This means that given the fact that there are fellows in the domain A whose research interest is the Semantic Web, its corresponding RDF-triple would be ⟨*fellow*; *interest*; *SemanticWeb*⟩ and its corresponding output target would be ⟨1; 0; 0⟩: only the first vector value (that represents Domain A is equal to 1) indicating that this triple can be found on domain A ontology. The second training pattern indicates that the RDF-triple ⟨*project*; *is-about*; *ontologies*⟩ can be found on domain B (⟨0; 1; 0⟩), because the second value of the target vector is equal to 1.

The MLP model parameters are set according to typical values, randomly initialized. The number of input neurons for the MLP model is set to a standard RDF-triple. The hidden layer neurons number is set empirically, according to the training data and a desired accuracy for the matching. At the output, there is a specialized output neuron in the model for each domain, that recognizes when a domain ontology label or instance is presented to the model. The allowed values for each output neuron are 1 or 0, meaning that the neuron recognizes/does not recognizes a concept belonging to the domain it represents.

The good generalization property of an ANN model means the ability of a trained network to correctly predict a response to a set of inputs not seen before. It says that a trained network must perform well on a new dataset distinct from the one used for training.

The ANN-based ontology-matching model here proposed is trained with each domain ontology RDF-annotations and their corresponding instances. Our basic assumption is that knowledge is captured in an arbitrary ontology encoding, based on a consistent semantics. From this, it is possible to derive additional knowledge such as, in our case, similarity of concepts in different ontologies. Understanding that labels describe concepts in natural language one can derive that concepts/instances having the same labels are similar. This is not a rule which always holds true, but it is a strong indicator for similarity. Other constructs as subclass relations or type definition can be interpreted similarly.

We have used a small set of patterns (34) for ANN model training, because at the moment we are working with small domains and with not highly populated ontologies. For testing model effectiveness, several ANN models have been tested, considering different number of hidden neurons and performance on training and validation patterns, using the cross-validation procedure combined with the Levenberg–Marquardt [22] training algorithm, which is a quasi-Newton method, designed to approach second-order training speed without having to compute a Hessian matrix. When the ANN model performance function has the form of a sum of squares (typical in feedforward networks training), then the Hessian matrix can be approximated as $H = J^T J$ and the gradient can be computed as $g = J^T e$, where J is the Jacobian matrix that contains first derivatives of the network errors with respect to the weights and biases, and e is a vector of network errors. The Jacobian matrix can be computed through a standard backpropagation technique that is much less complex than computing the Hessian matrix [14]. The ANN model is built and trained off-line, and its parameters are tuned and re-trained periodically when data changes or new domains are added to the system. However, the time needed for this processes can be disregarded because the ANN model is used on-line. Examples of model use for matching are presented in the next subsection.

2.5.2 ANN-Based Ontology-Matching Model: Matching Phase

The Knowledge Source Discovery agent uses the ANN model on-line once the model has been trained, producing and instant response, each time a mobile agent carrying a request knocks on its door. The query is expressed in natural language by an end-user, and it is processed at the mobile agent, until only the keywords remain. These keywords, represented as a RDF-triple, are used to consult on the ANN model, as shown in the example of Fig. 2.6. In the presented example, the ANN model indicates that the domain ontologies of A and B contain some ontology labels or instances that are similar to the presented request. Therefore, the Knowledge Source Discovery agent should return to the agent a Domain-list containing the domains A and B to be visited by the mobile agent. According to the ANN model of the KSD agent, those domains are very likely to be able to provide the required information.

Because of how neural models work (interpolating data) and the properties associated to a three-layer MLP model (generalization ability), the model would always

Fig. 2.6 Querying the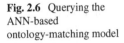
ANN-based
ontology-matching model

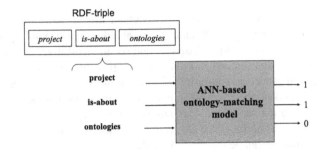

Table 2.1 Query RDF-triplets examples

Query RDF-triplets	Matching domain ontologies RDF-triplets
(1) ⟨fellow, interest, semanticWeb⟩	Domain A: ⟨fellow, interest, semanticWeb⟩
(2) ⟨researcher, topic, –⟩	Domain B: ⟨researcher, topic, semanticWeb⟩
(3) ⟨miembro, tema, gobierno⟩	Domain C: ⟨miembro, tema, gobiernoElectronico⟩
(4) ⟨project, is-about, ontologies⟩	Domain A: ⟨fellow, interest, ontologies⟩,
	Domain B: ⟨researchProject, is-about, ontologies⟩
(5) ⟨researcher, topic, web⟩	Domain B: ⟨researcher, topic, semanticWeb⟩
(6) ⟨–, –, semanticGrid⟩	Domain A: ⟨fellow, interest, semanticGrid⟩

provide a response [14]. Besides, standard learning algorithms can be used for the model, for which stability and convergence is guaranteed. If the request contains concepts totally unknown to the model, it shows that fact answering with values very different from the training patterns.

The ANN-based ontology-matching model has been tested on six query-examples, presented in Table 2.1. Note that the query triplet (4) ⟨project, is-about, ontologies⟩ has a translation in both domain A and domain B ontologies, therefore the ANN model should indicate that the domain ontologies of *A* and *B* contain some ontology labels or instances that are similar to the presented request. Therefore, the KSD agent should return a Domain-list containing the domains *A* and *B* to be visited by the mobile agent carrying the request, because according to the ANN model of the KSD agent, those domains are very likely to be able to provide the required information. Another interesting test query is represented by (3) ⟨miembro, tema, gobierno⟩ and (5) ⟨researcher, topic, web⟩, where the matching model must recognize an instance name which is part of an ontology instance name. For all of these examples the ANN-based ontology matching model has provided a satisfactory result.

The number of query triplets is fixed a priori for each query category, however the final number of ontology triplets for training the ANN-model is dependent on how populated the ontologies are. Therefore, triplets must be created off-line for training the model, but it then can be used on-line for query resolution purposes. Linguistic terms can be mapped into ontology classes (i.e., researcher) or instances (i.e., semanticWeb, agents).

2.6 Conclusions

This chapter has presented some basic concepts and foundations regarding the new Semantic Web, how it will be populated with ontologies and why ontology-matching techniques are needed. The idea of software agents that travel the web carrying query request from users has also been addressed. The web knowledge source discovery task has been explained in detail and some motivating scenarios were introduced.

A condensed literature review on these subjects has been presented, and the advantages of combination of Artificial Intelligence techniques and models, such as agent-based technologies and Artificial Neural Networks (ANN), that can be used for intelligent web knowledge source discovery in the emergent Semantic Web, have been highlighted.

In summary, this chapter has presented the benefits of combining Artificial Neural Networks with Semantic Web Technologies, and an ANN-based software agent with capabilities for discovering distributed knowledge sources has been presented.

References

1. Baeza-Yates, R.: Web mining. In: Proc. LA-WEB Congress, p. 2 (2005)
2. Berners-Lee, T., Hendler, J., Lassila, O.: The Semantic Web. Scientific American **5**(1), 29–37 (2001)
3. Breitman, K., Casanova, M.A., Truszkowski, W.: Semantic Web: Concepts, Technologies and Applications. Springer, London (2007)
4. Castano, S., Ferrara, A., Montanelli, S.: Dynamic knowledge discovery in open, distributed and multi-ontology systems: techniques and applications. In: Web Semantics and Ontology. Idea Group Inc, London (2006)
5. Chortaras, A., Stamou, G.B., Stafylopatis, A.: Learning ontology alignments using recursive neural networks. In: Proc. Int. Conf. on Neural Networks (ICANN), Poland. Lecture Notes in Computer Science, vol. 3697, pp. 811–816. Springer, Berlin (2005)
6. Cybenko, G.: Neural networks in computational science and engineering. IEEE Computational Science and Engineering **3**(1), 36–42 (1996)
7. Curino, C., Orsi, G., Tanca, L.: X-SOM: Ontology mapping and inconsistency resolution. In: 4th European Semantic Web Conference (ESWC'07), 3–7, June 2007
8. Davies, J., Studer, R., Warren, P.: Semantic Web Technologies: Trends and Research in Ontology-Based Systems. Wiley, London (2007)
9. Doan, A., Madhavan, J., Domingos, P., Halevy, A.: Ontology matching: A machine learning approach. In: Handbook on Ontologies in Information Systems, pp. 385–403. Springer, New York (2004)
10. Ehrig, M., Sure, Y.: Ontology mapping—an integrated approach. In: Proc. 1st European Semantic Web Symposium (ESWS 2004), Greece. Lecture Notes in Computer Science, vol. 3053, pp. 76–91. Springer, Berlin (2004)
11. Euzenat, J., Barrasa, J., Bouquet, P., Bo, J.D., et al.: State of the art on ontology alignment. D2.2.3, Technical Report IST-2004-507482, KnowledgeWeb, 2004
12. Euzenat, J., Shvaiko, P.: Ontology Matching. Springer, London (2007)
13. Gómez-Pérez, A., Fernández-López, M., Corcho, O.: Ontological Engineering—with Examples from the Areas of Knowledge Management, e-Commerce and the Semantic Web. Springer, London (2004)

14. Haykin, S.: Neural Networks: A Comprehensive Foundation, 2nd edn. Prentice-Hall, New York (1999)
15. Hornik, K., Stinchcombe, M., White, H.: Multilayer feedforward networks are universal approximators. Neural Networks **2**(5), 359–366 (1989)
16. Hendler, J.: Agents and the Semantic Web. IEEE Intelligent Systems **16**(2), 30–37 (2001)
17. Huang, J., Dang, J., Vidal, J., Huhns, M.: Ontology matching using an artificial neural network to learn weights. In: Proc. IJCAI Workshop on Semantic Web for Collaborative Knowledge Acquisition (SWeCKa-07), India (2007)
18. Lam, T., Lee, R.: iJADE FreeWalker—an intelligent ontology agent-based tourist guiding system. Studies in Computational Intelligence **72**, 103–125 (2007)
19. Li, W., Clifton, C.: SEMINT: a tool for identifying attribute correspondences in heterogeneous databases using neural networks. Data and Knowledge Engineering **33**(1), 49–84 (2000)
20. López, V., Motta, E., Uren, V.: PowerAqua: fishing the semantic web. In: Proc. 3rd European Semantic Web Conference, Montenegro. Lecture Notes in Computer Science, vol. 4011, pp. 393–410. Springer, Berlin (2006)
21. Maes, P.: Intelligent software. Scientific American **273**(3), 84–86 (1995)
22. Marquardt, D.: An algorithm for least-squares estimation of nonlinear parameters. SIAM Journal on Applied Mathematics **11**, 431–441 (1963)
23. Nejdl, W., Wolf, B., Qu, C., Decker, S., Sintek, M., Naeve, A., Nilsson, M., Palmér, M., Risch, T.: EDUTELLA, A P2P networking infrastructure based on RDF. In: Proc. 11th World Wide Web Conference (WWW2002), USA, pp. 604–615 (2002)
24. Peis, E., Herrera-Viedma, E., Montero, Y.H., Herrera, J.C.: Ontologías, metadatos y agentes: Recuperación semántica de la información. In: Proc. II Jornadas de Tratamiento y Recuperación de la Información, España, pp. 157–165 (2003)
25. Pinkus, A.: Approximation theory of the MLP model in neural networks. Acta Numerica **1**, 143–195 (1999)
26. Rumelhart, D.E., Hinton, G.E., Williams, R.J.: Learning representations by back-propagating errors. Nature **323**, 533–536 (1986)
27. Russell, S., Norvig, P.: Artificial Intelligence: A Modern Approach. Prentice-Hall, New York (2002)
28. Stegmayer, G., Caliusco, M.L., Chiotti, O., Galli, M.R.: ANN-agent for distributed knowledge source discovery. In: On the Move to Meaningful Internet Systems 2007: OTM 2007 Workshops. Lecture Notes in Computer Science, vol. 4805, pp. 467–476. Springer, Berlin (2007)
29. Werbos, P.: The Roots of Backpropagation. From Ordered Derivatives to Neural Networks and Political Forecasting. Wiley, New York (1994)
30. Wermter, S.: Neural network agents for learning semantic text classification. Information Retrieval **3**(2), 87–103 (2000)
31. Wooldridge, M.: An Introduction to Multiagent Systems. Wiley, New York (2002)
32. Wray, J., Green, G.: Neural networks, approximation theory and precision computation. Neural Networks **8**(1), 31–37 (1995)
33. Zhu, X., Huang, S., Yu, Y.: Recognizing the relations between Web pages using artificial neural network. In: Proc. ACM Symposium on Applied Computing, USA, pp. 1217–1221 (2003)

Chapter 3
Computing Similarity of Semantic Web Services in Semantic Nets with Multiple Concept Relations

Xia Wang, Yi Zhao, and Wolfgang A. Halang

Abstract The similarity of semantic web services is measured by matching service descriptions, which mostly depends on the understanding of their ontological concepts. Computing concept similarity on the basis of heterogeneous ontologies is still a problem. The current efforts only consider single hierarchical concept relations, which fail to express rich and implied information on concepts. Similarity under multiple types of concept relations as required by many application scenarios still needs to be investigated.

To this end, first an original ontological concept similarity algorithm in a semantic net is proposed taking multiple concept relations into consideration, particularly fuzzy-weight relations between concepts. Then, this algorithm is employed to promote computing the similarity of semantic web services. An experimental prototype and detailed empirical discussions are presented, and the method is validated in the framework of web service selection.

3.1 Introduction

Ontologies formally define concepts and concept relationships in a machine-understandable way with the goal to enable sharing and re-use of knowledge. Although this increases the level of understanding and flexibility of computerized systems, it also adds new complexity if independent, heterogeneous ontologies describing the same or similar domains are being used. This introduces the problem of understanding the relationship of ontological concepts. A key relationship in this problem domain to look at is concept similarity which tries to define conceptual overlaps. If two concepts can be identified to be similar, and this similarity can be measured and expressed quantitatively, then a heterogeneous concept space can be "harmonized".

X. Wang (✉)
Fernuniversität, 58084 Hagen, Germany
e-mail: xia.wang@fernuni-hagen.de

Y. Badr et al. (eds.) *Emergent Web Intelligence: Advanced Semantic Technologies,*
Advanced Information and Knowledge Processing,
DOI 10.1007/978-1-84996-077-9_3, © Springer-Verlag London Limited 2010

sws1: ServiceName: ZipCodeLookup
   operation: GetZipByCityState
     input: StateCode, CityName
     output: Body

sws3: ServiceName: DistanceBetweenTwoZipCodes
   operation: CalcDistTwoZipsKm
     input: ZipCode1, ZipCode2
     output: Body

sws5: ServiceName: Zip4
   operation1: FindZipPlus4
     input: Address, City, State
     output: Body
   operation2: FindCityState
     input: Zip
     output: Body

sws2: ServiceName: CityStateByZip
   operation: GetCityStateByZip
     input: ZipCode
     output: Body

sws4: ServiceName: ZipCodeService
   operation: FindZipCodeDistance
     input: Code1, Code2
     output: Body
   operation2: FindZipDetails
     input: Code1
     output: Body

Fig. 3.1 Examples for descriptions of semantic web services

In the context of semantic web services (SWS), it is a key functionality to enable service discovery, selection, and composition under the assumption that services are described using heterogeneous ontologies—a situation occurring under many circumstances. In particular, concept similarity is important when the selection of services is based on the similarity of descriptions of semantic services.

Similarity of semantic services is measured by the conceptual overlap of service capabilities, including non-functional information such as service name, service categories, and service qualities, and functional properties, i.e., service operations. In order to illustrate this, Fig. 3.1 shows an example of five services related to postal codes (taken from the *Semantic Web Services Repository* of University College Dublin (http://moguntia.ucd.ie/repository/). The services are used to look up zip codes or to calculate distances between two places given their zip codes.

Taking *sws4* and *sws5* of Fig. 3.1 as examples, we assume that *zip* and *code* are similar to a certain extent in a specific application. By comparing service names and service operation names, services can be regarded as similar from the signature level. In addition, by matching their operations and inputs/outputs we can conclude that the services *sws4* and *sws5* are similar—both services can provide information on a city according to a given zip code. Furthermore, if we assume that a machine can understand that there is some similarity between {*zip, ZipCode, code, Zip_Code_1, code1*} or {*CalcDisTwoZipsKm, findZipCode-Distance*}, then we can derive that *sws1:operation* is similar to *sws5:operation1*, *sws2:operation* is similar to *sws5:operation2* and *sws4:operation2*, and *sws3:operation* is similar to *sws4:operation1*. As it becomes obvious from this example, ontological concept similarity based on both syntactic and semantic approaches is the basis for service similarity.

In the above service descriptions, there are some special concept features appearing in semantic services. They cause the following problems.

- Concepts are of two types: some are formal ones and the others are composite ones combined of several concepts, which are not formal vocabularies indexed by dictionaries such as WordNet.[1] For such composite concepts, e.g., *findZip-CodeDistance* and *CalcDistTwoZipsKm*, the traditional methods (e.g., *Edit Dis-*

---

[1]WordNet is a lexical reference system at http://wordnet.princeton.edu/.

tance of strings) are not applicable to measure their semantic similarity. Therefore, the similarity of composite concepts constitutes a considerable problem.

- A concept has a specific sense in a given service application description, e.g., *code* in our above service examples does not mean *cipher* nor *computer code*, but is actually used as synonym for *zip code*. Therefore, word disambiguation is required before considering concept similarity.
- Information among concepts should be more than what is represented by small pieces of service ontologies, which are currently used by semantic service descriptions. And there should be more concepts relations than just the *is-a* relation. Therefore, mining implied information and concept relations is necessary and contributes to the assessment of service similarity.

Although concept similarity is a well studied topic in the fields of ontology engineering, artificial intelligence (AI), knowledge management, and information retrieval (IR), it is still a problem for semantic web services with the above conceptual features. Moreover, a service does not only use single domain ontologies to define its applications but may, in fact, use several domain ontologies. A travel service, for instance, may involve concepts from the finance and the transportation domain. The relations between concepts turn very complex. Therefore, the application ontology for a kind of semantic services cannot simply be structured in form of traditional tree-like networks, which only emphasize the *subtype* or *is-a* relations between concepts of one domain, but as a hybrid semantic net including multiple kinds of concept relations. That is the main reason for the limited usefulness of the existing concept similarity algorithms in semantic web service scenarios.

Our approach to determine concept similarity aims to solve the above problems. In essence, it consists of two parts: (1) building a unified application ontology ($\mathcal{AO}$) as a knowledge base for a kind of semantic services [37], and (2) calculating concept similarity in such unitary $\mathcal{AO}$ to improve the measurement of semantic service similarity, which is elaborated in this chapter. To this end, first an original ontological concept similarity algorithm in a semantic net will be proposed taking multiple concept relations into consideration, particularly fuzzy-weighed relations between concepts. Then, this algorithm will be employed to promote computing the similarity of semantic web services.

3.2 Ontologies in the SWS Context

3.2.1 Ontology Levels

Guarino [10] suggested to use different generality levels of ontologies as shown in Fig. 3.2. *Top-level ontologies* describe very general concepts which are independent of particular problems or domains. *Domain ontologies* describe vocabularies related to generic domains by specializing the concepts introduced by top-level ontologies. *Task ontologies* describe vocabularies related to generic tasks or activities by specializing top-level ontologies. *Application ontologies* finally define the concepts in

Fig. 3.2 Different kinds of
ontologies and their
relationships

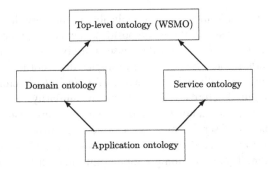

applications often corresponding to rôles played by domain entities while performing certain activities in applications.

For semantic web services, several major generic ontologies have been proposed, such as OWL-S [26] and WSMO [33]. Although they use different conceptual frameworks to model services, they both apply similar approaches for the description of service ontologies and service capabilities [29]. Without lack of generality, we employ WSMO as our generic ontology.

Analogously, we distinguish between the other three ontologies: service ontology ($\mathcal{SO}$), domain ontology ($\mathcal{DO}$), and application ontology ($\mathcal{AO}$). Specifically, the small piece of ontology attached to a service description is named service ontology (and denoted as $\mathcal{SO}$), and usually defined with a certain service ontology language, e.g., OWL [28] or WSML [16]. Any semantic service relates to a specific application. All concepts of an *application ontology* ($\mathcal{AO}$) belong to a specific application domain of services. For example, a *tourism ontology* consists of any concept used by travel-related applications, and may involve the finance domain, transposition domain, and some others. The *domain ontology* generally models a specific domain and represents the particular meanings of terms as they are applied to that domain. Therefore, the relations between these three ontologies are described as:

- An *application ontology* may involve several domain ontologies in order to define a specific application, i.e., $\mathcal{AO} \subset \bigcup_{i=1}^{m} DO_i$, $i, m \in \mathcal{N}$.
- An *application ontology* consists of *service ontologies* of the same kind as the service application, i.e., $\mathcal{AO} \doteq \bigcup_{j=1}^{n} SO_j$, $j, n \in \mathcal{N}$.

3.2.2 Ontologies in WSMO

In order to be independent of any specific web ontology language, we re-considered the definition of ontology structures proposed by [9] as:

Definition 3.1 (Ontology with datatypes) An ontology with datatypes is a structure $O := (C, \leq_C, T, R, \sigma_R, A, I)$ consisting of a set of concepts C aligned in a hierarchy $\leq_C$, a set of relations R, the signature $\sigma_R : R \to C \times C$, a set of datatypes T with type transition functions, sets of attributes A and instances I. For

Table 3.1 Ontology
definition in WSMO

class Ontology
hasConcept **ofType** (0 *) concept
hasRelation **ofType** (0 *) relation
hasAxiom **ofType** (0 *) axiom
hasInstance **ofType** (0 *) instance
class concept **subConceptOf** wsmoElement
hasType **ofType** (1) datatype
hasAttribute **ofType** (0 *) attribute
hasDefinition **ofType** logicExpression
multiplicity = single-valued

a relation $r \in R$, we define its domain by $dom(r) := \pi_1(\sigma_R(r))$ and its range by $range(r) := \pi_2(\sigma_R(r))$.

Definition 3.2 (Ontology knowledge base) A knowledge base is a quadruple $\mathcal{KB} := \{\mathcal{O}, \mathcal{I}, inst, instr\}$ consisting of an ontology $\mathcal{O}$, a set $\mathcal{I}$ of instances, a function concept instantiation $inst : \mathcal{C} \to 2^{\mathcal{I}}$ called concept instantiation, and a relation instantiation function $instr : \mathcal{R} \to 2^{\mathcal{I} \times \mathcal{I}}$.

Table 3.1 shows Definition 3.1 expressed in WSMO. Based on this, the similarity of two ontology concepts can be measured by counting their concept relations, concept types, attributes and instances. The similarity of concept instances, however, is out of this chapter's scope.

3.3 An Ontology-Based Selection Framework of SWSs

Our work is motivated by the question of how to select semantic web services. On one side there is a user defining service requirements in S_R (say, a *WSMO-goal* in the WSMO framework), and on the other side there are already many available candidate services, $S_{A_1}, S_{A_2}, \ldots, S_{A_n}$ published, (say, *WSMO-web services*). As shown on the right-hand side of Fig. 3.3, a service selection engine compares each pair (S_R, S_{A_i}), $i \in \mathcal{N}$ by matching/filtering their *non-functional* (including service qualities) and *functional* service requirements with service advertisements, and ranks them by semantic similarity.

The current service selection approaches are, however, mostly based on the assumption that all service descriptions use a single ontology. Unfortunately, this assumption is unrealistic in real-world scenarios when services are free to use their own ontologies. Thus, the interoperation of heterogeneous ontologies is a big challenge in selecting, as well as in composing and discovering semantic services.

In Fig. 3.3, the part on the left-hand side presents a component for building an application ontology as solution to the problem of integrating services with different ontologies. This issue has been addressed in detail in [37], and will be briefly

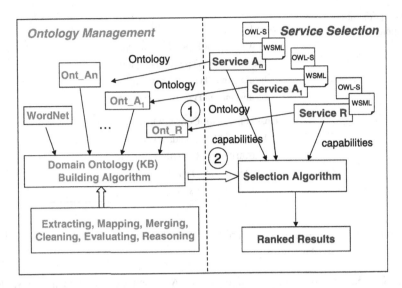

Fig. 3.3 Ontology-based framework for selecting semantic services

outlined in Sect. 3.3.1. In a nutshell, the output of step (2) is the application on-tology ($\mathcal{AO}$), which can be used by the *selection algorithm* as a common ontol-ogy. In fact, the *Application Ontology Building* component is transparent to ser-vice providers and users when service descriptions would deem using one single ontology inappropriate. This approach of building an application ontology reduces misunderstandings between services descriptions and prevents difficulties in service interoperation.

3.3.1 Building Application Ontologies

Assuming that a set of semantic web services is from the same application domain, $S_{A_1}, S_{A_2}, \ldots, S_{A_n}$, $n \in \mathcal{N}$, and SO_i is the service ontology of S_{A_i}, $i \leq n$, then the application ontology ($\mathcal{AO}$) is defined as $\mathcal{AO} = \bigcup_{i=1}^{n} \{SO_i | \mathcal{W}\}$, where $\mathcal{W}$ denotes WordNet (in our algorithm, WordNet is used as the knowledge base to retrieve con-cepts/concept relations and for word sense disambiguation). Building $\mathcal{AO}$ is an it-erative process [37], which consists of

1. Loading $\mathcal{AO}$. If $\mathcal{AO} = NIL$, then initialize $\mathcal{AO}_0 = \emptyset$.
2. Importing a service ontology SO_i ($1 \leq i \leq n$), and re-organizing it into the on-tology structure defined in Table 3.1.
3. Preprocessing each concept of SO_i through WordNet. The possible operations include:

   • word sense disambiguation by *WSD Algorithm*;

- extracting concept *synonymy, hyponymy,* and *meronymy* by the *WordNet Concept Extraction Algorithm (WCEA)*;
- adding the retrieved information to $\mathcal{SO}_i$ and obtaining a new $\mathcal{SO}_i'$.

4. Merging $\mathcal{SO}_i'$ and $\mathcal{AO}_{i-1}$ by following seven rules defined in the *WordNet Ontology Merging Algorithm (WOMA)*. It addresses the way how to merge/copy/add/delete concepts and remove concepts conflicts. Finally, this yields a new $\mathcal{AO}_i$.
5. Managing the application ontology $\mathcal{AO}_i$ by removing conflicts, updating, and storing.
6. Steps 2 through 5 are repeated until $i = n$; then the building process is stopped.

3.4 Semantic Net with Multiple Concept Relations

As we have mentioned in Sect. 3.2, in the context of semantic web services an $\mathcal{AO}$ may involve several $\mathcal{DO}$s to describe a certain application. Therefore, $\mathcal{AO}$ cannot intuitively be structured in a hierarchical tree-like fashion, which can only express the strict superconcept and subconcept relations of a single domain, but as a semantic net with any possible concept relations.

Here, we extend the *relation* as defined in Table 3.1 by four concept relations, viz., *Specialization/Generalization* (or "*is-a*"), *Meronym/Holonym* (or "*is-a-part-of*"), *Hyponym/Hypernym*(or "*is-a-kind-of*"), and *Similar* (which contains *Synonym*). Although *Generalization* generalizes *Holonym* and *Hypernym*, we still keep the *Generalization* relation, because it is inherited from its original service ontology during the ontology merging process, and how to specify them is out of our work's scope. The relations *Holonym, Hypernym* and *Synonym* are the new concept relations retrieved from WordNet during the process of building $\mathcal{AO}$.

Using multiple types of concept relations in a semantic net, the $\mathcal{AO}$ is represented by a fuzzy-weighted graph [6] $\tilde{G} = (V, E, \tilde{c})$, which consists of a set V of nodes v_i and a binary relation E of edges $e_k = (v_i, v_j) \in V \times V$, where $head(e_k) = v_i$ and $tail(e_k) = v_j$. Each edge is associated with a weight, say $\tilde{c}_{i,j} = \tilde{c}(v_i, v_j)$, $\tilde{c}_{i,j} \in \tilde{c}$. Then, an edge with its relation $r_k \to v_i \times v_j$, $r_k \in R$, is represented as a tuple $\langle v_i, v_j, r_k, \tilde{c}_{ij} \rangle$. In this case, there are four types of concept relations, which are specified as $R = \{r_s, r_i, r_m, r_h\}$, and their respective relation weights are $\tilde{c} = \{\tilde{c}_s, \tilde{c}_i, \tilde{c}_m, \tilde{c}_h\}$. In Fig. 3.4, for instance, the triple $\langle 8, 6, s, \tilde{c}_s \rangle$ on edge $e_{8,6}$ shows that concepts C_8 and C_6 have a *specialization* relation with weight $\tilde{c}_s$.

Also, a path p from node v_i to v_j is defined in this semantic net as $p = \{v_0, v_1, v_2, \ldots, v_l\}$ (where v_0 denotes v_i as the start of the path, and v_l denotes v_j) with l edges. Therefore, the weights' sum of the path is defined as $wp = \sum \tilde{c}_k l_k$, where $k \in \{s, h, m, i\}$, $\tilde{c}_k$ is the weight value of relation k, and l_k is the number of relations k of this path.

All the relation weights are between 0 and 1, which are parameters given by users or derived from experiments testing with concrete datasets of the application domain. Then, the weights' sum of a path between two concepts is considered as measure of two concepts' similarity.

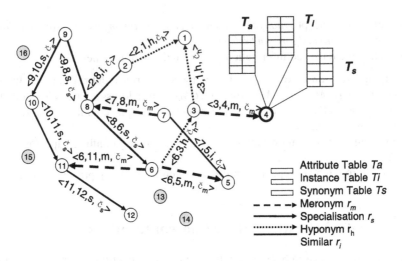

Fig. 3.4 Conceptual ontological semantic net

As shown in Fig. 3.4, a semantic net with 16 connected nodes and 4 isolated nodes (in *grey* color) is depicted. The semantic net has 4 concept relations, *Specialization* (depicted as a solid direct edge, r_s), *Meronym* (depicted as a dashed direct edge, r_m), *Hyponym* (as a dotted direct edge, r_h), and *Similar* (r_i) depicted as a line annotated with a similarity value $sim(c_1, c_2) \in [0, 1]$. If $sim(c_1, c_2) = 1$, then two concepts c_1, c_2 are synonyms; if $sim(c_1, c_2) = 0$, then they are completely dissimilar. Each concept c_i may have attribute table T_{Ai}, instance table T_{Ii}, and a synonym table T_{Si}.

3.4.1 Ontological Concept Similarity Algorithm (OCSA)

In the context of semantic web services, concept similarity is calculated both from the point of view of ontology structure, in which *conceptual distance* is the shortest path between two linked concepts in the semantic net of hierarchical relations, as $Distance_s$, and from the point of view of ontology information content, i.e., the more properties two concepts have in common, the more closely related they are, as $Distance_c$ [4, 17, 19, 32].

Agreeing with Rada's statement [30] "*Distance is a metric on the sets of concepts (single and compound) defined on a semantic net*", we propose a novel algorithm as:

$$Distance(c_1, c_2) = w_s \cdot Distance_s(c_1, c_2) + w_c \cdot Distance_c(c_1, c_2), \quad (1)$$

where c_1 and c_1 are two concepts of semantic nets, and w_s and w_c are, respectively, the weights of structure similarity and content similarity, and $w_s + w_c = 1$.

From the structural point of view, concept similarity does not depend on the path length (l) together with concept depth (h) and density (d) of ontologies as proposed in [18]. In our semantic net, it relates to path length and ontology concept depth, which is defined as $sim(c_1, c_2) = f(l, d)$. As a metric, the function $f(x, y)$ must have properties such as (1) $f(x, x) = 0$ (reflexivity), (2) $f(x, y) = f(y, x)$ (symmetry), and (3) $f(x, y) \geq 0$ (non-negativity). This function does not, however, satisfy the triangular inequality as discussed in [30], because there is more than one single relation involved in our case.

When various concept relations exist in the semantic net, then different tags should be assigned to different links to indicate the importance (or strength) of the links between connected concept nodes. In Fig. 3.4, for example, element $\langle 8, 6, s, \tilde{c}_s \rangle$ on edge $e_{8,6}$ shows that concepts c_8 and c_6 have a *Specialization* relation with weight $\tilde{c}_s$. Then, we assume that semantic relatedness or semantic distance of concepts is measured by weight values on their paths, which is unrelated to the number of directed edges connecting concept nodes, i.e., the edge length has no semantic meaning in our context. According to this discussion, we define *Distance*$_s$ as

$$Distance_s(c_1, c_2) = f(f_1(l), f_2(d)) \tag{2}$$

where f_1 and f_2 are two functions related to path and ontology structure, respectively. The characteristics of this semantic net is that, when the path of two concepts tends to infinity, the similarity tends to 0; otherwise the similarity tends to 1. Hence, we take an exponential function to define

$$f_1(l) = e^{-wp} = e^{-\sum \tilde{c}_k l_k}. \tag{3}$$

If only one relation is considered, then $f_1(l) = e^{-\tilde{c} \cdot l}$, which is consistent with [9].

Furthermore, we propose a simplified method to compute the shortest path. If the similarity between two concepts on a path has been evaluated to be "small", we do not consider such path as valid for our approach. Therefore, we define that a concept similarity value should not be less than a threshold τ. We set $\tau = 0.2$ and then consider equation (3): $e^{-0.8 \cdot l} = 0.2$, then $l \doteq 2.012$ when $\tilde{c}_s = 0.8$ (the similarity between a concept and its superclass is assumed to be 0.8). Therefore, in our approach we assign $l = 3$ corresponding to human intuition, i.e., if two concepts are similar, their distance is not too high.

If there is no path between nodes c_i and c_j in the semantic net, but instead there is a common superconcept that subsumes the two concepts being compared, then the conceptual similarity can be measured based on the maximum depth (h) to their common parent node. This is also possible for our approach, however, we consider 4 different relations. Thus, we use the function of [9] as $f_2(h) = \frac{e^{\beta h} - e^{-\beta h}}{e^{\beta h} + e^{-\beta h}}$.

In summary, based on (2),

$$Distance_s(c_1, c_2) := \begin{cases} e^{-\sum \tilde{c}_k l_k} \cdot \frac{e^{\beta h} - e^{-\beta h}}{e^{\beta h} + e^{-\beta h}}, & c_1 \neq c_2, \\ 1, & \text{otherwise} \end{cases} \tag{4}$$

where $\beta \geq 0$ is a parameter used to scale the contribution of depth h in a concept hierarchy. Consistent with previous work, equation (4) considers the shortest path and concept depth of their common superconcept.

From the point view of information content held by concepts, if concepts have rich information as concept attributes, instances and given synonyms, then the concept distance is measured as

$$Distance_c(c_1, c_2) = \frac{|c_1 \cap c_2|}{|c_1 \cap c_2| + \gamma|c_1/c_2| + (1-\gamma)|c_2/c_1|} \tag{5}$$

where $|c_1 \cap c_2|$ is the intersection of the two concepts indicating the concepts' common characteristics and $|c_2/c_1|$ is their difference; $|\ |$ is the cardinality of a concept information set, and γ $(0 \leq \gamma \leq 1)$ is a weight that defines the relative importance of concepts' non-common characteristics.

3.4.2 Algorithm and Implementation

To test the quality and feasibility of our proposed algorithm under various real-world conditions, we built an experimental prototype, the *wsao* tool (web service application ontology, at http://wsao.deri.ie).

As shown in Table 3.2, several methods have been defined to calculate the similarity of any two concepts of $\mathcal{AO}$. If a concept is an isolated node, then the concept similarity is $s = 0$, according to Method 1. If two concepts are not isolated nodes, then Method 2 is used to count any possible paths between them, and Method 5 is applied to calculate the distance of each path. Methods 3 and 4 are used when two concepts have a common parent, and finally return their distance. Method 6 computes, from the point of view of ontology structure, the sum distance, and the shortest path is taken as their distance. Method 7 calculates concept distance from the point of view of concept information. Method 8 yields the final similarity of two concepts.

In the subalgorithm, a method of counting paths between two concepts is listed, say $path(c_1, c_2)$. This method goes through the loop from line 2 to 6 to track and mine any possible indirected relations between concepts c_1, c_2 and their related concepts which are the ones collected into the array lists $rs1[\ ][\ ]$ and $rs2[\ ][\ ]$. Basing on the optimization policy, $l = 3$, the loop then only needs to run once as Table 3.2 shows.

We have built an experimental prototype. Figure 3.5 shows the part of building a zip-related application ontology. The input is a zip-related service ontology. Referring to WordNet, there are 2 more meronym relations and 11 more synonym relations. Figure 3.6 shows the ranked result of concept similarity simulated by our algorithm. It imports the relations of concepts (where concepts are indexed by numbers), and considers the shortest path of concepts involving different relations. All relation weights are set between 0.8 and 0.95 as recommended in [12]. In Fig. 3.7 an example of a *zip-related* application ontology is visualized by the *wsao* tool. It has four types of concept relations, and different relation types are indicated by different colors. It also has concept attributes (blue rectangles) and instances (green triangles) attached to concepts.

Table 3.2 Concept similarity algorithm

	Algorithm: Semantic net based *OCSA*

Inputs: Concepts c_1, c_2, and the application ontology $\mathcal{AO}$;

Output: The concept *similarity s* of concepts c_1 and c_2;

Initialization: Relation weights $\tilde{c}_s, \tilde{c}_h, \tilde{c}_m \in (0, 1), \tilde{c}_i = 1.0$;

Methods:

1. *isolated(c)*;
   // If one concept is an isolated node, then $s = 0.0$.
2. *path*(c_1, c_2);
   // Calculate paths between c_1 and c_1.
3. *hasParent*(c_1, c_2);
   // If there is no path between c_1 and c_2, but they
   // have a common parent, the depth h is the
   // maximum number of edges to the parent concept.
4. *similarityD*(c_1, c_2, h);
   // Calculate concept similarity by depth h.
5. *similarityR*$(c_1, c_2, path_i)$; $(i \in \{1, \dots, k\})$
   // If there are k paths between concepts c_1 and c_2,
   // then calculate the similarity of each path.
6. *similarityS*$(c_1, c_2) = \max(similarityR) \cdot similarityD$;
7. *similarityC*(c_1, c_1);
   // Check the similarity of c_1 and c_2 by their
   // common attributes and instances.
8. $s = w_s \cdot similarityS + w_c \cdot similarityC$;

Subalgorithm of ***path***(c_1, c_2);

1. if (*similar*(c_1, c_2) == true) then path[i];
2. rs1 [ ][ ] = *relationSet*(c_1);
3. rs2 [ ][ ] = *relationSet*(c_2);
4. if (*linkBySimilar*(rs1, rs2) = true) then pathS[j];
5. else if (*linkByRelation*(rs1, rs2) == true)
6. then pathR[k];
7. pathNumber = $i + j + k$;

3.4.3 Service Similarity

In the selection model for semantic web services proposed in [36] service similarity is based on ontological concept similarities measured by *non-functional, functional*, and *quality* properties. Concept similarity was defined there as $sim(c_i, c_j) = \{f(c_i, c_j) \mid c_i \in SO_i \land c_j \in SO_j\}$, where $f(c_i, c_j) = dis(c_i, c_j)$. As in [30], the fol-

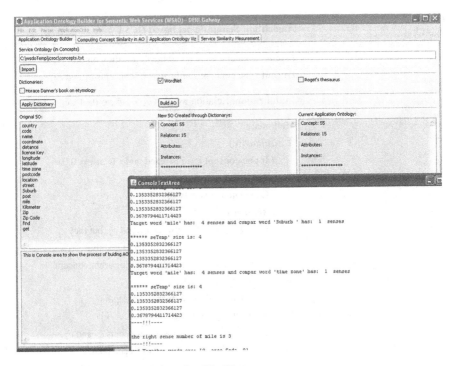

Fig. 3.5 Building a zip-related $\mathcal{AO}$ using WordNet

lowing three cases are distinguished to calculate concept distances in the context of semantic services:

1. If concepts c_i and c_j are single concept terms, e.g., *Zip* and *Code*, then

$$dis(c_i, c_j) = \text{the shortest distance between } c_i \text{ and } c_j. \tag{6}$$

2. If concepts c_i and c_j are compound or conjunctive ones, e.g., *CalcDisTwo-ZipsKm* or *findZipCodeDistance*, then $Distance(c_i, c_j)$ is defined as

$$dis(x_1 \wedge \cdots \wedge x_k, y_1 \wedge \cdots \wedge y_m) = \frac{1}{km} \sum_{i=1}^{k} \sum_{j=1}^{m} dis(x_i, y_j), \tag{7}$$

where $\{x_1, x_2, \ldots, x_k\}$ are subconcepts of c_i and $\{y_1, y_2, \ldots, y_k\}$ are subconcepts of c_j, e.g., *CalcDisTwoZipsKm* = {*Calculate, Distance, Two, Zip, Kilometer*}.

3. If only one concept C_i or C_j is conjunctive, then $dis(c_i, c_j)$ is defined as

$$dis(x_1 \wedge \cdots \wedge x_k, c_j) = \frac{1}{k} \sum_{m=1}^{k} dis(x_m, c_j). \tag{8}$$

Based on these, we propose an ontology-based method to determine similarity of semantic web services as

$$sim_{Service} = \sum sim_{Concept} + \sum sim_{Operation}, \tag{9}$$

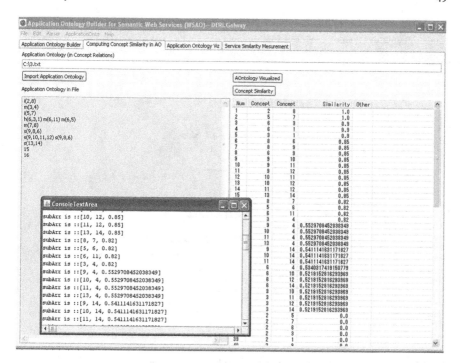

Fig. 3.6 Ranked result of concept similarity

where the summations are extended over the similarities of all service concepts, and the similarities of the operation parameters with their data types, respectively.

3.5 Experimental Evaluation and Discussion

A test-bed for service selection has also been set up as part of the *wsao* tool aiming to evaluate our approach. The test dataset is similar to the ones used in [8, 14, 15, 38, 39]. Web services for this dataset are initially modeled as OWL-S services, and each of them consists of five documents, viz., *_service.owl*, *_profile.owl*, *_process.owl*, *_Grounding.owl*, and *_Concepts.owl*, and its *WSDL* file.

First, we needed to prepare the data by translating them from OWL-Lite into WSML-DL. Basing on Definition 3.1, we defined some translation rules as shown in Table 3.3. Finally, we obtained 17 valid *zip*-related services in the WSML language. During the translation process several problems were encountered:

1. The real semantic information provided by service *_Concepts.owl* is not well modeled with respect to OWL syntax which, in turn, limits the possibilities of service matching. In particular, definitions of many concepts are missing, and some concepts are not well defined. For example, a concept "*city*" is defined as *concept* and *relation* at the same time.

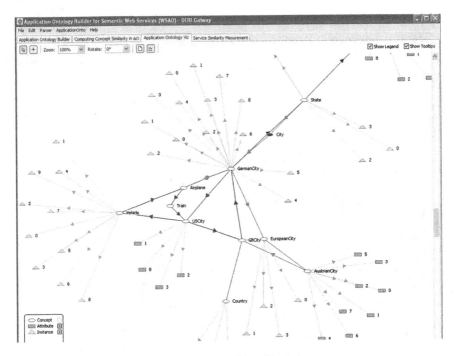

Fig. 3.7 Ontology visualization of semantic net with multi-relations

Table 3.3 Translation from OWL-Lite to WSML-DL

concept	*owl:class*
	rdf:domain
type	*rdf:datatypes*
cardinality	*owl:cardinality*
attribute	*owl:ObjectProperty*
	owl:DatatypeProperty
	rdf:Property
	rdfs:subPropertyOf
axiom	*owl:Restriction*
	owl:subClassOf
	owl:allValuesFrom
	owl:someValuesFrom
synonym (relation)	*owl:equivalentClass*
synonym (relation)	*owl:sameAs*
specialization (relation)	*owl:subClassOf*
instances	*owl:individuals*

Table 3.4 Data collection

	Initial dataset	New dataset
Normal concepts	39	46
Composite concepts	76	67
Concepts (Attributes)	30 (79)	28 (74)
Relation types	2	4
Relations	47	29
Service names	17	17
Service operations (Messages)	59 (118)	59 (118)

2. Only a limited number of modeling constructs is used in _Concepts.owl, such as *owl:class*, *owl:ObjectProperty*, *owl:DatatypeProperty*, *rdfs:range*, *rdfs:domain*, *rdfs:sub*, *ClassOf*, and *rdfs:subPropertyOf*. They are translated to *concept*, *sub-ConceptOf*, *attribute*, and *type* in WSML-DL.

This modeling deficiency of practical service ontologies was out of our expectation, and increases the difficulties in evaluation. Most likely, this problem is caused by semantic services being created by service providers who often lack ontology engineering skills. It also shows that a uniform formal application ontology is necessary for semantic web services to be modeled.

After translation and several manual cleanings (e.g., deleting meaningless concepts), we obtained 17 service ontologies in WSML-DL. Applying the ontology building algorithm described in [37] yielded an application ontology of *zip* services. Table 3.4 shows the initial and the new dataset. In the initial one, there are many compound concepts, and the two relation types defined are *Specialization* and *Hyponym*. These 17 services have 59 service operations and 118 input/output messages. In the new dataset, the number of concepts, of concepts with attributes, and of concept relations is higher, because our algorithm separates compound concepts into terms, and uses WordNet to identify more relations, such as *Synonym*, *Meronym*, and *Hyponym*.

We focus on the 17 *zip-related* services in the application domain as listed in Table 3.5, and carried out two types of experiments with our similarity algorithm: (1) name-based service similarity and (2) operations-based service similarity. We calculated the parameters precision and recall by comparing them with the manually generated results. In Table 3.6, our results are compared with the average precisions and recalls of similar work [15]. In these experiments we assumed that 4 concept relations have the same weights of 0.85. Although using weights weakens the different influences of multiple relations, we selected this set-up to provide feasible results for comparison with the precision/recall of related work.

As shown in Table 3.6 and Fig. 3.8 our method renders good results. The main reasons are that (1) our similarity evaluation is not limited to small pieces of ontologies but uses a well structured application ontology with enriched semantics, (2) our ontology-based service similarity is based on multiple concept relations, and

Table 3.5 Experimental data

Service name	Service operations
ZipCode	ZipCodeToCityState
	CityToZipCode
	CityStateToZipCode
	ZipCodeToAreaCode
	ZipCodeToTimeZone
	CityStateToAreaCode
ZipCodeService	findZipCodeDistance
	findZipCoordinates
	findZipDetails
	getCodeSet
DistanceService	getLocation
	getState
	getCity
	getDistance
	getLatitude
	getLongitude
...	...

Table 3.6 Parameters precision and recall

	Recall (average)	Precision (average)	F-measure
Keyword-based [15]	19.8%	16.4%	23.7%
Semantic matching of [27]	62.6%	63.2%	62.89
Interface-based [15]	78.2%	71%	74.43
Our approach in service names	100%	76.47%	86.66%
Our approach in service operations	70.24%	88.06%	78.15%

that (3) our method correctly deals with compound concepts which are often used in the context of semantic web services.

3.6 Related Work

Measuring concept similarity of ontologies, taxonomies, or schemas has widely been studied in the fields of ontology engineering, information retrieval, and database schema matching. Generally, different approaches have been applied to measure the semantic similarity of objects, which are organized in hierarchical ontology structures. They can be classified into the two categories [13] edge-based

Fig. 3.8 Comparison of
experimental results

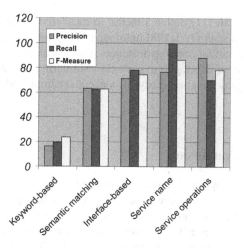

approach [17] (measuring a shorter path from one node to another) and node-based
approach [32] (measuring the amount of shared information content).

There is plenty of related work on ontology mapping, integration, merging, and
alignment [5]. Although these researches use different mechanisms (e.g., generating
a new ontology from two or more original ones, creating mappings between original
ontologies, or schema matching), different measurement methods (e.g., Bayesian
net [25], vector space [35], similarity matrix [7, 21], cosine distance [22]), and different metrics (distance, scores, measure degree, or a set of bridge rules using $\supseteq$,
$\subseteq$, $\equiv$, $*$ (related), $\perp$ (unrelated) [3]), they basically take ontology mapping as foundation, i.e., they use calculated concept similarity to find mapping pairs of concepts
between ontologies.

In the field of information retrieval, Bernstein et al. [2] present five different distance measures for ontologies, where *ontology distance* considers the shortest path
through a common ancestor in a directed acyclic graph. However, the computational
degree and weights of edges are not considered. The *vector space approaches* [1,
24, 34] computing cosine or Euclidean distances of k-dimensional vectors do not
easily apply to nominal concepts, as it is difficult to represent plenty of concepts
as computable vectors. The *Full-text Retrieval Method* (TF/IDF) is mostly used in
information retrieval [1, 34] to compare entire documents considered as bags of
words. For structured concepts, however, it is inadequate as semantic relations between concepts are ignored. In contrast to this, our approach combines structure-
and information-based methods to measure similarity in the context of semantic
services.

There is some related work on schema matching, e.g., [23, 31], which focuses on
finding the matching pairs between two schemas. Its basic idea is that "two nodes
match if nodes in their neighborhood also match". We argue that such structure-
depended approach without semantic consideration is not efficient enough. Related
work in the field of the semantic web or semantic web services is [8, 11] and [20].
Maedche et al. [20] propose an approach to cluster ontology-based concepts, using the hierarchical clustering algorithm to consider instances of concept similarity.

Hau et al. [11] define a metric to measure the similarity of semantic services annotated with OWL [28] ontologies. They use an information-theoretic approach to match similar ontology instances. Dong et al. [8] compute the common information content of ontologies to scale their similarity. In summary, most of these researches disregard the complexity of concept relations and the deficiencies of information content.

3.7 Conclusion

A novel approach based on application ontologies is proposed to improve the selection of semantic web services. After building an application ontology by merging semantic service ontologies, we represent this application ontology as a fuzzy-weighted semantic net with multiple ontological concept relations, and calculate formal/compound concept similarity on it. The ontological concept similarity is finally used to calculate similarity of semantic services. We have built a prototype to evaluate our work, and the experiments performed show that our approach is very effective as compared to related work.

References

1. Baeza-Yates, R., Ribeiro-Neto, B.: Modern Information Retrieval. ACM, New York (1999)
2. Bernstein, A., Kaufmann, E., Buerki, C., Klein, M.: How similar is it? Towards personalized similarity measures in ontologies. In: Proc. Intl. Tagung Wirtschaftsinformatik (2005)
3. Bouquet, P., Serafini, L., Zanobini, S.: Semantic coordination: A new approach and an application. In: Proc. 2nd Intl. Semantic Web Conf (2003)
4. Budanitsky, A., Hirst, G.: Semantic distance in WordNet: An experimental, application-oriented evaluation of five measures. In: Proc. Workshop on WordNet and Other Lexical Resources (2001)
5. Choi, N., Song, I., Han, H.: A survey on ontology mapping. SIGMOD Record 35(3), 34–41 (2006)
6. Cornelis, C., de Kesel, P., Kerre, E.E.: Information retrieval based on conceptual distance in IS-A hierarchies. International Journal of Intelligent Systems 19(11), 1051–1068 (2004)
7. Doan, A., Madhavan, J., Dhamankar, R., Domingos, P., Halevy, A.: Learning to match ontologies on the semantic web. VLDB Journal 12(4), 303–319 (2003)
8. Dong, X., Alon, Y., Madhavan, J., Nemes, E., Zhang, J.: Similarity search for web services. In: Proc. VLDB (2004)
9. Ehrig, M., Haase, P., Hefke, M., Stojanovic, N.: Similarity for ontologies—a comprehensive framework. In: Proc. ECIS (2005)
10. Guarino, N.: Formal ontology and information systems. In: Guarino, N. (ed.) Formal Ontology in Information Systems. IOS Press, Amsterdam (1998)
11. Hau, J., Lee, W., Darlington, J.: A semantic similarity measure for semantic web services. In: Proc. WWW2005 (2005)
12. Jarmasz, M., Szpakowicz, S.: Roget's thesaurus and semantic similarity. In: Proc. Conf. on Recent Advances in Natural Language Processing (2003)
13. Jong, K., Candan, K.: CP/CV: Concept similarity mining without frequency information from domain describing taxonomies. In: Proc. CIKM (2006)
14. Kokash, N.: A comparison of web service interface similarity measures. In: Proc. European Starting AI Researcher Symposium (2006)

15. Kuang, L., Deng, S.G., Li, Y., Shi, W., Wu, Z.H.: Exploring semantic technologies in service matchmaking. In: Proc. ECOWS (2005)
16. Lausen, H., de Bruijn, J., Polleres, A., Fensel, D.: WSML—a language framework for semantic web services. In: Proc. W3C Workshop on Rule Languages for Interoperability (2005)
17. Lee, J.H., Kim, H., Lee, Y.J.: Information retrieval based on conceptual distance in IS-A hierarchies. Journal of Documentation **49**, 188–207 (1993)
18. Li, Y.H., Bandar, Z., McLean, D.: An approach for measuring semantic similarity between words using multiple information sources. IEEE Transactions on Knowledge and Data Engineering **15**(4), 871–882 (2003)
19. Lin, D.: An information-theoretic definition of similarity. In: Proc. 15th Intl. Conf. on Machine Learning (1998)
20. Maedche, A., Staab, S.: Measuring similarity between ontologies. In: Proc. European Conf. on Knowledge Acquisition and Management (2002)
21. Maedche, A., Motik, B., Stojanovic, L., Studer, R., Volz, R.: Ontologies for enterprise knowledge management. IEEE Intelligent Systems **18**(2), 26–33 (2003)
22. Mao, M.: Ontology mapping: An information retrieval and interactive activation network based approach. In: Proc. 6th Intl. Semantic Web Conf. Lecture Notes in Computer Science, vol. 4825. Springer, Berlin (2007)
23. Milo, T., Zohar, S.: Using schema matching to simplify heterogeneous data translation. In: Proc. Intl. Conf. on Very Large Databases (1998)
24. Mitchell, T.M.: Machine Learning. McGraw-Hill, New York (1997)
25. Mitra, P., Noy, N.F., Jaiswals, A.: OMEN: A probabilistic ontology mapping tool. In: Proc. Intl. Semantic Web Conf (2005)
26. OWL-S: Semantic markup for web services, W3C member submission (2004)
27. Paolucci, M., Kawamura, T., Payne, T., Sycara, K.: Semantic matching of web services capabilities. In: Proc. Intl. Semantic Web Conf. Lecture Notes in Computer Science, vol. 2342. Springer, Berlin (2002)
28. Patel-Schneider, P.F., Hayes, P., Horrocks, I. (eds.): OWL web ontology language semantics and abstract syntax, W3C recommendation (2004)
29. Polleres, A., Lara, R. (eds.): A conceptual comparison between WSMO and OWL-S, WSMO Working Group working draft (2005)
30. Rada, R., Mili, H., Bicknell, E., Blettner, M.: Development and application of a metric on semantic nets. IEEE Transactions on Systems, Man, and Cybernetics **19**(1), 17–30 (1989)
31. Rahm, E., Bernstein, P.: A survey of approaches to automatic schema matching. VLDB Journal **10**(4) (2001)
32. Resnik, P.: Semantic similarity in a taxonomy: An information-based measure and its application to problems of ambiguity in natural language. Journal of Artificial Intelligence Research **11**, 95–130 (1999)
33. Roman, D., Keller, U., Lausen, H., et al.: Web service modeling ontology. Applied Ontology **1**(1), 77–106 (2005)
34. Salton, G., McGill, M.J.: Introduction to Modern Information Retrieval. McGraw-Hill, New York (1983)
35. Tous, R., Delgado, J.: A vector space model for semantic similarity calculation and OWL ontology alignment. In: Bressan, S., Kueng, J., Wagner, R. (eds.) Proc. DEXA. Lecture Notes in Computer Science, vol. 4080. Springer, Berlin (2006)
36. Wang, X., Ding, Y.H., Zhao, Y.: Similarity measurement about ontology-based semantic web services. In: Proc. Ws. on Semantics for Web Services (2006)
37. Wang, X., Vitvar, T., Hauswirth, M., Foxvog, D.: Building application ontologies from descriptions of semantic web services. In: Proc. IEEE/WIC/ACM Intl. Conf. on Web Intelligence (2007)
38. Wang, Y., Stroulia, E.: Semantic structure matching for assessing web service similarity. In: Service-Oriented Computing. Lecture Notes in Computer Science, vol. 2910. Springer, Berlin (2003)
39. Zhuang, Z., Mitra, P., Jaiswal, A.: Corpus-based web services matchmaking. In: Proc. AAAI (2005)

Chapter 4
General-Purpose Computing on a Semantic Network Substrate

Marko A. Rodriguez

Abstract This article presents a model of general-purpose computing on a semantic network substrate. The concepts presented are applicable to any semantic network representation. However, due to the standards and technological infrastructure devoted to the Semantic Web effort, this article is presented from this point of view. In the proposed model of computing, the application programming interface, the run-time program, and the state of the computing virtual machine are all represented in the Resource Description Framework (RDF). The implementation of the concepts presented provides a computing paradigm that leverages the distributed and standardized representational-layer of the Semantic Web.

4.1 Introduction

This article discusses computing in semantic networks. A semantic network [41] is also known as a directed labeled graph or multi-relational network. The thesis of this article is that the state of a computing machine, its low-level instructions, and the executing program can be represented as a semantic network. The computational model that is presented can be instantiated using any semantic network representation. However, given the existence of the Resource Description Framework (RDF) [30, 33] and the popular Web Ontology Language (OWL) [24, 32], this article presents the theory and the application in terms of these constructs.

The computing model that is proposed is perhaps simple in theory, but in application, requires a relatively strong background in computer science. This article discusses a wide breadth of concepts including those from computer architecture, the Semantic Web, and object-oriented programming. In order to accommodate all interested readers, each discipline's concepts will be introduced at a tutorial level in

M.A. Rodriguez (✉)
T-5, Center for Nonlinear Studies, Los Alamos National Laboratory, Los Alamos, NM 87545, USA
e-mail: marko@lanl.gov

Y. Badr et al. (eds.) *Emergent Web Intelligence: Advanced Semantic Technologies,*
Advanced Information and Knowledge Processing,
DOI 10.1007/978-1-84996-077-9_4, © Springer-Verlag London Limited 2010

this introduction. The remainder of the article presents a more in-depth practical application of the proposed model. The practical application includes a specification for an RDF virtual machine architecture (RVM) called Fhat (pronounced făt, like "fat") and an RDF programming language designed specifically for that architecture called Neno (pronounced nēnō, like "knee-know").

The introduction to this article is split into three subsections. Section 4.1.1 provides a brief introduction to the field of computer architecture in order to elucidate those concepts which will be of primary interest later in the article. Section 4.1.2 discusses the Semantic Web and the RDF semantic network data model. Finally, Sect. 4.1.3 provides an overview of object-oriented programming and its relation to OWL.

4.1.1 General-Purpose Computing and the Virtual Machine

A general-purpose computer is one that can support any known computation. The meaning of computability and what is required to compute was first developed by Alan Turning in the late 1930s [43]. Since then, and with the large leaps in the engineering of computing machines, most computers of today are general-purpose computing machines. The two primary components of a computing machine are the central processing unit (CPU) and the main memory (RAM).

The purpose of the CPU is to perform calculations (i.e. execute algorithms on data). Generally, the CPU reads instructions and data from RAM, performs a calculation, and re-inserts its results back into RAM. Most CPUs maintain a relatively small set of instructions that they can execute [19]. Example instructions include add, sub, load, store, branch, goto, etc. However, these primitive instructions can be composed to perform any computing task desired by the programmer.

Currently, the smallest unit of information in a digital computer is the bit. A bit can either be a 0 or a 1. Bits are combined to form bytes (8-bits) and words (machine architecture dependent). Most desktop machines of everyday use have a 32-bit word and are called 32-bit machines. 32-bits can be used to represent 2^{32} different "things". For example, an unsigned 32-bit integer can represent the numbers 0 to 4,294,967,295. While instructions, like data, are represented as a series of 0s and 1s, it is possible to represent the instructions in a more human readable form. The abstraction above binary machine language is called assembly language [11]. For example, the following three assembly instructions

```
load 2, 3
load 1, 2
add 1, 2, 3
store 3, 2
```

instruct the CPU to (1) read the word at memory address 2 in RAM and store it in CPU register 3, (2) read the word at memory address 1 and store it in register 2, (3) add the contents of register 1 and 2 and store the result in register 3, and finally (4) store the word in register 3 into memory address 2 of RAM.

Modern day computer languages are written at a much higher level of abstraction than both machine and assembly language. For instance, the previous instructions could be represented by a single statement as

```
z = y + x
```

where register 1 holds the value of variable y, register 2 holds the value of variable x and memory address 3 holds the value of variable z.

To the modern-day programmer, the low-level CPU instructions are hidden. It is the role of the language compiler to translate the human readable/writable source code into the machine code of the CPU. Simply stated, a compiler is a computer program that translates information written in one language to another language [2]. In practice, the compiler translates the human code to a list of CPU instructions that are stored in RAM and executed by the CPU in sequential order as pointed to by the CPU's program counter (PC). In some instances, the compiler will translate the human code to the native language of the CPU (the instruction set of the CPU). In other cases, the compiler will translate the human code to another language for a virtual machine to compute [14]. Virtual machine language is called byte-code. A virtual machine is, for all practical purposes, a CPU represented in software, not hardware. However, depending on the complexity of the implementation, a virtual machine can either do a hard implementation (where an exact software replica of hardware is instantiated) or a soft implementation (where more of the hardware components are black-boxed in software). The virtual machine computes its byte-code instructions by using the underlying hardware CPU's instruction set. Finally, to complete the computation stack, the CPU relies on the underlying physical laws of nature to compute its instructions. The laws of physics drive the CPU from state to state. The evolution of states and its effects on the world is computing.

Perhaps the most popular virtual machine is the Java virtual machine (JVM) [27] of the Java programming language [16]. The JVM is a piece of software that runs on a physical machine. The JVM has its own instruction set much like a hardware CPU has its own instruction set. The JVM resides in RAM and requires the physical CPU to compute its evolution. Thus, the JVM translates its instructions to the instruction set of the native CPU. The benefit of this model is that irrespective of the underlying hardware CPU, a JVM designed for that CPU architecture can read and process any Java software (i.e. any Java byte-code). The drawback, is that the computation is slower than when instructions are represented as instructions for the native CPU.

4.1.2 The Semantic Web and RDF

The previous section described the most fundamental aspects of computing. This section presents one of the most abstract levels of computing: the Semantic Web. The primary goal of the Semantic Web effort is to provide a standardized framework for describing resources (both physical and conceptual) and their relationships to one another [18]. This framework is called the Resource Description Framework (RDF) [30].[1]

RDF maintains two central tenets. The first states that the lowest unit of representation is the Universal Resource Identifier (URI) [8], the blank node, and the literal (e.g. strings, integers, floating point numbers, etc.). A URI unambiguously identifies a resource. When two resources share the same URI, they are the same resource. However, when two resources do not share the same URI, this does not necessarily mean that they are not the same resource. In practice, URIs are namespaced to ensure that name conflicts do not occur across different organizations [10]. For example, the URI http://www.newspaper.org/Article can have a different meaning, or connotation, than http://www.science.net/Article because they are from different namespaces.[2]

The second tenet of RDF states that URIs and literal values are connected to one another in sets of triples, denoting edges of a directed labeled graph. A triple is the smallest relational fact that can be asserted about the world [42]. For instance, the statement "I am", can be denoted (I, am, I) in triple form. The first element of the triple is called the subject and can be any URI or blank node. The second element is called the predicate, and it can be any URI. Finally, the third element is called the object, and it can be any URI, blank node, or literal. If U is the set of all URIs, B is the set of all blank nodes, and L is the set of all literals, then an RDF network denoted G can be defined as

$$G \subseteq ((U \cup B) \times U \times (U \cup B \cup L)).$$

RDF has attracted commercial and scholarly interest, not only because of the Semantic Web vision, but because RDF provides a unique way of modeling data. This enthusiasm has sparked the development and distribution of various triple store applications dedicated to the storage and manipulation of RDF networks [26]. Some triple stores can support computations on RDF networks that are on the order of 10^{10} triples [1, 22]. A triple store is analogous to a relational database. However, instead of representing data in relational tables, a triple store represents its data as a semantic network. A triple store provides an interface to an RDF network for the purpose of reading from and writing to the RDF network. The most implemented query language is the SPARQL Protocol and RDF Query Language (SPARQL— pronounced spär-kel, like "sparkle") [36]. SPARQL, loosely, is a hybrid of both SQL (a relational database language) and Prolog (a logic programming language) [29]. As an example, the following SPARQL query returns all URIs that are both a type of ex:CognitiveScientist and ex:ComputerScientist.

```
SELECT ?x
WHERE {
```

---

[1] Note that RDF is a data model, not a syntax. RDF has many different syntaxes like RDF/XML [30], Notation 3 (N3) [6], the N-TRIPLE format [5], and TRiX [12].

[2] For the sake of brevity, prefixes are usually used instead of the full namespace. For instance, http://www.w3.org/1999/02/22-rdf-syntax-ns# is prefixed as rdf:.

Fig. 4.1 An example RDF network

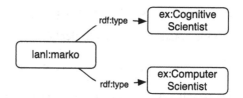

```
?x <rdf:type> <ex:ComputerScientist> .
?x <rdf:type> <ex:CognitiveScientist> }
```
The example SPARQL query will bind the variable ?x to all URIs that are the subject of the triples with a predicate of rdf:type and objects of ex:Computer-Scientist and ex:CognitiveScientist. For the example RDF network diagrammed in Fig. 4.1, ?x would bind to lanl:marko. Thus, the query above would return lanl:marko.[3]

The previous query can be represented in its more set theoretic sense as

$$X = \{?x \mid (?x, \text{rdf}:\text{type}, \text{ex}:\text{ComputerScientist}) \in G$$

$$\wedge (?x, \text{rdf}:\text{type}, \text{ex}:\text{CognitiveScientist}) \in G\},$$

where X is the set of URIs that bind to ?x and G is the RDF network represented as an edge list. The above syntax's meaning is: "X is the set of all elements ?x such that ?x is the head of the triple ending with rdf:type, ex:ComputerScientist and the head of the triple ending with rdf:type, CognitiveScientist, where both triples are in the triple list G". Only recently has there been a proposal to extend SPARQL to support writing and deleting triples to and from an RDF network. SPARQL/Update [38] can be used to add the fact that lanl:marko is also an rdf:type of ex:Human.

```
INSERT { <lanl:marko> <rdf:type> <ex:Human> .}
```

In a more set theoretic notation, this statement is equivalent to

$$G = G \cup (\text{lanl}:\text{marko}, \text{rdf}:\text{type}, \text{ex}:\text{Human}).$$

The meaning of the previous statement is: "Set the triple list G to the current triple list G unioned with the triple (lanl:marko, rdf:type, ex:Human). Finally, it is possible to remove a triple using SPARQL/Update. For instance,

---

[3]Many triple store applications support reasoning about resources during a query (at run-time). For example, suppose that the triple (lanl:marko, rdf:type, ex:ComputerScientist) does not exist in the RDF network, but instead there exist the triples (lanl:marko, rdf:type, ex:ComputerEngineer) and (ex:ComputerEngineer, owl:sameAs, ex:ComputerScientist). With OWL reasoning, ?x would still bind to lanl:marko because ex:ComputerEngineer and ex:ComputerScientist are the same according to OWL semantics. The RDF computing concepts presented in this article primarily focus on triple pattern matching and thus, beyond direct URI and literal name matching, no other semantics are used.

```
DELETE { <ex:I> <ex:am> <ex:I> . }
```

In set theoretic notation, this is equivalent to

$$G = G \setminus (\texttt{ex:I}, \texttt{ex:am}, \texttt{ex:I}),$$

where the meaning is: "Set the triple list G to the current triple list G minus the triple $(\texttt{ex:I}, \texttt{ex:am}, \texttt{ex:I})$".

4.1.3 Object-Oriented Programming and OWL

OWL is an ontology modeling language represented completely in RDF. In OWL, it is possible to model abstract classes and their relationships to one another as well as to use these models and the semantics of OWL to reason about unspecified relationships. In OWL semantics, if ex:Human is a class and there exists the triple (lanl:marko, rdf:type, ex:Human), then lanl:marko is considered an instance of ex:Human. The URI ex:Human is part of the ontology-level of the RDF network and the URI lanl:marko is part of the instance-level (also called the individual-level) of the RDF network. In OWL, it is possible to state that all ex:Humans can have another ex:Human as a friend. This is done by declaring an owl:ObjectProperty named ex:hasFriend that has an rdfs:domain of ex:Human and an rdfs:range of ex:Human. Furthermore, it is possible to restrict the cardinality of the ex:hasFriend property and thus, state that an ex:Human can have no more than one friend.[4] This is diagrammed in Fig. 4.2.[5]

A class specification in object-oriented programming is called an application programming interface (API) [39]. OWL ontologies share some similarities to the object-oriented API. However, OWL ontologies also differ in many respects. OWL is a description logic language that is primarily focused on a means by which to reason on RDF data, where reasoning is determining which instances are subsumed by which descriptions. An object-oriented API is primarily focused on concretely defining classes and their explicit relationships to one another and is thus, more in line with the frames modeling paradigm [44]. Furthermore, OWL ontologies can contain instances (i.e. individuals), allow for multiple inheritance, do not support the unique name assumption, nor the closed world assumption [35, 44].

---

[4]This is interpreted in OWL semantics as saying: "A human is something that has a single human as a friend." In OWL, given that it is a description logic [4], an ontology defines descriptions and the purpose of the OWL reasoner is to determine which instances are subsumed by which descriptions.

[5]In this article, ontology diagrams will not explicitly represent the constructs rdfs:domain, rdfs:range, nor the owl:Restriction anonymous URIs. These URIs are assumed to be apparent from the diagram. For example, the restriction shown as [0..1] in Fig. 4.2 is represented by an owl:Restriction for the ex:hasFriend property where the owl:maxCardinality is 1 and ex:Human is an rdfs:subClassOf of this owl:Restriction.

Fig. 4.2 An ontology and an instance is represented in an RDF network

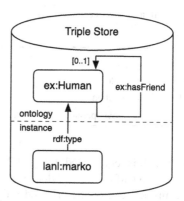

Another aspect of OWL that differs from object-oriented APIs is that object-oriented APIs include the concept of a method. The method is an algorithmic "behavior" that forms the foundation of the evolutionary processes that drive the instances of these classes from state to state. One of the primary purposes of this article is to introduce an OWL ontology for modeling methods and their low-level machine instructions. While process information can be represented in Frame Logic (i.e. F-Logic) [21] as well as other rule languages such as the Semantic Web Rule Language (SWRL) [20], this article is primarily interested in modeling methods in much the same way that they are represented in modern day object-oriented languages such as Java and C++. This modeling is in terms of their syntax, semantics, and low-level representation.

In Java and C++, a method is defined for a class and is used to manipulate the properties (called fields) of an instance of that class. For example,

```
class Human {
  Human hasFriend;
  void makeFriend(Human h) {
    this.hasFriend = h;
  }
}
```

declares that there exists an abstract class called Human. A Human has one field called hasFriend. The hasFriend field refers to an object of type Human. Furthermore, according to the class declaration, a Human has a method called makeFriend. The makeFriend method takes a single argument that is of type Human and sets its hasFriend field to the Human provided in the argument. The this keyword makes explicit that the hasFriend field is the field of the object for which the makeFriend method was invoked.

In many object-oriented languages, an instance of Human is created with the new operator. For instance,

```
Human marko = new Human();
```

creates a Human named (referenced as) marko. The new operator is analogous to the rdf:type property. Thus, after this code is executed, a similar situation

Table 4.1 The relationship between object-oriented programming, OWL, and the section example

	Object-oriented	OWL	Example
class specification	API	ontology	Human
object property	field	`rdf:Property`	hasFriend
object method	method		makeFriend
instantiate	new operator	`rdf:type` property	new/`rdf:type`

exists as that which is represented in Fig. 4.2. However, the ontological model dia-
grammed in the top half of Fig. 4.2 does not have the makeFriend method URI.
The relationship between object-oriented programming and OWL is presented in
Table 4.1.

It is no large conceptual leap to attach a method URI to a class. Currently, there
is no strong incentive to provide a framework for representing methods in OWL.
RDF was originally developed as a data modeling framework, not a programming
environment *per se*. However, in a similar vein, the Web Ontology Language for
Services (OWL-S) has been proposed as a web services model to support the discovery, execution, and tracking of Semantic Web services [3, 31]. An OWL-S service
exposes a service profile that describes what the service does, a service grounding
that describes how to invoke the service, and a service model that describes how
the service works. While OWL-S does provide the notion of object-oriented method
invocation on the Semantic Web, OWL-S is more at the agent-oriented level and
its intended use is for more "client/server" type problems. Another interesting and
related idea is to use RDF as a medium for communication between various computing devices and thus, utilize the Semantic Web as an infrastructure for distributed
computing [17]. Other object-oriented notions have been proposed within the context of RDF. For instance, SWCLOS [23] and ActiveRDF [35] utilize RDF as a
medium for ensuring the long-term persistence of an object. Both frameworks allow
their respective languages (CLOS and Ruby) to populate the fields of their objects
for use in their language environments. Once their fields have been populated, the
object's methods can be invoked in their respective programming environments.

4.1.4 Contributions

This article unifies all of the concepts presented hitherto into a framework for computing on RDF networks. In this framework, the state of a computing virtual machine, the API, and the low-level instructions are all represented in RDF. Furthermore, unlike the current programming paradigm, there is no stack of representation.
The lowest level of computing and the highest level of computing are represented in
the same substrate: URIs, literals, and triples.

This article proposes the concept of OWL APIs, RDF triple-code, and RDF virtual machines (RVM). Human readable/writable source code is compiled to create

Table 4.2 The various levels of abstraction in current and proposed computing paradigms

Level	Machine paradigm	Virtual machine paradigm	RDF paradigm
high-level code	source code	source code	source code
machine code	native instructions	byte-code	triple-code
instruction units	bits	bits	URIs and literals
machine state	hardware	software	RDF
machine execution	physics	hardware	software

an OWL ontology that abstractly represents how instructions should be united to form instruction sequences.[6] When objects and their methods are instantiated from an OWL API, RDF triple-code is created. RDF triple-code is analogous to virtual machine byte-code, but instead of being represented as bits, bytes, and words, it is represented as URIs and triples. In other words, a piece of executable software is represented as a traversable RDF network. The RVM is a virtual machine whose state is represented in RDF. The RVM's stacks, program counter, frames, etc. are modeled as an RDF network. It is the role of the RVM to "walk" the traversable RDF triple-code and compute.

In summary, software is written in human readable/writable source code, compiled to an OWL API, instantiated to RDF triple-code, and processed by a computing machine whose state is represented in RDF. However, there is always a homunculus. There is always some external process that drives the evolution of the representational substrate. For the JVM, that homunculus is the hardware CPU. For the hardware CPU, the homunculus is the physical laws of nature. For the RVM, the homunculus is some host CPU whether that host CPU is another virtual machine like the JVM or a hardware CPU. Table 4.2 presents the different levels of abstraction in computing and how they are represented by the physical machine, virtual machine, and proposed RDF computing paradigms.

4.2 A High-Level Perspective

Assume there exists an RDF triple store. Internal to that triple store is an RDF network. That RDF network is composed of triples. A triple is a set of three URIs, blank nodes, and/or literals. Those URIs can be used as a pointer to anything. This article presents a model of computation that is represented by URIs and literals and their interrelation to one another (triples). Thus, computation is represented as an RDF network. Figure 4.3 presents a high-level perspective on what will be discussed throughout the remainder of this article. What is diagrammed in Fig. 4.3 is

---

[6]While OWL has many features that are useful for reasoning about RDF data, the primary purpose of OWL with respect to the concepts presented in this article is to utilize OWL for its ability to create restricted data models. These restricted models form the APIs and ensure that instance RDF triple-code can be unambiguously generated by an RVM.

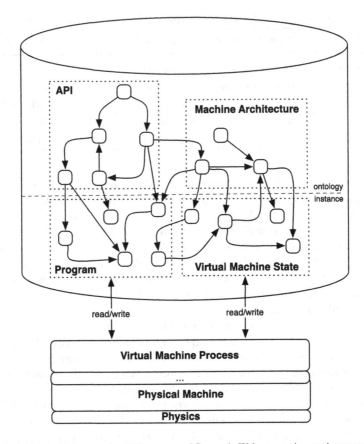

Fig. 4.3 A high-level perspective of the proposed Semantic Web computing environment

a very compartmentalized model of the components of computing. This model is in line with the common paradigm of computer science and engineering. However, less traditional realizations of this paradigm can remove the discrete levels of representation to support multi-level interactions between the various computing components since all the components are represented in the same RDF substrate: as URIs, blank nodes, literals, and triples.

Figure 4.3 shows 6 primary components. Two of these components are at the ontological level of the RDF network, two are at the instance level of the RDF network, and two are at the machine level external to the RDF network. While there are many benefits that emerge from this computing model that are currently seen and as of yet unseen, established interesting aspects are enumerated below.

1. The total address space of the RVM is the space of all URIs, blank nodes, and literals. In the RVM model of computing, the RVM state has no concept of the underlying hardware CPU's address space because instructions and data are represented in RDF. This idea is discussed in Sect. 4.3.1.

2. The Semantic Web is no longer an information gathering infrastructure, but a distributed information processing infrastructure (the process can move to the data, the data doesn't have to move to the process). An RVM can be "GETed" from a web-server as an RDF/XML document or "SELECTed" from an RDF triple store. RDF programs and RVM states are "first-class" web-entities. The ramifications of this is that an RVM can move between triple store environments and can compute on local data sets without requiring moving the data to the processor. This idea is discussed in Sect. 4.4.2.

3. This model maintains the "write once, run anywhere" paradigm of the JVM. The RVM model ensures that human readable/writable source code is compiled down to an intermediate language that is independent of the underlying hardware CPU executing the RVM process.

4. Languages built on a semantic network substrate can have unique constructs not found in other languages (e.g. inverse field referencing, multi-instance fields, field querying, etc.). While it is theoretically possible to add these constructs to other languages, they are not provided in the core of the languages as these languages do not have an underlying semantic network data model. These novel language constructs are discussed in Sect. 4.3.2.

5. Currently, there already exists an infrastructure to support the paradigm (triple stores, ontology modeling languages, query languages, etc.) and thus, requires very little investment by the community. The primary investment is the development of source-to-OWL API compilers, RVMs, and the standardization of RDF triple-code and RVM distribution/security protocols.

6. An RVM can be engineered at any level of complexity. It is possible to move the complexity to the software implementing the RVM process to ease machine architecture development and speed up computing time. This idea is discussed in Sect. 4.4.4.

7. In this model, language reflection exists at the API, software, and RVM level (everything is represented in RDF). This idea is discussed in Sect. 4.4.3.

4.2.1 The Ontological Level

The ontological level of the RDF network diagrammed in Fig. 4.3 is represented in OWL. This subsection will discuss the two primary ontological components: the API, and the RVM architecture.

4.2.1.1 The API

OWL supports the specification of class interactions. However, class interactions are specified in terms of property relationships, not method invocations. OWL has no formal way of specifying class behaviors (i.e. methods). However, in OWL, it is possible to define method and instruction classes and formally specify restrictions that dictate how instructions should be interrelated within a method. The method and instruction ontology presented in this article makes RDF a programming framework and not just a data modeling framework.

4.2.1.2 The Machine Architecture

The RDF machine architecture is modeled in OWL. The machine architecture ontology is an abstract description of an instance of a particular RVM. Depending on the level of abstraction required, different machine architectures can be implemented at varying levels of detail.

4.2.2 The Instance Level

The instance level of an RDF network is constrained by the requirements specified in the ontological level of the RDF network. This subsection will present the two components of the instance layer of the diagram in Fig. 4.3.

4.2.2.1 The Program

An API abstractly defines a software application. When an API is instantiated, instance RDF triple-code is created. Triple-code represents the instructions used by an RVM to compute.

4.2.2.2 The Virtual Machine

An instance of the machine architecture is an RDF virtual machine (RVM). The purpose of the RVM is to represent its state (stacks, program counter, etc.) in the same RDF network as the triple-code instructions. However, the RDF-based RVM is not a "true" computer. The RVM simply represents its state in RDF. The RVM requires a software implementation outside the triple store to compute its instructions. This requires the machine level discussed next.

4.2.3 The Machine Level

The machine level is where the actual computation is executed. An RDF network is a data structure. RDF is not a processor in the common sense—it has no way of evolving itself. In order to process RDF data, some external process must read and write to the RDF network. The reading and writing of the RDF network evolves the RVM and the objects on which it is computing. This section discusses the machine level that is diagrammed in Fig. 4.3.

4.2.3.1 The Virtual Machine Process

The virtual machine process is represented in software on a particular host machine. The RVM processor must be compatible with both the triple store interface (e.g. SPARQL/Update) and the underlying host machine. The RVM's host machine can be the physical machine (hardware CPU) or another virtual machine. For instance, if the RVM's machine process is implemented in the Java language, then the machine process runs in the JVM. This is diagrammed in Fig. 4.3 by the . . . component in between the virtual machine process and the physical machine.

4.2.3.2 The Physical Machine

The physical machine is the actual hardware CPU. The RVM implementation translates the RDF triple-code to the host machine's instruction set. For example, if the RVM process is running on the Intel Core Duo, then it is the role of the RVM process to translate the RDF triple-code to that specified by the Intel Core Duo instruction set. Thus, portability of this architectural model relies on a per host implementation of the RVM. Finally, to complete the computational stack, the laws of physics compute the hardware CPU. Much like the RDF representation of the RVM is a "snap-shot" representation of a computation, the hardware CPU is a silicon/electron "snap-shot" representation of a computation.

4.3 The Neno Language

This section presents the specification of a programming language designed to take advantage of a pure RDF computing environment. This language is called Neno. Neno is a high-level object-oriented language that is written in a grammar similar to other object-oriented languages such as Java and C++. However, Neno provides some functionality that is not possible with other languages (i.e. not explicit in the constructs of other object-oriented languages). This functionality is not due to the sophistication of the Neno language, but instead, is due to the fact that it is written for an RDF substrate and thus, can take advantage of the flexibility of RDF and its read/write interfaces. For this reason, Neno is in a class of languages that is coined semantic network programming languages. Neno is Turing complete and thus, can perform any classical (non-quantum) computation.

Neno source code is written in human readable/writable plain-text like the source code of many other high-level programming languages. Neno source code is compiled by a NenoFhat compiler. The NenoFhat compiler compiles Neno source code to a Fhat OWL API. The Fhat OWL API is analogous to the `jar` file of Java. A Fhat RVM instantiates (loads) aspects of the API into the instance layer of the RDF network. This instantiated aspect of the API is executable RDF triple-code. A Fhat RVM processes the triple-code and thus, computes. The analogies between the Neno and Java components are presented in Table 4.3.

Table 4.3 The mapping between Neno and Java components

Artifact	Neno	Java
source code	AClass.neno	AClass.java
compiler	nenofhat	javac
API	AClass.owl	AClass.class
virtual machine	fhat	java
program	RDF network	JVM memory

Table 4.4 The mapping between the terms in OWL and object-oriented programming

OWL	Object-oriented languages
owl:Class	Class
neno:Method	Method
rdf:Property	Field
subject of rdf:type	Object

The following examples will only explicitly denote the namespace of those resources that are not in http://neno.lanl.gov. In other words, the default namespace is http://neno.lanl.gov (prefixed as neno). The Neno programming language is engineered to be in compliance with OWL and the XML Schema Definition (XSD) namespaces. OWL provides the concept of classes, inheritance, datatype and class properties, and property restrictions. However, Neno restricts its compiled Fhat OWL APIs to single-parent classes (i.e. multiple-inheritance is not supported) and holds the closed world assumption (i.e. only properties that are stated in the ontology can be computed on in a Neno object). This is similar to what is assumed in Java. XSD provides the specification for the literal data types (e.g. string, integer, float, double, date, time, etc.). The XSD URI namespace prefix is xsd.

The lexicon that will be used to express the following concepts is drawn from object-oriented programming, not OWL. OWL parlance will only be used when completely describing the "back-end" of a particular aspect of the language. Table 4.4 states the relationship between OWL terms and object-oriented programming terms.

4.3.1 The Universally Unique Identifier Address Space

Throughout the remainder of this article, Universally Unique Identifiers (UUIDs) will be continually used [25]. The set of all UUIDs is a subset of the set of all URIs. A UUID is a 128-bit (16-byte) string that can be created in disparate environments with a near zero probability of ever being reproduced. To understand the number of UUIDs that are possible at 128-bits, it would require 1 trillion unique UUIDs to be created every nanosecond for 10 billion years to exhaust the space of all possible UUIDs.[7] A UUID can be represented as a 36 character hexadecimal string. For example, 6c3f8afe-ec3d-11db-8314-0800200c9a66, is a UUID. The hexadecimal representation will be used in all the following examples. However, for the sake of brevity, since 36 characters is too lengthy for the examples and diagrams, only the first 8 characters will be used. Thus, 6c3f8afe-ec3d-11db-8314-0800200c9a66 will be represented as 6c3f8afe. Furthermore, UUIDs, when used as URIs are namespaced as

```
urn:uuid:6c3f8afe-ec3d-11db-8314-0800200c9a66
```

and for diagrams and examples, is abbreviated as `urn:uuid:6c3f8afe`.

When Neno source code is compiled to Fhat triple-code, a UUID is created for nearly everything; every instruction class and instruction instance is identified by a UUID. When a Fhat is instantiated, a UUID is created for all the resources that compose the machine (i.e. stacks, frames, etc.). In typical programming environments, the programming language and its computing machine are constrained by the size of RAM (and virtual memory with most modern day operating systems). For a 32-bit machine, the maximum size of RAM is approximately 4 gigabytes. This means that there are only 2^{32} possible addresses and thus, words in RAM. However, for Neno, no such constraints exist. The space of all UUIDs is the address space of a Fhat RVM (more generally, the space of all URIs and literals is the address space). Fhat does not use RAM for storing its data and instructions, Fhat uses an RDF network. Thus, Fhat does not have any hard constraint on how much memory it "allocates" for its processing.

4.3.2 Class Declarations in Neno Source Code

Neno source code has a grammar that is very similar to other object-oriented languages. For instance, suppose the following simple class written in the Java programming language:

```
package gov.lanl.neno.demo;

import java.lang.*;
import java.util.*;

public class Human {
  private String hasName;
  private ArrayList<Human> hasFriend;

  public Human (String n) {
    this.hasName = n;
```

---

[7]This fact was taken from Wikipedia at http://en.wikipedia.org/wiki/UUID.

```
   }

   public void makeFriend(Human h) {
     if(h != this)
       this.hasFriend.add(h);
   }

   public void setName(String n) {
     this.hasName = n;
   }
}
```

The Human class has two fields named hasName and hasFriend. The field hasName takes a value of String (or java.lang.String to be more specific) and hasFriend takes a value of Human. The Human class has one constructor and one method. A constructor is used to create an object and is a type of method. In Java, a constructor tells the JVM to allocate memory for the object on the heap (i.e. an object "pool") and set the object's field values according to the statements in the body of the constructor. The constructor for Human takes a String called n and creates a new Human instance called an object. The Human constructor sets that object's hasName field to n. The Human method is called makeFriend. This method takes a Human with variable name h as an argument. If the object referenced by h is not the Human for which this method was invoked, then the object for which this method was called has h added to its hasFriend field. Note, that unlike the example in Fig. 4.2, it is possible for a Human object to have multiple friends because of the use of the ArrayList<Human>.[8]

The Neno programming language is similar to Java. The following source code demonstrates how to declare nearly the same class in Neno.[9]

```
prefix owl: <http://www.w3.org/2002/07/owl>;
prefix xsd: <http://www.w3.org/2001/XMLSchema>;
prefix demo: <http://neno.lanl.gov/demo>;

owl:Thing demo:Human {
  xsd:string hasName[1];
  demo:Human hasFriend[0..*];

  !Human(xsd:string n) {
    this.hasName = n;
  }

  makeFriend(demo:Human h) {
    if(h != this)
```

---

[8]Java generics as represented by the < > notation is supported by Java 1.5+.

[9]When there are no ambiguities in naming, the class declaration can be written without prefixes.

```
      this.hasFriend =+ h;
  }

  setName(xsd:string n) {
    this.hasName = n;
  }
}
```

While the Human class declaration in Java and in Neno are nearly identical, there are a few constructs that make the two languages different. For one, instead of "importing" packages, in Neno, namespaces are declared and ontologies are imported. To ease namespace declarations, prefixes are used (e.g. owl, xsd, and demo). All constructors are denoted by the class name prefixed by the ! symbol. Similarly, though not in the above example, all destructors are denoted by the class name prefixed by the ~ symbol. Notice that all datatype primitives (e.g. xsd:string) are from the XSD namespace. The Fhat RVM is engineered specifically for these datatypes. Perhaps the most unique aspect of the Neno language is the cardinality restriction specifier in the field declaration (e.g. [0..*]). Because Neno was designed for a semantic network substrate, there is nothing that prevents the same property (i.e. field) to point to multiple different URIs. In order to demand that there exist one field, the [1] notation is used. Note that demo:Human is an rdfs:subClassOf owl:Thing as specified by the owl:Thing demo:Human class description. Class inheritance is specified by the prefix to the declaration of the class name. Note that in Neno, a class can only have a single parent even though OWL supports multiple-inheritance.[10] Furthermore, note that all class properties have a universal restriction on the class or datatype value. For example, in the above demo:Human class, the hasName property must have an xsd:string value and all hasFriend properties must have Human values.

In order to demonstrate the relationship between Neno source code and its compiled OWL API, a simple class example is presented. The class

```
prefix owl: <http://www.w3.org/2002/07/owl>;
prefix xsd: <http://www.w3.org/2001/XMLSchema>;
prefix demo: <http://neno.lanl.gov/demo>;

owl:Thing demo:Example {
  xsd:integer t[0..1];

  test(xsd:integer n) {
    for(xsd:integer i=0; i < n; i++) {
      this.t = this.t + 1;
    }
```

---

[10]This constraint does not apply to owl:Restrictions as Neno classes utilize owl:Restrictions to make explicit property restrictions. Thus, excluding owl:Restriction subclassing, a Neno object class can only be the subclass of a single class.

```
    }
}
```

has the following OWL RDF/XML representation:

```
<rdf:RDF
    xmlns:rdf="http://www.w3.org/1999/02/22-rdf-syntax-ns#"
    xmlns:rdfs="http://www.w3.org/2000/01/rdf-schema#"
    xmlns:owl="http://www.w3.org/2002/07/owl#">
  <owl:Ontology rdf:about="http://neno.lanl.gov"/>
  <owl:Ontology rdf:about="http://neno.lanl.gov/demo">
    <owl:imports rdf:resource="http://neno.lanl.gov"/>
  </owl:Ontology>
  ...
  <!-- A PUSHVALUE INSTRUCTION -->

  <owl:Class rdf:about="http://neno.lanl.gov/demo#2271ea72-877c-4090-...">
    <rdfs:subClassOf rdf:resource="http://neno.lanl.gov#PushValue"/>
    <rdfs:subClassOf>
      <owl:Restriction>
        <owl:onProperty rdf:resource="http://neno.lanl.gov#hasValue"/>
        <owl:allValuesFrom>
          <owl:Class rdf:about="http://neno.lanl.gov/demo#9792cc3c-5600-..."/>
        </owl:allValuesFrom>
      </owl:Restriction>
    </rdfs:subClassOf>
    <rdfs:subClassOf>
      <owl:Restriction>
        <owl:onProperty rdf:resource="http://neno.lanl.gov#nextInst"/>
        <owl:allValuesFrom>
          <owl:Class rdf:about="http://neno.lanl.gov/demo#a80ba54c-5344-..."/>
        </owl:allValuesFrom>
      </owl:Restriction>
    </rdfs:subClassOf>
  </owl:Class>

  <!-- THE PUSHED VALUE -->

  <owl:Class rdf:about="http://neno.lanl.gov/demo#9792cc3c-5600-4660-...">
    <rdfs:subClassOf rdf:resource="http://neno.lanl.gov#LocalDirect"/>
    <rdfs:subClassOf>
      <owl:Restriction>
        <owl:hasValue rdf:datatype="http://www.w3.org/2001/XMLSchema#integer"
        >1</owl:hasValue>
        <owl:onProperty rdf:resource="http://neno.lanl.gov#hasURI"/>
      </owl:Restriction>
    </rdfs:subClassOf>
  </owl:Class>

  <!-- THE NEXT INSTRUCTION AFTER PUSHVALUE: AN ADD INSTRUCTION -->

  <owl:Class rdf:about="http://neno.lanl.gov/demo#a80ba54c-5344-4df1-...">
    <rdfs:subClassOf rdf:resource="http://neno.lanl.gov#Add"/>
    <rdfs:subClassOf>
      <owl:Restriction>
        <owl:onProperty rdf:resource="http://neno.lanl.gov#hasLeft"/>
        <owl:allValuesFrom
         rdf:resource="http://neno.lanl.gov/demo#4c715d16-..."/>
      </owl:Restriction>
    </rdfs:subClassOf>
    <rdfs:subClassOf>
      <owl:Restriction>
        <owl:onProperty rdf:resource="http://neno.lanl.gov#hasRight"/>
        <owl:allValuesFrom
         rdf:resource="http://neno.lanl.gov/demo#fdde7f6f-..."/>
      </owl:Restriction>
    </rdfs:subClassOf>
```

```
<rdfs:subClassOf>
  <owl:Restriction>
    <owl:onProperty rdf:resource="http://neno.lanl.gov#nextInst"/>
    <owl:allValuesFrom
     rdf:resource="http://neno.lanl.gov/demo#e3b8a797-..."/>
  </owl:Restriction>
</rdfs:subClassOf>
</owl:Class>
...
</rdf:RDF>
```

The most important idea to take away from the above Fhat OWL API subset is that the role of the compiler is to generate UUID-named instruction classes that are subclasses of particular Fhat instructions (e.g. PushValue). These generated instruction classes have owl:Restrictions on them that ensure that instances of these classes are connected to one another in an unambiguous way (e.g. owl:Restrictions on their respective nextInt property) and that their operand values are made explicit (e.g. owl:Restrictions on their respective operand properties). This unambiguous instantiation is the RDF triple-code that is created when a Fhat RVM instantiates the API.

For example, in the above Fhat OWL API snippet, any demo:2271ea72 PushValue instruction instance must have one and only one hasValue property. The value of that property must be a demo:9792cc3c LocalDirect value with a hasURI property value of "1"^^<xsd:integer>. The instance of demo:2271ea72 must also have a nextInst property that is of rdf:type demo:a80ba54c, where demo:a80ba54c is an rdfs:subClassOf Add. An instance of this demo:a80ba54c Add instruction instructs the Fhat RVM to add its hasLeft operand and its hasRight operands together. This demo:a80ba54c Add also has a nextInst property value that must be an instance of demo:e3b8a797. Though not shown, the demo:e3b8a797 is an rdfs:subClassOf Set. In this way, through strict owl:Restrictions, the flow of triple-code can be generated in an unambiguous manner by the Fhat RVM.

The remainder of this section will go over the more salient aspects of the Neno programming language.

4.3.2.1 Declaring Namespaces

Namespaces promote the distributed nature of the Semantic Web by ensuring that there are no URI name conflicts in the ontologies and instances of different organizations [10]. The Java language has a similar construct called packaging. The package specification in Java supports organizational namespacing. Neno supports the prefixing of namespaces. For example, demo:Human resolves to http://neno.lanl.gov/demo#Human.

4.3.2.2 Datatypes

Fhat is engineered to handle xsd:anySimpleType and provides specific support for any of its derived types [9]. The XSD namespace maintains, amongst others:

`xsd:string`, `xsd:double`, `xsd:integer`, `xsd:date`, etc. Example operations include,

```
"neno"^^xsd:string + "fhat"^^xsd:string
"2007-11-30"^^xsd:date < "2007-12-01"^^xsd:date
"1"^^xsd:integer - "0"^^xsd:integer
```

Neno has low-level support for high-level datatype manipulations such as string concatenation, data and time comparisons, date incrementing, etc. Exactly what operations are allowed with what datatypes will be discussed later when describing the Fhat instruction set.

4.3.2.3 The **this** Variable

The `this` variable is used in many object-oriented languages to specify the field to be accessed or the method to be invoked. All methods inherently have `this` as a variable they can use. The same construct exists in Neno with no variation in meaning.

4.3.2.4 Field Cardinality

While Neno is an object-oriented language, it is also a semantic network programming language. Neno is more in line with the concepts of RDF than it is with those of Java and C++. One of the major distinguishing features of an object in Neno is that objects can have multi-instance fields. This means that a single field (predicate) can have more than one value (object). For instance, in Java

```
Human marko = new Human("Marko Rodriguez");
marko.setName("Marko Antonio Rodriguez");
```

will initially set the `hasName` field of the `Human` object referenced by the variable name `marko` to "Marko Rodriguez". The invocation of the `setName` method of `marko` will replace "Marko Rodriguez" with "Marko Antonio Rodriguez". Thus, the field `hasName` has a cardinality of 1. All fields in Java have a cardinality of 1 and are universally quantified for the specified class (though taxonomical subsumption is supported).

In Neno, it is possible for a field to have a cardinality greater than one. In Neno, when a class' fields are declared, the cardinality specifier is used to denote how many properties of this type are allowed for an instance of this class. Thus, in the Neno code at the start of this section,

```
xsd:string hasName[1];
```

states that any `Human` object must have one and only one field (property) called `hasName` and that `hasName` field points to some `xsd:string`. Therefore, it is illegal for the Fhat RVM to add a new `hasName` property to the class `marko`.

The original property must be removed before the new property can be added. The general grammar for field restrictions in Neno is [# (..(# | *))], where # refers to some integer value.

Currently, Neno does not adopt any of the OWL semantics regarding cardinality and "semantically distinct" resources. The owl:sameAs relationship between resources is not considered when determining the cardinality of a property and thus, only the explicit number of properties (explicit triples) of a particular type (predicate) are acknowledged by the NenoFhat compiler and Fhat RVM.

4.3.2.5 Handling Fields

Neno provides the following field and local variable operators: =+, =-, =/, and =. These operators are called "set plus", "set minus", "set clear", and "set", respectively. The definition of these operators is made apparent through examples that demonstrate their use. For instance, from the class declarations above, the Human class has the field hasFriend. For the Java example, the hasFriend field can have more than one Human value only indirectly through the use of the ArrayList<Human> class. In Neno, no ArrayList<Human> is needed because a field can have a cardinality greater than 1. The cardinality specifier [0..*] states that there are no restrictions on the number of friends a Human can have. In order to add more friends to a Human object, the =+ operator is used. If the Human instance has the URI urn:uuid:2db4a1 and the provided Human argument has the URI urn:uuid:47878d then the =+ operator instructs Fhat to execute

```
INSERT { <urn:uuid:2db4a1> <demo:hasFriend>
         <urn:uuid:47878d> .}
```

on the triple store. On the other hand, if the = operator was used, then Fhat would issue the following commands to the triple store:

```
DELETE { <urn:uuid:2db4a1> <demo:hasFriend> ?x .}

INSERT { <urn:uuid:2db4a1> <demo:hasFriend>
         <urn:uuid:47878d> .}
```

For a multi-instance field, the = is a very destructive operator. For a [0..1] or [1] field, = behaves as one would expect in any other object-oriented language. Furthermore, for a [0..1] or [1] field, =+ is not allowed as it will cause the insertion of more than one property of the same predicate.

In order to control the removal of fields from a multi-instance field, the =- and =/ operators can be used. For example, suppose the following method declaration in Neno

```
makeEnemy(Human h) {
    this.hasFriends =- h;
}
```

The makeEnemy method will remove the Human object identified by the variable name h from the hasFriend fields. If the h variable is a reference to the URI urn:uuid:4800e2, then at the Fhat level, Fhat will execute the following command on the triple store:

```
DELETE { <urn:uuid:2db4a1> <demo:hasFriend>
          <urn:uuid:4800e2> .}
```

Finally, assume that there is a rogue Human that wishes to have no friends at all. In order for this one man army to sever his ties, the =/ operator is used. Assume the following overloaded method declaration for a Human.

```
makeEnemy() {
  this.hasFriends =/;
}
```

The above statement would have Fhat execute the following delete command on the triple store:

```
DELETE { <urn:uuid:2db4a1> <demo:hasFriend> ?x }
```

4.3.2.6 Field Querying

In many cases, a field (i.e. property) will have many instances. In computer programming terms, fields can be thought of as arrays. However, these "arrays" are not objects, but simply greater than one cardinality fields. In Java, arrays are objects and high-level array objects like the java.util.ArrayList provide functions to search an array. In Neno, there are no methods that support such behaviors since fields are not objects. Instead, Neno provides language constructs that support field querying. For example, suppose the following method

```
boolean isFriend(Human unknown) {
  if(this.hasFriend =? unknown) {
    return true;
  }
  else {
   return false;
  }
}
```

In the above isFriend method, the provided Human argument referenced by the variable name unknown is checked against all the hasFriend fields. Again, the owl:sameAs property is not respected and thus, "sameness" is determined by exact URIs. The =? operator is a conditional operator and thus, always returns either "true"^^xsd:boolean or "false"^^xsd:boolean. At the Fhat level, if this references the UUID urn:uuid:2d3862 and unknown references urn:uuid:75e05c, then the Fhat RVM executes the following query on the triple store:

```
ASK { <urn:uuid:2d3862> <demo:hasFriend>
        <urn:uuid:75e05c> . }
```

Similarly, imagine the following method,

```
boolean isFriendByName(Human unknown) {
  if(this.hasFriend.hasName =? unknown.hasName) {
    return true;
  }
  else {
   return false;
  }
}
```

Assuming the same UUID references for this and unknown from the previous examples, the =? operation would have the Fhat execute the following query on the RDF network

```
ASK { <urn:uuid:2d3862> <demo:hasFriend>   ?x .
       ?x <demo:hasName> ?y .
       <urn:uuid:75e05c> <demo:hasName> ?y }
```

Again, there is no reasoning involved in any of these triple store operations; only "raw" triple and URI/literal matching is used.

4.3.2.7 Looping and Conditionals

Looping and conditionals are nearly identical to the Java language. In Neno, there exists the for, while, and if/else constructs. For example, a for statement is

```
for(xsd:integer i = "0"^^xsd:integer;
    i<"10"^^xsd:integer; i++)
{ /* for block */ }
```

a while statement is

```
while(xsd:integer i < "10"^^xsd:integer)
  { /* while block */ }
```

and an if/else statement is

```
if(xsd:integer i < "10"^^xsd:integer)
  { /* if block */ }
  { /* else block */}
```

It is important to note that these statements need not have the literal type specifier (e.g. xsd:integer) on every hardcoded literal. The literal type can be inferred from its context and thus, is automatically added by the compiler. For example, since i is an xsd:integer, it is assumed that 10 is also.

4.3.2.8 Field Looping

In many cases it is desirable to loop through all the resources of a field for the purposes of searching or for manipulating each resource. For instance, suppose the following Human method:

```
namelessFaces() {
  for(Human h : this.hasFriend) {
    h.hasName = "..."^^xsd:string;
  }
  for(xsd:integer i=0; i<this.hasFriend*; i++) {
    Human h = this.hasFriend[i];
    h.hasName = "."^^xsd:string;
  }
}
```

The above namelessFaces method demonstrates two types of field looping mechanisms offered by Neno. The first is analogous to the Java 1.5 language specification. With the first for loop, the variable h is set to a single hasFriend of this. The second for loop uses the index i that goes from index 0 to the size of the "array" (this.hasFriend*). The * notation in this context returns the number of hasFriend properties of the this object. In other words * returns the cardinality of the this.hasFriend field.

Finally, as field values are not stored in a vector, but instead as an un-ordered set, the field "arrays" in Neno are not guaranteed to be ordered. Thus, this.hasFriend[1] may not be the same value later in the code. Ordering is dependent upon the triple store's indexing algorithm and stability of a particular order is dependent upon how often re-indexing occurs in the triple store. It is worth noting that higher-order classes can be created such as specialized rdf:Seq and rdf:List classes to provided ordered support for arrays.

4.3.2.9 Type Checking

The typeof operator can be used to determine the class type of a URI. For instance, the following statement,

```
xsd:boolean isType = urn:uuid:2db4a1d2 typeof Human
```

would set isType to true if urn:uuid:2db4a1d2 is rdf:type Human or rdf:type of some class that is an rdfs:subClassOf Human. Also,

```
xsd:boolean isType = urn:uuid:2db4a1d2 typeof
                rdfs:Resource
```

always returns true. Thus, RDFS subsumption semantics are respected and thus, Neno respects the subclassing semantics employed by modern objected-oriented languages. Similarly the typeOf? operator returns the type of the resource. For instance,

```
xsd:anyURI type = urn:uuid:2db4a1d2 typeof?
```

would set `type` to http://neno.lanl.gov/demo#Human.

4.3.2.10 Inverse Field Referencing

In object-oriented languages the "dot" operator is used to access a method or field of an object. For instance, in `this.hasName`, on the left of the "dot" is the object and on the right of the "dot" is the field. Whether the right hand side of the operator is a field or method can be deduced by the compiler from its context. If `this` resolves to the URI `urn:uuid:2db4a1d2`, then the following Neno code

```
Human h[0..*] = this.hasFriend;
```

would instruct Fhat to execute the following query:

```
SELECT ?x
  WHERE { <urn:uuid:2db4a1d2> <demo:hasFriend> ?x . }
```

According to the previous query, everything that binds to `?x` will be set to the variable h. The above query says: "Locate all `Human hasFriends` of `this` object." However, Neno provides another concept not found in other object-oriented languages called the "dot dot" operator. The "dot dot" operator provides support for what is called inverse field referencing (and inverse method invocation discussed next). Assume the following line in some method of some class,

```
Human h[0..*] = this..hasFriend;
```

The above statement says, "locate all `Humans` that have `this` object as their `hasFriend`." At the Fhat level, Fhat executes the following query on the triple store:

```
SELECT ?x
  WHERE { ?x <demo:hasFriend> <urn:uuid:2db4a1d2> . }
```

Furthermore, if the statement is

```
Human h[0..3] = this..hasFriend;
```

Fhat would execute:

```
SELECT ?x
  WHERE { ?x <demo:hasFriend> <urn:uuid:2db4a1d2> . }
        LIMIT 3
```


4.3.2.11 Inverse Method Invocation

Like inverse field referencing, inverse method invocation is supported by Neno. Inverse method invocation will invoke all the methods that meet a particular requirement. For instance,

```
this..hasFriend.makeEnemy(this);
```

will ensure that all objects that have this as their friend are no longer friends with this.

4.3.2.12 Variable Scoping

Variable scoping in Neno is equivalent to Java. For example, in

```
xsd:integer a = "11"^^xsd:integer;
if(a < "10"^^xsd:integer) {
  xsd:integer b = "2"^^xsd:integer;
}
else {
  xsd:integer c = "3"^^xsd:integer;
}
```

the true and false block of the if statement can read the variable a, but the true block cannot read the c in the false block and the false block cannot read the b in the true block. Also, methods are out of scope from one another. The only way methods communicate are through parameter passing, return values, and object manipulations.

4.3.2.13 Constructors and Destructors

Constructors and destructors are used in object-oriented languages to create and destroy object, respectively. The concept of a constructor in Neno is similar to that of Java and C++. The concept of a destructor does not exist in Java, but does in C++. It is very important in Neno to provide the programmer an explicit way of performing object destruction. Again, unlike Java, Neno is intended to be used on a persistent semantic network substrate. Thus, when a Fhat RVM stops executing or an object is no longer accessible by a Fhat RVM, that object should not be automatically removed. In short, Fhat does not provide automatic garbage collection [29]. It is the role of the programmer to explicitly remove all unwanted objects from the RDF network.

In order to create a new object, the constructor of a class is called using the new operator. For example,

```
Human marko = new Human("Marko"^^xsd:string);
```

will generate a sub-network in the RDF network equivalent to Fig. 4.4. The algorithm by which Fhat creates the RDF sub-network will be discussed in the next section. For now, understand that in the variable environment of a Fhat instance there exists a variable named marko that points to the newly created Human instance (e.g. (marko, rdf:type, Human)).

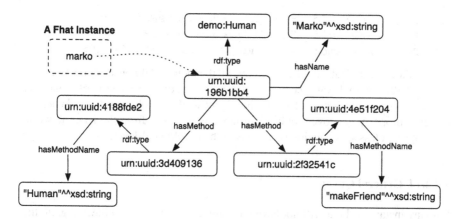

Fig. 4.4 A Fhat instance maintains a variable reference to an object

A destructor will instruct Fhat to destroy an object. A destructor is specified in the class declaration. For instance, suppose the following specification for
demo:Human:

```
owl:Thing Human {
  string hasName[1];
  Human hasFriend[0..*];

  !Human(string n) {
    this.hasName = n;
  }

  ~Human() {
    this.hasName =/
    this.hasFriend =/
    this..hasFriend =/
  }
}
```

In the above class declaration !Human(string n) is a constructor and
~Human() is a destructor. A destructor is called using the delete operator. For
instance,

```
delete marko;
```

calls marko's ~Human() destructor.

A class can only have at most one destructor and the destructor takes no arguments. The ~Human() destructor removes the reference to the object's name,
removes all the references to the object's friends, and removes all hasFriend
references to that object. Thus, if the Human object has the URI urn:uuid:
55b2a3b0, Fhat would execute the following commands on the triple store:

```
DELETE { <urn:uuid:55b2a3b0> <demo:hasName> ?x .}
DELETE { <urn:uuid:55b2a3b0> <demo:hasFriend> ?x .}
DELETE { ?x <demo:hasFriend> <urn:uuid:55b2a3b0> .}
```

Behind the scenes, Fhat would also remove all the method references of urn:uuid: 55b2a3b0, internal variable references to urn:uuid:55b2a3b0, and the rdf:type relationships that relate the object to the ontological-layer. When an object is properly destroyed, only its instance is removed from the RDF network. The object's class specification still exists in the ontological-layer.

4.3.2.14 General Query

In many instances, Fhat will not have a reference to a particular object. Again, the environment anticipated is one in which objects persist in the RDF network. Thus, when code is executed, it may be necessary to locate the URI of a particular object for processing. In order to make this easy for the programmer, a query operator is defined called the "network query" operator and is denoted by the symbol <?. For example,

```
xsd:string x = "Marko Antonio Rodriguez"^^xsd:string;
xsd:string query =
    "SELECT ?x WHERE { ?x <demo:hasName> <" + x + "> }
     LIMIT 1"^^xsd:string;
Human h[0..1] <? query;
```

will query the RDF network for at most one Human named "Marko Antonio Rodriguez". Note that three statements above could have been written as one. However, to demonstrate string concatenation and variable use, three were used.

4.3.3 Starting a Program in Neno

In Neno, there are no static methods. Thus, there does not exist something like the public static void main(String[] args) method in Java. Instead, Fhat is provided a class URI and a method for that class that takes no arguments. The class is automatically instantiated by Fhat and the specified no-argument method is invoked. For example, if Fhat is pointed to the following Test class and main method, then the main method creates a Human, changes its name, then exits. When main exits, Fhat halts.

```
owl:Thing demo:Test {
  main() {
    demo:Human h = new Human("Marko Rodriguez");
    h.setName("Marko Antonio Rodriguez");
  }
}
```

4.3.4 Typical Use Case

This section describes how a developer would typically use the Neno/Fhat environment. The terminal commands below ensure that the NenoFhat compiler translates Neno source code to a Fhat OWL API, loads the Fhat OWL API into the triple store, instantiates a Fhat RVM, and points the RVM to the demo:Test class with a main method. Note that the third command is broken into four lines for display purposes. Do not assume that there is a newline character at the end of the first three lines of the third statement.

```
> nenofhat Human.neno -o ntriple
                      -t http://triplestore.net/sparql
> nenofhat Test.neno -o xml -t http://triplestore.net/sparql
> fhat -vmc http://neno.lanl.gov/neno#Fhat
       -c http://neno.lanl.gov/neno/demo#Test
       -cm main
       -t http://triplestore.net/sparql
```

The first terminal command compiles the Human.neno source code into a Fhat OWL API represented in N-TRIPLE format and then inserts the Human.ntriple triples into the triple store pointed to by the "-t" URL. The second terminal command compiles the Test.neno source code and generates a Fhat OWL API in RDF/XML called Test.xml. That RDF/XML file is then loaded into the triple store. Finally, a Fhat processor is initiated. The virtual machine process (fhat) is called with a pointer to an ontological model of the desired machine architecture. The machine architecture is instantiated. The instantiated Fhat then instantiates a Test object and calls its main method. The instantiated Test main method is executable RDF triple-code.

In some instances, a Fhat RVM state may already exist in the triple store. In such cases, the following command can be invoked to point the Fhat RVM process to the stored RVM state. In the example below, assume that urn:uuid:60ab17 is of rdf:type Fhat.

```
> fhat -vmi urn:uuid:60ab17
       -t http://triplestore.net/sparql
```

When the Fhat RVM state is located, fhat processes the current instruction pointed to by its programLocation.

The following list outlines the flags for the nenofhat compiler,

- -o: output type (ntriple | n3 | xml)
- -t: triple store interface

and the fhat RVM process,

- -vmi: virtual machine instance URI
- -vmc: virtual machine class URI
- -c: start class URI
- -cm: start class no-argument method
- -t: triple store interface.

Table 4.5 Different VM implementation types, their requirements, and an example

Implementation type	Requirements	Example
soft	hardware methods	Java Virtual Machine, r-Fhat
semi-hard	high-level components	Fhat
hard	low-level components	VHDL designs

4.4 The Fhat Virtual Machine Architecture

Fhat is an RVM that was specifically designed for RDF-based semantic network languages. Fhat is a semi-hard implementation of a computing machine. Table 4.5 presents an explanation of the various levels of virtual machine implementations. The concept of soft, semi-hard, and hard implementations are developed here and thus, are not part of the common lexicon. In the JVM, all of the "hardware" components are represented in software and the state of the machine is not saved outside the current run-time environment. For VHSIC Hardware Description Language (VHDL) machines, the hardware components are modeled at the level of logic gates (AND, OR, XOR, NOT, etc.) [13]. In Fhat, the hardware components are modeled in RDF (the state), but component execution is modeled in software (the process).

There are many reasons why a semi-hard implementation was desired for Fhat and these reasons will be articulated in the sections discussing the various components of the Fhat architecture. However, while this section presents the semi-hard implementation, a soft implementation of Fhat called reduced Fhat (r-Fhat) will be briefly discussed. In short, r-Fhat is faster than the Fhat virtual machine, but does not support run-time machine portability and machine-level reflection. In other words, r-Fhat does not support those functions that require an RDF representation of the machine state.

Any high-level language can be written to take advantage of the Fhat architecture. While Neno and Fhat were developed in concert and thus, are strongly connected in their requirements of one another, any language that compiles to Fhat RDF triple-code can use a Fhat RVM. This section will discuss the Fhat RVM before discussing the Fhat instruction set. Figure 4.5 presents the Fhat machine architecture. This machine architecture is represented in OWL and is co-located with other resources in the ontology layer of the RDF network.

4.4.1 Fhat Components

There are 8 primary components to the Fhat RVM. These are enumerated below for ease of reference. Each component will be discussed in more detail in the following subsections.

1. `Fhat`: the virtual machine that interprets instructions and uses its various components for processing those instructions.
2. `halt`: suspends Fhat processing when false, and permits processing when true.

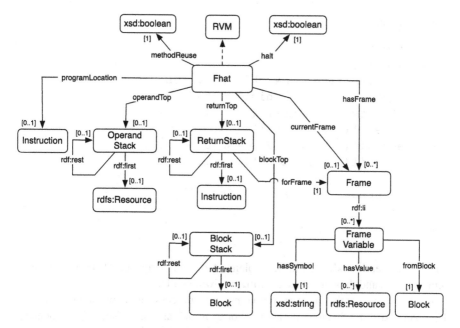

Fig. 4.5 The ontological model of the Fhat RDF virtual machine

3. methodReuse: determines whether or not method triple-code is reused amongst object instances.
4. programLocation: a pointer to the current instruction being executed (i.e. a PC).
5. BlockStack: an rdf:List that can be pushed and popped for entering and exiting blocks.
6. OperandStack: an rdf:List that can be pushed and popped for arithmetic computations.
7. Frame: a Method unique environment for storing local variables.
8. ReturnStack: an rdf:List that provides a reference to the instruction that called a method and the frame of that method.

While all of these components are represented in RDF, only Fhat has an external software component. The software implementation of Fhat is called the "virtual machine process" in Fig. 4.3.[11]

4.4.1.1 Fhat

Fhat is the primary component of the Fhat RVM. Fhat is the most complicated component in the entire Fhat architecture. The high-level Neno pseudo-code for the

---

[11]When the term Fhat is used, it is referring to the entire virtual machine, when the teletyped term Fhat is used, it is referring to the virtual machine process identified by the URI Fhat.

Fhat component is

```
owl:Thing Fhat {
  execute() {
    while(!this.halt && this.programLocation != null) {
      Instruction i = this.programLocation
      if(i typeof Block) { ... }
      else if(i typeof If) { ... }
      else if(i typeof Expression) { ... }
      else if(i typeof Set) { ... }
      ...
      /* update programLocation */
    }
  }
}
```

The above pseudo-code should be implemented in the language of the virtual machine process and thus, for the executing hardware CPU.

It is worth noting that a Fhat virtual machine process can be written in Neno as demonstrated in the Neno code above. For example, assume a Neno implemented Fhat instance called Fhat1. In such cases, another Fhat, called Fhat2, is processing Fhat1. Fhat2 can be run on yet another Fhat, called Fhat3, or grounded into some other language that is translating code to the native machine language. This is possible because Neno/Fhat is Turing complete and thus, can run a simulation of itself. When a simulation of itself is run, a complete RDF virtual machine is created. In this simulation environment, both the state and process of the Fhat RVM are represented in RDF.

Fhat supports common uses of the xsd:anySimpleType and a few of these uses are summarized below:

- xsd:boolean: Not, Equals
- xsd:integer, xsd:float, xsd:double: Arithmetic, Compare
- xsd:string: Add, Compare
- xsd:date, xsd:dateTime: Add, Subtract, Compare
- xsd:anyURI: Compare.

4.4.1.2 halt

At any time, Fhat can be forced to halt by setting the halt property of Fhat to true^^xsd:boolean. Multi-threading can be simulated in this way. A Neno program can be engineered to run a master Fhat that has a reference to the halt property of all its slave Fhats. By setting the halt property, the Fhat master can control which Fhat slaves are able to process at any one time. In essence, the master Fhat serves as an operating system.

4.4.1.3 methodReuse

When methodReuse is set to true^^xsd:boolean, Fhat will instantiate new objects with unique instructions for each method. When methodReuse is set to false^^xsd:boolean, Fhat will reuse method triple-code amongst the same methods for the different objects. This will be discussed in more detail in Sect. 4.5.2.

4.4.1.4 programLocation

The programLocation is a pointer to the current instruction being executed by Fhat. Fhat executes one instruction at a time and thus, the programLocation must always point to a single instruction. The "while" loop of Fhat simply moves the programLocation from one instruction to the next. At each instruction, Fhat interprets what the instruction is (by its rdf:type "opcode") and uses its various components appropriately. When there are no more instructions (i.e. when there no longer exists a programLocation property), Fhat halts.

4.4.1.5 BlockStack

The BlockStack is important for variable setting. When a new variable is created in a block of code, it is necessary to associate that variable with that block. When the thread of execution exits the block, all variables created in that block are "deallocated".

4.4.1.6 OperandStack

The OperandStack is a LIFO (i.e. "last in, first out") stack that supports any rdfs:Resource. The OperandStack is used for local computations such as x = 1 + (2 * 3). For example, when x = 1 + (2 * 3) is executed by Fhat, Fhat will

1. push the value 1 on the OperandStack
2. push the value 2 on the OperandStack
3. push the value 3 on the OperandStack
4. pop both 2 and 3 off the OperandStack, multiply the two operands, and push the value 6 on the OperandStack
5. pop both 1 and 6 the OperandStack, add the two operands, and push the value 7 on the OperandStack
6. set the current Frame FrameVariable x to the value 7 popped off the OperandStack.

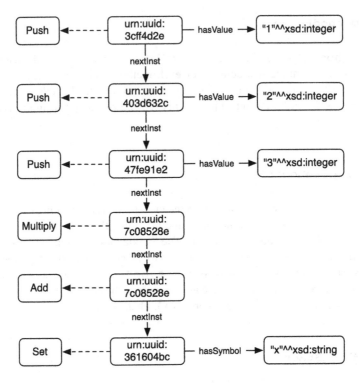

Fig. 4.6 The triple-code representation of the statement x = 1 + (2 * 3)

The Neno statement x = 1 + (2 * 3) is actually multiple instructions when compiled to Fhat triple-code. The NenoFhat compiler would translate the statement to the triple-code represented in Fig. 4.6.

It is very important to represent such components as the OperandStack component in RDF and not simply in the memory of the host CPU. Suppose that a Fhat instance is to move to another physical machine or, by chance, lose its process "back-end". If any of these two scenarios were the case, the state of the machine is always saved in RDF and thus, would simply "freeze" to await another virtual machine process to continue its execution. If the OperandStack was represented in software and thus, in RAM, then when the software halted, the OperandStack would be lost and the state of the machine would be inconsistent with its programLocation. With an RDF state, the RAM representation of the virtual machine process has a negligible effect on the consistency of the machine.

4.4.1.7 Frame

Fhat is a frame-based processor. This means that each invoked method is provided a Frame, or local environment, for its variables (i.e. FrameVariables). Due to how variables are scoped in object-oriented languages and because Neno does not support global variables, each method can only communicate with one another through parameter (i.e. method arguments) passing, return value passing, or object manipulations. When method *A* calls method *B*, the parameters passed by method *A* are stored in method *B*'s Frame according to the variable names in the method description. For example, assume the following method,

```
xsd:integer methodB(xsd:integer a) {
    return a + "1"^^xsd:integer;
}
```

If method *A* calls method *B*, with the statement,

```
xsd:integer x = marko.methodB("2"^^xsd:integer);
```

the value 2 is placed into the Frame of method *B* with the associated variable a. Method *B* adds 1 to the value and pushes the value 3 on the OperandStack. Method *A* pops one value off the OperandStack and sets the local variable x to the value 3. The OperandStack is used for the placement of method return values.

4.4.1.8 **ReturnStack**

The ReturnStack is a LIFO stack that maintains pointers to the return location of a method and the method Frame. To support recursion, the ReturnStack maintains a pointer to the specific Frame that is being returned to.

In order to explain how the ReturnStack is used, an example is provided. When method *A* calls method *B*, the next instruction of method *A* following the method invocation instruction is pushed onto the ReturnStack. When method *B* has completed its execution (e.g. a return is called), Fhat pops the instruction off the ReturnStack and sets its programLocation to that instruction. In this way, control is returned to method *A* to complete its execution. When return is called in method *B*, Fhat will delete (i.e. deallocate) all triples associated with the method *B* Frame. If return has a value (e.g. return 2), that value is pushed onto the OperandStack for method *A* to use in its computation.

4.4.2 Migrating Fhat Across Different Host CPUs

An interesting aspect of Fhat is the ability to migrate a Fhat process across various host CPUs. A Fhat implementation has two primary components: an RDF state representation and a software process. Because both the RDF triple-code and the complete state of a Fhat instance are represented in the RDF network, it does not matter which Fhat process is executing a particular Fhat state. The Fhat RDF state representation ensures that there are no global variables in the software process. The only variables created in the software process are local to the instruction being executed. Because there are no global variables in the software process, any software

Fig. 4.7 Migrating a Fhat
execution across multiple
host CPUs

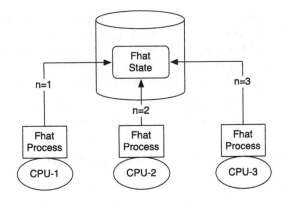

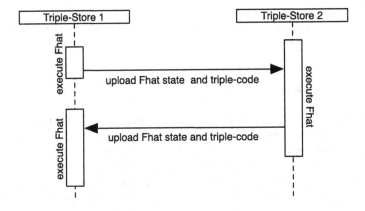

Fig. 4.8 Migrating a Fhat state across different triple stores

process can execute the Fhat RDF state without requiring inter-software process communication. For example, one host CPU can be running the Fhat software process and halt. Another CPU can then start another Fhat software process that points to the URI of the originally halted Fhat RDF state and continue its execution. This concept is diagrammed in Fig. 4.7 where $n = 1$ refers to instruction 1.

In principle, each CPU can execute one instruction and then halt. In this way, it is possible to migrate the Fhat RVM across different host CPU's. Thus, if a portion of the Semantic Web is needed for a particular computation, it may be best to have the physical computer supporting that RDF sub-network host the Fhat RVM. Once the Fhat RVM has completed computing that particular RDF sub-network, it can halt and another CPU can pick up the process on yet another area of the Semantic Web that needs computing by the Fhat RVM. In this model of computing, data doesn't move to the process, the process moves to the data. This idea is diagrammed in Fig. 4.8, where both triple store servers have Fhat process implementations.

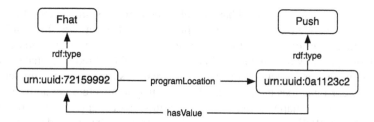

Fig. 4.9 A Fhat processor can process itself

4.4.3 Fhat Reflection

A Fhat RVM and the triple-code that it is executing are in the same address space and thus, can reference one another. It is the UUID address space of Neno/Fhat that makes it a unique programming environment in that Neno is not only a completely reflective language, but also that it removes the representational stack found in most other programming environments. Language reflection means that the program can modify itself during its execution. Many scripting languages and even Java (through the java.lang.reflect package) support language reflection. However, not only does Neno/Fhat support language reflection, it also supports machine reflection. A Fhat RVM can modify itself during its execution. There are no true boundaries between the various components of the computation. This idea is represented in Fig. 4.9, where a Fhat RVM has its program counter (programLocation) pointing to a Push instruction. The Push instruction is instructing Fhat to push a reference of itself on its operand stack. With a reference to the Fhat instance in the Fhat operand stack, Fhat can manipulate its own components. Thus, the Fhat RVM is executing triple-code that is manipulating itself.

4.4.4 r-Fhat

The primary drawback of the RVM is computing time because a virtual machine must not only read the RDF network to interpret the program instructions, it must also read/write to the RDF network to manipulate data (i.e. instance objects) in the RDF network. Moreover, the virtual machine must read and write to that subnetwork of the RDF network that represents the virtual machine's state (e.g. program counter, operand stack, etc.). In doing so, many read/write operations occur in order for the virtual machine to compute. However, much of this issue can be resolved through the use of r-Fhat.

What has been presented thus far is a semi-hard implementation of Fhat. The semi-hard implementation explicitly encodes the state of a Fhat instance in RDF. While this has benefits such as fault tolerance due to virtual machine process failures, support for distributed computing in the form of processor migration, and support for machine-based evolutionary algorithms, it requires a large read/write overhead. Each instruction requires the virtual machine process to explicitly update the virtual machine state. A faster Fhat virtual machine can be engineered that does not explicitly encode the state of the machine in the RDF network. In such cases, the only read/write operations that occur are when an object is instantiated, destroyed, or a property manipulated. This faster Fhat is called reduced Fhat (r-Fhat). In r-Fhat, the operand stack, return stack, etc. are data structures in the implementing language. r-Fhat does not have an OWL machine architecture nor an RDF state. However, there is a mapping that can take the in-memory representation of r-Fhat and generate an RDF representation of it. Thus, r-Fhat can be mapped to a standard Fhat instance.

4.5 The Fhat Instruction Set

In order for Neno software to run on a Fhat RVM instance, it must be compiled to a Fhat OWL API that is compliant with the Fhat instruction set (the Fhat OWL API `owl:imports` the Fhat instruction set ontology). A Fhat RVM uses the Fhat OWL API as a "blueprint" for constructing the instance-level representation of the RDF triple-code. It is the instance-level triple-code that the Fhat RVM "walks" when a program is executing.

4.5.1 The `Method`

In Neno, the only process code that exists is that which is in a `Method` `Block`. Figure 4.10 defines the OWL ontology of a `Method`.

A `Method` has an `ArgumentDescriptor` that is of `rdfs:subClassOf` `rdf:Seq` and a return descriptor that is of type `rdfs:Resource`. The sequence of the `ArgumentDescriptor` `Argument` denotes the placement of the `Method` parameter in the method declaration. For instance,

`xsd:integer exampleMethod(xsd:string n, Human h) { ... }`

would set the object of the `hasReturnDescriptor` property to the URI `xsd:integer` and the `ArgumentDescriptor` to the `Arguments` n (`rdf:_1`) and h (`rdf:_2`).

The `hasHumanCode` property can be used, if desired, to point to the original human readable/writable source code that describes that class and its methods. By using the `hasHumanCode` property, it is possible for "in-network" or run-time compiling of source code. In principle, a Neno compiler can be written in Neno and be executed by a Fhat RVM. The Neno compiler can compile the representation that results from resolving the URI that is the value of the `xsd:anyURI`.

4.5.1.1 A `Block` of Fhat Triple-Code

A `Method` has a single `Block`. A `Block` is an `rdfs:subClassOf` `Instruction` and is composed of a sequence of `Instructions`. The `Instruction`

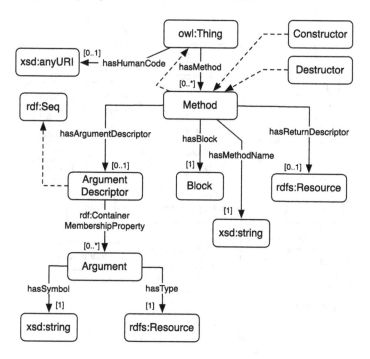

Fig. 4.10 The OWL Method ontology

sequence is denoted by the nextInst property. The Instruction rdf:type is the "opcode" of the Instruction. The set of all Instructions is the instruction set of the Fhat architecture. Figure 4.11 provides a collection of the super class Instructions that can exist in a Block of code and their relationship to one another.

Examples of these super classes are itemized below.[12]

- Arithmetic: Add, Divide, Multiply, Not, Subtract.
- Condition: Equals, GreaterThan, LessThan.
- Setter: NetQuery, Set, SetClear, SetMinus, SetPlus, SetQuery.
- Invoke: Construct, Destruct.

The Value class has a set of subclasses. These subclasses are itemized below.

- Direct: LocalDirect, PopDirect.
- Variable: LocalVariable, FieldVariable, ObjectVariable.

When a Fhat instance enters a Method it creates a new Frame. When a Variable is declared, that Variable is specified in the Frame and accord-

---

[12]Conditions are unique in that they have a trueInst and a falseInst property. If the Condition is true, the next Instruction is the one pointed to by the trueInst property, else the next Instruction is the one pointed to by the falseInst property.

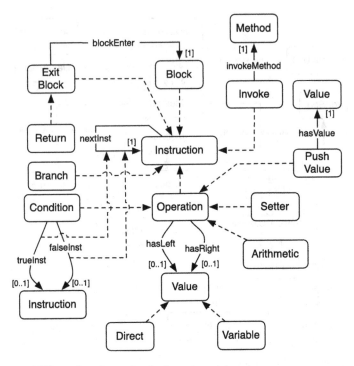

Fig. 4.11 The OWL ontology for a `Block` of `Instructions`

ing to the current `Block` of the `Fhat` instance as denoted by `Fhat`'s `blockTop` property. A `Block` is used for variable scoping. When Fhat leaves a `Block`, it destroys all the `FrameVariables` in the current `Frame` that have that `Block` as their `fromBlock` property (refer to Fig. 4.5). However, entering a new `Block` is not exiting the old `Block`. Parent `Block` `FrameVariables` can be accessed by child `Blocks`. For instance, in the following Neno code fragment,

```
xsd:integer x = "1"^^xsd:integer;
if(x > 2) {
  xsd:integer y = x;
}
else{
  xsd:integer y = x;
}
```

the two `y` `Variables` in the if and else `Blocks` are two different `FrameVaria-bles` since they are from different `Blocks`. Furthermore, note that both the if and else `Blocks` can access the value of x since they are in the child `Block` of the `Block` declaring the variable x. When Fhat leaves a `Method` (i.e. returns), its `Frame` and its `FrameVariables` are destroyed.

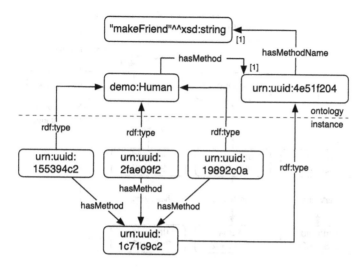

Fig. 4.12 Multiple object's of the same type will share the same Method instance

4.5.2 A *Method Instance*

There are two ways in which a Method instance is handled by Fhat: global and local instance models. In the global instance model, when a new object is instantiated, its methods are also instantiated. However, if the instantiated Method already exists in the RDF network, the newly created object points its hasMethod property to a previously created Method of the same hasMethodName and UUID. Thus, only one instance of a Method exists for all the objects of the same class type. While it is possible to have a unique Method instance for each object, by supporting method reuse amongst objects, Fhat limits the growth (in terms of the number of triples) in the RDF network. Furthermore, this increases the speed of the Fhat RVM since it does not need to create a new Method from the Fhat OWL API. The global instance model is diagrammed in Fig. 4.12. To ensure global instances, the methodReuse property of the Fhat instance is set to "true"^^xsd:boolean (refer to Fig. 4.5).

In the local instance model, the methodReuse property of a Fhat instance is set to "false"^^xsd:boolean. In such cases, a new Method instance is created with each new instance of an owl:Thing. The benefit of this model is that method reflection can occur on a per-object basis. If an object is to manipulate its Method triple-code at run-time, it can do so without destroying the operation of its fellow owl:Things. The drawback of the local instance model is triple store "bloat" and an increase in the time required to instantiate an object relative to the global instance model. The local instance model is diagrammed in Fig. 4.13.

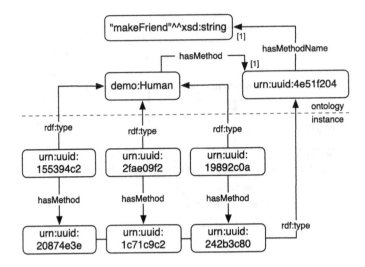

Fig. 4.13 Multiple object's of the same type each have a unique Method instance

4.5.2.1 An Example Method Instance

Suppose the following code,

```
owl:Thing Human
{
  xsd:int example(xsd:string a) {
    if(a == "marko"^^xsd:string) {
      return "1"^^xsd:int;
    }
    else {
      return "2"^^xsd:int;
    }
  }
}
```

When this code is compiled, it compiles to a Fhat OWL API. When an instance of Human is created, the Fhat RVM will start its journey at the URI Human and move through the ontology creating instance UUID URIs for all the components of the Human class. This includes, amongst its hard-coded properties, its Methods, their Blocks, and their Instructions. When the Human class is instantiated, an instance will appear in the RDF network as diagrammed in Fig. 4.14.

4.6 Conclusion

Imagine a world where virtual machines are as easy to distribute as an HTML document (e.g. an RDF/XML encoding of the virtual machine sub-network). Given

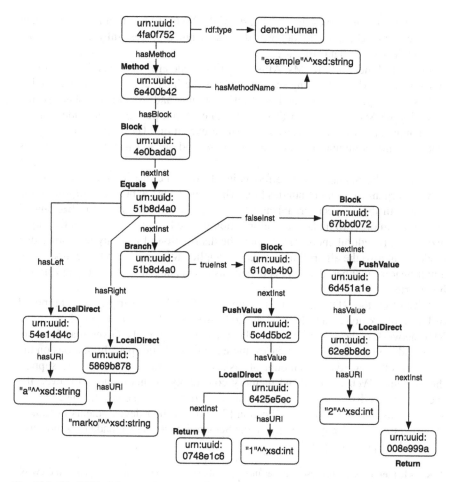

Fig. 4.14 The RDF triple-code for the `example(xsd:string)` method

that a virtualized machine encodes its state in the RDF network, think about how RVMs can "move" between physical machines in mid-execution. There is complete hardware independence as no physical machine maintains a state representation. Physical machines compute the RVM by reading its program location, its operand stack, its heap, etc. and update those data structures. In such situations, a personal computer can be encoded in the RDF network and be accessed anywhere. Thus, the underlying physical machine is only a hardware shell for the more "personal" machine encoded in the RDF network. These ideas are analogous to those presented in [37]. With respect to the Linked Data initiative [7], where all RDF data sets are interconnected to form a global "Web of Data", what emerges is a "Web of Data and Process". Currently the Web of Data is a pull-based environment much like the World Wide Web of documents. By providing a means to compute on Web of Data data sets in their local environment, a distributed computing model emerges that is more efficient than harvesting large parts of the Web of Data to a remote machine for processing. Thus, this model provides a distributed process infrastructure to the existing distributed data structure.

In the RDF network, RVMs, APIs, and triple-code are "first-class" web entities. What happens when archiving services such as the Internet Archive, search engine caches, and digital libraries archive RDF programs and "snap-shot" states of the executing RVMs [28, 34]? In theory, the state of computing world-wide, can be saved/archived and later retrieved to resume execution. The issues and novelties that archiving computations presents are many and are left to future work in this area.

Much of the Semantic Web effort is involved in the distribution of knowledge between organizational boundaries [15]. This is perhaps the primary purpose of the ontology. In this respect, organizations of a similar domain should utilize shared ontologies in order to make their information usable between their respective organizations. Procedural encodings support the distribution of not only the knowledge models, but also the algorithms that can be applied to compute on those models. In a non-disjoint manner, data and code are easily exchanged between organizational boundaries.

Given that the RDF network is composed of triples and triples are composed of URIs, blank nodes, and literals, the address space of any virtual machine in the RDF network is the set of all URIs, blank nodes, and literals. Given that there are no bounds to the size of these spaces, there are no realistic space limitations on the RVM. In other words, the amount of disk-space provided world-wide to support the Semantic Web is the actual memory constraints of this model. However, the success of this distributed computing paradigm relies on the consistent use of such standards as the Link Data specification [7]. With further developments in Linked Data and the RVM computing model, the Semantic Web can be made to behave like a general-purpose computer.

Acknowledgements   This research was made possible by a generous grant from the Andrew W. Mellon Foundation. Herbert Van de Sompel, Ryan Chute, and Johan Bollen all provided much insight during the development of these ideas. Neno/Fhat was originally designed in the fall of 2006. At the completion of this article, the author was introduced to the Ripple RDF programming language being developed by Joshua Shinavier [40]. The similarity in ideas has fostered a close collaboration.

References

1. Aasman, J.: Allegro graph. Technical Report 1, Franz Incorporated (2006). http://www.franz. com/products/allegrograph/allegrograph.datasheet.pdf
2. Aho, A.W., Sethi, R., Ullman, J.D.: Compilers: Principles, Techniques, and Tools. Addison-Wesley, Reading (1986)
3. Alesso, H.P., Smith, C.F.: Developing Semantic Web Services. A.K. Peters Ltd, Wellesley (2005)
4. Baader, F., Calvanese, D., Mcguinness, D.L., Nardi, D., Patel-Schneider, P.F. (eds.): The Description Logic Handbook: Theory, Implementation and Applications. Cambridge University Press, Cambridge (2003)

5. Beckett, D.: N-Triples. Technical Report, University of Bristol (2001). http://www.dajobe.org/2001/06/ntriples/

6. Berners-Lee, T.: Notation 3. Technical Report, World Wide Web Consortium (1998). http://www.w3.org/DesignIssues/Notation3

7. Berners-Lee, T.: Linked data. Technical Report, World Wide Web Consortium (2006). http://www.w3.org/DesignIssues/LinkedData.html

8. Berners-Lee, T., Fielding, R., Software, D., Masinter, L., Systems, A.: Uniform Resource Identifier (URI): Generic Syntax (2005). http://www.ietf.org/rfc/rfc2396.txt

9. Biron, P.V., Malhotra, A.: XML schema part 2: Datatypes second edition. Technical Report, World Wide Web Consortium (2004). http://www.w3.org/TR/xmlschema-2/

10. Bray, T., Hollander, D., Layman, A., Tobin, R.: Namespaces in XML 1.0. Technical Report, World Wide Web Consortium (2006). http://www.w3.org/TR/REC-xml-names/

11. Britton, R.: MIPS Assembly Language Programming. Prentice-Hall, Englewood Cliffs (2003)

12. Carroll, J.J., Stickler, P.: RDF triples in XML. In: Extreme Markup Languages. IDEAlliance, Montréal, Québec (2004)

13. Coelho, D., Stanculescu, A.: A state-of-the-art VHDL simulator. In: Thirty-Third IEEE Computer Society International Conference, pp. 320–323. San Francisco, CA (1988)

14. Craig, I.D.: Virtual Machines. Springer, Berlin (2005)

15. Davies, J., Fensel, D., van Harmelen, F.: Towards the Semantic Web: Ontology-Driven Knowledge Management. Wiley, New York (2003)

16. Eckel, B.: Thinking in Java. Prentice-Hall, Englewood Cliffs (2002). http://www.mindview.net/Books/TIJ/

17. Fensel, D.: Triple-space computing: Semantic web services based on persistent publication of information. In: Proceedings of the International Conference on Intelligence in Communication Systems, pp. 43–53. Bangkok, Thailand (2004)

18. Fensel, D., Hendler, J.A., Lieberman, H., Wahlster, W. (eds.): Spinning the Semantic Web: Bringing the World Wide Web to Its Full Potential. MIT Press, Cambridge (2003)

19. Hennessy, J.L., Patterson, D.A.: Computer Architecture: A Quantitative Approach. Morgan Kaufmann, San Mateo (2002)

20. Horrocks, I., Patel-Schneider, P.F., Boley, H., Tabet, S., Grosof, B., Dean, M.: SWRL: A Semantic Web rule language combining OWL and RuleML. Technical Report, World Wide Web Consortium (2004). http://www.w3.org/Submission/SWRL/

21. Kifer, M., Lausen, G., Wu, J.: Logical foundations of object-oriented and frame-based languages. Journal of the ACM **42**(4), 741–843 (1995)

22. Kiryakov, A., Ognyanov, D., Manov, D.: OWLIM—a pragmatic semantic repository for OWL. In: International Workshop on Scalable Semantic Web Knowledge Base Systems. Lecture Notes in Computer Science, vol. 3807, pp. 182–192. Springer, New York (2005)

23. Koide, S., Kawamura, M.: SWCLOS: A Semantic Web processor on Common Lisp object system. In: Proceedings of the International Semantic Web Conference, Hiroshima, Japan (2004)

24. Lacy, L.W.: OWL: Representing Information Using the Web Ontology Language. Trafford Publishing, Victoria (2005)

25. Leach, P.: A Universally Unique IDentifier (UUID) URN Namespace. Technical Report, Network Working Group (2005). http://www.rfc-archive.org/getrfc.php?rfc=4122

26. Lee, R.: Scalability report on triple store applications. Technical Report, Massachusetts Institute of Technology (2004)

27. Lindholm, T., Yellin, F.: The Java Virtual Machine Specification. Addison-Wesley, Reading (1999)

28. Lorie, R.A.: Long term preservation of digital information. In: Proceedings of the 1st ACM/IEEE-CS Joint Conference on Digital Libraries, pp. 346–352. ACM, New York (2001). doi:10.1145/379437.379726

29. Louden, K.C.: Programming Languages: Principles and Practice. Brooks/Cole–Thomson Learning (2003)

30. Manola, F., Miller, E.: RDF primer: W3C recommendation (2004). http://www.w3.org/TR/rdf-primer/

31. Martin, D., Burstein, M., Hobbs, J., Lassila, O., McDermott, D., McIlraith, S., Narayanan, S., Paolucci, M., Parsia, B., Payne, T., Sirin, E., Srinivasan, N., Sycara, K.: OWL-S: Semantic markup for web services. Technical Report, World Wide Web Consortium (2004). http://www. w3.org/Submission/OWL-S/

32. McGuinness, D.L., van Harmelen, F.: OWL web ontology language overview (2004)

33. Miller, E.: An introduction to the Resource Description Framework. D-Lib Magazine (1998). http://dx.doi.org/hdl:cnri.dlib/may98-miller

34. Nelson, M.L., McCown, F., Smith, J., Klein, M.: Using the web infrastructure to preserve web pages. International Journal on Digital Libraries (2007). doi:10.1007/s00799-007-0012-y

35. Oren, E., Delbru, R., Gerke, S., Haller, A., Decker, S.: ActiveRDF: Object-oriented semantic web programming. In: Proceedings of the International World Wide Web Conference WWW07, Banff, Canada (2007)

36. Prud'hommeaux, E., Seaborne, A.: SPARQL query language for RDF. Technical Report, World Wide Web Consortium (2004). http://www.w3.org/TR/2004/WD-rdf-sparql-query-20041012/

37. Satyanarayanan, M., Gilbert, B., Toups, M., Tolia, N., Surie, A., O'Hallaron, D.R., Wolbach, A., Harkes, J., Perrig, A., Farber, D.J., Kozuch, M.A., Helfrich, C.J., Nath, P., Lagar-Cavilla, H.A.: Pervasive personal computing in an Internet suspend/resume system. IEEE Internet Computing 11(2), 16–25 (2007)

38. Seaborne, A., Manjunath, G.: SPARQL/Update: A language for updating RDF graphs. Technical Report, Hewlett-Packard (2007). http://jena.hpl.hp.com/~afs/SPARQL-Update.html

39. Sebesta, R.W.: Concepts of Programming Languages. Addison-Wesley, Reading (2005)

40. Shinavier, J.: Functional programs as linked data. In: 3rd Workshop on Scripting for the Semantic Web, Innsbruck, Austria (2007)

41. Sowa, J.F.: Principles of Semantic Networks: Explorations in the Representation of Knowledge. Morgan Kaufmann, San Mateo (1991)

42. Sowa, J.F.: Knowledge Representation: Logical, Philosophical, and Computational Foundations. Course Technology (1999)

43. Turing, A.M.: On computable numbers with an application to the entscheidungsproblem. Proceedings of the London Mathematical Society 42(2), 230–265 (1937)

44. Wang, H.H., Noy, N., Rector, A., Musen, M., Redmond, T., Rubin, D., Tu, S., Tudorache, T., Drummond, N., Horridge, M., Sedenberg, J.: Frames and OWL side by side. In: 10th International Protégé Conference, Budapest, Hungary (2007)

Part II
Collaboration, Semantic and Intelligence

Chapter 5
Agent Technology Meets the Semantic Web: Interoperability and Communication Issues

Anastasia Karanastasi and Nikolaos Matsatsinis

Abstract This overview paper is a survey of recent research on agent technologies and how this technology can serve the scopes of the Semantic Web project. In a short time, Web has become the dominant database for information retrieval. Due to the exponential growth of the Web and the information it provides, finding accurate information is becoming more and more difficult. In the near future, access to Web will be mediated by intelligent applications and software agents that will assist users in finding accurate information and complete transactions successfully. Concisely, the Semantic Web means ontologies and semantics, software agents means multi-agents systems (MASs) built in FIPA 2002 and other agent platforms with their own standards, and Web services means XML. We will try to investigate the way these technologies can cooperate without changing their specifications.

5.1 Introduction

Agent Technologies are becoming open and heterogeneous with final scope to increase inter-connectivity and capability of collaboration. To achieve this goal, there is a need for agents that can manage multiple agent communication languages, content languages and multiple ontology representations.

The vision of the Semantic Web according to [3] was to enrich web pages with meaning and to enable automation, so that information will be accessed programmatically. By this way, the Web will gradually be transformed from being simply a collection of web pages to a collection of programs that offer combined functionality over standard protocols.

The Semantic Web promises to change the way agents navigate and utilize information over the Internet. By providing a structured, distributed representation for expressing concepts and relationships defined by multiple domain ontologies, it is now possible for agents to read and reason about knowledge without the need of

A. Karanastasi (✉)
Decision Support Systems Laboratory, Technical University of Crete, Chania, 73100, Greece
e-mail: natasha@ergasya.tuc.gr

Y. Badr et al. (eds.) *Emergent Web Intelligence: Advanced Semantic Technologies,*
Advanced Information and Knowledge Processing,
DOI 10.1007/978-1-84996-077-9_5, © Springer-Verlag London Limited 2010

centralized ontologies. But, in order to exploit the benefits of the collaboration of multi-agent systems with the semantics of the web we need first to solve the interoperability issues between different MASs and investigate how to integrate the technology with the available information over the Internet.

The Semantic Web is a mesh of information linked up in such a way as to be easily processable by machines, on a global scale. It is an efficient way of representing data on the World Wide Web, or we may say a globally linked database.

The Semantic Web was though up by Tim Berners-Lee, inventor of the WWW, URIs, HTTP, and HTML. There is a dedicated team of people at the World Wide Web consortium (W3C) working to improve, extend and standardize the system, and many languages, publications, tools and so on have already been developed.

The problem with the majority of data on the Web is that it is difficult to use on a large scale, because there is no global system for publishing data in such a way as it can be easily processed by anyone. The Semantic Web can be seen as a huge engineering solution. The Semantic Web uses syntaxes called "Resource Description Framework" syntaxes, which are triples based structures. RDF XML [25] is considered to be the standard interchange format for RDF [24] on the Semantic Web. Once information is in RDF form, it becomes easy to process it, since RDF is a generic format, which already has many parsers. The benefit of using RDF in comparison with XML is that the information maps directly and unambiguously to a decentralized model. In an RDF application, you know which bits of data are the semantics of the application and which are syntactic.

To facilitate automated processing on the Web and enable applications to communicate and work with each other, we need programmatic interfaces, named web services. A web service is a collection of functions that are packaged as a single entity and published on the network to be used by other programs. The Web Services model relies on a service oriented architecture [9] based on three main categories of actors: the *service providers* which are entities responsible for the Web Service, the *clients* acting as intermediaries for the services' users and the *directories* offering to suppliers the possibility to publish their services and to customers the means for locating their requirements in term of services. Specifically, a web service is a software system identified by a Uniform Resource Identifier, (URI), whose public interfaces and bindings are defined and described using the eXtended Markup Language (XML) [30]. Its definition can be discovered by other software systems. These systems may then interact with the web service as described in its definition, using XML-based messages oven standard Internet protocols. The power of web services lies in that they can interact seamlessly and transparently to achieve combined functionality and produce the overall required result. In this way, programs providing simple services can be combined to deliver sophisticated value-added services. To put it in another way, web services are building blocks for creating open distributed systems.

In the following section we are going to analyze why web services could not serve the scopes of the Semantic Web by confronting their specifications with the ones of agents. The benefits that agents present are also the reason for their interoperability problems that need to be solved in order to integrate with success their technology with the Semantic Web.

5.2 Main Differences Between Web Services and Agents

Given a request for a service from a user, web services need first to be located, matched against the particular request and then executed. Ideally, to achieve the full potential of Web Services and the Semantic Web, users—individuals and organizations—should be able to identify their needs and delegate them to software agents who can then locate the appropriate web services. Thus, agents can facilitate the seamless integration of web services so that the complexity of the execution of the request is transparent to the user—by hiding the underlying complexity. Although web services and agents encapsulate functionality, they are different in that [27]:

- A service is static and unable to adapt. It only knows about itself and its own functionality. On the other hand, agents can learn about the user, other agents and services and may be able to adapt and offer personalized services according to the user's needs. Agents can also take advantage of new information to best serve the user.

- Services are passive until they are invoked. Agents, on the other hand, are autonomous and proactive, and thus can actively seek to help the user, for instance, by checking periodically for new information on a topic that the user is interested in, or notifying her when a new product has arrived at a particular store. An agent may invoke a service at regular intervals to check the price of the stocks in the user's portfolio, but only alert the user when the price falls below a certain threshold. Once a service is invoked with the correct parameters, it will be executed, i.e., a service does not have control over its execution, whereas an agent can decide on its own whether to execute a request or not.

- The communication between services is at a low, syntactic level; services can exchange data, but they do not understand them. Thus, services are not designed to use and work with ontologies. If a requester and a service provider use different ontologies, the result of the web service invocation would be incomprehensible to the requester. Agents can take advantage of ontologies and the Semantic Web and resolve possible incompatibilities.

- Although a service can interact with other services, composed functionality among services can only be achieved if orchestrated by a third party; services *per se* do not have a social ability and they cannot coordinate to deliver composed functionality. On the other hand, agents can cooperate with one another and can form groups so that they can provide combined functionality and more comprehensive services.

5.3 Web Agents

Web agents are complex software systems that operate in the world wide web, the Internet, and related corporate, government, or military intranets. They are designed to perform a variety of tasks from caching and routing to searching, categorizing, and filtering.

The ideal web agent needs to satisfy four requirements:

- Communicative: able to understand the user's scope, preferences and constraints.

A problem with the most well known search engines is that they have no knowledge of the domains of interest. Solutions to this problem usually involves the use of ontologies, a formal definition of a body of knowledge. The most typical type of ontology used in building agents involves a structural component. It is essentially a taxonomy of class and subclass relations coupled with definitions of the relationships between the terms of the ontology.

If an ontology is well structured and uses a machine readable vocabulary, it allows a software program to manipulate the terms used in the ontology, terms that make sense to users who understand this information. A software program can manipulate terms that the user understands. Software components, like agents promote this communication, by reflecting users' needs, preferences and constraints.

- Capable: able to take actions rather than simply provide advice.

Either we refer to an autonomous agent or a multi-agent system, the agent needs to be capable not only to recommend but also to take action in order to fulfill tasks assigned by a user. It needs to take actions so to make things simpler and automated for the user. For this scope, it is necessary the agent to be able to overcome the syntactic elements in order to extract the semantic elements of a web page. Here is one of the major problems for the web agents. While agreement is starting to emerge, a lot of engineering is still to be done to encode information about Internet sources and about finding the appropriate way to manipulate them.

- Autonomous: able to act without the user being in control the whole time.

A truly effective web agent or a web multi-agent system, needs to be able to take some sort of action and work for the user. The key to autonomy is finding the right level for the task at hand. The autonomy is a difficult programming task, because it is very dependent on the characteristics of the domain a program is operating. The level of autonomy also depends on the group of users that use the proposed service and their constraints. It is difficult to predefine what a specific user would like to take action for and what he/she wants to be done automatically without knowing any details.

- Adaptive: able to learn from experience about both its tasks and about its users preferences.

It is very important for the system to succeed its goal by meeting user's criteria and not overstep his/her constraints. To do that it needs to "understand" user's preferences on a particular application environment. A web agent with a predefined number of pages to visit, is limited and needs to be able to adapt its behavior based on a combination of user feedback and environmental factors. Enabling autonomy is not an easy programming task, particularly because each system depends on the context of the area that operates. The ways of achieving such a behavior are many. Theories from machine learning, collaboration filtering etc. can be adapted.

5.4 Characteristics of Multi-Agent Systems

Definition A multi-agent system consists of a network of loosely-coupled computational autonomous agents who can perform actions, have resources at their disposal and possess knowledge, capabilities or skills. They are situated in a common environment and they can interact through a set of rules, namely an interaction protocol.

Well known problems with MASs are how to enable agents to interact with one another, how agents can find others in open environments, such as the Internet and how to enable agents to dynamically form teams in order to solve complex problems.

In an open MAS, the system often has no prior static design, only single agents within. Agents are not necessarily aware of others or the expertise and services that they can offer. Therefore, a mechanism for locating other agents within the system is required. Agents may be non-cooperative, malicious or untrustworthy. An example of an open MAS is an electronic marketplace. Agents representing customers may not necessarily be aware of providers and to obtain services and products they need yo be able to locate such agents. This is usually done through specially designed middle agents that act as a directory.

One of the advantages of open MASs is that single agents or groups are designed separately. Such systems are more flexible and fault tolerant, since failure of one agent even if this agent is an expert in a particular area/task, does not mean failure of the entire system; another expert agent can be located ant take on the task. Such a MAS is easier to maintain since no single individual/organization/team is responsible for the maintenance of the entire system. The system is dynamic like an open society, and may evolve according to the changing needs of the agents and the users they represent. The agents may adapt and evolve. However, since the individual entities within the system may be developed by different developers using different languages and frameworks, heterogeneity is inherent. As a result, communication protocols, languages and ontologies, may vary across agents. Agents and their interaction protocols need to be designed carefully in order to allow interoperation. Malicious behavior is difficult to avoid and consequently the overall behavior of the system is not predictable while at times, as there is no explicit global control, the behavior may be incoherent.

Multi-agent systems are becoming increasingly popular as a new software engineering paradigm that provides the right abstraction level and the right model to build a lot of distributed applications. The basic components, agents, interact with one another to achieve their individual design objectives. Interactions are the results of communicative actions or physical actions that transform the environment and are carried out by at least two agents. More often, we are not interested in random interactions, but in interactions that enable agents to coordinate themselves in achieving their tasks, whether by cooperating or competing. Therefore, it is useful to have interaction protocols in place, that is, rules that guide the interaction that takes place between agents. These rules define the messages or actions that are possible for any particular interaction situation. This set of possible messages or actions that an agent can perform as part of an interaction protocol is finite. In agreeing to use a particular protocol, an agent agrees to conform to its rules and conventions.

Interaction protocols may be communication protocols, cooperation protocols or negotiation protocols. Cooperation protocols provide a framework within agents can coordinate their actions to achieve a complex task or to solve a problem in a cooperative way. Negotiation protocols help the parties involved to reach a compromise and resolve the conflict by way of an agreement. Communication protocols provide rules that structure message-passing and produce meaningful dialogues or conversations. Alternatively, such protocols can be thought of as constraints on the possible valid exchanges of communication primitives, very much as in meaningful conversations among humans. To sum up, when we talk about interoperability we need to distinguish 3 levels:

- the technological level
- the syntactical level
- the semantical level

Communication has three aspects:

1. *syntax*: how the symbols of communication are structured;
2. *semantics*: what the symbols denote;
3. *pragmatics*: how the symbols are interpreted.

So, meaning is a combination of semantics and pragmatics.

5.5 Agent Communication Languages

An agent communication language is defined at three levels: the lower level, which specifies the method of interconnection; the middle level, which specifies the format or syntax; and the top level, which specifies the meaning or semantics.

An agent communication language has three components: the outer and inner languages and the vocabulary. The 'outer' language is the language that is used in order to express the primitives, i.e. the performatives that an agent is permitted to use in communicating with other agents. It defines an 'envelope' format for using messages and is used by the agent to explicitly state the intended illocutionary force of a message. The 'inner' or 'content' language (syntax) is the (logical or representation) language which is used to write the message itself. In other words, it is the syntax used for the message. This layer allows for knowledge sharing. The vocabulary describes the domain of discourse in terms of concepts and their relationships and prescribes meaning to the terms used, i.e. it is the semantics.

Labrou and Finin [15] identified a number of features as essential for a good ACL. First of all, a good ACL should be declarative and syntactically simple. Secondly, the ACL needs to have a well-defined set of primitives and also needs to distinguish between the communicative language which expresses the primitives, and the content language which expresses the message itself, although it should not commit to a content language. Thirdly, the semantics for the primitives should be clearly defined, preferably through a formal description, as in modal logic. Another desirable feature is that the implementation of the language should be efficient, both in terms of speed and bandwidth, with simple interfaces. Moreover, as networking is prevalent, a good ACL should support all of the basic connections, i.e. point-to-point, multicast and broadcast, and both synchronous and asynchronous communication. Given the heterogeneity of environments, programming languages and frameworks, a good ACL should provide tools for dealing with heterogeneity and support interoperability with other languages and protocols. Finally, an ACL should support reliable and secure communication among agents, including authentication facilities and error detection.

5.5.1 Knowledge and Query Manipulation Language (KQML)

The Knowledge and Query Manipulation Language (KQML), is a high-level, message-oriented, communication language and set of protocols for information exchange [14, 16]. KQML emanated as the result of the DARPA-funded Knowledge Sharing Effort (KSE) in the early 1990s which concentrated on developing a methodology for distributing information among heterogeneous intelligent systems [21].

In essence, KQML is an 'outer' language and is based on speech act theory. It consists of three layers: the *content* layer, the *message* layer and the *communication* layer. The communication layer encodes a set of message features that describe the lower-level communication parameters, such as the identities of the sender and addressee(s) and a unique identifier associated with the message. The message layer is used to encode the message to be sent. This layer specifies the speech act or performative that the sender attaches to the content and sends to the addressee. It also includes optional features, such as the content language or the ontology used, among others. The content layer includes the content of the message itself. This can be in any representational language. In KQML there is a separation of protocol semantics from content semantics. All the information required to understand the message is independent of the transport mechanism (TCP/IP, CORBA, etc.), the content language (KIF, SQL, etc.) or the ontology assumed by the content.

5.5.2 FIPA ACL

As part of the standardization effort for agent interaction protocols, FIPA proposed the FIPA Agent Communication Language [11] or else FIPA ACL. Similar to KQML, FIPA ACL is based on speech acts, and messages are considered to be communicative acts. Communicative acts are described in both a narrative form and a formal semantics based on modal logic. The syntax of FIPA ACL is very similar to that of KQML. It contains a core of primitive communicative acts, and additional acts can be defined in terms of two core ones: **inform** and **request**. In a similar way to KQML, FIPA ACL upkeeps the distinction between outer and inner languages and is independent of the content language.

Semantics in FIPA ACL is defined through the *Semantics Language* (*SL*), which is a quantified multi-modal logic with operators for beliefs (*B*), uncertain beliefs (*U*), desires (*D*) and persistent foals or intentions (*PG*). *SL* is based on the theory of speech acts of Cohen and Levesque [6]) and, in particular, its extension by Sadek [4, 26]. The semantics of each communicative act is defined in terms of two sets of *SL* formulas: *Feasibility Preconditions* and *Rational Effects*. For a communicative act *a*, the feasibility preconditions *FP*(*a*) describe the necessary conditions that need to hold true in order for the sender to send the act *a*. The feasibility precondition expresses a constraint which describes what the sender of the message must satisfy, if it is to be considered as conforming to FIPA ACL. Although the agent is not obliged to perform *a*, if *FP*(*a*) holds, it may choose to do so. The rational effect of a communicative act represents the effect that an agent can expect to occur as a result of it performing the act, and it may also specify conditions that should hold true for the receiver. In other words, the rational effect describes the purpose of the message, i.e. that it is that the sender attempts to achieve by sending it. However, as agents are autonomous, the rational effect of a communicative action cannot be guaranteed. Therefore, the receiver of the message does not have to condom to the rational effect of the message.

FIPA provides the specification for a number of communication exchange protocols, such as the *Request*, *Query* and *Request When* interaction protocols, among others. Similar to KQML, the current FIPA specification does not provide any particular mechanisms for secure agent communications. An approach to deal with security issues in FIPA agents including communication has been suggested in [22]. FIPA ACL compliant systems include JADE [2], Agent Factory [7, 8], Grasshopper [1] and JACK Intelligent Agents [5].

5.5.3 Comparing KQML and FIPA ACL

Although KQML and FIPA ACL look syntactically similar and ascribe to the same theory, there are fundamental differences between them. The first and most prominent is that of semantics. In KQML, semantics is described in terms of pre, post and completion conditions, whereas FIPA ACL semantics is based on speech acts as rational actions [4, 6, 26] that have feasibility preconditions and rational effects. Each ACL uses different languages to describe the propositional mental attitudes, e.g. KQML's *BEL operator* is not the same as FIPA ACL's *B operator*. Although the FIPA ACL primitives can be approximated using the KQML performatives and vice versa, a direct transformation between the two languages is not possible. Both languages claim that they are independent of the use of content language. However, in order to be able to process some incoming communicative acts in FIPA ACL such as **request**, the agent needs to have a basic understanding of the *SL* language.

Other differences between the two languages include the use of different keywords, for instance, KQML uses **tell**, whereas FIPA ACL uses **inform** for the same communicative act. Even though the two performatives syntactically are almost identical, their semantics differ as well. A further difference has to do with the treatment of the 'administration' and 'facilitation' primitives. These are important as they allow an agent to register itself so that it can locate and be located in an open multi-agent system by other agents. In KQML such communicative acts are treated as first-class objects and constitute primitives. In FIPA ACL **register** and **unregister** are treated as requests for actions with reserved (natural language) meaning, while facilitation primitives such as **broker, recommend** and **recruit** are not part of the FIPA ACL specification.

Communication can take place among agents that reside in the same agent platform or among agents on different platforms. In the latter case, the message will have to be transported using the underlying network infrastructure. To enable effective agent communication among agents platforms, a layered approach is required.

Above the message envelope there is the agent communication language layer which defines which agent communication language is used to write the message, i.e. FIPA ACL or KQML. The content language layer defines the inner language used to write the content of the message itself such as, for instance, KIF or Prolog. It goes without saying that ontologies need to be explicitly defined so that the message content can be understood by all participants in the communication exchange. Finally, the top layer is the dialogue or interaction protocol layer. The interaction protocol essentially identifies the sequence of messages hat need to be exchanged, or in other words the structure of the conversation, for agents to have meaningful interactions. It is crucial that interaction protocols are well-designed and efficient while they minimize unnecessary message exchange. A badly designed interaction protocol means that the interaction will take longer to bring about a successful conclusion.

5.6 Ontologies

Web services might be one of the most powerful uses of Web ontologies and a key enabler for Web agents [13]. Businesses, especially those in supply chain management for business-to-business e-commerce, have been discussing the role of ontologies in managing machine-to-machine interactions. The problem till now has been the approach of using the ontologies. The approach before the Semantic Web vision was that the development presupposed the use of ontologies to ensure that everyone will agree on terms, types, constraints and so forth. On the Semantic Web there are machine-readable ontologies that can be used by agents to find the appropriate Web services and automate their use.

The Semantic Web envisions that almost every company, university or organization will want their Web resources linked to ontological content because of the many powerful tools that will be available for using that content. Data and services will be exchanged between applications. On top of this infrastructure as Hendler declares, agent-based computing will become much more practical. The Semantic

Web ontologies are straightforward for their purpose of use. By creating service advertisements in an ontological language, we will be able to use the hierarchy and conform with the constraints, to find matches through class and subclass properties or other semantic links. By using a combination of Web markup and ontology languages we can put advertisement into ontologies but also include a machine-readable description of service and some explicit logic describing the consequences of using the service. Such service descriptions and service logic will lead us to the integration of agents and ontologies.

Agents that communicate and understand each other need despite the common language, also a common terminology. Confusion and misunderstandings may arise if agents use the same language to communicate, but refer to the same concept employing different terms. Confusion may also arise when agents refer to different concepts using the same term. If agents are not aware of this distinction, they will not be able to enter into a meaningful dialogue. Consequently, a shared representation is essential for successful communication and interaction to take place between heterogeneous agents.

This common vocabulary or shared terminology can be captured and crystallized in an ontology. An ontology is a specification of the concepts, objects and their attributes, and relationships, in a specific knowledge domain. The subject of ontology s the study of the classes of things, their attributes and relationships that exist in some domain D. The product, an ontology, is a specification of the types of things that exist in D from a particular perspective, using a language L. As an ontology represents a domain from a particular perspective, conforming to an ontology means committing to seeing the world in a particular way.

An ontology defines a common vocabulary for those who need to share information in a domain. In other words, an ontology constitutes common ground for those wishing to engage in meaningful interactions. This is one of the primary reasons why we need to develop ontologies.

Ontologies are also important because they enable the reuse of domain knowledge [18]. For instance, models of many different domains need to represent the notion of time. If such an ontology is developed in sufficient detail once, then it can be deployed in many other domains. Existing ontologies that describe only parts of a domain and no its entirety, can also be integrated into one large domain ontology. Although this may not always be straightforward, it is still possible and allows for the reuse of domain knowledge.

Ontologies also allow us to encode assumptions about the domain explicitly. These encodings can be easily changed if our domain assumptions change. It is much easier to change domain assumptions when there are encoded in ontologies, rather than when they are hard-coded in a program. Consequently m i is also easier to share the changes in the domain assumptions.

Furthermore, ontologies allow us to separate semantics from operational knowledge. Finally, explicit specifications of domain knowledge are useful for new users who must learn the meanings of the terms in the domain.

5.6.1 OWL

OWL [20] is an ontology language that can formally describe the meaning of terminology used in Web documents. OWL extends and is a revision of the DARPA Agent Markup Language + Ontology Inference Layer (DAML + OIL) web ontology language.

The Resource Description Framework (RDF) is a datamodel for resource objects on the Web and the relations between them. It is mainly intended for representing metadata about resources but also in general about things that can be identified on the Web, even if they cannot be directly retrieved. RDF provides the means to represent graphs which express the structure of a given document. RDF documents are written in XML. But the RDF primitives themselves are rather sparse. RDF Schema is a basic vocabulary for describing properties and classes of RDF resources along with a semantics for generalization-hierarchies of such properties and classes. RDF Schema does not provide actual application-specific classes and properties, instead it provides the framework to describe them. Classes in RDF Schema are much like classes in object-oriented programming languages. This allows resources to be defined as instances of classes, and subclasses of classes.

OWL builds on RDF and proposes a specific vocabulary that provides selected frame and description logic primitives to capture ontologies. Thus, it has an enriched vocabulary which allows for describing classes and properties including relation between classes, cardinality, equality, richer typing of properties and enumerated classes. OWL and RDF are much of the same thing, but OWL is a stronger language with greater machine interoperability than RDF. Similar to RDF, OWL is written in XML.

OWL provides three sublanguages with increasing expressiveness:

- OWL Lite supports those users primarily needing a classification hierarchy and simple constraints. OWL Lite has the lower formal complexity among the OWL sublanguages.
- OWL DL supports those users who want the maximum expressiveness while retaining computational completeness (all conclusions are guaranteed to be computable) and decidability (all computations will finish in finite time). OWL DL includes all OWL language constructs, but they can be used only under certain restrictions (for example, while a class may be a subclass of many classes, a class cannot be an instance of another class). OWL DL is so named due to its correspondence with description logics, a field of research that has studied the logics that form the formal foundation of OWL.
- OWL Full is meant for users who want maximum expressiveness with no computational guarantees. OWL Full allows an ontology to augment the meaning of the pre-defined (RDF or OWL) vocabulary. It is unlikely that any reasoning software will be able to support complete reasoning for every feature of OWL Full.

5.7 Specifications for Open Multi-Agent Systems

Despite the many challenges that open MASs raise, they will become increasingly prevalent because of their flexibility and because they are fully distributed. Even though open MASs have no prior static design, such systems are not just simply collections of agents that are situated in a common environment. Agents come together in order to make use of the services of other agents, share resources, expertise and information, perform a complex task or solve a difficult problem. For these causes a general infrastructure is required. A MAS infrastructure consists of the set of services and knowledge that facilitate agent interactions [28]. The set of services that are considered essential for the enactment and support of an open MAS are described in what follows.

At the most basic level a MAS depends on the operating environment. The operating environment is comprised by the machines and their operating systems, the network infrastructure and the transport protocols such as TCP/IP, etc.

A MAS also requires an underlying communication infrastructure. Messages between agents as well as between the agents and the MAS itself, need to be transferred through appropriate communication channels. The communication infrastructure should support different modes of communication. Also the communication infrastructure should be independent of the Agent Communication Language (ACL) used by the MAS and the transport protocol. This means that systems that deploy different ACLs should be able to employ the same underlying communication infrastructure.

A suitable ACL is required in order agents to communicate with each other, which enables the agents to send different types of messages depending of the situation. An ACL should describe the syntax of the messages to be exchanged as well as their semantics. In addition to an ACL, a common terminology—an ontology—that enables the agents to understand and be understood is also essential. Conversational policies and protocols should also be defined at this level.

A MAS infrastructure should also provide performance and management services. These are services that enable one to monitor the system's activities as well as performance. A performance module can monitor the performance of the system as a whole and that of individual agents. Such information could be used, for instance, to optimize the execution of a task and the allocation of resources identify bottlenecks and take appropriate action such as assign more agents to a specific task.

Security and trust management services are also required in order to ensure that agents are who they claim to be and their behavior is checked upon and regulated so as to avoid harmful interactions.

In order agents in open MASs to know other agents based on their services and capabilities a MAS infrastructure should offer appropriate description and discovery services. When agents enter a MAS they should be able to make themselves known through some process of registration with the system, and also describe their capabilities.

Another important service is that of discovery and matching. Agents need to be able to advertise themselves and describe their capabilities or services to a middle agent who can then match them with incoming requests from requester agents.

Finally, a MAS infrastructure should allow for the interoperation between different MASs. This is the most important part of the infrastructure as far as it concerns the interoperability of MASs. Translation services may be required in order to allow agents across different MASs to communicate and exchange services and information when using different ACLs.

5.8 Interoperability Issues

Research in the agent field revealed that co-operating agents require access to unambiguous semantic description of the same concept, entity of object. For example, the DARPA Knowledge Sharing Effort (KSE) tackled the problem of interoperability between heterogeneous knowledge sources by dividing the problem into three layers: a language translation layer, a communications layer and an ontology layer in which semantic consistency is preserved within the domain in which the application work [19]. The idea behind this is that a shared domain ontology is developed in advance and is being used by the agents, who can choose or extend the elements that best suit their own perspective. In this scenario, knowledge can be shared, because agents understand the language of the shared ontology. Agent communication languages such as KQML and FIPA assume a shared ontology between communication agents. In KQML, the message layer allows the agent to specify an ontology service to allow agents to reason about domain knowledge.

As we have already mentioned, one of the key objectives of the Semantic Web project is to enable processing of web resources by distributed, intelligent entities such as software agents [3]. Along with this project, several specifications have been introduced such as RDF (http://www.w3.org/RDF/), OIL (http://www.ontoknowledge.org/oil/), DAML (http://www.daml.org) and OWL (http://www.w3.org/TR/owl-features/), which allow domain ontologies to be produced. The approach based on the methodologies proposed by the Semantic Web is a top-down approach to the problem of the semantic agreement. However, the difficulty in this approach is how agreement is reached on the correct knowledge representation for a particular domain. If two or more ontologies are used for a particular domain, agents who wish to communicate will require a translation service between ontologies. Even worst, where agreement is not reached, each agent uses a knowledge representation based on local semantics and communication between agents requires a translation service between each pair of agents.

As analyzed in [12], despite the obvious benefits of an agreed semantic framework, the take-up on Semantic Web proposals to date has been slow. Instead, simpler, 'bottom-up' initiatives have become much more successful as for example, the RSS, which has become the standard mean of allowing information providers to publish up-to-date data on the web, without requiring explicit semantic mark-up. The proliferation of these 'bottom-up' approaches appears to be stimulated by the lack of centralized co-ordination required for their deployment. This suggests that web content providers prefer minimal constraints on the local definition of semantics.

Other approaches of heterogeneous schema matching are based on machine learning [23] but the problem still remains; where agents have heterogeneous knowledge representations, such approaches require a mapping between representations for every pair of agents. On the contrary, we want to research how the information agents, that are part of multi-agent systems, can learn to refer to common objects inside and outside their environment, without having to formally define or learn a particular semantic framework.

Work has also been done for the semantic integration of FIPA compliant agent platforms [10]. The research included the implementation of an infrastructure that allowed the semantic matching of remote platforms and was proposed as an extension to FIPA abstract architecture specification. The results were quite promising, but the methodology did not address the problem of interoperability between different agent platforms.

A good approach for solving the interoperability problem in agent environments can be found in [29]. To deal with heterogeneity, authors propose an abstract ontology representation (AOR) of the agent's internal knowledge representation. They use this AOR to capture abstract models of communication related knowledge (domain models, agent communication languages, content languages and models of how these interact). The methodology is quite promising, but a number of issues rise. It is not clear if the abstraction can be performed in general with communication languages. It is also not clear that there will always be neat 1–1 mappings between language concepts. There is also an issue about the plenitude of the languages when represented as ontologies. A lot of work must also be done in the linking of ontology definitions. It appears to be useful to identify a set of common concepts which act as bridging points between ontologies. The question is which concepts these should be, how many should there be and at what granularity.

Another work done in this area is described in [17]. In this work a conceptual and architectural framework for the multi-agent systems' interoperability based on Web Services is presented. Agents publish their abilities as Web Services that can be used by other agents, independently of conceptual (e.g. architecture) or technical (e.g. platform, programming language) aspects. The proposed interoperability environment, Web-MASI, is composed of two elements: an encapsulation of MAS in the functional model of the Web Services and an interoperability module which constitutes the interface between the MAS and the Web Services environment. The next step in this approach is the integration of OWL-S ontologies in the semantic description of the agents' goals.

5.9 Conclusions

The expected outcome of the collaboration of all the well known platforms and architectures of the multi-agent systems technology is the development of a protocol prototype and a communication software engineering framework that will ensure the communication of heterogeneous multi-agent systems in order to serve successful user interactions with the Semantic Web.

With the development of such a prototype, software community will achieve to place the right foundations of valid communication of systems of software agents and through the recording of problems to simulate the ideal model for the implementation such systems.

The Semantic Web promises to change the way agents navigate and utilize information over the Internet. By providing a structured, distributed representation for expressing concepts and relationships defined by multiple domain ontologies, it is now possible for agents to read and reason about knowledge without the need of centralized ontologies. It still remains to see this potential in action.

References

1. Baumer, C., Breugst, M., Choy, S., Magedanz, T.: Graussshopper: A universal agent platform based on OMG MASIF and FIPA Standards. Technical Report, IKV++, GmbH (2000)
2. Bellifemine, F., Poggi, A., Rimassa, G.: JADE: A FIPA-compliant agent framework. In: Proceedings of the Fourth International Conference and Exhibition on the Practical Application of Intelligent Agents and Multi-Agent Technology (PAAM-99), London, UK (1999)
3. Berners-Lee, T., Hendler, J., Lassila, O.: The Semantic Web. Scientific American **284**(5), 34–43 (2001)
4. Bretier, P., Sadek, D.: A rational agent as the kernel of a cooperative spoken dialogue system: implementing a logical theory of interaction. In: Muller, J., Wooldridge, M., Jennings, N. (eds.) Intelligent Agents III: Agent Theories, Architectures and Languages (ATAL). Lecture Notes in Artificial Intelligence, vol. 1193, pp. 189–203. Springer, Berlin (1997)
5. Busetta, P., Ronnquist, R., Hodgson, A., Lucas, A.: JACK intelligent agents: Components for intelligent agents in Java. AgentLink Newsletter, 2–5 (1999)
6. Cohen, P.R., Levesque, H.J.: Communicative actions for artificial intelligence. In: Proceedings of the First International Conference on Multi-Agent Systems (ICMAS-95), San Francisco, CA (1995)
7. Collier, R.W.: Agent factory: A framework for the engineering of agent-oriented applications. PhD Thesis, University College Dublin (2001)
8. Collier, R.W., O'Hare, G.M.P., Lowen, T., Rooney, C.: Beyond prototyping in the factory of the agents. In: Multi-Agent Systems and Applications III: Proceedings of the Third Central and Eastern European Conference on Multi-agent Systems (CEEMAS-03). Springer, Berlin (2003)
9. Curbera, F., Nagy, A., Weerawarana, S.: Web services: Why and how? In: Proceedings of the OOPSLA 2001 Workshop on Object-Oriented Web Services (2001)
10. Erdur, R.C., Dikenelli, O., Seylan, I., Gurcan, O.: An infrastructure for the semantic integration of FIPA compliant agent platforms. In: AAMAS, pp. 1316–1317 (2004)
11. FIPA: Communicative Act Library Specification. http://www.fipa.org/specs/fipa00037/ (2002)
12. Hayes, C., Avesani, P., Cova, M.: Language games: Learning shared concepts among distributed information agents. In: Proceedings of the 1st IJCAI Workshop on Multi-Agent Information Retrieval and Recommender Systems, pp. 11–17 (2005)
13. Hendler, J.: Agents and the semantic web. IEEE Intelligent Systems **16**(2), 30–37 (2001)
14. Labrou, Y., Finin, T., Mayfield, J.: KQML as an agent communication language. In: Brandshaw, J. (ed.) Software Agents. MIT Press, Cambridge (1997)
15. Labrou, Y., Finin, T.: Semantics for an agent communication language. In: Singh, M.P., Rao, A., Wooldridge, M.J. (eds.) Intelligent Agents IV: Agent Theories, Architectures and Languages (ATAL). Lecture Notes in Artificial Intelligence, vol. 1365, pp. 209–214. Springer, Berlin (1998)

16. Labrou, Y., Finin, T., Peng, Y.: Agent communication languages: The current landscape. IEEE Intelligent Systems **14**(2), 45–52 (1999)
17. Melliti, T., Haddad, S., Suna, A., Fallah-Seghrouchni, A.E.: Web-MASI: Multi-agent systems interoperability using a web services based approach. In: Proceedings of the IEEE/WIC/ACM International Conference on Intelligent Agent Technology (IAT'05) (2005)
18. Noy, N.F., McGuinness, D.L.: Ontology development 101: A guide to creating your first ontology. http://www.ksl.stanford.edu/people/dlm/papers/ontology101/otology101-noy-mcguiness. html (2001)
19. Neches, R., Fikes, R., Finin, T., Gruber, T., Patil, R., Senator, T., Swartout, W.R.: Enabling technology for knowledge sharing. AI Magazine **12**(3), 36–56 (1991)
20. OWL: The OWL web ontology language. http://www.w.org/TR/owl-features/ (2008)
21. Patil, R.S., Fikes, R.E., Patel-Schneider, P.F., McCay, D., Finin, T., Gruber, T., Neches, R.: The DARPA knowledge sharing effort: Progress report. In: Hunhs, M., Singh, M.P. (eds.) Readings in Agents. Morgan Kaufmann, San Mateo (1997)
22. Poslad, S., Charlton, P., Calisti, M.: Specifying standard security mechanisms in multi-agent systems. In: Falcone, R., Barber, K.S., Korba, L., Singh, M.P. (eds.) Trust, Reputation, and Security: Theories and Practice, AAMAS 2002 International Workshop, Selected and Invited Papers. Lecture Notes in Artificial Intelligence, vol. 2631, pp. 163–176. Springer, Berlin (2002)
23. Rahm, E., Bernstein, P.A.: A survey of approaches to automatic schema matching. VLDB Journal **10**(4), 334–350 (2001)
24. RDF. http://www.w3.org/RDF/ (2008)
25. RDF-XML. http://www.w3.org/TR/rdf-syntax-grammar/ (2008)
26. Sadek, M.D.: A study in the logic of intention. In: Proceedings of the Third International Conference on Principles of Knowledge Representation and Reasoning (KR'92), Cambridge, MA (1992)
27. Singh, M.P., Huhns, M.N.: Service-Oriented Computing: Semantics, Processes, Agents. Wiley, Chichester (2005)
28. Sykara, K.P., Paolucci, M., Van Velsen, M., Giampapa, J.A.: The RETSINA MAS infrastructure. Autonomous Agents and Multi-Agent Systems **7**(1–2), 29–48 (2003)
29. Willmott, S., Constantinescu, I., Calisti, M.: Multilingual agents: Ontologies, languages and abstractions. In: Proceedings of the Workshop on Ontologies in Agent Systems, Fifth International Conference on Autonomous Agents, Montreal, Canada (2001)
30. XML. http://www.w3.org/XML/ (2008)

Chapter 6
Mining of Semantic Image Content Using Collective Web Intelligence

C.H.C. Leung, J. Liu, A. Milani, and W.S. Chan

Abstract Human users spend a vast amount of time in interacting with image contents on the Web. Their interaction entails the exercise of considerable perceptive intelligence, visual judgment and mental evaluation. For high-level semantic image features and concepts, such processes of intelligent judgment cannot be mechanized or carried out automatically by machines. In this chapter, an indexing method is described whereby the aggregate intelligence of different Web users is continuously transferred to the Web. Such intelligence is codified, reinforced, distilled and shared among users so as to enable the systematic mining and discovery of semantic image contents. This method allows the collaborative creation of image indexes, which is able to instill and propagate deep knowledge and collective wisdom into the Web concerning the advanced semantic characteristics of Web images. This method is robust and adaptive, and is able to respond dynamically to changing usage patterns caused by community trends and social networking.

6.1 Cumulative Web Intelligence for Image Mining

With the expanded diversity of devices that can capture high resolution images, it is estimated that new digital images are generated at close to a billion per day [10]. Like all forms of data collection, images are produced in order to be used, viewed or shared. The purpose of image generation will be defeated if the data so obtained cannot be retrieved or discovered. Thus, effective exploration and retrieval of images on the Web become an increasingly critical issue, and locating a particular image from it with high precision presents a significant challenge.

In text-oriented Web search activities, the PageRank algorithm and its variants focus on ranking query results based on scoring and the link structure of the Web [3–5, 13, 14, 16, 17, 22]. In this way, the relevance and relative importance of Web pages may be quantified and ranked accordingly. On the other hand, image search is

C.H.C. Leung (✉)
Department of Computer Science, Hong Kong Baptist University, Kowloon Tong, Hong Kong
e-mail: clement@comp.hkbu.edu.hk

Y. Badr et al. (eds.) *Emergent Web Intelligence: Advanced Semantic Technologies,*
Advanced Information and Knowledge Processing,
DOI 10.1007/978-1-84996-077-9_6, © Springer-Verlag London Limited 2010

significantly more difficult compared with the relatively well-developed algorithms of text-oriented Web page searches, and one reason is that, unlike text-based documents, the features and characteristics of photographs and images are not automatically extractable and some form of annotation is necessary [2, 6, 24, 28–31]. In addition, unlike text documents, there is no measure of image prestige on the Web and direct links among images are relatively uncommon. Research in image retrieval may be divided between two main categories: "concept-based" image retrieval, and "content-based" image retrieval [1, 7, 8, 11, 15, 18, 19, 21, 23, 26, 30]. The former focuses on higher-level human perception using words to retrieve images (e.g. keywords, captions), while the latter focuses on the visual features of the image (e.g. color, texture). One aspect in Web image retrieval which that needs to be overcome is the semantic gap [9, 20, 25, 27, 29], which signifies the "lack of coincidence between the information that one can extract from the visual data and the interpretation that the same data have for a user in a given situation". This implies the necessity of some form of manual indexing. However, intensive dedicated manual indexing are labor intensive, error prone, and time consuming and are unable to keep up with the rapid creation rate of digital images.

The ability to recognize and extract semantic patterns and concepts from images and photographs is an important and unique human trait which machines cannot yet perform. Since human users, with their unique perception and judgmental abilities, spend an increasing amount of time in interacting with and viewing Web contents, of which images form an important and voluminous component, it is advantageous to establish a mechanism to capture and encapsulate such intelligence and codify it on the Web. Such a mechanism enables the intelligent perception and visual judgment of one user to be passed on to other users in such a way that the collective perceptive evaluations and knowledge of individual users may be gradually transferred and accumulated on the Web. This method allows the collaborative creation of image indexes, which is able to instill and propagate deep knowledge and collective wisdom into the Web concerning the advanced semantic characteristics of Web images, enabling them to be meaningfully mined and discovered.

The next section explains the underlying structure for the indexing method. In Sects. 6.3 and 6.4, the index scoring and creation mechanisms respectively are described. In Sect. 6.5, the ability of the method to impart deep wisdom and advanced semantics is indicated, and some empirical observations are given in Sect. 6.6.

6.2 Attaining Intelligence Through Adaptive Indexing

Here, we primarily concentrate on the indexing of semantic contents of images although some form of metadata may also be incorporated. We consider a set of images $\{O_j\}$, each of which has an *index set*. The index set is made up of a number of index elements:

$$I_j = \{e_{j1}, e_{j2}, \ldots, e_{jM_j}\}. \tag{1}$$

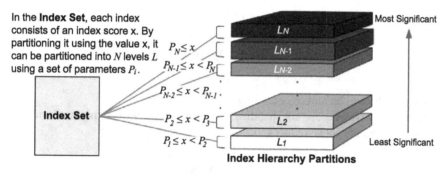

In the **Index Set**, each index consists of an index score x. By partitioning it using the value x, it can be partitioned into N levels L using a set of parameters P_i.

Fig. 6.1 Partitioning of the index set

Each index element is a triple

$$e_{jk} = (t_{jk}, s_{jk}, o_j), \tag{2}$$

where t_{jk} is an index term, s_{jk} is the score associated with t_{jk}, and o_j represents the ImageID. The value of the score induces a partition of the associated index term into N levels $L_1, L_2, \ldots, L_N$ according to a set of parameters $P_1, P_2, \ldots, P_N$ (see Fig. 6.1). For a given index term with score x, the index term will be placed in level L_i if

$$P_i \leq x < P_{i+1}, \quad i = 1, \ldots, N-1, \tag{3}$$

and will be placed in level N if

$$P_N \leq x. \tag{4}$$

The index sets of all the images in the database are collectively referred to as the *index hierarchy*. In general, terms in the higher levels are more significant than those in the lower levels, and thus the top level will be searched first; in some situations, the lower levels may not need to be probed at all.

Suppose a Web user enters a series of search terms $T_1, T_2, \ldots, T_n$ in an image query $Q(T_1, T_2, \ldots, T_n)$, and furthermore suppose a series of corresponding weights $W_1, W_2, \ldots, W_n$ are also specified, which indicate for this particular query the relative importance of the different features. We calculate the *query score* $S(Q|O_j)$ for a particular image O_j as follows. We first look up the score for a particular term T_i in the index hierarchy for that image. In SQL notation, this will be

SELECT Score
FROM Index_Hierarchy
WHERE Image = "ImageID" and Index_Term = "T_i"

In cases where an index term is absent for a particular image, the score is taken to be zero. Each score s_{jk} so obtained will then be weighted by the corresponding query weight W_i and then aggregated over all index terms to form the image aggregate score for a particular image O_j:

$$S(Q|O_j) = \sum_{k=1}^{n} W_k S_{jk} \tag{5}$$

and the results will be ranked according to $S(Q|O_j)$.

If the query weights are not specified, we may take them to be the same and set $W_i = 1, \forall i$, and the above reduces to

$$S(Q|O_j) = \sum_{k=1}^{n} S_{jk}. \tag{6}$$

In returning images resulting from query processing, the returned images will be ranked in accordance with the aggregate image score.

6.3 Reinforcing Collective Judgment

An index term may be enforced or nullified according to whether the social communities who collectively use the images collaboratively agree on its adoption. This will result in either incrementing the score or decrementing it.

6.3.1 Incrementing the Score

Suppose a user issues a query including a query term T. Then typically all images having that term in their index hierarchy will be included in the retrieval results, ranked according to a the query score computed above, though not all of them will be considered relevant to this query by the user. In typical image retrieval, the user will go through a number of iterations using relevance feedback (Fig. 6.2).

Thus, the final results R may include three sets:

1. S_2, a set of images having the index term T is present in the top level L_N of its index hierarchy,
2. S_1, a set of images having the index term T is present in one of the levels $L_1, L_2, \ldots, L_{N-1}$ of its index hierarchy,
3. S_0, a set of images where the index term T is absent from any of the levels of the index hierarchy.

Thus we have,

$$R = S_2 \cup S_1 \cup S_0, \quad \text{with } S_i \cap S_j = \emptyset, \text{ for } i \neq j. \tag{7}$$

In the cases of S_2 and S_1 the score of T will be incremented by a predetermined amount Δ. This may cause the promotion of T to the next higher level. In the case

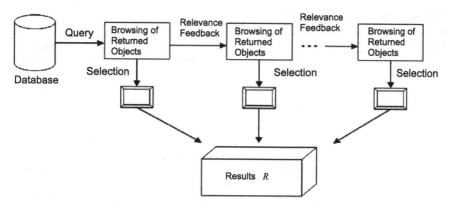

Fig. 6.2 Iterative retrieval with relevance feedback

of S_0, the index term T will be added to the lowest level of the index hierarchy with an initial score of P_1. (Note: Here for simplicity, we use a fix amount of increase Δ. In general cases, different amounts may be incremented depending on which stage the image is selected for inclusion in the final results. Maximum increment will occur in the first stage of selection.)

6.3.2 Decrementing the Score

Let U_T be the set of images having the term T at some level in its index hierarchy. Now, some images of U_T may not be included in the final selected results R. This suggests that term T may not be very useful as an index term for that image. Possible reasons may be that the particular feature described by term T is not sufficiently prominent or significant in the multimedia image (e.g. a particular actress, although included in the index of a movie, is given an insignificant role in that movie). Thus, denoting the score of T by $|T|$, for images in the set $U_T - R$, the following can occur:

1. $|T| \geq P_1 + \Delta$ in which case $|T|$ is decremented by the amount Δ, and the updated $|T|$ is still greater than P_1 after the decrement, and hence remains in the index hierarchy,
2. $|T| < P_1 + \Delta$ in which case $|T|$ is decremented by the amount Δ, and the updated $|T|$ is less than P_1 after the decrement, and hence it will be dropped from the index hierarchy.

We shall refer to an increment as *positive feedback*, and a decrement as *negative feedback*. We shall illustrate the case where $N = 3$, $P_1 = 0$, $P_2 = 10$, $P_3 = 25$, $\Delta = 3$ (Table 6.1). We physically separate the three levels of the index hierarchy into three tables as follows (other physical organizations are possible such as using a single table to store all three levels). The primary key in all three tables will be the composite key (Index Term, ImageID). All scores in the Main Index Table will

Table 6.1 Physical implementation of the index hierarchy

Main Index Table

Index Term	Score	ImageID
Tl	27	#20
T2	42	#167
Tl	30	#39
...	...	...

Potential Index Table

Index Term	Score	ImageID
T5	9	#20
T7	0	#167
Til	3	#61
...	...	...

Pre-Index Table

Index Term	Score	ImageID
T19	24	#71
T2	12	#277
T78	18	#71
...	...	...

have score ≥ 25; those in the Pre-Index Table will have scores less than 25 but ≥ 10, and those in the Potential Index Table will have scores less than 10 but ≥ 0. Here, a positive feedback to T5 will cause it to be deleted from the Potential Index Table and added to the Pre-Index Table (since $9 + 3 \geq 10$). Conversely, a negative feedback to T1 for image #20 will cause it to be deleted from the Main Index Table and added to the Pre-Index Table (since $27 - 3 < 25$). Furthermore, a negative feedback to T7 will cause it to be dropped from the index hierarchy altogether.

6.4 Expanding Intelligence Through Evolution

An image which is *minimally indexed* is one having the following properties: (i) it has only a single index term T, and (ii) T is *simple* (i.e. T consists of only a single word). An index term which is not simple is referred to as a *compound* index term. An image for which there is no index term associated with it is referred to as *unindexed*. In image collections, it is often minimally indexed (or slightly better) from the automatic keyword extraction of some kind of caption information provided alongside the image. Sometimes, however, it is completely unindexed as no caption information is available.

6.4.1 Augmentation of an Existing Index Term

Consider a particular image J, which is minimally indexed with term $T = w$ (i.e. T consists of the single word w, e.g. "swan"). Suppose a user enters a query using $w \oplus u$, which signifies a situation where $w \oplus u$ forms a single meaningful compound index term (e.g. "black swan"). In general, u may be added before or after w and serves to further qualify w (hence narrowing down the search possibilities). From this query, all images with w in its index will be returned—there may be some images with $w \oplus u$ or $w \oplus u'$ (e.g. white swan or black swan). After some browsing through these returned images, the user finally selects a particular image. As a result of this selection, it is inferred that the selected image will have the property represented by the more complete index term $w \oplus u$ (i.e. black swan). Thus the term $w \oplus u$ will be added to the index hierarchy of this image, and if this happens many times, the score of $w \oplus u$ will increase and this will cause $w \oplus u$ to be installed along with w in the index of the image so that the retrieval results will be much more accurate. The original index term w will remain in the index hierarchy, and may be retained or gradually dropped in accordance with the score updating algorithm. In general, an image which is minimally indexed with term $T = w$ may be successively augmented to $w \oplus u_1 \oplus \cdots \oplus u_k$ through this mechanism.

6.4.2 Addition of New Index Terms

Consider a particular image J, which is indexed with term T (which may, for example, be extracted from its caption), where T may be simple or compound. When a query is entered using the term T, many images of different types will be returned, all of which will have the term T in their index. Among this results set is the required image J, and this is the only relevant image for the user. Other images that have been returned are not relevant for this user query. Due to the volume of images returned, it will take considerable time and effort for the user to navigate through them to get to the target image J, which is inefficient.

Next, suppose the same image J can have another index term T' which is not yet included in the current index but represents an additional property of J. Occasionally, users would include both terms T and T' in a query with a view of increasing the precision of the search. Since T' is not indexed, the initial search results will still be the same as before. As the user is interested in J and not other images, he will eventually select J from among the images returned. This suggests that T' may be a potential index term and will enter the index hierarchy at the lowest level with a score of P_1. Once it has been installed in the index hierarchy, repeated search using it and subsequent selection will serve to raise its score and may eventually elevate it to the main index. In so doing, an image which is indexed with a single term may subsequent have a number of index terms associated with it. In general, an image having an initial set of index terms $T_1, T_2, \ldots, T_n$, may have new index terms $T'_1 T'_2, \ldots, T'_m$ added to it through repeated usage.

a Images with index term "London" ONLY.

b Image with index terms "London" and "River Thames".

Fig. 6.3 Addition of index term

As an example, consider the searching of a particular image of "River Thames" (in London) at dawn (Fig. 6.3b). Let us assume that only the term "London" has been initially indexed for this particular image. When a query is entered using the term "London", many images, all of which will have the term "London" in their index, will be returned (Figs. 6.3a and 6.3b). Among this results set is the required image of River Thames, and this is the only relevant image for the user (Fig. 6.3b). However, some queries may be more specific, with both "London" and "River Thames" specified, but the initial search results will still be the same as before as "River Thames" has not been indexed. The user will eventually select this image, and this suggests that the term "River Thames" may also be included in the index of this image. Thus "River Thames" would be included in the index hierarchy for this image. Thus, every time the terms "London" and "River Thames" are both specified in a query, and if the user subsequently selects that image, the index score of this new term "River Thames" will be increased. When this score reaches the required threshold, then "River Thames" will be installed as a proper index term of this image. Similarly, other terms may be added to the index in a dynamic way.

Using a combination of the above two mechanisms, the number and precision of index terms of an image will evolve and be enriched as usage progresses. This will increase search effectiveness as time goes on. The main principle is that human users—through their considerable time spent in interacting with the system and their visual judgment—has progressively transferred and instilled their intelligence into the system so that the index of images is gradually enriched, which cannot be achieved by purely automatic means as current technology does not allow image objects to be meaningfully recognized. As the images reside collectively on the Web, then the intelligence of the Web will be enhanced through such process.

In this way, richer image semantics, particularly *entities*, *attributes* and *relationships*, may be incorporated into the query processing algorithms of images. For example, an image with a boy riding on an elephant is initially minimally indexed with only the term "elephant" (an entity). As time goes on, using the mechanisms indicated above, "boy" (a further entity) will be added to the index of the image. Still later, the term "riding" (relationship) will also be added. Thus, after progressive usage, the three terms "boy", "riding", "elephant" (representing entities and relationship) will all be part of the index of this particular image, even though at the beginning, only "elephant" was in the index. Similarly, attributes such as "brown elephant", and "small boy" may be added. Through the incorporation of all three terms with relevant attributes in the index, and through the inclusion of all three terms with relevant attributes in a query, a much more precise retrieval can occur, reducing time and effort in navigating a large number of irrelevant images.

6.4.3 Maximal Indexing

For a given image, which may for example be unindexed or minimally indexed, the number of its index terms will increase through usage. As time goes on, the number of index terms associated with it will converge to a given level and will remain there after which no further increase will take place. Such an index will be referred to as a *stable maximal index*. In more general situations, even the maximal index will change over time and is dictated by changing usage patterns and user preference; this

Fig. 6.4 An unstable index
caused by oscillating social
community trends

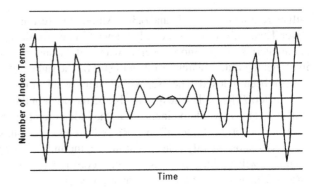

is referred to as an *unstable index*. A diagrammatic illustration of an unstable index
is illustrated in Fig. 6.4; such a situation may occur due to changing usage patterns
caused by social community trends. In our study, we shall be mostly concerned with
stable index.

6.4.4 Probability of Image Recovery

In relation to information recovery, where one wishes to retrieve a specific known
image, let us consider the recovery rate ρ, which gives the probability of successful
image recovery, for a situation where $z\%$ of the collection is maximally indexed.
Here, we suppose that an image will be retrieved when some or all of its indexed
terms match some or all of the terms specified in a query. Assuming all the image
accessed activities are uniformly distributed (i.e. each query is equally likely to
target any of the images with no special preference for any particular ones), then
for a given query Q, there are four cases. Denoting the set of maximally indexed
terms of a given image by X, the set of indexed terms included in the query Q by
X_q, where we assume $X_q \neq \emptyset$, and the set of indexed terms included in the target
image by X_o, then the four cases are:

1. $X_q = X_o = X$, i.e. the target image is maximally indexed, and the query Q specifies all the maximally indexed terms
2. $X_q \subset X_o = X$, i.e. the target image is maximally indexed, but the query Q specifies only some, but not all, of the maximally indexed terms (unlike "$\subseteq$", here
   "$\subset$" excludes improper subset, i.e. X_q and X_o are not permitted to be equal)
3. $X_o \subset X_q = X$, i.e. the target image is not maximally indexed, but the query Q
   specifies all the maximally indexed terms
4. $X_o \subset X$, and $X_q \subset X$, i.e. the target image is not maximally indexed, and Q does
   not specify all the maximally indexed terms.

   Cases 1 and 2 will result in the successful retrieval of the target image. Since $z\%$
of the images are maximally indexed, and since all images sustain the same amount
of access activity, these two cases will account for $z\%$ of the queries. Thus, for $z\%$

of the queries, the recovery rate $\rho = 100\%$. Hence, even assuming the recall of other queries is 0%, the recovery rate averaged over all queries is $z\%$.

However, the recovery rate of Cases 3 and 4 are not necessarily 0%. In Case 3, since the query is maximally indexed, and if the target image is not unindexed, i.e. $X_o \neq \emptyset$, then matching of indexed terms will take place between the query and the target image (i.e. $X_q \cap X_o \neq \emptyset$), and so successful retrieval of the target image will result. That is, Case 3 will result in unsuccessful retrieval only if $X_o \neq \emptyset$. In Case 4, if there are coincidences between the terms given in the query and the indexed terms of the image (i.e. $X_q \cap X_o \neq \emptyset$), then matching will take place, and the target image will be retrieved. If $X_q \cap X_o = \emptyset$, then no matching will take place and the target image is not retrieved. Thus, Case 4 will yield 0% recovery only if there is no overlap between the query terms and the indexed terms of the target image. Thus, we conclude that the recovery rate $\rho \geq z\%$, and most likely strictly greater than $z\%$.

6.5 Collective Wisdom Indexing for Advanced Image Semantics

Depending on the users knowledge and experience, the perception and interpretation of semantic image contents can have varying degrees of richness, which may be distinguished into the following levels:

- The *primary level* offers an objective, factual description of image content, including any entities, attributes, and relationships that every user will basically agree on
- The *secondary level* involves a basic level of interpretation or summary of some or all of the entities in the picture which may exhibit variations among individual users of the community

Human wisdom and prior knowledge may be brought to bear on the indexing of different levels. In moving from the primary level to the secondary level, in particular, basic knowledge of, say, the particular news event associated with the image may be incorporated. To go beyond the two levels entails drawing copiously upon the background, history, or even technical knowledge and theoretical developments of the domain. The characteristics of this will be:

- The *tertiary level* consists of a knowledge-based element as well as elements of emotions and feelings. This level includes background information; historical knowledge; expert knowledge; lateral and loosely correlated knowledge; abstract concepts; objective, inter-subjective, and subjective wisdom; technical details; theoretical framework; feelings; emotions; sentiments; reactions; and inferred or observed behavior.

As the amount of information encoded in an image can be potentially unlimited, considerable knowledge and wisdom can be *read into* it for the purpose of indexing and for the benefit of the community of users. Collectively, the amount of wisdom encapsulated in the index structure of Web images can therefore be extremely rich and diverse. Such *wisdom indexing* will not undermine the effectiveness of retrieval

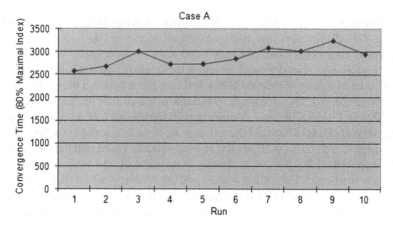

Fig. 6.5 Indexing convergence time (hours) for Case A

based on lower level semantics, since these would augment, rather than supersede, other index terms.

6.6 Index Convergence

Experiments have been carried out to determine the evolution time and feasibility of such indexing process, and the following cases are considered.

6.6.1 Case A

Initial number of index terms per image $= 0$ (unindexed). Maximal number of index terms per image $= 3$. Database size $= 10,000$ images. Access rate follows a Poisson distribution with parameter $\lambda = 10$ accesses per hour [12]. Each access has a probability of 0.05 of incrementing the index set by one index term. Figure 6.5 shows the time for the database to achieve 80% maximal indexing capability (i.e. 8,000 images in the database will have reached 3 index terms).

Here, the mean time to achieve 80% maximal indexing capability is 2897.75 hours which is about 17 weeks. The standard deviation is 209.31 hours or about 8.7 days.

6.6.2 Case B

Initial number of index terms per image $= 3$. Maximal number of index terms per image $= 8$. Database size $= 10,000$ images. Access rate follows a Poisson distribution with parameter $\lambda = 10$ accesses per hour. Each access has a probability of

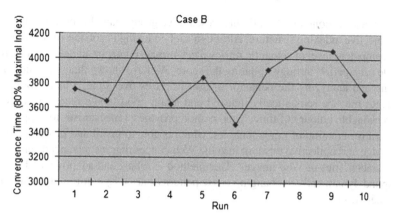

Fig. 6.6 Indexing convergence time (hours) for Case B

0.05 incrementing the index set by one index term. Figure 6.6 shows the time for the database to achieve 80% maximal indexing capability (i.e. 8,000 images in the database will have reached 8 index terms).

Here, the mean time to achieve 80% maximal indexing capability is 3830.86 hours which is about 23 weeks. The standard deviation is 221.45 hours or about 9.2 days. Thus, even allowing two standard deviations from the mean value (23 weeks + 18.4 days), there is a high probability—over 95% using the Central Limit Theorem approximation to a normal distribution [12]—that 80% maximal indexing capability can be achieved within six months.

6.7 Conclusions

The efficient identification of Web documents in the past has made use of user retrieval patterns and access characteristics. We have presented a method whereby the indexing of images can be done by similarly keeping track of the users querying behavior. By analyzing the users' search, relevance feedback and results selection patterns, our method allows semantic concepts to be gradually discovered and migrated through an index hierarchy. Our method also includes a robust scoring mechanism which enables faulty indexing to be rectified over time. This includes the following properties: (i) repeated and sustained corroboration of specific index terms is required before their installation, and (ii) the flexibility not only for the index score to be incremented but also for it to be decremented (which may lead to the eventual deletion of the index term).

Given that the automatic recognition of semantic image contents, and hence their automatic indexing, is not possible, such a semi-automatic evolutionary approach will allow human intelligence and judgment to be progressively transferred to the Web and will bring substantial benefits. In particular, this will obviate the need to perform time-consuming, intensive, dedicated manual indexing which has shown to be costly and, if done by a small unrepresentative group, can also produce a biased and subjective indexing structure. Although such indexing is not one-off or immediate, a competent level of semantic retrieval performance may be achieved over a reasonable time period through updating the score. We have shown that, by judiciously tracking and analyzing the behavior of user accesses over time, a large collection of images may be semantically indexed and attain good image recovery rates after a reasonable amount of time. This method provides a mechanism to support the collaborative creation of image indexes, which is able to instill and propagate deep knowledge and collective wisdom into the Web concerning the advanced semantics and characteristics of Web images. This method is robust and adaptive, and is able to respond dynamically to changing usage patterns caused by community trends and social networking.

References

1. Azzam, I., Leung, C.H.C., Horwood, J.: Implicit concept-based image indexing and retrieval. In: Proc. of the IEEE Int'l Conf. on Multi-media Modeling, Brisbane, Australia, pp. 354–359 (2004)
2. Bertini, M., Bimbo, A.D., Torniai, C., Grana, C., Vezzani, R., Cucchiara, R.: Sports video annotation using enhanced HSV histograms in multimedia ontologies. In: Proc. of the 14th Int'l Conf. of Image Analysis and Processing—Workshops, pp. 160–170 (2007)
3. Chakrabarti, S., Joshi, M.M., Punera, K., Pennock, D.M.: The structure of broad topics on the web. In: Proc. of the 11th Int'l World Wide Web Conf., Honolulu, Hawaii, USA, pp. 251–262 (2002)
4. Diligenti, M., Gori, M., Maggini, M.: Web page scoring systems for horizontal and vertical search. In: Proc. of the 11th Int'l World Wide Web Conf., Honolulu, Hawaii, USA, pp. 508–516 (2002)
5. Dwork, C., Kumar, R., Naor, M., Sivakumar, D.: Rank aggregation methods for the web. In: Proc. of the 10th Int'l World Wide Web Conf., Hong Kong, pp. 613–622 (2001)
6. Fan, J., Gao, Y., Luo, H.: Hierarchical classification for automatic image annotation. In: Proc. of the 30th Annual Int'l ACM SIGIR Conference on Research and Development in Information Retrieval, Amsterdam, The Netherlands, pp. 111–118 (2007)
7. Finkelstein, L., Gabrilovich, E., Matias, Y., Rivlin, E., Solan, Z., Wolfman, G., Ruppin, E.: Placing search in context: The concept revisited. In: Proc. of the 10th Int'l World Wide Web Conf., Hong Kong, pp. 406–414 (2001)
8. Funkhouser, T., Min, P., Kazhdan, M., Chen, J., Halderman, A., Dobkin, D., Jacobs, D.: A search engine for 3D model. ACM Transactions on Graphics $22(1)$, 83–105 (2003)
9. Ganguly, P., Rabhi, F.A., Ray, P.K.: Bridging semantic gap. In: Proc. of the 2002 Conference on Pattern Languages of Programs, Melbourne, Australia, vol. 13, pp. 59–61 (2003)
10. Gantz, J.F., et al.: The diverse and exploding digital universe: An updated forecast of worldwide information growth through 2011. IDC White Paper (March 2008)
11. Gevers, T., Smeulders, A.W.M.: Image search engines: An overview. In: Emerging Topics in Computer Vision, pp. 1–54. Prentice-Hall, Englewood Cliffs (2004)
12. Ghahramani, S.: Fundamentals of Probability with Stochastic Processes, 3rd edn. Prentice-Hall, Englewood Cliffs (2005)
13. Haveliwala, T.H.: Topic-sensitive PageRank. In: Proc. of the 11th Int'l World Wide Web Conf., Honolulu, Hawaii, USA, pp. 517–526 (2002)
14. Haveliwala, T.H.: Topic-sensitive PageRank: A context-sensitive ranking algorithm for web search. IEEE Transactions on Knowledge and Data Engineering $15(4)$, 784–796 (2003)

15. Hawarth, R.J., Buxton, H.: Conceptual-description from monitoring and watching image sequences. Image and Vision Computing **18**, 105–135 (2000)
16. Jeh, G., Widom, J.: Scaling personalized web search. In: Proc. of the 12th Int'l World Wide Web Conf., Budapest, Hungary, pp. 271–279 (2003)
17. Kamvar, S.D., Haveliwala, T.H., Manning, C.D., Golub, G.H.: Extrapolation methods for accelerating PageRank computations. In: Proc. of the 12th Int'l World Wide Web Conf., Budapest, Hungary, pp. 261–270 (2003)
18. Leung, C.H.C., Liu, J.: Multimedia data mining and searching through dynamic index evolution. In: Proc. of the 9th Int'l Conf. on Visual Information Systems, Shanghai, China, pp. 298–309 (2007)
19. Leung, C.H.C., Liu, J., Chan, W.S., Milani, A.: An architectural paradigm for collaborative semantic indexing of multimedia data objects. In: Proc. of the 10th Int'l Conf. on Visual Information Systems, Salerno, Italy, pp. 216–226 (2008)
20. Millard, D.E., Gibbins, N.M., Michaelides, D.T., Weal, M.J.: Mind the semantic gap. In: Proc. of the 16th ACM Conf. on Hypertext and Hypermedia, Salzburg, Austria, pp. 54–62 (2005)
21. Müller, H., Müller, W., Squire, D.M., Marchand-Maillet, S., Pun, T.: Performance evaluation in content-based image retrieval: Overview and proposals. Pattern Recognition Letters **22**(5), 593–601 (2001)
22. Nie, L., Davison, B.D., Qi, X.: Topical link analysis for web search. In: Proc. of the 29th Annual Int'l ACM SIGIR Conf. on Research and Development in Information Retrieval, Seattle, Washington, USA, pp. 91–98 (2006)
23. Over, P., Leung, C.H.C., Ip, H., Grubinger, M.: Multimedia retrieval benchmarks. IEEE Multimedia **11**(2), 80–84 (2004)
24. Shi, R., Lee, C., Chua, T.: Enhancing image annotation by integrating concept ontology and text-based bayesian learning model. In: Proc. of the 15th Int'l Conf. on Multimedia, Augsburg, Germany, pp. 341–344 (2007)
25. Smeulders, A.W., Worring, M., Santini, S., Gupta, A., Jain, R.: Content-based image retrieval at the end of the early years. IEEE Transactions on Pattern Analysis and Machine Intelligence **22**(12), 1349–1380 (2000)
26. Tam, A.M., Leung, C.H.C.: Structured natural-language descriptions for semantic content retrieval of visual materials. Journal of the American Society for Information Science and Technology **52**(11), 930–937 (2001)
27. Wang, C., Zhang, L., Zhang, H.: Learning to reduce the semantic gap in web image retrieval and annotation. In: Proc. of the 31st Annual Int'l ACM SIGIR Conf. on Research and Development in Information Retrieval, Singapore, pp. 355–362 (2008)
28. Wang, J.Z., Geman, D., Luo, J., Gray, R.M.: Real-world image annotation and retrieval: An introduction to the special section. IEEE Transactions on Pattern Analysis and Machine Intelligence **30**(11), 1873–1876 (2008)
29. Wang, M., Zhou, X., Chua, T.: Automatic image annotation via local multi-label classification. In: Proc. of the 2008 Int'l Conf. on Content-Based Image and Video Retrieval, Niagara Falls, Canada, pp. 17–26 (2008)
30. Wong, R.C.F., Leung, C.H.C.: Automatic semantic annotation of real world Web images. IEEE Transactions on Pattern Analysis and Machine Intelligence **30**(11), 1933–1944 (2008)
31. Yang, C., Dong, M., Fotouhi, F.: Region based image annotation through multiple-instance learning. In: Proc. of the 13th Annual ACM Int'l Conf. on Multimedia, Hilton, Singapore, pp. 435–438 (2005)

Chapter 7
Suited Support for Distributed Web Intelligence Cooperative Work

Dominique Decouchant, Sonia Mendoza,
and José Rodríguez

Abstract Researches and efforts currently being developed within the World Wide Web environment, whose aim is to provide cooperative supports, are mainly performed in the field of the "Semantic Web". These efforts are based on technological components such as the XML, RDF, and OWL languages that allow the cooperative definition of distributed ontologies. From these components, it is possible to develop "reasoning" programs that are able a) to infer information from data described with these languages and b) to exploit the defined ontologies. Moreover, programs may also be defined to provide supports to collaborators to cooperatively exploit the defined ontologies. However, all theses efforts remain developed at the application level. Thus, no suited distributed support for Web cooperative work had been investigated that deals with the unreliability of such a distributed environment.

In this chapter, we present the PIÑAS infrastructure which provides means for supporting cooperative work on the Web. Using cooperative applications that are built employing the services of this infrastructure, several users can access and modify replicated shared entities in a consistent and controlled way. PIÑAS provides suited features, such as: user identification, multi-site user definition, user and entity naming, shared entity fragmentation and replication, storage, consistency, and automatic distributed updating. We propose seamless extensions to standard Web services that can be fully integrated within the Web environment. Moreover, the innovative PIÑAS features provide reliable support for temporarily disconnected and nomadic work.

D. Decouchant (✉)
Laboratoire LIG de Grenoble, Grenoble, France
e-mail: Dominique.Decouchant@imag.fr

D. Decouchant
UAM-Cuajimalpa, México D.F., México

Y. Badr et al. (eds.) *Emergent Web Intelligence: Advanced Semantic Technologies,*
Advanced Information and Knowledge Processing,
DOI 10.1007/978-1-84996-077-9_7, © Springer-Verlag London Limited 2010

7.1 Introduction to Web Cooperative Work

Initially the Web was developed in order to allow users distributed over the Internet to access a large and increasing amount of information. Thus, using relatively simple but efficient functions, any client site was able to download HTML documents from remote HTTP Web servers in order to access a rich and varied documentation information. As correctly observed in 2001 and reported in Tim Berners Lee et al. [2], the Web content was only designed for users to access documentation.

Progressively, the possibility to perform accesses to this distributed space of information appeared not only interesting for end-users but also for computer programs. In this way, the computer programs became able to define specific information and to make them understandable to other programs: the Semantic Web was born. As clearly said by Tim Berners-Lee: *"The Semantic Web will bring structure to the meaningful content of Web pages, creating an environment where software agents roaming from page to page can readily carry out sophisticated tasks for users"*. As highlighted in Feigenbaum et al. [15], the Semantic Web is based on three technological components: (a) the XML (eXtensible Markup Language) and RDF (Resource Description Language) languages, (b) the ontologies, and (c) the possibility to develop "reasoning" programs. These programs are then able to discover and to reason about information described with such languages and exploit the defined ontologies. The XML and RDF languages provide supports to users or programs (a) to define and create their own document structure and content, and (b) to establish relations between information parts.

Ontology has to be considered as *"a set of statements—that translate information from disparate databases into common terms"* [15]. In practice, an ontology attempts to represent the knowledge of a given domain by (a) proposing a data model that is representative of the domain concepts and (b) establishing/managing relations among these concepts through specific functions. The development, management and endorsement of an ontology constitutes a main task [42] that has to be regularly and cooperatively performed by the concerned communities. Thus, the development of dedicated applications to manage ontologies and their evolutions are required. This constitutes a first step towards the definition of cooperative Web applications: users can cooperatively define and merge various sources of heterogeneous data that are integrated within potentially distributed ontologies. This cooperation principle is successfully applied in many domains such as the life sciences (e.g., medicine [13] or biology [31]), and in many other application or research domains (natural sciences, social sciences, groupware systems, engineering technologies, etc.).

Moreover, in recent years considerable efforts have been made to support cooperation over the Web including synchronous browsing [25], cooperative learning [3], casual interaction environments [32], among others. However, similar to the developments in the field of the "Semantic Web", all these efforts have been addressed towards the application level and/or towards the communication protocol level (see Sect. 7.1.1). Thus, despite the fact that some initial limitations of the Web environment have already been well identified [42], there exist only a few proposals that provide suited, efficient and reliable support for distributed Web cooperative work.

Thus, analyzing the available Web infrastructures, we can note that there is neither adequate support for clearly managing users, nor for identifying user actions. There is also a need for shared entity replication to deal with link failures and site disconnections. In such an unreliable environment, nomadic work in a disconnected or degraded mode is a useful feature given the work practices of current users.

Many current research efforts in Web authoring focus on providing elaborate functions for accessing and publishing documents on remote servers. A user is able to get documents, to modify them, and finally to send them back to the servers. This approach is followed by the WebDAV project [46] that defines functions to support cooperative authoring of shared documents managed by Web servers. However, these functions do not provide reliable support for cooperative authoring of remotely stored documents.

The work presented in this chapter builds upon the experience gained from the design and implementation of the AllianceWeb cooperative editor/browser [9]. During its design stage, we have come to the conclusion that the current Web technology lacks flexible and reliable support for distributed cooperative work. Thus, we have defined the requirements of services that have to be offered to achieve this goal. These requirements gave birth to PIÑAS, a Platform for Interaction, Naming And Storage. The services provided by PIÑAS are suitable not only for cooperative authoring, but could also be used by other kinds of cooperative applications with similar requirements.

7.1.1 Some Efforts at Protocol Level

A representative effort to support Web cooperative work is the WebDAV project that has been developed by IETF [46, 47]. By extension of the HTTP protocol, special functions are added (document versioning, collection management, access control, overwrite prevention, document properties, and namespace management) for supporting concurrent and cooperative authoring of an entire document. Using these functions, a user can load a Web document, locally modify it and send it back to the remote HTTP server. To ensure the consistency of a co-authored document, WebDAV provides functions for handling exclusive and shared locks on remote resources. The production of a shared document follows these steps (see Fig. 7.1):

1. The client-side authoring application sends to the HTTP server a request to set a lock on the document.

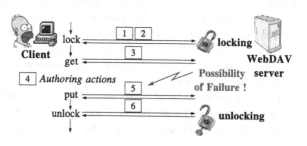

Fig. 7.1 WebDAV cooperative authoring principle

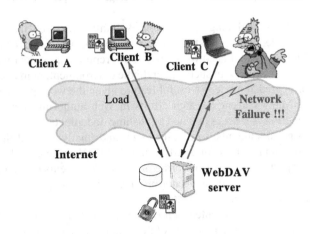

Fig. 7.2 WebDAV potential problem

2. If the locking operation succeeded, the document properties are returned.
3. The authoring application gets a copy of the remote document.
4. The document copy is locally modified by using an interactive authoring tool (e.g., Amaya [19]) or simply a HTML/XML "tag" based tool.
5. Once the authoring process is accomplished, the new version is transmitted and updated on the HTTP server.
6. Finally, the client-side application unlocks the remote document.

Cooperative work support provided by WebDAV is based on the well known *"hybrid storage/processing"* (also called client/server, see Sect. 7.2.4) distribution architecture (local processing and remote data storage) that makes difficult maintaining consistency of remotely accessed resources in an unreliable distributed environment. This problem mainly comes from the potential unreliability of its three components: the client site, the remote storage site and the communication link.

This architecture is commonly used in the Web environment to support browsing operations. In the case that authoring actions and modifications are concurrently performed on a shared document, we have to ensure the document consistency. Many problems may occur and several kinds of solutions should be performed depending on failure sources (client, server and/or network) and on their associated characteristics (nature, time, locked resources).

As established (see Fig. 7.2) and discussed in Sect. 7.1.2, WebDAV solution is not really suited for cooperative authoring of large resource collections on a wide area network as Internet because of the potential high frequency of network failures. However, WebDAV does not constitute a bad solution at all as it can be satisfactorily applied over a reliable network (e.g., a local area network in an industrial environment). In this way, in the field of wide area network, new elaborated solutions have to be designed and developed to ensure consistency and reliability of the distributed shared authored resources.

This new solution based on a *"fully distributed architecture"* (see Sect. 7.2.3) has been combined with the WebDAV solution to obtain a complete and suited Web solution. Before examining these different distribution architectures in details (see

Sect. 7.2), we first present the requirements that the proposed solution must satisfy to efficiently and consistently support distributed cooperative work on the Web.

7.1.2 Requirements for a Suited Web Cooperative Infrastructure

Cooperation implies a powerful interaction model, which needs to rightly identify all the partners and resources of the cooperative work process: this mutual user identification is required to control accesses and cooperative contributions, and to support group awareness. More specifically, a cooperative application on the Web environment must be viewed as a system in which each user identifies and locates each other to send events, to cooperatively produce, to establish a synchronous session, to transfer information, etc. In addition, users outside the cooperating group may eventually be able to access public versions of the different produced resources.

Thus, the design of the Web groupware infrastructure we target is guided by the following requirements:

User identification Because the Web environment provides only anonymous and solitary support for a user to publish and consult information (HTML/XML documents), new features (e.g., user definition) are required to establish cooperation of several users distributed around the world.

Resource sharing Although the Web does not constitute a reliable environment for supporting the distributed cooperative work, the relevant resources of a project should be partially or totally shared among collaborators in a consistent way.

Resource availability The Web technology provides client/server support to consult, modify and send back remote resources. However, Internet provides unreliable communication support, and so we must provide solutions to allow users to work in a disconnected (network or server failures, nomadic work) or degraded mode (transmission delay and slowness). Thus, as presented in Sect. 7.2, resource replication constitutes a suited mechanism to satisfy this need.

Resource consistency As highlighted, we are interested in implementing replication mechanisms in order to guarantee resource availability. Consequently, it is required to provide dedicated principles and mechanisms to also ensure replicated resource consistency. Thus, we will demonstrate that we can define efficient and automatic functions based on information structuring to ensure resource consistency.

Collection consistency A Web document should be treated as a container of resources. In this way, elaborated and suited operations should allow to correctly share, modify, copy, move, rename or delete the document or its component resources within a distributed cooperative Web environment.

Relationship integrity The correctness of relationships among both distributed Web documents and their associated shared resources should be guaranteed whenever a collaborator carries out manipulations on resource collections (e.g., adding/suppressing an element to/from a collection or moving an element from a collection to another).

Nomadic cooperative work By replicating the shared resources on different sites, we increase their availability. From one side, the replication of user definitions is required to support disconnected cooperative work, but moreover it also provides a basis to support nomadic cooperative work.

This chapter is organized in two main parts:

- First, in Sect. 7.2, we study the different ways by which a distributed groupware can be structured and implemented. This study is focalized on centralization/distribution of the two central groupware components: the shared entities and the treatments applied on such entities. Section 7.2 also provides a detailed analysis of the architectures and solutions that can be successfully applied to design and implement the coordination function whose goal, within a groupware system, is to take in charge all inconsistency problems related to the cooperative production.
- Then, enlighted by the characteristics of the different architectures studied in Sect. 7.2, and taking into account the limitations of the Web (see Sect. 7.1.1), our goal is to extend the Web environment to support distributed cooperative work. Section 7.3 presents the PIÑAS (Platform for Interaction Naming And Storage) project that aims at providing elaborated features to support distributed groupware systems on the Web in an efficient and reliable way. Multi-site user definition and identification, user and entity naming, event transmission, sharing and updating of replicated entities, among others, are the advanced features provided by the PIÑAS Web infrastructure. This service layer is not only dedicated to support a specific application domain, but it is designed as generic as possible in order to support several kinds of Web distributed cooperative applications.

7.2 What Architecture for What Groupware?

The distribution architecture of a groupware system defines the components and the associated management mechanisms that are executed or used on the different cooperating sites, location of their execution or use. In the particular case of distributed groupware we are especially focusing on providing suited solutions, the distribution architecture constitutes the keystone that describes the logical link between the involved sites [39]. The choice of a specific distribution architecture has a direct main influence on the groupware development and use [11, 35]. From the point of view of the groupware system development, the distribution architecture directly conditions the implementation effort and easiness, as well as the possibility to reuse existent code. From the groupware system use point of view, the distribution architecture directly influences the provided functionalities (e.g., performance, efficiency, fault tolerance and scalability).

7.2.1 Classification Model

For studying the distribution architectures, we used the extensible classification model, proposed by Roth and Unger [39], initially designed to classify synchronous groupware systems. In contrast to other previous models (e.g., the Patterson's taxonomy [34] or the Dewan's generic architecture [10]), the extensible classification model takes into account groupware distribution characteristics such as the communication between components. This model consists in an application scheme and a distribution scheme that respectively defines (1) the groupware components and (2) the distribution/replication of these components on the cooperating sites.

7.2.1.1 Application Scheme

The application scheme for the analysis of the distribution architectures is defined (1) from the Arch scheme [6] that is intended to design mono-user applications and (2) from some other schemes such as multi-user MVC[1] [26], AVL[2] [21, 22], and PAC*[3] [4] that are intended for the design of groupware. These schemes focus on decomposing a system in sub-systems that individually contain some components of the *groupware core*[4] as well as of the user interface. This separation allows to uncouple the application and the user interface developments. Moreover, this uncoupling allows to define and implement several kinds of user interfaces (e.g., table or graphic) that constitute different interaction ways with the application data (e.g., statistical data).

More particularly, the application scheme allows to represent a groupware system as a software that is distributed among the cooperating sites, and more important it is structured and built as interconnected distributed components. The organization and distribution of the components on the different sites depend on the selected distribution scheme, and more specifically on the adopted architecture. In the next sections, we present the different kinds of possible architectures that the developer may select for designing his distributed groupware system. Thus, depending on the chosen distribution scheme, some sites may only be dedicated for the interactions of the collaborators, while some other sites may only act as servers (storage, treatments and/or coordination). The private and shared entity spaces that are manipulated by the groupware system are not explicitly defined by the model, but they are rather introduced as parts of other components. However, the detailed specification and analysis of these components and their inter-relations are required for a correct and complete global understanding of distribution architectures. To answer to this requirement, we extended the application scheme adding the concept of state component of the Interlace model [35] and thus, we represented *the space of shared entities* and *the space of private entities* as full fledged components.

More generally, as illustrated in Fig. 7.3 that shows the general component structure of a groupware system, the architecture of a groupware system (distributed or not) includes the following three main components:

---

[1]MVC: "Model-View-Controller" paradigm.

[2]AVL: "Abstract-Link-View" paradigm.

[3]PAC: "Presentation-Abstraction-Control" paradigm.

[4]The "groupware core" term refers to the functional kernel of the groupware.

Fig. 7.3 Component
structure of a groupware
system

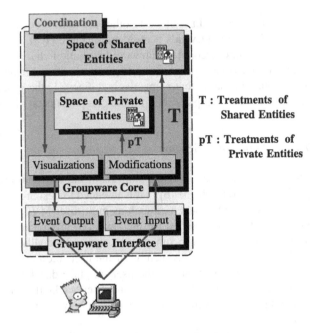

- the **Space of Shared Entities** component contains all entities that are shared and
  appear within the collaborators' perception/working spaces. This component offers functionalities to permanently store, replicate and update the different distributed copies of shared entities.
- the **Groupware Core** component refers to the functional kernel of the groupware system that contains all the data and functions to implement for instance
  the structure of the shared document and the authoring functions, in the case of
  a cooperative authoring tool. This macro-component includes three elementary
  components and two functional modules (see Fig. 7.3):
  - the **Space of Private Entities** component encapsulates all user private entities
    which can be used during a cooperative session. Possibly, while the session
    is going on, some entities may migrate to the Space of Shared Entities and
    reciprocally,
  - the **Modifications** component interprets and transforms the events coming
    from the user interface in actions that are then applied on the entities of the
    private and/or shared spaces,
  - the **Visualizations** component is in charge to create or actualize the user inter-
    action views when the states of shared or private entities are modified,
  - the **T** functional modules (see Fig. 7.3) gathers all treatment functions that can
    be applied on the shared entities,
  - and finally, the **pT** functional modules gathers all treatment functions that can
    be applied on the private entities.
- the **Groupware Interface** component allows the collaborator to interact with the
  groupware core. This macro-component includes two elementary components:

- the **Event Input** component transforms all user interactions via physical or logical devices in events that are transmitted to the groupware core (see Fig. 7.3),
- the **Event Output** component provides and updates an interaction view understandable by the user. These views are displayed on output devices (e.g. monitor, windows, and speakers).

It is important to note that this decomposition is incomplete if we do not mention the **Coordination** component whose objective is to ensure the consistency of the shared entity space which can be concurrently accessed and modified by collaborators. The design and implementation of this component, that may be either centralized or distributed, constitutes a specific research topic that is discussed later in Sect. 7.2.5.

Modifications applied on the Space of Shared Entities component may imply some effects on the Space of Private Entities component, and vice versa. For example, considering a cooperative editor, the produced document is naturally shared/distributed between collaborators, but each collaborator owns a private cursor (position and aspect). However, the Modifications component will perform dedicated actions on both the private and the shared entity spaces if a collaborator suppress a paragraph on which another collaborator's work is focused on.

7.2.1.2 Distribution Scheme

The presented application scheme, as structured in the form of inter-connected components, does not depend on the aspects related to the distribution of these components. The groupware designers discharged of these aspects can then concentrate on the specific problems of the application domain [35].

However, distributed groupware systems are obviously designed and developed as distributed systems. Thus, a specific distribution of the components may unfavorably influence the performances and usability of the groupware functions. We put in evidence the second part of the extensible classification model [39] that precisely allows to define these aspects. More particularly, a distribution scheme describes the organization and placement (at runtime) of the groupware components on the cooperating sites.

The collaborators' working sites have to be considered as peer sites, while other sites must be perceived as servers. Components located on peer sites are referred as "decentralized components" and components located on server sites are named as "centralized components".

As we will see in Sects. 7.2.2–7.2.4, the centralization or replication of the different components define different groupware distribution architectures that generate specific constraints and/or provide new interesting collaboration possibilities.

7.2.2 Centralized Architecture

Groupware systems that follow the centralized architecture (see Fig. 7.4) allow collaborators to work from remote client sites that have to be considered as X terminals:

D. Decouchant et al.

Fig. 7.4 Collaboration based
on a centralized architecture

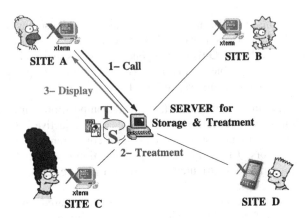

both data persistent storage and processing are respectively managed and performed
within a unique central server site.

Thus, if we analyze a collaborator's working session (see Fig. 7.4), each action
that the user wants to perform on the shared environment is divided into three steps:
(1) via his user interface, the collaborator invokes a treatment T (data processing)
that will be applied within the central server site; data persistent storage S is also
managed by this site; (2) required treatments are locally performed by the server
site; and finally (3) the results (graphical events) are transmitted back to the client
site.

According to this totally centralized architecture, as shown in details in Fig. 7.5,
the complete Groupware Core and the Space of Shared Entities components are
centralized on the server site, while the Groupware Interface component is always
located on the client site. Thus, for each collaborator, the server site administrates
a particular instance set including the three components (Visualizations, Modifications and Space of Private Entities) while each client site owns the Event Input and
Event Output corresponding components.

Since on the particular Visualizations, Modifications, and Space of Private Entities components are associated to each collaborator, the groupware systems that
follow the centralized architecture are able to handle relaxed WYSIWIS[5] views
[43] for displaying the shared entities. The Event Input component communicates
with the Modifications component by mean of user interface events, while the Visualizations component communicates with the Event Output component via display
requests. Each client site transmits its events to the server which then is able to
diffuse them to all other client sites.

The main advantage of the centralized architecture resides in the facility to implement the storage and synchronization services of the shared entities, as only one
instance of each entity exists in the system that is managed by the server [28, 30].
This architecture easily provides support to manage session "latecomers"[6] because

---

[5]WYSIWIS: What You See Is What I See.

[6]"Latecomers" refer to collaborators who join a session in progress.

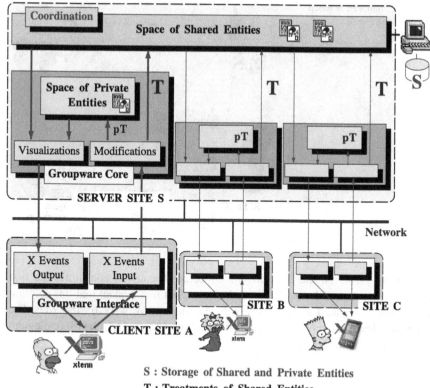

S : Storage of Shared and Private Entities
T : Treatments of Shared Entities
pT : Treatments of Private Entities

Fig. 7.5 The centralized architecture

of the unicity and centralization of the shared entities [29]. Moreover, groupware developers do not have to treat eventual distribution problems because its support is provided by the toolbox that supports the interactions at the user interface level, e.g., system X Windows. In fact, as shown in Fig. 7.5, the only required distribution functions are dedicated to the generation, transport and integration of user interaction events with the groupware components that are running on the server site.

The main disadvantages of this architecture reside in its high bandwidth consumption and its sensibility to network latency because the clients–server communication is based on event transmission [35]. However, used over high speed networks, the performances of this solution may be acceptable [44].

The existence of a unique server site nevertheless constitutes a real problem of scalability because the treatments T applied on shared entities inevitably imply some other treatments on all client sites [22]. Consequently, if the Visualizations and Modifications components require intensive processing or if some costly entities have to be stored and treated, the server resources may rapidly be consumed.

Fig. 7.6 Collaboration based
on a fully distributed
architecture

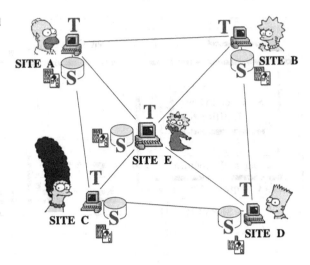

We have presented the centralized architecture because it constitutes the first
alternative to manage distributed shared entities, but it is evident that this solution
is completely unsuited to support distributed cooperative work on the Web. The
groupware development infrastructures Rendezvous [22] and Clock [18] implement
the centralized architecture.

7.2.3 Fully Distributed Architecture

The fully distributed architecture proposes a solution to structure the collaboration process completely in opposition with the centralized architecture: all treatment components and all shared entities are replicated on all cooperating sites (see
Fig. 7.6). Hence, server sites do not exist anymore, and thus each site acts in the
same way as the others.

The groupware systems that follow this architecture may correctly and efficiently
provide relaxed WYSIWIS views [43] because of the existence of the private entities
on each peer site. Synchronization is only required to update the space of shared
entities. Instead of transmitting events to a server site, all local components create
and manage them internally. Then, the events are transmitted to other peer sites
using a dedicated notification service. By receiving notification events, all peer sites
locally update their entity replicas and their user interfaces.

The main advantage of this architecture resides in the reactivity improvement of
the user interface because the accesses (processing and displaying) are performed
on local replicas. As shown in Fig. 7.7, each peer site includes all components of
the architecture, treatment components (Visualizations and Modifications) and application components (Space of Shared Entities), that allow it to be considered autonomous and able to work in temporarily disconnected mode. For instance, apply-

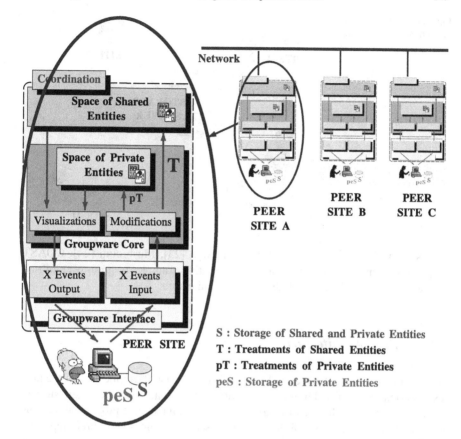

Fig. 7.7 The distributed architecture

ing an optimistic policy for the concurrency control, updating of shared entities can be performed, locally and independently of the network latency.

Moreover, because of the distribution of all treatment components and data components, this solution avoids processing overload as bottlenecks of the network communications that inevitably appear when using centralized servers. Usually, the distributed architecture provides better scalability than the centralized one. This advantage directly depends on the different costs related to the synchronization of the distributed replicas (e.g., complexity of the implemented solution, distributed processing and delays) [35].

The major inconvenience of the fully distributed architecture resides (1) in the management of the distributed replicas and (2) in the definition of an efficient synchronization service. As argued in the Alliance project [36], the structuring of the shared entities and its fragmentation in independent parts constitute a suited way to provide an efficient and reliable synchronization support.

Fig. 7.8 Collaboration based
on an hybrid architecture

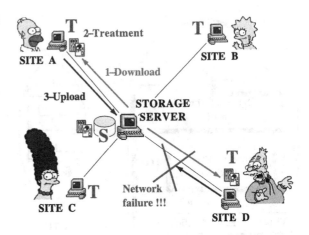

Research efforts like GINA [1], GroupDesign [23], Mushroom [24], COAST
[41], and DreamTeam [38] constitute representative examples of groupware infrastructures that implement the full distributed architecture.

7.2.4 Hybrid Architecture

The hybrid (or semi-replicated) architecture is based on a) the replication of the processing components T and b) the centralization of the shared data persistent storage
S within a server site. In order to participate to the collaborative process, all actions
performed by each client site follow a generic scheme composed of three steps (see
Fig. 7.8):

1. the client site downloads the required shared entity from the central server repository S. To avoid the production of concurrent versions, a lock has to be initialized
   on this site,
2. the client site can then edit/modify the local version obtained by applying the
   treatments T,
3. finally, after the client site application finished working with the shared entity, it
   uploads the new version to the server site and unlocks it.

The Web, as we use it daily, is a distributed world wide infrastructure based on
the hybrid architecture: all clients download the different Web pages from remote
server sites and treat them locally producing some nice presentations that eventually
allow users to interact with. This is the basic widespread scheme. More rarely, users
are authorized to modify the downloaded pages, and after he has terminated his
production, he has to upload the new page versions. The WebDAV project modifies
the Web working scheme extending the interaction protocol to add functionalities to
lock/unlock and author remote pages. The cooperative authoring principle remains
based on the hybrid architecture that includes a potentially important problem that
may enhance troubles especially in the field of the distributed cooperative work.

For instance, the collaborator on site D (see Fig. 7.8) has downloaded a shared entity on which he/she wants to locally apply some special actions. Now, supposing that during the authoring process, the network link with the server falls down. He/she is unable to validate the modifications that has produced during maybe several hours. This is a big problem that could become even more debatable if a lock has been established on the server site. How can we consistently revoke this lock? And after revoking the lock, if the network link is re-established, what about the user production? In the case of failure, the applied solutions may become more problematic than the initial problem. This point constitutes the first limitation of the hybrid architecture that can be strongly minimized if used in a quite local and reliable distributed environment (e.g., a LAN connecting different buildings).

The hybrid architecture takes advantages of both centralized and fully distributed architectures reducing their respective disadvantages. The hybrid architecture is simpler to develop and install than the fully distributed architecture as it is easier to maintain the consistency of the shared entities by means of a centralized algorithm that does not require a sophisticated procedure to synchronize the distributed replicas.

Moreover, within the hybrid architecture, if the peer sites and server sites communicate via a standard protocol, then different kinds of applications can concurrently gain access to the shared entities [7].

The hybrid architecture supports better scalability than the centralized architecture because the Visualizations and Modifications components are executed on the peer sites [18]. Because the treatments T are distributed on all peer sites, an important limitation of the hybrid architecture comes from the fact that the different shared entities have to be downloaded from the centralized server site before being used on the client sites. In the case of the existence of latencies within the network links that inter-connect the client and server sites, the global efficiency may be strongly reduced. This efficiency degradation effect can be reduced if the use of the hybrid architecture is limited to a high-speed reliable LAN. That constitutes the key point for the success of using the hybrid architecture for designing and implementing distributed collaborative environments.

However, if the characteristics of the network link are not so good as required, solutions based on the use of shared entity caches can improve the global performance of the distributed groupware system (see Fig. 7.9).

We can also highlight that in the case of the hybrid architecture, the Space of Private Entities component can be either placed on the client site or on the server site. These two possibilities are illustrated in the two client sites presented in Fig. 7.9. Selecting one possibility rather the other one is not fundamental, but the choice could be conditioned by: (a) the characteristics of the network links that connect the different sites and (b) the planned load of the cooperating sites.

To conclude on the hybrid architecture, it can be successfully used in a reliable and efficient distributed local environment (i.e., a LAN network) and it can be successfully combined with the fully distributed architecture to ensure this same reliability and efficiency within a wide distributed environment (i.e., a WAN network

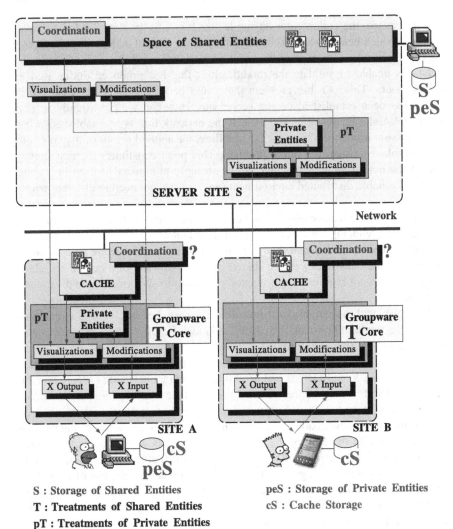

S : Storage of Shared Entities   peS : Storage of Private Entities
T : Treatments of Shared Entities   cS : Cache Storage
pT : Treatments of Private Entities

Fig. 7.9 The hybrid architecture

such as Internet). The PIÑAS platform presented in Sect. 7.3 shows one practical way to combine the hybrid and the full distributed architectures to especially support groupware systems or applications on the Web.

The groupware development infrastructures Suite [12], Weasel [17], DOLPHIN [45], Clock [18], GroupKit [37], and DreamTeam [38] successfully use the hybrid architecture.

7.2.5 Coordination Architectures

Coordination has been defined by Ellis et al. [14] as one of the three components of the functional clover that allows to identify and classify the functions provided by a groupware system. According to Ellis et al. and more clearly explained by Salber et al. [40], coordination constitutes a space that:

1. defines the actors in terms of persons, groups, roles, or "intelligent" software agents;
2. identifies the activities and tasks, and more particularly their temporal relations;
3. defines the actors who are in charge of the activities and tasks.

While the "production space" presents a static view of a groupware system, the "coordination space" defines its dynamics.

The "coordination space" includes functions whose goal is to ensure (a) the integration of modifications on the shared entities and (b) the production of consistent versions for these entities. Two classes of functions can be distinguished:

- the first class of functions is based on social interactions, and so offers mechanisms to allow users to coordinate themselves in order to determine the rules and ways to produce consistent versions of the shared entities. This class of functions is mainly centered on coordinating the interaction among collaborators, who explicitly define the consistent versions.
- the second class of functions takes advantage of some specific property of the shared entities to define mechanisms to automatically produce stable and consistent versions of the distributed shared entities.

As we will see later in this section, we can fruitfully use the shared entity structure to define powerful automatic distributed coordination functions.

The coordination functions take in charge all inconsistency problems related to the cooperative production: from the more elementary functions (e.g., definition and management of the sharing grain and locking of shared entity fragments) to the very elaborated functions of the user level (e.g., definition of the social roles and tasks associated to collaborators). The variety of the coordination tools is wide and rich, but their support may require the definition and use of artifacts that represent actual entities (e.g., telepointer) and logical ones (e.g., turn-taking).

7.2.5.1 Centralized Coordination: A Dedicated Server Site

The easiest solution to implement the Coordination component of a groupware system, in centralized or distributed environment, consists in encapsulating its functions within a dedicated server site.

The undeniable advantage of the centralized coordination component resides in the simplicity of administration. Thus, the Coordination component that is deployed on the coordination server (see Fig. 7.10) locally applies the Coordination Treatments on the Shared Coordination Entities.

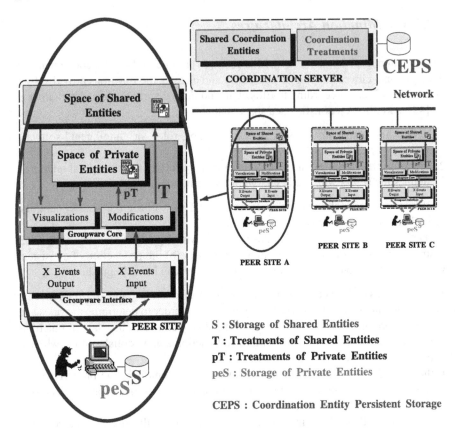

Fig. 7.10 Centralized coordination architecture

Within the coordination server, the operations to be applied on the Shared Coordination Entities (SCE) are treated following the First Come, First Served (FCFS) policy. The locking strategy is also easy to implement especially because the SCE are centralized on an unique server site.

The main disadvantage of the centralized coordination solution is precisely to use a single server site especially in the case of a distributed groupware system implemented on an unreliable environment. Effectively, if the server site fails or if it becomes unaccessible (e.g., network failure) for some cooperating sites, the consistency of the distributed productions cannot be assured anymore. In addition, the correctness of activities, which are being performed, is compromised (e.g., site blocking or disconnection, lost or inconsistent productions, inoperability of the distributed groupware system). In summary, implementing the Coordination component of a distributed groupware system, within a centralized server site, negates all advantages that we obtained by replicating both the Space of Shared Entities and Groupware Core components. Without any doubt, it is not at all the solution to be applied within the Web environment.

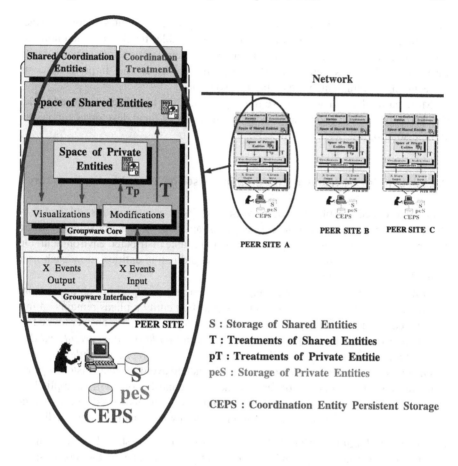

Fig. 7.11 Distributed/replicated coordination architecture

7.2.5.2 Distributed Coordination: Cooperation of Peer Sites

The second solution that seems to be suited to deploy the Coordination component of a distributed groupware system, consists in replicating on all cooperating sites: (a) the Shared Coordination Entities and (b) the Coordination Treatments. Figure 7.11 illustrates the replication principle of the coordination entities and functions.

However, the design and implementation of the Coordination Treatments are obviously more elaborated and complex than the ones presented for the centralized solution: additional specific notification/updating algorithms and mechanisms have to be defined and implemented for the distributed synchronization of the replicas of the Shared Coordination Entities.

Moreover, if some optimistic distributed algorithms are used, it is also required to employ other very complex algorithms to invalidate or to undo the disordered operations. Thus, a distributed coordination architecture constitutes a more satisfactory solution to provide users with a more comfortable, flexible and autonomous cooperative working environment (e.g., allowing them to cooperate in temporarily disconnected but consistent way). However, all these advantages imply extra costs in designing and implementing elaborated solutions.

More particularly, if we analyze the approaches that have been proposed to define and support Web cooperative work, the majority of them developed simple but limited solutions.

7.2.5.3 Defining Distributed Coordination Based on Shared Entity Structure

As we introduced it, replicating both the Shared Coordination Entities and the Coordination Treatments on the different peer sites, appears like a really suited solution to deploy the Coordination component on an unreliable distributed environment. On each peer site, the replicated application and coordination entities allow each user to work in an autonomous way.

However, designing and implementing a coordination algorithm able to ensure the automatic updating of the distributed application entity replicas remains an important requirement. The key element to satisfy this need is to give answer to the following question: "*According to what principle can I authorize concurrent and distributed productions on the distributed application entity replicas, while of course ensuring the consistency of such an entity?*" In fact, to avoid the inconsistency problem, we must ensure that the different concurrent contributions will be applied on "independent" regions of the shared application entity. In this way, the entity structure may allow to define a suited solution if the following principles are satisfied:

Shared entity fragmentation Following its structure, the shared entity can be splitted into fragments that can be independently modified, i.e., without processing any consistency control in cooperation with other peer sites.

Fragment value extraction for diffusion The value of a modified entity fragment can be easily extracted from a full replica of the entity in order to be diffused to the other peer sites.

Fragment value updating The diffused fragment value can be integrated within all peer site entity replicas in an autonomous way, i.e. without requiring any information exchange with other peer sites.

Independent fragment updating The various new versions of fragments can be integrated in any order within any entity replica producing the same final version.

Assuming that these conditions are satisfied, we can then better complement the principles required by such distributed coordination mechanism:

Master fragment copy Although each shared entity fragment is replicated on all peer sites, only one copy allows modifications that can be applied on the site that owns it. This copy is called the "master copy".

Slave fragment copy All other peer sites own copies that only permit consultation. Such copies are called "slave copies".

Fragment migration On demand or for management purpose, the master copy can migrate from one peer site to another. In fact, the master and slave copies are exchanged between the peer sites. To avoid potential inconsistencies, this operation is performed using a traditional transaction mechanism [5].

The last introduced "fragment migration" principle does not absolutely constitute a requirement. Thus, for some kind of shared entities, the fragments cannot migrate from one peer site to another (e.g., this is the case for the PIÑAS user definition entities that are explained in detail in Sect. 7.3.5). In addition, it is important to note that, depending on the entity type, fragmentation may be fixed (e.g., modifications/updates of the PIÑAS user definition entities in Sect. 7.3.5) or highly variable (e.g., cooperative authoring of structured documents [36]).

Applying the distributed coordination architecture to design and implement a groupware system, we can establish a similarity between synchronous and asynchronous coordination systems and synchronous and asynchronous group awareness functions [20]. Thus, we can distinguish groupware systems that requires either a synchronous or an asynchronous coordination support.

7.2.5.4 Synchronous Distributed Coordination

By defining and using synchronous coordination functions, a groupware system mainly emphasizes on the notifications and Coordination Treatments (CT) than on the validation, diffusion, and storage of the modifications applied on the Shared Coordination Entities (SCE). Thus, on each collaborator's site, the priority is then: (1) to apply treatments on the local replicas of the SCE and (2) to notify as soon as possible the other collaborators' CT of the applied modifications ... and of course to relegate with low priority the diffusion and updating of these modifications on the distributed persistent storage sites of the SCE.

For instance, a distributed cooperative white-board application not only requires an efficient synchronous group awareness function, but also the real-time execution of the distributed Coordination Entities. To define and manage the white-board logical sharing between distributed collaborators, we have to define a dedicated coordination entity able to provide the white-board with some structure, from which we can develop and apply sophisticated sharing principles and provide efficient synchronous cooperative work mechanisms.

Thus, this coordination entity can manage the fragmentation of the white-board in different working regions as shown in Fig. 7.12. Of course, as a distributed cooperative white-board is a dynamic groupware system from the fragmentation point of view, this coordination entity must support dynamic creation, deleting or fusion of white-board fragments that in this case represent working regions.

In Fig. 7.10 and Fig. 7.11, we have respectively presented the organization of the centralized and distributed coordination architectures. In order to provide a quite complete panorama to design and implement the Coordination component, we will now study the synchronous coordination approach followed by the hybrid architecture (see Fig. 7.13): the Coordination Treatments (CT) are distributed on the collaborator's sites and the Coordination Entity Persistent Storage (CEPS) that organizes

Fig. 7.12 Fragmentation of a white-board in working regions

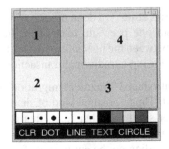

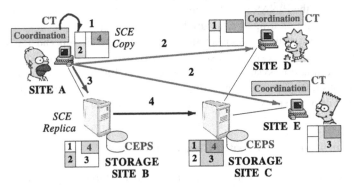

CEPS: **Coordination Entity Persistent Storage**
CT: **Coordination Treatments**

Fig. 7.13 Principle of the synchronous distributed coordination

the white-board fragmentation (see Fig. 7.12) is managed by dedicated server sites that own replicas of the Shared Coordination Entities (SCE) and that regularly communicate to update them.

In this way, according to the hybrid architecture, the synchronous coordination approach performs modification actions on the distributed Shared Coordination Entities (SCE) replicas applying the following steps (see Fig. 7.13):

1. A user working on his client site modifies the working copy of the Shared Coordination Entities (SCE) that previously downloaded from the remote Coordination Entity Persistent Storage (CEPS) repository. The SCE define a specific structure of the white-board that allows to logically fragment it, so that concurrent productions can be carried out on the different regions. Thus, as the user on site *A* obtained the control of the white-board fragment #4 defined by the associated SCE (see Fig. 7.13), he can: (a) produce on the corresponding white-board region and/or (b) fragment the associated SCE in smaller regions to increase the possibility of concurrent productions.

2. Modification of a white-board region dispatches a coordination event that has to be notified as soon as possible to other remote collaborators' application instances via the associated Shared Coordination Entities (SCE). Each collaborator's site (see sites *D* and *E* in Fig. 7.13) that receives such a notification in-

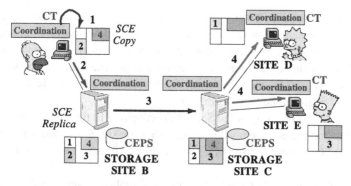

CEPS: Coordination Entity Persistent Storage
CT: Coordination Treatments

Fig. 7.14 Principle of the asynchronous distributed coordination

tegrates the modifications within the SCE working copy and updates the user interface.

Thus, the urgent inter-sites notification is supported by the Coordination Treatments (CT) components that are only present on the collaborators' sites (see Fig. 7.13).

3. Once the collaborators' sites had been notified, site *A* working copy of the Shared Coordination Entities (SCE) has to be validated within the corresponding persistent storage site. Thus, on site *B*, the "master" fragment #4 of the SCE replica is updated with the uploaded fragment #4 of site *A* working copy.

4. Finally, the updated "master" fragment #4 of the SCE replica on site *B* is diffused to all persistent storage sites (see site *C* in Fig. 7.13) in order to maintain the consistency of the distributed replicas of the SCE.

7.2.5.5 Asynchronous Distributed Coordination

By contrast, if the required distributed coordination support emphasizes much more on the updating and storage of the Shared Coordination Entities (SCE) than on the Coordination Treatments (CT) and inter-site notifications, while ensuring the persistence of the validated modifications, then an asynchronous coordination approach is required.

For instance, if a user asks and finally obtains the rights/roles to act on a whiteboard region, after waiting for quite a long time, the distributed groupware system mainly emphasizes to make valid and consistent this right obtention in the whole system. Notification of this right/role acquisition to collaborators remains of low priority and is asynchronously performed.

According to the hybrid architecture, a support that follows the asynchronous distributed coordination approach performs modification actions on distributed Shared Coordination Entities (SCE) applying the following steps (see Fig. 7.14):

1. A user working on his client site (e.g., site A) modifies the working copy of the Shared Coordination Entities (SCE) that previously downloaded from one of his Coordination Entity Persistent Storage (CEPS) repository. Because the user on site A has obtained the control on the white-board fragment #4 defined by the SCE (see Fig. 7.14), can: a) produce on the corresponding white-board region and/or b) fragment the SCE in smaller pieces.

2. The site A working copy of the Shared Coordination Entity (SCE) has to be validated within the persistent storage sites. Thus, on site B, the "master" fragment #4 of the SCE replica is updated with the uploaded fragment #4 of site A working copy.

3. The updated "master" fragment #4 of the SCE replica on site A is diffused to all persistent storage sites (see site C in Fig. 7.14) in order to maintain the consistency of the distributed replicas of the SCE.

4. After diffusing and updating the white-board fragment #4 in all distributed replicas managed by the different Coordination Entity Persistent Storage (CEPS) repositories, the Coordination Treatments (CT) component notifies all remote collaborators' application instances.

   Each collaborator's site (sites D and E in Fig. 7.14) that receives such notification integrates the modifications within its SCE (Shared Coordination Entity) working copy and updates the user interface.

It is important to note that in contrast with the synchronous coordination architecture (see Fig. 7.13), the asynchronous coordination architecture requires the full distribution of the coordination functions to all sites (see Fig. 7.14).

7.2.5.6 In Summary

In both synchronous and asynchronous distributed coordination principles that we have presented: (a) it had been defined a structuring of the shared coordination entity (fragmentation) and (b) the content of each of these fragments can be easily extracted and independently replaced/updated within another working copy or replica of the shared entity. Thus, we demonstrated that it is possible to clearly define and structure the different kinds of architectures: (1) to clearly organize, distribute and access to shared entities, and (2) to define and efficiently implement distributed coordination functions.

The studied architectures allow: (1) to organize shared entity distribution and sharing (Sects. 7.2.2–7.2.4), and (2) to define distributed coordination functions (Sect. 7.2.5). These architectures for which we highlighted the main characteristics will be integrated within the PIÑAS development infrastructure in order to define and efficiently implement distributed groupware functions that allow to define and support Web collaborative work in a reliable and flexible.

7.3 The PIÑAS Web Infrastructure

The PIÑAS infrastructure aims at providing support for the development of cooperative applications on the Web. More specifically, it has been designed to support cooperative production of Web documents. PIÑAS offers a set of groupware services for the identification, naming and management of authors, documents, resources, sessions, projects, applications and events. These groupware services are available for cooperative applications through standard interfaces (e.g., HTTP protocol) and through more specialized interfaces (e.g., proprietary extensions and conventions with standard protocols). On one hand, "PIÑAS-aware" applications are capable of requesting services, thus gaining access to the features of the infrastructure (e.g., richer contents) that they are capable to handle. On the other hand, "non-PIÑAS-aware" applications are capable of requesting services using standard interfaces, thus gaining access to specific features, while avoiding sending them information (e.g., proprietary formatting information) that they will not be able to deal with.

Requirements   For the design of the PIÑAS infrastructure, we have identified the requirements for pertinent document and resource sharing, availability and consistency. We have also identified additional issues that need to be solved: the need for user, document and resource identification, development of specific access mechanisms, access time specification and access site specification.

To achieve these requirements, we define and use the following mechanisms: fragmentation, access control, concurrency control, replication, automatic updating and virtual naming of users, documents and resources. These mechanisms are developed and mapped into the software architecture of the PIÑAS infrastructure, which is further discussed in the following subsection.

Software Architecture   The PIÑAS software architecture is structured in layers that integrate key components to provide support for cooperative work on the Web. In order to be homogeneous with the Web environment, PIÑAS is based on a client/server communication model, whose server side consists of three main layers (see bottom block in Fig. 7.15). The bottom layer offers a set of HTTP-based communication functions. The middle layer contains the key cooperative entities offered by the infrastructure, as well as their corresponding management services (that are not shown). Finally, for developing and supporting cooperative applications, the top layer provides a synchronous API (Application Programming Interface) that allows them to access the services.

The PIÑAS infrastructure manages different types of entities, such as Users, Documents and their Resources, Sessions, Projects, Events, Applications and Group Awareness [33], which are essential to the collaboration support. The User entity manages information allowing to identify a collaborator at the system and social levels. Thus, once a user is identified, it becomes possible to grant access rights to him on shared documents and resources, to determine his contributions and to coordinate his actions. The Document entity represents a Web document, which can be divided into several fragments following the logical structure of the document.

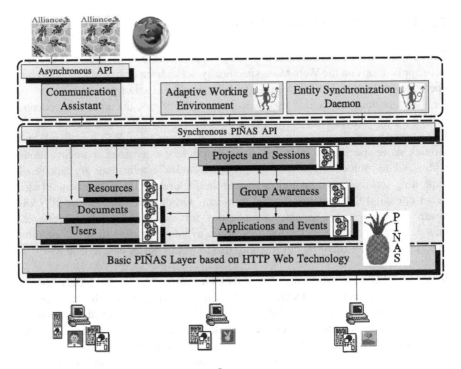

Fig. 7.15 The software architecture of the PIÑAS infrastructure

Each fragment can contain several instances of the Resource entity, which represents a multimedia resource. The Application entity represents a cooperative application that allows users to work on shared documents, whereas the Event entity represents state information (e.g. presence, availability, and location in the shared workspace) of users and documents. The Project entity maintains static information about the User and Document entities involved in a collaborative project. Finally, the Session entity handles dynamic information of a Project entity associated to an Application entity.

The upper block in Fig. 7.15 separates the applications interacting with the infrastructure through the synchronous API from the applications interacting by means of the asynchronous API. Applications use the asynchronous API when they lack communication support to interact with the infrastructure services. The assistant module carries out all communications with the synchronous API by means of function calls of the required entities and services at the server side. The PIÑAS infrastructure supports three types of applications: PIÑAS-based groupware applications (e.g. AllianceWeb), standard Web browsers (e.g. Firefox) and dedicated applications (e.g. inference engine tool). Particularly, standard Web browsers have limited access to the infrastructure entities and services.

As we will see in Sect. 7.3.2, the PIÑAS infrastructure proposes an approach mixing the hybrid architecture with the fully replicated architecture already experimented in the Alliance project [36]. This approach merges the flexibility of the hybrid architecture with the reliability of the fully replicated architecture. Moreover, it is important to note that the document replication principle constitutes the first step to offer nomadic work features.

The PIÑAS infrastructure does not impose constraints on the document structure that is application-dependent. Web documents have to be considered as a generic information entity from which distributed collaborative applications can define their principles and mechanisms for supporting cooperative production of shared information (e.g., report documents for cooperative document authoring, or a board document for a distributed white-board application).

7.3.1 PIÑAS Naming Space

The PIÑAS infrastructure is designed to provide a naming space in which each user is clearly identified. Moreover, this naming space is able to uniquely name and provide access to user's entities. PIÑAS ensures unambiguous user authentication and naming to control entity accesses and to protect them against unauthorized actions. User naming is based on the following principles:

- Each user is able to identify, contact or send information to other users regardless of whether they are working at the same time or not.
- User names are unique and cannot be re-allocated. These names constitute the basis for entity protection and, depending on the entity type, they are handled by the corresponding management system (e.g., document renaming and moving, or more generally document base reorganization).

PIÑAS distinguishes between the working site where a user's actions are performed and the storage site where stable versions of his entities are persistently saved. This working principle may look similar to the one commonly proposed in the Web environment, but differs on the following essential points:

- Each individual user is free to decide whether or not to store and access entities from a remote Web site. This possibility allows users to share the same entity server site on a more reliable environment (e.g., LAN).
- Entities are basically replicated on HTTP server sites to enhance their availability, providing support for Web cooperative working in disconnected, degraded, or nomadic modes.

As shown in Fig. 7.16, a PIÑAS user employs services of two different server sites: (1) one that is in charge of entity storage management (his entities and copies of his collaborators' entities), and (2) a site that receives events from other users to support group awareness, cooperation negotiation, or communication.

The identification of the storage and working sites is based on the URL [27] standard Web naming space. This characteristic constitutes the requested condition to be able to extend existing Web services without need to create a new, specialized, and heterogeneous naming space.

Fig. 7.16 User working and storage sites

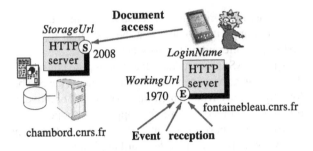

```
User        Maggie

StorageUrl  http://chambord.cnrs.fr:2008
WorkingUrl  http://fontainebleau.cnrs.fr:1970
LoginName   msimpson

End
```

Fig. 7.17 Basic user definition

Figure 7.17 shows the definition of user *Maggie* who is logged and working on the site called *fontainebleau.cnrs.fr*, and whose entities (e.g., documents or resources) are stored and managed by the Web server of the site *chambord.cnrs.fr* at the port 2008. This site association constitutes the basic principle for user definition. The complete *Maggie*'s multi-site user definition is provided in Fig. 7.21.

7.3.1.1 Virtual Naming Space

In order to well manage (eventually shared) Web entities, we define a virtual naming space that offers two functions: (a) to allocate a name for each entity that allows to designate it, and (b) to locate an entity in order to perform accesses. The Web standard naming system mainly uses the URL schema [27] that mixes (1) the identification of the considered resource and (2) its physical location within the server repository space. Using such kind of naming service, it is quite difficult for the consistent management of Web entities: for instance, the modification of the name or location of a standard Web resource does not allow clients that own the old name to access it anymore. To cope with this important limitation, our proposition avoids such kind of problems by defining a global naming space that is totally compatible with the standard URL-based Web naming system.

Using the proposed naming system, the already existing Web browsers and the targeted cooperative applications can perform accesses (in a fully homogeneous and transparent way) to the distributed shared entities. More specifically, the global naming space of shared entities focus on satisfying some clearly identified requirements:

- unambiguous identification of shared entities,
- availability of the shared distributed entities,
- support for remote collaborators to gain access to shared entities,

- coordination of concurrently applied distributed operations,
- access to consistent and updated shared entities,
- notification and updating of distributed concurrent productions,
- consistency of inter-entity relations,
- possibility to share entities between collections.

Taking into account these requirements, we define a global naming space that is composed of three well identified levels:

1. **Logical level**: the names or identifiers are explicitly associated by users to the entities (e.g., "Report" or "myCV"). These names can be reallocated but are unique within a given context that is called a "naming space". The naming space concept is fundamental for the name definition because the unicity on entity logical names can only be ensured within this space (e.g., a global site, a document, a directory or a resource catalog). A logical name is a string of alphanumeric characters that does not contain any information about the entity location within the persistent storage space.
2. **Virtual level**: a virtual name is a unique system identifier that is associated to an entity at creation time. Its scope is the entire distributed PIÑAS infrastructure. This name is unique, non re-allocatable and entity location-independent. From the implementation point of view, a virtual name is the combination of several units of information: (a) the IP address of the storage site on which the entity was created, (b) a unique integer label delivered by a storage site distributor (e.g., 172.56.102.3_#103).
3. **Physical level**: the storage space defines and manages unique and non re-allocatable identifiers that allow to locate the corresponding entities within the storage repositories. A physical entity name is composed of three information units: (a) a MIME[7] [16] prefix that provides information about the entity type, (b) the entity virtual name, and (c) a suffix that presents the MIME subtype. All these information units are combined in order to organize and facilitate the storage and searching operations within the storage space.

In opposition with the logical names that are associated to entities by users, the virtual and physical names are attributed by the PIÑAS infrastructure, and so they are not visible at the user level.

Figure 7.18 presents the organization of the three naming levels, and more particularly the different names that are respectively associated with user *Maggie*, one of her documents, and a resource of this document. "Maggie", "Report" and "Diagram01.gif" are respectively the user, document and resource logical names that are provided by *Maggie* to designate them.

As shown in Fig. 7.18, a dedicated storage Web entity base is allocated for user "*Maggie*" in which all her entities are well organized. Thus, the resource "Diagram01.gif" is a component of the document "Report" owned by *Maggie*'s Web entity base.

---

[7]MIME: Multipurpose Internet Mail Extensions.

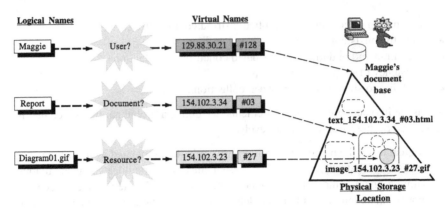

Fig. 7.18 Virtual naming space

Each virtual identifier is unique, not re-allocable and valid for the entity lifetime. The correspondences between logical, virtual and physical names are dynamic and user transparent. For instance, the resource logically named "Diagram01.gif" corresponds to the entity virtually named "154.102.3.23_#27" and stored in the file "image_154.102.3.23_#27.gif".

7.3.2 Web Document Replication

Inside the PIÑAS storage space, each Web document is represented by a set of files which contain document fragments and some metadata, e.g. the user roles for each fragment, the order of all fragments in a document, and the current state of each fragment.

To allow each user to work on a shared document, even in case of a network failure, documents are replicated on each HTTP server site where they are needed. All document fragments and their corresponding management information are replicated on all of these sites. Each user can then work independently. To allow cooperation, local copies must be updated when remote users perform modifications. Depending on the document nature, the associated updates are carried out in either synchronous or asynchronous mode.

Document consistency is based on a simple principle. In the whole system, there is always one master copy for each fragment, which is the reference; there are as many slave copies as needed. On a given HTTP server site where at least one user works on the document, all fragments of that document are available and each fragment copy is either the master or a slave copy:

- The master copy allows the user to act on it with the writer role. As the master copy is unique, only one user can play this role for a given fragment at a given time.

- A slave copy only allows the reader role, even if a role with writing rights is assigned to the user on that fragment.

According to this principle, the set of all master copies constitutes the current document state. As a site usually does not own the master copies of all fragments of a given document, each site and each user may have a delayed perception (asynchronous mode) of the document state. However, these different perceptions of the document are regularly corrected by the asynchronous transmission of updating messages, when a site owning the master copy of a fragment produces a new version of that fragment.

The document management principles (replication, master and slave copies, copy diffusion, and automatic synchronous or asynchronous updating) constitute the keystones to provide a reliable support for disconnected or nomadic work. Following these principles, the PIÑAS storage system automatically manages replicated document copies, ensuring their consistency.

7.3.2.1 Combining Local and Distributed Document Storage

Two architectures have already been used within the field of the Internet and/or Web environments:

- **The fully distributed architecture** (see Sect. 7.2.3). Experimented in the Alliance [8] cooperative editor on Internet, it is based on the document replication among the user's sites. This solution is well suited to support failure-tolerant applications and disconnected cooperative work.
- **The hybrid architecture** (see Sect. 7.2.4). Following this principle, documents are remotely loaded from the server site, locally modified on the user client site, and then sent back to the server site. This solution allows for the sharing of storage between several sites in a simple and easy way, but remains really applicable in a reliable network environment.

Taking into account some experiences already developed in the field of the Internet, our approach mixes the hybrid and distributed architectures (see Fig. 7.19). Each user involved in the distributed cooperative work, can choose between these two document store and access solutions to cooperate and interact with other users.

As shown in Fig. 7.19, a group of users working on sites A and B (resp. sites C and D) are connected in a reliable network environment (e.g., LAN), where they share and access the same Web documents. By contrast, these two groups of users (sites A–B and C–D) are inter-connected by the less reliable Internet network. Thus, all documents shared between these two users must be replicated to prevent network failures from disrupting the joint work and to support cooperative work in temporarily disconnected mode. In our example, storage of document copies is managed by sites A and C.

In this way, on each LAN, it is necessary to install an HTTP server and dedicated scripts to handle access requests to documents. These access requests are sent to the storage communication port (S).

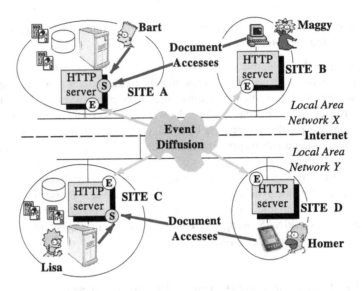

Fig. 7.19 A realistic PIÑAS configuration

The inter-application events (e.g., lock/unlock fragment, update or modify fragment, get and put information, partition of fragment) are exchanged via the event communication ports (E). Events are asynchronously transmitted to the editing application. Thus, each site that participates in the cooperative work architecture, needs to run an HTTP server: they are dedicated to event transmissions and/or storage management. To access document copies, a user on side B does not necessarily own a login on site A.

7.3.3 Multi-Site User Work Organization

To illustrate the assignment principle of working and storage to collaborators via user definitions and more especially, the association between "storage sites–working sites", we examine now a practical example that we will progressively modify and enrich in the next sections.

7.3.3.1 The Practical Example

Suppose that the potential collaborators *Maggie, Lisa, Homer,* and *Bart* are distributed around the world and can use different sites to produce and interact. *Bart* can work on shared entities from the working sites *chichenitza.unam.mx, versailles.cnrs.fr* and *neuschwanstein.gmd.de* (see Fig. 7.20). In addition, *Bart* can upload/download shared entities from/to the storage sites *uxmal.unam.mx, chambord.cnrs.fr, blois.cnrs.fr* and *linderhof.gmd.de. Bart*'s working and storage sites

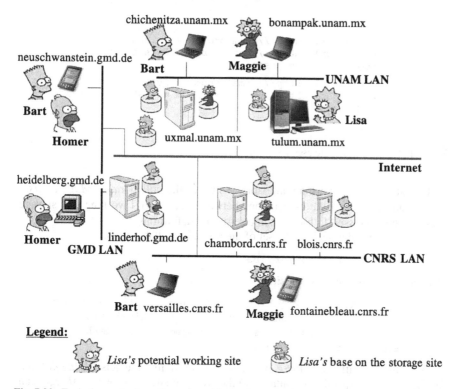

chichenitza.unam.mx   bonampak.unam.mx

neuschwanstein.gmd.de

Bart   Maggie

UNAM LAN

Bart

Homer   uxmal.unam.mx   tulum.unam.mx

Lisa

Internet

heidelberg.gmd.de

Homer   linderhof.gmd.de   chambord.cnrs.fr   blois.cnrs.fr
GMD LAN

CNRS LAN

Bart versailles.cnrs.fr   Maggie fontainebleau.cnrs.fr

Legend:

Lisa's potential working site   *Lisa's* base on the storage site

Fig. 7.20 Typical organization of users' working and storage sites

are located within different institutions from different countries (UNAM in México, CNRS in France, and GMD in Germany). This organization of working and storage sites allows *Bart* to work in a nomadic way, moving from a site to another during his different trips. Depending on *Bart's* current location (e.g., *chichenitza.unam.mx*), he can access the shared entities managed on the associated UNAM storage site (e.g., *uxmal.unam.mx*). Thus, this site association allows *Bart* to move from an Internet working point to another while using and taking benefits of a more reliable working environment: each time, the working and storage sites are co-located within the same local area network (see Fig. 7.20).

In the particular case of *Maggie*, she can start cooperative working sessions from sites *bonampak.unam.mx* and *fontainebleau.cnrs.fr* that are respectively located within UNAM and CNRS institutions. As represented in Fig. 7.20, from these sites, *Maggie* can download/upload entities from/to her storage sites *uxmal.unam.mx* and *chambord.cnrs.fr*. *Maggie's* multi-site user definition is presented in Fig. 7.21. In a same way as for *Bart*, the PIÑAS distributed infrastructure will allow *Maggie* to move from a working point to the another, remaining aware of the evolution of the cooperative process without loosing any information. As shown in Fig. 7.21, *Maggie* may use completely different login names to start a cooperative session on her different working sites.

```
User  Maggie

StorageUrl    http://chambord.cnrs.fr:2008
WorkingUrl    http://fontainebleau.cnrs.fr:1970
LoginName     msimpson

StorageUrl    http://uxmal.unam.mx:2005
WorkingUrl    http://bonampak.unam.mx:1959
LoginName     mag

End
```

Fig. 7.21 Maggie's multi-site user definition

The attribution of working and storage sites to the collaborators *Maggie*, *Lisa*, *Homer*, and *Bart*, and the associations between each user's working and storage sites, can be expressed following some set-based definitions.

First of all, we define U as the set of the potential collaborators:

```
U := {Maggie, Lisa, Homer, Bart}
```

and S as the set of the different sites:

```
S := {bonampak.unam.mx, chichenitza.unam.mx, tulum.unam.mx,
      uxmal.unam.mx, chambord.cnrs.fr, fontainebleau.cnrs.fr,
      versailles.cnrs.fr, heidelberg.gmd.de, linderhof.gmd.de,
      neuschwanstein.gmd.de}
```

From the definitions of these two sets, we can define the sets *ft(Maggie)* and *fs(Maggie)* that respectively contain: (a) the working sites from which *Maggie* can start a working session and (b) the storage sites from/to which she is able download/upload entities. Finally, the set *ts(Maggie)* contains the "working site–storage site" associations that are established between the sets *ft(Maggie)* and *fs(Maggie)*:

```
ft(Maggie) := {bonampak.unam.mx, fontainebleau.cnrs.fr}
fs(Maggie) := {uxmal.unam.mx, chambord.cnrs.fr}
ts(Maggie) := {bonampak.unam.mx ↦ {uxmal.unam.mx},
               fontainebleau.cnrs.fr ↦ {chambord.cnrs.fr}}
```

In a same way, the sets *ft(Lisa)* and *fs(Lisa)* respectively contain *Lisa*'s working and storage sites, whereas the set *ts(Lisa)* defines the associations between these site:

```
ft(Lisa) := {tulum.unam.mx}
fs(Lisa) := {tulum.unam.mx, uxmal.unam.mx}
ts(Lisa) := {tulum.unam.mx ↦ {tulum.unam.mx, uxmal.unam.mx}}
```

For *Bart* and *Homer* the associated sets are respectively defined as followed:

```
ft(Bart) := {chichenitza.unam.mx, versailles.cnrs.fr,
             neuschwanstein.gmd.de}
fs(Bart) := {uxmal.unam.mx, chambord.cnrs.fr, blois.cnrs.fr,
             linderhof.gmd.de}
ts(Bart) := {chichenitza.unam.mx ↦ {uxmal.unam.mx},
             versailles.cnrs.fr ↦ {chambord.cnrs.fr,
                                    blois.cnrs.fr},
```

```
                    neuschwanstein.gmd.de  ↦  {linderhof.gmd.de}}

ft(Homer)  := {heidelberg.gmd.de, neuschwanstein.gmd.de}
fs(Homer)  := {linderhof.gmd.de}
ts(Homer)  := {heidelberg.gmd.de ↦ {linderhof.gmd.de},
                    neuschwanstein.gmd.de ↦ {linderhof.gmd.de}}
```

7.3.3.2 Working Site Sharing

Although it may appear evident, several users can use the same working site at different moments. For example, *Bart* and *Homer* can potentially use the same site *neuschwanstein.gmd.de* to start a working session. From this site, the shared entities will be downloaded/uploaded from/to the *linderhof.gmd.de*. As shown in Fig. 7.20 legend, *Bart*'s and *Homer*'s replicas of their Web entity base are represented on the site *linderhof.gmd.de* by a small disk surmounted of the corresponding small icon.

7.3.3.3 Storage Site Sharing

Several users who are acting from working sites of the same reliable organization can share some common storage sites. Thus, as shown in Fig. 7.20, at a given moment, if *Bart* and *Homer* are respectively working on *neuschwanstein.gmd.de* and *heidelberg.gmd.de*, they are using the same storage site while download-ing/uploading entities from/to *linderhof.gmd.de*. In the same way, *Maggie*'s site *bonampak.unam.mx*, *Lisa*'s site *tulum.unam.mx*, and *Bart*'s site *chichenitza.unam.mx* use the common storage site *uxmal.unam.mx*.

Thus, several users whose working sites are located within a reliable environment (e.g, a LAN) can share the storage capabilities of a common site. Of course, it is possible for a storage site (e.g., *blois.cnrs.fr*) to be associated to a single user (*Bart*) and even to a single working site (*versailles.cnrs.fr*).

7.3.3.4 Several Storage Sites Associated to a Same Working Site

For several reasons (e.g., mirroring, administration, and load), a user who started a working session from a specific site (e.g., *Bart* on site *versailles.cnrs.fr*) may indif-ferently access shared entities as his own private entities from several storage sites (e.g., *chambord.cnrs.fr* and *blois.cnrs.fr*) on which these entities are replicated. Ini-tially, we can imagine that *Bart* is working using the storage site *chambord.cnrs.fr*. Depending on different reasons (e.g., unavailability or overloading of this site and network link failure), the PIÑAS infrastructure may choose to switch to the storage site *blois.cnrs.fr*. This operation remains transparent for the user.

7.3.3.5 Dual Storage/Working Site

Finally, we must highlight the fact that a unique site acting as both working and storage site constitutes a really interesting working support: the user can work in an autonomous and highly reliable way, downloading and uploading entities from/to his local site. Thus, at the same time, the site *tulum.unam.mx* can offer services to *Lisa*: (1) to connect and start a working session, and (2) to make local accesses to her entities and to her collaborators' entities that are locally replicated. Thus, *Lisa*'s working session becomes completely autonomous. This possibility for a site to act at the same time as a working and storage site constitutes the first way to support disconnected or degraded cooperative work.

To conclude on the proposed site organization, we have provided an essential notion of multi-site user: (1) to identify and represent the future collaborators on Internet, and (2) to administrate and locate them during working sessions. As a user definition entity is dynamic, collaborators may add/delete both working and storage sites. Thus, despite users are collaborating within such an unreliable Internet environment, the principles of this site organization allows them to benefit from highly available shared entities that are replicated among collaborator's storage sites.

This site organization offers to users the possibility to work from different physical locations, moving from one working site to another. In the same way, on all their working sites, they can access shared entities. Moving from one working site to another, services offered by the PIÑAS infrastructure allow them to evolve within the same working environment. These services not only take in charge the designation, duplication and persistence of the shared entities, but more their updating and consistency.

Finally, the proposed infrastructure is homogeneous, and thus the user definition is fully integrated within the provided distributed/replicated model of shared entities. In the next Sect. 7.3.4, we show how the multi-site user definition constitutes a suited notion to easily establish cooperation between users.

7.3.4 Establishing the Cooperation

Following any social protocol for meetings or putting in touch, a group of persons decides to establish a cooperation in order to interact and produce a given entity in a concerted way (e.g., a technical documentation). Let us suppose that during a consultation meeting among collaborators, a project leader is chosen. This collaborator can then create in his working environment an initial document, whose value can be reduced to a preliminary version of its structure (e.g., main sections and subsections). In addition, the group members define different goals and roles to produce this entity.

Based on the initial attribution of roles to collaborators on the various component entities of the document (i.e., fragments and resources), the phase for establishing cooperation among the different involved sites takes place. The main goal of this phase consists in: (1) the identification and location of the cooperating sites; and (2) the location of the entities that have to be shared. More particularly, during this phase, the user definition of each collaborator is interchanged among the sites involved in the cooperative process. These fundamental shared entities represent the different collaborators and contain their corresponding storage and working multisite definitions.

In order to implement mechanisms for the distribution of shared entities as well as for the concurrent modification, updating and consistency of the different replicas, it is required that each one of these systems has knowledge of the different collaborators involved in the project, no matter the number and location of working and storage sites associated to each collaborator. The PIÑAS infrastructure is based on the Internet naming domains to carry out the distribution of entities to the involved sites.

7.3.4.1 Practical Example

In order to illustrate the different steps for the distribution and sharing of an entity, let us suppose that *Maggie*, *Bart* and *Lisa* decided to collaborate in the production of a shared document named "report". As manager of this cooperative process, *Maggie* asks their collaborators (i.e., *Lisa* and *Bart*) to transmit her their respective user definitions. To carry out this request, *Maggie* can use any working environment tool that may be integrated within the groupware application (e.g., email).

Once *Maggie* received *Lisa*'s and *Bart*'s user definitions (cf. transitions 1 and 2 in Fig. 7.22), she requests the establishment of cooperation among the involved sites (i.e., *Lisa*'s, *Bart*'s and *Maggie*'s sites) from her working site *bonampak.unam.mx*.

First, on the site *bonampak.unam.mx*, *Maggie*'s local user definition is analyzed in order to select one storage site. In relation to the definitions of *Maggie*'s working and storage sites and the associations between them (*ts(Maggie)*, see Sect. 7.3.3): (a) only the storage site *uxmal.unam.mx* is available for holding and managing *Maggie*'s entities within the UNAM naming domain and (b) the site *bonampak.unam.mx* is her only possible working site.

In this way, the site *bonampak.unam.mx* sends a request to the storage site *uxmal.unam.mx* (cf. transition 1 of Fig. 7.23) that includes all collaborators' user definitions (i.e., *Maggie*, *Lisa*, *Bart*) of the document "report".

The collaborators' user definitions must not only be diffused and stored on the site *uxmal.unam.mx*, but also they have to be diffused to all collaborators' storage sites (i.e., *uxmal.unam.mx*, *tulum.unam.mx*, *linderhof.gmd.de*, *chambord.cnrs.fr* and *blois.cnrs.fr*).

Thus, when all collaborators' storage sites have finally obtained all user definitions, each one is able to determine the storage and potential working sites of everybody. This information potentially allows each collaborator: (a) to perform accesses to any user's Web entity base, and (b) to locate and contact a specific collaborator acting from any of his declared working sites.

Instead of updating these storage sites following a site per site policy, the diffusion process starts from the site *uxmal.unam.mx* that is the current *Maggie*'s storage

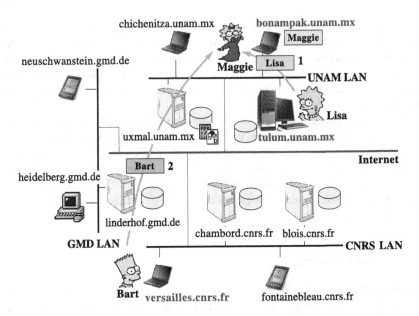

Fig. 7.22 Bart and Lisa transmit their user definitions to Maggie

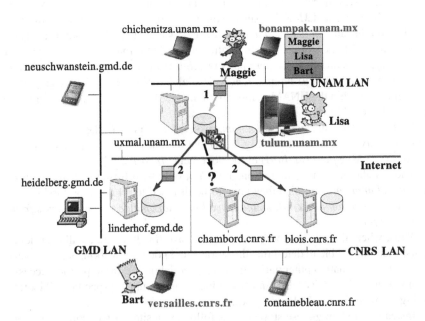

Fig. 7.23 Diffusion of Maggie's, Lisa's and Bart's user definitions

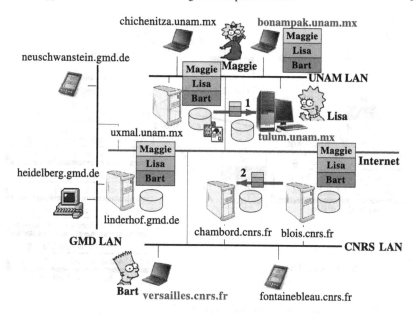

Fig. 7.24 Diffusion per domain of the users' definitions

site that now stores the three updated collaborators' definitions. Then, this site is in charge of updating one storage site per Internet naming domain. In this way, the distribution support determines the user definitions that have to be diffused to the three sets of storage sites corresponding to the three different naming domains: (1) *uxmal.unam.mx* and *tulum.unam.mx* in the UNAM naming domain, (2) *linderhof.gmd.de* in the GMD naming domain, and finally (3) *chambord.cnrs.fr* and *blois.cnrs.fr* in the CNRS naming domain.

The *uxmal.unam.mx* site is already updated (cf. transition 1 of Fig. 7.23) thus, the UNAM naming domain is already contacted. It remains to determine one storage site to update for the GMD and CNRS naming domains. In the case of the GMD naming domain, there is no need to select because it only includes one storage site, *linderhof.gmd.de*. In contrast, within the CNRS naming domain, two storage sites can be contacted. Let us suppose that the site *chambord.cnrs.fr* is temporarily unavailable (failed transition "?" in Fig. 7.23) and only the site *blois.cnrs.fr* is operational. Thus, the collaborators' definitions are then diffused to the sites *linderhof.gmd.de* and *blois.cnrs.fr* (cf. transitions 2 of Fig. 7.23).

Finally, the three updated sites (i.e., *uxmal.unam.mx*, *linderhof.gmd.de* and *blois.cnrs.fr*), behave as "relay" sites, which are in charge of diffusing the collaborators' definitions within their respective Internet naming domain. Thus, as illustrated in Fig. 7.24, the sites *uxmal.unam.mx* and *blois.cnrs.fr* propagate the collaborators' definitions respectively to the sites *tulum.unam.mx* (transition 1 in Fig. 7.24) and *chambord.cnrs.fr* (transition 2 in Fig. 7.24). In the case of this last propagation, it will take place as soon as the site *chambord.cnrs.fr* becomes operational.

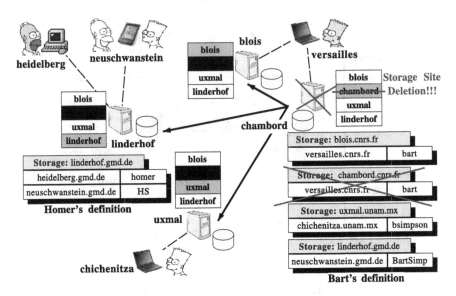

Fig. 7.25 User modification and distributed updating

At the end of this distribution process, all storage sites own every collaborator's user definition and more precisely, their associated storage and potential working sites. Then, cooperation can effectively start.

7.3.5 Disconnected and Nomadic Cooperative Work

As introduced in Sect. 7.3.3, the PIÑAS multi-site user definition allows the corresponding user to organize his work defining and using several storage and working sites that can be widely distributed among the Web. Thus, each user or system administrator who is in charge to organize and manage a community of collaborators is able to determine a suited and reliable configuration for the user's storage and working sites. This configuration is determined by taking into account the local environment structure (e.g., building, office, communities) and the quality of their interconnections. For instance, if the connection between two remote buildings remains quite unstable, he can decide to install two repository servers: one within each building area.

Moreover, for administration and/or reliability purposes, it is also possible to install more than one single repository site within the same institution. Thus, the different sites act as mutual mirrors that facilitate some administration tasks avoiding storage service disruption, e.g., temporary stop, execution of an administration task, restarting, removing or adding a site, or migration of the storage service from one site to another.

Relatively to our example (see Fig. 7.25), *Bart* can start a working session and act within the CNRS environment downloading and uploading entities either from *chambord.cnrs.fr* or *blois.cnrs.fr*. Entities can be indifferently accessed from any of these two sites. Moreover during a working session, an entity can be downloaded from one of these sites and later saved on the other one: the entity access is fully application independent and only managed by the PIÑAS infrastructure.

Thus, in a general way, acting and producing within a quite sophisticated working environment, the user have to be perceived no more as the active entity attached to only one working/storage site, but as the actor who can work from different working sites, under different login names, as well as store and access documents and other kinds of elaborated shared entities from different storage sites. In this way, the "*N* working sites–*M* storage sites" user definition constitutes a central notion allowing him to use the same cooperative working environment independently of his location.

7.3.5.1 User Definition: A Replicated Concurrently Modifiable Entity

During all stages of cooperative work, the representation of a user and its attributes may evolve over time. To cope with the evolution of each user's working environment, the user definition is a dynamic entity. Thus, a user definition can be easily modified in order to be adapted to the physical environment changes or to plan/organize modifications of his working environment: modification of a storage service name, installation of a new (possibly temporary) storage service, deleting or adding a new working site, creation of a new storage/working site, etc.

For instance, as we will see later, the possibility to extend the user definition installing a temporary storage service on a laptop provides the user with the possibility to cooperatively work in a temporarily disconnected nomadic mode. Of course, the installation of a new storage service requires the possibility for a user definition to be concurrently and consistently modified.

7.3.5.2 Fragmentation, Modification and Consistency of User Definitions

To allow dynamic access and modification of user attributes (working sites, login names, storage sites), in a similar way as for all shared entities, it is necessary to replicate the corresponding definition within all environments in which the user might work. This replication requires a method for supporting concurrent, consistent and possibly distributed modifications of user attributes.

Analyzing a user definition, we can easily notice that it is composed of a sequence of storage site records. Each of them associates a list of couples ⟨*working site*, *login*⟩ to a specified storage site: they are the working sites from which the user may connect using the corresponding login name to start a working session downloading/uploading entity replicas from/to the considered storage site.

In order to support concurrent modifications of user definitions, the PIÑAS infrastructure takes advantage of the already introduced entity structure-based principle (see Sect. 7.2.5) that authorizes concurrent and consistent modifications of a distributed shared entity. In this way, it is required to well define the structure and the way by which a user definition entity can be modified:

- The structure of a user definition entity in storage site records allows to define fragments that can be independently modified one from the others.
- Each modified fragment value can be integrated within every user definition version without any inter-fragment consistency concern.
- On each storage site that participates in the cooperative process, there exists a user definition replica of all collaborators. Each user definition replica includes "master" and "slave" fragments. Only a "master" fragment can authorize modifications.

The sequence of storage site records constitutes a natural and powerful way to structure a user definition entity. Each fragment corresponds to one storage site record that can only be modified on this site.

Continuing with our example, *Bart*'s user definition describes his possibilities (storage and working site associations, and login names) to work and cooperate with *Homer*. *Bart* starts a working session from the site *versailles.cnrs.fr*, but potentially he is also able to work from *neuschwanstein.gmd.de* or from *chichenitza.unam.mx* (represented by ghost *Bart*'s pictures in Fig. 7.25).

Bart's user definition is composed of four fragments that respectively own the attributes associated with his four storage sites (i.e., *blois.cnrs.fr*, *chambord.cnrs.fr*, *linderhof.gmd.de*, and *uxmal.unam.mx*). *Bart*'s user definition is replicated on all these storage sites (on each site, the "master" fragment that allows modifications is grey colored).

Bart decides to modify his working configuration. From the working site *versailles.cnrs.fr*, he decides to delete the site *chambord.cnrs.fr*, which serves as storage site (see Fig. 7.25). To carry out this operation, the site *chambord.cnrs.fr*: (1) transfers all fragments of *Bart*'s user definition from this site to the others, (2) deletes local *Bart*'s Web entity base, and finally (3) diffuses the new *Bart*'s user definition in which the record *chambord.cnrs.fr* has been deleted. The modified *Bart*'s user definition is then diffused to all other *Bart*'s storage sites, which integrate the modification by deleting the record *chambord.cnrs.fr*.

It is important to note that the diffusion process of *Bart*'s user definition is not only limited to his storage sites, but it also has to be diffused to all storage sites of *Bart*'s collaborators. Our example is a special case because *Bart* and *Homer* share the same storage site *linderhof.gmd.de*.

In conclusion, applying a similar fragmentation technique as the one used for documents, we can logically fragment a user definition into pieces, which will be replicated (master and slave copies) on all storage sites. As we will see in next subsection, the possibility of dynamically modifying the multi-site user definition is central and constitutes the required and suited base to support both temporarily disconnected and nomadic cooperative work on the Web.

7.3.5.3 Temporarily Disconnected and Nomadic Cooperative Work

A user working on a shared entity (e.g., a shared white-board, a document) is able to locate and contact other users on any site where they might be working on. A shared entity managed by the PIÑAS infrastructure refers to the list of users that are potential users. In this way, a shared entity can be considered as a meeting point to establish contact with other users and exchange their respective user definitions. This meeting principle provided by PIÑAS limits the scope of the information that a given user needs to handle.

Each time a new user is invited to join a cooperative work project, his attributes are explicitly added to the shared entity user list by a trusted user of the cooperative group (e.g., the leader). The attributes are then automatically sent / distributed to all other collaborators via the entity itself. The user list must be considered as metadata information associated to the entity.

As previously briefly introduced, the replication and the distributed periodic updating of shared structured user definitions (see Fig. 7.25) and other kinds of entities constitute the keystone to develop principles and mechanisms to support temporarily disconnected and/or nomadic cooperative work on the Web.

To explain these essential principles and mechanisms, let us consider the practical example that we are developing throughout this chapter.

Homer and *Bart* are cooperating on the production of a shared entity (e.g., a Web document) that is replicated on three storage sites: *linderhof.gmd.de* of GMD, *blois.cnrs.fr* of CNRS, and *uxmal.unam.mx* of UNAM (see Fig. 7.26). The different "master" fragments of this shared entity are distributed as follows: the site *linderhof.gmd.de* owns the master fragment #2 that allows *Homer* to edit it from his working site *heildelberg.gmd.de*, while the site *blois.cnrs.fr* (resp. site *uxmal.unam.mx*) owns the master fragments #1 and #3 (resp. master fragment #4). *Bart* is working on his laptop called *versailles.cnrs.fr* from which he can edit the fragments #1 and #3 downloading/uploading them from/to the storage site *blois.cnrs.fr*.

From this state, *Bart* plans to make a trip from France to México, passing from the CNRS institution to the UNAM university. *Bart*'s trip will take a quite long time and so, he would like to continue producing during his travel. Of course, during his flights, it could not be possible for him to communicate because he will be disconnected of any network, but he wants to continue producing on some part(s) of the shared document.

Bart's disconnected and nomadic cooperative authoring work process can be organized according to the following steps (see Fig. 7.26):

1. *Bart* has to prepare his laptop to support temporarily disconnected and nomadic work. First of all, he must modify his user definition declaring his laptop as new working-storage site. We can note that the site *versailles.cnrs.fr* previously was only a working site. Thus, using a dedicated PIÑAS function, he edits his user definition adding the following a new storage site record:

```
StorageUrl http://versailles.cnrs.fr:2000
WorkingUrl http://versailles.cnrs.fr:2000
LoginName theBart
```

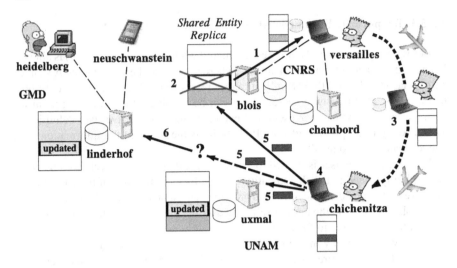

Fig. 7.26 Well organized disconnected and nomadic work

After validation, as all shared replicated entity, the new version of his user definition is diffused to: (a) all *Bart*'s storage sites, and (b) all his collaborators' storage sites. On each of these sites, the new storage site record (user definition fragment) is integrated into the local version of *Bart*'s user definition entity. For mutual inter-storage sites updating purpose, all his collaborators' sites know the new *Bart*'s storage site from/to which their associated storage sites can automatically download/upload versions of shared entity replicas.

At the same time, the new storage site Web entity base is installed on *Bart*'s laptop, and the target shared document is replicated on the new storage site *versailles.cnrs.fr*.

2. From this point, starting a working session on his laptop, *Bart* is able to gain access on the local replica of the shared entity. However, the shared entity fragments are only "slave" ones that do not allow authoring actions.

   Bart uses a special PIÑAS function to migrate the requested fragment #3 from the site *blois.cnrs.fr* to his laptop *versailles.cnrs.fr*. This function is performed in a transactional way that ensures the correctness of the "slave–master" fragment exchange between the storage sites.

3. *Bart* disconnects his laptop from the CNRS LAN and begins his trip. During his flight, he is able to consult all document fragments and more interesting, he can edit the fragment #3 that he locally owns in "master" mode.

4. Arriving at destination, he would like to restart his collaborative work with his collaborators, and in a first step he wants to exchange their respective productions with them.

   This operation is quite simple and only requires to declare his laptop as the site *chichenitza.unam.mx*. However, he also has to extend again his user definition declaring the *chichenitza.unam.mx* as a new storage site. This operation is performed in a same way as the declaration of *versailles.cnrs.fr* as a new storage site (see previous step 1). For efficiency reasons, it can be better to perform these storage site record creations at the same time.

Once the new storage site *chichenitza.unam.mx* is created, *Bart* can integrate his laptop to the UNAM LAN. Connectivity between *Bart* and *Homer* (and may be other) is re-established.

5. In an autonomous and unattended way, *Bart*'s *chichenitza.unam.mx* laptop starts diffusing the fragment #3 value to all storage sites (*blois.cnrs.fr*, *chambord.cnrs.fr*, *uxmal.unam.mx*, and *linderhof.gmd.de*) involved in the distributed cooperative authoring process. Fragment #3 contains the information that *Bart* has produced during his flight.

However, the site *linderhof.gmd.de* is temporarily unreachable and so the updating transmission of fragment #3 is differed.

6. At that moment, *Bart*'s laptop currently named *chichenitza.unam.mx* can re-contact the *Homer*'s storage site, and finally the shared entity replica of *linderhof.gmd.de* is successfully updated.

In this section, we presented the principles by which user definitions can be concurrently and independently modified in order to make inter-user cooperative working sessions that are easy to establish and to manage. The possibility of performing distributed modifications of collaborators' multi-site user definitions constitutes the keystone to define and administrate temporarily disconnected and/or nomadic cooperative work making the distributed cooperative process failure tolerant.

7.4 Conclusions

We presented the advanced solutions provided by the PIÑAS Web infrastructure to support distributed cooperative work on the World Wide Web. The proposed principles and mechanisms directly take benefits from the experience in designing and developing the AllianceWeb authoring application that allows users to directly author HTML/XML documents within the Web environment. This research work highlighted the importance and the suitability of structuring the shared replicated information in order to enhance the global efficiency and reliability of the distributed groupware system. In parallel with this experience, we started fundamental studies of the distributed architectures able to support distributed cooperative work.

Thus, the PIÑAS infrastructure proposes a new innovative and really realistic approach to support Web cooperative work. This approach is based on the combination of the hybrid architecture with the fully replicated architecture: it merges the flexibility of the hybrid approach, that can be successfully applied in a quite reliable environment (e.g., LAN network connections), with the reliability offered by the fully replicated architecture that have to be applied for wide area network connections such as provided by Internet.

This distributed infrastructure proposes new Web features that among others allow to uniquely identify users over the Internet network. Each user can define himself under the form of a multi-site user definition that permits him to start collaboration from several working points downloadind/uploading shared entities from/to reliable closest storage sites on which shared entities are replicated.

Moreover, it is important to note that both the shared entity replication principle and the multi-site user definitions constitute the essential base to support and offer disconnected and nomadic cooperative work features. In this way, users can easily: start a cooperative working session from a site, and then stop and continue it from another possibly remote site. The user environment that is composed of shared and private entities is automatically replicated and regularly updated on all collaborators' storage sites. From this point of view, PIÑAS offers a powerful and innovative framework to efficiently design and develop Web distributed cooperative applications. Dedicated "seamless" features to support Web mobile distributed cooperative work are being designed to be seamlessly integrated within the current PIÑAS infrastructure.

References

1. Berlage, T., Spenke, M.: The GINA interaction recorder. In: Larson, J.A., Unger, C. (eds.) Proc. of the IFIP TC2/WG2.7 Working Conference on Engineering for Human Computer Interaction, Ellivuori, Finland, 10–14 August 1992, pp. 69–80. North-Holland, Amsterdam (1992)
2. Berner-Lee, T., Hendler, J., Lassila, O.: The semantic web. Scientific American 284(5), 34–43 (2001)
3. Bourimi, M., Lukosch, S., Kühnel, F.: Leveraging visual tailoring and synchronous awareness in web-based collaborative systems. In: Proc. of CRIWG'2007, the 13th International Workshop on Groupware: Design, Implementation, and Use, Bariloche, Argentina, 16–20 September 2007. Lecture Notes in Computer Science, vol. 4715, pp. 40–55. Springer, Berlin (2007)
4. Calvary, G., Coutaz, J., Nigay, L.: From single user architectural design to PAC*: A generic software architecture model for CSCW. In: Proc. of CHI'97, the Conference on Human Factors in Computer Systems, Atlanta, GE, USA, 1997, pp. 242–249. ACM/Addison-Wesley, New York (1997)
5. Coulouris, G., Dollimore, J., Kindberg, T.: Distributed Systems: Concepts and Design, 4th edn. Addison-Wesley, Reading (2005)
6. Coutaz, J.: A metamodel for the runtime architecture of an interactive system. SIGCHI Bulletin 24(1), 32–37 (1992)
7. Day, M.: What synchronous groupware needs: Notification services. In: Proc. of HotOS-VI, the 6th IEEE Workshop on Hot Topics in Operating Systems, Cape Cod MA, USA, 5–6 May 1997, pp. 118–122. IEEE Comput. Soc., Los Alamitos (1997)
8. Decouchant, D., Quint, V., Romero Salcedo, M.: Chapter 13: Structured and distributed cooperative editing in a large scale network. In: Rada, R. (ed.) Groupware and Authoring, pp. 265–295. Academic Press, London (1996)
9. Decouchant, D., Martínez, A.M., Martínez, E.: AllianceWeb: Cooperative authoring on the WWW. In: Proc. CRIWG'99, Fifth International Workshop on Groupware, Cancun, México, 15–18 September 1999. IEEE Comput. Soc., Los Alamitos (1999)
10. Dewan, P.: Multiuser architectures. In: Bass, L.J., Unger, C. (eds.) Proc. of IFIP TC2/WG2.7, the Working Conference on Engineering for Human–Computer Communication, Yellowstone Park, USA, August 1996, pp. 247–270. Chapman & Hall, New York (1996)
11. Dewan, P.: Architectures for collaborative applications. In: Beaudouin-Lafon, M. (ed.) Computer Supported Cooperative Work. Trends in Software, vol. 7, pp. 169–193. Wiley, New York (1999)

12. Dewan, P., Choudhary, R.: A high-level flexible framework for implementing multi-user user-interfaces. ACM Transactions on Information Systems **10**(4), 345–380 (1992)
13. Dieng-Kuntz, R., Minier, D., Ruzicka, M., Corby, F., Corby, O., Alamarguy, L.: Building and using a medical ontology for knowledge management and cooperative work in a health care network. Computers in Biology and Medicine **36**(7–8), 871–892 (2006)
14. Ellis, C.S., Gibbs, S.J., Rein, G.L.: Groupware: Some issues and experiences. Communications of the ACM **34**(1), 38–58 (1991)
15. Feigenbaum, L., Herman, I., Hongsermeier, T., Neumann, E., Stephens, S.: The semantic web in action. Scientific American **297**(6), 90–97 (2007)
16. Freed, N., Borenstein, N.: Multipurpose Internet Mail Extensions (MIME) Part Two: Media Types, RFC 2046, IETF Standard (1996)
17. Graham, T.C.N., Urnes, T.: Relational views as a model for automatique distributed implementation of multi-user applications. In: Proc. of CSCW'92, the ACM Conference on Computer-Supported Cooperative Work, Toronto, Canada, 31 October–4 November 1992, pp. 59–66. ACM, New York (1992)
18. Graham, T.C.N., Urnes, T., Nejabi, R.: Efficient distributed implementation of semi-replicated synchronous groupware. In: Proc. of UIST'96, the ACM Symposium on User Interface Software and Technology, Seattle WA, USA, November 1996, pp. 1–10. ACM, New York (1996)
19. Guetari, R., Quint, V., Vatton, I.: Amaya: An authoring tool for the web. In: Proc. of MCSEAI'98, the Maghrebian Conference on Software Engineering and Artificial Intelligence, Tunis, Tunisia, 8–10 December 1998
20. Gutwin, C., Greenberg, S.: A descriptive framework of workspace awareness for real-time groupware. Computer-Supported Cooperative Work **11**(3–4), 411–446 (2002)
21. Hill, R.D.: The abstract-link-view paradigm: Using constraints to connect user interfaces to applications. In: Proc. of SIGCHI'92, the ACM Conference on Human Factors in Computing Systems, Monterey, CA, USA, 3–7 May 1992, pp. 335–342. ACM, New York (1992)
22. Hill, R.D., Brinck, T., Rohall, S.L., Patterson, J.F., Wilner, W.: The rendezvous architecture and language for constructing multi-user applications. ACM Transactions on Computer–Human Interaction **1**(2), 81–125 (1994)
23. Karsenty, A., Tronche, C., Beaudouin-Lafon, M.: GroupDesign: Shared editing in a heterogeneous environment. Computing Systems **6**(2), 167–195 (1993)
24. Kindberg, T., Coulouris, G., Dollimore, J., Heikkinen, J.: Sharing objects over the Internet: The Mushroom approach. In: Proc. of IEEE Global Internet'96 Mini-conference at GLOBECOM'96, London, 20–21 November 1996, pp. 67–71. IEEE Comput. Soc., Los Alamitos (1996)
25. Kobayashi, M., Shinozadi, M., Sakairi, T.: Collaborative customer services using synchronous web browser sharing. In: Proc. CSCW'98, ACM Conference on Computer Supported Cooperative Work, Seattle, Washington, 14–18 November 1998, pp. 99–108 (1998)
26. Krasner, G.E., Pope, S.T.: A cookbook for using the model-view-controller user interface paradigm in Smalltalk-80. Journal of Object-Oriented Programming **1**(3), 26–49 (1988)
27. Lee, S.H., Kim, S.J., Hong, S.H.: On URL normalization. In: Gervasi, O., et al. (eds.) Proc. of ICCSA'2005, the International Conference on Computational Science and Its Applications Conference, Singapore, 9–12 May 2005. Lecture Notes in Computer Science, vol. 3481, pp. 1076–1085. Springer, Berlin (2005)
28. Lukosch, S.: Transparent and flexible data sharing for synchronous groupware. PhD thesis, FernUniversität, Germany (2003)
29. Lukosch, S.: Transparent latecomer support for synchronous groupware. In: Favela, J., Decouchant, D. (eds.) Proc. of CRIWG'03, the 9th International Workshop on Groupware, Autrans, France, September 2003. Lecture Notes in Computer Science, vol. 2806, pp. 26–41. Springer, Berlin (2003)
30. Lukosch, S.: Flexible and transparent data sharing for synchronous groupware. International Journal of Computer Applications in Technology **19**(3–4), 215–230 (2004)
31. Mainz, D., Paulsen, I., Mainz, I., Weller, K., Kohl, J., Von Haeseler, A.: Knowledge acquisition focused cooperative development of bio-ontologies—a case study with BIO2Me. In:

Bioinformatics Research and Development, Proc. of the 2nd International Conference BIRD 2008, Vienna, Austria, 7–9 July 2008. Communications in Computer and Information Science, vol. 13, pp. 258–272. Springer, Berlin (2008)

32. McEwan, G., Greenberg, S.: Supporting social worlds with the community bar. In: Proc. of GROUP'2005, the International ACM SIGGROUP Conference on Supporting Group Work, Sanibel Island, FL, USA, 6–9 November 2005, pp. 21–30. ACM, New York (2005)

33. Morán, A.L., Decouchant, D., Favela, J., Martínez Enríquez, A.M., González Beltrán, B., Mendoza, S.: PIÑAS: Supporting a community of co-authors on the web. In: Proc. of DCW'02, the 4th International Conference on Distributed Communities on the Web, Sydney, Australia, 3–5 April 2002. Lecture Notes in Computer Science, vol. 2468, pp. 114–125. Springer, Berlin (2002)

34. Patterson, J.F.: A taxonomy of architectures for synchronous groupware applications. SIGOIS Bulletin 15(3), 27–29 (1995)

35. Phillips, W.G.: Architectures for synchronous groupware. No. 1999-425, Department of Computing and Information Science, Queen's University, Kingston, Ontario, Canada (1999)

36. Romero Salcedo, M., Decouchant, D.: Structured cooperative authoring for the world wide web. Computer-Supported Cooperative Work 6(2/3), 157–174 (1997)

37. Roseman, M., Greenberg, S.: Building real-time groupware with GroupKit, a groupware toolkit. ACM Transactions on Computer–Human Interaction 3(1), 66–106 (1996)

38. Roth, J.: The resource framework for mobile applications: Enabling collaboration between mobile users. In: Proc. of ICEIS, the 5th International Conference on Enterprise Information Systems, Angers, France, 22–26 April 2003, pp. 87–94 (2003)

39. Roth, J., Unger, C.: An extensible classification model for distribution architectures of synchronous groupware. In: Proc. of COOP'2000, the 4th International Conference on the Design of Cooperative Systems, Sophia Antipolis, France, 23–26 May 2000, pp. 113–127. IOS Press, Amsterdam (2000)

40. Salber, D., Coutaz, J., Decouchant, D., Riveill, M.: De l'observabilité et de l'honnêteté dans la communication homme-homme médiatisée". In: Proc. of IHM'95, Septièmes Journées sur l'Ingénierie de l'Interaction Homme-Machine, Cépaduès, Toulouse, France, 11–13 October 1995, pp. 27–33 (1995) (in French)

41. Schuckmann, C., Kirchner, L., Schummer, J., Haake, J.M.: Designing object-oriented synchronous groupware with COAST. In: Proc. of CSCW'96, the ACM Conference on Computer-Supported Cooperative Work, Boston, MA, USA, 16–20 November 1996, pp. 30–38. ACM, New York (1996)

42. Shadbolt, N., Hall, W., Berners-Lee, T.: The semantic web revisited. IEEE Intelligent Systems Journal 21(3), 96–101 (2006)

43. Stefik, M., Bobrow, D.G., Foster, G., Lanning, S., Tatar, D.: WYSIWIS revised: Early experiences with multi-user interfaces. ACM Transactions on Office Information Systems 5(2), 147–167 (1987)

44. Stødle, D., Bjørndalen, J.M., Anshus, O.J.: Support for collaboration, visualization and monitoring of parallel applications using shared windows. In: Proc. of PARA'06, the Workshop on State-of-the-art in Scientific and Parallel Computing, Umeå, Sweden, 18–21 June 2006. Lecture Notes in Computer Science, vol. 4699, pp. 228–238. Springer, Berlin (2006)

45. Streitz, N.A., Geißler, J., Haake, J.M., Hol, J.: DOLPHIN: Integrated meeting support across liveboards, local and remote desktop environments. In: Proc. of CSCW'94, the ACM Conference on Computer-Supported Cooperative Work, Chapel Hill, NC, USA, 22–26 October 1994, pp. 345–358. ACM/Addison-Wesley, New York (1994)

46. Whitehead, E.J. Jr., Goland, Y.Y.: WebDAV: A network protocol for remote collaborative authoring on the Web. In: Proc. of ECSCW'99, the 6th European Conference on Computer-Supported Cooperative Work, Copenhague, Denmark, 12–16 September 1999, pp. 291–310. Kluwer, Dordrecht (1999)

47. Whitehead, E.J. Jr., Wiggins, M.: WEBDAV: IETF standard for collaborative authoring on the web. IEEE Internet Computing 2(5), 34–40 (1998)

Chapter 8
Web Services and Software Agents for Tailorable Groupware Design

Nader Cheaib, Samir Otmane, and Malik Mallem

Abstract We present a new groupware architecture model called $U D^3$ that explicitly introduces the notion of tailorability in designing collaborative applications. This model is based on the integration of web services and software agents technologies, thus using protocols of each while reinforcing their individual strengths in the context of tailorable groupware design. In our work, web services are dynamically invoked by software agents in order to bring new behaviors, and hence, enhancing the collaboration process by dynamically adapting the services offered in the system to the users' preferences and not the other way around. Web services and agents were originally developed with different standards, thus their integration becomes important in the context of groupware tailorability, giving a totally innovative approach in the area of CSCW (Computer Supported Cooperative Work). We apply our model on the DIGITAL OCEAN project for the creation and distribution of multimedia files on the Internet.

8.1 Introduction

As the use of the Internet and the services offered with it are emerging more and more, people are in an increasing need of flexible and agile applications. The emergence of collaborative work over the Internet was a solution to the high complexity of systems and the technical difficulties that could arise from their use, as users, geographically distributed want more and more to work together on a single task, but using rigid and often incompatible applications that may lead to interoperability problems. The aim of CSCW (Computer Supported Cooperative Work) is to find ways for groupware to enhance collaboration between individuals. For [36], groupware invention is a challenge, as the nature of collaborative work continually changes as a consequence of changing work needs, but also as a consequence of how the systems themselves tend to change work relationships and processes. As a

N. Cheaib (✉)
IBISC CNRS FRE 3190, University of Evry, 91020 Evry Cedex, France
e-mail: nader.cheaib@ibisc.fr

Y. Badr et al. (eds.) *Emergent Web Intelligence: Advanced Semantic Technologies,*
Advanced Information and Knowledge Processing,
DOI 10.1007/978-1-84996-077-9_8, © Springer-Verlag London Limited 2010

consequence, the author argues that systems must themselves adapt to reflect the unpredictable differences between the requirements of support for collaborative work on the Internet during analysis and the actual requirements.

Hence, research about tailorability for groupware originated from the gap between the design and use of collaborative systems. Making the system and the services offered within, tailorable by users is an essential and ongoing research field that needs much attention to yet be concrete. For this reason, tailorability has shown to be an essential property that should be taken in consideration, as it offers to users the possibility to adapt the application based on their needs and not the other way around. In this work, we present a new groupware architectural model called UD^3 (Universal Directory for Description and Discovery), which is based on the integration of web services technologies with software agents. The aim is to design a tailorable groupware architecture using the integration of both technologies, thus using properties of each while reinforcing their individual strengths. In fact, agent-oriented technology is claimed to become the next breakthrough in the development and implementation of large-scale complex systems, while web services are fast emerging technologies for connecting remotely executing programs via well established Internet protocols. Web services and agents were originally developed with different standards, thus their integration becomes important in the context of groupware tailorability, giving a totally innovative approach for designing collaborative applications on the Internet.

In fact, with the emergence and advancement of Internet technologies and the Web 2.0 [11], universal interoperability between collaborative applications is becoming a reality, while geographically distributed people are highlighting the flexibility of cooperation by exchanging universally accessible services on the web. However, these types of systems do not take in consideration the evolving and excessive need of users' to dynamically integrate new components in order to enhance collaboration with others. On one hand, web services have become one of the most important architectures for the cooperation of heterogeneous systems and have ushered in a new era of software design that focuses on implicit and explicit collaboration between organizations [11]. While computer networks have been able to pass data between different hosts, it was the emergence of web services that allowed these remote hosts to offer services in a more flexible and dynamic way. However, with this flexibility comes systems complexity. On the other hand, the autonomy and intelligence of agents have considerably increased software automation of some operational areas. An important benefit in the use of software agents in designing software and groupware applications is their ability to help, through collaboration, human beings and softwares' execution, while their concept is even older than web services and has been used successfully for the implementation of distributed applications. We present an innovative approach for a tailorable groupware architecture integrating web services with software agents. The idea is to exploit agents' proactive interaction capabilities in order to improve the behavior of web services in a service-oriented architecture, hence creating a cohesive entity that attempts to surpass the weaknesses of each technology, while reinforcing their individual advantages in the context of tailorable groupware design.

We will proceed as follows: In Sect. 8.2, we give a motivating scenario explaining the problem, and we explain the concept of tailorability with the need of a new architecture supporting it. In Sect. 8.3, we talk about few approaches in the literature that attempt to introduce tailorability in their design of groupware applications. In Sect. 8.4, we give a background on web services and software agents', along with the JADE platform [36] for deploying software agents. Section 8.5 presents our own approach for a tailorable architecture; we call it the UD^3 model. Section 8.6 describes system's implementation on an ongoing project for the exchange of multimedia information over the Internet, Oce@nyd. The last section presents a conclusion and future work in the field.

8.2 Motivating Scenario

Let us consider a scenario where users geographically distributed are using a collaborative application over the Internet, thus using Internet protocols and standards in order to collaborate and exchange messages between each other. In order to achieve tailorability, we should think of a way in order to make users able to search, invoke and use new components that could be directly integrated in their system to satisfy their needs according to the task being done. If we imagine the components of the system built using web services standards, then we should enable users to invoke new web services and dynamically integrate them into their applications. As a concrete example, if users in collaboration need a video stream mechanism, we imagine a web service deployed somewhere in public registries on the Internet and containing this mechanism as a part of the services it offers, and thus the system should be designed in a way to seamlessly search, invoke and integrate this web service into the application. By tailoring here we mean dynamically adding/modifying web services during runtime of the application without interrupting its execution, and thus of users' collaboration with others. However, for [25], current techniques for publishing and finding web services rely on static descriptions of service interfaces, forcing consumers to find and bind services at design time. This motivated us to make the process dynamic in the essential purpose of enhancing collaborative applications, in particular making them tailorable by users. In our research, we found that software agents are a promising technology that could solve such problems. Unfortunately web services and agents were originally developed separately with different standards and features, therefore their integration becomes important in this context. With this paradigm, groupware components, each representing a web service and an agent in collaboration, will interact to provide unified services according to users' preferences, and thus achieve groupware tailorability.

8.2.1 Tailorability and the Need of a New Architecture

Some definitions exist in the literature for the concept of tailorability, but it is still ambiguous in putting it forward in CSCW systems, where the technologies for implementing such concept are still not explicitly identified. We retained few definitions that seemed most interesting to our work, as in [35] that defines a tailorable application as a system that can be adapted properly according to changes and the diversity of users' needs, or [32] that defines tailorability as the capacity of an information system to allow a person to adjust the application based on personal preferences or different tasks. For [10] tailoring is the continued development of an application by making persistent modifications to it. It is in fact initiated in response to an application being inefficient to use. However it remains to determine the mechanisms of evolution of tailorability. Morch [22] defines the concept in terms of customization, integration and extension. Tailorability by customization is limited by a set of predetermined number of components, tailorability by integration is to insert a new component in the architecture of the application, and tailorability by extension or radical tailoring is offering means to change or extend the components' implementation in order to derive the same flexibility as an "initial" application design. These mechanisms offer more flexibility but require more and more from the user computer skills, which partly explains why most of the current CSCW systems generally steer their tailorability to developers and expert users rather than end users that, paradoxically and from social sciences and humanities research, are those who need it the most. In our work we focus on the third type of tailorability, hence extending program code by new components depending on users' preferences. We assume that a component is a web service and an agent collaborating together in order to offer unified and dynamic services to users.

In groupware, a mismatch between the task done by users and the corresponding technology they are using could affect the co-operating people [33], thus tailoring by end-users themselves is generally regarded as a suitable means to solve this problem. Due to a lack of a theoretical framework for tailorability and the corresponding evaluation methods, results of different studies for groupware tailorability are hard to compare. Our research is mainly concentrating upon:

- Development of a collaborative architecture supporting tailorability.
- Integration of Internet technologies that has not been exploited before in the context of groupware tailorability.

In the next section, we talk about few approaches in the literature that aim to introduce tailorability in the design of groupware.

8.3 Tailorability Approaches

Various approaches aiming to integrate tailorability in CSCW systems have received much attention in the literature [3, 32, 35]. However, most of these approaches apply only to certain specific domains, as support for synchronous groupware, workflow-based or collaborative writing, and it is not certain whether these approaches could be applied to generic domains as well. In our research, we found that introducing tailorability in the design of groupware is still very limited and theoretical, as there exist various approaches without a sufficient support for comparison and classification. For this reason, we thought that providing a global view on some of these approaches is already a contribution for building a concise study of the problem, and finding suitable technologies to implement a solution. In the rest of this work, we will begin by building a global view on some approaches for tailorability in CSCW systems. We will mention respectively the activity theory [2], component-based [30] and building blocks [32] approaches, and finally we will see how we can use the Service-Oriented Architecture (SOA) for building collaborative applications [7].

8.3.1 Activity Theory

The author in [3] justifies that tailorability possesses a theoretical foundation enabling to apprehend it using fundamental properties of human activity. They propose a set of properties for constructing a conceptual model for a generic environment of CSCW systems, based on a fundamental theory, reflectivity. This environment is called DARE (Distributed Activities in a Reflexive Environment) [2]. In the realization of DARE, they propose a framework based on the concepts and mechanisms of the activity theory, which permits to distinguish two essential properties of the human activity:

- Reflexivity, that enables to access and modify the structure of the application during its execution.
- Crystallization or the reutilization of user's experiences. These experiences could be, for example, a specification of roles in a particular activity.

Based on the activity theory, all mediator elements influence the course of activity and thus it is impossible to predict its impact on a certain activity [3]. This is why, for the authors, the tool should be considered a fully mediator element, meaning that if it could influence the collaborative activity, then it should be modified by it. The authors were inspired by the Meta-Object Protocol (MOP) [2] for realizing DARE, as the reflexivity takes place with the introduction of a meta model whose main entity is the 'task,' that is a specification of the activity that describes the objectives, resources and roles that should take place in collaboration between actors.

8.3.2 Component-Based Architecture

A lot of research has been made for the design of component-based architecture for groupware [30, 32, 35]. The concept of a component-based architecture is independent of any application domain, and thus it is highly probable to adopt this kind of architecture to integrate tailorability in the design of groupware [30]. In a component-based approach, a groupware is designed as a collection of components in which they could be added, modified, or deleted. This type of applications will be able to support the evolution that tailorability tries to introduce. The authors in [30] argue that an ideal collaborative system should be designed as a composable system where the integration of new components is build on top of a neutral basis. We will see here two component-based approaches, each using different ways and mechanisms to reach tailorability: A reflexive computational system [35] and building blocks architecture [32].

8.3.2.1 Reflective Computational System

The authors in [35] define a tailorable system as one that can be adapted for eventual modifications in its structure according to diversity of user's needs. The authors use the term adaptability to identify tailorability in its technical aspects. Here, the authors reused the notion of reflexivity in the activity theory seen in the first approach [3], by insisting that an adaptable application should include a representation of aspects of itself, and this self representation should be changeable by internal or external influences, and connected to certain aspects of the application. If the representation changes, the application changes as well, and only aspects included in the self representation of the application are susceptible to be affected by tailorability activities. As a simple example, consider an application with an initialization file that specifies the application's background color [35]. In this case, this initialization file is the self representation of the application, and the color is the adaptable aspect. This type of applications is seen as a "Reflective computational system." Note that a reflexive system is one that contains both representations of aspects of the real world, and representations of its own activities. In consequence, this type of application is capable of examining its own state and structure, and able to modify it according to user's and the context's needs, which implies that every modification of the (meta) representation is automatically shifted towards the behavior of the system.

8.3.2.2 Building Block Architecture

The authors in [32] propose an approach based on building blocks for constructing tailorable CSCW systems. They argue that the evolution in the utilization of groupware is nowadays one of the main reasons for designing tailorable systems. In fact, the authors consider a tailorable system as one that permits for its users to perform modifications on the technical structure of the application, after its implementation according to their needs, personal preferences or different tasks. For the simple reason that all the modifications could not be predicted in the design phase by the application designers, it would be possible, according to the authors, to equip the users with means to accommodate these changes.

The authors introduce the concept of tailoring to the extreme [32]. This concept implies the extension of the set of functions in the system with new modules that could be integrated dynamically. An example of this concept is to permit the user to download modules from the Internet and plug them directly into the system (plug-ins, widgets, etc.). However, this approach requires that functional modules (building blocks) should be analyzed before integrating them in order to determine the functions that they could offer and the way in which they will communicate and interconnect to other modules for minimizing interference in the system. The authors here insist that interoperability standards are therefore essential between the building blocks that will be integrated into the system, probably resulting from different vendors, in order to standardize and facilitate the process of integration with other building blocks already existing, and therefore, insure the stability of the system as a whole. The authors implemented their concepts in the CooPS (Cooperative People and Systems) [32] project that describes the types of building blocks that form groupware applications and the relations between them.

8.3.3 Service-Oriented Architecture (SOA)

The demand for collaborative and flexible services is becoming more urgent as the competition in the marketplace is getting fiercer between service providers. For this reason, the authors in [7] propose the utilization of a Service-Oriented Architecture (SOA) for the construction of collaborative services. For the authors, SOA is becoming a new paradigm that aim at implementing loosely-connected applications which are extensible, flexible and integrate well with existing systems. Collaborative platforms have the potential of offering services on different layers of abstraction as their role is to offer a support tool for collaboration of activities [14].

SOA [7, 14] is a paradigm in full expansion that could be adapted to offer extensible services integrated in a platform for different users to collaborate between each other. Web services could facilitate the collaboration between groups or organizations, and can be defined by, for example, resource sharing, communication and interaction between collaborators (synchronous, asynchronous, communication channels, etc.), virtual rooms, organization management (calendar, mail, etc.). The support for web services offers interoperability between different collaborative or single-user systems [14], as they can be viewed as modular applications. The architecture considers a model of integrated services, where the interfaces of web services are described with a standardized language definition WSDL (Web Service Definition Language), and interact with each other using SOAP (Simple Object Access Protocol), while having their definitions saved in some norms of a web service catalogue using UDDI (Universal Description, Discovery and Integration).

In what follows, we give a brief a background on the CSCW domain, with a description of web services and software agents. We justify our choice for using the JADE platform in implementing software agents as a part of system's core. Our idea is to show that the CSCW domain can be leveraged by using web technologies in order to enhance collaboration between users.

8.4 Background

8.4.1 Ellis's 3C Model

We refer to the 3C model [8] for further understanding of the term collaboration and the functionalities behind it. In fact, according to [8], a groupware system covers three domain specific functions, production/cooperation, communication and coordination as we can see below: The production space designates the objects resulting from the activity of the group (ex: word document, paint, etc.). For Ellis [8], this production space is concerned with the result of common tasks to be achieved and it is the space where the productivity will take place. The coordination space defines the actors and their social structure, as well as different tasks to be accomplished in order to produce objects in the production space. Ellis eventually completed the model with the communication space that offers to actors in the coordination space means to exchange information in which the semantics concern exclusively the actor, and where the system only acts as a messenger.

We will use this decomposition of groupware's functionalities in order to introduce a collaborative architecture supporting the functional decomposition of services that can be present in a groupware system.

8.4.2 Web Services and the World Wide Web

W3C defines a web service as follows: "It is a software system that acts as an interoperable support in the machine–machine interaction. The system has an interface described in a form understood by the machine (specifically WSDL). Other systems interact with the web service depending on its description using SOAP messages that are typically transported through HTTP with an XML serialization in conjunction with other web standards." In fact, service-oriented architecture (SOA) emerged due to its simplicity, clarity and normalized foundations. The concept of web services currently revolves around three acronyms [24], as we can see in Fig. 8.1:

- SOAP (Simple Object Access Protocol) is a protocol for inter-application exchanging that is independent of any platform and based on XML. A SOAP service call is an ASCII flow embedded in XML tags and transported to the HTTP protocol.
- WSDL (Web Services Description Language) gives the XML description of web services by specifying the methods that can be invoked, their signatures and access point (URL, port, etc.). It is therefore equivalent in a way to the IDL language for CORBA distributed programming.
- UDDI (Universal Description, Discovery and Integration) is a standard of a distributed directory of web services, allowing both publishing and exploration. UDDI acts as a web service itself, whose methods are called using the SOAP protocol.

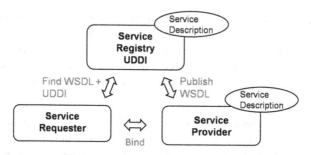

Fig. 8.1 Service-oriented architecture

Our choice of using web services in our system is driven by the fact they are: Language and platform independent (separation of specification from implementation), deployed over the Internet (no centralized control, use of established protocols), loosely coupled (using synchronous and asynchronous interactions) and interoperable (using standards already deployed and functional to support systems interoperability).

8.4.3 Software Agents

There exist several definitions of software agents in the literature. Khezami [15] has identified the agent as a computing object (in the sense of object-oriented languages) whose behavior can be described by a script with its own means of calculation, and can move from a place to another in order to communicate with other agents. The authors explain that some researchers have given the definition of agent through a good description of its functioning, where an agent must necessarily have the necessary motivation to achieve a certain goal for its existence to be worthwhile in its environment. An agent can communicate with other agents in the environment and must have means which enable it to achieve its goals. According to [19], an agent is a piece of software that acts on an autonomous basis to initiate charges on behalf of users. The authors here say that the design of many software agents is based on the approach that users need to only indicate a high level goal instead of issuing explicit instructions, leaving the decisions to the agent. The agent shows a number of features that makes it different from other traditional components, including self-direction, collaboration, continuity, character, communication, adaptation, mobility and temporal continuity.

8.4.4 JADE Platform

Java Agent DEvelopment framework (JADE) [36] is a middleware written in Java and conforms to the specifications of FIPA [9]. This environment simplifies the development of software agents by providing basic services as well as a set of tools for the deployment. The platform contains a runtime environment where the JADE agents may evolve while being active on a given host, a library of classes used to develop agents and a suite of graphical tools that allow the administration and supervision of agents' activities at runtime. In fact, the main container contains two special agents:

- AMS (Agent Management System) which provides a service Namespace (i.e. it ensures that every agent in the platform has a unique name) and represents the authority in the platform (it is possible to create or kill agents in remote containers by calling the AMS).
- DF (Directory Facilitator), on the other hand, is analogous to the UDDI used by web services, and offers the Yellow Pages service through which an agent can find other agents that are providing the services it needs in order to achieve its goal. JADE defines a generic agent model that can perform any type of architecture while fully integrating the FIPA [9] communication model: interaction protocols, wrapping, ACL (Agent Communication Language), languages content and transport protocols. In what follows, we proceed with some related work exposing researchers' motivation in this domain affecting many applications areas.

8.4.5 Related Work—Web Services and Agents' Integration

According to [10], web services have become one of the most important architectures for the cooperation of heterogeneous systems. They present a platform that provides a runtime environment of a lightweight agent that is located within a web container, which adds agents' functionalities to existing web servers. The components of the platform are deployed as web services, where SOAP (Simple Object Access Protocol) over HTTP acting as a communication channel through standard XML messages. In this way, the support for mobile agents can be added to the existing web infrastructure, without the need to replace components or installing client software. In [20], the authors propose a solution for the selection and composition of web services with software agents. The use of the concept allows an agent to support the pro activity and autonomy of the composition process in which clients and suppliers can take an active role through autonomous operation and negotiation. The proposed architecture provides flexibility and scalability in the development of different solutions, while offering a set of integrated tools.

For the authors in [18], it is widely admitted that web service composition is essential rather than accessing only a unique service. Searching for web services, integrating them into a composite service, triggering and monitoring their implementation are among the operations that users will handle, whereas most of these operations are complex and repetitive, with a large portion adapted to the computer tool and automation. Therefore, for the authors, software agents are appropriate candidates to assist users in their operations, and therefore the integration of software agents and web services in the same environment raises the importance of a specific approach. The authors employ a three-tiered approach: intrinsic, functional and behavioral, where each level has multiple properties that vary according to the component whose tier is applied, whether it is the agent or the web service. For the software agents' properties, the intrinsic level properties consist of an identifier, role, and type. For web services, the intrinsic level consists of identifier properties, description, type, input and output arguments, and cost and time of implementation. In [34], the Do-I-Care application has been designed to help users discover interesting changes on the web, using both technical means and social rights. Do-I-Care agents automate periodic visits to selected pages for detecting interesting changes on behalf of users, where they must keep their agents informed of the relevant pages and the quality of reported changes. Once an agent detects an interesting change, the user is notified by e-mail, and the change is attached to the web page associated with the agent. This web page is also used for the relevance of comments and the activity of cooperation.

Clearly, there is still no work in the literature that emphasizes the use of the two technologies in the domain of groupware tailorability. This gives originality to our approach and motivates us to present a model designed to tackle specifically the problem of tailorability along with interoperability problems between heterogeneous applications deployed on the Internet.

8.4.6 *Purpose of Integration*

For [25], current techniques for publishing and finding services (such as WSDL and UDDI) rely on static descriptions of service interfaces, forcing consumers to find and bind services at design time. However, web services are becoming one of the most important architectures used in heterogeneous cooperative information systems, as it was the appearance of web services that permitted Internet sites to offer services in a more flexible manner [10]. However, the concept of software agents is even older than web services, and it has been employed with success for executing distributed applications. Agents are defined briefly as is a piece of software that acts autonomously to undertake tasks on behalf of users. For [18], it is based on the fact that users only need to specify a high-level goal instead of issuing explicit instructions, leaving the how and when decisions to the agent. The same authors say that software agents exhibit a number of features that make them different from other traditional components including autonomy, goal-orientation, collaboration, flexibility, self-starting, temporal continuity, character, communication, adaptation, and mobility.

The reason behind our motivation to integrate software agents with web services is driven by the fact that agents put in practice the concept of mobile code, and through coordination with their flexible architectures, can easily be adapted to highly dynamic and heterogeneous environment as the web. Web services however are the fast emergence of dominant means for connecting distributed applications through well established Internet protocols.

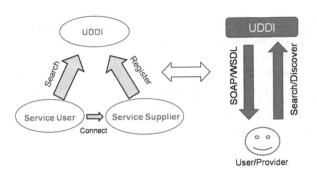

Fig. 8.2 Classical SOA vs. tailorable SOA

Furthermore, software agents can be one of the essential developments to web services for the fact that they are functional entities instead of being just simple interaction delegations or communication means [31]. To sum up, the idea is to explore the capacities of agents' proactive interactions to enhance the behavior of web services in a service-oriented architecture (SOA). With this paradigm, software components, where each one is representing a service and an agent in collaboration, can interact with each other for providing unified services in a specified environment, as for example the exchange of multimedia applications on the Internet (we are currently working on such system, we call it Oce@nyd). This is aligned with the authors in [31]: "agents will become an essential part of most web-based applications, serving as the 'glue' that makes a system as large as the web manageable and viable."

8.4.6.1 Classical SOA vs. Tailorable SOA

In Fig. 8.2, we can see the transformation of the classical SOA found in the literature to our vision of a tailorable SOA. In the classical SOA, there exist two actors: the service provider that registers the definitions of web services (WSDL) in the public registry (UDDI). The user in this kind of architecture has only the possibility to send SOAP requests to interrogate the UDDI about a needed service, but does not have the possibility to modify the UDDI by adding new services that could satisfy more his or her needs. This limits the use and the flexibility of the approach, as users would only be limited to use the services already existing in the system, and thus wouldn't be able to adapt the application to their needs, but rather the other way around.

In the tailorable SOA, the idea is to modify the structure of the classical SOA in a way that the service user is the service provider himself, as we can see in Fig. 8.2. In other words, the user will then have the privilege to interrogate the UDDI (self representation of the application, as seen in the reflexive computational system in Sect. 8.3.2) using standard SOAP requests, but also modify it using the same type of messages formats by adding the new web services definitions into the UDDI with mechanisms that will assure this type of modification. The protocols provided

(SOAP) in the SOA will be in charge of reconfiguring the links between the services added and the services already present in the system. In fact, the self representation part could be seen as an open implementation mechanism [16] where the users would be able to modify the structure of the application (inserting new service definitions through their WSDL files) without recompiling the system and stopping its execution. Also, this kind of system will satisfy the evolution of the system's use due to temporal or behavioral changes. In this case, the classical Service-Oriented Architecture will be transformed into a tailorable Service-Oriented Architecture by giving the user tools to accommodate these changes. In fact, the dynamic integration of new web services will be the task of software agents, where comes the main purpose of integrating software agents with web services in our system, and that is to insure service tailorability in a collaborative environment, as we will see in the next section.

8.5 The UD^3 Theoretical Model

As mentioned earlier, the aim behind our model is to integrate software agents and web services into a cohesive entity that attempts to surpass the weakness of each technology, while reinforcing their individual advantages [31]. W3C clearly expresses the notion that, "software agents are the running programs that drive web services—both to implement them and to access them as computational resources that act on behalf of a person or organization." In fact, the concept of software agents is older than web services and it has been employed with success for executing distributed applications, while their main aim is based on the fact that users only need to specify a high-level goal instead of issuing explicit instructions, leaving the how and when decisions to the agent to discover web services deployed on the Internet and integrate them in the system. This reinforces the reason behind our motivation to integrate software agents with web services, and is driven by the fact that agents put in practice the concept of mobile code, and through coordination with their flexible architectures, can easily be adapted to the highly dynamic and heterogeneous environment as the web.

We extend the work in [4] for the use of SOA in the design of a tailorable groupware, as it offers the needed interoperability and reconfigurability between system components, and the importance of using software agents in order to enhance the discovery of web services by making them proactive and dynamic. Moreover, we rely on the Arch model [1] by offering a canonical decomposition of the main structure of the system into five main components (Functional core, Functional core adapter, Physical Interaction, Logical Interaction and Dialog Controller components), each having a specific functionality in the system. However in our work we will concentrate on the design of the functional core which is the main component of the system, along with the system interfaces, and we will make no assumption about the other components. We rely also on Dewan's model [5] that structures a groupware system into a variable number of layers, each representing

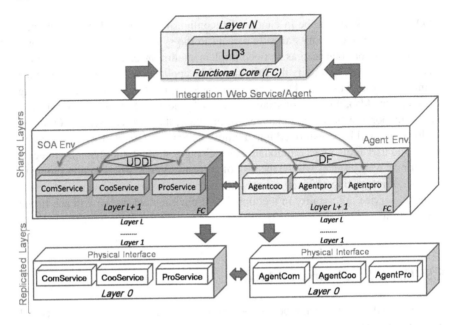

Fig. 8.3 The UD^3 model

specific levels of abstraction, where the highest layer is the semantic layer that corresponds to the functional core of the system (coincides with the one of the Arch model), and the lowest layer representing the material or the hardware level (Arch's Physical Interaction component), and eventually we compare our model with the clover model [17] that is itself built using the later models. Note that Fig. 8.3 representing our proposed architecture shows only the functional core of the system, along with the physical interaction layer that implements the interactions with the user. In the next section, we implement the physical component as a web interface serving as a case study of our model.

8.5.1 Description of the Functional Core (FC)

The overall architecture as we can see in Fig. 8.3 is constituted of a root representing shared layers, meaning that it is shared among all the users in the system, and several branches constituted by replicated layers for every user. The layers communicate vertically using interaction events, and use collaboration events for communication between layers of different branches. However, in contrast to the clover model [17] where the functional core is also split into two layers: one private and shared, while the other is replicated and public, the functional core in our model is represented by two layers that are both shared and constitute the root of the system: The first layer of the Functional Core (FC) at the level N represents the highest semantic level in the system, while the other FC layer at the level $N - 1$ is divided into two distinct parts: a service oriented environment (SOA), and a JADE agent layer. One can imagine two different environments evolving in parallel, while having a layer on the level N with the essential requirement of projecting the two environments on the level $N - 1$, hence integrating web services with the corresponding software agents. The use of two shared layers as a functional core is to increase the separation of functionalities, and thus to increase the modularity of the code. In this article, we will skip the details about the layers between the functional core and the physical interaction components, and we will concentrate on the essence of the architecture represented by its functional core composed of web services and agents, and the interfaces that residing on the lowest layer (Layer 0) of the system.

8.5.2 FC Decomposition

The shared layers of the architecture constituting the system's FC enable all users to manipulate domain objects and have access to various services during the interaction with the system, while the replicated layers handles the set of services and the state of the system that is private for every user in collaboration. We extend this layer abstraction as in [17] by decomposing each layer of the architecture into sub-components, each dedicated to one facet of Ellis' 3C model, while providing and managing specific services for communication, coordination and production (defined by the term cooperation in [8]). However, we suppose that only the layers on the level $N - 1$ and on the lowest level (Layer 0) satisfy these three main classifications, while we have made no assumption till now about the decomposition of the highest semantic layer in the architecture, that is for us mainly composed of one single component for integrating web services with agents, as we will see later in the description of our model. The sub-components on the level $N - 1$ are enclosed in a software interface exposing its functionalities to the clients, by dividing the services in the system into three main services: communication, coordination and production services.

Indeed, for [28], a component is a distributable and executable software module that provides and receives services through a well-defined interface. Specifically, a component is a module, an object, a unit of calculation or data. Hence we concretize the notion of component by defining it as a web service and a software agent interacting together and creating a dynamic environment for groupware tailoring, by offering common and unified services to satisfy users' preferences. We will explain in more details the FC of our system, beginning with the layer $N - 1$ that encloses an SOA environment and a JADE agents' environment respectively.

8.5.3 SOA Environment

As we can see in Fig. 8.3, the first component on the level $N - 1$ is based on an SOA environment. This component contains all the web services in the system grouped into 3 main services: communication services, coordination services and production services. By classifying services in the system into these three main categories, the main spaces of the software collaboration process defined by the 3C model [8], as we have mentioned, are satisfied. Note that we use the term 'Production' to mean 'Cooperation' of activities (used in the 3C model: Communication, Coordination and Cooperation):

- ComService: contains all services offering means of communication between users in collaboration (videoconference service, voice recorder service, etc.).
- CoorService: contains services implementing rules of coordination by codifying their interaction (i.e. workflow).
- ProService: contains services that are the collaborative product of using the architecture. (Ex: Paint application, Word document, etc.).

These services can be considered as orchestrations of various other services in the system [29], and include services based on the functionalities they offer. Compared to the architecture proposed in [4], the UDDI is viewed as a dynamic registry for web services description enhanced with software agent's capabilities, and containing definitions of services running in the system that are susceptible of undergoing tailorability activities. The definitions of these web services are provided using the standardized language for web services description (WSDL) and are connected to adaptable aspects that are the services themselves, residing in the SOA environment.

8.5.4 JADE Agents' Environment

In parallel to the SOA environment, a JADE environment constitutes the other part of the FC on the level $N - 1$. This layer is populated with software agents that are deployed on a JADE environment using its libraries for implementing agents' behaviors. The adopted paradigm of communication between layers is an asynchronous message passing with a format specified by the ACL (Agent Communication Language) defined by FIPA [9]. This format includes a number of fields, more specifically the sender of the message, the list of recipients, the communication intention that indicates the purpose of sending the message, the message content and its language i.e. the used syntax to explain the content that could be understood by the sender and the recipient, and finally the ontology i.e. the vocabulary of symbols used in the contents and their meanings that also should be understood both by the sender and the recipient of the message. As in the SOA environment, all agents are grouped into three main classes: communication, coordination and production agents. The use of agents, as we have mentioned before, is to make the discovery of new services in the system dynamic, meaning that new web services will be actively integrated into the FC without stopping the execution of the system. These services are normally used by users on the physical layer, which is the lowest layer in the architecture. The functional decomposition of the layer into three main sub-components corresponding to the 3C model will fasten the interaction with web services in the system, while every agent in one particular sub-component would know exactly where to search for a particular web service in the SOA environment that best suits the functionalities it can offer. Each sub-component in this layer manipulates semantic objects dedicated to one of the 3C model functionalities, and performs specific processing functions on its services.

8.5.5 Universal Directory for Description and Discovery

We describe the highest semantic layer of the architecture constituting the core component in the proposed model. The name of the UD^3 model is derived from integrating the UDDI [24] (Universal Description Discovery and Integration) used by web services and the DF [36] (Directory Facilitator explained in Sect. 8.4.4) used by software agents. Hence emerges the Universal Directory for Description and Discovery, or the UD^3 model. In fact, building a model using both technologies would constitute a new approach built on integration's synergy, which is still not been exploited till now in the context of tailorable groupware design. We can view this component on the highest level of the architecture as a shared registry with dynamic interaction mechanisms for the discovery of web services. We visualize a scenario where a client agent searches for a service in the system. The model can then trigger a mechanism to look up for available services in the web service environment. Hence the advantages of classifying web services into three main services (Communication, Coordination and Production) for making the search for available web services faster and more efficient by separation of their functionalities. If the web service is found, its corresponding ontology and interaction models are generated, then the agent registers the corresponding web service as its own service, and communication between the invoking agent and the service would be able to start. Hence, the aim of this part of the FC is for:

- Software agents to discover publish and invoke web services in web service registries (UDDI).
- Web service clients to discover software agents services in the Directory Facilitator (DF) of the JADE Platform.
- Web services to be published in the Directory Facilitator (DF) as a agent service.
- Web service clients to invoke Software Agents in order to integrate new web services in the system.

8.5.6 Dynamic Discovery and the Semantic Web

Existing syntax based on SOA standards such as WSDL allows for dynamic invocation of web services. However, this is only true for web services that have already been discovered, as WSDL does not allow attachment of semantic meaning to data in order to discover external web services on the fly. Dynamic discovery, on the other hand, needs to deal with unknown services on the Internet. It will hence require the use of semantic metadata that software agents can understand and interpret without human intervention. Hence a specific language should be used to add semantics to inputs and outputs of the web service by attaching semantic metadata that reference ontology concepts. Agents can then understand service descriptions without intervention from the human user, thus enabling dynamic discovery as well as dynamic invocation of web services, and hence tailoring groupware services in relation to user's preferences. The W3C community developed the Web Ontology Language (OWL) to address this problem [26]. It is a machine-understandable description language that is capable of describing resources in a richer manner than traditional flat taxonomies and classification systems, by providing a set of concepts specifically for describing web services inputs, outputs, operations, and categorization. However, UDDI is not capable of storing and processing semantic service descriptions written in OWL. Therefore it is clear that a registry that supports semantic annotation and matchmaking of web services will produce much more refined search results, invocation and integration mechanisms which we are exploiting in our model by implementing services' tailorability.

8.5.7 FC Implementation

As we have mentioned earlier, the FC on the level N of the architecture as shown in Fig. 8.4, should allow mechanisms for translating web services' invocations into a language understood by software agents, and vice versa. In fact, few related work in the literature have been identified dealing with such translation mechanisms. The authors in [25] present their tool, WS2JADE, that is based on two distinct layers: An interconnection layer that glues agents and web services together, and a static management layer that creates and controls these interconnection entities called WSAG (Web Service Agents), that are able to communicate and deliver web services as their own services by producing and deploying WSAG at runtime. For [21], agents can represent service consumers and providers that are independent, and collaborate together in order to dynamically configure and reconfigure service-based applications. Their approach implements an agent-based architecture and is realized in a web service agent platform (WSAF) that uses QoS ontology and an XML language enabling consumers and service providers to expose their preferences.

Our primary concern in the design of our model is to have a tool translating web services' and agents' invocation messages, and creating interaction mechanisms in order to tailor web services in the system. In fact, a useful tool in using JADE is the WSIG ('Web Service Integration Gateway') that meets our needs by providing means to register web services in the JADE DF [36] (see Sect. 8.4.4) "mapped" with descriptions of agents. In our case, registered web services can be called by agents by directing the invocation to the WSIG. Thus, a web service is published as JADE agent service, and an agent service can be symmetrically published as an "end-point" of a web service. As shown in Fig. 8.4, the highest level of the FC

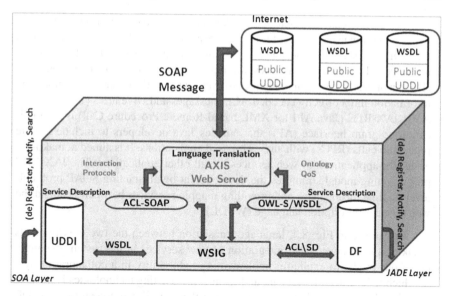

Fig. 8.4 FC implementation

contains a WSIG consisting of several components, each linked either directly or indirectly to two registries, the DF that is not visible outside the platform, and the UDDI that is visible internally to the WSIG, and externally to web services and web service clients, but not directly to agents, and hence the WSIG acts as the interface point between the agents and SOA environment.

In order to be visible in both environments, WSIG is registered as a special agent service in DF (Directory Facilitator) and a special web service endpoint in the UDDI directory, where any service description registered with either the DF or UDDI is automatically translated into an entry for the other. The purpose is to ensure that any registered web service is visible to agents via the DF and any registered agent is visible to web service clients via the UDDI. We describe the local components of the WSIG [13] of the JADE platform:

- OWL-S/WSDL codec (OWL-S is the semantic markup for web services [12]) that has the purpose of generating OWL ontologies from WSDL specifications. In fact, WSDL is known to have limited ability in order to express semantic information about the web service in order for it to be manipulated by an agent in the system. And thus, a specific need is to have a codec mapping WSDL elements or operations into OWL-S atomic processes, and alternatively, OWL-S class types of the inputs and outputs of an atomic process mapped onto WSDL elements. Of course, not all the operations in the WSDL can be mapped into OWL descriptions, therefore some descriptions would be added manually by the programmer. A scenario of use is described in Sect. 8.6.3 for further understanding of the invocations process between an agent and a web service.
- ACL-SOAP codec that is responsible for parsing ACL (Agent Communication Language [36]) messages received from the DF in order to extract the encoded

service descriptions (SD) held within their content, then translating them into a web service invocation and returning the results to the WSIG for registration in the UDDI. It is also responsible for parsing ACL messages sent to the WSIG to invoke a web service into a corresponding SOAP message. This codec operates also in a bidirectional manner in order to translate SOAP and service specification information into correctly encoded ACL messages and DF entries [13].

- Axis' JAX-RPC (Java API for XML based Remote Procedure Call) is an application program interface (API) that enables Java developers to include remote procedure calls (RPCs) with any web-based applications. It is aimed at making it easier for applications or web services to call other applications. The JAX-RPC programming model simplifies the development by abstracting SOAP protocol-level runtime mechanisms and providing mapping services between Java and the web services description language (WSDL).

As we can see in Fig. 8.4, language translation between the two environments for making the discovery and integration of new services in the system dynamic, leads in our model to explicitly implementing tailorability in a collaborative system, which is leveraged by reusing and identifying existing technologies instead of reinventing the wheel [25], with the use of the WSIG [13] component in the JADE platform. In the next section we will see how the UD^3 model can be put into practice in the Oce@nyd project.

8.6 Case Study—Oce@nyd

Figure 8.5 illustrates the application of the UD^3 on an ongoing project in our laboratory, Oce@nyd, which is a part of a national project DIGITALOCEAN [6] for the distribution and creation of multimedia applications (audio, video, text, etc.). In fact, it is designed to enable the public to discover, online, underwater environments. Our aim is to deal with the collaboration aspects of the project, as well as questions concerning its integration, interoperability and mainly tailorability.

Moreover, as the nature of collaborative work in this domain continually changes as a consequence of changing work needs, the system must adapt to reflect the unpredictable requirements of users' in collaboration. Hence emerges the need for a new architectural model that could satisfy these requirements in a real application. We have applied our model on Oce@nyd in order to satisfy these problems.

At the conceptual level we applied the FC shown in Fig. 8.3 that includes two shared layers. At the implementation level, Oce@nyd is a client–server application deployed on a Netbeans [23] platform using JADE libraries, along with other libraries for implementing the web services environment in the system. Both shared layers of the FC are deployed on the server side and other layers are replicated on users' machines, while the client/server communication is based on network streams. We will discuss mainly the FC of the model in a real application along with the physical interaction layer and the services offered that are tailored by users, while we make no assumptions, as we have mentioned before, for the other layers between the FC core and the physical interaction.

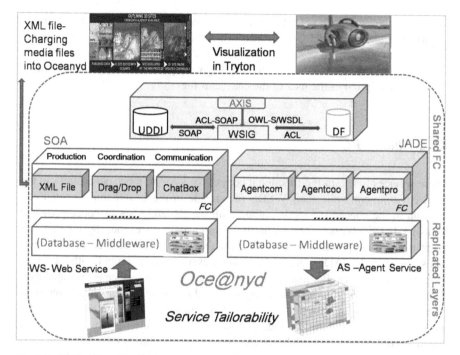

Fig. 8.5 Case study—Oce@nyd

8.6.1 Physical Layer

At the physical layer of the application, lays a web interface manipulated by users in collaboration. This web interface enables users to drag/drop multimedia files on a map of a specified underwater site taken by another partner for the project, using sensors, cameras and a GPS. The aim is to enrich this map with multimedia files by professional divers or users having real photos taken underwater when scuba diving in this particular location. We assume for now that the interface offers three mechanisms implemented with web services technologies, each dedicated to one aspect of the 3C model as follows:

- Communication: the application provides a chat mechanism enabling users to exchange information about the files dragged onto the loaded map.
- Coordination: a service is encapsulated into the system that divides the map into variable zones, and which will detect the coordinates of the dragged file onto the shared zone that is showing a loaded map of a particular underwater site (the number of zones dividing the map will be defined by the user, hence insuring tailorability of coordination capabilities in the system).
- Production: the system provides a mechanism for dumping the information of the multimedia applications dropped by users, into an XML file defining data attributes for every file dragged onto the map: date/time, nature (image, video or text), description (user's description of a particular file), and coordinates: the

user will be prompt to enter the exact coordinates of the file (x, y, z) taken in a particular underwater site. In the case where the actual coordinates are missing, the system will give an (x, y) coordinates of the file dropped by the user on the 2D loaded map, while a (z) coordinate will be given by the administrator depending on the description of the user of the particular file.

8.6.2 Shared FC

These services reside in the functional core of the system, more particularly in the SOA environment while their WSDL files reside in the UDDI implemented one level up in the conceptual model, along with the DF and a set of codec provided by using JADE libraries. The main aim is to ensure consistency by binding one agent to its corresponding web service via the WSIG as described in the previous section. In the JADE part of the system, every agent is bound with its corresponding web service. For example, a communication web service is managed by a communication agent insuring its integration and invoking in the system's physical interface. The part constituting the FC that contains all the agents are handled by the WSIG and JADE tools, providing basic methods for the registration of agents and their communication with the SOA. The agents use classes inherited from various behaviors offered by JADE libraries for implementing interaction protocols between agents: CyclicBehaviour that listens to messages exchanged between various agents, AchieveREInitiator/AchieveREResponder that provides an effective implementation for all the FIPA-Request-like interaction protocols, Contract NetInitiator/ContractNetResponder that offer various API and functionalities [13], etc.

8.6.3 Invocation of an External Web Service by an Agent

In the case where the system is prompted for an external web service, an agent handling the particular class of the web service (communication, coordination or production) sends an ACL Request message to the WSIG containing the identity, name or any parameters identifying the web service to be invoked. Received ACL messages are parsed and a SOAP message is constructed in order to prompt external public registries for this particular web service, using the WSDL of the service to be invoked. If the web service is found and a response is expected, a temporary endpoint is established on the web server in order to receive responses, where the incoming SOAP message is parsed into an ACL Inform message and sent to the invoking agent, while registering the service in the local UDDI as a regular web service. This particular agent will then be responsible for offering the requested web service to the user directly integrated into the web interface.

Hence, on the design level, web services can act as semi-autonomous agents that can be employed for describing the external behaviors and services offered by software agents, and where every agent works in relation to the environment as a regular web service. In consequence, agents are used to establish high level, flexible and dynamic interaction models, while the web services will be more appropriate for resolving the problems of interoperability in the system. At the execution level, UDDI WSDL and SOAP will provide capacities such as the discovery, deployment and communication.

8.6.4 Properties and Discussion

The originality of our model is the use of existing technologies' synergy in order to create a tailorable and interoperable architecture for groupware. Moreover, our model is inspired by the Arch and Dewan's model for separating the core functionality (logic of the application) of its interfaces, and thus carrying with it many essential properties such as modifiability, which is also crucial in the HCI domain. However, the two layers constituting the FC are both shared and handle exclusively the services and their dynamic integration, which is different from the clover model [17] that advocates a replicated functional core for every user by managing their private domain-dependent objects. We thought that a functional core adapter situated between the functional core and the physical layer (which was not discussed in our work presented) is more suited to handle this type of data, while dedicating the core of the application solely to handle tailoring system's services, and hence every newly added service will be shared by all users' participating in a particular session.

The functional core breakdown according to Ellis' 3C model contains several properties. In fact, from the implementation perspective, the functional breakdown will result in a greater modularity which reduces the complexity of groupware's implementation. For example, In the Oce@nyd system, it would be easy to add a new communication web service by adding, for example, a video stream service without affecting existing web services in the system. In addition, we have made no assumptions about the other layers in the system according to the functional decomposition of Ellis' model. This could reduce the development cost and computational time, while enabling the addition of independent and heterogeneous layers to improve the distribution of features and increase the modularity of code, and also by insuring interoperability on every layer of the architecture (by using FIPA and W3C specification and standards). As for the branching point discussed in [27], we have fix it after the FC layers, which induce a lower replication degree than the Clover model, but convenient in order to ensure state consistency of services, as well for collaborating users to share discovered services and reusing them when needed. Finally, our model identifies the implementation architecture that is deduced from the theoretical model in order to achieve tailorability in collaborative applications, where opposed to other models, it identifies explicitly a component as a web service and a software agent collaborating together to offer unified services in a specified environment, and where agents implement the concept of mobile code, while coordination with their flexible architecture would enable them to easily adapt to highly dynamic and heterogeneous environments as the web. Furthermore, this model accepts equity between roles of agents and web services to support tailorability, which is different from the traditional view that agents are considered on an upper level from web services and take solely the roles of web services providers and consumers.

8.7 Conclusion

In this work, we have proposed a new architectural model that supports tailorability in CSCW domain, where existing models are still lacking in putting it forward and identifying technologies supporting it in the field. Our model relies on the integration of web services and software agents that build system's components, and offers interoperability between heterogeneous applications by providing a synergy of technology used for the dynamic discovery and integration of web services. This leads us to conceive a totally innovative approach, where research about web services and agent's integration is, until now, never been exploited in the context of groupware tailorability, and hence bringing innovation in both the CSCW domain and the web. Moreover, our model relies on the Arch and Dewan's model, offering a canonical separation of the application's core from its interfaces, thus greater modularity, and also on Ellis' model by decomposing system's functionality into three facets: communication, coordination and production, which satisfies various properties in the HCI (Human–Computer Interaction) and CSCW (Computer Supported Cooperative Work) domains. However, storing and processing semantic service descriptions (OWL-S) in existing UDDI registries may not be the ideal solution in the long run, while compared to registries specifically designed to handle semantic service description and queries, it will have drawbacks with respect to some functionalities as well as efficiency in terms of both speed and storage. However, our approach will provide a cost effective and functional short-term solution that builds on top of existing registry infrastructure.

In our future work, we aim to complete our implementation for the UD^3 model. Our concern will be to modify incoming SOAP messages' headers of external web services in order to fasten their integration into the architecture according to their functionalities (communication, coordination and production). We believe that our preliminary approach for groupware tailorability will continue to mature through the use of web services and software agents, which revealed to be appropriate to bring this concept from theory to practice.

References

1. Bass, L.: A metamodel for the runtime architecture of an interactive system. SIGCHI Bulletin **24**(1), 32–37 (1992). User Interface Developers' Workshop
2. Bourguin, G.: Un support informatique a l'activite cooperative fonde sur la Theorie de l'Activite- le projet DARE. Thesis in computer science, University of Lille, France (2000)

3. Bourguin, G.: Les lecons d'une experience dans la realisation d'un collecticiel reflexif. In: Proc. of 15th IHM Conference, pp. 24–28 (2003)
4. Cheaib, N., Otmane, S., Mallem, M.: Integrating Internet technologies in designing a tailorable groupware architecture. In: Proc. of 12th IEEE CSCWD, Xi'an, China, pp. 141–147 (2008)
5. Dewan, P.: Architectures for collaborative applications. Computer-Supported Cooperative Work 7, 169–193 (1999)
6. Dinis, A., Fies, N., Cheaib, N., Otmane, S., Mallem, M., Nisan, N., Boi, J.M., Noel, C., Viala, C.: DIGITAL OCEAN: A national project for the creation and distribution of multimedia content for underwater sites. In: Proc. of 14th International Conference on Virtual Systems and Multimedia (VSMM'08), Limassol, Cyprus (2008)
7. Dustdar, S., Gall, H., Schmitt, R.: Web services for groupware in distributed and mobile collaboration. In: Proc. of 12th Euromicro Conference on Parallel, Distributed and Network-Based Processing, pp. 241–247 (2004)
8. Ellis, C.A., Wainer, J.A.: Conceptual model of groupware. In: Proc. of CSCW, pp. 79–88. ACM, New York (1994)
9. FIPA: http://www.fipa.org/ (2008)
10. Foukarakis, I.E., Kostaridis, A.I., Biniaris, C.G., Kaklamani, D.I., Venieris, I.S.: Webmages: An agent platform based on web services. Computer Communications 30(3), 538–545 (2007)
11. Gannod, G.C., Burge, J.E., Urban, S.D.: Issues in the design of flexible and dynamic service-oriented systems. In: Proc. of SDSOA'07: ICSE. IEEE Comput. Soc., Washington (2007)
12. http://www.w3.org/Submission/OWL-S/
13. JADE Board: JADE Web Services Integration Gateway (WSIG) Guide, Whitestein Technologies AG, Zürich (2005)
14. Jorstad, I., Dustdar, S., Thanh, D.V.: A service oriented architecture framework for collaborative services. In: Proc. of 14th IEEE International Workshops on Enabling Technologies, Infrastructure for Collaborative Enterprise, pp. 121–125. IEEE Press, New York (2005)
15. Khezami, N.: Vers un collecticiel basé sur un formalisme multi-agent destiné à la téléopération collaborative via Internet. Phd thesis, University of Evry Val d'Essone, Evry, France (December 2005)
16. Kiczales, G., Lamping, J., Lopes, C., Maeda, C., Mendhekar, A.: Open implementation design guidelines. In: Proc. of 19th International Conference on Software Engineering, pp. 481–490. ACM, New York (1997)
17. Laurillau, Y., Nigay, L.: Clover architecture for groupware. In: Proc. of the 2002 ACM Conference on Computer Supported Cooperative Work, pp. 236–245. ACM, New York (2002)
18. Maamar, Z., Akhter, F., Lahkim, M.: An agent-based approach to specify a web service-oriented environment. In: Proc. of WET ICE, pp. 48–49. IEEE Comput. Soc., Washington (2003)
19. Maamar, Z., Sheng, Q.Z., Benatallah, B.: Interleaving web services composition and execution using software agents and delegation. In: AAMAS Workshop (2003)
20. Matskin, M., Küngas, P., Rao, J., Sampson, J., Petersen, S.A., Link, I., Back, J.: Enabling web services composition with software agents. In: Proc. of IASTED, pp. 15–17 (2005)
21. Maximilien, E.M., Singh, M.P.: A framework ontology for dynamic web services selection. IEEE Internet Computing 8(5), 84–93 (2004)
22. Morch, A.: Three levels of end-user tailoring: customization, integration, and extension. In: Computers and Design in Context, pp. 51–76. MIT Press, Cambridge (1997)
23. Netbeans Platform. http://www.netbeans.org/
24. Newcomer, E.: Understanding Web Services: XML, WSDL, SOAP, and UDDI. Pearson Education, Boston (2002)
25. Nguyen, T.X., Kowalczyk, R.: WS2JADE: Integrating web service with Jade agents. In: Service-Oriented Computing: Agents, Semantics, and Engineering, pp. 147–159. Springer, Berlin (2007)
26. OWL Web Ontology Language Reference. Copyright W3C. http://www.w3.org/TR/owl-ref/ (2004)
27. Patterson, J.F.: A taxonomy of architectures for synchronous groupware applications. SIGOIS Bulletin 15(3), 27–29 (2005)

28. Payet, D.: L'enrichissement de message comme support pour la composition logicielle. Phd thesis, University of Monptellier, France (2003)
29. Peltz, C.: Web services orchestration. A review of emerging technologies, tools and standards. Hewlett Packard White Paper (January 2003)
30. Roseman, M., Greenberg, S.: Simplifying component development in an integrated groupware environment. In: Proc. of 10th Annual ACM Symposium on User Interface Software and Technology, New York, pp. 65–72 (1997)
31. Shen, W., Hao, Q., Wang, S., Li, Y., Ghenniwa, H.: Agent-based service-oriented integration architecture for collaborative intelligent manufacturing. Robotics and Computer-Integrated Manufacturing 23(3), 315–325 (2007)
32. Slagter, R., Biemans, M., Hofte, H.T.: Evolution in use of groupware: Facilitating tailoring to the extreme. In: Proc. of CRIWG, pp. 68–73 (2001)
33. Slagter, R., Biemans, M.: Designing tailorable groupware for the healthcare domain. In: Proc. of CRIWG, pp. 58–73. Springer, Berlin (2003)
34. Starr, B., Ackerman, M.S., Pazzani, M.: Do- I-Care: A collaborative web agent. In: Conference on Human Factors in Computing Systems, pp. 273–274. ACM, New York (1996)
35. Stiemerling, O., Cremers, A.: Tailorable component architectures for CSCW-systems. In: Proc. of 6th Euromicro Workshop on Parallel and Distributed Programming, pp. 21–24 (1998)
36. Telecom Italia Lab: JADE (Java Agent Development Framework). http://sharon.cselt.it/projects/jade/

Part III
Knowledge, Text, Semantic and Intelligence

Chapter 9
Toward Distributed Knowledge Discovery on Grid Systems

**Nhien An Le Khac, Lamine M. Aouad,
and M-Tahar Kechadi**

Abstract While massive amounts of data are being collected and stored from not only science fields but also industry and commerce fields, the efficient mining and management of useful information of this data is becoming a challenge and a massive economic need. This led to the development of distributed data mining techniques to deal with huge multi-dimensional datasets distributed among several sites.

Besides, to cope with large, graphically distributed, high dimensional, multi-owner, and heterogeneous datasets, Grid platforms are well suited for data storage and they provide an effective computational support for distributed data mining applications. Although Grid platforms allow to share resources distributed in large, heterogeneous environments, there are still many challenges on carrying these distributed data mining techniques on Grid because of lacking efficient distributed data mining systems.

In this chapter, we present a new DDM system basing on a Grid/P2P middleware tools to execute new distributed data mining techniques on very large and distributed heterogeneous datasets.

9.1 Introduction

During the last decade or so, we have had a deluge of data from not only science fields but also industry and commerce fields. Although the amount of data available to us is constantly increasing, our ability to process it becomes more and more difficult. Efficient discovery of useful knowledge from these datasets is therefore becoming a challenge and a massive economic need. This led to the need of developing large-scale data mining (*DM*) techniques to deal with these huge datasets either from science or economic applications.

Moreover, these large volumes of data that are collected daily are often heterogeneous, geographically distributed and owned by different organizations. In a

N.A. Le Khac (✉)
School of Computer Science and Informatics, University College Dublin, Belfield, Dublin 4, Ireland
e-mail: an.lekhac@ucd.ie

Y. Badr et al. (eds.) *Emergent Web Intelligence: Advanced Semantic Technologies,*
Advanced Information and Knowledge Processing,
DOI 10.1007/978-1-84996-077-9_9, © Springer-Verlag London Limited 2010

distributed environment, datasets are distributed among different sites for various reasons. For example, an application by its nature is distributed such as a multinational company that has customers worldwide—the datasets concerning its products and customers are distributed and heterogeneous (different customers, different legislation from country to country, etc.). In scientific applications, for instance, the data may be collected in different locations using different instruments, and therefore these separate datasets may have different formats and features. Concretely, the datasets we produce today are by nature distributed both in content and in administrative policies. What is perceived by the end user as a single data collection (dataset or database or data warehouse) is in fact composed of different collections of data administered by different authorities and owned by a variety of organizations with diverse or competing business models and strategies. Traditional centralized data management and mining techniques are not adequate anymore. More precisely, traditional *DM* techniques do not consider all the issues of data-driven applications such as scalability in both response time and accuracy of solutions, distribution and heterogeneity. In addition, transferring a huge amount of data over the network is not an efficient strategy and may not be possible for security and protection reasons. For example, in some fields such as physics (e.g., LHC at CERN, nanotechnology), bioinformatics (predicting gene, mapping/sequencing DNA, etc.), digital business ecosystem, meteorology, digital forensic, and telecommunication, where the data is produced and stored locally (distributed data) the users (scientists or data analysts) need to unite their effort to mine and analyze the data. At the same time they need to share the access to the data of interest. This puts a huge stress on the data integrity and protection for following main reasons: (i) different organizations have different policies for the access rights; (ii) the current Internet and other Global computers are very vulnerable to attacks, such as viruses, hacking, and Denial of Service attacks; (iii) network failure and temporarily heavy traffic.

Distributed data mining techniques constitute a better alternative as they are scalable and can deal efficiently with data heterogeneity. So distributed data mining (DDM) has become necessary for large and multi-scenario datasets requiring resources, which are heterogeneous and distributed. There are two major strands of research into DDM. The first strand considers homogeneous data sites and consists of combining different models of data from different sites. The second strand considers a broader range of distribution, where the datasets located in different sites may record different features. Most research effort is concentrated on the first strand and several techniques can be found in the literature. There exists very little that addresses the second strand (DDM on heterogeneous datasets). Moreover, existing methods are limited, particularly when additional requirements are needed and complexity (distribution, heterogeneity, large volume of data) of real-world data-driven applications increases.

Besides, to cope with large, graphically distributed, high dimensional, multi-owner, and heterogeneous datasets, Grid platforms [28] are well suited for data storage and they provide an effective computational support for distributed data mining applications. Because recent Grid platforms, which benefits from Web Services through its Open Grid Service Architecture [29] and Web Service Resource Framework [21], is an integrated infrastructure that efficiently supports the sharing and coordinated use of resources in dynamic heterogeneous distributed environments. Actually, only few projects that consider Grid as a platform for distributed data mining have been initiated [9, 15, 20] so far. Most of them use some basic Grid services and they are based on Globus Tool Kit [31]. However, they only provide means of managing and controlling the resources of the Grid but they are not focused on how to take advantage of the data-driven application features to efficiently execute their corresponding distributed algorithms.

In this chapter, we present a new *DDM* system combining dataset-driven and architecture-driven strategies. Data-driven strategies will consider the size and heterogeneity of the data, while architecture driven will focus on the distribution of the datasets. This system is based on a Grid middleware tools that integrate appropriate large data manipulation operations. Therefore, this allows more dynamicity and autonomicity during the mining, integrating and processing phases. The following section presents issues related to a *DDM* system. Section 9.3 deals with our system architecture. Section 9.4 presents new *DDM* algorithms, the core of this system. One of its key layers, Knowledge Map (KM), will be described in Sect. 9.5; and then the exploitation of this system will be showed in Sect. 9.6. We make a résumé of related works of *DDM* systems on Grid platforms in Sect. 9.7. Finally, we conclude on Sect. 9.8.

9.2 *DDM* Systems

In this section we firstly resume different aspects of *DDM* systems and then we discuss on problems related to an efficient *DDM* system on Grid platform.

A *DDM* system normally includes main components such as: data preprocessing, mining algorithms, communication subsystem, resource and task management, user interface. The main role of a *DDM* system is to provide an environment for accessing distributed data, mining algorithms and computing resource, monitoring the entire mining process, interpreting results to users. A *DDM* system should offer a flexible environment to adapt various kind of distributed mining applications. The architecture of a *DDM* system is also a important issue. Early researches on this subject are based on cluster of high-performance workstations or three-tier client/server model [18]. However, these approaches are appropriate for *PDM* tasks. Another approach is based on agent-based model addressing to scalable mining over large distributed datasets. Most of these systems require a supervisory agent that handles and facilitates the mining process.

9.2.1 *DDM* Issues

9.2.1.1 Centralised DM vs. *DDM*

Today, traditional centralized DM is not suitable for exploring a huge amount of data distributed in large scale environments. Some of the main problems can be listed

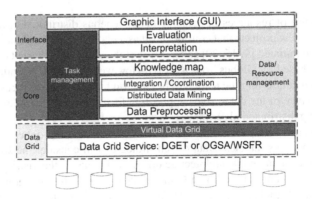

Fig. 9.1 System's architecture

as the communication cost, bottleneck, using of distributed resources, privacy and security, etc. In a distributed environment, data may be distributed among different sites for various reasons: an application by its nature is distributed or sometimes data are artificially distributed for better scalability and disk space management. Centralized DM techniques do not consider all the issues of data-driven applications such as scalability in both response time and accuracy of solutions, distribution and heterogeneity. Meanwhile, *DDM* approaches, as shown in Fig. 9.1, perform local data analysis followed by the generation of a global model by aggregating the local results. Precisely, *DDM* techniques which base on the availability of the distributed resources can be able to learn models from distributed data without exchanging the raw data.

9.2.1.2 Parallel Data Mining and *DDM*

The objective of Parallel Data Mining (PDM) is to perform fast mining of large datasets by using high performance parallel environments. We can find some related works on PDM in the literature such as [3, 30, 35]. This approach assumes existence of high-speed network connection between the computing nodes. That is not always available in many of the *DDM* applications. In spite of the development of *DDM* has been influenced by PDM, this approach is not in the scope of this book chapter where we investigate *DDM* techniques scaling well on large environments without existing of high-speed network connection.

9.2.1.3 Homogeneous vs. Heterogeneous

As mentioned in Sect. 9.1, there are two major strands of research into *DDM*. The first strand considers homogeneous data sites and consists of combining different models of data from different sites. The second strand considers a broader range of distribution, where datasets located in different sites may record different features.

This strand is also called *DDM* on heterogeneous datasets. Most research effort is concentrated on the first strand and several techniques can be found in the literature. For instance, [8, 24, 39] proposed ensemble learning for distributed classifier learning. Meta-learning [17] offers another approach for learning classifiers from homogeneous distributed data. Distributed Association Rule mining and distributed clustering for this homogeneous case can be found in [1, 27].

There exists very little research in the literature that addresses to the second trend (*DDM* on heterogeneous datasets). Most of them uses special-purpose algorithms. The WoRLD system [7], for example, is based on the "activation spread" approach. It first computes locally the cardinal distribution of the feature values of datasets. In the second phase, this knowledge is propagated across different sites. Features with strong correlations to the space model are identified and selected, to be use for learning the distribution. However, this technique may not be always appropriate for a given space model.

9.2.2 Toward an Efficient DDM System on Grid Platform

Traditional approaches of *DM*, as resumed above, are limited, particularly when the additional requirements and complexity (distribution, heterogeneity, large volume of data) of real-world data-driven applications are included. These requirements constitute challenges in this research area. Today, the development of Grid technologies allows to share resources distributed in large, heterogeneous environments. However, the sharing and transferring of a huge amount of data is not efficient and sometimes is not impossible because of the performance aspects. *DDM* becomes a remarkable solution for mining applications distributed on Grid platform. There are many challenges concerning both *DDM* techniques and the infrastructure that allow efficient and fast processing, reliability, quality of service, integration, and extraction of knowledge from this mass of data.

In order to become an efficient platform to explore and analysis huge data distributed on the Grid environment, a *DDM* system needs to combine dataset-driven and architecture-driven strategies. Dataset-driven will take into account the size and heterogeneity of data while architecture-driven will take into account the distribution of datasets. Concretely, an efficient *DDM* framework is consisted of the following main features:

- Providing a set of *DDM* algorithms that are robust, adaptive, flexible, low cost communication and scalable. *DDM* algorithms are heart of *DDM* system. However, most of the current approach of *DDM* framework for mining data on Grid platform [9, 15, 20] only propose services to handle distributed resources, process and knowledge. None of them offers any specific *DDM* algorithm. Besides, the integrating of traditional *DM* algorithms in these framework raises a question about the performance in real-world applications.
- Offering an effective knowledge management. As mentioned above, the process of local mining (build local knowledge) and then integrating all the results to

create new knowledge is seen to be one of the most effective solutions for mining applications distributed over Grid platforms. This will lead to the problem of managing efficiently the mined results, so called knowledge, which becomes more and more complex and sophisticated. This is even more critical when the local knowledge of different sites are owned by different organizations. Besides, two steps of *DDM* (local mining and integrating) are not independent since naive approaches to local analysis may produce incorrect and ambiguous global data models. In order to take advantage of the mined knowledge at different locations, *DDM* framework should have a view of the knowledge that not only facilitates their integration but also minimizes the effect of the local results on the global models. Briefly, an efficient management of distributed knowledge is one of the key factors affecting the outputs of these techniques.

- Managing efficiently distributed resources across Grid environment. Actually, most of the Grid Data Mining Projects in literature are based on Globus ToolKit (GT) [9, 15]. The use of a set of Grid services provided by this middleware helps the developer to deal with heterogeneous of resources. However, they also depend on GT's performance and problems such as security overhead. An efficient *DDM* framework needs to be more flexible with regards to many existing data grid platform developed today.
- Giving an user-friendly interface that helps users to build their mining applications and evaluate mining results easily and transparently over Grid platform.

In this section, we have just discussed important issues related to *DDM* systems. In the following sections, we will present a new *DDM* system for developing novel and innovative data mining techniques to deal with very large and distributed heterogeneous datasets in Grid environment.

9.3 Architecture of a New *DDM* System

This architecture includes three main layers: core, virtual data grid and interface. In this section we present the first two layers. Meanwhile, the interface layer will be described in Sect. 9.6.

9.3.1 Core Layer

The core layer is composed of three components: knowledge discovery, task management and data/resource management.

The role of the knowledge discovery component is to mine the data; integrate and consolidate the data; and discover new knowledge. It is key component of this layer and it contains three modules: data preprocessing; distributed data mining (*DDM*) with two sub modules: local data mining (*LDM*) and integration/coordination; knowledge map.

The first module carries out locally data pre-processing of a given tasks such as data cleaning, data transformation, data reduction, data project, data standardization, data density analysis, etc. These pre-processed data will be the input of the *DDM* module. Its *LDM* component performs locally data mining tasks. The specific characteristic of our new system compared with other current *DDM* systems is the ability of integrating different mining algorithms in a local *DM* task to deal with different kind of data. The local results will be integrated and/or coordinated by the second component of DDM module to produce global models. Distributed algorithms of for mining data are heart of the system and some of them will be presented in Sect. 9.4 below. At the interface level, user can choose *DDM* algorithms from a set of pre-defined ones in the system. Moreover, users can publish new algorithms to increase the performance.

The results of local DM such as association rules, classification, and clustering, etc. should be collected and analyzed by domain knowledge. This is the role of the last module: knowledge map. This module will generate significant, interpretable rules, models and knowledge. Moreover, the knowledge map also controls all the data mining process by proposing different strategies for mining as well as for integrating and coordinating all the jobs to achieve the best performance. Details of the knowledge map can be found in Sect. 9.5.

The task management component plays an important role in this system. It manages all the schedules created from the interface layer. This reads an executing schema from the task repository and then schedules and monitors the execution of corresponding tasks. According to the scheduling, this task management component carries out the resource allocation and then finds the best and appropriate mapping between resources and task requirements. This part is based on services supplied by Data Grid layer (e.g. DGET [33]) in order to find the best mapping. Next, it will activate these tasks (local or distribution). This component is also responsible for the coordination of the distributed execution that is, it manages communication as well as synchronization between tasks in the case of cooperation during the preprocessing, mining or integrating stages.

The role of data/resource management component is to facilitate the entire *DDM* process by providing an efficient control over remote resources in a distributed environment. This component creates, manages and updates information about resources in the dataset repository and the resource repository. The data/resource management component goes with the data grid layer to provide an transparent access to resources across heterogeneous platforms.

9.3.2 Data Grid Layer

The upper part of this layer, called virtual data grid, is a portable layer for data grid environments. Actually, most of the Grid Data Mining Projects in literature are based on Globus ToolKit (GT) [9, 15]. The use of a set of Grid services provided by this middleware gives some benefits. For instance, the developer do not waste time for dealing with heterogeneity of organizations, platforms, data sources, etc.; distributing of software is more easier because GT is the most widely used middleware in Grid community. However, this approach depends on GT problems such as security overhead, GT's organization of system topology.

In order to make our system more portable, and more flexible with regards to many existing data grid platforms developed to date, we build this portable layer as an abstraction of virtual Grid platform. It supplies a general services operations interface to upper layers. It unifies different grid middlewares by mapping *DM* tasks from upper layer to grid services according to OGSA/WSRF standard or to entities [33] in DGET model. The portable layer implements two groups of entities: data and resource entities. The first group deals with data and meta-data used by upper layers and the second deals with resources used. The DGET system guarantees the transparent access of data and resources across any heterogeneous platform. By using this portable layer, our system can be carried easily on many kind of Data Grid platforms such as GT and DGET.

9.4 Distributed Algorithms for Mining Large Datasets

The system should not only be a platform based on *Grid* [28] infrastructure for implementing *DDM* techniques but also it should provide new distributed algorithms for exploring very large and distributed datasets. The first step of the development of these algorithms concern distributed clustering techniques which are well studied by the community in comparison with distributed association rules and distributed classification. In this section, we present some important *DDM* algorithms of clustering, frequent items set generation that can be integrated in the system. Other traditional *DM* algorithms such as K-means clustering and a range of its variants are also implemented in our system.

9.4.1 Variance-Based Clustering

Clustering is one of the basic tasks in the data mining area. Basically, clustering groups data objects based on information found in the data that describes the objects and their relationships. The goal is to optimize similarity within a cluster and the dissimilarities between clusters in order to identify interesting structures in the underlying data. There is already a large amount of literature on clustering ranging from models, algorithms, validity and performances studies, etc. However, there are still several open questions about the clustering process. These include:

- What is the optimal number of clusters?
- How to assess the validity of a given clustering strategy?
- How to allow different shapes of the clusters rather than spherical shapes generated by the given distance functions?

- How to prevent the algorithms initialization and the order in which the features vectors are read from affecting the clustering output?
- How to find which clustering structure for a given dataset, i.e. why would a user choose an algorithm instead of another?

Answering these questions appropriately will guarantee the success of a clustering algorithm. Several algorithms have been developed to find several kinds of clusters (spherical, linear, dense, drawnout, etc.) depending on the data and its application.

In distributed environments, clustering algorithms have to deal with additional issues of distributed datasets, large number of nodes and domains, plural ownership and users, and scalability. It has been stated before that moving the entire data to a single location for performing a global clustering is not always possible due to different reasons. Moreover, communication issues are the key factors in the implementation of any distributed algorithm. It is obvious that a suitable algorithm for high speed network can be of little use in WAN-based platforms. Generally, it is considered that an efficient distributed algorithm minimizes the data exchange and tries to avoid synchronizations as much as possible.

For this purpose, lightweight distributed clustering techniques are the best choice for these systems. This was shown to improve the overall clustering quality and finds the number of clusters and the global inherent clustering structure of the global datasets. The variance-based clustering is developed in this way and it is presented below.

9.4.1.1 Algorithm Foundations

The most used criterion to quantify the homogeneity inside a cluster is the variance criterion, or sum-of-squared-error. The traditional constraint used to minimize this criterion is to fix the number of clusters to an a priori known number, as in the widely used k-means and its variants [41, 51, 52], etc. This constraint is very restrictive since this number is most likely not known in most cases. However, many approximation techniques exist including the gap statistic which compares the change within cluster dispersion with that expected under an appropriate reference null distribution [40, 49], or the index of Calinski and Harabasz [14], among many others. The imposed constraint here states that the increasing variance of the merging, or union, of two subclusters is below a given dynamic limit. This parameter depends on the dataset and is computed using a global assessment method. This allows to find the proper value of the variance increasing by varying it without violating the locality principle of this algorithm. This parameter can also be available from the problem domain for a given data.

The key idea behind this algorithm is to choose a relatively a high number of clusters in local sites which are referred to as subclusters. An optimal local number of clusters using approximation techniques can be considered. Then, the global merging is done according to an increasing variance criterion requiring a very limited communication overhead. The algorithm finds the proper variance criterion for each dataset based on a statistical global assessment. This preserves the locality criterion for each dataset.

In each node (site), the clustering can be done using different algorithms depending on the characteristics of the dataset. This may include k-means, k-harmonic-means, k-medoids, the statistical interpretation using the expectation-maximization algorithm, etc. The merging of local subclusters exploits the locality in the feature space, i.e. the most promising candidates to form a global cluster are subclusters that are the closest to each other in the features space. Each node can perform the merging and deduce global clusters, i.e. which subclusters are subject to form together a global cluster.

Another notion used in this algorithm is the border of a global cluster which represents local subclusters at its border. These subclusters are susceptible to be isolated and added to another global cluster in order to contribute to an improvement of the clustering output with respect to the variance criterion, i.e. that minimizes the sum-of-squared-error. These subclusters are referred to as perturbation candidates. The initial merging order may affect the clustering output, as well as the presence of non well-separated global clusters. This process is intended to reduce the input order impact. The global clusters are then updated. The border is collected by computing the common Euclidean distance measure. The b farthest subclusters are then the perturbation candidates, where b is deduced depending on the local number of subclusters at each site and their global composition. Multi-assigned subclusters are naturally affected by this process.

The aggregation part of the algorithm starts with $\sum_{i \in s} k_i$ subclusters, where s is the number of nodes involved and k_i, for $i = 1, \ldots, s$, are the local numbers of clusters in each node. Each node has the possibility to generate a global merging. An important point here is that the merging is a labeling process, i.e. each local node can generate the correspondences between local subclusters, without necessarily constructing the overall clustering output. This is because the only bookkeeping needed from the other nodes are centers, sizes and variances of the clusters. The aggregation is then defined as a labeling process between local subclusters. No data move is needed at this stage. On the other hand, the perturbation process is activated if the merging operation is no longer applied. The perturbation candidates are collected for each global cluster from its border, which is proportional to the overall size composition as quoted before. Then, this process moves these candidates by trying the closest ones first and with respect to the gain in the variance criterion when moving them from the neighboring global clusters. Formal definitions of this algorithm, and all notions and criterions, are given in [4].

9.4.1.2 Complexity and Evaluation

The complexity of this distributed algorithm depends on the algorithm used locally, the global assessment algorithm, the communication time which is a gather operation, and the merging computing time. If the local clustering algorithm is k-means, the clustering complexity is $O(N_{max}k_{max}d)$, where d is the dimension of the dataset, i.e. number of attributes. The assessment complexity depends on the size of local statistics. If the gap statistic is used on local centers, this will be $O(B(\sum_{i \in s} k_i)^2)$, where B is the number of reference distributions. The communication time is the reduction of $3d \sum_{i \in s} k_i$ elements. If t^i_{comm} is the communication cost of moving one element from node i to the aggregation node j, then the communication complexity is $3d \sum_{i \in s, i \neq j} t^i_{comm} k_i$. Since k_i is much smaller than N_i ($k_i \ll N_i$), the generated communication overhead is very small.

The merging process is executed a number of times, say u. This is the number of iterations until the merging condition is no longer applied. This cost is then equal to $u \cdot t_{newStatistics} = O(d)$. This is followed by a perturbation that costs $O(bk_g k_{max})$. This process computes for each of the b chosen subclusters at the border of a given cluster C_i, k_i distances for each of the k_g global clusters. The total cost is then $O(dN_i(\sum_{i \in s} k_i)^2)$ (with $T_{comm} \ll O(N_i k_i d)$).

This algorithm was tested on a range of simulated and real datasets including large Gaussian distributions, the well-known Iris dataset, the animal dataset, and the PUMS census dataset available from the UC Irvine KDD Archives. The algorithm finds the right global number of clusters by varying the maximum variance constraints, independently of the local clustering algorithm and the number of subclusters. An example using the Iris dataset, where the maximum variance constraint was twice the highest individual variance, is shown in Fig. 9.2. In this case, since the k-harmonic-means does not impose a variance constraint it finds a lower sum-of-squared-error locally. However, the variance-based clustering finds the 3 initial classes based on 5 and 7 subclusters locally. More experiments and evaluation are shown in [4, 5].

9.4.2 Distributed Frequency Itemsets Generation

The frequent itemset mining task is at the core of various data mining applications. Since its inception, many frequent itemset mining algorithms have been proposed [2, 11, 32, 44, 47], among many others. Many of them are based on the Apriori or the FP-Growth principals. Basically, frequent itemsets generation algorithms analyze the dataset to determine which combination of items occurs together frequently. For instance, considering the commonly known market basket analysis; each customer buys a set of items representing his/her basket. The input of the algorithm is a list of transactions giving the sets of items among all existing items in each basket. For a fixed support threshold s, the algorithm determines which sets of items of a given size k are contained in at least s transactions.

The focus here is on mining frequent itemsets on distributed datasets over the grid. The grid-based approaches are motivated by the inherent distributed nature of these applications, and by the challenge of developing scalable solutions for the data mining field, which is highly computationally expensive and data intensive. Effective distributed approaches for large scale data mining should take into account both the challenges raised by the underlying grid system and the complexity of

Fig. 9.2 The output using
5 (**a**) and 7 (**b**) subclusters,
and a centralized clustering
using k-harmonic means
in (**c**)

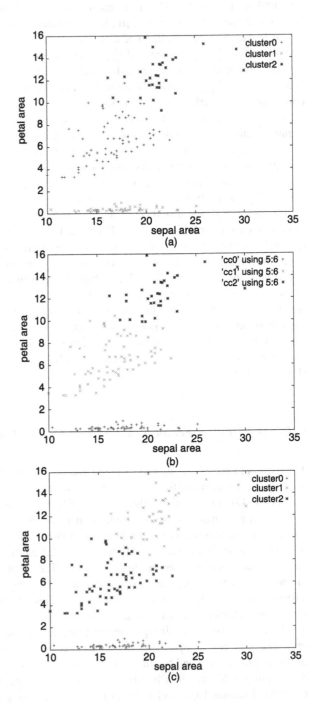

the task itself. For the purpose of developing well-adapted grid implementations, a performance study of frequent itemsets mining of large distributed datasets on the grid, based on the Apriori principle is required.

The study of the distributed aspect and the performance of Apriori-based approaches is done both theoretically and experimentally. The theoretical study presents a performance model of distributed algorithms based on the Apriori principal. Note that the main factor of an Apriori-based distributed algorithm is the number of candidates generated at each step or level. This factor, which governs the algorithm complexity, can be exponential of the size of the input. In the distributed version of this type of algorithms, one tries to maximize the number of concurrent activities (or parallel activities) and reduce the overheads of the communications and synchronizations. We show that local pruning strategies are sufficient and that global phases in classical distributions affect directly the performance of the system.

The approach introduces in [6] has two main phases. The first phase consists of generating frequent itemsets on each node based only on their local datasets. This phase is a *local mining phase* and it uses the traditional sequential Apriori algorithm. After this phase, the result will be the set of all locally frequent itemsets in each node. This information is sufficient for determining all globally frequent itemsets, using a top-down search. The second phase is the *global collection phase*. Each node broadcasts its frequent itemsets, of size k and maximal ones, to the others nodes of the system and asks for their respective support counts. The globally frequent itemsets are then identified by merging local support counts from each node. Then, the algorithm iterates on the subsets of itemsets that fail the global frequency test. More precisely the globally frequent itemsets are generated as follows:

1. Initially collect support counts of frequent itemsets of size k (the requested size) and all smaller frequent itemsets that are not subsets of any larger frequent itemset (maximal itemsets).
2. Generate globally frequent itemsets, and put all the itemsets that are not globally frequent in a set F.
3. If F is not empty, collect support counts of subsets of itemsets in F and go to 2.

This top-down search has been shown to be efficient, and the overheads due to synchronizations and communications are significantly reduced. This leads to much fewer communication passes. Also, the global pruning steps add extra computational costs in local nodes and therefore affects the global system performance.

9.4.2.1 Discussion and Evaluation

Comparisons with a classical Apriori-based distributed approach, namely the Fast Distributed Mining of association rules (FDM), show that in terms of computation, both algorithms perform approximately the same amount of work as they have the same amount of candidates in the local Apriori generation. However, in terms of communication, the proposed top-down approach performs better and has only two communication passes on both synthetic and real datasets; the PUMS census

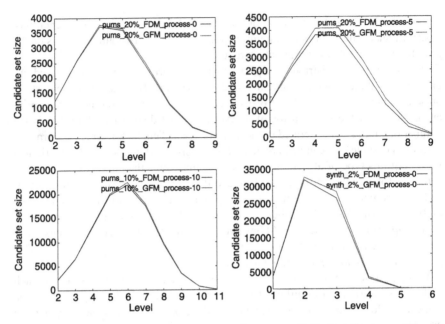

Fig. 9.3 The difference between some generated candidate sets using both approaches on different processes

dataset, and datasets generated using the IBM Quest code respectively. The IBM Quest code is a simulation model for supermarket basket data. It has been used in several frequent itemsets generation studies such as [32, 46, 48], etc.

As example, Fig. 9.3 shows plots of different candidates sets on different nodes using various support thresholds, on the two mentioned datasets. The lower bound, which is the ratio between the number of candidate sets of the two techniques, is 0.78. This value is close to 1 in most cases, with an average value of 0.93. If we look at the ratio of the number of 1-itemsets for the two techniques we can see the same behavior with an average value of 0.94. One can conclude that the difference in terms of candidate set generation between the two techniques is not significant. In terms of processing time, this is in the order of few seconds in all cases. For the overall computation costs, the proposed technique has a gain factor of up to 82%. However, this highly depends on the size of frequent itemsets and the number of communication passes. Also, the input and output requirements were not considered in this model for simplicity. This is likely to be more costly in the case of classical distributed approaches since the proposed approach generates less important overall sets for remote support count collection.

Basically, the results show that distributed implementations of the Apriori algorithm do not need global pruning strategies. Therefore, classical distributions are less efficient than the adopted global strategy in our approach, starting from the requested size and using a top-down search. Note that remote support counts computations can be very expensive in classical distribution, especially in lower levels where the number of locally frequent itemsets is high. This was avoided and reduced to a minimum in the proposed approach since only a few passes of remote computations are required and with smaller sizes. Formal definitions and more detailed results are presented in [6]. This method is intended not only to reduce synchronization and communication overheads but also the grid tools overheads which are due to jobs preparation or scheduling for instance. Efficient grid implementations should avoid multiple communication and synchronization steps as much as possible.

9.5 Knowledge Map

Today, the problem of managing efficiently the mined results, so called knowledge, which becomes more and more complex and sophisticated. This is even more critical when the local knowledge of different sites are owned by different organizations. Usually existing *DDM* techniques perform partial analysis on local data at individual sites and then generate global models by aggregating these local results. These two steps are not independent since naive approaches to local analysis may produce incorrect and ambiguous global data models. In order to take advantage of the mined knowledge at different locations, *DDM* should have a view of the knowledge that not only facilitates their integration but also minimizes the effect of the local results on the global models. Briefly, an efficient management of distributed knowledge is one of the key factors affecting the outputs of these techniques.

A "knowledge map" can be used to handle knowledge of *DDM* tasks on large scale distributed systems and also supporting the integration views of related knowledge. The concept of knowledge map has been efficiently exploited for managing and sharing knowledge [42] in different domains but not yet in *DDM* field. The main goal here is to provide a simple and efficient way to handle a large amount of knowledge built from *DDM* applications in Grid environments. This knowledge map helps to explore quickly any results needed with a high accuracy. This will also facilitate the merging and coordination of local results to generate global models. This knowledge map is also one of the key layers of the *DDM* system. This section starts with a background of knowledge representation and knowledge map concept. We present then architecture of knowledge map layer. Next, following paragraph deal with implementation issues. An evaluation of this approach is also presented to terminate this section.

9.5.1 From Knowledge Representation to Knowledge Maps

9.5.1.1 Representation of Knowledge Mined

There are many different ways of representing mined knowledge, such as decision tables, decision trees, classification rules, association rules, instance-based, and clusters. Decision table [25] is one of the simplest ways of representing knowledge.

The columns contain a set of attributes including the decisions and the rows represent the knowledge elements. This structure is simple but it can be sparse because of some unused attributes. Decision tree [25] approach is based on "divide-and-conquer" concept where each node tests a particular attribute and the classification is given at the leaves level. However, it has to deal with missing value problem. Classification rules' approach [25] is a popular alternative to decision trees. It uses production rules [12], called cause-effect relationships, to express the knowledge. Association rules [25] are kind of classification rules except that they can predict any attribute and this gives them the freedom to predict combinations of attributes too. Moreover, association rules are not intended to be used together as a set, like classification rules. The instance-based knowledge representation uses the instances to represent what is mined rather than inferring a rule set and store it instead. The problem is that they do not make explicit the structures of the knowledge. In the cluster approach, the knowledge can take the form of a diagram to show how the instances fall into clusters. There are many kinds of cluster representations such as space partitioning, Venn diagram, table, tree, etc. Clustering [25] is often followed by a stage in which a decision tree or rule set is inferred that allocates each instance to its cluster. Other knowledge representation approaches, such as Petri net [45], fuzzy Petri nets [19] and G-net [23] were also developed and used.

9.5.1.2 Knowledge Map Concept

A knowledge map is generally a representation of "knowledge about knowledge" rather than of knowledge itself [22, 26, 50]. It basically helps to detect the sources of knowledge and their structures by representing the elements and structural links of the application domains. Some kind of knowledge map structures that can be found in the literature are: hierarchical/radial knowledge map, networked knowledge map, knowledge source map and knowledge flow map.

Hierarchical knowledge map, so-called concept map [42], provides a model for the hierarchical organization of the knowledge: top-level concepts are abstractions with few characteristics. Concepts of the levels below contain detailed traits of the super concept. The links between concepts can represent any type of relations as "is part of", "influences", "can determine", etc. A similar approach is radial knowledge map or mind map [13], which consists of concepts that are linked through propositions. However, it is radially organized (star topology). Networked knowledge map is also called causal map which is defined as a technique "for linking strategic thinking and acting, making sense of complex problems, and communicating with others what might be done about them" [13]. This approach is normally used for systematizing knowledge about causes and effects. Knowledge source map [26] is a kind of organizational charts that does not describe functions, responsibility and hierarchy, but expertise. It helps experts in a specific knowledge domain. The knowledge flow map [26] represents the order in which knowledge resources should be used rather than a map of knowledge.

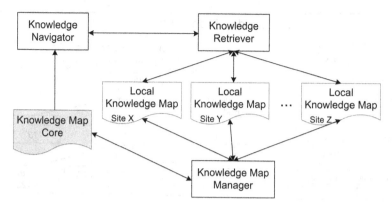

Fig. 9.4 Knowledge map system [37]

9.5.2 Knowledge Map Layer Structure

The knowledge map (*KM*) does not attempt to systematize the knowledge itself but rather to codify "knowledge about knowledge". In our context, it facilitates the deployment of *DDM* by supporting users coordination and interpretation of the results. The objectives of our *KM* architecture are: (1) provide an efficient way to handle a large amount of data collected and stored in large scale distributed system; (2) retrieve easily, quickly, and accurately the knowledge; and (3) support the integration process of the results. A *KM* architecture is proposed as shown in Figs. 9.4, 9.5 and 9.6 to achieve these goals. *KM* consists of the following components: knowledge navigator, knowledge map core, knowledge retrieval, local knowledge map and knowledge map manager (Fig. 9.4). From now on, we use the term "mined knowledge" to represent for knowledge built from applications.

9.5.2.1 Knowledge Navigator

Usually, users may not exactly know what they are looking for. Thus, knowledge navigator component is responsible for guiding users to explore the *KM* and for determining the knowledge of interest. The result of this task is not the knowledge but its metadata, called ***meta-knowledge***, which includes related information such as data mining task used, data type, and a brief description of this knowledge and its location. For example, a user may want to retrieve some knowledge about tropical cyclone. The application domain "meteorology" is used by this component to navigate the user through tropical cyclone area and then a list of information related to it will be extracted. Next, based on this meta-knowledge and its application domain, the users will decide which knowledge and its location are to be retrieved. It will interact with knowledge retrieval component to collect all the results from chosen locations.

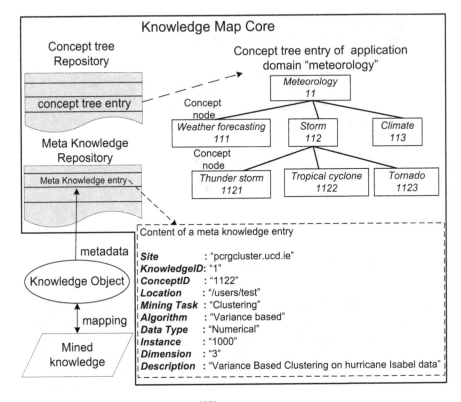

Fig. 9.5 Knowledge map core structure [37]

9.5.2.2 Knowledge Map Core

This component (Fig. 9.5) is composed of two main parts: *concept tree repository* and *meta-knowledge repository*. The former is a repository storing a set of application domains. Each application domain is represented by a *concept tree* that has a hierarchical structure such as a concept map [42]. A node of this tree, so called *concept node* represents a sub-application domain and it includes a unique identity, called *concept Id*, in the whole *concept tree* repository and the name of its sub-application domain. The content of each *concept tree* is defined by the administrator before using *KM*. The concept tree repository could also be updated during the run-time. In our approach, a mined knowledge is assigned to only one sub-application domain and this assignment is given by the user. By using *concept tree*, we can deal with the problem of knowledge context. For instance, given the distributed nature of the knowledge, some of them may have variations depending on the context in which it is presented locally.

Meta-knowledge repository (Fig. 9.5): this handles metadata of the mined knowledge from different sites. A knowledge is mapped to a ***knowledge object*** and its metadata is represented by a meta-knowledge entry in this repository. Figure 9.5

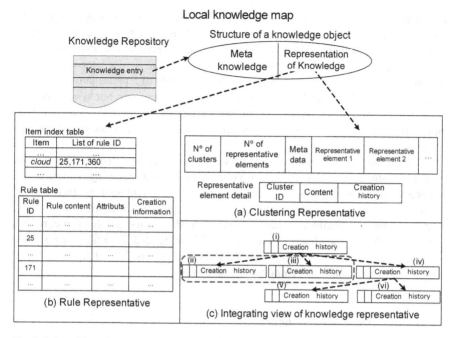

Fig. 9.6 Local knowledge map [37]

also shows an example of a meta-knowledge entry. Based on this information, users could determine which mined knowledge they want to extract.

The goal of the *KM* core, is not only detecting the sources of knowledge and information but also representing their relationships with concepts of a given application domain. This component could be implemented in a master site depending on the topology of the system that will be discussed below.

9.5.2.3 Knowledge Retrieval

The role of this component is to seek the knowledge that is potentially relevant. This task depends on the information provided by the users after navigating through application domains and getting the meta-knowledge needed. This component is similar to a search engine which interacts with each site and collects the local knowledge.

9.5.2.4 Local Knowledge Map

This component (Fig. 9.6) is local to each site of the system. *Local knowledge map* is a repository of knowledge entries. Each entry, which is a knowledge object, represents a mined knowledge and contains two parts: *meta-knowledge* and a *representative*. *Meta-knowledge* includes information such as the identity of its mined knowledge that is unique in this site, its properties, and its description. These attributes were already introduced in Sect. 9.5.2.2. This *meta-knowledge* is also submitted to the **Knowledge map core** and will be used in *meta-knowledge entry* of its repository to be used at the global level. The *representative* of a knowledge entry depends on a given mining task. KM supports two kinds of representatives: one for clustering task and another for rule-based knowledge. Moreover, our system has the capacity of adding more representative types for other mining tasks. Figures 9.6a and 9.6b show respectively the representatives of clustering and rule-based knowledge.

Besides, another important information of cluster representative is the creation type which shows how this cluster was created: by either a clustering process or an integration process which merges sub-clusters from different sources. In the integration case, the cluster representative shows its integration link representing all information needed to build this cluster. Figure 9.6c shows an example of integration link. In this figure, the cluster at the root level is integrated from three other sub-clusters where the last one is also integrated from two others. Note that in Fig. 9.6c, representatives (ii) and (iii) belong to the same knowledge.

9.5.2.5 Knowledge Map Manager

Knowledge map manager is responsible for managing and coordinating the local knowledge maps and the knowledge map core. For *local knowledge map*, this component provides primitives to create, add, delete, update knowledge entries and their related components (e.g. *rule net* and *item index table*) in knowledge repository. It also allows to submit local meta knowledge to the its repository in *knowledge map core*. This component provides also primitives to handle the meta-knowledge in the repository as well as the concept node in the concept tree repository. One key role of this component is to keep the coherence between the *local knowledge map* and *the knowledge map core*.

9.5.3 Evaluation

This tool is used in the system described in [36, 37]. It is difficult to evaluate our approach by comparing it to other systems because it is unique so far. Therefore, this new approach is validated by evaluating different aspects of the system architecture for supporting the management, mapping, representing and retrieving the knowledge. First, we evaluate the complexity of search/retrieve the knowledge object of the system. This operation includes two parts: searching relative concept and search/retrieve the knowledge. Let N be the number of *concept tree* entries and n be the number of *concept nodes* for each *concept tree*. The complexity of the first part is $O(\log N + \log n)$ because the concept tree entries are indexed according to a tree model. However, the number of concept entries as well as of concept nodes of a concept tree is negligible compared to the number of knowledge entries. So this complexity depends strongly on the cost of search/retrieve operations. Let M be the number of meta-knowledge entries in the *KM core*, so the complexity of searching a meta-knowledge entry at this level is $O(\log M + C_s)$, where C_s is the communication cost between a node s and the host node where the meta-knowledge repository is stored. This depends on the bandwidth between two nodes and the size of the data size. The complexity of retrieving a knowledge object is the same as for the search operation. However, the retrieve operation depends on the number of knowledge entries m in the *local KM*.

Some tests have been launched to evaluate the search/retrieve performance. More details about these tests can be found in [37]. Next, we estimate the performance of the knowledge map architecture. Firstly, the structure of *concept tree* is based on the concept map [42], which is one of the advantages of this model. We can avoid the problem of semantic ambiguity as well as reduce the domain search to improve the speed and accuracy of the results. In the 1–n model (one server–n client nodes), the concept tree is implemented either only at the server node or at each client node. The client–server communication is needed when we interact with concept tree via the operations add, search, delete concept nodes or get the concept identity when adding new knowledge. In a large distributed system, this concept tree can be cached at each local node to reduce the communication cost because the number of operations of add/delete a concept node is very small compared to the number of search operations.

Secondly, the division of knowledge map into two main components (local and core) has some advantages: (i) the core component acts as a summary map of knowledge and it is a representation of knowledge about knowledge when combined with local *KM*; (ii) avoiding the problem of having the whole knowledge on one master node (or server), which is not feasible on very large distributed systems such as Grid. By representing knowledge meta-data by their relationship links, the goal is to provide an integration view of these knowledge.

Finally, this approach offers a knowledge map with flexible and dynamic architecture where users can easily update the *concept tree* repository as well as meta-knowledge entries. The current index technique used in a rule representative is an inverted list. However, we can improve it without affecting to whole system structure by using other index algorithms [38] or by applying compressed technique as discussed in [53]. Moreover, flexible and dynamic features are also reflected by mapping a knowledge to a *knowledge object*. The goal here is to provide a portable approach where knowledge object can be represented by different techniques such as an entity, an XML-based record, or a record of database, etc.

Another important discussion is the implementation of knowledge core. In the 1–n model, this component is implemented at the server node. However, as explained in the second paragraph of this section, the search operation time is higher than retrieve operation time because of the number of meta-knowledge entries. This will become a crucial bottleneck in a large-scale distributed system where only one server is dedicated to handle meta-knowledge of all other client nodes. An efficient solution is to use some nodes that can act as servers; i.e. each site handles the meta-knowledge of a group of client nodes. Nevertheless, which nodes will be chosen

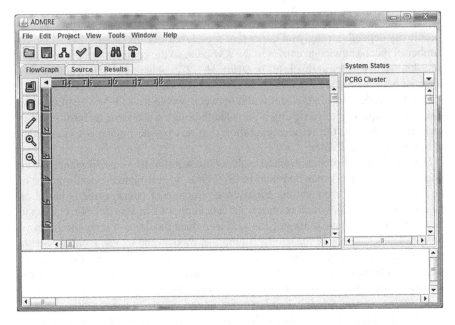

Fig. 9.7 *DDM* system interface

and under which criteria is not a straightforward task because one should satisfy the
constraints related to the network topology, nodes' performance, etc.

9.6 Exploitation

9.6.1 Interface

The upper of the interface layer is a graphical user interface (GUI) (Fig. 9.7) allowing the development and the execution of DDM applications. By using this interface,
users can build an *DDM* job including one or many tasks via building an executing
flow chart. A task contains either one of the DM techniques such as classification,
association rules, clustering, prediction or other data operations such as data preprocessing, data distribution. Firstly, users choose a tasks and then they browse and
choose resources that are represented by graphic objects, such as computing nodes,
datasets, DM tools and algorithms correspondent to DM technique chosen. These
resources are either on local site or distributed on different heterogeneity sites with
heterogeneous platforms. However, this system allows users to interact with them
transparently at this level. The second step in the building of a DDM job is to establish links between tasks chosen, i.e. the execution order. By checking this order, this
system can detect independent tasks that can be executed concurrently. Furthermore,
users can also use this interface to publish new DM tools and algorithms. Besides,

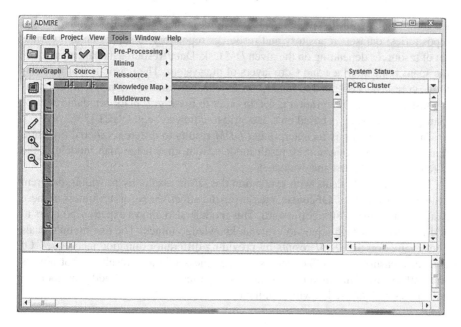

Fig. 9.8 System tools

users can separately execute mining and preprocessing tasks provided (e.g for testing purposes) by choosing appropriate tools supplied by the system (Fig. 9.8).

This layer allows to visualize, represent as well as to evaluate results of a *DDM* application too. The discovered knowledges will be represented in many defined forms such as graphical, geometric, etc. This system supports different visualization techniques which are applicable to data of certain types (discrete, continual, point, scalar or vector) and dimensions (1-D, 2-D, 3-D). It also supports the interactive visualization which allows users to view the *DDM* results in different perspectives such as layers, levels of detail and help them to understand these results better. Besides the GUI, there are four modules in this layer: *DDM* task management, Data/Resource management, interpretation and evaluation.

The first module spans both Interface and Core layers of the system. The part in the Interface layer of this module is responsible for mapping user requirements via selected *DM* tasks and their resources to an executing schema of tasks correspondent. Another role of this part is to check the coherence between *DM* tasks of this executing schema for a given *DDM* job. The purpose of this checking is, as mentioned above, to detect independent tasks and then this schema is refined to obtain an optimal execution. After verifying the executing schema, this module stores it in a task repository that will be used by the lower part of this task management module in the core layer to execute this *DDM* job.

The second module allows to browse necessary resources in a set of resources proposed by system. This module manages the meta-data of all the available datasets and resources (computing nodes, *DM* algorithms and tools) published. The part in the Interface layer of this module is based on these meta-data that are stored in two repositories: datasets repository and resources repository to supply an appropriate set of resources depending on the given *DM* task. Data/Resource management module spans both Interface and Core layers of the system. The reason is that modules in the core layer also need to interact with data and resources to perform data mining tasks as well as integration tasks. In order to mask grid platform, data/resource management module is based on a data grid middleware, e.g. DGET [33].

The third module is for interpreting *DDM* results to different ordered presentation forms. Integrating/mining result models from knowledge map module in the core layer is explained and evaluated.

The last module deals with evaluation the *DDM* results by providing different evaluation techniques. Of course, measuring the effectiveness or usefulness of these results is not always straightforward. This module also allows experienced users to add new tools or techniques to evaluate knowledge mined. The last module deals with evaluation the *DDM* results by providing different evaluation techniques. Of course, measuring the effectiveness or usefulness of these results is not always straightforward. This module also allows experienced users to add new tools or techniques to evaluate knowledge mined.

9.6.2 An Example of Exploiting the DDM System via Knowledge Map

KM (cf. Sect. 9.5) is implemented and integrated in the *DDM* system (Fig. 9.9). In this version, repositories of *KM core* and *Local KM* are in XML format. *KM* daemons are initially created by using the primitive "*init*". The primitive "*stop*" will terminate all the *KM Daemons*. A *KM* application can send requests to one or many remote sites.

As shown in Fig. 9.10, for example, we first search all the meta-knowledge needed via primitive "find". The user can launch this task via either a command line or graphical user interface (Fig. 9.10). We extract knowledge via primitive "retrieve". As an example with the system's GUI, Fig. 9.11 shows a screenshot of meta-knowledge found in DBDC [34] clustering task. The user can decide which knowledge to be retrieved by selecting an appropriate row and then click on the retrieve button. In Fig. 9.12 an example of a retrieved knowledge which is represented by a tree is shown. An important remark is that the users do not take into account the location of knowledge when searching/retrieving it.

Next, we present two scenarios of using knowledge map in the system. In the first one, the mined knowledge already exist at different sites of the system. In the second scenario, a distributed data mining task is executed on a system such as cluster or gird. In the first scenario, if the meta-knowledge of those mined knowledge have not been handled by the knowledge map, then the first step is to use knowledge map tool to create knowledge objects and store them in each site (*local KM*). Their *meta-knowledge* will be automatically submitted to the *meta-knowledge repository*

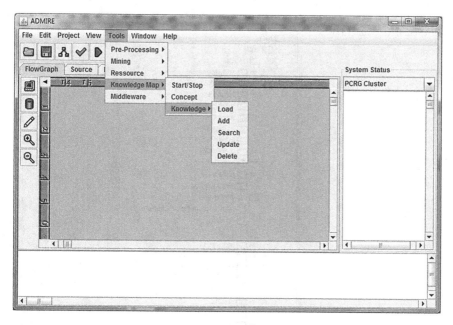

Fig. 9.9 Knowledge map integrated in the *DDM* system

Fig. 9.10 Screenshot of searching meta-knowledge [37]

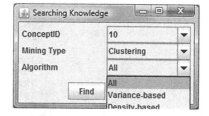

Fig. 9.11 Screenshot of retrieving knowledge basing on meta-knowledge chosen [37]

at the *knowledge core map*. The users can also add more appropriate concepts to their knowledge. This step needs more interactions with the user. The user, then, can exploit these meta-knowledge and knowledge object in their integration process or only explore the knowledge. In the second scenario, after the local mining processes have been completed, the local mined knowledge is built in each site. Its meta-

Fig. 9.12 Knowledge
retrieved, tree format [37]

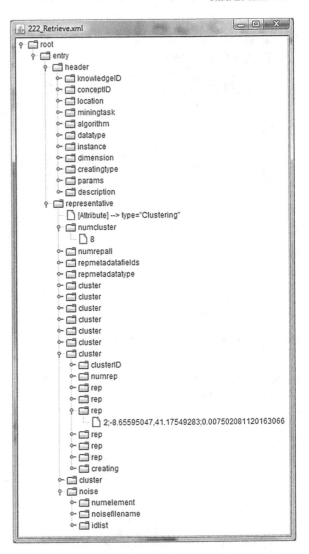

knowledge is created and stored in local repository. Then, the integration process
uses these meta-knowledge to retrieve information required.

9.7 Related Works of DDM Frameworks on Grid Platforms

We present three most recent *DDM* projects for heterogeneous data and platforms:
Knowledge Grid [15, 16], Grid Miner [9, 10] and Discovery Net [20]. The first two
projects use Globus Toolkit [31] as a Grid middleware.

9.7.1 Knowledge Grid

Knowledge Grid (KG) is a framework for implementing distributed knowledge discovery. This framework aims to deal with multi-owned, heterogeneous data. This project is developed by Cannataro el al. at University "Magna Graecia" of Catanzaro, Italy. The architecture of KG is composed of two layers: Core K-Grid and High level K-Grid.

The first layer includes Knowledge Directory service (KDS), Resource allocation and execution management service (RAEMS). KDS manages metadata: data sources, data mining (DM) software, results of computation, etc. that are saved in KDS repositories. There are three kinds of repositories: Knowledge Metadata Repository for storing data, software tool, coded information in XML; Knowledge Base Repository that stores all information about the knowledge discovered after parallel and distributed knowledge discovery (PDKD) computation. Knowledge Execution Plan Repository stores execution plans describing PDKD applications over the grid. RAEMS attempts to map an execution plan to available resource on the grid. This mapping must satisfy users, data and algorithms requirements as well as their constraints.

High level layer supplies four service groups used to build and execute PDKD computations: Data Access Service (DAS), Tools and Algorithms Access Service (TASS), Execution Plan Management Service (EPMS) and Results Presentation Service (RPS). The first service group is used for the search, selection, extraction, transformation, and delivery of data. The second one deals with the search, selection, download DM tools and algorithms. Generating a set of different possible execution plans is the responsible of the third group. The last one allows to generate, present and visualize the PDKD results.

The advantage of KG framework that it supports distributed data analysis and knowledge discovery and knowledge management services by integrating and completing the data grid services. However this approach only concerns the distributed architecture but not *DDM* algorithms. Besides, KG does not provide a management of knowledge metadata in their relationships to support the integration view of the knowledge as well as the coordination of different local mining processes. There is moreover no distinct separation in between resource, data, and knowledge.

9.7.2 GridMiner

GridMiner is an infrastructure for distributed data mining and data integration in Grid environments. This infrastructure is developed at Institute for Software Science, University of Vienna. GridMiner is a OGSA-based data mining approach. In this approach, distributed heterogeneous data must be integrated and mediated by using OGSA-DAI [43] before passing data mining phase. Therefore, they have divided data distribution in four data sources scenarios: single, federate horizontal partitioning, federate vertical partitioning and federate heterogeneity.

The structure of GridMiner consists of some elements: Service Factory (GMSF) for creating and managing services; Service Registry (GMSR) that is based on standard OGSA registry service; DataMining Service (GMDMS) that provides a set of data mining, data analysis algorithms; PreProcessing Service (GMPPS) for data cleaning, integration, handling missing data, etc.; Presentation Service (GMPRS) and Orchestration Service (GMOrchS) for handling complex and long-running jobs.

The advantages of GridMiner is that it is an integration of Data Mining and Grid computing. Moreover, it can take advances from OGSA. However, it depends on Globus ToolKit as well as OGSA-DAI for controlling data mining and other activities across Grid platforms. Besides, distributed heterogeneous data must be integrated before the mining process. This approach is not appropriate for complex heterogeneous scenarios.

9.7.3 Discovery Net

Discovery Net project proposes an architecture to support the knowledge discovery process on Grid platforms.

Discovery Net (*DN*) architecture is composed of three main components: Knowledge Servers, Resource Discovery Server and Meta-information Server. The first component is a warehouse of information about discovery process performed by *DN*. It provides three main functions: storage service, reporting service and application generation service. The Resource Discovery Server component is a registry server which is used to deploy and map services to computational resources for execution. The last component is responsible for the management of data types used by services in the system.

A remarkable pros of this architecture is that it is based on the service model concept and can be used on any service-based Grid platforms. However, as Knowledge Grid resumed above, this approach does not concerns *DDM* algorithms.

9.8 Conclusion

In this chapter, we have presented a *DDM* system based on Grid environments to execute new distributed data mining techniques on very large and distributed heterogeneous datasets. The architecture and motivation for the design have been presented. We have also discussed some related projects and compared them with our approach. We have developed prototypes for each layer of the system to evaluate the system features, test each layer as well as whole framework and building simulation and *DDM* test suites.

Knowledge map layer, key layer of this system, is integrated in this framework. Experimental results on real-world applications are also produced [37] and allow us to test and evaluate the system robustness and the distributed data mining approaches at very large scale. Throughout estimations of each component and its functionality, we can conclude that knowledge map is an efficient system in a large-scale and distributed environment. It satisfies the needs for managing, exploring, and retrieving the mined knowledge of *DDM* in large distributed environment.We are currently working on the knowledge map structure that takes in account the network and the distributed system (such as Grid) features. These features include the mapping of the knowledge map onto a virtual network topology such as *TreeP*.

DDM algorithms presented in Sect. 9.4 above are also being integrated in the system in the module of distributed data mining techniques. The preliminary evaluation of our approach shows that it is efficient and flexible.

In the future works, more *DDM* algorithms will be developed and integrated in this system. Besides, a workflow engine will also be built on the top of the system in order to conduct efficient implementations on the Grid at both the application level and the knowledge management level.

References

1. Agrawal, R., Shafer, J.C.: Parallel mining of association rules. IEEE Transactions on Knowledge and Data Engineering **8**, 962–969 (1996)
2. Agrawal, R., Srikant, R.: Fast algorithms for mining association rules. In: VLDB'94: Proceedings of the 20th Int. Conf. Very Large Data Bases, Santiago de Chile, Chile, September 12–15, 1994
3. Alsabti, K., Ranka, S., Singh, V.: A one-pass algorithm for accurately estimating quantiles for disk-resident data. In: Proceedings of the VLDE'97 Conference, pp. 346–355. Morgan Kaufmann, San Francisco (1997)
4. Aouad, L.M., Le-Khac, N.-A., Kechadi, M.-T.: Lightweight clustering technique for distributed data mining applications. In: The 7th Industrial Conference on Data Mining ICDM 2007. Lecture Notes in Artificial Intelligence, vol. 4597. Springer, Berlin (2007)
5. Aouad, L.M., Le-Khac, N.-A., Kechadi, M.-T.: A multi-stage clustering algorithm for distributed data mining environments. In: COSI 2008, Colloque sur l'Optimisation et les Systèmes d'Information (2008)
6. Aouad, L.M., Le-Khac, N.-A., Kechadi, M.-T.: Performance study of distributed apriori-like frequent itemset mining, University College Dublin, Technical report (2008)
7. Aronis, J., Kulluri, V., Provost, F., Buchanan, B.: The WoRLD: Knowledge discovery and multiple distributed databases. In: Proceedings of Florida Artificial Intelligence Research Symposium (FLAIRS-97) (1997)
8. Bauer, E., Kohavi, R.: An empirical comparison of voting classification algorithms: Bagging, boosting, and variants. Machine Learning **36**, 105–139 (1999)
9. Brezany, P., Hofer, J., Tjoa, A., Wohrer, A.: GridMiner: An infrastructure for data mining on computational grids. In: Data Mining on Computational Grids APAC'03 Conference, Gold Coast, Australia, October 2003
10. Brezany, P., Janciak, I., Woehrer, A., Tjoa, A.: GridMiner: A framework for knowledge discovery on the Grid—from a vision to design and implementation. In: Cracow Grid Workshop, Cracow, December 2004, pp. 12–15 (2004)
11. Brin, S., Motwani, R., Ullman, J.D., Tsur, S.: Dynamic itemset counting and implication rules for market basket data. In: SIGMOD'97: Proceedings ACM SIGMOD Int. Conf. on Management of Data, Tucson, Arizona, USA, May 13–15, 1997
12. Buchanan, B.G., Shortliffe, E.H.: Rule-Based Expert Systems: The MYCIN Experiments of The Standford Heuristic Programming Projects. Addison-Wesley, Reading (1984)
13. Buzan, T., Buzan, B.: The Mind Map Book. Plume, New York (1996)

14. Calinski, R.B., Harabasz, J.: A dendrite method for cluster analysis. Communication in Statistics Journal **3**(1), 1–27 (1974)
15. Cannataro, M., et al.: A data mining toolset for distributed high performance platforms. In: Proc. of the 3rd International Conference on Data Mining Methods and Databases for Engineering, Finance and Others Fields, pp. 41–50. WIT Press, Southampton (2002)
16. Cannataro, M., Talia, D., Trunfio, P.: Distributed data mining on the grid. Future Generation Computer Systems **18**(8), 1101–1112 (2002)
17. Chan, P., Stolfo, S.: Toward parallel and distributed learning by meta-learning. In: Working Notes AAAI Workshop in Knowledge Discovery in Databases, pp. 227–240. AAAI Press, Menlo Park (1993)
18. Chattratichat, J., et al.: An architecture for distributed enterprise data mining. In: HPCN Europe, pp. 573–582. Springer, Heidelberg (1999)
19. Chen, S.M., Ke, J.-S., Chang, J.-F.: Knowledge representation using fuzzy Petri nets. IEEE Transactions on Knowledge and Data Engineering **2**(3), 311–319 (1990)
20. Curcin, V., Ghanem, M., Guo, Y., Kohler, M., Rowe, A., Syed, J., Wendel, P.: Discovery net: towards a grid of knowledge discovery. In: Proceedings of the Eighth ACM SIGKDD International Conference on Knowledge Discovery and Data Mining, Edmonton, Alberta, Canada, pp. 658–663. ACM, New York (2002)
21. Czajkowski, K., et al.: The WS-resource framework, Version 1.0. http://www-106.ibm.com/developerworks/library/ws-resource/ws-wsrf.pdf
22. Davenport, T.H., Prusak, L.: Working Knowledge. Harvard Business School Press, Cambridge (1998)
23. Deng, Y., Chang, S.-K.: A G-net model for knowledge representation and reasoning. IEEE Transactions on Knowledge and Data Engineering **2**(3), 295–310 (1990)
24. Dietterich, T.G.: An experimental comparison of three methods for constructing ensembles of decision trees: Bagging, boosting and randomization. Machine Learning **40**, 139–158 (2000)
25. Dunham, M.H.: Data Mining Introductory and Advanced Topics. Prentice-Hall, Englewood Cliffs (2002)
26. Eppler, M.J.: Making knowledge visible through intranet knowledge maps: Concepts, elements, cases. In: Proceedings of the 34th Hawaii International Conference on System Sciences (2001)
27. Forman, G., Zhang, B.: Distributed data clustering can be efficient and exact. In: SIGKDD Explorations, vol. 2 (2000)
28. Foster, I., Kesselman, C.: The Grid: Blueprint for a New Computing Infrastructure, pp. 593–620. Morgan Kaufmann, Los Altos (2004)
29. Foster, I., Kesselman, C., Nick, J., Tuecke, S.: The physiology of the grid: An open grid services architecture for distributed systems integration. http://www.globus.org/research/papers/ogsa.pdf
30. Freitas, A.A., Lavington, S.H.: Mining Very Large Databases with Parallel Processing. Kluwer Academic, Dordrecht (1998)
31. Globus Tool Kit website: http://www.globus.org
32. Han, J., Pei, J., Yin, Y.: Mining frequent patterns without candidate generation. In: Proceedings of the 2000 ACM SIGMOD International Conference on Management of Data, Dallas, Texas, USA (2000).
33. Hudzia, B., McDermott, L., Illahi, T.N., Kechadi, M.-T.: Entity based peer-to-peer in a data grid environment. In: Proc. of 17th IMACS World Congress Scientific Computation, Applied Mathematics and Simulation, Paris, France, July 2005, pp. 11–15 (2005)
34. Januzaj, E., Kriegel, H.-P., Pfeifle, M.: DBDC: Density-based distributed clustering. In: Proc. of 9th Int. Conf. on Extending Database Technology (EDBT), Heraklion, Greece, pp. 88–105 (2004)
35. Joshi, M., et al.: Parallel algorithms for data mining. In: CRPC Parallel Computing Handbook. Morgan Kaufmann, San Francisco (2000)
36. Le-Khac, N.-A., Aouad, L.M., Kechadi, M.-T.: An efficient support management tool for distributed data mining environments. In: 2nd IEEE International Conference on Digital Information Management (ICDIM'07), Lyon, France, October 28–31, 2007

37. Le-Khac, N.-A., Aouad, L.M., Kechadi, M.-T.: An efficient knowledge management tool for distributed data mining environments. International Journal of Computational Intelligence Research **5**(1), 5–15 (2009)
38. Martynov, M., Novikov, B.: An indexing algorithm for text retrieval. In: Proceedings of the International Workshop on Advances in Databases and Information System (ADBIS'96), Moscow, pp. 171–175 (1996)
39. Merz, C.J., Pazzani, M.J.: A principal components approach to combining regression estimates. Machine Learning **36**, 9–32 (1999)
40. Mingjin, Y., Keying, Y.: Determining the number of clusters using the weighted gap statistic. Biometrics **63**(4), 1031–1037 (2007)
41. Ng, R.T., Han, J.: Efficient and effective clustering methods for spatial data mining. In: VLDB, Proceedings of 20th International Conference on Very Large Data Bases, Santiago de Chile, Chile, September 12–15, 1994
42. Novak, J.D., Gowin, D.B.: Learning How to Learn. Cambridge University Press, Cambridge (1984)
43. OGSA-DAI website: http://www.ogsadai.org.uk/
44. Park, J.S., Chen, M.-S., Yu, P.S.: An effective hash-based algorithm for mining association rules. In: SIGMOD'95: Proceedings of the 1995 ACM SIGMOD International Conference on Management of Data, San Jose, California, USA (1995)
45. Peterson, J.-L.: Petri nets. ACM Computing Surveys **9**(3), 223–252 (1977)
46. Purdom, P.W., Van Gucht, D., Groth, D.P.: Average-case performance of the Apriori algorithm. SIAM Journal on Computing **33**(5) (2004)
47. Savasere, A., Omiecinski, E., Navathe, S.B.: An efficient algorithm for mining association rules in large databases. In: VLDB'95: Proceedings of the 21st International Conference on Very Large Databases, Zurich, Switzerland (1995)
48. Schuster, A., Wolff, R., Trock, D.: A high-performance distributed algorithm for mining association rules. In: ICDM'03: Proceedings of the Third IEEE International Conference on Data Mining, Melbourne, Florida, USA (2003)
49. Tibshirani, R., Walther, G., Hastie, T.: Estimating the number of clusters in a dataset via the gap statistic. Stanford University (2000)
50. Wexler, M.N.: The who, what and why of knowledge mapping. Journal of Knowledge Management **5**, 249–263 (2001)
51. Xu, R., Wunsch, D.: Survey of clustering algorithms. IEEE Transactions on Neural Networks **16**(3), 645–678 (2005)
52. Zhang, B., Hsu, M., Dayal, U.: k-harmonic means—A data clustering algorithm, HP Labs (1999)
53. Zobel, J., Moffat, A.: Inverted files for text search engines. ACM Computing Surveys **38**(2), Article 6 (2006)

Chapter 10
Metamodel of Ontology Learning from Text

Marek Wisniewski

Abstract Ontologies play a pervasive role in many areas of IT. Over the last decade a substantial number of ontologies have been developed. However, while looking for a specific ontology it is difficult to find the right one because of the problems of the ontology unavailability or inadequacy. Although many ontology learning methods already exist, there are no comprehensive models of the whole process of the ontology learning from text. In this article, the metamodel of the ontology learning from text is presented. The approach is based on the survey of the existing methods, while evaluation is provided in the form of a reference implementation of the introduced metamodel.

10.1 Motivation

Electronic commerce was one of the first domains of IT that took advantage of the Internet's potential. A family of EDI standards allowed parties to run business on an unprecedented scale. Standardization initiatives on a technical level enable convenient and efficient data exchange [68]. But moving a traditional provisioning scheme to the Internet requires seamless and secure information and knowledge flow. Therefore, it is necessary to understand in what ways the conceptualizations, which comprise the subject of an electronic market exchange, are to be gathered, represented, shared and processed both by human users and intelligent agents.

The Semantic Web vision [10] lays out foundations for an information exchange among parties collaborating on an electronic market. Exchange, in which ontologies provide shared vocabularies (conceptualisms) that precise the meaning of data, and intelligent agents which, on behalf of the users, gather and exchange semantically enriched information.

Achievements in the ontology domain allow for an unambiguous representation of concepts that are understood both by human users and appropriately constructed

M. Wisniewski
Poznan University of Economics, Al. Niepodleglosci 10, Poznan, Poland

Y. Badr et al. (eds.) *Emergent Web Intelligence: Advanced Semantic Technologies,*
Advanced Information and Knowledge Processing,
DOI 10.1007/978-1-84996-077-9_10, © Springer-Verlag London Limited 2010

computer programs [50]. Ontology languages, such as RDF[1] and OWL[2] are the standards of W3C[3] organization which disseminates the most important technologies related to the information systems interoperability on a technical and semantic level.

The semantic e-commerce is the commerce that is run with the help of electronic means, in which the exchanged information is enriched with semantics. The semantic e-commerce is the approach to knowledge management in the processes that occur on the electronic market by the systematic application of Semantic Web technologies [90].

Electronic commerce consists of a few segments which acronyms relate to the class of involved parties. The motivation for the presented work continues with the B2C (business-to-customer) segment.

B2C segment includes four distinct perspectives:

- Consumer perspective whose aim is to search for product or service information.
- Deliverer perspective that delivers products and services information taken from different producers.
- Producer perspective that manufactures products or delivers services.
- Broker perspective that mediates between producers and consumers (e.g. auction platforms).

All the above mentioned actors interoperate on the electronic market. The nature of their collaboration and the State-of-the-Art technologies applied in the B2C segment implicates a variety of problems, i.e.:

Product or service search E-commerce allowed for a faster and cheaper access to products and services. Barriers of a physical and time nature have been minimized in comparison with a traditional access. However, finding a particular product or service is still a time consuming activity, especially when unknown web sites are visited or a product does not have a standard set of constraints. Scenarios related to searching illustrate the problems of terms and concepts ambiguity. Terms ambiguity relates to the situation where a term relates to many concepts, whereas concept ambiguity relates to the situation where a concept is represented by many terms. For instance, when looking for a handheld device, we expect the search engine to return not only devices from class "handheld device", but also "PDA" or even "Smartphone".

Filtering Websites collect all sorts of information about users, either directly (forms) or indirectly (navigation or interaction history). This information is represented as a user profile. Profile building processes are dedicated to the specific deliverers. A user profile that is constructed by the deliverer cannot be applied in other places. There are no shared vocabularies that allow for a standardization of building and managing user profiles across many web applications.

---

[1] http://www.w3.org/RDF/.

[2] http://www.w3.org/2004/OWL/.

[3] http://www.w3.org/.

Market transparency E-commerce drastically increased the market transparency. However, a product comparison is still inconvenient because of ambiguity problems. A smart construction of deliverers' application or additional information can precise the meaning. But still, these methods are auxiliary, ineffective in a case of machine processing.

Services maturity The majority of deliverers not only allow for browsing and navigating product catalogs, but also transaction processing. The next level of development is the process automation, e.g. the automation of goods delivery. Many businesses allow for this kind of the automation purely on technical and organizational levels. Exchanged data hardly ever conveys any semantics which are needed for the process automation.

Negotiations E-commerce requires parties to negotiate the terms for a service provisioning (e.g. SLAs). Tools for negotiations that involve an electronic data exchange need to use a standardized, common and shared conceptualization.

The crucial challenge for the tools used in electronic commerce is building a formal, shared conceptualization, i.e. ontology. The thesis has been confirmed both in cognitive [58] and technical science [36, 99].

Ontologies comprise an active branch of research in IT [50, 51]. The first commonly used definition of ontology was popularized by Thomas Gruber in 1993 [42]: "An ontology is a shared specification of a conceptualization". The elaboration of this definition is provided in [43].

Ontologies are different, which results from different sources of ontology research including philosophy and Artificial Intelligence. A popular classification includes three levels of ontologies [73]:

1. Upper level ontologies reflecting philosophical relations among entities, such as SUMO [77].
2. Domain ontologies that reflect entities and relations in key application domains, such as IT or biology. Their utilization is constrained to the domain applications, but they are not specific enough to satisfy the needs of a particular application.
3. Application ontologies that define the entities for a specific subdomain or a particular application.

The more detailed a domain is, the less ontologies one can actually use. For instance, it is much more feasible to use upper level ontology in e-commerce (although only a few concepts are really helpful) than ontology related to molecular biology (a specific domain with no common concepts at all). As a result, the fine-grained ontology for e-commerce is difficult to find.

The existing ontology repositories, such as SchemaWeb,[4] DAML library[5] or Swoogle[6] provide a possibility to search through many already existing and ready to use ontologies.

---

[4] http://www.schemaweb.info.

[5] http://www.daml.org/ontologies/.

[6] http://swoogle.umbc.edu/.

The SchemaWeb library allows for browsing through 240 ontologies.[7] Unfortunately, the majority of ontologies are related to standards. One may find ontologies for RDF, OWL-S, vcard, BibTeX, ACL, WordNet, etc.

The DAML library hosts links to 282 ontologies.[8] The repository allows for a convenient navigation by a few well defined attributes, including URI, key words, date of submission or a responsible organization. The DAML library provides CYC—the well-known upper level ontology. The number of domain ontologies in comparison to SchemaWeb is much higher.

Swoogle is not a classic library. Swoogle is a search engine for semantically annotated documents. Annotated documents make use of concepts and relations that are part of some ontologies. The relation is explicit. As a result, a user can easily track the ontologies that stand behind the semantically annotated documents. Swoogle is an important source, because the number of hosted documents amounts to 878 462 that consists in total of 609 639 517 statements.[9]

The repositories make an illusory impression that the much needed ontologies are at hand. Unfortunately, there are several problems with getting the right ontology:

1. In most cases the domain of an application is specific and ready to use ontologies simply do not exist.
2. Even if similar ontologies exist, their scope is not covering exactly the same part of the domain. For instance, there is one well known ontology for e-commerce, namely eClassOWL that covers the relations among concepts such as IT products and services [49]. However, constraints defined by the typical scenarios in B2C segment make eClassOWL ontology difficult to accept. The problem is more general as the exact shape of the ontology will be different from application to application, even within the same domain.
3. The level of the ontology might not meet the desired level (the ontology might be too general or too detailed).

Therefore, the problem of ontology unavailability or inadequacy appears. As a result, the researchers turn to ontology building methods as the only ones capable of providing the right ontologies.

The process of the ontology building has been called the ontology engineering. There are two classes of ontology engineering methods: manual and automatic. Manual methods of the ontology engineering [29, 81] allow for a fine-grained and precise definition of an ontology, but they are expensive to construct. For the purposes of a cost estimation some authors proposed specific models [89].

The ontology engineering process can be partly or fully unsupervised. Semisupervised or unsupervised ontology engineering has been called the ontology learning [14]. The level of supervision is dependent on the expert involvement or the necessity of model training.

---

[7]Last updated: 4.04.2008.

[8]Last updated: 4.04.2008.

[9]Last updated: 4.04.2008.

10.2 A Survey of Ontology Learning Methods

A comprehensive approach to a definition of the ontology learning process has been conducted twice. Both the process defined in [63] and the one depicted in [23] concern a sequence of subsequent tasks that have to be run in order to construct a full ontology, but they both concern a different set of layers.

The process introduced by [63] is more general. It is comprised of the extraction phase, the construction phase and the ontology pruning. The process dictates a clear but strict division between the linguistic analysis phase (term extraction), actual ontology construction and the phase where resulting ontology is adjusted to the real needs of an application. The last phase is characteristic as it stresses an importance for a final pruning of an ontology for a particular task, application or domain. In most modern approaches for the ontology learning these phases are overlapping, for instance, a domain term filtering is part of a linguistic analysis [69] or a linguistic analysis is performed during the ontology construction phase [65].

The process defined in [23] is more detailed and it classifies identified and researched problems better. The ontology learning process is composed of the following, subsequent extraction tasks:

- terms,
- synonyms,
- concepts,
- taxonomic relations,
- non-taxonomic relations,
- rules.

The illustration of the ontology learning process as defined by [23] is depicted in Fig. 10.1 and shows a symbolic reduction in the number of analyzed objects. An analysis of terms results in the highest number of outcomes. Layer by layer,

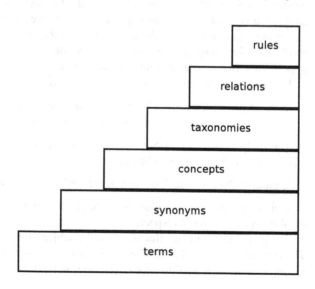

Fig. 10.1 The layered approach to the ontology learning process [23]

the number of results is lower. The last layer produces the least number of objects. However, many current approaches to the ontology learning treats this dependency rather loosely. For instance, some approaches perform the term or concept extraction along with the relation extraction ([4] as a notable example). Surprisingly, there are still only a few approaches that cover all the phases. In most cases, solutions focus on a particular phase.

10.2.1 Terms

Terms are basic objects in the ontology learning process. They express a semantically uniform phrase within a text in the form of a word or a group of words. Terms can be extracted by applying methods based on NLP or statistical analysis. Most current approaches combine both of these method classes, thus applying the hybrid approach. Usually, a linguistic method is called for an actual term extraction and a statistical method is used to perform an evaluation of terms usefulness for a domain or an application.

Statistical methods are the most popular since they are dependent only on statistical measures which are simple to implement and apply. They also do not require a linguistic annotation which is quite often a very compelling attribute. However, the linguistic methods are in most cases more effective [104].

10.2.1.1 Linguistic Methods

Linguistic methods consist in performing a linguistic analysis to a text [67] and then applying extraction patterns on the generated linguistic information. The linguistic analysis results in linguistic information in the form of an annotated text or annotation sets. This information presents a valuable source not only for the term extraction, but also for any subsequent phase of the ontology learning process. The mechanism for a linguistic method is built on rules or extraction patterns. The most popular pattern classifies all found nouns as terms.

Linguistic methods utilize two classes of extraction methods:

- based on part of speeches (POS tagging), also referred as shallow text processing,
- based on text structure dependencies, also known as deep text processing.

The analysis based on POS relies on a classification of each word. The linguistic information of the following phrase:

Canonical(NP) intends(VB) to(TO) merge(VB) two(CD) distributions(NNS)

classifies the words to the following word classes: proper noun, verb, to, verb, cardinality and noun plural, respectively.

The prepared linguistic information is the subject of a surface patterns definition. These patterns use POS classification and an order of words. The linguistic information prepared for shallow processing does not consist of any information on the

Table 10.1 A set of linguistic information for a deep text processing

	Token	POS	Head	Relation to head
1	Canonical	proper noun	–	–
2	intends	verb	1	noun-verb
3	to	preposition	4	verb-preposition
4	merge	verb	2	verb-verb
5	two	cardinal number	5	noun-cardinality
6	distributions	noun plural	4	verb-noun

logical relations in a sentence. The example surface pattern defines a noun phrase as a sequence of occurring nouns (e.g. NN, NN). The usual practice is to apply the lemmatization to analyze only the base form of a word.

The analysis based on POS is the basic method in the popular NLP systems [30, 52, 70, 82]. Surface patterns can be defined in specific rule languages, such as JAPE [31].

The analysis based on structure dependencies is more complex. Apart from the linguistic information about a word, its position within a sentence and a POS classification, it additionally utilizes the information about a phrase, i.e. a structure that lies behind the sequence of words. This relation is represented by a binary relation between words, e.g. a head of a word and a modifier. For instance, the example phrase might result in the set of linguistic information depicted in Table 10.1.

The last column is the binary relation that is produced between the head and the modifier, two logically connected words. This relation is the basic element of extraction methods based on a dependency structure. Patterns that are built on a dependency structure are called syntactic patterns as opposed to surface patterns (only POS).

The term extraction task is heavily dependent on the natural language. Each natural language needs it own linguistic tools, such as tokenizers, lemmatizers and structure dependency processing tools.

Term extraction based on surface and syntactic patterns are domains that evolve rapidly. Research aimed at the increase of effectiveness is conducted in many natural languages. English is traditionally a subject of most investigations but most other popular languages are also studied.

10.2.1.2 Statistical Methods

In general, statistical methods rely on the frequency of words. The methods can vary from a co-occurrence analysis to a distribution of a word occurrence within a domain or a corpus. For instance, the terms *computer* and *table* are equally popular in general, but their frequency of occurrence within IT and carpentry domains is substantially different.

The most popular measures for statistical term extraction are:

• Mutual information—co-occurrence analysis,

- TFIDF, KFIDF [107],
- C/NC [39],
- χ^2.

TFIDF is the most popular measure:

$$\text{TFIDF}(w) = \text{tf}(w) \cdot \log \frac{N}{\text{df}(w)} \tag{1}$$

where:

- TFIDF(w) is the relative importance of a word within the document,
- tf(w) is the frequency of a word (the number of occurrences within the document),
- df(w) is the frequency of a document (the number of documents containing a word),
- N is the number of documents.

TFIDF measure describes the term relevance in the document based on its frequency of occurrences within a document and a corpus. The higher frequency in the document and lower in the corpus, the more important a term is. TFIDF is extremely popular in document indexing, where the uniqueness of a term guarantees its distinction within a corpus. The classic TFIDF measure, serves rather an auxiliary role in term extraction because the distinction criteria are sometimes not important. Still, TFIDF is a popular choice but it is used in conjunction with other methods.

10.2.2 Synonyms

The second task of ontology learning process deals with an analysis of terms. Terms quite often refer to the same concept which is determined by their similarity. A similarity is a relational characteristic. The exact degree of a similarity between given terms is dependent on the actual context. For instance, the terms: "handheld device", "PDA" and "Smartphone" are very similar from the perspective of biology. But from the perspective of an electronic goods producer they are a completely different class of products. The problem is difficult, because 100% synonyms do not exist. We can say about some level of a similarity that holds under certain conditions.

The synonym extraction task analyzes terms and defines sets of terms that are characterized by their high degree of similarity. The basic methods for synonym extraction are classification and clustering algorithms [11, 12, 72, 74, 85]. The classification consists in an assignment to a certain class. The majority of methods use WordNet's synset classes [35] or equivalent linguistic sources with a synonymy relation present. The clustering methods apply popular statistical methods that measure the distribution of term attributes (e.g. a co-occurrence measure, such as Jaccard, Dice or cosine).

The task of synonym extraction also includes identification and translation of multilingual terms where additional linguistic sources are utilized (dictionaries).

Fig. 10.2 The meaning
triangle [96]

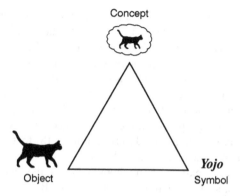

Alike synonyms translations are determined by a certain level of similarity and context attributes among different natural languages. In most multilingual approaches the extraction is a combination of approaches to different natural languages and an application of specific filters that increase the precision of extracted terms [41]. As a result, the effectiveness of term and synonym extraction methods is still the most important part.

10.2.3 Concepts

In the famous meaning triangle [78] a concept according to the upper level classification is an abstraction form [95]. A concept is a certain idea about the objects that exist and is depicted with symbols (Fig. 10.2).

The interpretation of meaning triangle is based on three levels of an abstraction. The actual black cat is represented by an object. A reference to the object is indicated by a symbol. Symbols are what is actually used in natural or formal languages. In the case of Fig. 10.2 the object is represented with the word *Yojo*. A symbolic representation is not constrained and in result, mapping from a symbol to an object or a concept is difficult. A class of objects, i.e. an abstract form of all objects is represented as a concept. The meaning triangle generates two fundamental problems:

- an ambiguity of terms (symbols), which means that a term can represent many objects (a term possess many meanings),
- a concept can be represented by many terms (a concept posses many designations).

These problems are a result of imprecise mapping of objects into concepts. The most likely cause is the improper symbol. In the case of ontology learning from text the processed symbols are basic constituents of text, namely tokens. The perfect concept extraction method aims at as precise as possible mapping of objects (represented by symbols, i.e. tokens) into ontology concepts.

Concept extraction methods come from abstract form definitions as depicted in [95]. The definition of an abstract form can be twofold. First of all, a concept can be defined as a combination of two or more already present concepts. It is semantically irrelevant whether a word "grandfather" is replaced by a phrase "father of father". This kind of a definition is useful whenever a fast and precise communication channel is required and present approaches make the channel noisy. A definition by a combination is known as *explicit definition*. The other method of a definition is in contradiction called *implicit definition*. It is not created from any other particular concepts, instead it defines a new concept based on certain conditions. A term might become a concept once it meets certain conditions. A popular formalism to perform such classifications is a description logic [8] that allow for a concept classification based on the actual value of their attributes.

Concept extraction methods rely on the explicit definition from linguistic sources, such as dictionaries or thesauri. By far the most used linguistic resource is WordNet [35] and its national equivalents (e.g. EuroWordNet [102] or GermaNet [46]).

10.2.4 Taxonomic Relations

The next phase of the ontology learning process is the extraction of taxonomic relations. The extraction process includes two types of relations: hypernymy and hyponymy. The former denotes the relation of class and its subclass, whereas the latter depicts the opposite relation. The currently used methods fall into one of the following categories:

- lexical-syntactic patterns [6, 47, 48, 60, 97],
- clustering [18, 19, 24, 26],
- linguistic approaches [15, 100],
- document subsumption [38, 87],
- taxonomy extensions [5, 63, 105, 106],
- combination of the above approaches [18, 20, 25, 93].

10.2.5 Non-taxonomic Relations

Existing relation extraction methods relate to a lexical-syntactic and linguistic analysis. The most popular methods consist in discovering *named non-taxonomic relations*. In this respect, also taxonomic relations are treated as named relations (*is-a*). The same principle applies to any new type of relations which are first named and only then extracted. As a result, most approaches are specific to one type of a relation.

The research has been conducted in the following four classes of approaches:

- Meronymy relation (*part-of*) which causes a problem of its exact definition that differs from one approach to the other. The meronymy can have a physical meaning as in *car-engine*, but also in *team-team members* and as well in *person-personality*. Therefore, the basic problem that a method should deal with is the precise definition of its scope and a subject. Chronologically first approach to the meronymy extraction is based on the surface pattern *X consists of Y* [22].

- Methods based on a *qualia structure* that defines the following four roles: formal, constitutive, telic and agentive [28, 108].
- A causation method based on an extraction of the pattern: *X leads to Y* [40].
- An attribute extraction on the basis of the pattern: *the X of Y* [83].

The utilization of a linguistic structure also allows for the extraction of *named non-taxonomic relations*. Similar approaches retrieve relations by an analysis of linguistic patterns. For instance, OntoLT [16] assigns a linguistic pattern represented as an XPath expression to an ontology object (a concept or a relation). TextToOnto [64] allows for a dependency between the concepts analysis and then its generalization.

10.2.6 Rules

The last phase of the ontology learning cycle consists in the information extraction that points to the axiomatic relations within a domain. Every domain has its own axioms, e.g. in an academic domain one can say that if a person works at the university she is either an academic staff or an administrative staff. Rules extraction methods are not bound to any specific logic formalism, however the most widely used is the first order logic and especially its Horn subset.

Unfortunately, there are not many methods that deal with the axiom extraction. Methods that use axioms treat them mainly as an input for other extraction tasks (as a supportive source of domain information). Approach presented in [62] suggests using frequently occurring relations between concepts as an indication for rule definition. A statistical analysis in [44] is used to generate exclusion rule definitions.

10.2.7 Ontology Learning Maps

In order to summarize the survey of the ontology learning from text approaches we have developed the ontology learning maps that depict recognized methods and relations among them. The ontology learning maps were built on the survey of approximately 50 relevant approaches.

According to the defined ontology learning process one can identify 6 different extraction tasks. In order to classify the methods into functionally cohesive areas and sketch a chronological order of relations and mainstreams of a research, we have decided to classify methods according to one of the extraction tasks. This classification is sometimes difficult to follow as some methods relate to more than just one task. In extreme cases, methods cover all extraction tasks [7].

The ontology learning maps are divided into a classification of terms, synonyms, concepts and a classification of relations.

10.2.7.1 Term, Synonym and Concept Extraction Methods

A survey of term, synonym and concept extraction methods is depicted on Fig. 10.3 which represents the most important methods and relations among them (source and development).

The most popular linguistic issues used in the process of the term, synonym and concept extraction are word sense disambiguation [109], collocation analysis [92] and anaphora resolution [84]. In a general case, all linguistic approaches over the years can be classified as term extraction methods. For clarity reasons we are excluding some of them as indicated in the metamodel in Sect. 10.3.2.1. The first method that introduced both linguistic and statistical analysis was [33].

The term, synonym and concept extraction for the ontology learning has been seriously treated since 2000. In 2000 the work presented in [86] as first serialized linguistic analysis results into a conceptual graphs introduced by John Sowa [94].

The presented survey shows that the map and the directions were shaped by individual research units.

The first research unit that contributed to the introduction of complex term and concept extraction methods was the team from Karlsruhe University under Rudi Studer's leadership. This team in 2000 worked out a number of methods based on linguistic, statistical and lexical analysis and put it into a tool On-To-Knowledge [37] that was the first publicly available application that allowed for method comparison. The team evolved up to now with tools such as TextToOnto [65, 66] and Text2Onto [27] being currently one of the most popular among researchers.

The next center that contributed substantially to the development of ontology learning extraction methods is the *Linguistic Computing Laboratory* at the University of Rome under a leadership of Paola Velardi.[10] The work of LCL is based on the flexible NLP tool Ariosto+Chaos [9] and relates to a definition and utilization of a domain relevance [100] and multi token analysis. The results of the work can be examined by using OntoLearn tool [69, 73, 75].

The last research unit that contributes to the general evolution of this field is DFKI that produced the OntoLT environment [16]. OntoLT is particularly interesting because of the linguistic annotation format and a convenient rule building mechanism.

These well-known approaches were created with the purpose of assisting users with the task of ontology creation with a given corpus. For this task, they provide specialized methods, e.g. OntoLT allows for user formalization of linguistic rules based on XPath expressions [15].

10.2.7.2 Relation Extraction Methods

A survey of the second group of methods, i.e. taxonomic and non-taxonomic relation extraction methods, is depicted in Fig. 10.4. A division between taxonomic and non-

---

[10]http://lcl.di.uniroma1.it/people.jsp. Last accessed: 15.05.2008.

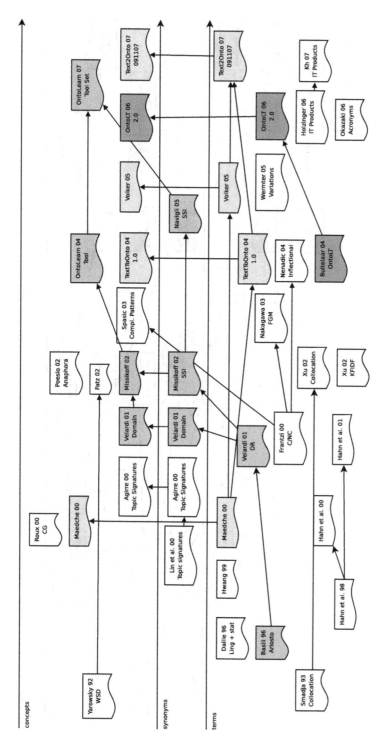

Fig. 10.3 A survey of term, synonym and concept extraction methods

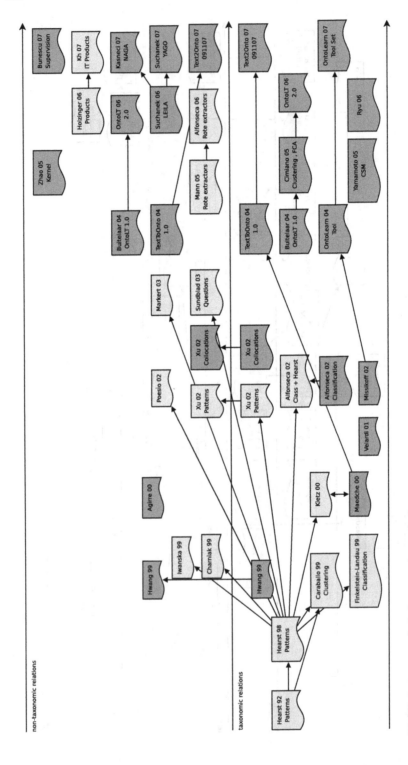

Fig. 10.4 A survey of relation extraction methods

taxonomic relation extraction is easier than the previous classification. Due to lack of rule extraction methods, this kind of task is not reflected on the map.

The methods depicted in Fig. 10.4 can be divided into two separate groups:

- methods derived from linguistic and statistical analysis,
- methods based on lexical-syntactic patterns.

The first method for relation extraction was developed in 1992 by Marti Hearst [47, 48] and is based on lexical-syntactic patterns. Since then, a vast amount of methods have followed the same principle.

In the central point of Fig. 10.4 one can find two methods related to On-To-Knowledge tool: [60] and [64]. These are the first methods that related both approaches to relation extraction, i.e. Hearst patterns and linguistic-statistical approaches.

A combination of clustering algorithms with linguistic analysis introduced by [60, 64] and developed by [23, 25, 26] show that the current level of efficiency is at a satisfactory level.

A non-taxonomic relation survey indicates that some of the methods (especially these extracting the named relations) provide a reasonable efficiency. However, their main drawback is that the ontology creator is assumed to be a domain expert, i.e. it is assumed to know exactly what kind of relations are relevant for the domain. The problem has been recently pointed out in the literature. Work presented in [17] tries to tackle this by proposing the kernel-based methods to minimize supervision. However, the main drawback stays the same—the user is still required to be a domain expert, even for stating a few positive and negative examples. In practice, it means that it is extremely difficult to run the extraction process. Other approaches to the problem focus on integration of different sources. For instance, [53] introduce popularity and uniqueness measures for relation classification.

10.2.8 Conclusions

The survey of the current ontology learning methods leads to the following conclusion:

> There is no general model of ontology learning from text. Only models of particular methods or layers exist, e.g. [91], but the whole cycle of the ontology learning from text process is described only conceptually, e.g. [23]. Therefore, the need for a complete and formal model for ontology learning from text arises.

The particular tasks within the ontology learning from text process can be depicted as models. The model of these particular models is therefore called a metamodel. The reasoning is consistent with MOF specification[11] and provides a clear separation between a particular task model and a general model.

---

[11] http://www.omg.org/mof/.

10.3 Metamodel

A metamodel describes a general method of the ontology learning from text that includes the models of the particular extraction tasks and the relations between them. The metamodel of the ontology learning from text M is therefore:

$$M = \{D, LA, T, S, C, A, TR, NTR\}. \tag{2}$$

D is a set of documents, $D = \{d_1, \ldots, d_n\}$. The set D defines a corpus for the whole process of the ontology learning from text, describing among all: a domain, a narration style and a natural language. A selection of this set is crucial for obtained results and differs from one approach to another.

The set D is not directly used in the extraction processes because of efficiency and interoperability issues. The set D is converted to annotation sets. LA is the set of linguistic annotation for the set D obtained by using the function Λ:

$$\Lambda : D \times \lambda \times LR \times EC \to LA \tag{3}$$

where D is the set documents, λ represents a set of methods for annotation building, LR stands for a set of linguistic tools that are used in the annotation building process and EC means an expert classifier.

The expert classifier EC is an annotation performed by an expert that is considered to be model. It is used in the extraction processes for method evaluations. The expert classifier is the optimization parameter of Λ function. The most frequently occurring attributes of EC are:

- a size and a relation of training and testing data sets,
- an optimization quality, e.g. with respect to a compliance to annotation requirements (guidelines and fault tolerance),
- a number of expert indications deciding about the classification with an assumption that the document d_i is annotated by more than one expert.

The LA set is open in theory but in practice one has to follow a certain set of recognized linguistic annotation standards. A selection of the LA set is crucial for the evaluation purposes. An abstract LA model consists of the following three parts: morphosyntactic annotation related to the particular tokens, phrase analysis (chunks) and grammatical functions of phrases. The presence and utilization of each of these parts denotes a distinct application. In a general case, the richer the linguistic information is, the higher efficiency but the method is more domain constrained.

T denotes a set of terms $T = \{t_1, \ldots, t_n\}$ that is a subject of the extraction process from the set LA using Γ function:

$$\Gamma : LA \times \gamma \times K_{\text{term}} \to 2^T \tag{4}$$

where LA is the set of linguistic annotation, γ denotes a set of term extraction methods and K_{term} represents a set of thresholds for term classifications. Γ function results in a set of all subset of T set (a power set of T).

According to ISO normalization standards [54, 55] terms denote a designate or a label for a concept. A term is a set of tokens within a set of documents D that identifies an unknown concept. A concept is represented in a document by a term occurrence. This definition of a relation between a term and a concept is consistent with a valid definition from the knowledge representation domain [95] and current ISO standards [56].

S is a set of synonyms $S = \{s_1, \ldots, s_n\}$ in which each s_n is a non-empty set of terms related by a certain degree of similarity. In the WordNet's terminology [35], it should have been called a synset. The set S results from the function Φ:

$$\Phi : 2^T \times LR \times K_{\text{sim}} \times \phi \to S \tag{5}$$

where 2^T denotes a power set of T, LR is a set of linguistic resources, K_{sim} represents a set of synonym classification thresholds (a strength of similarity relation that is taken to group the set S) and ϕ denotes a set of actual synonym extraction methods. The strength of a similarity relation is a part of standard linguistic resources, such as a family of WordNet tools [35, 80, 102]. The distinguishing feature of each synonym extraction model is a value from the set ϕ.

C is a set of concepts $C = \{c_1, c_2, \ldots, c_n\}$ that results from the concept extraction function Δ:

$$\Delta : S \times LR \times \delta \times K_{\text{con}} \to C \tag{6}$$

where S stands for a set of synonyms, LR denotes a set of linguistic resources, δ is a set of concept extraction methods and K_{con} represents a set of concept classification thresholds.

A denotes a set of domain axioms:

$$A = \{A_1 \Rightarrow B_{11}, B_{12}, \ldots, B_{1m}; \ldots A_n \Rightarrow B_{n1}, \ldots, B_{nm}\} \tag{7}$$

where each A_n represents a head of the statement n and each $B_{n1}, \ldots, B_{nm}$ is a body of n.

TR is a set of taxonomic relations that hold among the elements of the set C:

$$TR = \{isa(c_{i1}, c_{j1}), \ldots isa(c_{in}, c_{jm})\} \tag{8}$$

where $c_{i1}, \ldots, c_{in}$ denotes a set of isa relation subjects, $c_{j1}, \ldots, c_{jm}$ is a set of isa relation objects and $\forall isa\ i \neq j$.

NTR denotes a set of named non-taxonomic relations:

$$NTR = \{rel_1(c_{x_1}, c_{y_1}), rel_2(c_{x_2}, c_{y_2}), \ldots, rel_n(c_{x_n}, c_{y_n})\} \tag{9}$$

where $rel_1, \ldots, rel_n$ is a set of named non-taxonomic relations, $c_{x_1}, \ldots, c_{x_n}$ are subjects of NTR, $c_{y_1}, \ldots, c_{y_n}$ are objects of NTR. Each element of NTR represents a relation for a given domain. For instance, a meaning of the named non-taxonomic relation $worksAt(x, y)$ should be interpreted as a binary relation with the first argument as an instance of the *Person* class and the second argument as an element of the set *Organization*.

10.3.1 Model Duality

The presented extraction models include two distinct forms of similar functions— the one denoted by a small Greek letter is an argument of the function represented by a capital Greek letter. For instance, (4) consists of both Γ function, as well as γ function.

The duality of each model comes from the following two reasons:

- The aim of the metamodel is to provide an abstraction layer over the existing extraction models and methods. Particular extraction models need not to be bound to any existing method or model (regardless of how good they are). Therefore, the small letter denotes the changing methods of a given extraction model, whereas the capital letter represents general characteristics of the particular extraction model.
- Each extraction model includes elements that are independent of a particular shape of extraction method (e.g. there are a substantial number of methods that are based on the same WordNet).

From the following reasons, a function denoted by a small Greek letter stands for a concrete extraction method (in a case of (4)—the term extraction method). Both the shape of this function, as well as, their arguments can be different in each extraction approach. A capital Greek letter denotes a function that is independent of a particular extraction method. The term extraction model Γ is exactly the same, nonetheless the shape of γ function.

The resulting layer of abstraction implies that a utilization of different extraction methods does not influence the shape of the models. This characteristic is crucial, especially while performing method evaluation.

10.3.2 Extraction Models

Each of the presented metamodel elements (2) requires a functionally distinct extraction process. These processes are represented by the extraction models. In this section, each model is examined to constrain its scope and define possible solutions.

10.3.2.1 Term Extraction

Term extraction according to (4) is the function that maps a linguistic annotation set LA into a set of all subsets of T using a term extraction method γ.

The following tasks are not part of the γ function:

- collocation extraction [33],
- anaphora resolution [84, 101],
- acronym extraction [3, 21, 79, 88, 98],
- Named Entities extraction [45, 57, 67].

The reasons for a separation of these tasks from the term extraction model is theirs distinct characteristics and approaches, something that is widely indicated [79, 84, 104]. Furthermore, methods that are subjects of these tasks can be used separately to boost the effectiveness of a term extraction. Therefore, an application of these tasks does not influence the model of actual implementations of γ function.

The term extraction task is handled by the combination of statistic (frequency-based) and linguistic approaches as highlighted in Sect. 10.2.1.

Linguistic approaches are based on linguistic information in the form of annotation sets. The necessary information is retrieved according to the linguistic rules. In most cases linguistic rules need to be constructed manually by a domain expert. Extraction can be based on shallow linguistic information, i.e. morphosyntactic, derivational and compound analysis, including POS classification or deeper information, e.g. phrases, chunk analysis and clauses. Most of these approaches result in quite high efficiency but their major drawback are the supervision and huge effort required for handcrafting linguistic rules.

An excellent evaluation of linguistic approaches, especially compared to frequency measures is presented in [104]. The application of one such approach is present in OntoLT tool where the user is able to construct linguistic rules based on XPath expressions and a specialized precondition language [16].

The following frequency measures have been used in the term extraction task:

- TFIDF, KFIDF [76, 107];
- C-value/NC-value [39];
- χ^2, LogLike, MI, Co-occurrence analysis [33, 34].

Frequency based methods are fairly simple to implement and evaluate. They produce reasonable results but do not allow for fine grained control over the extraction process. One of the best-known tools to provide a means for frequency-based extraction is Text2Onto and its predecessor [27].

Machine Learning (ML) approaches allow for the unsupervised construction of rules. n-gram models have been a cornerstone of modern ML applications in text processing. The classic n-gram approach to the term extraction is based on a word sequence (w_n denotes nth word):

$$P(w_n | w_1, \ldots, w_{n-1}) \tag{10}$$

or its POS counterpart.

ML approaches have been widely used in the term extraction task. Surprisingly, for a long time n-gram models were based on words. The first classic approach based on a words n-gram model was introduced by [92]. More recent approaches such as [103] use n-gram models for the separation of domain terms from non-specific, common terms to extract multi-word terms. Modern approaches take other non-syntactic classes of tokens into account, such as POS tags but still follow the same principle.

An example term extraction model based on ML approach is presented in [2]. The method is particularly recommended, because it is evaluated to outperform the classic approaches. In this method, the term classification task of a sequence of words w_n is the conditional probability function based on POS (pos_n) for particular words within a sequence:

$$P(X) = P(term_k | pos_1, \ldots, pos_n) \tag{11}$$

where:

- n denotes the number of nodes in n-gram model,
- k denotes the position of node indicated as term, $1 \leq k \leq n$,
- *term* denotes the node indicated as term,
- *pos* denotes the POS label of a node.

The presented method is based on the following extending assumptions to the classic Markov model:

1. The term classification function is based on the sequence of adjacent POS of words.
2. The term classification function depends on the direct context of word sequence.
3. Word sequence context is not determined, i.e. information capacity for context words classification function is variable.
4. The model works on shallow linguistic information which means that it can handle annotation sets with data of low quality.

The main difference is that the model is based on a context model, not directly on n-grams.

10.3.2.2 Synonym Extraction

The synonym extraction according to (5) is the function that maps a set of all subsets of T into a set of synonyms S by using a set of linguistic resources LR with defined synonym relations and a synonym extraction method ϕ. Linguistic resources such as WordNet [35], FrameNet [71], Roget [61] or solutions adjusted to the specific needs of other languages (e.g. [80]) include synonym indications among terms that turned out to be useful on most occasions. The method ϕ in a general case consists in checking all term combinations and linking these terms that have a degree of similarity higher than a declared similarity threshold k_{sim}. The most popular approach is reduced to the classic clustering with an agglomerate method.

Therefore, the efficiency of synonym extraction models Φ depends to a large degree on a quality of synonym relations defined in the set of linguistic resources LR.

10.3.2.3 Concept Extraction

According to (6) the concept extraction task is the function that maps a set S consisting of elements of T into a set C by using linguistic resources LR and concept extraction methods δ. δ is the concept classification function. The actual shape of δ can vary with different approaches applied (see Sect. 10.2.3).

For a model implementation of a δ function it is recommended to use an extension test [13]. It means that δ classifies the element s_n in a case of a lexical realization of s_n or consisting terms ($2^T \rightarrow S$).

In the concept extraction task it is convenient to also extract concept instances.[12] In a case of a negative result of an extension test, a POS classification of s_n or consisting terms can be looked up to indicate a possible concept-instance relation. For instance, while using WordNet [35] and ANNIE [59] as elements of *LR* the instance classification proceeds when extension test in WordNet fails and s_n is classified in ANNIE as Person, Organization, Location, Address, Date or Money.

10.3.2.4 Taxonomic Relation Extraction

According to (8) the taxonomic relation extraction task is a function that maps a set of concepts *C* into a set of taxonomic relations *TR*. In the introduced model it is assumed that the model is built with one of the methods presented in Sect. 10.2.4.

10.3.2.5 Non-taxonomic Relation Extraction

An extraction of non-taxonomic relations is a function that maps a set of concepts *C* into a set of *NTR* (equation (9)). The metamodel does not dictate any particular relation extraction method (see Sect. 10.2.5 for a brief survey of the existing methods).

For a reference metamodel implementation, it is recommended to use a relation extraction method that minimizes the degree of a supervision. The approach presented in [1] consists of a new relation extraction method based on a feedback cycle assumption between domain axioms and linguistic information in the set *LA*. By minimizing the required degree of an expert's supervision it maps a set of domain axioms *A* and a set of *LA* into a set of non-taxonomic relations *NTR*.

10.3.3 Reference Architecture

The metamodel is a theoretical and abstract model of the ontology learning from text. This abstract metamodel can be realized in terms of classic system engineering design methods including a functional and technological partitioning. The functional partitioning results in a functional architecture, whereas the technological partitioning leads to mapping a functional architecture to the concrete technologies.

10.3.3.1 Functional Partitioning

The functional partitioning consists in a separation of functionally uniform components, so called architectural building blocks (ABB) and a definition of relations that

---

[12]Some authors prefer to exclude an instance extraction from a concept extraction task from historical divisions into terminological (TBox) and assertional knowledge (ABox). Still, the methods used for these two tasks in the ontology learning are similar.

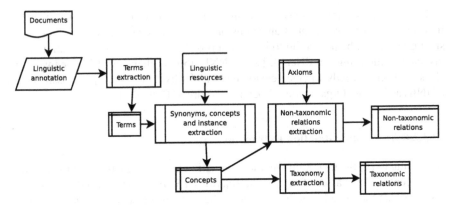

Fig. 10.5 General functional partitioning

hold among ABBs. A general functional partitioning is depicted in Fig. 10.5. A standard flow chart notation indicates that the diagram is at the same time a behavioral model.

The components placed on the left hand side of Fig. 10.5 denote the set D, i.e. a corpora of documents and the set of linguistic annotation LA built on the basis of the function Λ. The Λ realization by the presented metamodel includes the following tasks:

- sentence boundary detection,
- tokenization,
- POS annotation,
- morphological analysis, including inflectional, compound and derivational analysis,
- lemmatization,
- Named Entity recognition,
- phrases detection,
- analysis of grammatical functions of phrases.

Linguistic analysis is performed by using tools: ANNIE [32], Ballie [70] (for English) and SProUT [82] (for German and Polish).

The linguistic annotation format in the set LA is selected in such a way that a reliable and objective evaluation is feasible and the metamodel is supplied with suitable attributes of a corpus (D). Choosing the OntoLT annotation format [15] is caused by its popularity and a clear separation of different types of linguistic information. A modular structure additionally allows for a clear selection of a linguistic information scope for different applications and corpus features.

The task of term extraction is performed by using the Γ function (4) as indicated earlier and is classified as a separate functional unit.

A functional similarity of synonym, concept and instance extraction tasks leads to grouping all these three elements into one functional ABB in Fig. 10.5. The synonym and concept extraction functions (Φ and Δ respectively) make a heavy use of

Table 10.2 Architectural partitioning

ABBs	Technologies applied
Linguistic annotation *LA*	ANNIE, Ballie, SProUT
Linguistic annotation format	OntoLT
Term extraction	Linguistic, statistical, ML
Concept classification	ANNIE, WordNet, EuroWordNet, PLWordNet
Axioms serialization	SWRL
Ontology construction	Jena
Ontology language	OWL DL
SWRL-based reasoning	Pellet

linguistic resources *LR*. The quality of these resources to a large degree shapes the quality of the actual extraction functions.

The set of concepts *C* is a basis for an extraction of both taxonomic and non-taxonomic relations. There are a few methods that use domain axioms (*A*) for the relation extraction. In the reference implementation of the metamodel it is recommended to implement the relation extraction method presented in [1]. The set of axioms *A* is serialized to a suitable form of the SWRL file.[13]

10.3.3.2 Technological Partitioning

The architectural partitioning is designed for suggesting concrete technologies in order to deliver functionalists included in ABBs. Table 10.2 depicts the mapping between the most crucial functionalists and the concrete technologies. The proposed map is general which means that the technologies and tools allow for building solutions that are compliant with the metamodel, for instance different corpora or natural languages.

The functionalists depicted in Table 10.2 does not map directly to the ABBs defined in the functional partitioning. The only criterion that was taken into consideration is the technological autonomy.

10.4 Evaluation

The evaluation of the metamodel is based on the proof of building ontologies based on the different sets of its constituents, i.e. particular extraction models and theirs arguments. In order to provide such an evaluation we have provided a reference implementation of the metamodel.

---

[13]http://www.w3.org/Submission/SWRL/.

The reference implementation of the metamodel comes with a number of models, methods and tools to boost certain ontology learning from text tasks. In the course of metamodel design we have implemented the following metamodel elements:

- corpora,
- term extraction methods,
- synonym and concept extraction methods,
- relation extraction methods.

In is crucial to point out that the main point of the evaluation is to show that the presented metamodel can represent many diverse ontology learning methods. The aim of the research is to provide a general model of the ontology learning in order to provide a common base for an objective method of comparison and an evaluation framework. Therefore, it is not vital to depict a particular method effectiveness.

However, a presence of these methods makes it possible for a reference implementation to bootstrap initial ontologies. As an example, we have bootstrapped an initial ontology for academic events that consists of:

- 417 classes, e.g.: Colleague, PilotProject, University, etc.,
- 579 instances of types specified in standard ANNIE's NE tags,
- labels for instances that correspond to the lexical occurrence of terms in the text,
- 685–26 442 relations between concepts—the exact number depends on the threshold level with a classic trade-off between precision and recall.

10.4.1 Corpora

The metamodel (2) includes sets of D and LA as first elements. These elements both relate to a corpus—a set of D describes its elements, a set of LA formalizes it in a form of a linguistic annotation set.

Corpora are usually quite different because of the three main features: domain, natural language and narration style. With respect to these features, the reference implementation includes two substantially different corpora. The outlook of these corpora is depicted in Table 10.3.

The first corpus is the KMi (Knowledge Media Institute) electronic newsletter. The text used in the news articles is unstructured, e.g. the writers sometimes use slang, break grammatical rules, incorrectly use punctuation, etc. This makes it difficult to successfully apply heuristics to any extraction task. The KMi corpus consists of 273 text documents in English (62 303 tokens). The linguistic annotation was provided by GATE and ANNIE standard linguistic resources [30].

The other corpus consists of text documents in Polish that describe IT product specifications. It contains a lot of specialized, domain specific terms and its quality is also very low. The corpus comprises all products from one of the IT product distribution sites[14] and consists of 6789 text documents (481 455 tokens). The linguistic annotation was provided by SProUT [82].

---

[14]http://znak.pl.

Table 10.3 Comparison of two corpora: *KMi* and *IT Product*

	KMi	IT Product
Domain	academic news	e-commerce
Natural language	English	Polish
Narration style	free, e-mail	technical specifications
Number of documents	273	6789
Number of tokens	62 303	481 455
POS annotation	GATE/ANNIE	SProUT
Named entities	GATE/ANNIE	–
Annotation format	OntoLT	OntoLT
Expert classifier	expert	expert group

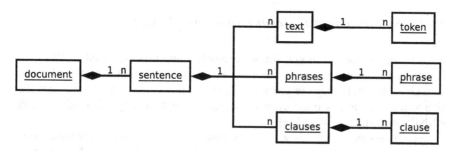

Fig. 10.6 Annotation format structure

Metamodel is also an evaluation framework which means that it is possible to test different corpora without interfering with other constituents. This results in different corpora having exactly the same annotation format. We have chosen the OntoLT format as it is an open, XML-based, well structured and easily extensible [15]. The structure of the annotation format is depicted in Fig. 10.6.

Expert classifiers to both corpora were provided manually by a group of 30 experts during an Information Extraction course. The annotation included proper names, single and multi-token terms complying with the definition in ISO 1087-1:2000 [54].

10.4.2 Term Extraction Methods

In the metamodel reference implementation we have implemented a number of representative term extraction methods, namely:

- standard TFIDF based on documents similarity,
- TFIDF based on corpora similarity (comparing corpus to common language words),

- KFIDF [107],
- C-value/NC-value [39],
- classic POS n-gram model,
- POS n-gram model based on a proximity context window [2].

A detailed evaluation of all these methods is performed and presented in [2]. In general, n-gram based models reach better results but only in limited threshold levels, which means that optimization procedures need to be applied. Frequency based methods, particularly KFIDF and C-value/NC-value, indicate a reasonably good performance on all occasions.

For a metamodel evaluation it is vital that all these methods can be compared and evaluated on a standard set of other metamodel elements, e.g. corpora and linguistic annotation sets.

10.4.3 Synonym and Concept Extraction Methods

For a synonym classification a simple disambiguation method based on WordNet [13] is implemented. Terms are checked against each other in synsets and based on a given threshold they are grouped into synonyms. For a concept formation the simple intention test is provided and for Named Entity Recognition—the default ANNIE linguistic resources [13].

In both groups of methods we have extensively used third-party linguistic tools, such as GATE and ANNIE [30] for English and SProUT [82] for Polish. The effectiveness of these methods is strictly related to a quality of these tools.

10.4.4 Relation Extraction Methods

The reference implementation also includes the relation extraction method presented in [1] which is based on a feedback cycle between a set of domain axioms and linguistic features of a text.

The general rules for academic domain (A) were provided by an expert that did not have access to the KMi corpus but knew the organization well.[15] The resulted set A consists of 25 rules that are ready for relation extraction methods.

10.5 Conclusion

The main goal of the presented metamodel was to formalize a variety of methods for ontology learning from text. We have surveyed a representative set of methods that

---

[15]We had the pleasure to welcome a KMi researcher from Open University as a guest at our university.

were grouped according to ontology learning from text phases, i.e. term, synonym, concept, taxonomy and relation extraction.

The early stage of research in this field leads to usual problems of lack of evaluation frameworks and comparison methodologies. We did solve some of these problems by the introduction of the metamodel for ontology learning from text. We believe that from now on, every method could be described with its elements.

We have applied a qualitative evaluation by implementing some of the current state-of-the-art methods and showing they can be described with a metamodel notation. Two substantially different corpora, 6 representative term extraction methods, synonym, concept and relation extraction methods were all implemented to show that the model is general enough. As a result, it is possible to evaluate some of the metamodel elements while keeping others intact.

Of course, there are some methods which cannot be described with a metamodel notation. These are basically methods that are classified to more than one extraction phase (e.g. [4]). However, we believe that the level of metamodel generality is enough to include most of the current and still-to-be-developed ontology learning from text methods.

References

1. Abramowicz, W., Vargas-Vera, M., Wisniewski, M.: Axiom-based feedback cycle for relation extraction in ontology learning from text. In: DEXA '08: Proceedings of the 19th International Conference on Database and Expert Systems Applications. IEEE Comput. Soc., Los Alamitos (2008)
2. Abramowicz, W., Wisniewski, M.: Proximity window context method for term extraction in ontology learning from text. In: DEXA '08: Proceedings of the 19th International Conference on Database and Expert Systems Applications. IEEE Comput. Soc., Los Alamitos (2008)
3. Adar, E.: Sarad: A simple and robust abbreviation dictionary. Bioinformatics 20(4), 527–533 (2004)
4. Agirre, E., Ansa, O., Hovy, E., Martínez, D.: Enriching very large ontologies using the www. In: Proc. of the Ontology Learning Workshop, ECAI, Berlin, Germany (2000)
5. Alfonseca, E., Manandhar, S.: Extending a lexical ontology by a combination of distributional semantics signatures. In: Proceedings of the 13th International Conference on Knowledge Engineering and Knowledge Management (EKAW 2002) (2002)
6. Alfonseca, E., Manandhar, S.: Improving an ontology refinement method with hyponymy patterns. In: Language Resources and Evaluation (LREC-2002), Las Palmas, Spain (2002)
7. Aussenac-Gilles, N., Biébow, B., Szulman, S.: Revisiting ontology design: A methodology based on corpus analysis. In: Proceedings of the 12th European Workshop on Knowledge Acquisition, Modeling and Management. Springer, Berlin (2000)
8. Baader, F., Calvanese, D., McGuinness, D.L., Nardi, D., Patel-Schneider, P.F.: The Description Logic Handbook: Theory, Implementation, and Applications. Cambridge University Press, Cambridge (2003)
9. Basili, R., Pazienza, M.T., Velardi, P.: An empirical symbolic approach to natural language processing. Artificial Intelligence 85, 59–99 (1996)
10. Berners-Lee, T., Hendler, J., Lassila, O.: The semantic web. Scientific American 284(5) (2001)
11. Brody, S., Navigli, R., Lapata, M.: Ensemble methods for unsupervised WSD. In: ACL '06: Proceedings of the 21st International Conference on Computational Linguistics and the 44th

Annual Meeting of the ACL, pp. 97–104, Association for Computational Linguistics, Morristown, NJ, USA (2006)

12. Budanitsky, A., Hirst, G.: Evaluating WordNet-based measures of lexical semantic relatedness. Computational Linguistics **32**(1), 13–47 (2006)

13. Buitelaar, P., Cimiano, P.: Ontology learning from text: Tutorial. In: 11th Conference of the European Chapter of the Association for Computational Linguistics, Trento, Italy (2006)

14. Buitelaar, P., Cimiano, P., Magnini, B.: Ontology learning from text: An overview. In: Buitelaar, P., Cimiano, P., Magnini, B. (eds.) Ontology Learning from Text: Methods, Evaluation and Applications. Frontiers in Artificial Intelligence and Applications. IOS Press, Amsterdam (2005)

15. Buitelaar, P., Olejnik, D., Sintek, M.: A protege plug-in for ontology extraction from text based on linguistic analysis. In: Proceedings of the 1st European Semantic Web Symposium (ESWS) (2004)

16. Buitelaar, P., Sintek, M.: Ontolt version 1.0: Middleware for ontology extraction from text. In: Proceedings of the Demo Session at the International Semantic Web Conference (ISWC) (2004)

17. Bunescu, R., Mooney, R.: Learning to extract relations from the web using minimal supervision. In: Proceedings of the 45th Annual Meeting of the Association of Computational Linguistics, Association for Computational Linguistics, Prague, Czech Republic (June 2007)

18. Caraballo, S.A.: Automatic construction of a hypernym-labeled noun hierarchy from text. In: Proceedings of the Conference of the Association for Computational Linguistics (1999)

19. Caraballo, S.A.: Automatic construction of a hypernym—labeled noun hierarchy from text. PhD thesis, Providence, RI, USA, 2001. Adviser—E. Charniak

20. Cederberg, S., Widdows, D.: Using LSA and noun coordination information to improve the precision and recall of automatic hyponymy extraction. In: Proceedings of the Conference on Natural Language Learning (CoNNL) (2003)

21. Chang, J., Schutze, H.: Abbreviations in biomedical text. In: Ananiadou, S., Mcnaught, J. (eds.) Text Mining for Biology and Biomedicine, pp. 99–119. Artech House, Norwood (2006)

22. Charniak, E., Berland, M.: Finding parts in very large corpora. In: Proceedings of the 37th Annual Meeting of the ACL (1999)

23. Cimiano, P.: Ontology learning from text. PhD thesis, University of Karlsruhe (2006)

24. Cimiano, P., Hotho, A., Staab, S.: Learning concept hierarchies from text corpora using formal concept analysis. Journal of Artificial Intelligence Research **24**, 305–339 (2005)

25. Cimiano, P., Schmidt-Thieme, L., Pivk, A., Staab, S.: Learning taxonomic relations from heterogeneous evidence. In: Ontology Learning from Text: Methods, Applications and Evaluation, pp. 59–73. IOS Press, Amsterdam (2005)

26. Cimiano, P., Staab, S.: Learning concept hierarchies from text with a guided agglomerative clustering algorithm. In: ICML 2005 Workshop on Learning and Extending Lexical Ontologies with Machine Learning Methods (2005)

27. Cimiano, P., Völker, J.: Text2onto—a framework for ontology learning and data-driven change discovery. In: 10th International Conference on Applications of Natural Language to Information Systems (NLDB'2005) (2005)

28. Cimiano, P., Wenderoth, J.: Automatically learning qualia structures from the web. In: Proceedings of the ACL Workshop on Deep Lexical Acquisition (2005)

29. Cristani, M., Cuel, R.: A survey on ontology creation methodologies. International Journal on Semantic Web and Information Systems **1**(2), 49–69 (2005)

30. Cunningham, H., Maynard, D., Bontcheva, K., Tablan, V.: Gate: A framework and graphical development environment for robust NLP tools and applications. In: Proceedings of the 40th Annual Meeting of the ACL (2002)

31. Cunningham, H., Maynard, D., Tablan, V.: Jape: A java annotation patterns engine (2nd edn.). Technical report, Department of Computer Science, University of Sheffield (November 2000)

32. Cunningham, H., Maynard, D., Bontcheva, K., Tablan, V., Ursu, C., Dimitrov, M., Dowman, M., Aswani, N., Roberts, I., Li, Y., Shafirin, A.: Developing Language Processing Components with GATE Version 4. Department of Computer Science, University of Sheffield, 4.0-beta1 edition, April 2007
33. Daille, B.: Study and implementation of combined techniques for automatic extraction of terminology. In: Klavans, J., Resnik, P. (eds.) The Balancing Act: Combining Symbolic and Statistical Approaches to Language, pp. 49–66. MIT Press, Cambridge (1996)
34. Dunning, T.: Accurate methods for the statistics of surprise and coincidence. Computational Linguistics 19(1), 61–74 (1993)
35. Fellbaum, C.: WordNet: An Electronic Lexical Database. MIT Press, Cambridge (1998)
36. Fensel, D.: Ontologies: A Silver Bullet for Knowledge Management and Electronic Commerce. Springer, New York (2003)
37. Fensel, D., van Harmelen, F., Klein, M., Akkermans, H., Broekstra, J., Fluit, C., van der Meer, J., Schnurr, H.-P., Studer, R., Hughes, J., Krohn, U., Davies, J., Engels, R., Bremdal, B., Ygge, F., Lau, T., Novotny, B., Reimer, U., Horrocks, I.: Onto-knowledge: Ontology-based tools for knowledge management. In: Proceedings of the eBusiness and eWork 2000 (eBeW'00) Conference, Madrid, Spain (2000)
38. Fotzo, H.N., Gallinari, P.: Learning generalization/specialization relations between concepts—application for automatically building thematic document hierarchies. In: RIAO (2004)
39. Frantzi, K., Ananiadou, S., Mima, H.: Automatic recognition of multi-word terms: The C-value/NC-value method. International Journal on Digital Libraries 3(2), 115–130 (2000)
40. Girju, R., Moldovan, D.: Text mining for causal relations. In: Proceedings of the FLAIRS Conference (2002)
41. Grefenstette, G.: Cross-Language Information Retrieval. Kluwer International Series on Information Retrieval. Kluwer Academic, Boston (1998)
42. Gruber, T.R.: A translation approach to portable ontology specifications. Knowledge Acquisition 5(2), 199–220 (1993)
43. Gruber, T.: Ontology. In: Liu, L., Tamer Ozsu, M. (eds.) Encyclopedia of Database Systems. Springer, Berlin (2008)
44. Haase, P., Völker, J.: Ontology learning and reasoning—dealing with uncertainty and inconsistency. In: Proceedings of the Workshop on Uncertainty Reasoning for the Semantic Web (URSW) (2005)
45. Hammerton, J., Osborne, M., Armstrong, S., Daelemans, W.: Introduction to special issue on machine learning approaches to shallow parsing. Journal of Machine Learning Research 2002(2), 8 (2002)
46. Hamp, B., Feldweg, H.: Germanet—a lexical-semantic net for German. In: Proceedings of ACL Workshop Automatic Information Extraction and Building of Lexical Semantic Resources for NLP Applications, Madrid, Spain (1997)
47. Hearst, M.A.: Automatic acquisition of hyponyms from large text corpora. In: 14th International Conference on Computational Linguistics (1992)
48. Hearst, M.A.: Automated discovery of WordNet relations. In: Fellbaum, C. (ed.) WordNet: An Electronic Lexical Database and Some of its Applications, pp. 132–152. MIT Press, Cambridge (1998)
49. Hepp, M.: Products and services ontologies: A methodology for deriving owl ontologies from industrial categorization standards. International Journal on Semantic Web and Information Systems 2(1), 72–99 (2006)
50. Hepp, M.: Ontologies: State of the art, business potential, and grand challenges. In: Ontology Management, pp. 3–22. Springer, Berlin (2008)
51. Hepp, M., De Leenheer, P., de Moor, A., Sure, Y.: Ontology Management, Semantic Web, Semantic Web Services, and Business Applications. Semantic Web and Beyond Computing for Human Experience, vol. 7. Springer, Berlin (2008)
52. Hepple, M.: Independence and commitment: Assumptions for rapid training and execution of rule-based POS taggers. In: Proceedings of the 38th Annual Meeting of the Association for Computational Linguistics (ACL-2000), Hong Kong (2000)

53. Huang, J.-X., Shin, J.-A., Choi, K.-S.: Integrating relations for a domain ontology. In: Proceedings of the 6th International Semantic Web Conference, Busan, Korea (November 2007)

54. International Organization for Standardization. ISO 1087-1:2000 Terminology Work—Vocabulary—Part 1: Theory and Application (2000)

55. International Organization for Standardization. ISO 704:2000 Terminology Work—Principles and Methods (2000)

56. International Organization for Standardization. ISO 860:2007 Terminology Work—Harmonization of Concepts and Terms (2007)

57. Jurafsky, D., Martin, J.H.: Speech and Language Processing: An Introduction to Natural Language Processing, Computational Linguistics, and Speech Recognition. Prentice-Hall, Upper Saddle River (2000)

58. Kauffman, R.J., Walden, E.A.: Economics and electronic commerce: Survey and directions for research. International Journal of Electronic Commerce 5(4), 5–116 (2001)

59. Kenter, T., Maynard., D.: Using GATE as an annotation tool. Department of Computer Science, University of Sheffield (January 2005)

60. Kietz, J., Maedche, A., Volz, R.: A method for semi-automatic ontology acquisition from a corporate intranet. In: Workshop "Ontologies and Text", co-located with EKAW'2000 (2000)

61. Kipfer, B.A.: Roget new millennium thesaurus, 1st edn. (v 1.1.1), 2006-04-03 (2006)

62. Lin, D., Pantel, P.: Dirt—discovery of inference rules from text. In: Proceedings of ACM SIGKDD Conference on Knowledge Discovery and Data Mining (2001)

63. Maedche, A.: Ontology Learning for the Semantic Web. Kluwer Academic, Boston (2002)

64. Maedche, A., Staab, S.: Discovering conceptual relations from text. In: ECAI 2000. Proceedings of the 14th European Conference on Artificial Intelligence, Berlin, Germany. IOS Press, Amsterdam (2000)

65. Maedche, A., Staab, S.: Semi-automatic engineering of ontologies from text. In: Proceedings of the 12th International Conference on Software Engineering and Knowledge Engineering (2000)

66. Maedche, A., Staab, S.: The text-to-onto ontology learning environment. In: Proceedings of the 12th Internal Conference on Software and Knowledge Engineering, Chicago, USA (2000)

67. Manning, C.D., Schutze, H.: Foundations of Statistical Natural Language Processing. MIT Press, Cambridge (1999)

68. Medjahed, B., Benatallah, B., Bouguettaya, A., Ngu, A.H.H., Elmagarmid, A.K.: Business-to-business interactions: Issues and enabling technologies. The VLDB Journal 12(1), 59–85 (2003)

69. Missikoff, M., Navigli, R., Velardi, P.: Integrated approach to web ontology learning and engineering. IEEE Computer 35(11), 60–63 (2002)

70. Nadeau, D.: Balie—baseline information extraction. Multilingual information extraction from text with machine learning and natural language techniques. Technical report, School of Information Technology and Engineering, University of Ottawa, Canada (2005)

71. Narayanan, S., Petruck, M.R.L., Baker, C.F., Fillmore, C.J.: Putting FrameNet data into the ISO linguistic annotation framework. In: Proceedings of the ACL 2003 Workshop on Linguistic Annotation, pp. 22–29, Association for Computational Linguistics, Morristown, NJ, USA (2003)

72. Navigli, R.: Meaningful clustering of senses helps boost word sense disambiguation performance. In: ACL '06: Proceedings of the 21st International Conference on Computational Linguistics and the 44th Annual Meeting of the ACL, pp. 105–112, Association for Computational Linguistics, Morristown, NJ, USA (2006)

73. Navigli, R., Velardi, P.: Learning domain ontologies from document warehouses and dedicated web sites. Computational Linguistics 30(2), 151–179 (2004)

74. Navigli, R., Velardi, P.: Structural semantic interconnections: A knowledge-based approach to word sense disambiguation. IEEE Transactions on Pattern Analysis and Machine Intelligence 27(7), 1075–1086 (2005)

75. Navigli, R., Velardi, P., Cucchiarelli, A., Neri, F.: Quantitative and qualitative evaluation of the OntoLearn ontology learning system. In: COLING '04: Proceedings of the 20th International Conference on Computational Linguistics, p. 1043, Association for Computational Linguistics, Morristown, NJ, USA (2004)

76. Nenadic, G., Ananiadou, S., McNaught, J.: Enhancing automatic term recognition through recognition of variation. In: COLING '04: Proceedings of the 20th International Conference on Computational Linguistics, p. 604, Association for Computational Linguistics, Morristown, NJ, USA (2004)

77. Niles, I., Pease, A.: Towards a standard upper ontology. In: FOIS '01: Proceedings of the International Conference on Formal Ontology in Information Systems. ACM, New York (2001)

78. Ogden, C.K., Richards, I.A.: The Meaning of Meaning: A Study of the Influence of Language upon Thought and of the Science of Symbolism. International Library of Psychology, Philosophy, and Scientific Method. Harcourt Brace, New York (1923)

79. Okazaki, N., Ananiadou, S.: A term recognition approach to acronym recognition. In: Proceedings of the COLING/ACL on Main Conference Poster Sessions, Association for Computational Linguistics, Morristown, NJ, USA (2006)

80. Piasecki, M., Broda, B.: Semantic similarity measure of Polish nouns based on linguistic features. In: Proceedings of 10th International Conference on Business Information Systems, Poznan, Poland. Lecture Notes in Computer Science. Springer, Berlin (2007)

81. Pinto, H.S., Martins, J.P.: Ontologies: How can they be built? Knowledge and Information Systems **6**(4), 441–464 (2004)

82. Piskorski, J., Drozdzynski, W., Krieger, H.-U., Schafer, U.: Sprout—a general-purpose NLP framework integrating finite-state and unification-based grammar formalisms. In: Proceedings of the 5th International Workshop on Finite-State Methods and Natural Language Processing, Helsinki, Finland. Lecture Notes in Artificial Intelligence. Springer, Berlin (2005)

83. Poesio, M., Almuhareb, A.: Identifying concept attributes using a classifier. In: Proceedings of the ACL Workshop on Deep Lexical Acquisition (2005)

84. Poesio, M., Ishikawa, T., Schulte im Walde, S., Vieira, R.: Acquiring lexical knowledge for anaphora resolution. In: Proceedings of the 3rd Conference on Language Resources and Evaluation (2002)

85. Rinaldi, F., Yuste, E.: Exploiting technical terminology for knowledge management. In: Buitelaar, P., Cimiano, P., Magnini, B. (eds.) Ontology Learning from Text: Methods, Evaluation and Applications. Frontiers in Artificial Intelligence and Applications. IOS Press, Amsterdam (2005)

86. Roux, C., Proux, D., Rechenmann, F., Julliard, L.: An ontology enrichment method for a pragmatic information extraction system gathering data on genetic interactions. In: Proceedings of the ECAI2000 Workshop on Ontology Learning (OL2000), Berlin, Germany (2000)

87. Sanderson, M., Croft, B.: Deriving concept hierarchies from text. In: SIGIR '99. ACM, New York (1999)

88. Schwartz, A., Hearst, M.: A simple algorithm for identifying abbreviation definitions in biomedical texts. In: Proceedings of the Pacific Symposium on Biocomputing PSB 2003 (2003)

89. Simperl, E.P.B., Sure, Y., Tempich, C.: Ontocom: A cost estimation model for ontology engineering. In: Proceedings of the 5th International Semantic Web Conference, Athens, Georgia (November 2006)

90. Singh, R., Iyer, L.S., Salam, A.F.: Semantic ebusiness. International Journal on Semantic Web and Information Systems **1**(1), 19–35 (2005)

91. Sintek, M., Buitelaar, P., Olejnik, D.: A formalization of ontology learning from text. In: International Semantic Web Conference. Hiroshima, Japan (2004)

92. Smadja, F.: Retrieving collocations from text: Xtract. Computational Linguistics **19**(1), 143–177 (1993)

93. Snow, R., Jurafsky, D., Ng, A.Y.: Semantic taxonomy induction from heterogeneous evidence. In: ACL '06: Proceedings of the 21st International Conference on Computational

Linguistics and the 44th Annual Meeting of the ACL, pp. 801–808, Association for Computational Linguistics, Morristown, NJ, USA (2006)

94. Sowa, J.F.: Conceptual Structures: Information Processing in Mind and Machine. Addison-Wesley, Reading (1984)

95. Sowa, J.F.: Knowledge Representation: Logical, Philosophical, and Computational Foundations. Brooks/Cole, Pacific Grove (2000)

96. Sowa, J.F.: Ontology, metadata, and semiotics. In: Proceedings of the Linguistic on Conceptual Structures: Logical Linguistic, and Computational Issues. Springer, Berlin (2000)

97. Sundblad, H.: Automatic acquisition of hyponyms and meronyms from question corpora. In: Proceedings of the Workshop on Natural Language Processing and Machine Learning for Ontology Engineering at ECAI'2002. Lyon, France (2003)

98. Torii, M., Liu, H., Hu, Z., Wu, C.: A comparison study of biomedical short form definition detection algorithms. In: TMBIO '06: Proceedings of the 1st International Workshop on Text Mining in Bioinformatics, pp. 52–59. ACM, New York (2006)

99. Uschold, M., Gruninger, M.: Ontologies and semantics for seamless connectivity. SIGMOD Record 33(4), 58–64 (2004)

100. Velardi, P., Fabriani, P., Missikoff, M.: Using text processing techniques to automatically enrich a domain ontology. In: Proceedings of the International Conference on Formal Ontology in Information Systems (FOIS) (2001)

101. Vieira, R., Poesio, M.: An empirically based system for processing definite descriptions. Computational Linguistics 26(4), 539–593 (2000)

102. Vossen, P.: Introduction to EuroWordNet. Computers and the Humanities 32(2–3), 73–89 (1998)

103. Wermter, J., Hahn, U.: Paradigmatic modifiability statistics for the extraction of complex multi-word terms. In: HLT '05: Proceedings of the Conference on Human Language Technology and Empirical Methods in Natural Language Processing, pp. 843–850, Association for Computational Linguistics, Morristown, NJ, USA (2005)

104. Wermter, J., Hahn, U.: You can't beat frequency (unless you use linguistic knowledge): a qualitative evaluation of association measures for collocation and term extraction. In: ACL '06: Proceedings of the 21st International Conference on Computational Linguistics and the 44th Annual Meeting of the ACL, pp. 785–792, Association for Computational Linguistics, Morristown, NJ, USA (2006)

105. Widdows, D.: Unsupervised method for developing taxonomies by combining syntactic and statistical information. In: Proceedings of HLT/NAACL (2003)

106. Witschel, H.F.: Using decision trees and text mining techniques for extending taxonomies. In: Proceedings of Learning and Extending Lexical Ontologies by using Machine Learning Methods, Workshop at ICML-05 (2005)

107. Xu, F., Kurz, D., Piskorski, J., Schmeier, S.: A domain adaptive approach to automatic acquisition of domain relevant terms and their relations with bootstrapping. In: Proceedings of the 3rd International Conference on Language Resources an Evaluation (LREC'02), Las Palmas, Canary Islands, Spain (2002)

108. Yamada, I., Baldwin, T.: Automatic discovery of telic and agentive roles from corpus data. In: Proceedings of the 18th Pacific Asia Conference on Language, Information and Computation (PACLIC 18) (2004)

109. Yarowsky, D.: Word-sense disambiguation using statistical models of Roget's categories trained on large corpora. In: Proceedings of COLING-92, Nantes, France (1992)

Chapter 11
An Analysis of Constructed Categories for Textual Classification Using Fuzzy Similarity and Agglomerative Hierarchical Methods

Marcus V.C. Guelpeli,
Ana Cristina Bicharra Garcia,
and Flavia Cristina Bernardini

Abstract Ambiguity is a challenge faced by systems that handle natural language. To assuage the issue of linguistic ambiguities found in text classification, this work proposes a text categorizer using the methodology of Fuzzy Similarity. The clustering algorithms Stars and Cliques are adopted in the Agglomerative Hierarchical method and they identify the groups of texts by specifying some type of relationship rule to create categories based on the similarity analysis of the textual terms. The proposal is based on the methodology suggested, categories can be created from the analysis of the degree of similarity of the texts to be classified, without needing to determine the number of initial categories. The combination of techniques proposed in the categorizer's steps brought satisfactory results, proving to be efficient in textual classification.

11.1 Introduction

The access to means of information distribution is becoming easier day by day. Motivated by the great availability of computer resources and the ease of exchanging and storing information, institutions in the most diverse fields have produced and electronically stored a large amount of data. In light of this possibility, companies have started making their products available by these means of distribution, expanding their markets globally and maximizing profits. Until a short time ago, this fact was not seen as a competitive advantage or a support tool for decision-making with indicators of successes and failures. As such, the amount of information is currently very great and continues to grow every minute. As well as being large, the information is set up in a disorganized and non-standardized manner, making it difficult to locate and to access. For [32], more than 80% of the information is currently

M.V.C. Guelpeli (✉)
Departamento de Ciência da Computação, Instituto de Computação—IC, Universidade Federal Fluminense—UFF, Rua Passo da Pátria 156, Bloco E, 3° andar, São Domingos, Niterói, RJ CEP 24210-240, Brazil
e-mail: mguelpeli@ic.uff.br

Y. Badr et al. (eds.) *Emergent Web Intelligence: Advanced Semantic Technologies,* 277
Advanced Information and Knowledge Processing,
DOI 10.1007/978-1-84996-077-9_11, © Springer-Verlag London Limited 2010

found in a textual format. These textual documents are released on the web on a daily level, creating large collections of information, such as: a variety of reports, product specifications, error reports and software warning messages, summaries, notes, electronic mail, a multitude of documents (newsletters, newspapers, magazines, etc.) and all sorts of textual electronic publications (virtual libraries, a variety of document collections, etc.) [12].

One of the biggest problems in accessing these types of information consists in correctly identifying the subject of any given document. This identification, conducted for the purpose of indexation, is done manually by people, which leads to delay problems or imprecise indexations. Another problem encountered in this area is adapting the automatic systems to, based on words from the text, select a set of terms that is representative of the desired concept. People find it relatively easy to infer concepts from words in documents, because they possess a reasonable knowledge of grammar as well as knowledge of the world around them, which, in the literature, is also known as background knowledge. In contrast to humans, automatic systems do not have this natural ability and, yet, the language used to recover information has to be closer to the natural language. This language, which is less deterministic, more flexible and open, offers the user the possibility of formulating questions with great ease, so that they can locate the most relevant documents. However, language's semantic wealth imposes a few limitations to this type of categorization.

Having discussed some of the most decisive concerns in this area, most of which are related to the large amount of available information, it can be concluded that new means of access and manipulation of large quantities of textual information should be created. For example, the study conducted by [24] cites two main problems that result from the overload of information: one is related to the location of relevant information and the other concerns the knowledge identification and extraction present in the relevant information that was found. To identify the relevant information, it is often necessary to spend hours in front of a search engine. After having identified the relevant information, it is generally not found in isolation but, rather, accompanied by many other pieces of information or spread in a series of documents, making it necessary to analyze the content matter of the information, then filter or extract the data that is actually important.

At present, there is an emerging field, called Textual Data Analysis [24], that is concerned with studying and solving these two previously cited phases. Another field is called Knowledge Discovery from Texts, as described in [10, 18, 27, 32]. Both fields involve the process of recovering, filtering, manipulating and summarizing the knowledge extracted from large sources of textual information and presenting it to the final user by making use of a variety of resources, which usually differ from the originals. Hence, it is important that the analysis and processing mechanisms focus on this type of information that is contained in documents. Computational methods that automatically classify the available textual documents should be used in order to recovery information with greater speed and faithfulness (when it comes to the content matter of the texts), so that they can be useful to the decision-making process within organizations. There are a number of systems aimed at making systemic information storage and processing both socially and economically rational and profitable. Some methodologies have contributed to the appearance of computational systems that are capable of acquiring new knowledge, new abilities and new ways of organizing the existing knowledge [22].

Text Mining (TM) has been making it possible to transform this large volume of information, which is generally non-structured, into useful knowledge, which is often innovative, for the companies. Its use allows people to extract knowledge from non-structured brute textual information, providing elements of support to Knowledge Management, which, in turn, is the way of reorganizing how knowledge is created, used, shared, stored and evaluated. In terms of technology, TM supports knowledge management by transforming the content of information repositories into knowledge that can be analyzed and shared by the organization [34].

TM is a field of technological research whose main goal is to search for patterns, trends and regularity in texts written in natural language. It is normally involved with the process of extracting interesting and non-trivial information from non-structured texts. In this way, the aim is to transform implicit knowledge into explicit knowledge [9]. The process of Text Mining was inspired by the process of Data Mining, which consists of "non-trivial extraction of implicit information that is previously unknown and potentially useful data" [11]. For [5] this is called Text Data Mining. It is in fact a relatively new interdisciplinary field that encompasses: Natural Language Processing, in particular Computational Linguistics, Machine Learning, Information Recovery, Data Mining, Statistics and Information Visualization. For [13], TM is the result of the symbiosis of these fields. Applying a process of TM may have many purposes: creating summaries; clusterization (grouping texts according to similarities in their content matter); identifying languages; extracting terms; text categorization; managing electronic mail, managing documents and research and market investigation.

The focus of this work is to use techniques of text clusterization to categorize textual documents. Clusterization techniques are used when the classes in the elements of the available domain are unknown and, hence, one is looking to automatically separate the elements into groups by some affinity criterion or similarity. Clusterization aids in the process of uncovering in-text knowledge, thereby facilitating the identification of patterns in the classes.

The aim of this work is to propose a categorizer by using fuzzy similarity to improve the issue of linguistic ambiguities found in text classification and to use the agglomerative hierarchical method to create categories from the similarity analysis of textual terms. This is based on the hypothesis that categories can be created from the suggested methodology. In other words, the degree of similarity of the texts to be categorized improves the quality of the cluster representation, which increases their identification capacity, as well as facilitates the comprehension of the resulting clusters. The Eureka categorizer [37–39] groups the text in clusters according to the similarity among the words that compose each sentence. Results using Eureka categorizer is used to compare with the results obtained with categorizer proposed in this work. Our experiments were conducted using Temário, RSS_Terra and Reuters corpora.

The paper is organized as follows. In Sect. 11.2, we introduce the theoretical concepts of Fuzzy Similarity. Section 11.3 handles clusterization methods, especially the hierarchical ones, which are the focus of this work, as well as the algorithms used (Stars and Cliques). In Sect. 11.4 a method that uses fuzzy logic with a relative frequency calculation for the selection of characteristics is proposed in order to obtain the similarity matrix. In Sect. 11.5 we discuss the results that were obtained with the suggested categorizer, which are compared to results obtained with other categorizers in the literature. Finally, Sect. 11.6 presents the conclusions drawn about the proposed method and future works.

11.2 Fuzzy Similarity

Ambiguity is the greatest challenge that systems dealing with natural language have to face. Identifying the real meaning of a given word can be so complicated that sometimes the only way to do so is to ask the user. In the process of choosing a more adequate alternative to the mathematical treatment with regards to questions formulated in natural language, the use of fuzzy logic comes with a great advantage, because conventional logic presents some difficulties when it comes to representing abstract concepts. In conventional, or Boolean, logic, which is commonly used in computing, only two possible values are determined: true (1) or false (0). This logic is not ideal for systems that deal with natural language, since it is impossible to faithfully cover all of the representations of the linguistic context. These systems are based only on right or wrong, yes or no; that is, in only two values to represent an extremely complex world.

Fuzzy logic, on the other hand, is based on the theory of fuzzy sets, whose concepts and principles were first introduced by [40, 41]. Fuzzy logic is multivalued, meaning that there is a set of possible values. Hence, fuzzy logic can be defined as a logic that supports the approximate modes of reasoning, instead of exact ones. The mathematical treatment of fuzzy logic is more appropriate for dealing with imprecise information that is generally employed during human communication, allowing to infer the approximate answer to a question based on knowledge that is inexact, incomplete or not completely trustworthy. The use of fuzzy sets, which are naturally inclined to deal with the domain's linguistic knowledge, can produce easier to interpret solutions [23], which allows you to create specialist systems by using linguistic variables. Fuzziness is found precisely in information of this nature [19].

In fuzzy logic, a function must be generalized to be able to assume values in a given interval and the assumed value indicates the pertinence of an element in a particular set. In this way, the pertinence degree function μA of a fuzzy set A is in the form: $\mu A : X \rightarrow [0, 1]$. In other words, fuzzy set A is characterized by the pertinence function $\mu A(x)$, which assigns a real number in the interval $[0, 1]$ to each element in the set X. In this way, the value of $\mu A(x)$ represents the degree of pertinence of element $x \in X$ in set A [14].

There are important works that use fuzzy logic in data mining. In [21], this technique is used in decision-making systems and marketing systems. Fuzzy logic has also been used to analyze consumer behavior [16, 33]. [17] shows that fuzzy logic is the most adequate mathematical model for the treatment of data in a study that tried to reproduce consumer behavior in choosing brands in a virtual supermarket, when compared to conventional methods, such as boolean logic models relying on determinism and probability.

The problem of ambiguity in text processing can be tackled with the use of fuzzy logic, as its purpose is to deal with imprecise situations, providing improved results by way of the pertinence calculation of an element to a set. By using this technique, it is possible to define just how important and relevant a term is (or not) to any given category. There are a number of fuzzy functions that can be used to fulfill this end. The simplest fuzzy function is called set theoretic inclusion. [4] assesses the presence of words in two documents, which are compared to one another. If the term appears in both documents, the value of 1 is added to the counter; if not, 0 is added. At the end, the degree of similarity is a fuzzy value between 0 and 1, calculated by mean, i.e., the total value of the term counter divided by the total number of words that appear in both documents. This fuzzy value represents the degree in which one element is included in the other or the degree of equality between them. However, this function presents a problem, since it only weights the importance of a word appearing in both documents. The fact that a given word is more or less important in one document than in another, as it appears in different frequencies, is not taken into account. This problem can be partly resolved by using another function, which calculates the mean using fuzzy operators, which are similar to the above function, but assigning weights to the terms [25]. Thus, the fact that the terms appear with different levels of importance is taken into account. In this case, the weights of the terms may be based on the relative frequency or any other discriminating value. Both these functions are found in the literature and were used separately. However, in this work, they will be used together. More details can be found in Sect. 11.4.

The use of fuzzy logic in this work is focused on categorizing elements, not only in terms of pertinence or non-pertinence, as in the case of classical theory, but also in terms of varying degrees of pertinence. Hence, the fuzzy approach is used to categorize objects in accordance to a measure of similarity between them and the center of a conceptual space, whereby the closer to the center the object is, the more similar it is; the further away from the center, the less similar. Each text is represented by a set of characteristics that best define it, and fuzzy similarity is then used to define how similar two representative vectors are. Based on a set of characteristics of a text, composed here by the attributed relevance of the terms in relation to the text, the fuzzy approach is founded upon the notion of similarity of text and a category. The results that are supplied are partial classifications, where each category is assigned a degree of pertinence or relevance in relation to the analyzed text. To verify the similarity between a text and a category, all the terms that make up the set of characteristics of the text are compared to the terms that make up the set of characteristics of the category. A term is considered similar when it is found in the index of the category as well as in the index of the text. The degrees of equality of the terms are then used to determine the degree of similarity between the text index and the category index. In this way, the text is classified under the category in which it obtains the highest degree of similarity. Section 11.4 will explain this proposal, as well as the functions mentioned above, in more detail.

11.3 Agglomerative Hierarchical Methods

The clusterization process can be defined as a process that accept as input continuous regions of a space that has a large number of points and divides this regions into regions with smaller amount of points, called clusters. These clusters have the following properties: density, variance, dimension, form and separation. Based on these properties, different types of conglomerates emerge, which may be hyperspherical, curvilinear, elongated or they may have structures that are more differentiated [1, 3, 7]. According to their configuration, the clusters can be classified into the following categories: hierarchical agglomerative, hierarchical divisive, iterative partitioning, density search, factor analytic, clumping and graph-theoretic. When applied to a data set, these algorithms generate different results [1, 3, 6].

In hierarchical methods, the data are partitioned successively, producing a hierarchical representation of the clusters. This type of representation makes it easier to visualize the clusters at each stage, as well as facilitates the perception of the degree of similarity between them. Another interesting characteristic is that hierarchical methods does not require a definition of the number of clusters. The main advantage of this method [3] is that different similarity measures can be used, which augments the applicability of these methods to any type of attribute (numeric or categorical). The main disadvantages are the stop criterion and the non-refining of the results as the hierarchy is being constructed. With regards to the stop criterion, this can be defined when one reaches a given number of clusters or when some type of stop condition takes place. This criterion requires a distance matrix between the clusters, known as a similarity matrix [15]. This similarity matrix characterizes another problem in the hierarchical methods because it grows exponentially in the face of its database [35].

To calculate the distance in the similarity matrix, many methods can be used [2]. The most important ones are: Simple Connection (the distance between two more similar clusters); Complete Connection (the distance between two less similar clusters); Centroids (the distance between two clusters is obtained by their centroids); Connection Mean (the mean of the distance s between elements of each cluster); Connection group Mean (the distance of two clusters is obtained by the mean of the union of two related clusters) and Ward (finding partitions that minimize the loss associated to each cluster).

In this work, two approaches in hierarchical methods have been considered: agglomerative (Bottom-up) and divisive (Top-down) ones [1, 3, 7]. In the agglomerative hierarchical approach, the data are initially distributed in such a way that each example represents a cluster and, then, these clusters are recursively clustered taking into consideration some measure of similarity until all of the examples belong to one single cluster. Hence, in the beginning, the clusters exist in reduced numbers with a high degree of similarity between their elements, but throughout the process, these groups start to increase and their elements become dissimilar [30]. In Algorithm 1, the steps that are conducted in this approach are described. In this way, Fig. 11.1 can be interpreted as initially containing five clusters [A, B, C, D, E]. At the end of all the steps, a cluster called G1 is formed, wherein clusters [A, B] can be

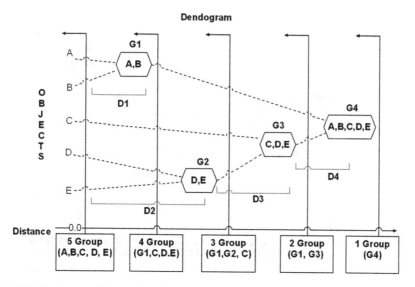

Fig. 11.1 Dendogram of the agglomerative hierarchical method

found and the similarity of the G1 cluster is measured by Distance D1. The cluster G2 is formed by the clusters [D, E], in which case the measure of similarity for G2 is equal to D2. In the next step, cluster G3 is formed by the cluster [C] and by the cluster G2 and the similarity distance of G2 to G3 is the distance D3. The next step is to create the cluster G4, formed by clusters G1 and G3, and the similarity distance is D4. An agglomerative hierarchical algorithm can basically be described in the following way:

Algorithm 1 Agglomerative algorithm

---

1. Look for the pair of clusters with the largest degree of similarity.
2. Create a new cluster that groups the selected pair in Step 1.
3. Decrease by 1 the number of remaining clusters.
4. Return to Step 1 until only one cluster is left.

The divisive hierarchical method, on the other hand, is the least common among the hierarchical methods, as it is inefficient and has high computational costs [1, 3, 6]. In the divisive hierarchical approach (Fig. 11.2), the process is initiated with only one cluster, which contains all the data, and continues to recursively divide according to a given metric that reaches a given stop criterion, usually the number of clusters that are wanted [17]. Figure 11.2 can be interpreted as, in the beginning, everyone is in the cluster [G4] making up one single cluster. This cluster is divided into two clusters [G1 and G3] and the similarity measure is represented by D1. In the next step, one can see that the cluster G3 is divided into [C and G2] and the measure of similarity between these clusters is D2. At this point there are

Dendogram

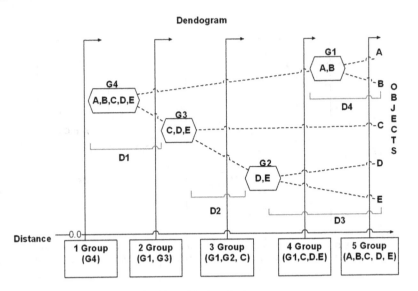

Fig. 11.2 Dendogram of the divisive hierarchical method

already three clusters [G1, G2 and C]. The cluster [G2] is divided into [D and E] and
the similarity between these clusters is the distance D3. In this case, four clusters remain [G1, C, D, E]. The next step is to divide cluster G1, creating clusters [A and B]
and the measure of similarity is expressed as the distance D4. At this point, we are
left with the five clusters [A, B, C, D and E]. The steps to this approach are described
in Algorithm 2.

Algorithm 2 Divisive algorithm
___
1. One single cluster containing all elements is constructed.
2. The similarity matrix is calculated between all pairs in the cluster.
3. A new cluster is created dividing the pairs with the lowest degree of similarity.
4. Return to Step 1 until each cluster contains a single element, or the desired number
of clusters is achieved.

The most important algorithms pertaining to the agglomerative hierarchical
method, according to [20], are: Cliques, Stars, Connected Components and Strings.

The biggest problem in Natural Language Processing methods is its complexity.
They involve the analysis of a series of issues such as text coherence and cohesion,
which could be related to cultural, social, situational and political issues and/or they
could be directly related to the author and the moment in which the text was written [8]. On algorithmic view, texts are analyzed in clusters for the purpose of information recovery or knowledge discovery. It is necessary that the groups constituted
by the texts (objects) have a certain cohesion amongst them. The clusters with very
different objects would not be admissible due to the lack of cohesion of their texts.

Fig. 11.3 Graphic representation of the Stars algorithm

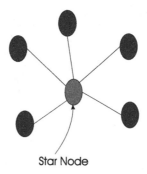

Star Node

The problem is that some of the algorithms, such as Connected Components and Strings, are not as restrictive as expected [37], because they allow objects with a small degree of similarity to be clustered simply because they have a strong relationship with one single object in the group, but not with all the objects found in the clusters. Hence, in this work, we choose using Cliques and Stars algorithms due to their ability to construct more cohesive clusters; that is, texts that are more coherent among themselves. In what follows, we describe in details both algorithms.

11.3.1 Stars Algorithm

The Stars algorithm [20] has this name precisely because the conglomerates that are formed have a shape that is similar to a star; that is, one central element with a variety of other elements connected to it, creating the tips of a star. In this case, the central element is the one that has a relationship to all the other elements of the star, which are interconnected. The elements at the tips are not necessarily related one to the other, which is precisely one of the algorithm's biggest shortcomings, seeing as the elements may not be similar. To minimize this problem of the lack of similarity between the elements located on the tips of the star, a similarity threshold must be established. Hence, the solution for the elements on opposing tips of the star not to be too dissimilar or distant consists of selecting a larger degree of similarity, seeing as the closer they are to the center, the more similar the elements will be amongst themselves, giving the group more coherence. The Stars algorithm is shown in Fig. 11.3. Algorithm 3 describes the steps in the Stars algorithm.

Algorithm 3 Stars algorithm

---

1. Select 1 (one) element and place all similar elements in the same cluster;
2. Elements that are not yet allocated/classified are placed as a cluster seed (repeat Step 1 for 1 element that is not yet allocated).

Fig. 11.4 Graphic
representation of the Cliques
algorithm

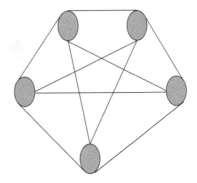

11.3.2 Cliques Algorithm

The Cliques algorithm [20], whose graph when formed is illustrated in Fig. 11.4, is similar to the Stars algorithm, however, the elements are only added to a cluster IF their degree of similarity is greater than the threshold for all the elements already present in the conglomerate, not only in relation to the central element. In this case, the conglomerates tend to be more cohesive and to have a higher quality, seeing as the elements are more similar or closer to one another. Algorithm 4 describes the steps of the Cliques algorithm.

Algorithm 4 Cliques algorithm

1. Select next object and add it to a new cluster;
2. Look for a similar object;
3. If this object is similar to all of the objects in the cluster, add it;
4. Stop criterion: while there is at least one object not allocated, come back to Step 2;
5. Return to Step 1.

11.4 An Approach to Text Categorization—A Proposal

This section proposes an approach to text categorization. This approach is divided into four steps, as illustrated in Fig. 11.5.

In the first step, a pre-text-processing stage is conducted, in which the texts are prepared for the second step. In this step (Step 1), a technique, called case folding, which consists of transforming all words into small case letters, is used. After, the stopwords[1] [26] are removed. The purpose of this step is to make the text more

---

[1]Stopwords are closed classes of words that do not carry meaning, such as articles, pronouns, interjections and prepositions.

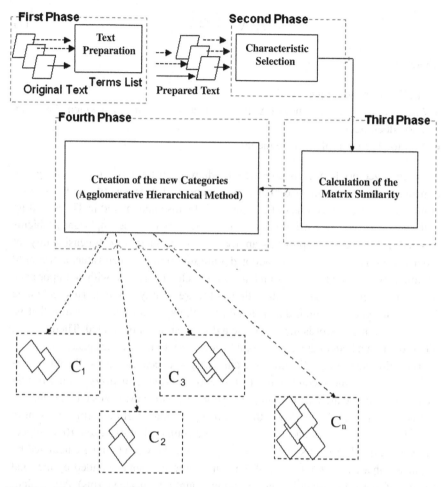

Fig. 11.5 Use of Stars and Cliques algorithms in the agglomerative hierarchical method

concise and the category index more succinct. The removal of stopwords as well as the case folding technique in Text Mining were proposed by [36].

In the second step, term characteristics in the text are selected by way of relative frequency. The latter defines the importance of a given term according to the frequency in which the term appears in the text. The more a term appears in a text, the more important it is in defining it. It is due to this definition of relative frequency that the removal of the stopwords is so important in the pre-processing step. The relative frequency is calculated by (1) [29]. This formula normalizes the result of absolute frequency of the terms by preventing small documents to be represented by small vectors and, conversely, large documents be presented by large vectors. After this normalization, all the documents will be represented by vectors of the same size.

$$F_{rel}X = \frac{F_{abs}X}{N} \tag{1}$$

where:

- $F_{rel}X$ = relative frequency of X;
- $F_{abs}X$ = absolute frequency of X, that is, the amount of times in which X appears in the document;
- N = total number of terms in the text.

Since a vectorial-space is considered, where each term is represented by one dimension, there are as many dimensions as there are different words. Even when we eliminate the stopwords, one of the biggest problems encountered in TM is dealing with the very large dimension spaces. In this way, one of the important problems handled in the second step of this approach is the reduction of dimensionality. In order to do this in this work, we adopted a minimum importance value, a threshold or similarity threshold [37], in which the words (characteristics) with an importance (frequency) below the given value (threshold) are simply ignored. This technique is important given the high dimensionality of the space of characteristics, that is, the large volume of words that compose a document must be treated. Therefore, in order to attain a better categorization, it is necessary to reduce the space.

The third step aims to identify the similarity between the terms (the characteristics selected in the second step). To this end, a measure of fuzzy similarity was used: a measure, called set theoretic inclusion [4], which evaluates the presence of words in the two elements (texts) that are being compared. If the term is present in both elements, a value of one (1) is added to the counter; if it isn't, zero (0) is added. At the end, the degree of similarity is a fuzzy value between 0 and 1 calculated by the mean; that is, the total value of the common term counter divided by the total number of words in both documents (without counting repeated terms). After calculated the fuzzy similarity, a matrix is generated that indicates the similarity values between every text present in the text database. In the main diagonal of the similarity matrix, the value is always 1, as the degree of similarity of a text when compared to itself is always 1. Based on this matrix, clustering algorithms are used to identify the text clusters, which specify some type of relationship rule.

The fourth and final step of the proposed approach consists of using the agglomerative hierarchical method, whose main advantage upon the other clustering methods is the non-definition of a prior number of clusters. Analyzing the constructed dendograms, it is possible to work out the appropriate number of clusters. We used the Cliques and Stars algorithms, as these algorithms are capable of constructing more cohesive clusters, as seen in Sect. 11.3.

In the next section, we will describe the experiments conducted with the approach proposed in this work, which are compared to the categorizer proposed by [37], called Eurekha.

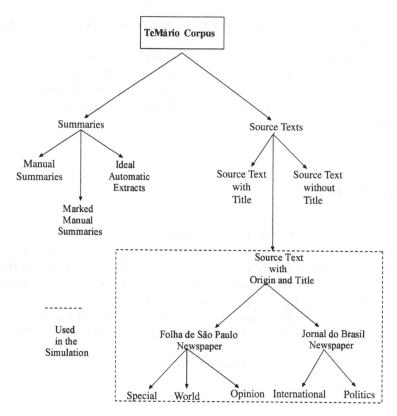

Fig. 11.6 Division of categories in the TeMário Corpus

11.5 Experiments

For the experiment with the Categorizer proposed in this work and Wives's Eurekha categorizer [37] the following Corpus were used: TeMário [26], Reuters-21578, Distribution 1.0 and Really Simple Syndication (RSS).[2]

Figure 11.6 illustrates the composition of the TeMário Corpus. This corpus is composed of two main sections: summaries and source texts. The source-text section is subdivided into source texts with titles, source texts without titles and source texts with subdivided titles. These were separated into two categories: Folha de São Paulo and Jornal do Brasil, two newspapers with major circulation in Brazil. In this summaries section, there are: manual summaries, ideal summaries and marked summaries. Marked summaries contain sections which an automatic summarizer should select from the original text. To conduct the experiments, we used source texts with the subdivided titles, illustrated in Fig. 11.6 in the box with dotted lines. Regarding to the subdivision, the texts of each newspaper with subdivided into 5 categories:

---

[2]Corpus extracted from Terra Networks Brasil S/A.

Special, World, Opinion, Politics and International. Each of these categories possesses a total of 20 texts.

The Reuters Corpus is made up of 100 texts in English, all in the field of economics.[3] The Distribution 1.0 corpus has 22 files. The RSS_Terra corpus is also made up of 100 texts, in Portuguese, classified in 7 categories: Brazil (22 texts), Cities (16 texts), Education (1 text), Police (36 texts), Politics (13 texts), Health (8 texts) and Traffic (4 texts).[4]

11.5.1 Hypothesis

The null hypothesis of this work consists in the statement that the Categorizer is equal to Eurekha when it comes to text distribution in the categories. This hypothesis is true for both the use of the Cliques algorithm as well as for the Stars algorithm and for each of the corpuses that were simulated. It relates the variance in the number of texts of each category constructed by the categorizers. In other words, if a categorizer found 3 categories, each with 3, 5 and 7 texts, the variance of this sample of the population is 4. Formally, this null hypothesis can be represented by

$$H_0: \quad \sigma \; Categorizer = \sigma \; Eurekha \qquad (2)$$

where:

- H_0 = null hypothesis,
- $\sigma \; Eurekha$—variance of the Eurekha sample,
- $\sigma \; Categorizer$—variance of the Categorizer sample.

If the null hypothesis is considered false, some other statement must be true. Hence, this work proposes an alternative hypothesis H_1 that represents the opposite of the null hypothesis H_0. The alternative hypothesis is formally represented by

$$H_1: \quad \sigma \; Categorizer \neq \sigma \; Eurekha. \qquad (3)$$

The methodology to test the hypothesis that was adopted in this work considers the populations, which were obtained in the generated categorizer simulations, independent and with the same variability. Hence, the F-test was chosen, where the populations were assumed to be normally distributed and the ration of the variance of the samples follow a distribution known as F [31].

---

[3]The complete collection has 1,578 texts, however, these files were not available for use in their totality. Hence, we used only the 100 texts that are available online.

[4]These files, which come from the most diverse RSS channels of Terra Networks Brasil S/A, were collected daily during the period comprising February to March 2008.

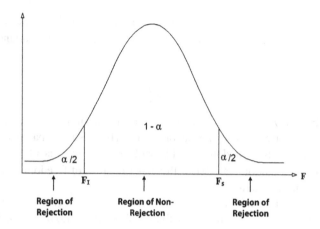

Fig. 11.7 Regions of rejection and non-rejection for the two-tailed F test

11.5.2 Decision Rule for the F-Test

The critical values of the F distribution depend on two sets of degrees of freedom. The degrees of freedom of the numerator of the fraction pertain to the first sample (Eurekha), and the degrees of freedom in the denominator pertain to the second sample (Categorizer).

The null hypothesis is rejected if the statistics of the F-test are calculated as being greater than the critical value of the upper tail, F_S, based on the distribution of F with $n_1 - 1$ degrees of freedom in the numerator, from Sample 1, and $n_2 - 1$ degrees of freedom in the denominator, from Sample 2.

The null hypothesis is also rejected if the statistics of the F-test are positioned below the critical value of the lower tail, F_I, of the distribution of F, with $n_1 - 1$ and $n_2 - 1$ degrees of freedom in the numerator and in the denominator, respectively.

Therefore, the decision rule is:

$$\text{Reject } H_0 \text{ if } F > F_S \text{ or } F < F_I.$$
$$\text{If not, do not reject } H_0.$$

Figure 11.7 shows the areas of rejection and non-rejection, keeping in mind that this is a two-tailed test and the area of rejection is shared between the lower and upper tails of the F distribution. Since, in this work, we have adopted the level of significance of 5% with a value of $\alpha = 0.05$, then the region of rejection will contain 0.025 of the distribution, in other words, $\alpha/2$.

11.5.3 Testing the Null Hypothesis

The procedure for testing the hypothesis of equality of the two variances is based on the following result: Let $x_{11}, x_{12}, \ldots, x_{1n}$ be a random sample of a normal population with a mean of μ_1 and variance of σ_1^2, and let $x_{21}, x_{22}, \ldots, x_{2n}$ be a random sample of a second normal population with a mean of μ_2 and variance of σ_2^2. Assume that both populations are independent. Let S_1^2 and S_2^2 be the variances of the samples. The ratio

$$F = \frac{S_1^2}{S_2^2} \qquad (4)$$

has a distribution F, with $n_1 - 1$ degrees of freedom in the numerator and $n_2 - 1$ degrees of freedom in the denominator. This result is based on the fact that $(n_1 - 1)S_1^2/\sigma_1^2$ is a random variable with $n_1 - 1$ degrees of freedom, that $(n_2 - 1)S_2^2/\sigma_2^2$ is a random variable with $n_2 - 1$ degrees of freedom and that both populations are independent.

The idea of the null hypothesis in this work H_0: σ *Categorizer* $= \sigma$ *Eurekha* where the ratio $F = S_1^2/S_2^2$ with a distribution $F = (n^1 - 1)/(n^2 - 2)$. Formally, this can be represented:

- $S_1^2 = $ variance of the sample of n_1 elements;
- $S_2^2 = $ variance of the sample of n_2 elements;
- Degree of freedom is given by:
  $F_S = n_1 - 1 = $ degree of freedom in the numerator;
  $F_I = n_2 - 1 = $ degree of freedom in the denominator.

The following formulas are obtained for the calculations:

$$F = F_{(\frac{\alpha}{2}, n_1-1, n_2-1)} = Critical\ limit\ of\ the\ uppertail, \qquad (5)$$

$$F = F_{(1-\alpha, n_1-1, n_2-1)} = Critical\ limit\ of\ the\ lowertail. \qquad (6)$$

Each corpus has a population of 100 texts. Their samples correspond to the distributions of each text in numbers of categories created by Eurekha and by the Categorizer, using the algorithm Stars and Cliques on each of the simulated corpora. As an example, consider the Reuters corpus and the Cliques algorithm, for which the Eurekha categorizer obtained 15 categories, while the Categorizer obtained 38. In this way, there are $(15 - 1)$ degrees of freedom for the Eurekha categorizer and $(38 - 1)$ degrees of freedom for the Categorizer.

The F_S of each corpus, the critical value of the upper tail of the F distribution is obtained by (5). In [28], one is able to locate the table showing the distribution values of F.

In F_I, the critical value of the lower tail of the F distribution, with $n_1 - 1$ degrees of freedom, from Sample 1 in the numerator and $n_2 - 1$ degrees of freedom from Sample 2 in the denominator, is calculated by taking the reciprocal of F_S*, a critical value of the upper tail of the F distribution, with "inverted" degrees of freedom, that is, $n_2 - 1$ degrees of freedom in the numerator and $n_1 - 1$ degrees of freedom in the denominator. This relationship is shown in (6).

Let us return to the example in order to show how the F test works. Recalling that the degrees of freedom are equal to 37 and 14, respectively, to obtain the critical value of 0.025 from the lower tail, you need to obtain the critical value of the lower tail, which, in this case, equals 2.27, with 37 degrees of freedom in the numerator

Table 11.1 Results of the F-test applied to the simulation corpuses with the Stars algorithm with a degree of significance of 5%

Corpus	TeMário	Reuters	RSS_Terra
F_I	0.42	0.05	0.5
F_S	2.34	19.44	2.00
F	3.17	102.08	1.86
H_0	*Reject($F > F_S$)*	*Reject($F > F_S$)*	*Accept*

Table 11.2 Results of the F-test applied to the simulation corpuses with the Cliques algorithm with a degree of significance of 5%

Corpus	TeMário	Reuters	RSS_Terra
F_I	0.55	0.41	0.57
F_S	1.80	2.27	1.75
F	0.44	3.38	11.66
H_0	*Reject($F < F_I$)*	*Reject($F > F_S$)*	*Reject($F > F_S$)*

and 14 degrees of freedom in the denominator. Hence, the value of $F_I = \frac{1}{2.43} = 0.412$. Using the decision rule, we have:

$$\text{Reject } H_0 \text{ if } F > F_S = 2.27 \text{ or } F < F_I = 0.412.$$
$$\text{If not, do not reject } H_0.$$

In (4), the ratio of the proportion of the two samples is calculated. Applied to the example of the Reuters corpus, we have: $F = \frac{10.809521}{3.20056} = 3.37738$. Therefore, in the example of the Reuters corpus we have $F_I = 0.412 < F = 3.37738$. As $F = 3.37738 > F_S = 2.27$, H_0 is rejected, a significant difference between the variability of Eurekha and of the Categorizer does exist in the text distribution for each of the categories created in the Reuters corpus simulation.

Tables 11.1 and 11.2 display the results of the F-test using the Reuters, TeMário and RSS_Terra corpuses and the algorithms Stars and Cliques. A 95% trust interval was established for this two-tailed test.

After analyzing the results shown in Tables 11.1 and 11.2, you can see that the null hypothesis was only accepted in the RSS_Terra corpus using the Stars algorithm. When the null hypothesis is accepted according to the F-test, a t-test is indicated for the difference between the two arithmetic means with the equal variances. For the t-test, assuming that there are two populations with unknown means of μ_1 and μ_2, we have:

$$H_0 \text{ (null hypothesis):} \quad \mu_1 = \mu_2;$$
$$H_1 \text{ (alternative hypothesis):} \quad \mu_1 \neq \mu_2.$$

The t-test is formally described by:

$$t = \frac{\overline{X_1} - \overline{X_2}}{S_a \sqrt{\frac{1}{n_1} + \frac{1}{n_2}}} \tag{7}$$

where:

Table 11.3 Results of the t-test applied to the RSS_Terra corpus of the simulation with the Stars algorithm with a degree of significance of 5%, which obtained equal variance

Corpus-Stars	RSS_Terra
S_a^2	15.22
t_l	-2.00
t_S	2.00
t	1.40
H_0	*Accept*

- n_1 = size of sample 1;
- n_2 = size of sample 2;
- $\overline{X_1}$ = mean of sample 1;
- $\overline{X_2}$ = mean of sample 2;
- S_1^2 = variance of sample 1;
- S_2^2 = variance of sample 2;
- S_a = clustered variance calculated by

$$S_a = \frac{(n_1 - 1)S_1^2 + (n_2 - 1)S_2^2}{n_1 + n_2 - 2}. \tag{8}$$

Cluster variance is given this name because the statistics of the test require that both variances of the sample, $S_1^2 = S_2^2$, be clustered or combined for the purpose of obtaining S_a^2, the best estimate of a variance that is common to both samples, under the premise that both variances of the two samples are equal.

The t-test statistics for cluster variance follows a t distribution with $n_1 + n_2 - 2$ degrees of freedom. In this way, the criteria for the rejection of the null hypothesis can be formalized as follows:

$$\text{Reject } H_0, \text{ if } t > t_{n_1+n_2-2} \text{ or } t < -t_{n_1+n_2-2}.$$

Table 11.3 shows the result after confirming the null hypothesis for the variances (H_0: $\sigma_1^2 = \sigma_2^2$) in the simulation of the RSS_Terra corpus, where we applied a t-test with a significance level of 5% to test the difference between the means (H_0: $\mu_1 = \mu_2$).

With the result obtained in the t-test, it became clear that the means of both populations were effectively equal. Hence, the probability of detecting a difference with this dimension or greater, between the two arithmetic means of the samples, corresponds to 0.19806804. Since the critical value is greater than $\alpha = 0.05$, there isn't sufficient evidence to accept the null hypothesis.

11.5.4 Qualitative Analysis of the Constructed Categories

In Fig. 11.8, the graph shows the number of categories created by Eurekha and by the Categorizer, using each of the three simulation corpuses with the use of the Stars and Cliques algorithms.

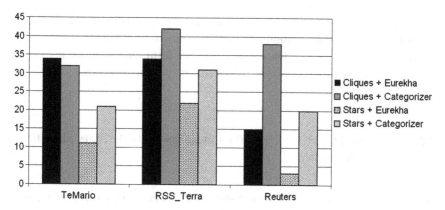

Fig. 11.8 Number of categories created by Eurekha and by Categorizer using the Stars and Cliques algorithm

Figure 11.8 shows that the Categorizer obtained in each of the simulated corpuses a greater number of categories in comparison to Eurekha.

The Categorizer obtained in the Reuters and RSS_Terra corpuses a greater number of categories as compared to Eurekha. In this way, Eurekha only had a higher number of categories in the TeMário corpus using the Cliques algorithm, which accounts for 16.66% of all the simulations.

After analyzing the results in Fig. 11.8, some important observations can be made regarding the amount of categories obtained in the Categorizer and in Eurekha:

The first aspect refers to the methodology adopted in this work, which opted for clusterization using the agglomerative hierarchical method. This technique is important in this work precisely due to the fact that it does not define the initial number of clusters since, in the context of Text Mining, the domain specialist would have to define how many categories there would be to later start categorizing. This process creates a certain degree of autonomy as there is no need for human intervention in the act of defining the number of categories, as these are automatically generated by way of the agglomerative hierarchy.

The second aspect worth noting refers to the other part of the methodology proposed in this work, where a minimum value of importance, a threshold (here, we used 0.05) or similarity threshold [37] was employed in which the words (characteristics) with an importance (frequency) below a given value are simply ignored. Along with the threshold, the use of fuzzy similarity, that is, the measure of set theoretic inclusion, determines the number of categories and sub-categories that will exist throughout the process and also determines the similarity distance between them.

The high number of categories represents the refinement of the texts. Texts categorized using our approach are added into one category only if its similarity rate is bigger than the boundary to all the texts present in the category and not only related to the main category. This factor is significant to indicate the high degree of similarity among the clustered texts and also shows that the greater the distance between the categories (depth level in the hierarchy tree), the greater will be the dissimilarity between them, thereby determining the higher degree of similarity between the texts grouped into each category. Hence, this proves the justification that the higher the number of categories, the greater the refinement among the categorized texts.

11.5.4.1 Details of the Results from the Categorizer with the Stars Algorithm Using the Reuters Corpus

Using the Stars algorithm, the Categorizer created 20 categories. Category C_1 was the one that obtained the highest number of texts—18 in total—and their topics were the economy. Categories C_{12}, C_{17}, C_{18}, C_{19} and C_{20} were the categories with only one allocated text. It was observed that for the texts that were clustered in pairs, as in the case of category C_{11}, there was no coherence with regards to their topics. Now with only two texts there is category C_{11} which appears to have texts that are closely related and handle the same topic.

There were 15 texts in category C_2, all of which related to political economy in general. In C_3 there was a total of 10 texts whose main topic involves types of investments. The Categorizer clustered into category C_5 11 texts on investments focused exclusively on companies looking for patents and new products. One can see that some of the files speak a lot of pharmaceutical labs. In category C_{10} there were 8 texts that talk generally about the economy in a variety of different countries. In category C_{14} there were 5 texts that deal essentially with production. Categories C_8, C_9 and C_{13} each had a total of 4 texts. The ones in C_3 covered mining, agriculture and the market; the Japanese economy was the topic of the texts in C_9 and, in C_{13}, no relationship was found between the texts.

With 3 texts grouped into each category, we have categories C_4, C_6, C_7, C_{15} and C_{16} although in categories C_7, C_{15} and C_{16} there was no relationship between the texts. However, the texts in category C_4 cover the world economy and cite Argentina, Tanzania and Africa. Category C_6 handles joint ventures with Japan.

11.5.4.2 Details of the Results from Eurekha with the Stars Algorithm Using the Reuters Corpus

In this simulation, the Eurekha categorizer created 3 categories, wherein C_1 obtained a total of 86 texts, C_2 clustered 12 texts and C_3 had 2 texts. By the analysis, it is not possible to establish a relationship between the texts clusters in C_1, C_2 and C_3, as there is no apparent relationship between the texts. We were unable to establish coherence in the texts within the referred clusters.

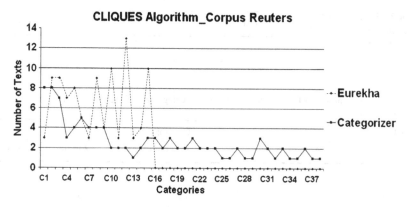

Fig. 11.9 Number of categories created in the Cliques algorithm with the simulation of the Reuters corpus in the Categorizer and in Eurekha

Table 11.4 Total number of categories created in the categorizers Eurekha and Categorizer in the RSS_Terra corpus

Eurekha	Categorizer
22	31

11.5.4.3 Graphically Comparing the Results of the Text Distribution in the Categorizer and in Eurekha with the Cliques Algorithm Using the Reuters Corpus

As we can see in Fig. 11.9, the Eurekha categorizer obtained a total of 15 categories, while the Categorizer had 38 categories. If we observe the text distribution in the Categorizer, we can see that there was no category with more than eight allocated texts, whereas using Eurekha, 13 texts were allocated to the C_{12} category.

We also can see that in the Categorizer there were 10 categories that only had one single allocated text, whereas in using Eurekha there were no categories with only one single text. However, the number of categories created by the Categorizer was more than double the amount of categories created by Eurekha.

11.5.4.4 Comparing the Results of the Text Distribution of the Categorizer and of Eurekha with the Stars Algorithm Using the RSS_Terra Corpus

According to Table 11.4 the Categorizer obtained a greater number of categories in comparison to Eurekha. In Table 11.6 you can see how the texts were distributed in the categories created by each of the categorizers when using the Stars algorithm.

Table 11.5 shows that the Categorizer had a distribution of 16 texts in one given category, while Eurekha obtained in a given category of cluster of 20 texts. In Eurekha there was no cluster in categories with 1, 8, 10 and 11 texts, whereas in the

Table 11.5 Text distribution in the categorizers created by Eurekha and Categorizer using the RSS_Terra corpus

Eurekha	Categorizer
34	42

Table 11.6 Total number of categories created in the categorizers Eurekha and Categorizer in the RSS_Terra corpus

Eurekha		Categorizer	
Amount of text	Amount of categories	Amount of text	Amount of categories
1	0	1	12
2	5	2	6
3	8	3	4
4	2	4	5
5	3	5	0
6	0	6	1
7	2	7	0
8	0	8	0
9	1	9	1
10	0	10	0
11	0	11	1
20	1	16	1

Categorizer this did not occur with the amounts of texts 5, 7, 8 and 10. The Eurekha categorizer did not have any category with only 1 text, but this occurred in 12 categories in the Categorizer.

11.5.4.5 Comparing the Results of the Text Distribution of the Categorizer and of Eurekha with the Cliques Algorithm Using the RSS_Terra Corpus

According to Table 11.6, the Categorizer obtained a greater number of categories in comparison to Eurekha. Table 11.7 shows how the texts were distributed in the categories created by each of the categorizers when using the Cliques algorithm.

The table shows that the Eurekha categorizer clustered 20 texts in only one single category, whereas the Categorizer placed in one given category 6 texts. None of the categories in Eurekha received only one text, whereas in the Categorizer there were 11 categories with only one single text. In Eurekha texts in pairs occurred in 24 categories, whereas in the Categorizer they were found in 14 categories. Eurekha did not create a single category in which the amount of texts was 1, 5 and 6, whereas in the Categorizer, each category that was created had at least one allocated text.

Table 11.7 Text distribution in the categorizers created by Eurekha and Categorizer using RSS_Terra corpus

Eurekha		Categorizer	
Amount of text	Amount of categories	Amount of text	Amount of categories
1	0	1	11
2	24	2	14
3	8	3	10
4	2	4	5
5	0	5	1
6	0	6	1
20	1	–	–

11.5.4.6 Comparing the Results of the Categorizer in the Distribution of Texts in Each Category Using the TeMário Corpus in Relation to the Stars and Cliques Algorithm

The use of the Cliques algorithm by the Categorizer generated 32 categories, as shown in Table 11.8. Category C_4 and C_{10} were the ones that obtained the highest number of texts using the Categorizer: 9 each. With the Stars algorithm, 23 categories were created. Category C_1 obtained a total of 21 texts. Categories C_{13}, C_{25}, C_{27} and C_{31} were categorized with only a single text. The remaining categories had their texts clustered in intervals ranging from 2 to 8, as indicated in Table 11.9. All of them are characterized by coherence in their subjects. In contrast, for the Stars algorithm, categories C_5, C_{10}, C_{11}, C_{17}, C_{18}, C_{19}, C_{20} and C_{23} were clustered with only one text, while the other categories had texts clustered in intervals between 2 and 21.

Another fact that must be observed in the Cliques algorithm is the lower number of categories created with only one text (4 in total) in contrast to the Stars algorithm (which created 8).

No incoherence was observed in the Cliques algorithm in the case of categories with only two texts, as seen with the Stars algorithm.

As seen in Fig. 11.10, the Cliques algorithm, in comparison to the Stars algorithm, didn't have any category with a cluster of over 10 texts. This is due to the fact that, in this algorithm, elements are only added to a category if their degree of similarity exceeds the threshold for all elements already present in the category and not only with regards to the central element.

11.5.4.7 Comparing the Results of Eurekha in the Distribution of Texts in Each Category Using the TeMário Corpus in Relation to the Stars and Cliques Algorithm

Eurekha generated 33 categories using the Cliques algorithm and 10 categories with the Stars algorithm. By analyzing the behavior of the Cliques algorithm in

Table 11.8 Texts clustered by the Categorizer using the Stars (S) and Cliques (C) algorithm in the TeMário corpus. *Folha de São Paulo* is abbreviated as FSP and *Jornal do Brasil* is abbreviated as JB

Categories created		FSP						JB				Total categories	
		Opinion		World		Special		Intern.		Politics			
S	C	S	C	S	C	S	C	S	C	S	C	S	C
C_1	C_1	13	3	2	–	5	–	–	–	1	–	21	3
C_2	C_2	2	4	–	–	–	1	–	–	–	–	2	5
C_3	C_3	2	2	2	–	3	–	2	–	6	–	15	2
C_4	C_4	2	2	2	–	3	–	2	–	6	–	15	2
C_5	C_5	1	3	–	2	–	1	–	–	–	–	1	6
C_6	C_6	–	1	–	–	3	–	–	1	–	–	3	2
C_7	C_7	–	1	6	1	1	–	5	–	1	–	13	2
C_8	C_8	–	–	–	–	2	3	2	–	2	–	6	3
C_9	C_9	–	–	–	–	3	3	–	–	–	–	3	3
C_{10}	C_{10}	–	–	–	3	1	2	–	4	–	–	1	9
C_{11}	C_{11}	–	–	–	–	1	3	–	–	–	4	1	7
C_{12}	C_{12}	–	–	1	–	–	4	1	–	–	–	2	4
C_{13}	C_{13}	–	–	1	–	–	1	3	–	–	–	4	1
C_{14}	C_{14}	–	–	1	1	–	1	–	1	1	–	2	3
C_{15}	C_{15}	–	–	1	–	–	1	1	–	3	1	5	2
C_{16}	C_{16}	–	–	–	2	–	–	1	1	1	–	2	3
C_{17}	C_{17}	–	–	–	3	–	–	1	–	–	–	1	3
C_{18}	C_{18}	–	–	–	1	–	–	1	4	–	–	1	5
C_{19}	C_{19}	–	–	–	3	–	–	1	–	–	–	1	3
C_{20}	C_{20}	–	–	–	1	–	–	1	1	–	–	1	2
C_{21}	C_{21}	–	–	–	1	–	–	–	2	2	–	2	3
C_{22}	C_{22}	–	–	–	1	–	–	–	1	2	–	2	2
C_{23}	C_{23}	–	–	–	–	–	–	–	1	1	1	1	2
–	C_{24}	–	–	–	–	–	–	–	1	–	–	–	1
–	C_{25}	–	–	–	–	–	–	–	1	–	–	–	1
–	C_{26}	–	–	–	–	–	–	–	1	–	2	–	3
–	C_{27}	–	–	–	–	–	–	–	1	–	–	–	1
–	C_{28}	–	–	–	–	–	–	–	–	–	2	–	2
–	C_{29}	–	–	–	–	–	–	–	–	–	3	–	3
–	C_{30}	–	–	–	–	–	–	–	–	–	2	–	2
–	C_{31}	–	–	–	–	–	–	–	–	–	1	–	1
–	C_{32}	–	–	–	–	–	–	–	–	–	2	–	2
Total		20	20	20	20	20	20	20	20	20	20	100	100

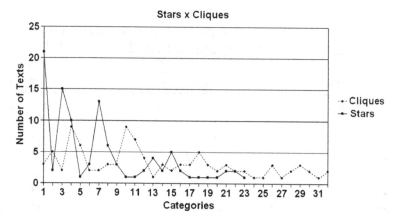

Fig. 11.10 Comparison between the stars and Cliques algorithm using the Categorizer on TeMário corpus

Table 11.9, one can see that there is a certain uniformity in the text distribution in each category, which is normal for this algorithm. The maximum was 6 (six) texts allocated per category and there was no case of a category that was allocated only a single text. In contrast, with the Stars algorithm there was a very high concentration of texts in category C_1 (with 32 texts) and in C_2, C_3 and C_6 (with 13, 18 and 10 texts, respectively).

Another fact that must be observed in the Cliques algorithm is the very high number of texts allocated in pairs, which occurred in 16 categories. Furthermore, the greatest text allocation took place in category C_{12}, with 6 texts, wherein five were in the international category and one in the world category.

In the Stars algorithm, the category that received the lowest number of allocated texts was C_8 with only two texts. The most noteworthy characteristic of this algorithm is the very high concentration of texts in the initial categories, as can be observed in Table 11.9.

As seen in Fig. 11.11, the Cliques algorithm, in comparison to the Stars algorithm, didn't have any category with a cluster of over 6 texts. This is due to the fact that, in this algorithm, elements are only added to a category if their degree of similarity exceeds the threshold for all elements already present in the category and not only with regards to the central element.

11.6 Conclusion

This work proposed a text categorization approach using fuzzy similarity to improve the issue of linguistic ambiguities found in text classification and using agglomerative hierarchical method to create categories based on the similarity analysis of textual terms.

Table 11.9 Texts clustered by Eurekha using the Stars and Cliques algorithm in the TeMário corpus. *Folha de São Paulo* is abbreviated as FSP and *Jornal do Brasil* is abbreviated as JB

Categories created		FSP						JB				Total categories	
		Opinion		World		Special		Intern.		Politics			
S	C	S	C	S	C	S	C	S	C	S	C	S	C
C_1	C_1	10	–	9	–	10	2	3	–	1	–	33	2
C_2	C_2	2	–	3	–	2	3	5	–	1	–	13	3
C_3	C_3	–	–	2	–	4	2	2	–	10	–	18	2
C_4	C_4	–	–	3	–	1	4	2	–	–	–	6	4
C_5	C_5	1	–	1	–	2	2	–	–	1	–	5	2
C_6	C_6	–	–	1	–	–	3	7	–	2	–	10	3
C_7	C_7	1	–	–	–	–	3	1	2	1	–	3	5
C_8	C_8	–	–	1	–	–	–	–	5	1	–	2	5
C_9	C_9	4	–	–	–	–	–	–	2	–	–	4	2
C_{10}	C_{10}	2	–	–	–	1	–	–	3	3	–	6	3
–	C_{11}	–	1	–	1	–	–	–	1	–	–	–	3
–	C_{12}	–	–	–	1	–	–	–	5	–	–	–	6
–	C_{13}	–	–	–	–	–	–	–	2	–	–	–	2
–	C_{14}	–	–	–	2	–	–	–	–	–	–	–	2
–	C_{15}	–	–	–	2	–	–	–	–	–	–	–	2
–	C_{16}	–	–	–	2	–	–	–	–	–	–	–	2
–	C_{17}	–	–	–	2	–	–	–	–	–	–	–	2
–	C_{18}	–	–	–	2	–	–	–	–	–	–	–	2
–	C_{19}	–	2	–	2	–	–	–	–	–	–	–	4
–	C_{20}	–	–	–	2	–	–	–	1	–	–	–	2
–	C_{21}	–	1	–	2	–	–	–	–	–	–	–	3
–	C_{22}	–	3	–	1	–	–	–	–	–	–	–	4
–	C_{23}	–	–	–	1	–	–	–	–	–	2	–	3
–	C_{24}	–	2	–	–	–	–	–	–	–	–	–	2
–	C_{25}	–	2	–	–	–	–	–	–	–	–	–	2
–	C_{26}	–	4	–	–	–	–	–	–	–	–	–	4
–	C_{27}	–	2	–	–	–	–	–	–	–	–	–	2
–	C_{28}	–	2	–	–	–	–	–	–	–	–	–	2
–	C_{29}	–	1	–	–	–	–	–	–	–	3	–	4
–	C_{30}	–	–	–	–	–	–	–	–	–	5	–	5
–	C_{31}	–	–	–	–	–	–	–	–	–	4	–	4
–	C_{32}	–	–	–	–	–	–	–	–	–	2	–	2
–	C_{33}	–	–	–	–	–	1	–	–	–	4	–	5
Total		20	20	20	20	20	20	20	20	20	20	100	100

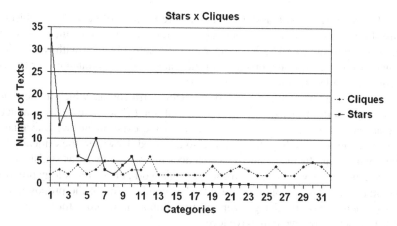

Fig. 11.11 Comparison between the Stars and Cliques algorithm using Eurekha on TeMário corpus

The technique of relative frequency adopted in the selection step allows the Categorizer to have the lists of the words that appear most often in the text. This technique was imperative in order to indicate which terms within the collection have a higher level of significance; that is, it established a threshold to decrease the dimensionality of the characteristics' vector space. The fuzzy similarity technique (set theoretic inclusion) used in the Categorizer, determined the inference function of the fuzzy logic, thereby allowing us to measure the similarity between the texts on the list. Stars and Cliques algorithms were employed in the Agglomerative Hierarchical methodology to identify the groups of texts by specifying some type of relationship rule. Although they obtained very similar results, the Cliques algorithm presented a slight advantage of the Stars algorithm in that it created a larger number of clusters.

With regards to the comparison between the two categorizers that were studied, Eurekha and the Categorizer, there is statistical evidence suggesting that the Categorizer is more significant that Eurekha. In all of the simulations conducted, Eurekha attained a higher number of created categories in only 16.66% of the corpuses. Even so, the difference between the categories created by Eurekha and the Categorizer was of only one unit, in only one corpus and using only the Cliques algorithm.

In the Reuters corpus the Eurekha categorizer had its worst performance: when using the Stars algorithm, Eurekha obtained only two categories, which made it impossible to carry on any sort of analysis looking to assess the relationship between the clustered texts.

On the other hand, the results with the TeMário corpus were very interesting, due to the fact that the corpus was developed with the purpose of summarizing texts that are very close and that are divided into previously established categories, which considerably facilitates the content analysis as well as the treatment of the file names.

The results of Eurekha and the Categorizer showed a very close proximity, up to the point where they were literally equal to one another. However, with the use of the F-test, it was seen that the variances were in fact different. As a subjective means of evaluation, we also verified a considerable advantage of the Categorizer in comparison to the Eurekha by comparing the results obtained with results from a human evaluator. The categorization of the Categorizer was much closer to what was considered ideal by the human evaluator.

Another interesting result was that of the RSS_Terra corpus, which in the F-test had its null hypothesis accepted. From that point, the t-Student test was conducted for equal variances after which the means from the experiments were evaluated. In the t-Student test, the hypothesis was also accepted. However, the critical-p was greater than its significance value α, which does not prove there was statistical evidence that the means were equal. To conclude this work, the methodology proposed in this study points to encouraging results. The combination of the proposed techniques in each step of the Categorizer was very important in order for the results to be able to reach a positive indicative level.

One of the greatest challenges in this field is the reduction of vector space; that is, the calculation of the similarity matrix. As a proposal for the future, we expect to exclude these calculations, thereby reducing vector space as well as reducing the computational complexity of the text categorization algorithms.

Another common problem in the field is the definition of the stop criterion, which still stands in the way of a truly autonomous process. A common practice is to establish these criteria based on observations of the classifier's behavior. Note however that this problem is quite serious from the viewpoint of knowledge discovery, since this scenario is made up of groups of texts that are considerably dense and lengthy. A future contribution could be to use an automatic learning process to make decisions on a variety of circumstances regarding the best stop criterion to be used.

References

1. Aldenderfe, M.S., Mark, R.K., Aldenderfe, S.: Cluster Analysis, p. 88. SAGE University, Beverly Hills (1978)
2. Arora, R., Bangarole, P.: Text mining: classification & clustering of articles related to sports. In: Proceedings of the 43rd Annual Southeast Regional Conference ACM-SE 43, vol. 1. ACM, New York (2005)
3. Berkhin, P.: Survey of clustering data mining techniques. Technical report, Accrue Software, San Jose, CA (2002)
4. Cross, V.: Fuzzy information retrieval. Journal of Intelligent Information Systems 3, 29–56 (1994)
5. Dagan, I., Feldman, R., Hirsh, H.: Keyword-based browsing and analysis of large document sets. In: Proceedings of the Fifth Annual Symposium on Document Analysis and Information Retrieval—SDAIR, Las Vegas, Nevada, pp. 191–208 (1996)
6. Everitt, B.S., Dunn, G.: Applied Multivariate Data Analysis, 2nd edn. Edward Arnold, London (2000). http://www.iop.kcl.ac.uk/iop/Departments/BioComp/MvBook.stm
7. Fasulo, D.: An analysis of recent work on clustering algorithms. Technical report, Univ. of Washington, Washington, DC (1999).
8. Fávero, L.: Coesão e Coerência Textuais. Ática, São Paulo (2000). In Portuguese
9. Fayyad, U., Uthurusamy, R.: Data mining and knowledge discovery in databases (introduction to the Special Issue) Editorial. Data Mining and Knowledge Discovery. Communications of the ACM 39(11), 24–26 (1996)

10. Feldman, R., Hirsh, H.: Exploiting background information in knowledge discovery from text. Journal of Intelligent Information Systems 9(1), 83–97 (1997)
11. Frawley, W.J., Piatestsky, S.G., Matheus, C.: Knowledge discovery in data bases: An overview. AI Magazine 13(3), 57–70 (1992). http://www.kdnuggets.com/gpspubs/aimag-kdd-overview-1992.pdf
12. Han, J., Kamber, M.: Data Mining: Concepts and Techniques, 1st edn. Morgan Kaufmann, New York (2001)
13. Hearst, M.A.: Automated Discovery of WordNet Relations. MIT University Press, Cambridge (1998)
14. Hellmann, M.: Fuzzy logic introduction. Université de Rennes (2001)
15. Jain, A.K., Dubes, R.C.: Algorithms for Clustering Data. Prentice-Hall, Englewood Cliffs (1988). http://www.cse.msu.edu/~jain/Clustering_Jain_Dubes.pdf
16. Jianan, W., Rangaswamy, A.: A fuzzy set model of consideration set formation calibrated on data from an online supermarket. EBusiness research Center Working Paper, No. 5, 1999
17. Karypis, G., Han, S.H.E.: Chameleon: Hierarchical clustering using dynamic modeling. IEEE Computer 32(8), 68–75 (1999)
18. Keogh, E., Kasetty, S.: On the need for time series data mining benchmarks: A survey and empirical demonstration. In: Proc. of 8th ACM SIGKDD International Conference on Knowledge Discovery and Data Mining, Edmonton, Alberta, Canada, 23–26 July 2002, pp. 102–111. ACM, New York (2002)
19. Klir, G.J., Folger, T.A.: Fuzzy Sets, Uncertainty, and Information. Prentice-Hall, Englewood Cliffs (1988)
20. Kowalski, G.: Information Retrieval Systems: Theory and Implementation. Kluwer Academic, Norwell (1997)
21. Kwok, R.C., Ma, J., Zhou, D.: Improving group decision making: A fuzzy GSS approach. IEEE Transactions on Systems, Man, and Cybernetics—Part C: Applications and Reviews 32, 54–63 (2002)
22. Mitchell, T.M.: Machine Learning. McGraw-Hill Series in Computer Science. McGraw-Hill, New York (1997)
23. Mitra, S., Acharya, T.: Data Mining: Multimedia, Soft Computing, and Bioinformatics. Wiley, New York (2003)
24. Moscarola, J., Bolden, R.: From the data mine to the knowledge mill: applying the principles of lexical analysis to the data mining and knowledge discovery process. Technical report, Université de Savoie (1998)
25. Oliveira, H.M.: Seleção de entes complexos usando lógica difusa. Dissertation (Masters in Computer Science), Instituto de Informática (1996). In Portuguese
26. Pardo, T.A.S.: Dmsumm: Um gerador automático de sumários. Master's thesis, Universidade Federal de São Carlos, São Carlos (2002). In Portuguese
27. Pottenger, W.M., Yang, T.: Dmsumm: Um gerador automático de sumários. Detecting emerging concepts in textual data mining. In: Berry, M. (ed.) Computational Information Retrieval. SIAM, Philadelphia (2001). In Portuguese
28. Rohf, F.J., Sokal, R.R.: Statistical Tables, 2nd edn. W.H. Freeman, San Francisco (1981)
29. Salton, G.: Introduction to Modern Information Retrieval. McGraw-Hill, New York (1983)
30. Silva, C.M., Vidigal, M.C., Vidigal Filho, P.S., Scapim, C.A., Daros, E., Silvério, L.: Genetic diversity among sugarcane clones (saccharum spp.). Scientiarum Agronomy 27, 315–319 (2005)
31. Snedecor, G.W.: Calculation and interpretation of analysis of variance and covariance (1934)
32. Tan, A.H.: Text mining: the state of the art and the challenges. In: Workshop on Knowledge Discovery from Advanced Databases. Lecture Notes in Computer Science, pp. 65–70. Springer, Berlin (1999)
33. Tsaur, S.H., Chang, T.Y., Yen, C.H.: The evaluation of airline service quality by fuzzy MCDM. Tourism Management 23(2), 107–115 (2007). Available at: http://mslab.hau.ac.kr/mgyoon/master_02/ahp8.pdf. Accessed on June 23, 2007. Lecture Notes in Computer Science, vol. 1574

34. Velickov, S.: Textminer theoretical background. http://www.delft-cluster.nl/textminer/theory/ (2004). Accessed on September 10, 2007
35. Vianna, D.S.: Heurísticas híbridas para o problema da logenia. PhD Thesis, Pontifícia Universidade Católica—PUC, Rio de Janeiro, Brazil (2004). In Portuguese
36. Witten, I.H., Moffat, A., Bell, T.C.: Managing Gigabytes. Van Nostrand Reinhold, New York (1994)
37. Wives, L.K.: Um estudo sobre agrupamento de documentos textuais em processamento de informações não estruturadas usando técnicas de clustering. Master's thesis, Universidade Federal do Rio Grande do Sul, Porto Alegre, Brazil (1999). In Portuguese
38. Wives, L.K.: Utilizando conceitos como descritores de textos para o processo de identificação de conglomerados (clustering) de documentos. PhD Thesis, Universidade Federal do Rio Grande do Sul.Programa de Pós-graduação em Computação, Porto Alegre, RS, Brazil (2004). In Portuguese
39. Wives, L.K., Rodrigues, N.A.: Eurekha. Revista Eletrônica da Escola de Administração da UFRGS (READ) **6**(5) (2000). In Portuguese
40. Zadeh, L.A.: Fuzzy sets. Information and Control **8**, 338–353 (1965)
41. Zadeh, L.A.: Outline of a new approach to the analysis of complex systems and decision processes. Transactions on Systems, Man and Cybernetics **3**, 28–44 (1973)

Chapter 12
Emergent XML Mining: Discovering an Efficient Mapping from XML Instances to Relational Schemas

Hiroshi Ishikawa

As a technology related to emergent XML mining, we propose an adaptable approach to discovery of database schemas for well-formed XML data such as EDI, news, and digital libraries, which we interchange, filter, or download for future retrieval and analysis. The generated schemas usually consist of more than one table. Our approach controls the number of tables to be divided by use of statistics of XML so that the total cost of processing queries is reduced. We generate schemas appropriate for complex data such as text formatting tags and child elements with the small maximum number of occurrences in order to reduce the number of tables. To this end, we introduce three functions NULL expectation, Large Leaf Fields, and Large Child Fields for controlling the number of tables to be divided. We described how to translate queries in XQuery into those in SQL. We also describe the concept of short paths contained by generated database schemas and their effects on the performance of query processing. We discuss when and how it is necessary to change the resultant database schemas in case of updates of the original XML data. We evaluate typical XML queries over the generated schemas and normalized schemas as another approach and measure and compare both of the costs in order to validate our approach.

12.1 Introduction

XML (Extensible Markup Language) [24] data are widely used especially in the Internet-related technologies such as Web-based e-commerce systems. As a salient feature, XML data have a hierarchical structure, that is, a tree-like structure. In order to make clear what "emergent XML mining" means, we will make a brief survey on mining in the context of Web and XML.

H. Ishikawa (✉)
Faculty of Informatics, Shizuoka University, 3-5-1 Johoku, Naka-ku, Hamamatsu, Shizuoka, Japan
e-mail: ishikawah@acm.org

Y. Badr et al. (eds.) *Emergent Web Intelligence: Advanced Semantic Technologies,*
Advanced Information and Knowledge Processing,
DOI 10.1007/978-1-84996-077-9_12, © Springer-Verlag London Limited 2010

12.1.1 Web Mining

Here we describe Web mining. In the context of data-intensive Web information systems such as e-commerce systems, the sources of a large amount of data are Web contents, Web back-end databases, and Web server access logs. The Web contents are pages consisting of data such as texts and images. The contents have a graph structure consisting of pages as nodes and hyperlinks between pages as edges. The back-end databases in the database servers such as relational database management systems constitute a "deep Web" together with "surface Web" contents within the Web servers. The Web server access logs are traces (sequences) of pages which the users visit within the Web sites.

In general, Web mining deals with a large amount of data except databases and is classified into three categories according to types of data sources:

1. Web content mining with respect to Web contents
2. Web structure mining with respect to the graph structures of Web contents
3. Web usage mining with respect to Web access logs

Real works are often combination of these categories such as search engines both based on Web content and structure mining. We more widely describe structure-related research works on Web mining instead of being confined to Web structure mining.

Ohta et al. [16] introduced hierarchical structures into a set of pages as a result of search engines. They hierarchically cluster pages only based on similarity of the contents (i.e., texts) and automatically generate labels of resultant clusters by choosing them based on TF (Term Frequency)-IDF (Inverse Document Frequency) weighted by page ranks within the search result.

Broder et al. [2] introduced the bow-tie model of macroscopic structures of Web by obtaining strongly-connected components of the whole Web graphs. Barabási et al. [1] empirically discovered the power law with respect to the cardinality of links going into and out of pages and theoretically verified the law by assuming that the Web graph evolves as edges are selectively attached to existent nodes. Page et al. [17] introduced the extended surfer model of the users browsing pages and discussed a method to calculate the PageRank of individual pages as Web microscopic structures by solving an eigenvalue problem with respect to a matrix corresponding to "converted" strongly-connected components of the whole Web graph. As a research work at the intermediate level between the macroscopic and microscopic structures of Web graphs, Flake et al. [6] discussed a method to discover Web communities by applying the max-flow min-cut theorem to Web graphs with the cohesively-connected pages.

Ishikawa et al. [12] aimed to improve Web site structures by using Web usage mining. They clustered access logs based on the similarity of patterns of accessed pages and discovered unexpected behaviors of the users caused by ill-structured Web sites. Analyzing this can help the Web site designer to remedy the inappropriate site design.

12.1.2 Emergent XML Mining

As we have covered Web mining, we will move to XML mining. As XML is used for describing contents and structures of Web pages such as XHTML [23], it can be considered as an emergent key technology for Web. We discuss mining XML or semi-structured data. The technologies related to XML mining have not been so fully systematized yet as Web mining although individual research works have increased recently. If we borrowed the framework from Web mining, we could classify such technologies for XML mining in the following way:

1. XML content mining with respect to XML contents
2. XML structure mining with respect to the hierarchical structures of XML contents
3. XML usage mining with respect to XML data access logs

However, this classification is not so meaningful partly because it is nonsense to discuss XML contents without hierarchical structures and partly because there is no natural way to keep XML access logs.

We assume that the principal purpose of emergent XML mining is to discover frequent patterns appearing in XML data. Then, we consider promising applications of emergent XML mining in order to clarify what it really means, as follows.

Efficiently Storing and Querying XML Data by Using Databases Such as Relational Databases If we find frequent combinations of XML elements and store them into one relation, we will be able to efficiently process XML data queries by reducing joins of separate relations.

Describing XML Queries and XML Views In general, it is difficult to formulate queries without sufficient knowledge about the structures of XML data. If we find frequent structures, we will be able to specify queries applicable to a wide range of XML data. Furthermore, if we keep such queries as views, we will be able to reuse them instead of formulating queries from scratch.

Indexing XML Data If we make indices on frequent XML structures, we will be able to efficiently access such structures.

Abstracting XML Data If we find frequent structures of a large amount of XML data, we will be able to consider such structures as outlines or abstracts of the original data.

Extraction of Rules for Classifying XML Data If we find common structures appearing in XML data which are manually given the same classes (i.e., categories) in advance, we will be able to use such structures as classification rules for unknown XML data.

XML Similarity and Clustering Based on the Similarity   If we define the measurement for similarity between two pieces of XML data, then we will be able to cluster or rank a given set of XML data such as a search result based on the similarity.

Compressing XML Data   If we find frequent structures from given XML data, we will be able to efficiently compress the XML data by taking advantage of such structures.

Mining Web Access Patterns   Access patterns are extracted from Web access logs. In general, access patterns are trees or graphs. XML data can be used to represent such patterns. If we find frequent patterns, we will be able to recommend Web pages or to remedy bad site designs by using the patterns more accurately than by using linear access patterns used in traditional Web usage mining.

12.1.3 Previous Works on Emergent XML Mining

We describe concrete research works related to emergent XML mining in this subsection.

Ishikawa et al. [13] aim to design efficient relational schemas for XML instances based on the statistical features of the instances collected in advance. This is the very theme of this chapter. We will describe our approach in the following sections in more detail.

Hammerschmidt [10] discusses the various approaches to indexing XML data in detail.

DataGuides [8], one of such approaches, also can help the users to formulate a query on XML data.

Tekli et al. [21] proposed the measurement for XML similarity which takes into account both tree structures and contents of XML data simultaneously. This approach aims to check similarity between instance-instance, instance-schema such as DTD (Document Type Definition), and schema-schema. This measurement can also provide clustering and ranking search results with a basis.

As an approach to XML compression, Ishikawa et al. [11] proposed a method to translate original XML data into compressed XML data by replacing the tags by new tags. A new tag is determined by the value "the length times the frequency" of the original tag within the original XML data. The larger the value is, the shorter tag is assigned. The compressed data remain to be XML data, so they can be queried without decompression.

Filtering by XPath [26], specified within XQuery [27], needs to evaluate many filter conditions for XML data. Therefore, Gupta et al. [9] proposed the automaton called XPush machine combining two or more filters in a bottom up fusion, which is not influenced by the number of filter conditions. However, an XPush machine has a big problem that it is impossible to update in the strict sense. Even if only one filter is to be deleted, re-calculation of the whole XPush machine is required. Then, the XPush machine which returned to NFA (Nondeterministic Finite Automaton) of an initial state decreases the throughput of filtering due to the lazy translation to DFA (Deterministic Finite Automaton). In order to solve this problem, Takekawa et al. [20] proposed a method to construct the whole automaton from a set of sub-XPush machines for queries without constructing it from scratch.

In Sect. 12.2, we describe issues in discovery of XML structures. We introduce general concepts and definitions needed to describe our approach in Sect. 12.3. In Sect. 12.4, we discuss our approach in detail. In Sect. 12.5, we explain our experiments to validate the effectiveness of our approach. In Sect. 12.6, we discuss schema change required in update of XML data.

12.2 Discovery of XML Structures

As a technique on emergent XML mining, we now focus on discovery of XML structures appropriate for efficiently storing and querying XML instances. Due to the proliferation of XML-enabled applications, we are surrounded by a lot of XML data. For example, we interchange electronic data for e-commerce, i.e., EDI (Electronic Data Interchange), receive updated news and blogs, and download digital libraries such as dblp.xml [3] as XML data in our everyday life. Therefore we must design database schemas to accommodate such voluminous XML data for future query and analysis. Of course, we assume that the system manages relational databases and helps the end-user to describe XML-to-database mappings extensively. In general, approaches to storing XML data into databases are generally divided into the following categories:

1. To store XML data into predefined schemas of databases
2. To store XML data into dynamically generated schemas from XML structures such as DTD or XML instances

The first category which we call a *static schema approach* includes some variations. Zhang et al. [30] take an approach to storing elements and strings (PCDATA) into separate tables together with locations within XML data. Florescu et al. [7] propose three approaches; an approach to edges and values of XML trees into separate tables, an approach to clustering data according to the kinds of edges into the same tables, and an approach to storing all elements into universal relations by viewing them as having the same set of tags virtually. Both Jiang et al. [14] and Yoshikawa et al. [29] decompose XML data into values, elements, and paths and store them into separate tables. Yokoyama et al. [28] also have proposed a method to store XML data as a stream of events suitable for SAX parsers.

All these approaches have the following merits:

1. It is possible to accommodate any XML data into the uniform schemas.
2. It is easy to preserve the ordering of various structures of XML data.
3. It is easy to automatically translate queries including hierarchical relationships (i.e., ancestor and descendants).

On the other hand, all these have the following demerits:

1. It is rather difficult to distinctively define basic data structures such as numerals and characters of XML values.
2. It is rather complex to formulate queries involving aggregate functions such as summation and average.
3. The fixed schemas don't necessarily take into consideration the inherent quantitative properties of individual databases such as depth of nesting and number of occurrences.

Note that Tian et al. [22] did a comparative study about some of the above methods.

In general, the second category which we call a *dynamic schema approach* solves the above demerits for the following reasons. It allows basic data structures to be represented according to each element value and allows aggregate queries to be evaluated in a straightforward manner. However, as the number of tables increases according to the number of element kinds, it is often necessary to join tables in queries. Therefore, the cost of query processing may be very high if database schemas are fully "normalized" like relational databases.

The remedy to the above issue is to reduce the number of tables constituting database schemas. The works along this line include methods of Deutsch et al. [4] and of Shanmugasundaram et al. [19]. However, both of them assume the existence of DTD (Document Type Definitions), which every end-user is not always expected to be able to describe, and reduce the coverage of applications. The approach of Klettke et al. [15] supports generation of ORDB (Object-Relational Databases) schemas by analyzing the number of occurrences of elements in DTD and XML data and analyzing frequent queries, but it takes no account of the efficient way of decomposing tables.

Further, since DTD are not intended to be used to succinctly describe relational schemas, they are insufficient to generate efficient schemas since it is not possible to determine appropriate data types and maximum number of occurrences of child elements in parent elements. In other words, XML data generated from DTD only are likely to be diverse and it is difficult to determine optimal database schemas from such XML data.

On the other hand, XML Schemas [25] are more expressive and are richer in information for generating database schemas than DTD. Therefore, it seems more promising to generate efficient database schemas by using XML Schemas if they are available, but not every end-user is expected to describe XML Schema.

Hereafter in this chapter, we propose an adaptable approach to generating database schemas based on statistics of XML data only, in which we can take the inherent quantitative properties into account. In other words, we don't assume the existence of XML schemas for adaptability of our approach. We assume the following criteria for deciding good schemas:

1. Databases (i.e., tables) containing unnecessary null values are redundant and undesirable.

2. Database schemas containing many tables are undesirable because many joins consuming large processing costs are needed.

Therefore, our objective is to dynamically generate as little number of tables and as little redundant tables as possible. Salient features of our approach are that it generates database schemas based on statistics such as number of occurrences of tags and maximum number of occurrences of child elements in parent elements, but neither DTD nor XML Schema. Our approach generates database schemas by combining the following methods:

1. Data from text formatting tags resulting in complex models and leaf elements more often than a predetermined threshold occurring in parent elements are stored as texts in order to reduce the number of referenced tables.
2. An evaluation function to determine the ratio of null values based on statistics of XML data is defined. Database schemas producing small value of the function are generated in order to reduce redundancy resulted from reduction of the number of tables.

Further, in this chapter, we describe how to translate queries expressed in XQuery [27] into those in SQL. We also describe the concept of short paths contained by generated database schemas and their effects on the performance of query processing. We discuss when and how it is necessary to change the resultant database schemas in case of updates of the original XML data.

12.3 Concepts and Definitions

12.3.1 Concepts

We mean by ideal database design that database schemas contain little data redundancy and little number of tables to be joined. However, reducing redundancy of databases will usually increase the number of tables and the times of joining such tables. On the other hand, reducing the number of tables for reducing the times of joining them will usually increase redundancy. There is a trade-off between these two objectives. One possible way is to apply normalization used for logical design of relational databases [5]. Recently, ORDB systems allow advanced data types such as arrays and objects to represent partially-normalized data. In other words, our proposed approach is to discover latent structures corresponding to such data types from XML data. However, availability of such data types depends on specific database systems (i.e., object relational databases or object-oriented databases). So we use data types only supported by pure relational database systems. We assume that it is more efficient to stores enumerated leaf elements and non-leaf elements occurring for less times than a prescribed threshold into one table. So we try to reduce the total number of tables by using the maximum number of occurrences of parent and child elements that are not expressed by DTD. We also try to reduce the number of tables by storing rather complex data such as text formatting as character strings.

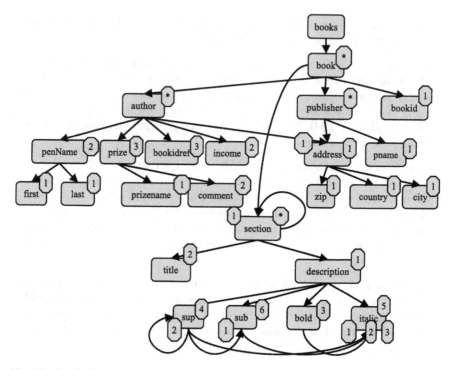

Fig. 12.1 Model for XML data

To reduce redundancy caused by storing different type of elements into one table, we define a function for evaluating redundancy related to the maximum number of occurrences.

12.3.2 Definitions

In general, rules expressing XML elements and parent-child relationships are called a model of XML data. We represent a model as a graph by corresponding elements and parent-child relationships to nodes and links in the graph, respectively. Schema definitions by DTD or XML Schema are examples of models. For example, a graph induced by DTD has links labeled "?", "*", "+" expressing the number of occurrences of parent and child elements. Instead, we represent the number of occurrences explicitly (see Fig. 12.1). Please not that if the number of occurrences is larger than or equal to ten, the link is labeled "*" similarly for the moment. A model which we mention hereafter in this chapter means a model in our proposal. We call XML elements simply nodes. They are divided into non-leaf nodes for elements having any descendants and into leaf nodes for elements having no descendants.

We use the following notations for a model M and a node A:

- $|M|$: the number of nodes contained by M
- $R(M)$: the root node of M
- $P(A)$: parent nodes of A
- $p(A)$: a parent node of A having a shortest path to the root of the model. If there are more than one, a node occurring most often is chosen among them.
- $C(A)$: child nodes of A
- $D(A)$: descendant nodes of A
- $L(A)$: leaf and descendant nodes of A

For example, if we take the model illustrated in Fig. 12.1 as M, the above parameters have the following values:

- $|M| = 24$
- $R(M) = book$
- $P(address) = \{author, publisher\}$
- $p(address) = \{author\}$; we assume that publisher elements occurs more often than address elements
- $C(author) = \{penName, prize, bookdlref, income\}$
- $D(author) = \{penName, first, last, prize, prizename.comment, bookdlref, income, address, zip, country, city\}$
- $L(author) = \{first, last, prizename.comment, zip, country, city\}$

Now we describe XML statistics. We calculate statistics for XML data by following rules:

1. We view attribute names and values as element names and values, respectively.
2. We views texts (i.e., character strings) not directly contained by elements as a child element <#PCDATA>.
3. We view child elements having the same attribute name and value as the same element only if the parent elements have the same name.

By assuming that e denotes an element, we define sub functions used by our evaluation functions as follows:

- $\mathrm{cnt}(e)$: the number of occurrences of the starting tag of e
- $\mathrm{mo}(p(e), e)$: the maximum number of occurrences of a child e in a parent $p(e)$
- $\mathrm{np}(p(e), e) = 1 - \mathrm{cnt}(e)/(\mathrm{cnt}(p(e)) \cdot \mathrm{mo}(p(e), e))$: Null probability

For example, assuming that cnt($author$) is 100 and cnt($penName$) for M illustrated in Fig. 12.1, the Null probability is calculated as follows:

$$\mathrm{np}(author, penname) = 1 - \frac{\mathrm{cnt}(penname)}{\mathrm{cnt}(author) \cdot \mathrm{mo}(author, penname)} = 0.25.$$

Here we summarize relations between models and database schemas. We call a sub-tree of a model a tree model. The number of tree models is equal to the number of tables in the database schemas. The name of the root node of a tree model is equal to the name of a table. The size of a tree model is determined by the number of the fields of a table. The name of a field is a concatenation of a name of an element and its order. Names of a parent and a child are delimited by ".".

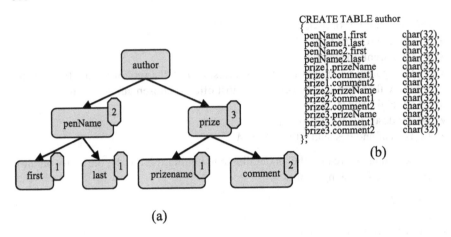

(a)

Fig. 12.2 (**a**) Sub-tree of a model. (**b**) Table schema

For example, Fig. 12.2(a) depicts a tree model for a model *M* in Fig. 12.1 with a node author as its root. From this tree model, table schemas expressed by SQL are generated as in Fig. 12.2(b).

12.4 Our Approach

12.4.1 Discovery of Complex Data

First, how we discover complex data such as text formatting is described. Complex data are elements where child elements such as <#PCDATA>, <sup>, <sub>, <italic>, <bold> occur recursively. Apparently, it is inefficient to mechanically divide such complex structures into different tables. Instead, we store them as character strings. We call such complex data raw data in this chapter. We discover raw data as complex data and simplify a final model.

We illustrate how we discover raw data by taking a character string as an example. The model depicted in Fig. 12.3(a) is a sub-tree of a model depicted in Fig. 12.1. We describe the algorithm by using this example. Figure 12.3(a) illustrates the maximum number of occurrences, too because the number is considered as important.

(Step 1) Candidate roots of raw data are {description, sub, italic} as character strings occur for more than or equal to two. Among the three, description has a shortest path to the root of the model, so the description node is chosen as the root of raw data.

(Step 2) Among candidate raw nodes are sub because the maximum number of occurrences of character strings is more than or equal to one. {bold, #PCDATA} are also among candidates because the number of kinds of child elements is less than two.

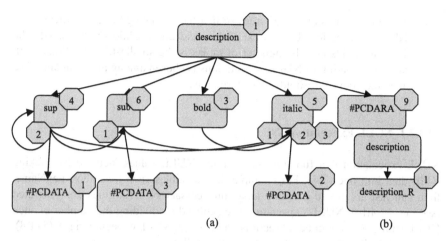

Fig. 12.3 (**a**) Complex data. (**b**) Transformed tree

(Step 3) From descendants of the raw root node description, candidate raw root nodes and candidate raw nodes are deleted.

(Step 4) A node description_R occurring only once at most is added as a child element of the raw root node description.

The resultant structure is illustrated in Fig. 12.3(b). We have successfully discovered <text> from standard.xml in the XML Benchmark Project [18] and <title> dblp.xml in DBLP [3] as complex data.

12.4.2 Division of Tables

Next, how to determine whether we should store elements occurring less often into one table or into separate tables is described. If we store elements occurring less often into one table, we can reduce the number of tables and increase unnecessary NULL values, too. So it is important to determine the target database schemas so that the number of tables is as small as possible and the function for evaluating unnecessary NULL values satisfies the prescribed threshold.

We describe XML structures to be divided when design database schemas. Nonleaf child and parent elements whose maximum number of occurrences is more than or equal to ten, annotated as "*" in our approach, are to be divided. Child elements with more than one parent element are also to be divided. Such structures are to be divided by other approaches, too. The resultant model is a forest (i.e., a set of trees).

For example, a parent element Book and a child element author in Fig. 12.1 are designed as separate tables because their maximum numbers of occurrences are more than or equal to ten (i.e., "*"). An element section is also designed as a separate table because it has more than one parent (i.e., book and section itself).

We describe how to divide tree models taking redundancy into consideration. The number of possible cuts of tree models is equal to the number of links. We select a candidate division of sub-trees so that the following three statistical functions (NULL expectation, Large Leaf Fields, and Large Child Fields) satisfy the prescribed thresholds and the number of tables is the smallest. A candidate with the smallest summation of NULL expectations is chosen among all candidates. We determined the above thresholds by experiments.

12.4.2.1 NULL Expectation (NE)

NULL expectation is a function for counting NULL values incurred by packing XML data into one table. For example, if four tables such as author, penName, first, and last are stored into one table, unnecessary NULL values are generated (see Fig. 12.4(b)). NULL expectation is calculated by dividing the number of such NULL values by the number of records. In this case, NULL expectation is 9/5 (1.8). In general, NULL expectation is calculated as follows:

$$
NE(T) = \sum_{l \in L(T)} \prod_{n=l}^{p(n)=r(T)} mo(p(n), n)
$$

$$
- \sum_{l \in L(T)} \prod_{n=l}^{p(n)=r(T)} mo(p(n), n)(1 - np(p(n), n))
$$

where

$$
\prod_{n=l}^{p(n)=r(T)} mo(p(n), n) = mo(p(l), l) \cdot mo(p(p(l)), p(l)) \cdot \cdots \cdot mo(p(n) = r(T), n).
$$

A database schema which has a lot of NULL values is considered as inefficient, so candidates to be divided, which contain tree models with NULL expectation higher than the threshold, are deleted.

12.4.2.2 Large Leaf Fields (LLF)

Large Leaf Fields is a function for counting most frequent leaf nodes, related to the cost of query processing. For example, if we retrieve comment nodes in the table structure described by Fig. 12.2(b), we have to retrieve six fields such as prize1.comment1, prize1.comment2, prize2.comment1, prize2.comment2, prize3.comment1, and prize3.comment2.

The largest number of fields needed to retrieve a particular node is the function Large Leaf Fields. In general, the function is calculated as follows:

$$
LLF(T) = \max_{l \in L(T)} \left(\prod_{n=l}^{p(n)=r(T)} mo(p(n), n) \right).
$$

For example, we assume that T is a tree model in Fig. 12.2(a).

author

authorID
1
2
3
4
5

penName

penNameID	authorID
1	1
2	3
3	3
4	4
5	4
6	5
7	5

first

penNameID	first
1	
2	
3	
4	
6	
7	

last

penNameID	last
1	
2	
3	
4	
5	

(a)

TagID	penName1.first	penName1.last	penName2.first	penName2.last
1			NULL	NULL
2	NULL	NULL	NULL	NULL
3				
4			NULL	
5		NULL		NULL

(b)

Fig. 12.4 (a) Tables to be merged. (b) Merged tables

$$\mathrm{LF}(T) = \max\{\mathrm{mo}(penName, first) \cdot \mathrm{mo}(author, penName),$$
$$\mathrm{mo}(penName, last) \cdot \mathrm{mo}(author, penName),$$
$$\mathrm{mo}(prize, prizeName) \cdot \mathrm{mo}(author, prize),$$
$$\mathrm{mo}(prize, comment) \cdot \mathrm{mo}(author, prize)\}$$

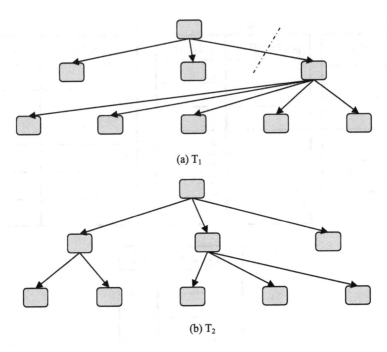

(a) T_1

(b) T_2

Fig. 12.5 Tree models

$$= \max\{1 \cdot 2, 1 \cdot 2, 1 \cdot 3, 2 \cdot 3\} = 6.$$

In this case, 6 is the count for the comment node. A database schema which has a lot of fields necessary to retrieve one node is considered to produce a lot of "or" conditions in SQL commands. This can make the cost for query processing high. So it is considered as better that such a database schema is to be divided. Therefore, candidates to be divided, which contain tree models with LLF higher than the threshold, are deleted.

12.4.2.3 Large Child Fields

Large Child Fields is a function for counting the most frequent child nodes in a parent node, related to good division of tables. For example, in two tree models T_1 and T_2 (see Fig. 12.5), we assume that $|T_1| = |T_2|$ and $\mathrm{NE}(T_1) = \mathrm{NE}(T_2)$ and $\mathrm{LLF}(T_1) = \mathrm{LLF}(T_2)$. Then we will decide either of T_1 or T_2 to be divided. In this case, T_1 is less balanced than T_2. T_1 is to be divided at a broken line.

To express such an imbalance of tree models, we count the most frequent child nodes in tree models. A tree model which has a lot of child nodes is considered to be unbalanced, so such child nodes are to be divided from the tree model. Therefore, candidates to be divided, which contain tree models with LCF higher than the threshold, are deleted. In general, LCF is calculated as follows:

$$\text{LCF}(T) = \max_{c \in C(T)} \left(\sum_{l \in L(c)} \prod_{n=l}^{p(n)=r(T)} \text{mo}\big(p(n), n\big) \right).$$

For example, LCF of a tree model T in Fig. 12.6 is calculated by using the above formula:

$$
\begin{aligned}
\text{LCF}(T) = \max\big\{ & (\text{mo}(penName, first) \cdot \text{mo}(author, penName) \\
& + \text{mo}(penName, last) \cdot \text{mo}(author, penName)), \\
& (\text{mo}(prize, prizeName) \cdot \text{mo}(author, prize) \\
& + \text{mo}(prize, comment) \cdot \text{mo}(author, prize)) \big\} \\
= \max & \{ 1 \cdot 2 + 1 \cdot 2, 1 \cdot 3 + 2 \cdot 3 \} = 9.
\end{aligned}
$$

In this case, the node prize is to be divided.

12.4.3 Resultant Database Schema and Short Path

Our approach generates database schemas which consist of a master table for containing information about a XML document and elements and of a file table for containing XML instances. For example, we consider a model for book.xml (see Fig. 12.1 again). We assume that book.xml is divided as in Fig. 12.6. The resultant database schemas are depicted in Fig. 12.7. The final design of schemas contains flags in each table for the match with the shortest path to the root. Such information helps to reduce the number of referenced tables and the number of joins.

We describe the concept of short paths appearing in final schemas. In general, the efficiency of query processing is largely affected by the number of tables involved in a given query. So we introduce the concept of a short (more accurately, shortest) path from the root to the element in order to reduce the number of tables involved the query. We call such a path the short path and store it in a master table named *MstTag*. Another master table called *MstRes* contains identifiers of XML documents. If there is more than one short path, the one with the largest *MaxOccurs* (i.e., maximum number of occurrences) in the parent element is chosen. The file table such as Address, which contains an individual element, has the field *isShort* to indicate whether its short path matches with the one contained in the corresponding master table.

12.5 Evaluation

We have done experiments in order to validate our approach. We describe the experiment settings and results for evaluation in detail in this section. We have processed

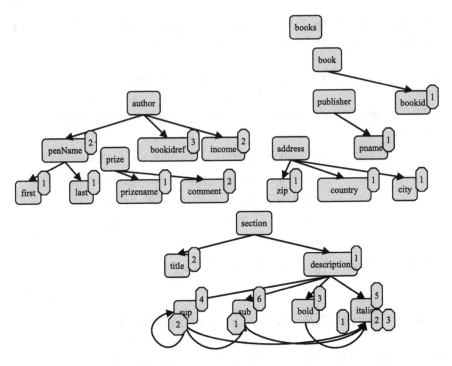

Fig. 12.6 Division of a model

queries over database schemas generated both by our approach and by the usual normalization theory [Elmasri et al.99] and measured and compared the needed costs.

12.5.1 Settings

Indeed, there are some available XML data for benchmarking, such as standard.xml in XMark [18]. However, they have the high largest number of occurrences of parent and child elements. As a result, the generated schemas are equivalent to the normalized ones only. Usual XML data such as personal contact information and EDI (electronic data interchange) have the low largest number of occurrences of parent and child elements. So we have decided to generate XML data for evaluation.

For experiments, we have generated XML data with the low largest number of occurrences. The generated XML documents have a size of 360 MB and 10.2 millions of elements. The level of the hierarchy is eight. In the normalized schema approach, we have divided parent and child elements with the largest number of occurrences more than one.

The database server machine has two Xeon 2.0 GHz CPUs and 1 G main memory. It has SQL Server 2000 on Windows 2000 server. The client machine has a Pentium4, 1.5 GHz CPU and 640 MB main memory. It has SQLQuery Analyzer on Windows XP. The server and client are connected with 100 M LAN.

Author	Prize	Address	Section
PosID	PosID	PosID	PosID
ParentID	ParentID	ParentID	ParentID
IsShort	IsShort	IsShort	IsShort
PenName1.first	prizeName	zip	title1
PenName1.last	comment1	country	title2
PenName2.first	comment2	city	Description R
PenName2.last			
income1			
income2			
bookidref1			
bookidref2			
bookidref3			

Fig. 12.7 Resultant table schemas

12.5.2 Queries

We have formulated three queries for evaluating our approach as follows:

(1) A basic query involving more than one field to evaluate the effect of increase in the number of referenced fields.
(2) A query returning all descendants of an element to evaluate the effect of increase in depth of the hierarchy.
(3) A query calculating an aggregate function to evaluate the overhead of computation.

We provide XQuery-based queries for the above queries. For (1), we used the following query:

"Retrieve the comments of authors whose last name begins by a letter T."

FOR $p IN document("book.xml")/books/book/author
WHERE $p/penname/last/text() LIKE 'T%'
RETURN $p/prize/comment/text()

For (2), we used the following query:

"Retrieve all information of authors whose last name which begins by a letter T."

	Process a document and non-table elements
1	Path: document("book.xml")/books/book/author/address/city $p= document("book.xml")/boks/book/author
	SELECT city *FROM MstRes INNER JOIN Address ON (MstRes.ResID=Address.ResID)* *WHERE MstRes.URI='book.xml'*
2	**In case of *RETURN*, repeat outer join with parent element until Path matches with $p**
	Path:document("book.xml")/books/book/author/address <>$p
	/* add to the from-table clause */ *LEFT OUTER JOIN Author ON (Author.ResID=Address.ResID* *AND Author.PosID=Address.ParentID*
	Path:document("book.xml")/books/book/author =$p
3	**Repeat natural join with the parent element until Path matches with the short path of the last element**
	Path:document("book.xml")/books/book/author =document("book.xml")/books/book/author
4	**Add the condition on IsShort of the last element**
	Path:document("book.xml")/books/book/author
	/* add to the where-clause */ *AND Author.IsShort=TRUE*

Fig. 12.8 XQuery translation

FOR $p IN document("book.xml")/books/book/author
WHERE $p/penname/last/text() LIKE 'T%'
RETURN $p/descendant-or-self::node()

For (3), we used the following query:

"Retrieve sum of salaries of all authors."
FOR $p IN document("book.xml")/books/book/author
RETURN SUM($p/income/text())

12.5.3 Query Translation

We describe how we translate queries in XQuery into those in SQL. We take the following query as a running example.

FOR $p IN document ("book.xml")/books/book/author
RETURN $p/address/city

We translate this query as follows (see Fig. 12.8).

(Step 1) The expression *document ("book.xml")* introduces the condition MstRes. URI = 'book.xml'. To return the city of address (i.e., non-table element),

Fig. 12.9 (a) Statistics of
database. (b) Query
processing costs (in seconds)

	Our approach	Normalization
# of tables	7	16
# of records	2,890,292	7,780,837
Data size (MB)	760	1801
Index size (MB)	71	296

(a)

	Our approach	Normalization
Basic query	0.99	26.28
Descendant	6.70	28.14
Aggregate	2.25	3.44

(b)

we add the natural join of the *MstRes* and *Address* tables on key *ResID* (omitted in the schemas) to the from-table clause and the *city* field to the target column list.

(Step 2) We initialize the variable *Path* by the path in the RETURN clause. We repeatedly add the outer join with the table for the parent and delete the last element of *Path* until it matches with the path indicated by $p.

(Step 3) We repeatedly add the natural join of the table for the last element of *Path* with the table for its parent element until its short path matches with *Path*.

(Step 4) We add the condition on the *isShort* field of the last element of *Path*.

We make a few comments on other aspects of query translation. We translate GROUP BY in XQuery into GROUP BY ParentID (i.e., parent identifier) in SQL. We use SQL procedures and DOM operations if necessary, such as structural retrieval of raw data.

12.5.4 Results

Figure 12.9(a) depicts statistics about the database schemas generated by our approach and normalization approach. The number of records corresponds to the total number of records contained by all the tables. Our approach has a smaller number

No.	XPath	Location	Referenced tables
1	/books/book/author/address/city	RETURN	MstRes, Author, Address
2	/books/book/author/address/city	WHERE	MstRes, Author
3	/books/book/publisher/address/city	WHERE	MstRes, Publisher, Address
4	/books/book/ /section/title	WHERE	MstRes, Section

Fig. 12.10 Tables referenced by XPaths

of tables than the normalization approach. The number of records in our approach is also smaller. This can reduce both the database size and index size. In summary, our approach can reduce the number of tables and can increase the number of fields to retrieve at the same time as it "partially" normalizes database schemas.

We translated the above queries into SQL queries systematically as described above and evaluated the execution time of them As for the result of the query (1), the time of our generated schemas, 0.99 sec, is rather small in comparison with 26.28 sec of the normalized schemas (see Fig. 12.9(b)). This supports our expectation that the number of referenced tables (two for our approach and four for the normalized approach) is a dominant factor. As the result of the query (2), the time of our generated schemas, 6.70 sec, is also small in comparison with 28.14 sec of the normalized schemas. This also comes from the fact the number of generated schemas for representing a hierarchy is small because the number is three for our approach and seven for the normalized approach. As the result of the query (3), the time of our generated schemas, 2.25 sec, is better than 3.44 sec of the normalized schemas. Summation of our approach is operated on two fields. Nevertheless, the result indicates that the overhead is small.

Now we describe the effects of short paths in the reduction of the number of tables involved in generated SQL queries. Figure 12.10 indicates XPath and the tables referenced in the corresponding SQL query. Please note that the prefix *document("book.xml")* is omitted because it is common to all XPaths. In case of XPath in the where clause, Step 2 is skipped. XPath 3 is a path different from XPath 2 in that the number of the tables of the former is larger than that of the latter.

We have evaluated the effects of short paths by using three versions of the following query 4.

FOR $p IN document ("book.xml")/books/book/author/address
WHERE $p/zip/text() LIKE '1%'
RETURN <address pref=$p/prefecture/text() num=$p/housenumber/text()/>

This query returns the address of the author whose zip code starts from "1". The three versions are different as follows:

1. No use of any short path
2. Use of the short path for author
3. Use of the short path for address

The result of the experiment shown on the Fig. 12.11 validates that short paths can drastically reduce the number of tables and the processing time of the corresponding queries.

	No use of short path	Use of the short path for author	Use of the short path for address
Processing time[sec]	1.50	0.95	0.25
# of referenced tables	4	2	1

Fig. 12.11 Evaluation results of short paths

12.6 Schema Change

We use the statistics about XML instances to discover efficient database schemas. It is necessary to change the resultant schemas in some cases where the original XML instances or the original XML schemas, which we don't take into account in determining the schemas, are updated. We discuss our approach to such cases.

In general, the XML schemas are changed, the corresponding database schemas must be changed. Especially, if the MaxOccurs of child elements increases, the corresponding database schemas are to be changed. If parent and child elements are stored in the same table such as author and PenName, the database schemas must be changed. Otherwise, we don't have to change the schemas because the values of the functions for controlling the division of the tables are already over the threshold. For example, if MaxOccurs of penname in author is changed from two to three, the fields *PenName3.fisrt* and *PenName3.last* are added to the current table *Author*. On the other hand, the MaxOccurs of address in author is changed from one to two, we don't have to change the corresponding tables because they are separate tables. Even if XML data are changed and are still valid to the original XML schemas, we don't have to change the database schemas.

12.7 Conclusions

We have briefly surveyed on Web and XML mining from the structural point of view in order to introduce the concept of emergent XML mining. As a structure-related work on emergent XML mining, we have proposed an adaptable approach to dynamically generating database schemas for well-formed XML data. Our approach controls the number of tables to be divided based on XML statistics so that the total cost of processing queries is reduced. We have devised schemas appropriate for complex data such as text formatting and child elements with the small maximum number of occurrences in order to reduce the number of tables. To this end, we have defined three functions NULL expectation, Large Leaf Fields, and Large Child Fields for controlling the tables to be divided. We have evaluated typical queries over the generated schemas and normalized schemas and measured and compared both of the costs. Through this, we have successfully validated our approach.

We described how we translate queries in XQuery into those in SQL. We also described the concept of short paths contained by generated database schemas and their effects on the performance of query processing. We discussed when and how it is necessary to change the resultant schemas in case of updates of the original XML data.

This work is rather a basic research in that we have devised basic methods for generating schemas and translating an XQuery query into an SQL query over the generated schemas, and have checked both of the feasibility. We have a plan to implement the two main program components materializing these methods:

1. The relational schema generator from XML data
2. The query translator from XQuery to SQL

By combining the above components, the end-user is expected to be able to efficiently retrieve XML data by XQuery.

Acknowledgements   This work is partially supported by the Ministry of Education, Culture, Sports, Science and Technology, Japan under Grants-in-Aid for Scientific Research (16 300 030, 19 300 026). We appreciate Mr. Takeyoshi Maku for his great efforts in the implementation and evaluation of the general ideas described in this chapter.

References

1. Barabási, A.-L., Albert, R.: Emergence of scaling in random networks. Science **286**(5439), 509–512 (1999)
2. Broder, A., Kumar, R., Maghoul, F., Raghavan, P., Rajagopalan, S., Stata, R., Tomkins, A., Wiener, J.: Graph structure in the web. In: Proceedings of the WWW International Conference, pp. 309–320 (2000)
3. DBLP (Digital Bibliography & Library Project): http://www.informatik.uni-trier.de/~ley/db/index.html. Accessed 2007
4. Deutsch, A., Fernandez, M., Suciu, D.: Storing semistructured data with STORED. In: Proceedings of the ACM SIGMOD International Conference, pp. 431–442 (1999)
5. Elmasri, R., Navathe, S.B.: Fundamentals of Database Systems, 3rd edn. Addison-Wesley, Longman, Boston (1999)
6. Flake, G.W., Lawrence, S., Giles, C.L.: Efficient identification of Web communities. In: Proceedings of the ACM SIGKDD International Conference on Knowledge Discovery and Data Mining, pp. 150–160 (2000)
7. Florescu, D., Kossmann, D.: Storing and querying XML data using an RDBMS. IEEE Data Engineering Bulletin **22**(3), 27–34 (1999)
8. Goldman, R., Widom, J.: DataGuides: Enabling query formulation and optimization in semistructured databases. In: Proceedings of the VLDB International Conference, pp. 436–445 (1997)
9. Gupta, A.K., Suciu, D.: Stream processing of XPath queries with predicates. In: Proceedings of the ACM SIGMOD International Conference, pp. 419–430 (2003)
10. Hammerschmidt, B.C.: Keyx: Selective Key-Oriented Indexing in Native XML-Databases. IOS Press, Amsterdam (2006)
11. Ishikawa, H., Yokoyama, S., Isshiki, S., Ohta, M.: Project Xanadu: XML- and active-database-unified approach to distributed e-commerce. In: Proceedings of the DEXA Workshops, pp. 833–837 (2001)
12. Ishikawa, H., Ohta, M., Yokoyama, S., Nakayama, J., Katayama, K.: On the effectiveness of web usage mining for page recommendation and restructuring. In: Proceedings of the NODe Web and Database-Related Workshops, pp. 253–267. Springer, Berlin (2002)

13. Ishikawa, H., Yokoyama, S., Ohta, M., Katayama, K.: On mining XML structures based on statistics. In: Proceedings of International Conference on Knowledge-Based Intelligent Information and Engineering Systems, pp. 379–390. Springer, Berlin (2005)
14. Jiang, H., Lu, H., Wang, W., Yu, J.X.: Path materialization revisited: An efficient storage model for XML data. In: Proceedings of the Australasian Database Conference, pp. 85–94 (2002)
15. Klettke, M., Meyer, H.: XML and object-relational database systems enhancing structural mappings based on statistics. In: Lecture Notes in Computer Science, vol. 1997, pp. 151–170. Springer, Berlin (2001)
16. Ohta, M., Narita, H., Katayama, K., Ishikawa, H.: Overlapping clustering methods for a Japanese meta search engine. In: Proceedings of the IASTED International Conference on Databases and Applications, pp. 100–106 (2004)
17. Page, L., Brin, S., Motwani, R., Winograd, T.: The PageRank citation ranking: Bringing order to the web, Stanford Digital Library Technologies Project (1998)
18. Schmidt, A.R., Waas, F., Kersten, M.L., Florescu, D., Manolescu, I., Carey, M.J., Busse, R.: The XML benchmark project. Technical report, INS-R0103, CWI (2001) http://monetdb.cwi.nl/xml/index.html. Accessed 2007
19. Shanmugasundaram, J., Tufte, K., He, G., Zhang, C., DeWitt, D., Naughton, J.: Relational databases for querying XML documents: Limitations and opportunities. In: Proceedings of the VLDB International Conference, pp. 302–314 (1999)
20. Takekawa, H., Ishikawa, H.: Incrementally-updatable stream processors for XPath queries based on merging automata via ordered hash-keys. In: Proceedings of the DEXA Workshops, pp. 40–44 (2007)
21. Tekli, J., Chbeir, R., Yétongnon, K.: Efficient XML structural similarity detection using subtree commonalities. In: Proceedings of the Brazilian Symposium on Databases, ACM SIGMOD DiSC, pp. 116–130 (2007)
22. Tian, F., De Witt, D.J., Chen, J., Zhang, C.: The design and performance evaluation of alternative XML storage strategies. SIGMOD Record 31(1), 5–10 (2002)
23. XHTML: http://www.w3.org/TR/xhtml1/ Accessed 2007
24. XML: http://www.w3.org/XML/ Accessed 2007
25. XML Schema: http://www.w3.org/TR/xmlschema-0/ Accessed 2007
26. XPath: http://www.w3.org/TR/xpath20/ Accessed 2007
27. XQuery: http://www.w3.org/XML/Query/ Accessed 2007
28. Yokoyama, S., Ohta, M., Katayama, K., Ishikawa, H.: An access control method based on the prefix labeling scheme for XML repositories. In: Proceedings of the Australasian Database Conference, vol. 39, pp. 105–113. ACM, New York (2005)
29. Yoshikawa, M., Amagasa, T.: XRel: A path-based approach to storage and retrieval of XML documents using relational databases. ACM Transactions on Internet Technology 1(1), 110–141 (2001)
30. Zhang, C., Naughton, J.F., DeWitt, D.J., Luo, Q., Lohman, G.M.: On supporting containment queries in relational database management systems. In: Proceedings of the ACM SIGMOD International Conference, pp. 425–436 (2001)

Chapter 13
XML Based Information Systems and Formal Semantics of Programming Languages

Thierry Despeyroux

Abstract Web sites and XML based information systems must be up to date and coherent. This last quality is difficult to insure because sites can be updated very frequently, may have many authors or be partially generated, and in this context, proof-reading is a real challenge. In this chapter, we make a parallel between programs and Web sites or information systems. Semantic constraints that one would like to specify (constraints between the meaning of categories and sub-categories in a thematic directory, consistency between the organization chart and the rest of the site in an academic site, etc.) are similar to semantic constraints in programs (for example coherence between the use of objects and their declared types). Human knowledge is often represented using ontologies. Ontologies can be seen as type systems. Semantic constraints and types have been heavily studied in the context of the semantics of programming languages. We explore how techniques used in this context can be used to enforce the quality of information systems.

13.1 Introduction

Starting as an amazing way of exchanging information, the Web is now a federative agent for a large number of information systems to which it provides a uniform man-machine interface. In fact, with the semantic Web, it becomes also a machine-machine interface.

Web sites are now ordinary products, and consumers are aware of the notion of quality of a Web site. For consumers, the quality of a site is linked to its graphic appearance, to the easiness of accessibility and also to other criteria such as the fact that the site is up to date and coherent. This last quality is difficult to insure because sites can be updated very frequently, may have many authors or be partially generated, and in this context, proof-reading is very difficult. The same piece of

T. Despeyroux (✉)
INRIA Paris-Rocquencourt, Domaine de Voluceau, B.P. 105, F-78153 Le Chesnay Cedex, France
e-mail: thierry.despeyroux@inria.fr

Y. Badr et al. (eds.) *Emergent Web Intelligence: Advanced Semantic Technologies,*
Advanced Information and Knowledge Processing,
DOI 10.1007/978-1-84996-077-9_13, © Springer-Verlag London Limited 2010

information may be found at different occurrences in a document, but also in meta-data, sometime by use of ontologies, leading to the need for consistency checking.

The coherence problem becomes even more accurate in the context of the se-mantic web as an error may be rapidly propagated to other information systems. An ad-hoc way of managing information systems is no more possible. Time is now to Web and information system engineering, using formal techniques as ontologies and formal semantics.

The life cycle of a Web site can be complex: many authors, frequent updates or redesigns. Very often they are heterogeneous objects: some parts are static, other parts may be generated, use databases, etc. As for other "industrial" products, one can think of the notion of quality of a Web site, and then look for methods to achieve this quality.

The main effort developed in the domain of the Web is the Semantic Web [3, 5]. Its goal is to ease computer based data mining, formalizing data which is most of the time textual. This leads to two main directions:

- Giving a syntactical structure to documents. This is achieved with XML, DTDs, XML-schema, style sheets and XSLT [40]. The goal is to separate the content of Web pages from their visual appearance, defining an abstract syntax to constrain the information structure. In this area, there is, of course, the work done by the W3C, but we can also mention tools that manipulate XML documents, taking into account the conformance to DTD: Xduce [21] and XM-λ [30]. This means that by using these languages we know that the documents which are produced will conform to the specific DTDs that they use, which is not the case when one uses XSLT.
- Annotating documents to help computerized Web mining. One will use ontologies with the help of RDF [4, 40], RDF-Schema or DAML+OIL [41]. The goal is to get a computer dedicated presentation of knowledge [12, 13, 38] to check the content of a page with the use of ontologies [39] or to improve information retrieval.

This is not sufficient. Web sites, as many other types of information systems, contain naturally redundant information. This is in part due to accessibility reasons. Web pages can be annotated and the same piece of information can exist in many different forms, as data or meta-data. We have to make sure that these different representations of the same piece of knowledge are consistent. Some parts of a Web site can also be generated, from one or more databases, and again, one have to make sure of the consistency between these databases and the rest of the site. With the development of Web based systems one now speaks of Web engineering [6, 19, 31, 35].

Obviously, traditional proof-reading (as it may be done for a book) is not pos-sible for Web sites. A book may contain a structure (chapters, sections, etc.) and references across the text, but its reading can be essentially linear. An information system such as a Web site looks more like a net.

These difficulties lead to the need for a better understanding of the formal prop-erties of Web sites. Many approaches can be used that call for different areas of computer sciences: model checking and linear temporal logic [15], term rewriting techniques [25], rules based approach [1, 2].

We propose to apply techniques from software engineering, in particular from semantics of programming languages and type theory to increase the quality level of Web sites. In the context of Web sites, it is not possible to make proofs as it is the case for some sorts of programs or algorithms, but we will see that some techniques used in the area of formal semantics of programming languages [18] can be successfully used in this context.

With this approach, we are concerned in the way Web sites are constructed, taking into account their development and their semantics. In this respect we are closer to what is called content management.

The work presented here is limited to static Web sites and documents. It can be easily extended to more general information systems as many of them provide a Web interface or at least can generate XML documents, answering the two questions that we try to solve:

- How can we define verification tools for Web sites an more generally information systems?
- How can we mechanize the use of these tools?

In the same way of thinking, we make a parallel between ontologies and types, expecting again to reuse some notions and formal techniques.

The following section presents in an informal manner some basic notions about syntax and semantics of programs. Section 13.3 makes a parallel between programs and Web sites. Section 13.4 presents the genesis of a specification formalism to specify semantic constraints in Web sites. Section 13.5 presents ontologies as a type systems. Finally Sect. 13.6 gives some examples of applications and some implementation notes.

13.2 Syntax and Semantics of Programming Languages

Drawing a line between syntax and semantics is not a trivial task. When giving names to objects in a program or to tags in an XML file, we try to use the syntax to reflect an intentional semantics. We will define syntax and semantics in term of local and global constraints.

13.2.1 Syntax Versus Semantics

To execute a program you have, most of the time, to use a compiler which translates the source code to executable code, unless you are the end-user and someone else did this for you.

The goal of a compiler is not only to generate object code but also to verify that the program is legal, i.e., that it follows the *static semantics* of the programming language. For example, in many programming languages one can find some declarative parts in which objects, types and procedures are defined before being used in some other places in statements or expressions. One will have to check that the use of these objects is compatible with the declarations.

The static semantics is defined by opposition to the *dynamic semantics* which describe the way a program is executed. The static semantics give some constraints that must be verified before a program is executed or compiled.

A particularity of such constraints is that they are not local but *global*: they may bind distant occurrences of an object in a unique file or in many different files. A second particularity is that these constraints are *not context-independent*: an "environment" that allows us to know what are the visible objects at a particular point in the program is necessary to perform the verifications.

Global constraints are defined by opposition to local constraints. As a program may be represented by a labeled tree, a local constraint is a relation between a node in this tree and its sons. For example, if we represent an assignment, the fact that the right hand part of an assignment must be an expression is a local constraint. On the other hand, the fact that the two sides of an assignment must have compatible types is a global constraint, as we need to compute the types of both sides using an environment.

Local constraints express what is called the (*abstract*) *syntax* of the programming language and global constraints express what is called its *static semantics*. The abstract syntax refers to the tree representation of a program, its textual form is called its *concrete syntax*.

Representing programs by means of a tree is quite natural. Using a B.N.F. to describe the syntax of a programming language gives already a parse tree. Most of the time this tree can be simplified to remove meaningless reduction level due to precedence of operators. The grammar rules express local type constraints on the parse tree and explain what is a syntactically correct program.

Some programming languages use trees as based objects, for example Lisp and Prolog. A straight way of representing a program in a language like Prolog is to use (completely instantiated, i.e., with no logical variables) terms, even if Prolog terms are not typed.

The following example shows how a statement can be represented as a Prolog term.

```
A := B + (3.5 * C);

assign(var('A'),
       plus(var('B'),
            mult(num(3.5),var('C')))))
```

A Prolog term can itself be represented into XML as shown in the following example:

```
<assign>
  <var name="A"/>
  <plus>
    <var name="B"/>
    <mult>
```

```
            <num value="3.5"/>
            <var name="C"/>
        </mult>
    </plus>
</assign>
```

By defining a DTD for our language, we can constrain XML to allow only programs that respect the syntax of the programming language.

```
<!ELEMENT assign (var, (plus|mult|num...))>
```

This is equivalent to giving a signature to the Prolog terms

```
assign : Var * Exp -> Statement
```

where `Var` and `Exp` are types containing the appropriate elements.

However, using types or DTDs it is not possible to express semantic constraints, as for example "The types of the left and right hand sides must be compatible". If the variable A has been declared as an integer, the statement given as example is not legal.

13.2.2 Formal Semantics

Three main methods are used to formalize the semantics of programming languages: denotational semantics, operational semantics and axiomatic semantics.

We will use here the *Natural Semantics* [7, 22] which is an operational semantics derived from the structural operational semantics of Plotkin [34] and inspired by the sequent calculus of Gentzen [37]. One of the advantages of this semantics is that it is an executable semantics, which means that semantic definitions can be compiled (into Prolog) to generate type-checkers or compilers. Another advantage is that it allows the construction of proofs.

In Natural Semantics, the semantics of programming languages are defined using inference rules and axioms. These rules explain how to demonstrate some properties of "the current point" in the program, named *subject*, using its subcomponents (i.e., subtrees in the tree representation) and an environment (a set of hypothesis).

To illustrate this, the following rule explains how the statements part of a program depends on the declarative one:

$$\frac{\emptyset \vdash Decls \rightarrow \rho \quad \rho \vdash Stmts}{\vdash \textbf{declare } Decls \textbf{ in } Stmts}.$$

The declarations are analyzed in an empty environment $\emptyset$, constructing ρ which is a mapping from variable names to declared types. This environment is then used to check the statements part, and we can see that in the selected example the statements part does not alter this environment.

These inference rules can be read in two different ways: if the upper part of the rule has been proved, then we can deduce that the lower part holds; but also in a more operational mode, if we want to prove the lower part we have to prove that the upper part holds.

The following rule is an axiom. It explains the fact that in order to attribute a type to a variable, one has to access the environment.

$$\rho \vdash \mathbf{var}\ X : T, \quad \{X : T\} \in \rho.$$

"Executing" a semantic definition means that we want to build a proof tree, piling up semantic rules which have been instantiated with the initial data.

As we have seen, there are two important points here: *declarations* and *environments*. Depending of the programming language, the type system can be more or less strong, allowing multiple declarations (that must be in general compatible) or not. The environment is the link between declarations and locations where objects are used. Managing this environment is of course more easy if locations in which declarations can appear is well restricted or even unique.

13.3 XML Files Viewed as Programs

XML files, in opposition to traditional text files, are structured documents as programs are. However they mix structures, natural languages, and references to other objects as images.

13.3.1 Similarities and Differences

Web sites (we define a Web site simply as a set of XML pages) are very similar to programs. In particular, they can be represented as trees, and they may have local constraints expressed by means of DTDs or XML-schemas. As HTML pages can be translated to XHTML, which is XML with a particular DTD, it is not a restriction to focus only to XML web sites.

There are also differences between Web sites and programs:

- Web sites can be spread along a great number of files. This is the case also for programs, but in this case, these files are all located on the same file system. With Web sites we will have to take into account that we may need to access different servers.
- The information is scattered, with a very frequent use of forward references. A forward reference is the fact that an object (or a piece of information) is used before it as been defined or declared. In programs, forward references exist but are most of the time limited to single files so the compiler can compile one file at a time. This is not the case for Web sites and as it is not possible to load a complete site at the same time, we have to use other techniques.
- The syntax can be poorly, not completely or not at all formalized, with some parts using natural languages.

- There is the possibility to use "multimedia". In the word of programs, there is only one type of information to manipulate: text (with structure), so let's say terms. If we want to handle a complete site or document we may want to manipulate images for example to compare the content of an image with its caption.
- The formal semantics is not imposed by a particular programming language but must be defined by the author or shared between authors as it is already the case for DTDs. This means that to allow the verification of a Web site along its life one will have to define what should be checked.
- We may need to use external resources to define the static semantics (for example one may need to use a thesaurus, ontologies or an image analysis program). In one of our example bellow, we call the `wget` program to check the validity of URLs in an activity report.

Meta-data are now most of the time expressed using an XML syntax, even if some other concrete syntax can be used (for example the N3 notation [4] can be used as an alternative to the XML syntax of RDF [24]). So, from a syntactic point of view, there is no difference between data and meta-data. Databases also use XML, as a standard interface both for queries and results.

As we can see, the emergence of XML gives us a uniform framework for managing heterogeneous data. Using methods from software engineering will allow a web-master or an author to check the integrity of its information system and to produce error messages or warnings when necessary, provided that they have made the effort to formalize the semantics rules.

Every programmer can relate some anecdote in which somebody forgets to perform an action as recompiling a part of a program, leading to an incoherent system. Formalizing and mechanizing the management of any number of files is the only way to avoid such misadventure.

Again, at least one solution already exists. It is a utility program named "make" [36], well known to at least Unix programmers. This program can manage the dependencies between files and libraries, and it can minimize the actions (such as the calls to the compilers) which must be done when some files have been modified. This means that each time a set of modifications is applied, or at least each time a set of files is installed on a server, the "make" program must be used to check the integrity of the whole system. However, this program can only manage files located on the same file system and must be adapted to handle URLs when a Web site is scattered over multiple physical locations.

13.3.2 Semantic Constraints in XML Documents

For a better understanding of the notion of semantic constraints we will now provide two examples.

- A thematic directory is a site in which documents or external sites are classified. An editorial team is in charge of defining the classification. This classification shows as a tree of topics and subtopics. The intentional semantics of this classification is that a subtopic "makes sense" in the context of the upper topic, and this semantics must be maintained when the site is modified.

To illustrate this, here is an example:

Category: Recreation
Sub-Category: Sports, Travel, Games, Surgery, Music, Cinema

The formal semantics of the thematic directory use the semantics of words in a natural language. To verify the formal semantics, we need to have access to external resources, maybe a thesaurus, a pre-existing ontology or an ontology which is progressively constructed at the same time as the directory; how to access to this external resource is not of real importance, the important point is that it can be mechanized.

In the former example, the sub-category "Surgery" is obviously a mistake.

- An academic site presents an organization: its structure, its management, its organization chart, etc. Most of the time this information is redundant, maybe even inconsistent. As in a program, one have to identify which part of the site must be trusted: the organization chart or a diary (which is supposed to be up to date) and can be used to verify the information located in other places, in particular when there are modifications in the organization. The "part that can be trusted" can be a formal document such as an ontology, a database or a plain XML document.

The issue of consistency between data and meta-data, or between many redundant data appears in many places, as in the following examples.

- Checking the consistency between an image and its caption; in this case we may want to use linguistic tools to compare the caption with annotations on the image, or to use image recognition tools.
- Comparing different versions of the same site that may exist for accessibility reasons.
- Verifying the consistency between a request to a database, with the result of the request to detect problems in the query and verify the plausibility of an answer (even when a page is generated from a database, it can be useful to perform static verifications, unless the raw data and the generation process can be proved, which is most of the time not the case).
- Verifying that an annotation (maybe in RDF) is still valid when an annotated page is modified.

One characteristic of Web or XML documents is that they contain pieces of natural languages, that is of course much more difficult to manipulate that programming languages. Concepts can be formalized using ontologies, and meta-data (also called semantic annotations) can easily refer to ontologies. However, this is not the case for plain text and to check some consistency between text and annotations some special techniques such as entity extraction coming from the information retrieval and extraction community are useful.

13.4 A Specification Language to Define the Semantics of XML Documents and Web Sites

In this section we first try to give a list of requirements to justify the design of a specific language dedicated to the definition of semantic constraints in XML documents. This language is also presented and will be used in some examples given in Sect. 13.6.

13.4.1 Formalizing Web Sites

First experiments have been made using directly Natural Semantics [9, 10]. These experiments showed that this style of formal semantics perfectly fits our needs, but it is very heavy for end-users (authors or web-master) in the context of Web sites. Indeed, as we can see in the former rules, the recursion is explicit, so the specification needs at least one rule for each syntactical operator (i.e., for each XML tag). Furthermore, managing the environment can be tedious, and this is mainly due to the forward declarations, frequent in Web sites. (Forward declarations means that objects can be used before they have been defined. This implies that the verifications must be delayed using an appropriate mechanism as coroutines, or using a two-passes process.)

It is not reasonable to ask authors or web-masters to write Natural Semantics rules. Even if it seems appropriate for semantic checking, the rules may seem too obscure to most of them. Our strategy now is to specify a simple and specialized specification language that will be compiled in Natural Semantics rules, or more exactly to some Prolog code very close to what is compiled from Natural Semantics [8].

We can make a list of requirements for this specification language:

- no explicit recursion,
- minimizing the specification to the points of interest only,
- simple management of the environment,
- allowing rules composition (points of view management),
- automatic management of forward declarations.

In a second step we have written various prototypes directly in Prolog. The choice of Prolog comes from the fact that it is the language used for the implementation of Natural Semantics. But it is indeed very well adapted to our needs: terms are the basic objects, there is pattern matching and unification directly available.

After these experiments, we are able to design a specification language. Here are some of the main features of this language:

- Patterns describe occurrences in the XML tree. We have extended the language XML with logical variables. In the following examples variable names begin with the "$" sign.

- A local environment contains a mapping from names to values. The execution of some rules may depend on these values. A variable can be read ("=") or assigned (":=").
- A global environment contains predicates which are assertions deduced when rules are executed. The syntax of these predicates is the Prolog syntax, but logical variables are marked with the "$" sign. The sign "=>" means that its right hand side must be added to the global environment.
- Tests enable us to generate warnings or error messages when some conditions do not hold. These tests are just now simple Prolog predicates. The expression "? pred / error" means that if the predicate `pred` is false, the error message must be issued. The expression "? pred -> error" means that if the predicate `pred` is true, the error message must be issued. Messages are general XML expressions. So in fact it is possible to use them to produce new pieces of information that are more results than error.

A semantic rule contains two parts: the first part explains when the rule can be applied, using patterns and tests on the local environment; the second part describes actions that must be executed when the rule applies: modifying the local environment (assignment), adding of a predicate to the global environment, generating a test.

Recursion is implicit. It is also the case for the propagation of the two environments and of error messages.

13.4.2 Definition of SeXML

In this section, we give a complete description of our specification language, called SeXML.

13.4.2.1 Patterns

As the domain of our specification language is XML documents, XML elements are the basic data of the language. To allow pattern-matching, logical variables have been added to the XML language (which is quite different from what is done in XSLT).

Variables have a name prefixed by the "$" sign, for example: $X. Their also exist anonymous variables which can be used when a variable appears only once in a rule: "$_". For syntactical reasons, if the variable appears in place of an element, it should be encapsulated between "<" and ">": <$X>.

In a list, there is the traditional problem of determining if a variable matches an element or a sublist. If a list of variables matches a list of elements only the last variable matches a sublist. So in

```
<tag> <$A> <$B> </tag>
```

the variable $A matches the first element contained in the body of <tag> and $B matches the rest of the list (which may be an empty list).

When a pattern contains attributes, the order of the attributes is not significant. The pattern matches elements that contain at least the attributes present in the pattern.

For example, the pattern

```
<citation year=$Y> <$T> <$R> </citation>
```

matches the element

```
<citation type="thesis" year="2003">
    <title> ... </title>
    <author> ... </author>
    ...
    <year> ... <year>
</citation>
```

binding $Y with "2003" and $T with <title> ... </title>. The variable $R is bound to the rest of the list of elements contained in <citation>, i.e., the list of elements

```
    <author> ... </author>
    ...
    <year> ... <year>
```

When this structure is not sufficient to express some configuration (typically when the pattern is too big or the order of some elements is not fixed), one can use the following "contains" predicate:

```
<citation> <$A> </citation>
    &   $A contains   <title> <$T> </title>
```

In this case the element <title> is searched everywhere in the subtree $A.

13.4.2.2 Rules

A rule is a couple containing at least a pattern and an action. The execution of a rule may be constrained by some conditions. These conditions are tests on values which have been computed before and are inherited from the context. This is again different from XSLT in which it is possible to get access to values appearing between the top of the tree and the current point. Here these values must explicitly be stored and can be the result of a calculus.

In the following rule, the variable $A is bound to the year of publishing found in the <citation> element while $T is found in the context.

```
<citation year=$Y > <$A> </citation>
    &   current year = $T
```

The effect of a rule can be to modify the context (the modification is local to the concerned subtree), to assert some predicates (this is global to all the site) and to emit error messages depending on tests.

The following example sets the value of the current year to what is found in the argument of the <activityreport> element.

```
<activity report year=$Y >
   <$A>
</activity report>
        => current year := $Y ;
```

The two following rules illustrate the checking of an untrusted part of a document against a trusted part.

In the trusted part, the members of a team are listed (or declared). The context contains the name of the current team, and for each person we can assert that it is a member of the team.

```
<pers firstname=$F lastname=$L>
   <$_>
</pers>
   & teamname = $P
        => teammember($F,$L,$P) ;
```

In the untrusted part, we want to check that the authors of some documents are declared as members of the current team. If it is not the case, an error message is produced.

```
<author firstname=$F lastname=$L>
   <$_>
</author>
   & teamname = $P
      ? teammember($F,$L,$P)
         / <li> Warning: <$F> <$L> is not
         member of the team
         <i> <$P> </i>
         </li>;
```

13.4.3 Dynamic Semantics

On each file, the XML tree is visited recursively. A local environment which is initially empty is constructed. On each node, a list of rules which can be applied (the pattern matches the current element and conditions are evaluated to true) is constructed, then applied. This means that all rules which can be applied are evaluated in the same environment. The order in which the rules are then applied is not defined.

During this process, two results are constructed. The fist one is a list of global assertions, the second is a list of tests and related actions. These are saved in files.

A global environment is constructed by collecting all assertions coming from each different environment files. Then using this global environment, tests are performed, producing error messages if there are some.

To produce complete error messages, two predefined variables exist: $Source-File and $SourceLine. They contain respectively, the name of the current file which is analyzed and the line number corresponding to the current point.

13.5 Ontologies as Types

An ontology is a way of representing human knowledge in a formal manner. One main goal of an ontology is to be shared between a group of people to fix a terminology and the relations between concepts. Ontologies are heavily used in semantic annotations to ease both human and machine interface and is one of the foundation of the semantic Web [3, 5].

An important word in this definition is "shared". It implies the fact that an ontology is a reference [17]. An ontology in the context of an information system can be compared to declarations or libraries in a programming context.

As for web pages, the evolution of ontologies and semantic annotations must be controlled. The process of evolution is studied for example in [26–29].

The size of ontologies (in particular definitions), leads to the emergence of ontology engineering to allow the management of the creation, modification and development of huge ontologies. Some specialized software as editors are helpful (Protégé for example), and sometime database technology are required [42]. In many aspects, the development of formal systems as ontologies is closed to the development of programs as it is already the case for web-based information systems [8, 31, 35]. Traditional development of ontologies description formalisms refers to the world of logic [12, 16, 20, 32]. In this section we show that ontologies can be seen as type systems. Type systems have been heavily studied in the context of the semantics of programming languages [18]. Thus it should be possible to reuse many results coming from the types community to create more powerful and more secure definition formalisms to describe human knowledge, and this is of course not incompatible with the logical vision. Following P.-H. Luong [26, 29] we take a small ontology and use it by means of semantics annotations, then modifying this ontology we see the effects of this evolution of the ontology on the semantics annotations. In a second step we endorse the suit of a programmer and will implement the same ontology as a type system, applying then the same evolution.

```
Concepts: Person, Trainee, PhdStudent, Manager,
     Researcher, Director, Team, Project;


Researcher is-a Manager;
Director is-a Manager;
```

```
Manager is-a Person;
PhdStudent is-a Person:
Trainee is-a Person;

Properties: work, manage;

Person work Team;
Manager manage Project;
```

Let's take a list of semantic annotations, given as RDF triplets:

```
1. (r1 work v1)(r1 type Person)
2. (r2 work v2)(r2 type PhdStudent)
3. (r3 work v3)(r3 type Manager)
4. (r4 manage v4)(r4 type Manager)
5. (r5 work v5)(r5 type Researcher)
6. (r6 manage v6)(r6 type Researcher)
7. (r7 work v7)(r7 type Director)
8. (r8 manage v8)(r8 type Director)
```

In these annotations, r_i and v_i are instances of concepts that are inferred from the properties definitions and from type restrictions that are included in the annotations.

In [28], the effects of modifying the ontology on this set of annotations are studied. The original ontology is modified, deleting the concept Director, merging PhdStudent and Trainee into the concept Student. The new ontology that is obtained is defined below:

```
Concepts: Person, Student, Researcher, Director,
    Team, Project;

Researcher is-a Person;
Director is-a Person;
Student is-a Person;

Properties: work, manage;

Person work Team;
Director manage Project;
```

A consequence of the modifications of the ontology is that the annotations 2, 3, 4 and 6 become inconsistent.

We can make a parallel between ontologies and semantic annotations with programs that are also formal systems. Concepts can be viewed as types and subsumptions as type inclusions. In this context, properties get signatures that define their domains and co-domains.

The initial ontology can be described as follows:

```
Person, PhdStudent, Trainee, Manager, Researcher,
    Director, Team, Project : type;

PhdStudent <= Person;
Trainee <= Person;
Manager <= Person;
Researcher <= Manager;
Director <= Manager;

work : Person -> Team;
manage : Manager -> Project;
```

The sign <= denotes type inclusion.

The semantic annotations can be seen as expressions in a programming language. Instances are represented by objects (let's say constants). Types of object can be inferred or declared. We prefer to declare them as it is the case in languages with strong typing to optimize type verification and obtain as much error messages as possible.

```
r1 : Person;
r2 : PhdStudent;
r3, r4 : Manager;
r5, r6 : Researcher;
r7, r8 : Director;
v1, v2, v3, v5, v7  : Team;
v4, v6, v8 : Project;
```

If we apply the same modifications to the ontology as previously, the type system looks now as follow

```
Person, Student, Researcher, Director, Team,
    Project : type;

Student <= Person;
Researcher <= Person;
Director <= Person;

work : Person -> Team;
manage : Director -> Project;
```

Applying a traditional type checker to our set of semantic annotations, will produce error messages.

In the following declarations

```
r2 : PhdStudent;
r3, r4 : Manager;
```

the types (concepts) PhdStudent and Manager are not declared and these declaration are not legal.

In the annotations 2, 3 and 4, r2, r3 and r4 are not of type Person as declared by the signatures of the properties work and manage. In the annotation 6, r6 is not of type Director.

[23] shows that modifying a part of an ontology can imply some inconsistencies somewhere else in this ontology or when it is used. [26] proposed some rules to detect these inconsistencies. Viewing an ontology as a type system, we can say that checking the consistency of ontologies and annotations can be done by a traditional type-checking

13.6 Applications

When defining a programming language, one will want to give its complete semantics. This semantics is given to the programmer by means of manuals. This is not possible for a Web site, we will rather try to give only some semantic constraints that we want to check. The designer itself or the authors of the pages have to chose this set of rules, with the possibility to specify some gravity levels as errors and warnings.

Our technologies can also be used to extract and re-compose pieces of information that are spread out in one or more documents, taking benefit of the environment.

This section illustrates these two points. Extraction has been also used with the help of a tagger to extract both textual and structural information in documents to perform different feature selections and classify these documents into clusters [11].

13.6.1 Verifying a Web Site

The following example illustrates our definition language. We want to maintain an academic site. The current page must be trusted and contains a presentation of the structure of an organization.

```
<department>
    <deptname><$X></deptname>
    <$_>
</department>
    =>     dept:=$X
```

The left hand side of the rule is a pattern. Each time the pattern is found, the local environment is modified: the value matched by the logical variable $X is assigned to the variable dept. This value can be retrieved in all the subtrees of the current tree, as in the following example. $_ matches the rest of what is in the department tag.

Notice that, unlike what happens in XSLT in which it is possible to have direct access to data appearing between the root and the current point in a tree, we have to store explicitly useful values in the local environment. In return, one can store (and retrieve) values which are computed and are not part of the original data, and this is not possible with XSLT.

```
<head><$P></head>
   &   dept=$X
        =>    head($P,$X)
```

We are in the context of the department named $X, and $P is the head of this department. head($P,$X) is an assertion which is true for the whole site, and thus we can add this assertion to the global environment. This is quite equivalent to building a local ontology. If, in some context, an ontology already exists, we can think of using it as an external resource. Notice that a triplet in RDF can be viewed as a Prolog predicate [33].

```
<agent><$P></agent>
        ? appointment($P,$X)
            / <li> Warning: <$P> line <$SourceLine>
                    does not appear in the current
                    staff chart.
            </li>;
```

This rule illustrates the generation of error messages. In the XML text, the tag agent is used to indicate that we have to check that the designated person has got an appointment in a department. The treatment of errors hides some particular techniques as the generated code must be rich enough to enable to locate the error in the source code.

13.6.2 Verifying a Document and Inferring New Data

As a real sized test application, we have used the scientific part of the activity reports published by Inria for the years 2001 and 2002 which can be found at the following URLs: http://www.inria.fr/rapportsactivite/RA2001/index.html and http://www.inria.fr/rapportsactivite/RA2002/index.html.

The sources of these activity reports are LaTeX documents, and are automatically translated into XML to be published on the Web.

The XML versions of these documents contain respectively 108 files and 125 files, a total of 215 000 and 240 000 lines, more than 12.9 and 15.2 Mbytes of data. Each file is the reflect of the activity of a research group. Even if a large part of the document is written in French, the structure and some parts of the document are formalized. This includes parts speaking of the people and the bibliography.

Concerning the people, we can check that names which appears in the body of the document are "declared" in the group members list at the beginning. If it is not the case, the following error message is produced:

```
Warning: X does not appear in the list of
   project's members (line N)
```

Concerning the bibliography of the group, the part called "publications of the year" may produce error messages like the following one:

```
Warning: The citation line 2176 has not been
 published during this year (2000)
```

We have also use Wget to check the validity of URLs used as citation, producing the following error messages:

```
Testing of URL
 http://www.nada.kth.se/ruheconference/
 line 1812 in file "aladin.xml" replies:
 http://www.nada.kth.se/ruheconference/:
 14:50:33 ERREUR 404: Not Found.

Testing of URL
 http://citeseer.nj.nec.com/ning93novel.html
 line 1420 in file "a3.xml" replies:
 No answer or time out during wget,
 The server seems to be down or does not
 exist.
```

Beyond these verification steps, using a logic programming approach allows us to infer some important information. For example we found out that 40 publications out of a total of 2816 were co-written by two groups, giving an indicator on the way the 100 research groups cooperate.

```
The citation  "Three knowledge representation
 formalisms for content-based manipulation of
 documents" line 2724 in file "acacia.xml" has
 been published in cooperation with
 orpailleur.
```

Our system reported respectively 1372 and 1432 messages for the years 2001 and 2002. The reasons of this important number of errors are various. There is a lot of misspelling in family names (mainly due to missing accents or to differences between the name used in publications and the civil name for women). Some persons who participated to some parts of a project but have not been present during all the year can be missing in the list of the team's members. There is also a lot of mistakes in the list of publications: a paper written during the current year can be published the year after and should not appear as a publication of the year. There are also a lot of errors in URLs and this number of errors should increase as URLs are not permanent objects.

It is to be noticed that we have worked on documents that have been generated, and that the original latex versions have been carefully reviewed by several persons. This means that proofreading is not feasible for large documents.

For future developments, other important indicators can also be inferred: how many PhD students are working on the different teams, how many PhD theses are published, etc. These indicators are already used by the management to evaluate the global performance of the institute but are compiled manually. An automatic process should raise the level of confidence in these indicators. They can also be compared mechanically with other sources of information as, for example, the data bases used by the staff office.

13.6.3 Implementation Notes

All the implementation has been done in Prolog (more exactly Eclipse) except the XML scanner which has been constructed with flex.

An XML parser has been generated using an extension of the standard DCG. This parser has been extended to generate our specification language parser.

The rule compiler as been entirely written in Prolog.

Concerning the execution of the specification, the main difficulty comes from the fact that we have a global environment. The traditional solution in this case is to use coroutines or delays. As our input comes from many files, this solution was not reasonable, and we have chosen a two passes process. For each input file, during the first pass we use the local environment and construct the part of the global environment which is generated by the current file and a list of delayed conditions which will be solved during the second pass. During the second pass, all the individual parts of the global environment are merged and the result is used to perform the delayed verifications, producing errors messages when necessary.

A special mention should be made concerning pages that are dynamically generated on demand. These should not to be mixed up with pages that are statically generated by a compilation process. For pages generated on demand, one can perform some checks on this pages, but two points must be stressed: first, they must be checked in a fix global environment, and if for some reason the environment is modified, the modifications must not have an impact on the rest of the system; second, such a verification is a bit late, as it will be difficult to tell the end-user that a site produces an erroneous information. Other techniques to prove that the dynamic generation process is correct should be used.

Performances are of course an issue. Performances depend on two parameters: the size of the pages (viewed as Prolog terms), and the number of rules that must be performed. However the choice of Prolog here is a good point, as modern Prolog compilers make a smart use of hash-coding for clauses indexing.

13.7 Conclusion

Web sites and ontologies are formal objects and we have shown how techniques used to define the formal semantics of programming languages can be used in the context of the Web. This work can be viewed as a complement to other researches which may be very close: for example in [14], some logic programming methods are used to specify and check integrity constraints in the structure of Web sites (but not to its static semantics). Our work which is focused on the content of Web sites and on their formal semantics, remains original. It can be extended to the content management of more general information system.

As we have seen, the techniques already exist and are used in some other domains. The use of logic programming, and in particular of Prolog as an implementation language, is very well adapted to our goals. Our goal is to make these techniques accessible and easily usable in the context of Web sites with the help of a specific specification language. We are now convinced that the technology is adequate.

The gap between information systems and programs, ontologies and types is small. The world of software engineering and the type community have already investigate some important notions such as overloading, polymorphism, type parameters, and more generally modularity. A next step should be a fertilization step, importing these notions to construct more powerful languages and tools for the Web and other information systems.

References

1. Alpuente, M., Ballis, D., Falaschi, M.: Rule-based verification of web sites. Software Tools for Technology Transfer **8**(6), 565–585 (2006)
2. Alpuente, M., Ballis, D., Falaschi, M., Ojeda, P., Romero, D.: Fast algebraic verification service. In: Proceedings of the First International Conference on Web Reasoning and Rule Systems. Lecture Notes in Computer Science. Springer, Berlin (2007)
3. Berners-Lee, T.: A Road Map to the Semantic Web. http://www.w3.org/DesignIssues/Semantic.html (1998)
4. Berners-Lee, T.: Ideas about web architecture—yet another notation: Notation 3. http://www.w3.org/DesignIssues/Notation3.html (2001)
5. Berners-Lee, T., Hendler, J., Lassila, O.: The Semantic Web. Scientific American **284**(5), 34–43 (2001)
6. Deshpande, Y., Olsina, L., Murugesan, S.: Third ICSE workshop on web engineering. In: Proceedings of ICSE'2002 (2002)
7. Despeyroux, T.: Executable specification of static semantics. In: Semantics of Data Types, Lecture Notes in Computer Science, vol. 173. Springer, Berlin (1987)
8. Despeyroux, T.: Practical semantic analysis of web sites and documents. In: Proceedings of the 13th World Wide Web Conference (WWW2004). ACM, New York (2004)
9. Despeyroux, T., Trousse, B.: Semantic verification of web sites using natural semantics. In: RIAO 2000, 6th Conference on Content-Based Multimedia Information Access, College de France, Paris, France (2000)
10. Despeyroux, T., Trousse, B.: Maintaining semantic constraints in web sites. In: AACE WebNet 2001 Conference, Orlando, Florida (2001)
11. Despeyroux, T., Lechevallier, Y., Trousse, B., Vercoustre, A.M.: Experiments in clustering homogeneous XML documents to validate an existing typology. In: Proceedings of the 5th International Conference on Knowledge Management (I-Know), Vienna, Austria (2005)
12. Fensel, D., Decker, R., Erdman, M., Studer, R.: Ontobroker: The very high idea. In: Proceedings of the 11th International FLAIRS Conference (FLAIRS-98) (1998)
13. Fensel, D., Angele, J., Decker, S., Erdmann, M., Schnurr, H.P., Studer, R., Witt, A.: On2broker: Lessons learned from applying AI to the web. Technical report, Institute AIFB (1998)

14. Fernandez, M.F., Florescu, D., Levy, A.Y., Suciu, D.: Verifying integrity constraints on web sites. In: IJCAI, pp. 614–619 (1999). citeseer.nj.nec.com/fernandez99verifying.html
15. Flores, S., Lucas, S., Villanueva, A.: Formal verification of websites. Electronic Notes in Theoretical Computer Science **200**(3), 103–118 (2008)
16. Grosof, B.N., Volz, R., Horrocks, I., Decker, S.: Description logic programs: Combining logic programs with description logic. In: Proceedings of the 12th World Wide Web Conference (WWW2003) (2003)
17. Gruber, T.R.: A translation approach to portable ontology specifications. Knowledge Acquisition **5**(2), 199–220 (1993)
18. Gunter, C.A.: Semantics of Programming Languages. MIT Press, Cambridge (1992)
19. Holck, J.: 4 perspectives on web information systems. In: Proceedings of the 36th Hawaii International Conference on System Sciences (2003)
20. Horrocks, I., Patel-Schneider, P.F., Harmelen, F.V.: From SHIQ and RDF to OWL: The making of a web ontology language. Journal of Web Semantics **1**(1), 7–26 (2003)
21. Hosoya, H., Pierce, B.: Xduce: A typed XML processing language. In: Proceedings of Third International Workshop on the Web and Databases (2000)
22. Kahn, G.: Natural semantics. In: Proceedings of the Symp. on Theoretical Aspects of Computer Science, TACS. Lecture Notes in Computer Science, vol. 247. Springer, Berlin (1987). Also Inria Research Report 601, February 1987
23. Klein, M., Fensel, D., Kiryakov, A., Ognyanov, D.: Ontology versioning and change detection on the web. In: 13th International Conference on Knowledge Engineering and Knowledge Management (EKAW02), pp. 197–212 (2002)
24. Klyne, G., Carroll, J.J.: Resource description framework (RDF): Concepts and abstract syntax. W3C Recommendation, http://www.w3.org/TR/rdf-concepts/ (2004)
25. Lucas, S.: Rewriting-based navigation of web sites: Looking for models and logics. Electronic Notes in Theoretical Computer Science **157**(2), 79–85 (2006)
26. Luong, P.H.: Gestion de l'évolution d'un web sémantique. PhD thesis, Ecole des Mines de Paris (2007)
27. Luong, P.H., Dieng-Kuntz, R.: A rule-based approach for semantic annotation evolution. The Computational Intelligence Journal **23**(3), 320–338 (2007)
28. Luong, P.H., Dieng-Kuntz, R., Boucher, A.: Evolution de l'ontologie et gestion des annotations sémantiques inconsistantes. In: Proceedings of Extraction et gestion des connaissances (EGC'2007). Revue des Nouvelles Technologies de l'Information. Cépaduès (2007)
29. Luong, P.H., Dieng-Kuntz, R., Boucher, R.: Managing semantic annotations evolution in the CoSWEN system. In: Proceedings of the Third National Symposium on Research, Development and Application of Information and Communication Technology (ICT.RDA'06) (2006)
30. Meijer, E., Shields, M.: XMλ: A functional programming language for constructing and manipulating XML document. Draft, http://www.cse.ogi.edu/~mbs/pub/xmlambda/ (1999)
31. Murugesan, S., Deshpande, Y., Hansen, S., Ginige, A.: Web engineering: A new discipline for development of web-based systems. In: Proceedings of the Web Engineering, Software Engineering and Web Application Development. Springer, Berlin (2001)
32. Patel-Schneider, P.F., Horrocks, I.: A comparison of two modelling paradigms in the semantic web. In: Proc. of the Fifteenth International World Wide Web Conference (WWW 2006), pp. 3–12. ACM, New York (2006)
33. Peer, J.: A logic programming approach to RDF document and query transformation. In: Workshop on Knowledge Transformation for the Semantic Web at the 15th European Conference on Artificial Intelligence, Lyon, France (2002)
34. Plotkin, G.D.: A structural approach to operational semantics. Technical report DAIMI FN-19, Aarhus University (1981)
35. Pressman, R.S., Lewis, T., Adida, B., Ullman, E., DeMarco, T., Gilb, T., Gorda, B., Humphrey, W., Johnson, R.: Can Internet-based application be engineered? IEEE Software **15**(5), 104–110 (1998)
36. Stallman, R.M., McGrath, R.: GNU Make: A Program for Directing Recompilation, Version 3.79. Free Software Foundation, Cambridge (2000)

37. Szabo, E.: The Collected Papers of Gerhard Gentzen. North-Holland, Amsterdam (1969)
38. van Harmelen, F., Fensel, D.: Practical knowledge representation for the web. In: Fensel, D. (ed.) Proceedings of the IJCAI'99 Workshop on Intelligent Information Integration (1999)
39. van Harmelen, F., van der Meer, J.: Webmaster: Knowledge-based verification of web-pages. In: Twelfth International Conference on Industrial and Engineering Applications of Artificial Intelligence and Expert Systems IEA/AIE'99 (1999)
40. W3C: XML, XSL, XML schema and RDF recommendations or submissions. http://www.w3.org/
41. W3C: DAML+OIL (March 2001) reference description. http://www.w3.org/TR/daml+oil-reference (2001)
42. Weithöner, T., Liebig, T., Specht, G.: Efficient processing of huge ontologies in logic and relational databases. In: Proceedings of Ontologies, Databases, and Applications of Semantics Conference (ODBASE'2004) (2004)

Part IV
Applications and Case Studies

Chapter 14
Modeling and Testing of Web-Based Systems

Ana Cavalli, Mounir Lallali, Stephane Maag,
Gerardo Morales, and Fatiha Zaidi

Abstract The success and the massive adoption of Web applications and services
are pushing the community to increase and enhance their developments. By that
way, the complexity and size of Web-based systems are definitely growing. Accordingly, the need for sophisticated and complete methods used to test the reliability
and security aspects of Web systems is increasing as well. Quality and relevant test
cases development can achieve up to 70% of the total cost of the project when these
test cases are hand crafted. Because of this, the industry and the research community are making big efforts to automate test cases generation. That is the reason
why the test generator must be supplied with a precise and unambiguous semantic
description of the implementation under test (IUT), i.e. a formal model. This chapter presents two methodologies to attain automatic test cases generation: The first
one applies extended finite state machines to model Web services composition described in WS-BPEL, while the other one uses UML to model Web applications.
Together with the formal models of the web systems, this chapter presents methods
for conformance and non-regression test generation.

14.1 Introduction

Web-based systems (services and applications) are gaining industry-wide accep-
tance and usage. They are very popular because they offer complete interoperability
between systems. Using Web-based systems is relatively easy and inexpensive for
companies and institutions. It makes it easier for them to share their expertise, cooperate by outsourcing tasks between them and making their incompatible software
systems interoperable. It hardly matters what operative system, database or other

---

Research supported in part by the French National Agency of Research within the WebMov
project: http://webmov.lri.fr.

A. Cavalli (✉)
SAMOVAR CNRS UMR 5157, Telecom & Management SudParis, 9 rue Charles Fourrier,
91011 Evry Cedex, France
e-mail: Ana.Cavalli@it-sudparis.eu

Y. Badr et al. (eds.) *Emergent Web Intelligence: Advanced Semantic Technologies,*
Advanced Information and Knowledge Processing,
DOI 10.1007/978-1-84996-077-9_14, © Springer-Verlag London Limited 2010

characteristics their systems rely on. The idea behind Web-based systems was to create an interface that describes what a system does. Every operation with its input to the system and output obtained from the system is described. Another system can access the Web-based system, viewing it as a black box, by using Internet as the channel of communication. As the Web-based system implementations grow in size and complexity, the necessity for testing their reliability and level of security are becoming more and more crucial.

Besides knowing whether a given Web-based system satisfies its functional requirements, it is also important for a user to know whether the system behaves appropriately when interoperating with others. Some of the questions that need be answered are: (i) does the host of a selected Web-based system behave correctly without any implementation error? (ii) does the Web-based system behave correctly when new services are integrated to the network? (iii) does the selected Web-based system tolerate erroneous behavior of other services with whom it must interoperate? (iv) does the selected Web-based system produce outputs that can cause other components to fail?

Frequently we can find hand crafted methodologies for conformance testing. Although in most of the cases the execution of the test cases is automated, the biggest part of the test cases generation process is hand made. Under these conditions, the production of quality and relevant test cases can be expensive compared with the cost of the global project (30% to 70%). Because of this, the industry and the research community have been working and making efforts to automate test cases generation. So that a machine can generate the test cases and the oracle to assign the verdict for the tests, one needs to feed it with a description of the implementation under test (IUT), as precise and less ambiguous as possible; i.e. a formal description with a precise semantic.

The main contribution of this chapter is the presentation of a methodology to model and test Web-based systems. For the modeling of Web-based systems, we have chosen UML (Unified Modeling Language) [34] to specify web applications. The Web Services Business Process Execution Language (WS-BPEL) [32] has been chosen to specify services. This last language is well adapted for service composition description. For testing purposes, we propose a model-based approach that relies on formal description languages. WS-BPEL descriptions are translated into another formalism, the Time Extended Finite State Machines for Web Services (WS-TEFSM), which is well adapted for the modeling and the testing of Web-based systems. Once the formal model has been designed (in WS-TEFSM or UML), based on formal testing relations and on a fault-model, we provide test methods and its associated algorithms to generate the test cases. Afterwards, the test cases can be automatically or manually executed on the real implementation, i.e. the deployed Web-based system.

The tests which are presented in this chapter, are conformance and non-regression tests. By conformance testing we mean the assessment that a product conforms to its specification. Test cases are designed to test particular aspects of the Web-based system, which are called test purposes. Non-regression testing consists of testing modified software to detect whether new errors have been introduced by the modifications, and provides confidence that the modifications do not change the system behavior.

The proposed methodology is composed of two approaches, one based on WS-TEFSMs models and the other on UML models. The methodology based on the UML models has been applied to a real case study, an open source e-learning platform dotLRN [11]. Then, test generation methods have been applied to them. Numerous experiments have been performed for conformance and non regression testing, based on automatic test generation but also with hand crafted tests using TCLwebtests.

In this chapter, we do not address the Web semantic. Our work is related to testing and in particular to automation of testing Web-based systems to establish their correctness with respect to their specifications. To perform the conformance and non regressions testing, it exists languages and standards of reference to describe the Web-based systems and from which we generate the tests and execute them on the real implementation. The languages that are used in that chapter are a subset of UML and WS-BPEL. The languages that are used in the domain of semantic Web are very specific and address particular objectives that are not those addressed by this chapter. Nevertheless, we give below some references and information about the semantic Web that can help to understand what this domain covers and to establish the differences with the work performed here.

The semantic Web is the abstract representation of data on the World Wide Web to make it easily processed by machines, offering more effective discovery, automation, integration, and reuse among various applications [54]. It is different from the Web that is essentially syntactic. It aims to facilitate the communication human-machine and machine-to-machine and the automatic data processing. The semantic Web is based on some standards Ontology is the core of the Semantic Web. It consists of a set of concepts, axioms, and relationships that describe a domain of interest (e.g. system model, data model, etc.). Ontology engineering is supported by primary semantic Web standards and languages (e.g. RDF (Resource Definition Framework) [49], Web Ontology Language (OWL) [48]).

The semantic Web and Web services are complementary. The former aims at providing a semantic interoperability of content, while Web services aim at giving a syntactic interoperability of data exchanges. In addition, several information needed by the automation of design and implementation of Web services (like description, publication, discovery, selection, execution, composition, monitoring, replacement, compensation, etc.) are either absent or described to be only used or interpreted by humans. Such information can be provided by the semantic Web in a way that machines can understand and process it.

Several semantic types can be considered in the Web services domain [5]: (i) functional semantics: (the semantics of service signature (inputs/outputs)); (ii) data semantics (annotation of data involved in Web service operation using ontologies); quality of service semantics (the semantics of different quality aspects, e.g. deadlines, cost of service); (iv) execution semantics (these semantics concern message sequence, flows, effects of service invocation, etc.); (v) domain semantics:

the use of domain-specific semantics can ameliorate the discovery and selection of services.

Some approaches [5] have been developed to introduce semantics to Web services by using: WSDL-S (Web Service Description Language with Semantics) [52], OWL-S language (Ontology Web Language for Services) [51], WSMO (Web Services Modeling Ontology) [53].

As stated before, the semantic Web and our work address different objectives. Indeed, Semantic Web service technologies are developed in order to give richer semantics to services leading to the automation of the Web Service usage process. Nevertheless, there exist some works that try to apply testing techniques to semantic Web services as in [39, 59], and especially in automatic composition of semantic Web Services [43, 60].

The chapter is organized as follows: in Sect. 14.2, basic concepts of Web-based systems and testing techniques are presented. This section also includes the presentation of related work. Section 14.3 presents model-based testing techniques starting with a presentation of the modeling languages WS-BPEL, WS-TEFSMs and UML, used to describe the expected requirements or properties of the Web-based systems. In Sect. 14.4, Web services composition mechanisms and the test generation algorithms to generate tests from WS-TEFSMs and UML models are presented. Section 14.5 presents the case study, the dotLRN system, and the test generation from an UML model of the system by the application of the methods described in Sect. 14.4. Finally, we conclude the chapter and illustrate some perspectives in Sect. 14.6.

14.2 Preliminaries

This preliminary section is devoted first to the presentation of basic concepts related to the Web-based systems. Then, the testing vocabulary is detailed especially in focusing on the formal aspects. Finally we present the related works in that domain in order to illustrate the contribution of the Web-based community.

14.2.1 Definitions

According to W3C definition, a Web service provides a standard means of interoperating between different software applications. Web services deal with making heterogeneous applications interoperate. A standardized way of integrating Web-based applications is ensured by the XML (eXtensible Markup Language) [47], SOAP (Simple Object Access Protocol) [55], WSDL (Web Service Description Language) [7] and UDDI (Universal Description, Discovery and Integration) [31] that are open standards over an Internet protocol backbone. XML is used to tag the data, SOAP is the protocol used to transfer the data, WSDL describes the available services and UDDI is a kind of registry.

Used primarily as a way for businesses to communicate with each other and with clients, Web services allow organizations to communicate data without intimate knowledge of each other system behind the firewall. The combination of services—internal and external to an organization—makes up a service-oriented architecture. The composition of Web services became this last decade a subject of interest as well as for researchers then for industrials. Several proposals of languages to program and/or to specify Web services composition came up and among them, as previously mentioned, the WS-BPEL language. This latter is well tailored to address the composition of Web services and it is also widely used [30]. The composition is also commonly known as *Orchestration* and this is carried on at a single partner level.

While Web services are dedicated to the interactions between different programs, Web applications are commonly defined as a collection of logically connected Web pages managed as a single entity reachable via a Web browser over a network such as the Internet or an Intranet [50]. A Web applications is like a software application implemented in a browser-supported language (such as HTML, JavaScript, Java, etc.) executed through a Web browser.

We can notice that both types of systems, i.e. Web service and Web application rely on their access and availability through Internet and on specific dedicated languages. In our case, we consider the composition of Web services in order to produce more complex ones. The language to describe the workflow of the composition is the WS-BPEL. The Web application language is the HTML and for the modeling we use UML diagrams.

14.2.2 Testing Techniques

After the system has been implemented, the implementation must be verified to conform to its specification, to ensure that the system will operate correctly. This procedure is known as conformance testing, and can be accomplished by applying a sequence of inputs to the implementation, by means of an external tester, and by verifying if the sequence of outputs is the one specified.

If a test sequence is capable of detecting all erroneous implementations, it is said to provide *full* fault coverage. There are many methods for generating automatically a test sequence to check a given implementation against a specification. Most of the methods used in this chapter have been developed in the framework of protocol engineering, since protocols are normally programs for which precise specifications can be defined. However, these techniques can be adapted and applied successfully to the test of Web services and applications.

14.2.2.1 Basic Concepts

A program specification is typically composed by a control part and a data part. This chapter deals with the control part only; other approaches are oriented to the analysis of control and data dependencies [18]. The control part of a program, which

Fig. 14.1 A graphical
representation of a FSM

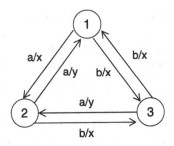

will be referred as program specification, can be modeled as a Finite State Machine (FSM) with a finite set of states $S = \{s_1, s_2, \ldots, s_n\}$, a finite set of inputs $I = \{a_1, a_2, \ldots, a_k\}$, and a finite set of outputs $O = \{x_1, x_2, \ldots, x_m\}$. The next state (σ) and output (φ) are given by a set of mappings $\sigma : S \times I \to S$ and $\varphi : S \times I \to O$. The FSM is usually also represented by a direct graph $G = (V, E)$, where the set $V = \{v_1, v_2, \ldots, v_n\}$ of vertices represents the set of states S, and a directed edge represents a transition from one state to another in the FSM. Each edge in G is labeled by an input a_r and a corresponding output x_q. An edge in E from v_i to v_j which has label a_r/x_q means that the FSM, in state s_i, upon receiving input a_r produces output x_q and moves to state s_j. A triplet $(s_i, a_r/x_q, s_j)$ is used in the text to denote a transition.

A FSM is said to be *fully specified* is from each state it has a transition for every input symbol, otherwise the FSM is said to be *partially specified*. If a FSM is partially specified and a non specified input is applied, under the *Completeness Assumption* the FSM will either stay in the same state without any output or signal an error. The initial state of a FSM is the state the FSM enters immediately after power-up.

State s_i is said to be weakly equivalent to state s_j if any specified *input/output* sequence for s_i is also specified for s_j. If two states are weakly equivalent to each other they are said to be strongly equivalent. A FSM is *deterministic*, if for each state $s_i \in S$, with two associated transitions $(s_i, a_r/x_q, s_j)$ and $(s_i, a_w/x_p, s_k)$ where $a_r \neq a_w$ and $s_j \neq s_k$.

A graph representation of a FSM is depicted in Fig. 14.1. For the FSM represented, $I = \{a, b\}$ and $O = \{x, y\}$.

14.2.2.2 Conformance

Since the implementation is tested as a black box (meaning that we do not have any internal views of the system), the strongest conformance relation that can be tested is *trace equivalence*: two FSMs are trace equivalent if the two cannot be distinguished by any sequence of inputs. That is, both implementation and specification will generate the same outputs (i.e. trace) for all specified input sequences. To prove trace equivalence it suffices to show that (i) there is a set of implementation states

Fig. 14.2 Conformance
testing scheme

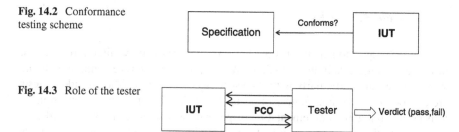

Fig. 14.3 Role of the tester

{$p_1, p_2, \ldots, p_n$} respectively isomorphic to specification states {$s_1, s_2, \ldots, s_n$}, and
(ii) every transition in the specification has a corresponding isomorphic transition in
the implementation. Figure 14.2 illustrates the goal of the conformance testing.

Conformance testing consists in making the implementation under test (IUT)
to interact with its environment. This environment is simulated by a tester (cf.
Fig. 14.3) that executes the test cases and stimulates the IUT. The interfaces of the
tester are called Points of Control and Observation (PCO).

14.2.2.3 Models of Faults

The types of faults detected by methods based on input/output FSMs are output and
transfer faults. An output fault occurs when a transition produces an unexpected output for a given input; that is, a transition specified as $(s_i, a_r/x_q, s_j)$ is implemented
as $(s_i, a_r/x_w, s_j)$ where $x_q \neq x_w$. A transfer fault occurs when a transition leaves the
implementation in the incorrect state; that is, a transition specified as $(p_i, a_r/x_q, p_j)$
is implemented as $(p_i, a_r/x_q, p_k)$ where p_j (the state that should implements s_j)
and p_k are not equivalent. Note that a single transition may incur into an output and
transfer fault.

14.2.2.4 Automatic Test Generation

The purpose of test generation is to produce a sequence of inputs (and corresponding
outputs), called a test sequence, which can be applied to an implementation to verify
that it correctly implements the specification.

There is a number of necessary assumptions that must be made in order to make
the experiment possible: (i) the specification FSM is strongly connected, so that all
states can be visited; (ii) the specification FSM does not have strongly equivalent
states (it is minimal); (iii) there is an upper bound on the number of states in the
implementation FSM (otherwise one could always construct a machine which would
pass a given test sequence by using as many states as there are transitions in the
sequence).

14.2.3 Related Works

Several techniques to perform testing have been proposed in the literature. We first describe what it exists in the domain of Web applications and we continue with the Web services and particularly with Web services composition. The considered tests are conformance and non regression tests. As mentioned previously, conformance tests establish that the implementation respects its specification. In other words, we interact with the implementation by feeding it with inputs and compare the outputs of the implementation to the expected answers. The relation that exists between the specification and the implementation is an implementation relation. The specification is produced from an informal description of what the system is expected to do, here the specification languages are UML and WS-BPEL. The second kind of test is regression testing, that is the process of validating modified software to detect whether new errors have been introduced into previously tested code, and provide confidence that modifications are correct.

As the use of the Web applications is growing up, the interest on testing these systems and the number of works is increasing as well. Among the recent works it can be quoted [1], work in which the authors survey several analysis modeling methods used in Website verification and testing. In [25], a methodology of Model-Driven Testing for Web application is presented. Moreover, concerning the testing needed to help maintaining the stability of Web applications, numerous works are using the regression testing approach. This testing technique as well as conformance testing is important to apply to the open source Web applications because of its continuous developing speed and changeable user demands. The work presented in [57] proposes a method based on Slicing to avoid the re-execution of all the regression test cases of a Web application, and selects just the test cases that will interact with the part of the Web application that have suffered a change with the insertion of the new code.

Several tools and methodologies have been developed to achieve an automatic regression testing on Web applications that do not have a formal specification. Among all the tools used to build the regression test cases, the ones that can record the interactions between the user and the Web application during a certain time, or a well defined number of interactions (e.g. to follow a link or to submit a form) are the most popular. Selenium [37], for example is a tool in which the trace of interactions (i.e. the record) is written as HTML tables. However, for our purpose it was needed to obtain a trace flexible enough to be changed and re-used in an easy and fast way, for example a trace written in a scripting language. Tclwebtest [41] is a tool to write tests for Web applications. It provides an API for issuing HTTP requests and processing results. It assumes specific response values, while taking care of the details such as redirects and cookies. It has the basic HTML parsing functionality to provide access to elements of the resulting HTML pages that are needed for testing, mainly links and forms. The execution of a test case written in Tclwebtest will simulate a user that is interacting with the Web application through a Web browser. Using the links and forms it is possible to add, edit or delete data of the Web application by executing the test case script. There exists also a lot of works that have focused their research on functional testing based on a formal model such as [23, 26, 42]. We can also mention some Web application tools (e.g. OpenSTA [38], WAPT [45], SOASTA [44]). The listing of load/performance test tools and Web functional/ regression test is presented in [46].

Regarding Web services, we survey the existing works for Web services composition. As previously stated, in the area of Web services, the design is the most important phase of the orchestration layer. This is where one describes the complete services behavior. The growing use of Web services makes it necessary to ensure that the behavior is correct. The common practice in the area is to generate unit and integration tests with tools such as SOAPUI [12] that are based on empirical approaches. In the last years, the software testing community has started to get involved in the Web services domain. As a consequence, several works have been published to try to bridge the gap between the usual Web testing practices and a formal testing process. The empirical approaches that are still used in the domain give acceptable results but they have become more and more costly and do not allow to cover all the problems raised by such systems. Moreover, when systems become complex, such approaches offer only partial verifications and validations. Consequently, if we want to validate Web systems with an improved test coverage, we need to introduce rigorous methods which nevertheless conform to the economical constraints of the Web services development process. The original nature of Web services requires to first validate them individually and test them when integrated. Industrial tools exist and are available to perform such kinds of tests. When complex Web services are considered, we also need to deal with the Web services composition or in other words, orchestration.

The current practice deals with the Web Service Description Language WSDL. WSDL is used to describe what a Web service can do, where it resides, and how to invoke it. In our case, we consider WS-BPEL that permits describing the control and data flows; thus, allowing to study the behavioral aspects of the Web service. Several WS-BPEL activities are related to time constraints. So, we need to take into account such constraints for their modeling. Currently, in the literature, we can find several papers dealing with WS-BPEL specification and formal models for Web services. Several models are described to transform the WS-BPEL specifications. In [56] a transformation of WS-BPEL in an annotated deterministic finite state machine (FSM) is proposed. This formalism does not allow to capture the timing aspects of some WS-BPEL activities and does not consider WS-BPEL variables. In [29] another formalism is proposed that deals with variables, the Extended Finite State Machine (EFSM), but no timing constraints are considered. In [21] a formalism taking into account timing constraints is proposed, the Web Service Timed Transition System (WSTTS). However, this formalism uses only clocks but no variables. We can also mention works that use different kinds of formalisms [4, 13, 16, 58]. In [16, 58] Petri nets are used to specify the Web services. This formalism is not well adapted for testing Web services composition because it results in a global description that lacks structure making it impossible to differentiate the service components.

In [4] an interesting approach is presented using RT-UML to model real time aspects of Web service choreographies but this does not consider orchestration and interoperability of services and components. The work presented in [13] is similar to this one: to design a methodology based on WS-BPEL. Formalization of WS-BPEL language semantics is necessary to eliminate ambiguities and make abstract operational specifications executable. Here an Abstract State Machine (ASM) model is used but unlike FSM or WS-TEFSM [24] (Web Services Timed Extended Finite State Machine) models used in this work, it is not directly executable and requires not so evident translations, making it more difficult to develop testing tools. The used Distributed ASM needs also to be extended with timing constraints and variables. Other not yet very advanced approaches exist, such as in [15] where WS-BPEL is translated to Promela which is the input language of the SPIN [17] model checker, allowing test generation. These approaches need to be developed and implemented in tools where scalability and usability can be evaluated.

14.3 Web-Based System Modeling

The proposed methodology is based on two main elements: the modeling language and the generation methods. This latter will be detailed in Sect. 14.4. The modeling step provides a precise representation of the system. The description language used here to describe the composition of Web services is the WS-BPEL language for the reasons that have been mentioned above. In the case of Web applications, the UML notation and in particular some diagrams have been chosen. This notation is well-suited to describe Web applications which are often developed using object concepts. With UML we can represent the navigation by means of a navigation map which provides information about the dynamic content of each Web page. Furthermore, the sequence diagrams that represent the exchange between the elements of the system are good candidate to express the test objectives.

We detailed below the modeling choices of both Web services and Web applications, note that the choices have been made taking into account the adequacy of the language to the system to be described and also for testing purposes. Let us note that both Web-based systems in our methodology need to be formally described for testing generation methods which is one of our problematics. The willing to deal with such an approach is issued from our own experience in industrial projects.[1] We notice that the delays to produce a software or a new release are becoming more and more short. Furthermore in a competitive market the clients request cost reduction in their management and maintenance costs. For all these reasons a more automated technique to generate tests is needed as hand-crafted tests are a time-consuming activity. Hence, as said, a model is the first step and represents the specification of the system inputs and can be handled at a very early stage of the development cycle of a Web-based system, i.e. from the requirement information.

---

[1]PLATONIS (http://www-lor.int-evry.fr/platonis), ASK-IT (http://www.ask-it.org/.) and WebMov (http://webmov.lri.fr).

14.3.1 Modeling of Web Services

To standardize the specification of a Web services composition, IBM and other companies have proposed the WS-BPEL language [32] that became in 2007 an OASIS Standard [30].

WS-BPEL is a coordination and composition language that captures business interactions between Web services. It can also be viewed as a workflow language for Web Services. WS-BPEL provides constructs to describe arbitrarily complex business processes. A WS-BPEL process can interact synchronously or asynchronously with its partners (i.e. client service or services that are invoked by the WS-BPEL process). The building blocks for a WS-BPEL process are the descriptions of the parts participating in the process, in terms of data and activities flow. A basic process in WS-BPEL is defined as a root element, consisting of one or more child elements describing *partners links*, a set of *variables* that records the state of the process, *correlation Sets*, *event handlers*, *fault handlers*, *compensation handlers* and *activities*. This latter defines the logical interactions of a process and its partners. The WS-BPEL activities that can be performed by a business process instance are categorized into basic (e.g. <wait>, <exit> and <assign> activities),communication (e.g. <receive>, <reply> and <invoke> activities) and structured activities (e.g. <sequence>, <flow> and <while> activities). For instance, the <receive> activity waits for a message from a partner, and the <reply> activity sends an answer for a message previously received with a <receive> activity. The <wait> activity waits for a specified amount of time before continuing while the <onAlarm> WS-BPEL construct corresponds to a timer-based alarm.

We present in the next section the timed modeling of the Web Services composition described in WS-BPEL.

14.3.1.1 WS-BPEL Timed Modeling Approach

A WS-BPEL process component implements a business process (i.e. Web service). The behavior of a Web service is described by sequences of activities, their execution time and their semantic. For instance, the <wait> activity is triggered when the timeout occurs, the <reply> of invocation may be considered as an instantaneous activity, while the <receive> activity may require an arbitrary amount of time. To model this temporal behavior, we propose the WS-TEFSM which extends EFSM with clock variables, state invariants on clocks and priorities on transitions. The time progresses in states, and transitions take no time to be executed. In order to represent the time progress, a local clock is added in the WS-TEFSM. It can be initialized at the beginning of each activity to be executed and can be reset at its end. Moreover, in order to model an absolute time, a global clock, denoted gc, is added in the WS-TEFSM. It can be explicitly set to a certain value at the beginning of the WS-BPEL process execution, and is never reset later. In order to control the time progress, we use time invariants in the states.

All WS-BPEL activities are modeled as instantaneous activities except <wait>, <receive>, <empty> (with *duration* attribute) and <onAlarm> that are related explicitly to a time notion. These instantaneous activities are modeled, as instant transitions called *action* transitions. These transitions are equivalent to assign the time invariant $c \leq 0$ (where c is a local clock initialized to *zero*) to the source state of the transition. In that case, the time cannot progress in this source state. Contrarily, the non instantaneous activities are modeled as *delay* transitions. They take certain amount of time represented by time increment in the state and followed by their immediate execution. It is semantically equivalent to add first a clock invariant to the source state of the transition depending on time, and secondly guards on the clock variables of transition guards on WS-BPEL process variables.

For instance, the <wait> activity and the <onAlarm> element are used to represent timeouts. These constructs have two forms. In the first one (with *for* attribute) they are triggered after a duration d. We associate in this case the invariant $c \leq d$ to the source state of the transition. In the second one (with *until* attribute), the transitions are triggered if the current absolute time has the specified value (i.e. deadline dl). We associate the invariant $gc \leq dl$ to the source state of the transition.

A transition priority is used to model interruptions in real-time systems. In this model, we use priority on transitions to model the fault handlers and the termination of the WS-BPEL process and its sub-activities. Each non atomic activity can be interrupted by adding an urgent transition from each state to a particular *stop* state. All the transitions of each WS-BPEL atomic activity have a highest priority and cannot be blocked or interrupted. A *delay* transition has a lowest priority.

In order to introduce the Timed Extended Finite State Machine with Priorities (WS-TEFSM), we need first to depict the clock valuation concept.

Let V a finite set of data variables. A valuation v over V is a function $v : V \mapsto D_V^{|V|}$ that assigns to each variable $x \in V$ a value in the data variables domain $D_V^{|V|}$. The initial data variables valuation is noted v_0. $v[\overrightarrow{v} := \overrightarrow{x}]$ denotes the data valuation which updates the variables $v_1, \ldots, v_n$ such that vector $\overrightarrow{v} = (v_1, \ldots, v_n)$ and keeps the rest of variables (i.e. $V \setminus \{v_1, \ldots, v_n\}$) unchanged.

A clock valuation u over the set of clocks C is a function $u : C \mapsto \mathbb{R}_+^{|C|}$ (noted by $u \in \mathbb{R}_+^{|C|}$) that assigns to each clock $c \in C$ a value in $\mathbb{R}_+$. The initial clock valuation u_0 corresponds to the initialization to 0 of all clock variables: $\forall c \in C, u_0(c) = 0$.

We introduce in the following the formal definition of the Timed Extended Finite State Machine with Priorities which is used to model the WS-BPEL process.

Definition 1 (WS-TEFSM) A machine WS-TEFSM M is a tuple $M = (Q, \Sigma, V, C, q_0, F, T, Pri, Inv)$ where:

- $Q = \{q_0, q_1, \ldots, q_n\}$: a finite set of states;
- $\Sigma = \{a, b, c, \ldots\}$: alphabet of the actions including symbols $!m$ (output action) and $?m$ (input action);
- $V = \{v_1, v_2, \ldots, v_m\}$: finite set of data variables where vector $\overrightarrow{v} = (v_1, v_2, \ldots, v_m)$;

- $C = \{c_1, c_2, \ldots, c_n\}$: finite set of clocks where vector $\vec{c} = (c_1, c_2, \ldots, c_n)$;
- $q_0 \in Q$: initial state;
- $F \subseteq Q$: finite set of end states;
- $T \subseteq Q \times A \times 2^Q$: transition relation that:
  A: set of transition actions $\Sigma \times P(V) \wedge \phi(C) \times \mu \times 2^C$ where:
  - $P(\vec{v}) \wedge \phi(\vec{c})$: guard condition is logical formula on data variables and clocks;
  - $\mu(\vec{v})$: data variables update function;
  - 2^C: set of clocks to be reset.
- $Pri : T \times D_C^{|C|} \mapsto N_{\geq 0}$ assigns to each transition its priority that respects the clock valuation u;
- $Inv : Q \mapsto \Phi(C)$ assigns a set of time invariants (logical formulas) to the states.

The actions in Σ represent an observable actions. The label $\tau \notin \Sigma$ denotes an *internal* action that is unobservable. We note Σ_τ the set $\Sigma \cup \{\tau\}$.

In the WS-TEFSM model, the states are associated with state invariants that express simple clock conditions. The invariants of a state should be *true* when the machine is in this state. This machine may remain in a state as long as the clock valuation satisfies the invariant condition of the considered state. We can assign a set of time invariants to one state because it can be the source state of several transitions such as <if> and <pick> activities. This set associated to a state q is denoted by $Inv(q) = \{e_1, e_2, \ldots\}$. We will write $u \in Inv(q)$ to denote that the clock valuation u satisfy $e_i \mid \exists e_i \in Inv(q)$.

Each transition $t = q_i \xrightarrow{\langle cond, a, [\vec{v} := \vec{x}; R] \rangle} q_j$ is annotated with a set of guards on data variables and clocks (e.g. *cond*), actions (e.g. *a*), data variable updates (denoted $\vec{v} := \vec{x}$) and a clock set to be reset (e.g. *R*). The transition priority depends of the time and can be dynamically updated with respect to time progress. It assigns a non-negative integer value to each transition priority with respect to a clock valuation. An enabled transition can block another one if it has a higher priority.

The WS-TEFSM semantic are defined as follows to be used in the description of the timed test case generation algorithm (presented in Sect. 14.4.1.2).

14.3.1.2 Semantic of WS-TEFSM

The *delay* transition indicates that if the other transitions outgoing from the same source state have a lower priority, then the any action. In other words, the state is not modified, but the machine increments the current value of the clocks d by $u \oplus d$ (that represents a valuation where all clocks have been incremented by the real value d from their value in u). A *delay* transition may affect the priority of other transitions through the function *Pri* and does not block any transition. The priority of the *delay* transition is a constant value *zero*.

The *action* transition having the highest priority, indicates that if the condition *cond* is evaluated to true, then the machine follows the transition by executing the action a, changing the current values of the data variables by the action $[\vec{v} := \vec{x}]$ (i.e. $v' = v[\vec{v} := \vec{x}]$), resetting the subset clocks R (the clock valuation u resets each clock in the set R) and moving to the next state q'. Particularly in the case of the internal action τ, the clocks remain unchanged and consequently $u' = u$.

Let $s, s' \in S$. In the following, we denote the *delay* transition by $s \xrightarrow{d} s \oplus d$, and the *action* transition by $s \xrightarrow{a} s'$.

Definition 2 (WS-TEFSM Semantic) Let M be a WS-TEFSM $M = (Q, \Sigma, V, C, q_0, F, T, Pri, Inv)$. The WS-TEFSM semantic is defined by a labeled transition system (LTS) $Sem_M = (S, s_0, \Gamma, \Rightarrow)$:

- $S \subseteq Q \times \mathbb{R}_+^{|C|} \times D_V^{|V|}$ is the set of semantic states (q, u, v) where:
  - q is a state of a machine M;
  - u is an assignment (i.e. clock values represented by clock valuation u) that satisfies one invariant of the state q (i.e. $u \in Inv(q)$);
  - v is a data values represented by data variable valuation v.
- $s_0 = (q_0, u_0, v_0)$ is the *initial* state;
- $\Gamma = \Sigma_\tau \cup \{d \mid d \in \mathbb{R}_+\}$ is the label set where d corresponds to the elapsed time.
- $\Rightarrow \subseteq S \times \mathbb{R}_+ \times S$ is the transition relation defined by:
  - *action* transition: Let (q, u, v) and (q', u', v') be two states. Then $(q, u, v) \xrightarrow{a} (q', u', v')$ if $\exists t = q \xrightarrow{\langle cond, a, [\vec{v} := \vec{x}; R] \rangle} q' \in T$ such that
    * $u \in cond$, $u' = u[R \mapsto 0]$, $u' \in Inv(q')$, $v' = v[\vec{v} := \vec{x}]$
    * $\forall t' = q \xrightarrow{\langle cond', a', [\vec{v'} := \vec{x'}; R'] \rangle} q'' \in T$, $u \in cond' \Rightarrow (Pri(t, u) > Pri(t', u)) \vee ((Pri(t, u) = Pri(t', u)) \wedge rand(t, t') = t)$
  - *delay* transition: Then $(q, u, v) \xrightarrow{d} (q, u \oplus d, v)$ if
    * $\forall 0 \leq d' \leq d$, $u \oplus d' \in Inv(q)$;
    * $\forall t = (q \xrightarrow{\langle cond, a, [\vec{v} := \vec{x}; R] \rangle} q') \in T$, $\forall 0 \leq d' \leq d$, $u \oplus d' \in cond \Rightarrow Pri(t, u \oplus d') = 0$.

After defining a WS-TEFSM and its semantic, an overview of the transformation of WS-BPEL into WS-TEFSM and two examples (e.g. activities) are presented.

14.3.1.3 Overview of WS-BPEL Mapping into WS-TEFSM

A WS-BPEL process always starts with the `<process>` element which contains the workflow definition. It is composed of the following optional children: `<partnerLinks>`, `<partners>`, `<variables>`, `<correlationSets>`, `<faultHandlers>`, `<compensationHandlers>` and `<eventHandlers>`. The execution of sub-activities is carried out in parallel because the fault, the event and the compensation handlers can be carried out independently of the principal `<process>` activity. If this is not the case, these sub-activities are synchronized by the tuple (sending, reception).

A transformation rule is defined for each WS-BPEL construct. The recursive mapping starts by transforming all the WS-BPEL constructs into partial WS-TEFSM. The WS-BPEL process model is based on the asynchronous product of the partial WS-TEFSMs of its sub-activities. This asynchronous product represents the parallel execution of the partial WS-TEFSMs where they are synchronized by the tuple (sending/receiving).

The recursion result is a partial WS-TEFSM *PM* which can be represented as a WS-TEFSM M by renaming the *initial* state q_0 by the *input* state q_{in}, adding the *output* states of Q_{out} to the final states set F and adding the *global* clock gc to the clocks set C. The data variables set V is the union of the transformation of the `<variables>`, `<partners>` and `<partnerLinks>` elements.

$$M = (Q, \Sigma, V, C \cup \{gc\}, q_{in}, F \cup Q_{out}, T, Pri, Inv),$$
$$PM = (Q, \Sigma, V, C, q_{in}, Q_{out}, F, T, Pri, Inv). \tag{1}$$

14.3.1.4 Examples of WS-BPEL Construct Transformation

The Wait Activity   The `<wait>` activity allows to wait for a given time period (i.e. duration d or until a certain deadline dl). One of the expiration criteria must be specified exactly [32]. The `<wait>` syntax is `<wait for=d>` or `<wait until=dl>`. Let $Pri_w = \{(t_1, \_, l_p)\}$ where l_p is a low priority.

- `<wait for=d>` is modeled as a partial WS-TEFSM *PM*

$$PM = (\{q_{in}, q_{out}\}, \emptyset, \emptyset, \{c\}, q_{in}, \{q_{out}\}, \emptyset, \{t_1\}, Pri_w, Inv),$$
$$t_1 = (q_{in}, \langle c = d, \_, [\_; \{c\}]\rangle, q_{out}), \tag{2}$$
$$Inv = \{(q_{in}, c \le d), (q_{out}, true)\}.$$

- `<wait until=dl>` is modeled as a partial WS-TEFSM *PM*

$$PM = (\{q_{in}, q_{out}\}, \emptyset, \emptyset, \emptyset, q_{in}, \{q_{out}\}, \emptyset, \{t_1\}, Pri_w, Inv),$$
$$t_1 = (q_{in}, \langle gc = dl, \_, \_\rangle, q_{out}), \tag{3}$$
$$Inv = \{(q_{in}, gc \le dl), (q_{out}, true)\}.$$

The partial WS-TEFSMs of the `<wait for>` and the `<wait until>` activities are illustrated in Fig. 14.4 and Fig. 14.5. Note that in these examples, there are not actions.

The Wait for Machine with Termination Handling   Each `<wait>`, for instance, can be interrupted and terminated prematurely. To terminate this activity, we add a stop transition t_2 to a `<wait>` machine (described above) which has an urgent priority and can interrupt the transition t_1. Let h_p be a highest priority. *stopProcess* is a global variable of the process that is assigned to *true* by the `<exit>` activity. *stopScope* is a local variable of each scope that is assigned to *true* by the scope

Fig. 14.4 The partial WS-TEFSM of the `<wait for>` activity

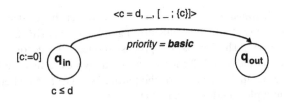

Fig. 14.5 The partial WS-TEFSM of the `<wait until>` activity

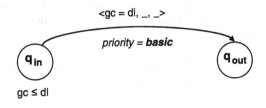

Fig. 14.6 The partial WS-TEFSM of the `<wait for>` activity with termination

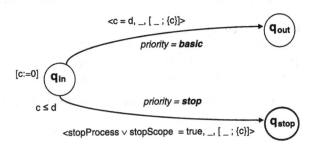

`<throw>` activity. These two boolean variables are used to handle the termination. The `<wait>` machine with termination is defined as:

$$PM = \big(\{q_{in}, q_{out}, q_{stop}\}, \emptyset, \emptyset, \{c\}, q_{in}, \{q_{out}\}, \emptyset, \{t_1, t_2\}, Pri_w, Inv\big),$$
$$t_1 = (q_{in}, \langle c = d, \_, [\_; \{c\}]\rangle, q_{out}),$$
$$t_2 = (q_{in}, \langle stopProcess \vee stopScope, \_, [\_; \{c\}]\rangle, q_{stop}),$$
$$Pri_w = \big\{(t_1, \_, l_p), (t_2, \_, h_p)\big\},$$
$$Inv = \big\{(q_{in}, c \leq d), (q_{out}, true), (q_{stop}, true)\big\}. \tag{4}$$

The partial WS-TEFSM of the `<wait for>` with termination is given in Fig. 14.6.

We can transform all the WS-BPEL constructs (elements and activities) in a similar way. While we have detailed how to model Web services, we tackle in the following the Web applications modeling.

14.3.2 Modeling of Web Applications

This methodology describes how UML diagrams developed in the analysis phase are used to automatically produce test cases. We will show how to check the graphical user interfaces but also the generated pages content.

14.3.2.1 UML Overview

The UML language is a standardized visual specification language for object modeling [34]; It is a general-purpose modeling language that includes a graphical notation used to create an abstract model of a system. Using UML, no one diagram can capture the different elements of a system in its entirety. Hence, UML 2.0 is made up of thirteen diagrams that can be used to model a system at different points of time in the software life cycle of a system. Nevertheless, in the methodology presented in this chapter only four UML diagrams, which constitute the input data, are needed to be applied for the Web application modeling and testing. The UML diagrams used in this approach are fully described in the next subsection.

14.3.2.2 Using UML to Model Web Applications

In order to derive the test cases, it is needed to grasp and describe the system functionality at least in a semi-formal way. A model-based approach of Web applications can be performed using UML techniques and UML notation. A design methodology based on a UML extension for Hypermedia [20] is used. It consists of three main steps that constitute the conceptual model, the navigation map, and the presentation model. The conceptual model is built taking into account the functional requirements captured with use cases [8]. The output of this step is not directly used as an input to the test suite but it is important in order to design the UML diagrams which actually constitute the input data.

From this conceptual model, the navigation space model is constructed, also represented as a static class model. It defines a view on the conceptual model showing which classes may be visited through navigation in the Web application. Finally, a dynamic presentation model is represented by UML sequence diagrams describing the collaborations and behaviors of the navigational objects and access primitives. In order to specify our model, the following diagrams are involved:

- Class Diagram to introduce the main classes of the system;
- Activity Diagram for each actor to display dependencies among the use cases;
- Navigation Map to provide information about the dynamic content of the Web pages;
- Sequence Diagram for each use case describing the main and the alternative scenarios of the use case to represent the dynamic presentation model.

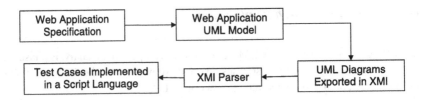

Fig. 14.7 Representation of the methodology

These diagrams are exported in an XMI format (XML Metadata Interchange format) [35] , i.e. an OMG standard for exchanging metadata information via XML. This activity is supported by all the modern CASE tools like ArgoUML [9] and Rational Rose [19]. Afterwards the XMI is parsed and it is produced a program which connects to the Web server and makes requests according to the given scenario in the Sequence Diagram. Finally, the response Web page is examined to verify if it conforms to the specification. Figure 14.7 presents briefly the different steps of our study.

14.3.2.3 From Conceptual Model to Navigation Map

In order to specify a Web application, first it is needed to build a conceptual model of the application domain taking into account the functional requirements captured with use cases. Techniques such as finding classes and associations, and defining inheritance structures are performed.

The Navigation Map of a Web application introduced in [3] is used because it provides information about the dynamic content of each Web page which is part of the system as well as the links between the different Web pages. This information is essential during the parsing of the HTML pages. Navigation Map is a Class diagram where each Web page is a class and a link between two pages is an association between the two respective classes. This extension of UML for Web applications introduces a number of tagged values, constraints and stereotypes (such as indexes, guided tours, queries and menus).

14.3.2.4 Modeling Use Case Dependencies

The use cases of a system are not independent. Apart from *include* and *extend* relationships, there are also sequential dependencies. In order to execute one use case, another should have taken place before. For instance, in any Web application such as an e-mail Web interface or e-learning platform, the user should login before being able to do anything else. Since testing automation procedure is also concerned, it is mandatory to describe somehow these dependencies. This is achieved by introducing an activity diagram where the vertices represent use cases and edges are sequential dependencies between the use cases.

An edge in such a diagram denotes that the use case in the tail has to be executed before the use case in the head. *Fork* and *join* are used when some use cases should be executed independently in order another one to take place. For instance, in an e-learning platform the addition of the subject and the addition of the term are two independent use cases which should be synchronized to allow the testing of the creation of a class.

14.3.2.5 Sequence Diagram

In UML, a Sequence diagram realizes the interaction of objects via the interchange of messages in time. Similarly, as in activity diagrams the objects are instances of a class described in the Class diagram. Usually the sequence diagrams describe a single scenario. The messages are enumerated in a way that allows to illustrate a number of alternative scenarios in the same diagram. According to this convention, capital letters denote alternatives (error messages). By adopting this tactic it is possible to derive easily the different Message Sequences [2] related to the same use case.

Now that the modeling of Web-based systems has been presented, that is: a proposed WS-TEFSM model for a Web services composition described in WS-BPEL, an overview of the WS-BPEL transformation into WS-TEFSM illustrated by an example and a methodology to model Web applications by using UML, we may present in the following techniques to test these Web-based systems from the formal models.

14.4 Web-Based System Testing

As previously mentioned, the main goal of Web-based systems modeling is to ease their testing. Therefore, this section presents testing techniques devoted to Web services and Web applications. The first method generates timed test cases and uses a timed-traces equivalence as conformance relation between a Web service implementation and its formal specification. The second method illustrates how to generate a test case for a Web application from the obtained UML diagrams.

14.4.1 Web Services Testing

To define a Web services composition testing methodology, a deterministic WS-TEFSM that models a composite Web service described in WS-BPEL and its semantic (see Sect. 14.3.1) are considered. First, the concept of timed sequences, timed traces, timed test cases and the conformance relation [14, 22] (between the specification and the implementation) to be used in this testing methodology are defined. Secondly, the timed test cases generation algorithm is detailed. Finally, an example of Web service modeling and testing is detailed.

14.4.1.1 Conformance Relation and Timed Test Cases

Let $M = (Q, \Sigma, V, C, q_0, F, T, Pri, Inv)$ be a WS-TEFSM and $[M] = (S, s_0, \Gamma, \Rightarrow)$ be the LTS describing the M semantic. Let $s, s_0, s_1, \ldots, s_n \in S$. Let $Seq(\Sigma) = (\Sigma \cup \mathbb{R})^*$ be the set of all finite timed sequences over Σ. A timed sequence $\sigma \in Seq(\Sigma)$ is composed of actions a and non-negative real d where: $s \xrightarrow{a} s'$ and $s \xrightarrow{d} s \oplus d$. $\sigma_\varepsilon \in Seq(M)$ is the <empty> sequence.

Let $\Sigma' \subseteq \Sigma$ and $\sigma \in Seq(\Sigma)$ a timed sequence. $\pi_{\Sigma'}(\sigma)$ denotes the projection of σ to Σ' obtained by deleting in σ all actions not present in Σ'. $Time(\sigma)$ denotes the sum of all delays in a sequence σ.

Let $\sigma = \sigma_1.\sigma_2 \ldots \sigma_n$ are a timed sequence, $s \xrightarrow{\sigma}$ is used to denote that there exists s_n and $s \xrightarrow{\sigma_1} s_1 \xrightarrow{\sigma_2} s_2 \cdots \xrightarrow{\sigma_n} s_n$. The observable timed traces of a WS-TEFSM M is defined by:

$$Tr(M) = \left\{ \pi_\Sigma(\sigma) \mid \sigma \in Seq(\Sigma_\tau) \wedge s_0 \xrightarrow{\sigma} \right\}. \tag{5}$$

Let M_S and M_I two WS-TEFSMs which model respectively the specification of a composite Web service (a WS-BPEL description) and its implementation (a WS-BPEL process instance). *Timed-traces equivalence* noted $\cong_{Tr}$ is considered as a *conformance* relation where the time delays is considered to be observable actions. First, the *timed-traces inclusion* relation noted $\preceq_{Tr}$ is defined. $M_I \preceq_{Tr} M_S$ requires each observable sequence of M_S to be an observable sequence of M_I:

$$(M_I \preceq_{Tr} M_S) \Leftrightarrow (Tr(M_S) \subseteq Tr(M_I)). \tag{6}$$

The $\preceq_{Tr}$ conformance relation (timed-trace inclusion) can be extended to $\cong_{Tr}$. This latter requires that each observable sequence of M_I is also an observable sequence of M_S. M_S *conforms* M_I, denoted $M_S \cong_{Tr} M_I$ if $Tr(M_S) = Tr(M_I)$:

$$(M_I \cong_{Tr} M_S) \Leftrightarrow (Tr(M_S) \preceq_{Tr} Tr(M_I) \wedge Tr(M_I) \preceq_{Tr} Tr(M_S)). \tag{7}$$

A timed test case is a timed trace that validates some timed requirements (e.g. timed test purposes) and generates a *pass* or *fail* verdict: the *pass* verdict if all test purposes are satisfied, the *fail* verdict else if.

Based on the WS-TEFSM semantic, a set of timed test purposes and the Hit-or-Jump exploration strategy [6]—the timed test case generation algorithm—is detailed in the following.

14.4.1.2 Timed Test Case Generation Algorithm

This algorithm generates timed test cases from a composite Web service specification given in WS-TEFSM and timed test purposes. For test case generation, the Hit-or-Jump strategy (a generalization of the exhaustive search technique and random walks) is adapted to WS-TEFSM model. The generated timed test cases are used to check the conformance of a composite Web service implementation to its specification. The test cases are a sequence of observable actions which have to be executed according to some time constraints.

Starting from the initial state of the WS-TEFSM and considering a search *depth limit* and a set of timed test purposes to be satisfied (represented by events or timed constraints), a partial search is conducted from the current state s_i of the reachability graph until:

A Hit step Reached a state s_j (a Hit state) where one or more test purposes are satisfied. Then the sequence from s_i to s_j is concatenated to the test sequence, the test purposes set is updated and the Hit step is repeated from s_j.

A Jump step Reached a search *depth limit* without satisfying any test purpose. Then one leaf node (i.e. a state s_j) of the partial search tree is selected, the sequence from s_i to s_j is concatenated to the test sequence, the state s_j is moved (a Jump state) and the Hit step is repeated from s_j.

The algorithm terminates when all the test purposes are satisfied or when there are no more transitions to explore. The main interest of this algorithm is that the construction of the complete WS-TEFSM reachability graph is not required. The test case generation algorithm is illustrated in Fig. 14.8.

14.4.1.3 Example of Web Service Modeling and Testing

In this section, The PICK Web service is applied to illustrate the WS-TEFSM resulting of the transformation of a WS-BPEL description, and the test cases generating from this WS-TEFSM by using the test generation algorithm detailed in the previous section.

The PICK process receives a loan application document from the user (e.g. the LOAN service). It invokes the asynchronous loan service (i.e. the ASYNCBPELSERVICE service) by sending this document and uses a BPEL `<pick>` activity to receive an asynchronous response from the partner service or to exit after a timeout (e.g. 30 seconds). This partner service sets the credit rating according the loan amount and returns the loan application document to the PICK service. If the loan amount is greater than 10000, it takes about 30 seconds for the partner service to process it and therefore a timeout will be raised. Finally, the PICK service sends the loan application document to its user.

The PICK Web service is illustrated in Fig. 14.9 (in BPMN Notation [33]). Its WS-BPEL description and the resulting WS-TEFSM (according to the methodology described in Sect. 14.3.1) are given in Appendix (respectively Figs. 14.18 and 14.19).

We want to test the two `<pick>` activity branches (see Fig. 14.9). We define, for instance, two test scenarios as following:

- The system is in an initial state $s_0 = (q_0, u_0, v_0)$;
- The Set of timed test purposes to be satisfied is $TP = \{tp_1, tp_2, \ldots, tp_m\}$.
- The timed test sequence seq is empty (i.e. $seq = \sigma_\varepsilon$).

The algorithm terminates when all the timed test purposes are satisfied, i.e. $TP = \emptyset$;

Repeat

① **Hit**: From the current system state s_i, conduct a search by exploring all possible transitions: *action* transition $s_i \overset{a}{\Rightarrow} s_{i+1}$ or *delay* transition $s_i \overset{d}{\Rightarrow} s_i \oplus d$ until ⓐ or ⓑ :

ⓐ Reach a state s_j such that $s_i \overset{\sigma}{\Rightarrow} s_j$ and
forall k such that $s_j \models tp_k : TP = TP \setminus \{tp_k\}$ — a Hit. **Then:**
  (i) Concatenate the sequence σ from s_i to s_j to the test sequence: $seq = seq.\sigma$;
  (ii) Move to ①.

ⓑ Reach a search *depth limit*. **Then** move to ②.

Until ($TP = \emptyset \vee$ "no transition to explore").

IF $TP = \emptyset$ **Then return** seq **else** "no test sequence!".

② **Jump**:

  (i) A partial searched tree has been constructed, rooted at s_i;
  (ii) Examine all the tree leaf nodes, and select one (s_j such that $s_i \overset{\sigma}{\Rightarrow} s_j$) uniformly and randomly;
  (iii) Concatenate the sequence σ from s_i to s_j to the test sequence: $seq = seq.\sigma$;
  (iv) Arrive at s_j — a Jump.
  (v) Move to ①.

Fig. 14.8 Timed test case generation algorithm

Scenario 1 Receive a ASYNCBPELSERVICE response after 10 seconds and reply this response to the user.
Scenario 2 Exit the BPEL process after waiting a ASYNCBPELSERVICE response 30 seconds.

For the two scenarios, we present below the test purposes used in the timed test case generation algorithm (defined in Sect. 14.4.1.2).

Test purposes for scenario 1 The PICK service receives the ASYNCBPELSER-VICE response (i.e. *response* variable) after 10 seconds. Finally, it sends this loan application document (i.e. *output* variable) to the user.[2] The test purposes for sce-

---

[2] A Web service that is involved in the WS-BPEL process is always modeled as a `<porType>` (i.e. abstract group of operations (noted op) supported by a service). These operations are executed via a `<partnerlink>` (noted by pl) that specifies the communication channel. In the following, the *input* message $pl\ ?op(v)$ denotes the receiving of the message $op(v)$ (constructed from the

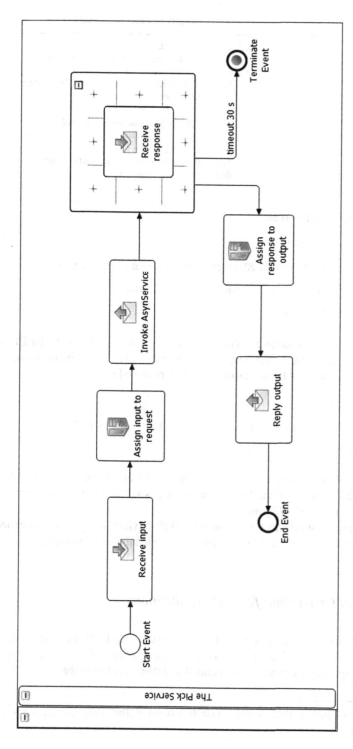

Fig. 14.9 The BPMN notation of the PICK Web service

Fig. 14.10 The timed test
cases for the two scenarios

Timed Test case for Scenario 1

```
1. client ?initiate(input)
2. AsyncBPELService !initiate(request)
3. delay = 10 seconds
4. AsyncBPELService ?onResult(response)
5. client !onResult(output)
```

Timed Test case for Scenario 2

```
1. client ?initiate(input)
2. AsyncBPELService !initiate(request)
3. delays = 30 seconds
```

nario 1 can be formulated as:

$$TP_1 = \{tp_1, tp_2, tp_3\},$$

$$tp_1 = \text{``}action: \texttt{AsyncBPELService ?onResult(response)}\text{''},$$

$$tp_2 = \text{``}action: \texttt{client !onResult(output)}\text{''},$$

$$tp_3 = \text{``}clock: \texttt{c4 = 10}\text{''}. \tag{8}$$

Test purposes for Scenario 2 The PICK service invokes the ASYNCBPELSER-
VICE service and waits its response for 30 seconds. After, it terminates its activity.
The timed test purposes for scenario 2 can be formulated as:

$$TP_2 = \{tp_1, tp_2\},$$

$$tp_1 = \text{``}action: \texttt{AsyncBPELService !initiate(request)}\text{''}, \tag{9}$$

$$tp_2 = \text{``}clock: \texttt{c4 = 30}\text{''}.$$

The two following timed test cases (presented in Fig. 14.10) are generated from
the WS-TEFSM model of the PICK Web service (see Fig. 14.19 in Appendix) and
the timed test purposes (TP_1 and TP_2).

After dealing with the test generation for Web services, an approach to generate
test cases from a parsed UML model for Web applications is presented.

14.4.2 Test Generation for Web Applications

To automate test generation, the goal is first to parse the UML diagrams obtained
from the previous steps. Therefore, based on these diagrams, the necessary requests
to the Web application server are generated and then checked if the server's replies

---

operation *op* and the WS-BPEL variable *v*) via the channel *pl*. The *output* message is denoted by
pl !*op*(*v*).

are as expected by the previous models. The requests are HTTP requests that simulate a user navigating the site through a Web browser. The possible actions are to fill and submit a form, to click on a link or to navigate to a given URL. Similarly the server's replies are HTTP Responses that can either contain an HTML page, a redirection to another URL or an error message. Assuming the first case, the HTML page of the response has to be parsed to see if its contents are the expected ones. Based on these requirements, it is needed to choose the components that were required to build the test suite.

Since we are dealing with UML, it would be more efficient to choose an object-oriented language as a test scripting language, which also serves to provide easy string handling and a high level of abstraction for network communications. For the reasons mentioned below, the chosen programming language as the most suitable is the Python scripting language. Python is a modern object-oriented language which combines remarkable power with very clear syntax. Its built-in modules provide numerous functions that facilitate string handling and networking.

14.4.2.1 Parsing and Executing the UML

To parse the UML diagrams it is possible either to use the API of a UML tool or to export the diagrams in an XMI format that would allow parsing them using an XML parser. Exporting to XMI was the preferred solution since it does not tie the methodology to a specific tool. Although having the possibility to use any XML parser to parse the XMI, due to the high complexity of the standard it was decided to use a specialized XMI parser.

The used one was the parser included in the System Modeling Workbench (SMW) tool [40]. It is free, open source and also written in Python, making it easier to integrate with the code.

14.4.2.2 Parsing the HTML Pages

Since HTML mixes presentation and content data, the HTML output of the Web application does not allow extracting the wanted information without first looking the implementation details. To avoid this, it is needed to change the page templates of the Web application in order to provide the data in a more formal way. This is achieved by adding id attributes to the tags we want to query. For example, to the td tag that contains the user's name in the user pages will have an attribute id=username. By this way it can query any page independently of the implementation of the page layout.

The approaches presented in this section are applied to a real case study illustrated in the following section.

14.5 Case Study: DotLRN

To exercise the testing generation methods previously presented, we consider
a real case study which is an open source e-learning platform (dotLRN) [11].
An open source platform is more demanding of testing aspects to maintain a correct e-learning Web application. Indeed, all the open source software are constantly
changing with addition of new features. Therefore new bugs may appear disabling
some functionalities. Then we need to re-execute all the previous tests that were
generated at the conformance testing phase in order to guarantee the stability of the
system. This step of testing is known as non-regression testing. We present the experiments that have been conducted on the e-learning platform. This case study is
representative enough to experience the approach. We have made the choice to deal
with only one real case study for both types of Web-based systems. This last point
is motivated by the growing convergence of these two types of systems. Indeed, we
can notice that the industrial market is more and more interested by editing its development as Web services to promote the use of its development. It can also allow
to use the Web application in the framework of new development by composition of
this application transformed into a web service with other available web services.
This aspect particularly holds for open source software that need to be used to get
feedback to improve the software.

We present in the following the model-based approach with the UML modeling
of dotLRN, the test objectives and how we execute the tests directly on the platform.
Afterwards, we also explain how hand tests can be produced for this particular application with TCL script when no formal model is provided. Finally, based on the
work described in [27] we explain how we can transform a Web application in a Web
service. This latter aspect is essential for certain kind of Web applications whose the
model is very tough to obtain (even using UML). Indeed, by migrating them to Web
services, the use of testing techniques based on WS-BPEL can be applied.

14.5.1 The DotLRN Framework

DotLRN is a learning management Web application [11]. It is an open source platform for supporting e-learning and digital communities. The tool was originally
developed at the Massachusetts Institute of Technology (MIT) as a virtual learning environment and it evolved into a comprehensive platform including not only
e-learning support but also generic Web resources.

The platform is based on the OpenACS Web application framework [36],
a toolkit for building scalable, community-oriented Web applications. The toolkit
structure is highly modular and dotLRN is a set of modules that provide the additional features to deploy an e-learning environment. The OpenACS (and therefore
dotLRN) is tightly integrated with a relational database, both PostgreSQL and Ora-

cle are currently supported. The Web server that handles requests at the basic level is AOLServer, the America Online's open source Web server. One of its main features is the integration in its core of a multi-threaded TCL interpreter which provides an effective solution for industrial strength type of services such as those present in large higher educational institutions [5].

As in most open source projects, there is a community around dotLRN/OpenACS involving nearly 11,000 registered users. The community portal is itself based on this platform and coordinates the interaction between developers, users, technical personnel employed by higher education institutions and anybody interested on exchanging ideas, solutions and information about the tool.

Several features make dotLRN an effective and powerful e-learning platform. Its modular structure allows for very fast customization and prototyping of new applications. The user space is organized through a customizable set of portlets, each of them offering access to one of the various services available. The underlying OpenACS toolkit provides an ever increasing set of Web functionality most of them suitable to be adopted by the e-learning platform.

The fact that OpenACS is a community-oriented toolkit has influenced and shaped dotLRN into what it could be called a "communication-oriented LMS" (Learning Management System). Most of the current LMS focused at the beginning of their existence on providing content management for teaching staff and learners. DotLRN, on the other hand, was conceived as a platform to facilitate communication among all the different actors in a learning experience.

14.5.2 Test Generation from the UML Model

In Sect. 14.3.2 are described the UML diagrams that are needed to model a Web Application, now it will be illustrated how these UML diagrams are used to model the dotLRN framework and how the test cases can be generated taking into account Sect. 14.4.2.

14.5.2.1 Modeling Use Case Dependencies

In the Class diagram the use case parameters are also included. The reason is that sometimes it is easier to realize the dependencies between the parameters of the use cases. For instance, in Fig. 14.11, in order to add a new class, the administrator should provide information about the term (Term.name) and the subject of the class (Subject.name). As a consequence, there is a dependency between the Add class, the Add Term and the Add Subject use cases.

Finally, in the diagram the use cases are organized in groups according to the objects they are associated with. These objects are instances of the classes in the Class diagram. Figure 14.11 shows the respective activity diagram for the Administrator. According to this latter, Add department should precede Add subject.

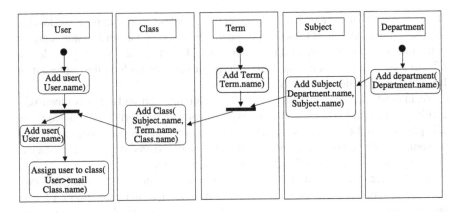

Fig. 14.11 The class diagram

Also, Add term and Add subject should occur before Add class, and Add user and Add class should take place before the execution of Assign user to class. Finally, Manage User depends on Add User since first the user should be added to the system and then the administrator can edit his profile and modify his permissions.

In the testing phase, before simulating the scenarios in the Sequence diagrams, these activity diagrams should be scanned to obtain the sequence in which the use cases will be tested.

14.5.2.2 Sequences Diagrams

The Sequence diagrams are also parameterized since input parameters can influence the execution and constitute separate choices [2]. Such a parameter can be the email of a user. Whether this email belongs to a registered user (exists in the database) or belongs to a new user (does not exist in the database) determines what is going to occur. In the former case the dotLRN page is displayed otherwise a warning appears in the Log In page. During the testing procedure, if there are such branches and parameters then the produced program has to fork to test all the different possibilities. Figure 14.12 shows the respective sequence diagram for the "Login" use case.

Table 14.1 summarizes the actions used in the Sequence diagram organized as HTTP requests of the user and possible HTTP responses returned to the user by the server, since the success or the failure of the tests depends upon these requests and the respective responses. The system under test being a Web application, there are three possibilities for the user: either (1) navigates to a URL or (2) requests a Web page through another one (clicks on a link to the wanted page) or (3) submits information by filling an HTML form. System answers either directly by returning the requested page (display) or by giving an error message.

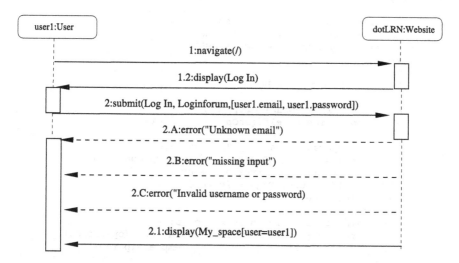

Fig. 14.12 HTTP sequences

Table 14.1 Actions of the sequence diagram

HTTP request	HTTP response
– navigate(url:String): User makes an HTTP request for an URL.	**– display(page:Webpage):** Web server returns the requested Web.
– link(target:String): User clicks in a HTTP link.	**– display(page:Webpage):** Web server returns the target Web page.
– Sublit(page:WebPage, form:Form,data:list): User submits an HTTP form.	**– display(page:Webpage):** In case of legitimate input the Web server responses with a new Web page.
	– error(msg:String): In case of wrong input the Web server responses with the previous page displaying a warning message.

14.5.2.3 dotLRN HTML Pages Parsing and Tests Execution

Figure 14.13 presents the skeleton of a possible result of the manner to parse the HTML and UML and then execute the UML. In the code we have left some code (mainly some functions) in order to reduce the size and increase clarity.

Function `execute` (line 24) is the main function of the class that reads the XMI code from the file defined in the variable `source` that is given as a parameter. It then isolates the sequence diagram (for this example we assume that only one exists) and then validates one by one all its messages (links).

All the getX functions (like `getLinks`) consist of navigating through the structure generated by SMW to get a specific data. They are assumed to be defined inside the class. The validation of each link depends on the operation.

```
1:  from urllib import urlopen
2:  from smw.io umport XMIStreamer
3:  from smw.metamodel import UML14
4:
5:  class TestSuite:
6:    returned page = None
7:
8:   def validateLink(self,link)
9:     operation = self.getOperation(link)
10:
11:    if operation.name == "navigate":
12:      url = self.getOperationParameters(operation)
13:      fd = urlopen(serverbase + url)
14:      self.returnedPage = fd.read()
15:      fd.close
16:
17:    elseif operation.nale == "display":
18:      params = self.getOperationParameters(operation)
19:      pageTemplate = generatePageTemplate(params)
20:
21:    parser = dotHTMLParser(pageTemplate)
22:    parser.feed(returnedPage)
23:
24:   def execute(self,source):
25:     xmi = XMIStreamer(UML14)
26:     fd = open(source,"r")
27:     model = xmi.loadFromStream(fd)
28:     fd.close()
29:
30:     sequenceDiagram = self.SequenceDiagram(model)
31:     for link in self.getLinks(sequenceDiagram)
32:       self.validateLink(link)
```

Fig. 14.13 Parsing and execution of UML

If the operation is navigate (lines 11–15) then we have to extract the destination URL from the parameters and then get the requested page. We assume that destination is a relative URL, so we use the serverbase variable (line 13) to make it absolute. The page is then kept in the returnedPage variable to be used by the following commands. In the case of a display operation (lines 17–22), we create a template of the page based on the operation parameters and then use the HTML parser to compare the returnedPage with the template. The skeleton of the parser is presented in Fig. 14.14.

The dotHTMLParser class inherits the HTMLParser class and overrides the handle_starttag function to search for elements that have an *id* attribute. Every such element will be validated according to the pageTemplate that was given during the instantiation. Similarly to the two example operations we can write the code to handle the rest of the supported operations.

Fig. 14.14 Parsing the
HTML

```
1:   from HTMLParser import HTMLParser
2:
3:   class dotHTMLParser(HTMLParser)
4:     pageTemplate = None
5:
6:     def init(self,pageTemplate):
7:       self.pageTemplate = pageTemplate
8:
9:     def handle_starttag(self,tag,attrs):
10:      for att in attrs
11:        if "id" in attr:
12:          validateElement(tag,attr)
```

14.5.3 Non-regression Testing for Web Applications

Besides and as this is above mentioned, the non-regression testing aims to verify if after the insertion of new source code into the application, all the functionalities still run correctly. Hence the first task for testing a Web application is to test if the behavior of the platform is conform to the blue-prints used to build it (i.e. its specification). Because of the lack of formal specification, the documentation of dotLRN and our expertise in OpenACS/dotLRN was used to build an informal specification (i.e. the list of requirements and standards that dotLRN must meet). By using this specification it is possible to interact with the platform and observe if it meets the standards or not. Now, to achieve the stability of the platform during its continuous development by applying a simple testing strategy, i.e. re-test all, requires an unacceptable amount of time and resources. It is needed then to automate the process to re-test the platform to improve the testing efficiency.

14.5.4 Alternative Method for the Test Generation of Web Applications

In order to test a Web application that does not have a formal specification, test cases may be manually developed. In this section the methodology followed to develop these test cases for dotLRN using the Tclwebtest recorder tool is illustrated. It will also introduce the acs-automated-testing, an OpenACS [36] package for the management of test cases execution and the verdict storage of each test case. Although the phase of the conformance testing was a hand made process, by using the TwtR plug in it is possible to obtain a record or static trace of the interaction of the user with the Web application, this static trace is the base for the development of the non-regression test cases. The process of obtaining a static trace is illustrated in Fig. 14.15.

The TwtR [41] is a recent tool based in the interaction recording as Selenium, by using this tool it is possible to obtain the trace written in a TCL script language, more specifically in Tclwebtest code. TwtR will produce a static trace that does not contain all the interactions between the user and the Web application, but only the

Fig. 14.15 Generation of the static traces used as a base for further non-regression testing

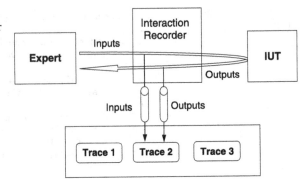

stimulations of the user to the Web application. This static trace is the basis for the part of the functional testing process presented in this article.

To build the tests for the dotLRN features, the information is first extracted from the OpenACS documentation and the dotLRN platform usability. Then the informal specification is built. After this, we interact with dotLRN to test its conformance while recording the static trace using TwtR.

If the result of this conformance test execution verdict is positive, the static trace can be re-used to serve as a basis to build the non-regression test case. This static trace must be modified by inserting variables instead of hard coded values (e.g. the id's and the URL's). Each test case will be finally described in Tclwebtest and composed by a set of concatenated scripts.

The generation of each test case using Tclwebtest is processed by following these steps:

1. Create the script of the test preamble, i.e. a sequence of operations that will lead the system to a state where the test case can be executed. For instance to test the edition of the user's name, first it is needed to corroborate the user existence and that it has already a name assigned, otherwise it is needed to create these elements;
2. Develop the script that will interact with the feature to be tested;
3. Develop the scripts that will analyze the reaction of the Web application to the interaction with the test case. This script will also assign the verdict (pass or fail); basically it will observe if the platform did what it was supposed to.

14.5.4.1 Example: The Addition of a Question and Answer from the faq Package of dotLRN

The trace produced during the addition of a Question and Answer (Q&A) of the FAQ is illustrated in Fig. 14.16. In this trace it can be observed that the elements such as the FAQ name and the Q&A is hard coded. In the first line it can be viewed that the user has followed a link named "Test faq" which is the name of the FAQ to be tested. After this in the third line the user followed the link to come to the page

```
1: ::tclwebtest::link follow Test faq ;#
                ~u {http://domain/faq/ad/one-faq?faq\_id=12}}
2: ::tclwebtest::assert text FAQ
3: ::tclwebtest::link follow Create New Q&A ;#
                ~u {http://domain/faq/ad/q-a-add?faq\_id=12}}
4: ::tclwebtest::form find ~n {new\_quest\_answ}}
5: ::tclwebtest::field fill What is your name? ;#
                    ~n {question} ;\# type of field = text}
6: ::tclwebtest::field fill Harry ;#
                    ~n {answer} ;\# type of field = password}
7: ::tclwebtest::form submit
```

Fig. 14.16 Static trace of the interactions of the user with dotLRN when creating a new Q&A

Fig. 14.17 Chunk of the test case that was extracted from the TwtR trace illustrated in Fig. 14.16

```
1: tclwebtest::link follow $faq_name
2: tclwebtest::link follow "Create New Q&A"
3: tclwebtest::form find ~n "new_quest_answ"
4: tclwebtest::field find ~n "question"
5: tclwebtest::field fill "$question"
6: tclwebtest::field find ~n "answer"
7: tclwebtest::field fill "$answer"
8: tclwebtest::form submit
9: aa_log "Faq Question Form submitted"
```

to create a new Q&A. Then from the lines four to seven the form was filled with the question "What is your name?" and the answer "Harry".

In replacing by variables all the texts to be inserted in the HTML forms and text of the links to be followed, the static trace is transformed into a dynamic script that will be the part of the test case for testing the addition of a Q&A. It will also be re-used and served as the preamble of other test cases, for example to the test "Edit a Q&A". Remember that before editing an item, it is mandatory that this item exists.

It is important to notice that the chunk of code of Fig. 14.17 will be just the part of the non-regression test case that will interact with the part of dotLRN that allows to add a new Q&A. The entire test case must include the preamble (log in of the user, creation of the FAQ, assign a value to the variables to be used, etc.) and the part of the test case that will analyze if the Q&A was correctly created and assign the verdict.

Besides, when a developer adds a new functionality to a system (in this case a Web application), most of the times he manually tests this new functionality to be sure that it works, to then release the new version of the system. However, not only the new functionality should be tested, but all the system functionalities to be sure that the new inserted implementation does not disturb the behavior of the rest of the system.

The OpenAcs framework has among its packages the acs-automated-testing, this package allows to execute the test cases and store the value of the verdict. In this way, it is possible to test dotLRN feature by feature and to store the verdict. The non-regression testing consists in executing the package A version x and then to test the package A version $x + 1$. As the verdicts of both tests are stored, it is possible to detect when a functionality that was working fine in the version x does not work anymore in the new version $(x + 1)$. By doing this it is possible to maintain the stability of all the features of the version x of the package A.

Next to the illustration of the methodologies to generate test suites for Web services and Web applications, we introduce in the following part of the chapter a method that allows to describe dotLRN in the Service Oriented Architecture (SOA). The goal of this method is to migrate from Web application into Web service. The main goal is of course to apply the methodology presented to testing Web services to dotLRN, and to generalize it to any other Web application.

14.5.5 Migrating Web Applications Functionalities into Web Services

Service Oriented Architecture (SOA) [28] is a paradigm for organizing and utilizing distributed capabilities that may be under the control of different ownership domains. It permits to encapsulate application logic in services with an uniformly defined interface and making these publicly available via discovery mechanisms. Software applications (offered by different providers) can be interconnected using the common SOA infrastructure for obtaining new services and applications. Some systematic approaches for exporting existing software applications towards the new service oriented architectures are proposed in the literature.

In [27], an approach based on wrapping techniques is proposed to migrate functionalities of existing Web applications into Web services. The main goal is to apply modeling and testing techniques used for Web services to Web application functionalities whose the formalization is often difficult to obtain. For instance, the Web application User Interface which is tough to model (even using UML) could be migrated towards a formal Web service and then be tested as mentioned in Sect. 14.4.1.

This migrating approach uses black-box reverse engineering techniques for modeling the Web application User Interface (i.e. a model of the interactions between a user and the Web application) for each functionality. A wrapper interacting with the Web application is used to transform the User Interface into Web service request/response interface (e.g. WSDL description [7]). This wrapper is constituted by the following four components:

i. Automaton which provides a model of the interactions associated with a given functionality. This model is a set of interaction states, actions and a set of transitions between these states;
ii. Web Application Interaction Executor which executes the interactions of the Automaton;
iii. Automaton Interpreter that coordinates the Web application execution (i.e. the execution of the actions associated to each state of the Automaton);
iv. Web Service Interface Manager that manages external Web service requests and responses.

This approach and a proposed migration platform are used to assist the migration of the dotLRN platform. Functionalities of each dotLRN module (e.g. forums, FAQs, calendar, file storage, etc.) can be migrated into a simple or a composite Web service. A selected dotLRN functionality can be captured by an use case. This latter can be decomposed in more elementary use cases which can be wrapped into single Web service. Therefore, the use case can be represented as a WS-BPEL process having as partners single services.

The process of this migration includes the following four steps:

1. Selection of the dotLRN functionality to be turned into a Web service;
2. Reverse engineering of the dotLRN User Interface: identification of execution scenarios and characterization of their states;
3. Design of the interaction model: evaluation of the modeling solutions and specification of the model in WSDL(for single automata) and eventually in WS-BPEL (for composite automata);
4. Wrapper validation and deploy: testing the wrapped Web service and publishing its WSDL description in an application server. The Web services composition testing approach is a used in this step to discover the execution failures of the wrapper Web service (e.g. unexpected output responses), unidentified Web pages, etc.

14.6 Conclusion

We have presented in this chapter two approaches to test a Web-based system. We have dealt with Web services composition and Web applications. We have proposed a stepwise methodology that consists first to describe formally the system that responds to the requirement information; then from the model we have developed methods to generate the tests and finally we have executed the tests on a real implementation, an e-learning platform.

The modeling step has been performed with two dedicated languages, i.e. WS-BPEL for the Web services composition and UML for Web applications. We have defined rules of mapping from WS-BPEL towards a formal specification, i.e. the Timed Extended Finite State Machines for Web Services (WS-TEFSM). The objective of this mapping is twofold: to give a semantic to the WS-BPEL composition and to dispose of a model from which the tests have been generated. For the Web applications, we have made the choice of UML as modeling language. This latter is well-suited to cope with object oriented applications and to model the test cases by means of sequence diagrams and also to represent the dynamic navigation between pages of the Web application.

Together with the formal models of the web systems, we have presented methods for conformance and non-regression test generation. The conformance is established by a conformance relation between an implementation and a specification. Two techniques have been developed for tests generation purpose, one to handle WS-BPEL specification and one for the UML model.

Finally, we have exercised the proposed methodology on a real case study, an open source e-learning platform dotLRN. We have carried on conformance and non-regression tests with the formal approach and also with a hand crafted methods based on TCL scripts. We have presented how to provide a Web service from a Web application. The obtained Web services can be composed with other available Web services and the WS-BPEL testing methods can be thus applied.

Appendix

```
<process>
  <sequence>
    <receive name="receiveInput" partnerLink="client"
         portType="tns:Pick" operation="initiate" />
                     variable="input" createInstance="yes"/>
    <assign>
     <copy>
       <from variable="input" part="payload"/>
       <to variable="request" part="payload"/>
     </copy>
    </assign>
    <invoke name="invokeAsyncService"
         partnerLink="AsyncBPELService"
         portType="services:AsyncBPELService"
              operation="initiate" inputVariable="request"/>
    <pick name="receiveResult">
     <onMessage partnerLink="AsyncBPELService"
          portType="services:AsyncBPELServiceCallback"
               operation="onResult" variable="response">
       <assign>
        <copy>
          <from variable="response" part="payload"/>
          <to variable="output" part="payload"/>
        </copy>
       </assign>
     </onMessage>
     <onAlarm for="'PT30S'">
       <terminate/>
     </onAlarm>
    </pick>
    <invoke name="replyOutput" partnerLink="client"
         portType="tns:PickCallback" operation="onResult" />
                                  inputVariable="output"/>
  </sequence>
 </process>
```

Fig. 14.18 The WS-BPEL description of the PICK Web service

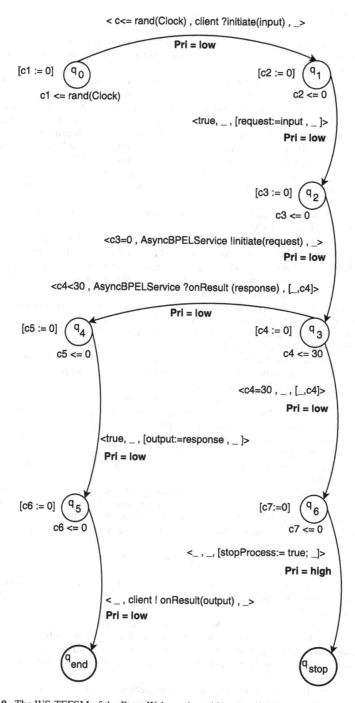

Fig. 14.19 The WS-TEFSM of the PICK Web service without termination handling

References

1. Alalfi, M.H., Cordy, J.R., Dean, T.R.: A survey of analysis models and methods in website verification and testing. In: Proc. Seventh International Conference on Web Engineering ICWE 2007, pp. 306–311 (2007)
2. Basanieri, F., Bertolino, A., Marchetti, E.: The cow_suite approach to planning and deriving test suites in UML projects. In: Jézéquel, J.M., Hussmann, H., Cook, S. (eds.) UML 2002— The Unified Modeling Language. Model Engineering, Languages, Concepts, and Tools, Proceedings of 5th International Conference, Dresden, Germany, September/October 2002. Lecture Notes in Computer Science, vol. 2460, pp. 383–397. Springer, Berlin (2002)
3. Bayse, E., Cavalli, A., Núñez, M., Zaidi, F.: A passive testing approach based on invariants: application to the WAP. Computer Networks and ISDN Systems **48**(2), 247–266 (2005)
4. Cambronero, M.E., Diaz, G., Pardo, J.J., Valero, V., Pelayo, F.L.: Rt-RT-UML for modeling real-time web services. In: Proc. IEEE Services Computing Workshops SCW 2006, pp. 131–139 (2006)
5. Cardoso, J.: Approaches to developing semantic web services. International Journal of Computer Science **1**(1), 8–21 (2006)
6. Cavalli, A.R., Lee, D., Rinderknecht, C., Zaïdi, F.: Hit-or-jump: An algorithm for embedded testing with applications to in services. In: FORTE XII / PSTV XIX 1999: Proc. of the IFIP TC6 WG6.1 Joint International Conference on Formal Description Techniques for Distributed Systems and Communication Protocols (FORTE XII) and Protocol Specification, Testing and Verification (PSTV XIX), pp. 41–56. Kluwer, Dordrecht (1999)
7. Christensen, E., Curbera, F., Meredith, G., Weerawarana, S.: Web Services Description Language (WSDL) 1.1. http://www.w3.org/TR/wsdl (March 2001)
8. Cockburn, A.: Writing Effective Use Cases, 1st edn. Addison-Wesley, Reading (2000)
9. CollabNet: Argouml. http://argouml.tigris.org/ (2008)
10. del Cid, J.P.E., de la Fuente Valentin, L., Gutierrez, S., Pardo, A., Kloos, C.D.: Implementation of a learning design run-time environment for the .LRN learning management system. Journal of Interactive Media in Education. Retrieved from ERIC database (2007)
11. dotLRN: Learn, research, network. http://www.dotlrn.org
12. EVIWARE: SOAPUI: The web services testing tool. http://www.soapui.org/ (2009)
13. Farahbod, R., Glasser, U., Vajihollahi, M.: Specification and validation of the business process execution language for web services. In: Abstract State Machines, pp. 78–94 (2004)
14. Fouchal, H., Petitjean, E., Salva, S.: Testing timed systems with timed purposes. In: Proc. Seventh International Conference on Real-Time Computing Systems and Applications, pp. 166–171 (2000)
15. García-Fanjul, J., Tuya, J., de la Riva, C.: Generating test cases specifications for BPEL compositions of web services using spin. In: Proc. International Workshop on Web Services— Modeling and Testing WS-MaTe 2006, pp. 83–94, Palermo, Italy (2006)
16. Hinz, S., Schmidt, K., Stahl, C.: Transforming BPEL to Petri nets. In: Business Process Management, pp. 220–235. Springer, Berlin (2005)
17. Holzmann, G.J.: The Spin Model Checker: Primer and Reference Manual. Addison-Wesley, Reading (2003)
18. Hong, H.S., Cha, S.D., Lee, I., Sokolsky, O., Ural, H.: Data flow testing as model checking. In: International Conference on Software Engineering, pp. 232–242. IEEE Comput. Soc., Washington (2003)
19. IBM: Rational rose. http://www-306.ibm.com/software/awdtools/developer/rose/index.html
20. Jones, C.A., Drake, F.L. Jr.: Python & XML, 1st edn. O'Reilly Media, Sebastopol (2001)
21. Kazhamiakin, R., Pandya, P., Pistore, M.: Timed modelling and analysis in web service compositions. In: Proc. First International Conference on Availability, Reliability and Security ARES 2006, p. 7 (2006)
22. Krichen, M., Tripakis, S.: An expressive and implementable formal framework for testing real-time systems. In: Proc. 16th IFIP International Conference on Testing of Communicating Systems TestCom 2005, pp. 209–225 (2005)

23. Kung, D.C., Liu, C.H., Hsia, P.: An object-oriented web test model for testing web applications. In: Asia-Pacific Conference on Quality Software, p. 111 (2000)
24. Lallali, M., Zaidi, F., Cavalli, A.: Timed modeling of web services composition for automatic testing. In: Proc. Third International IEEE Conference on Signal-Image Technologies and Internet-Based System SITIS 2007, pp. 417–426 (2007)
25. Li, N., Ma, Q.-q., Wu, J., Jin, M.-z., Liu, C.: A framework of model-driven web application testing. In: 30th Annual International Computer Software and Applications Conference, vol. 2, pp. 157–162 (2006)
26. Liu, C., Kung, D., Hsia, P., Hsu, C.: Structure testing of web applications. In: Proc. 11th Annual International Symposium on Software Reliability Engineering, pp. 84–96 (October 2000)
27. Lorenzo, G.D., Fasolino, A.R., Melcarne, L., Tramontana, P., Vittorini, V.: Turning web applications into web services by wrapping techniques. In: Working Conference on Reverse Engineering, pp. 199–208 (2007)
28. MacKenzie, C.M., Laskey, K., McCabe, F., Brown, P.F., Metz, R.: Reference model for service oriented architecture 1.0. oasis standard, 12 October 2006. http://docs.oasis-open.org/soa-rm/v1.0/soa-rm.pdf
29. Nakajima, S.: Lightweight formal analysis of web service flows. Progress in Informatics **2**, 57–76 (2005)
30. OASIS: Organization for the advancement of structured information standards. http://www.oasis-open.org/specs/index.php
31. OASIS: Universal description discovery and integration. http://uddi.xml.org/uddi-org
32. OASIS: WS-BPEL ver. 2.0. http://docs.oasis-open.org/wsbpel/2.0/OS/wsbpel-v2.0-OS.html (April 2007)
33. Object Management Group: BPMN, business process modeling notation. http://www.bpmn.org/ (2009)
34. OMG: Unified Modeling Language (UML). http://www.uml.org/
35. OMG: XML Metadata Interchange (XMI). http://www.omg.org/spec/XMI/2.1.1/
36. OpenACS Community: Openacs. http://openacs.org
37. OpenQA Community: Selenium ide. http://www.openqa.org/selenium-ide/
38. OpenSTA: Open system testing architecture. http://www.opensta.org/
39. Paradkar, A.M., Sinha, A., Williams, C., Johnson, R.D., Outterson, S., Shriver, C., Liang, C.: Automated functional conformance test generation for semantic web services. In: IEEE International Conference on Web Services ICWS, pp. 110–117 (2007)
40. probleme: System modeling workbench tool. http://www.abo.fi/~iporres/html/smw.html
41. Realfsen, A.S.: Tclwebtest recorder. http://www.km.co.at/km/twtr
42. Ricca, F., Tonella, P.: Analysis and testing of web applications. In: International Conference on Software Engineering, pp. 25–34 (2001)
43. Sheshagiri, M.: Automatic composition and invocation of semantic web services. Master's thesis, UMBC (2004)
44. SOASTA: Soasta CloudTest. http://www.soasta.com/
45. Softlogica: Wapt: Web application testing. http://www.loadtestingtool.com/
46. Software QA and Testing Resource Center: Web site test tools and site management tools. http://www.softwareqatest.com/qatweb1.html
47. W3C: Extensible Markup Language XML. http://www.w3.org/XML
48. W3C: Ontology Web Language (OWL). http://www.w3.org/TR/owl-features/
49. W3C: Resource Definition Framework (RDF). http://www.w3.org/RDF/
50. W3C: Web application formats working group. http://www.w3.org/2006/appformats/
51. W3C: Web ontology web language for services (OWL-S). http://www.w3.org/Submission/OWL-S/
52. W3C: Web service description language with semantics (WSDL-S). http://www.w3.org/Submission/WSDL-S/
53. W3C: Web services modeling ontology (WSMO). http://www.wsmo.org/
54. W3C: The world wide web consortium. http://www.w3.org/

55. W3C: Simple Object Access Protocol SOAP (version 1.1). http://www.w3.org/TR/soap/ (May 2000)

56. Wombacher, A., Fankhauser, P., Neuhold, E.: Transforming BPEL into annotated deterministic finite state automata for service discovery. In: Proc. IEEE International Conference on Web Services ICWS 2004, pp. 316–323 (2004)

57. Xu, L., Xu, B., Chen, Z., Jiang, J., Chen, H.: Regression testing for web applications based on slicing. In: Annual International Computer Software and Applications Conference, p. 652 (2003)

58. Yang, Y., Tan, Q., Yu, J., Liu, F.: Transformation BPEL to CP-nets for verifying web services composition. In: Proc. of International Conference on Next Generation Web Services Practices NWeSP 2005, p. 6 (2005)

59. Yu, Y., Huang, N., Luo, Q.: Owl-s based interaction testing of web service-based system. In: International Conference on Next Generation Web Services Practices, pp. 31–34 (2007)

60. Zhang, R., Arpinar, I.B., Aleman-Meza, B.: Automatic composition of semantic web services. In: International Conference on Web Services ICWS 2003, pp. 38–41 (2003)

Chapter 15
Web-Based Support by Thin-Client Co-browsing

**Matthias Niederhausen, Stefan Pietschmann,
Tobias Ruch, and Klaus Meißner**

Abstract As web applications are becoming ever larger, more complex and thus more demanding for their users, there is a growing need for customer support. Very often, it is provided by support centers via phone. However, the media break between browser and phone hampers the common understanding of user and consultant. As a result, support becomes ineffective and expensive, and users get frustrated. Screen sharing solutions are one possible solution for this problem, but they have major disadvantages like high bandwidth requirements, slow performance and, most importantly, the need for a client-side installation. These drawbacks are addressed by VCS, a concept and system for "instant co-browsing", that runs directly within the user's browser. It equally allows all participants of a support session to see and navigate the same web page on their screens, being aware of what the other person is currently doing on the page. People can directly interact with each other, jointly complete tasks and solve. The event-based nature of the synchronization approach to be presented further facilitates adaptation, so that users with heterogeneous end devices may collaborate. In this chapter, we present VCS and also discuss the special challenges that this approach entails.

15.1 Introduction

In the recent years, the Internet has changed dramatically. On top of a network of documents, a medium for entertainment, social interaction, communication and collaboration has evolved. Today, users are faced with an abundance of audio and video conferencing tools and social networks. They can upload photos, videos and other media, rate products, post in blogs and forums—the users' power to shape the virtual world they act in has increased significantly. However, collaboration over the Web has stayed asynchronous so far. Despite the efforts to create a "Social Web", web browsing itself is still a solitary activity. The need for actual real-time collaboration

M. Niederhausen (✉)
Chair of Multimedia Technology, Technische Universität Dresden, Dresden, Germany
e-mail: matthias.niederhausen@tu-dresden.de

Y. Badr et al. (eds.) *Emergent Web Intelligence: Advanced Semantic Technologies,*
Advanced Information and Knowledge Processing,
DOI 10.1007/978-1-84996-077-9_15, © Springer-Verlag London Limited 2010

becomes evident when we look at the large number of parallel communication networks that have been established: instant messaging, voice chat and many more are the result of peoples' wishes to share their online experiences.

Another trend we are experiencing is the increasing availability of rich web applications: more and more software companies offer software "as a service" over the Internet. While this has many advantages, users are facing a flood of ever more complex applications that in turn create a need for support.

To address these issues, a collaboration tool can couple users' browser views and enable communication with each other. There are already a number of systems that allow people to share applications running on their computer, e.g., web conferencing and remote desktop solutions (cf. Sect. 15.2). However, none of them truly address the problem of instant, real-time collaboration in the context of a web browsing application.

In this chapter, we introduce the concept and prototype of *Collaborative Context-Aware Browsing* (CoCAB), a new system for collaborative browsing. CoCAB aims at enabling unrestricted end-user collaboration on already existing web-based content, bridging the gap between social networking in real life and the online world.

After a state-of-the-art overview of collaborative browsing in Sect. 15.2, this chapter turns to the concept of CoCA-Browsing itself, which is divided in four parts. The first part (Sect. 15.3) illustrates the basic concepts, gives an architectural overview and provides information on the synchronization of co-browsing participants and on context-aware co-browsing. The second part (Sect. 15.4) outlines a number of application scenarios we have identified, in which CoCA-Browsing can help to improve the user experience. The third part (Sect. 15.5) focuses on the implementation of the concepts—more precisely, the prototype system VCS (*Virtual Consulting Services*). The fourth and last part (Sect. 15.6) of the overview discusses a number of challenges that emerge in a collaborative browsing system and how these challenges may be tackled. Finally, we give a prospect on the future of Co-CAB in Sect. 15.7.

15.2 State of the Art in Co-browsing

Co-browsing is an extension of traditional web browsing which allows users to jointly view and interact with web pages and to transfer awareness of these activities. Research on this field has been done since the mid 90s [16, 23, 29]. However, with the rise of Web 2.0 and the increasing availability of social web applications and rich Internet applications, this area of research has gained new acuteness. Next, we describe different existing approaches to collaborative browsing in more detail.

15.2.1 Related Co-browsing Approaches

There already exist a number of solutions, research prototypes as well as commercial products, that address the concern of enabling collaboration on the Web. They can be divided into two approaches, namely *application-sharing* and *co-browsing*.

Application-sharing tools allow for sharing arbitrary applications (i.e., desktop programs) over the Internet and are thus not bound to a web browser. However, all of them require a separate software client to be installed (e.g., NetMeeting[1]) or at least rely on previously installed browser plugins (e.g., WebEx[2]). Synchronization is achieved by transferring screenshots in fixed time intervals, which results in high latency and bandwidth required and thus negatively impacts the browsing experience. Their use of a separate client application further widens the gap between browsing alone and collaboratively.

Co-browsing tools, such as CoCAB, the system presented in this chapter, are designed with focus on the collaborative use of web content. They are commonly browser-based, so there is no need to toggle between applications when switching to collaboration mode. This is a key requirement of the "1-click collaboration" [12]. Due to their event-based synchronization, co-browsing systems are generally much faster than image-based application-sharing solutions. Furthermore, they offer superior presentation quality, as websites are rendered natively and not as compressed images.

In the last decade, different co-browsing systems have been presented that allow for the shared use of a web browser. Some of them are very application-specific, e.g., CoWeb [23], which supports synchronous filling of HTML forms, while others are more general in allowing a group of people to share the whole web page presented. Type and complexity of synchronization range from the purely navigational replication of URLs and their content to more sophisticated techniques such as shared mousepointers ("telepointer" [16] or "CoPointer" [27]), view slaving (following another user's scrolling position), annotations, synchronous form-filling (CoWeb) or whiteboard capabilities for web pages (PROOF [5]). While these systems do their best to provide a decent synchronization—even of streaming content, as in CoLab [21]—they rarely support domain-specific interaction techniques. Our system can be configured application-specifically and can therefore provide appropriate techniques for particular collaboration scenarios. As an example, we mention our concept of the "pencil tool" (cf. Sect. 15.3.4) for the use in consulting scenarios.

Finally, co-browsing tools are facing additional synchronization problems today. With the advent of Web 2.0, new forms of web applications have emerged that heavily use dynamic content. For future web-based collaboration, support for dynamic content is crucial. As many of the previously mentioned solutions are somewhat aged, they typically have no or at least insufficient support for dynamic pages, in contrast to CoCAB.

---

[1] http://www.microsoft.com/windows/netmeeting/.

[2] http://www.webex.com.

The majority of co-browsing solutions, e.g., academic prototypes like CoWeb and PROOF or products like BrowserFor2[3] and Bestscout,[4] claim to be thin-client; however, they rely on Java applets for interaction monitoring and communication between client and co-browsing proxy server. Thus, a client-side installation of the Java Runtime Environment is necessary. Many solutions, such as CoBrowser, further require the user to manually configure his browser to use a specific proxy server. This is inappropriate especially for computer-illiterate people—a relevant target group for online consultations. Other approaches like CoLab try to solve this by "automatic proxy configuration", but still require the user to manually adjust the browser settings.

The concept and system presented in this chapter provides two alternative approaches for the connection of client and proxy server, one of them being purely browser-based (Ajax), which makes CoCAB a "real" thin-client system. Similar work that is just as well only based on JavaScript has been presented in [12]. However, it only allows content to be co-browsed that is on the same server as the co-browsing system. Our concept supports co-browsing on arbitrary websites.

Only few co-browsing approaches take the heterogeneity of user groups and their devices into account at all. Most of them, e.g., GroupWeb and CoLab, implement "relaxed WYSIWIS" (What You See Is What I See), i.e., all participants see the same content, adapted only to their screen size [16]. This is done automatically by every modern web browser today and is no longer sufficient, taking into account the heterogeneity of Web-enabled devices, ranging from iPhone to multi-monitor desktop PCs. In WebSplitter [17], the author of the shared content needs to provide policy files to define access privileges for users (personalization) or devices (device-independence) to certain parts of a web page. The adaptation is performed by a proxy server, which then delivers the customized pages to the clients. [9] present a framework for multi-modal browsing on multiple clients, which heavily incorporates standards like XForms, XLink and XML Events. The requested content is not replicated, but every client is notified of a page change and requests the content itself, which results in individual views. As opposed to our approach, both systems do not support arbitrary HTML content, since they use proprietary content models for their shared pages which leads to extensive authoring. Thanks to its genericity, our adaptation approach works well with arbitrary existing web content and does not require an author to prepare the shared content.

The framework for co-browsing on heterogeneous devices presented in [8] does not use a specific content model. Instead, it employs automatic web page analysis and structure detection algorithms to provide all session members with a so-called Shared Viewpoint (SVP), i.e., the replica of the web page adapted to the smallest common denominator of all participating devices. Additionally, each user has a Personal Viewpoint (PVP), that is, the web page adapted to his personal interests and device capabilities. However, due to the heuristic nature of the utilized web page transcoding algorithms, the adaptation (and especially the quality or usability of the

---

[3]http://www.matthewssoftware.com/BrowserFor2.

[4]http://www.bestsella.com/produkte/bestscout.

resulting web pages) is often unpredictable [22] and cannot be controlled by the web site's author, as in our system.

15.3 CoCAB: Collaborative Context-Aware Browsing

In order to overcome the limitations of the previous solutions, we present the concept of *Collaborative Context-Aware Browsing* (CoCAB), which leverages existing web standards and a new synchronization paradigm.

15.3.1 Basic Concepts

First of all, CoCAB runs as a JavaScript application, embedded into the web pages a user requests. Therefore, it does not require the user to install a client software on his PC. As users on the Web have generally become more reluctant to install software from a website, this offers a significantly lower inhibition threshold for using CoCAB. The integration within the browser also entails a different synchronization approach. In contrast to the often-used transmission of screenshot sequences, CoCAB synchronizes DOM events that are triggered by the user's interaction with the website. This event-based synchronization offers very low latency, compared with the image-based processes. Furthermore, by relying on pure XHTML, CSS and JavaScript (Ajax) for all client-side modules, our concept easily provides cross-platform support. A great advantage of this approach is that, with new types of end devices being available for accessing the Web (like the iPhone), CoCAB systems can instantly support these devices if they implement said web standards.

15.3.2 Architectural Overview

The CoCAB system is based on a modular, proxy-based architecture, similar to UsaProxy [1]. Basically, it acts as a mediator between co-browsing users and content providers on the server side (Fig. 15.1), extending the common client–server architecture. To this end, the *CoCAB Server* synchronizes and bundles collaborative activities between the participating clients of one co-browsing session, but acts as a single client towards the external content server.

The CoCAB Server itself is also designed in a modular fashion. Its clients are offered two connection interfaces: one for regular HTTP page requests and one for the transmission of synchronization data. HTTP requests are relayed to the *Remote HTTP-Client* which retrieves the requested page from the Web or its own cache. To ensure that all subsequent HTTP requests are routed through the CoCAB Server, a *Content Assembly* component modifies the delivered web pages on-the-fly.

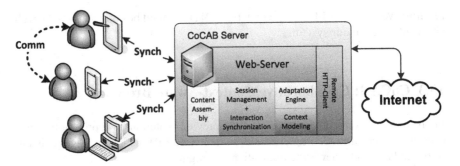

Fig. 15.1 CoCAB architecture

Every hyperlink contained in the web page is rewritten to point to the CoCAB Server. Further, the Content Assembly embeds a set of client-side components into every page. These are adapted to the specific client and constitute the whole functionality available on client-side. CoCAB also offers support for specialized application fields (cf. Sect. 15.4) and heterogeneous devices. To this end, a domain-dependent, component-based GUI is utilized to provide the user with an appropriate interface. A selection of client-side components is introduced in Sect. 15.5.5.2.

The *Session Management* and *Synchronization* components are responsible for synchronizing the state of different participants and managing all concurrent sessions running on the server. They also enforce the rights management, which is especially important for applications like consulting (see Sect. 15.4 for some examples). Finally, the *Adaptation Engine* tailors web pages to the specific needs and capabilities of both the user groups formed by a session and every single participant. Further details on the Adaptation Engine can be found in Sect. 15.3.5.

As stated previously, the client application is implemented in a thin manner, using only JavaScript. More precisely, it can be classified as a parasite [29], because it is embedded into the requested web pages and can control the behavior of the web browser as well as monitor user interactions. Since it is used in heterogeneous browser environments, the synchronization technology (cf. Sect. 15.5.6) is chosen depending on the client's capabilities.

Communication between participants plays an important role in any collaborative scenario. As Jensen et al. have shown, voice communication offers a superior quality to raw text-based chat [24]. Therefore, CoCAB allows users to communicate in many ways. However, a pure thin-client approach does not allow for any kind of voice chat. The default solution is to utilize either Adobe Flash or Skype (depending on what is already installed on the client) for communication—both allow for voice and even video chat. If neither Flash nor Skype are installed, CoCAB falls back to its default text chat which is based on Ajax technology.

15.3.3 Event-Based Synchronization

A crucial demand to co-browsing applications is the proper real-time synchronization of shared content and interactions of participating users. As we have shown in Sect. 15.2, a common answer to this demand is screen sharing, in which the entire view of a client is transferred to other participants on a pixel-by-pixel basis. This ensures that, regardless of the content, all shared views always look the same. However, this approach does not address the specific needs of real synchronous collaborative browsing. Today's web-enabled client devices, ranging from PDAs to Web TVs to desktop PCs, vary greatly in their capabilities. Even only a different screen resolution on PCs can ruin the co-browsing experience if one participant has to scroll his view constantly because his device can only display a part of other participants' screen. Just automatically resizing the transmitted images does not solve the problem, because it often renders details and small fonts—which are used quite frequently on the Web—unreadable. When it comes to even more heterogeneous situations, e.g., participants with mobile devices or visually impaired users, image-based applications fail to provide the necessary means for effective co-browsing.

To address these problems, CoCAB realizes an event-based approach for content synchronization. Whenever an event is triggered in a user's browser, for example, if someone points at a link, this event is intercepted by the client-side components. In a next step, the event is propagated to the server and, from there, distributed among the other clients in the session.

The flexibility of event-based synchronization comes at the cost of new challenges, which have to be addressed carefully. One difficulty is to ensure the consistency of shared content. A participant joining a co-browsing session has to receive not only the page that is currently viewed but also all changes which have been applied to the page during the session, e.g., filled form fields and script modifications. This task is accomplished by the Remote HTTP-Client on the server side which keeps track of the latest state of a web page and delivers that state whenever a new client enters the session. If synchronization messages are lost, e.g., due to network failure, a re-synchronization ensures consistency of the shared content.

A more complex problem is posed by non-deterministic content. More and more web applications deliver random or user-tailored images like advertisements; web shops show random offers of the day that vary every page request. Thus, co-browsing users might end up seeing different things on the same page—a situation which on no account may occur, if users are to talk about the same subject. The CoCAB architecture addresses this problem by caching a page on the first request within a session and delivering this page to all clients who request it afterwards.

One major advantage of event-based synchronization is that individual manifestations of the shared content (i.e., the page layout on the screen) need not be the same for all participants. Since user interactions are bound to specific elements of the underlying document, these events can be transparently reproduced for other participants, no matter where the underlying page elements are positioned or how they are rendered. Hence, the presentation can be adapted to the individual needs of the end user and his device while preserving the ability to collaborate.

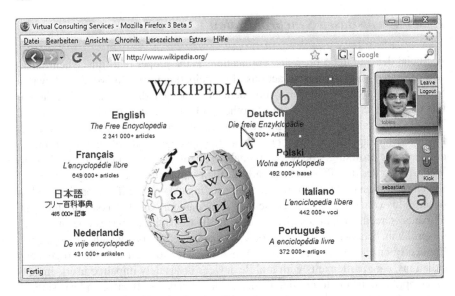

Fig. 15.2 CoCAB user bar (**a**) and radar view (**b**)

15.3.4 Co-browsing Awareness

Awareness is crucial element for any kind of collaboration. Because browsing the web is often a very fast-paced activity [18], awareness of other participant's activities and focus of interest is essential for users to keep track of what is going on. CoCAB provides many client-side components that support different notions of awareness within a co-browsing session. Here, a few awareness components of presence, activity, location and roles are presented.

First of all, users have to be aware of the presence of others. CoCAB offers this kind of information by showing a user bar (Fig. 15.2a) at the edge of the screen. On the bar, users can see all participants currently co-browsing in the same session with their name and avatar. Additionally, a click on somebody's photo provides you with additional information on that person and the option to start a chat.

However, awareness of the presence of other users alone is not enough. Another important information is knowing what another person is doing at the moment. This awareness is created by a number of different elements in CoCAB. The telepointer shows where on a page a participant currently is. There is one telepointer per user and they can be distinguished by the person's avatar floating next to it. Furthermore, an indicator at the telepointer shows whenever a user types text into a form field, even if his mouse has moved away. Finally, the user bar indicates whether someone has finished loading the current page or if a person is inactive and may have left the computer.

A different visualization of a user's position on a page can be provided by a radar view (Fig. 15.2b), which has the advantage of showing someone's position even if he is outside the own currently visible screen area. This is of special value in scenarios

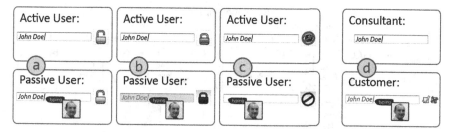

Fig. 15.3 CoCAB form protector (**a–c**) and pencil tool (**d**)

where long web pages are browsed or heterogeneous devices (with different screen sizes) are used.

In cases where private data (like passwords or credit card numbers) is entered into web forms, CoCAB allows awareness to be reduced in order to protect the participants' privacy. The form protector (Fig. 15.3a–c) enables users to select between (a) freely allowing everyone in the session to edit form fields, (b) claiming a form field so that nobody else can edit it, and (c) hiding the input of a form field from everybody. While other users are not able to see what exactly is entered into the field with option (c), they will still be aware that something is entered.

Finally, awareness of user's roles and capabilities is also supported. An example of this is the pencil tool (see Fig. 15.3d), which distinguishes between two groups of users in a session, usually a group with elevated rights and one with advisory function (like a consultant). Participants with elevated rights may fill out and submit any form on the current web page.

Advisory users may also fill out forms, but they cannot submit the form. Their input is displayed in grey to other participants who can either accept the suggestions or discard them. This resembles the procedures of contracting an insurance in real life, where insurance agents use their domain expertise to fill out a form, but the contract only becomes valid with the customer's signature.

15.3.5 Context-Awareness

Web-based cross-device collaboration requires adaptation of Web content to different client devices and user preferences while preserving the feeling for the users that they share the same web page. Yet, while a number of co-browsing systems have been proposed in the last decade, they only marginally address personalization and device independence. The co-browsing concept presented in this chapter facilitates context-awareness by utilizing Semantic Web technologies to address different issues of domain and context modeling as well as generic adaptation of shared web content.

An important trend co-browsing tools are facing is the increasing heterogeneity of web-capable devices. While in the 1990s the majority of PCs were rather similar in their capabilities, this has changed dramatically in the recent years. Target systems

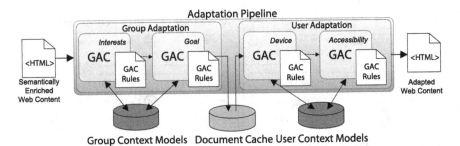

Fig. 15.4 CoCAB adaptation engine

for co-browsing tools nowadays range from Mobile Phones, PDAs and Ultra-Mobile PCs (UMPCs) to Desktop PCs, and thereby screen sizes, interaction modalities and computing power differ tremendously. Furthermore, besides the problem of device-independence, it can be useful to take the current situation (i.e., their context) of users into account. An example are web presentations, where the capability of taking private notes should be provided per-user, while buttons for moving backward and forward need only be seen by the presenter.

For all these reasons it is necessary to adapt content shared by a co-browsing group to the capabilities, preferences and needs of its individual members.

Thereby, co-browsing becomes context-aware. CoCAB introduces an adaptation process based on three related concepts: (a) semantically enriched web content, (b) user and group context models, and (c) the "Generic Adaptation Component" (GAC) [14]. While this section subsequently describes these concepts in more detail, Fig. 15.4 illustrates their interplay in the overall adaptation process.

15.3.5.1 Semantically Enriched Shared Content

As CoCAB aims at co-browsing on arbitrary Internet content, its main focus is on documents based on the HTML4 and XHTML standards. While these formats contain some intrinsic semantics which is apparent by the syntactical elements (e.g., an img tag indicates an image), such semantics does not allow for rich adaptation. Conventional transcoding systems, such as [3, 32] can, for example, extract all images on a web page, but they cannot decide whether two of them are alternatives. Thus, it is necessary to explicitly express semantic relationships between objects on a web page, e.g., one object describing or being an alternative to another one. While there have been various approaches to the enrichment of web content, e.g., microformats [26], the W3C has only recently addressed this issue with a Working Draft for RDFa [4]. This upcoming standard is defined as "a collection of attributes for layering RDF on XML languages". With the help of few elements (meta, link) and attributes (about, rel, rev, href, content) RDF (a standardized format to model information in the form of subject-predicate-object expressions) is embedded into HTML and thereby certain parts of web documents are

```
1  <div xmlns:wa="http://augmented.man.ac.uk/ontologies/wafa.owl">
2    <img id="logo" alt="Logo" src="logo.jpg"
3       about="#logo" rel="rdf:type" href="[wa:Logo]" />
4    <span style="…">
5      <link rel="rdf:type" href="[wa:Label]" />
6      <link rel="wa:is-label-for" href="#logo" />
7      TU Dresden
8    </span>
9  </div>
```

Fig. 15.5 Semantic annotation with RDF/A

linked to concepts in external ontologies (data models). The embedded semantics can describe the content as well as relationships between web page components. Examples include concepts like "technical image" or "navigation bar" and relations such as "is-alternative-for" or "is-more-detailed-than". Consequently, RDFa allows us to add semantics to shared, HTML-based content in a non-invasive and standards-compliant way. Thereby, a semantic basis is provided by external ontologies describing domain-specific concepts and their relationships.

As an example, Fig. 15.5 shows how the *Web Authoring for Accessibility* (WAfA) ontology can be used to enrich our content model. First, an image is linked to the concept "Logo" (line 3) by assigning it the rdf:type of wa:Logo, addressing the particular concept in the referenced WAfA ontology. Then the following text is defined to be of type "Label" in the same way. The link tag in line 6 establishes the relation is-label-for (which is provided by the ontology) between its parent element (the span) and the image above. Thereby, it eventually defines the logical relation between the label and the element with the ID "logo".

With the help of these annotations, the CoCAB server is able to "sense" the semantic relationship between the image and the text. This example shows how the basis for the later adaptation process is provided. Of course, authors are not limited to the use of the WAfA ontology, but can use arbitrary domain ontologies that cover the respective domain.

15.3.5.2 User and Group Context

The adaptation of web content, its layout, format, etc. always depends on a proper contextual basis [11], which is represented by a context model. To facilitate useful adaptation, it is crucial to have a rich, exhaustive and consistent representation of the context, i.e., the situation and environment of a user and—in our case—a co-browsing group. We now go into detail on how contextual information is stored and modeled in CoCAB.

Context Models In contrast to most prevalent, static XML-based approaches, we use an ontology-based model similar to [6] and [25]. This allows for the integration of external ontologies describing relevant contextual aspects (preferences, device

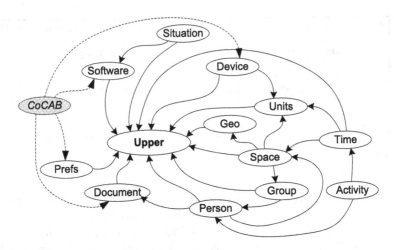

Fig. 15.6 Import relations between relevant parts of the Context Ontology

characteristics, location, time, etc.) as well as application-specific domain knowledge. Traditional approaches either directly store sensed contextual data, or they incorporate a static mapping from sensor data to context parameters. In contrast to this, an ontological basis provides machine-processable semantic metadata, domain-inherent integrity constraints and inferencing rules to derive higher-level contextual knowledge from basic sensor data. Thus, it becomes possible to model implicit knowledge and to establish a semantic context (meaning) on top of the purely technical context (parameters).

We have developed a generic, ontology-based context model, the *Context Ontology*, for the use in context-aware applications. As can be seen from Fig. 15.6, it consists of several sub-ontologies, that model different aspects of context, e.g., time, place, the user and his device. Therefore, we reused concepts from several well-known ontologies, such as SOUPA [7], PROTON[5] and the W3C Time Ontology.[6] Based on an Upper Ontology it is possible—and intended by all means—to extend the model and integrate application-specific domain knowledge. Depending on the usage scenario, relevant information of this domain can be modeled and added to the context model.

In the domain of co-browsing, characteristics not only of single users but also of user groups play an important role. For the use in context-aware co-browsing scenarios, we have extended, that is, specialized the Context Ontology with the *CoCAB Ontology*—a domain description containing co-browsing-specific concepts, some of which are shown in Fig. 15.7. As an example, it allows us to model that a user has a specific "SystemProfile" representing his hard- and software, e.g., his browser ("WebBrowserInstallation"), and that he is participant of a co-browsing session

---

[5]http://proton.semanticweb.org/.

[6]http://www.w3.org/TR/owl-time/.

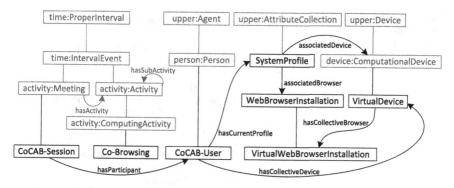

Fig. 15.7 Part of the concepts and relations modeled in the CoCAB domain

("CoCAB-Session"). These "Sessions" represent the group context of all participating members. They provide information on the lowest common denominator of all users (regarding their end device capabilities) as well as higher-level information that directly results from the combination of all users' parameters, e.g., "all project members are participating in the session", either by properties or relationships to such concepts. This information is used by the adaptation logic explained later. If, for example, all members of a co-browsing session are working on the same project and this is modeled as a shared (group) property, it might result in the inclusion of confidential project information into the shared content.

Context Modeling We have developed an ontology-based *Context Modeling Component* (CMC) responsible for inferring contextual information from basic sensor data based on the Context Ontology. This generic component allows arbitrary *context providers* to submit, and *context consumers* to request context data via specific service interfaces. In our scenario, CoCAB clients act both as providers and consumers. With the help of consistency and inferencing rules, higher-level information that may not be provided by any sensor is derived by the CMC and serves as a basis for the later adaptation process. As an example, we can adapt web content directly to the users' age, so that inappropriate content is filtered out. However, the age of consent differs from country to country, so, as a matter of course, we need to bind the adaptation to the semantic concept of *adulthood*, which can be dynamically reasoned from other contextual information of a user, such as his age and location.

Figure 15.8 shows the basic architecture of the CMC. It follows the blackboard design pattern, similar to DAIDALOS [33] and CoBrA [6]. This model promotes a data-centric approach in which external processes can post context information on a blackboard, or subscribe for change notifications [2]. Thus, it is rather easy to add new context providers and consumers, as is desirable for our component.

The CMC has three responsibilities: *(context) data management, consistency checking and reasoning*, and *context data update and provision*.

Data management consists of two parts: the *Context History* (CH), which contains the history of updates to the context model, and the *Context Store*. The latter comprises the *Consistent Context* (CC) representing the currently valid, consistent

Fig. 15.8 Architecture of the Context Modeling Component

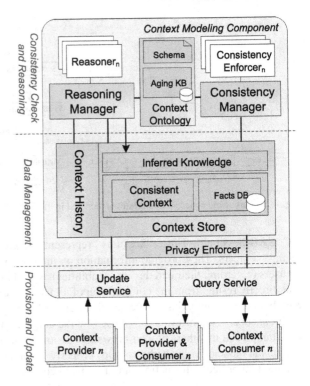

contextual data, a *Facts Database* which stores facts about the domain, and the *Inferred Knowledge* (IK) which encapsulates all information derived, i.e., reasoned from the current context information with the help of the facts. Consumers always request data from the *Context Store* by which the division of CC and IK becomes transparent to external components. The CH is completely hidden, though, and is only used internally for statistical analysis or by context reasoners that include the time-variation of context data into their inferencing process.

Consistency checking is done by the *ConsistencyManager* (CM), which is triggered every time new contextual data is added to the context model. An arbitrary number of *ConsistencyEnforcers*, each responsible for ensuring consistency of a certain aspect (e.g., data type or cardinality), can register at the CM to carry out consistency checks and conflict detection.

Reasoning is carried out by a *ReasoningManager* (RM). Similar to the CM, arbitrary *Reasoners* can register at the RM, which invokes them to start the reasoning process once relevant data changes. Context reasoning is done by checking facts stored in a *Facts Database* on the data available in the *Consistent Context*. Its result is, of course, subject to subsequent consistency checks. Since inferred data must not overwrite existing data—simply because it would interfere with the Confidence mechanism—it is stored separately in the IK base. This also facilitates the dynamic integration of additional reasoners at run time without negative impact on the *Consistent Context*.

Finally, to support context data update and provision, the CMC provides two services: the *ContextUpdate-* and *ContextQueryService*. The former facilitates updates and changes to the context model, while the latter provides both a synchronous and an asynchronous way to retrieve context information from the CMC. Context Consumers, i.e., any system that is interested in context changes (just like a CoCA-Browsing system) can register for specific context data, so that they are notified by a callback handler once it changes. Of course, consumers can also request data synchronously. These two different approaches facilitate the use of the CMC in different application scenarios. In any case, it is ensured that consumers have the necessary authorization to access data.

15.3.5.3 Generic Adaptation Rules

After describing the CoCAB content and context models, we now turn to the question of **how** adaptation is performed. For that purpose, we use the *Generic Adaptation Component* [15], a transcoding tool facilitating adaptation in XML-based web applications. The key observations behind the GAC are that generating hypermedia presentations is typically implemented as a series of data transformations and that adaptation-specific transformations can be separated well from the rest of the generation process. Accordingly, the GAC acts as an independent adaptation module that can be plugged-in into existing web architectures.

The CoCAB adaptation engine, as seen in Fig. 15.4, utilizes a series of GAC transformers, each of which is configured to perform a specific adaptation aspect, such as device independence, security, accessibility, etc. In this concrete example, the first GACs in the adaptation pipeline are responsible for adjusting the available web content to the group context model. The result of this *group adaptation process* is then subsequently processed by a second set of GACs that further adjust it to individual preferences of users. The advantage of this twofold configuration is the fact that the partially adjusted pages delivered by the group adaptation GACs can be cached and thus reused for different individuals. In general, the modularization of the adaptation pipeline (by using a series of groups of GACs) allows for a flexible reconfiguration of the adaptation behavior by the inclusion, exclusion or reordering of GACs. In [20] we have already presented a concept for this kind of adaption of a web processing pipeline.

In previous work, the rule-based adaptation configuration language of the GAC has already been extensively described [15]. Figure 15.9 shows an example adaptation rule being responsible for accessibility (which is used to configure the 4th GAC in Fig. 15.4). Based on our content model example shown in Fig. 15.5, it prescribes to exclude all elements of the type wa:Logo from the processed web documents for iPhones with a horizontal screen resolution of less than 300 pixel.

Due to the genericity of the rules, the Adaptation Engine works with any XML-based content, even standard HTML documents. Thereby, we not only support adaptation of RDFa-flavored, but of arbitrary (XML-based) web content. We further believe that such content will be increasingly extended with semantics, especially as

```
1   <gac:ExclusionRule priority="1" selector="//">
2    <gac:rdfa-selector>
3     <gac:type:>wa:Logo</gac:type:>
4    </gac:rdfa-selector>
5    <gac:conditions>
6     <gac:condition when="($client=iPhone)" />
7     <gac:condition when="($WindowWidth<300)" />
8    <gac:conditions>
9    <gac:ExclusionRule>
```

Fig. 15.9 Example of an exclusion rule

Fig. 15.10 Context-aware co-browsing on a desktop PC and iPhone

a result of automated authoring processes being part of Web 2.0, as in blogs or wikis.

Figure 15.10 shows a web page co-browsed with a desktop PC and an iPhone. While the desktop user can see the company logo, it is replaced with a textual label on the iPhone to achieve a better presentation. Additional adaptation rules and alternative CSS definitions are used to further tailor the page to the smartphone. Despite the changed design of the homepage, users are still presented with the same content and their actions remain synchronized.

With the concepts described above, CoCAB allows for the flexible adaptation of shared web content. We do not presume a proprietary content model, but support any XML-based documents such as standard HTML pages. Thereby, heterogeneous co-browsing of arbitrary web applications becomes possible, as the adaptation concept facilitates personalization, device independence, accessibility, and many more. In addition, our system can exploit other information, such as the user's location, preferences, characteristics or roles to present the shared content accordingly. Besides the adaptation to single users, our Adaptation Engine also facilitates transformations of web content depending on the context of a whole co-browsing group. This helps to provide a more consistent view and to improve the overall system performance.

15.4 Fields of Application

Co-browsing offers a promising and exciting approach towards a more social and useful Internet. Many collaborative scenarios known from the offline world can now be transferred to the Web. In the following we explain the benefits of co-browsing to four selected scenarios: co-shopping, consulting, presentation and online communities. However, many more possible fields of use exist, like e-learning or guidance through virtual manuals for on-site supporters.

15.4.1 Consulting

In the field of customer support, co-browsing poses an excellent and flexible alternative to the common helpdesk hotline. For companies that offer complex online transactions, like booking a flight or changing the modalities of an insurance contract, proper support is a crucial element to success. Until now, call centers have been the designated way to address this issue. However, in their current form, call centers have two significant drawbacks that can be addressed by co-browsing. First, a media break occurs when customers grab the phone: they have to use a different communication channel to request help. Second and most important, call centers are inefficient in that they simply lack a shared view between customer and operator, thus hampering common understanding. Very often, customers calling a help desk lack the domain knowledge to explain what actually their problems are. The operator then has the laborious task to reconstruct the customer's view in his mind by asking several questions. Then again, the operator has to navigate customers without seeing what they actually do. The described situation is still the ideal: as many of us have personally experienced, often enough the situation is misunderstood by the operator, leaving the customer puzzled.

With co-browsing techniques, support can be provided directly on the Web, avoiding the media break. Operator and customer share the same view and can act on the same web page to resolve the problem. Overall, this leads to an easier and far more convenient way of handling support requests, but also to more satisfied and confident customers because they can more easily understand and retrace the steps suggested by the support agent. Ultimately, this leads to lower numbers of repeated help requests. Co-browsing should, however, include domain-specific tools that closely resemble real-life interaction. An example within a consulting scenario is the pencil tool, which was previously explained in Sect. 15.3.4. Like in real life, it allows to get help with filling out a form without surrendering the freedom to decide what and when to submit it.

All above arguments about facilitating co-browsing for consulting purposes are especially valid for e-government applications. Today, public authorities provide online services for registration and tax return to achieve higher efficiency, faster processing of requests and lower costs. By moving services to the Web, long waiting queues and the workload of civil servants in government agencies can be reduced. Because of the legally required accessibility to government resources, direct support is even more critical than for companies as mentioned above. Co-browsing techniques can be utilized here to improve accessibility.

15.4.2 Co-shopping

While shopping on the Web has become a common way of buying goods, the traditional way of shopping still has one decisive advantage over e-commerce: consumer goods are often evaluated and bought together with friends or family. Thereby, shopping comprises a social component. Though e-shopping is convenient, takes less time and is often cheaper, going to the mall offers this social component which cannot be reproduced by web shops yet. Another advantage of retail stores is the availability of sales assistants. If you are looking for a present, want to know if a certain product is available and where it is located, or simply need a recommendation, an assistant can help and guide you through the store. Proof for the importance of this fact is given by the recent study "E-Shopping-Trend 2006",[7] which concludes that German e-businesses lose 9 Billion Euros every year because customers miss helpful advice and feel left alone. By addressing this deficiency in web-based shops, Internet businesses can raise their income and attractiveness. Further, by using collaboration features, a web shop becomes more distinguishable compared to other shops and attracts new customers [28]. As [13] state, people generally prefer shared browsing to single browsing when shopping. Even if this "social service" offered by web shops does not directly result in increased sales, it can still contribute much to the loyalty of customers towards a shop [10]. While it is obvious that co-browsing can enhance online shopping in general, the application of co-browsing to web shops can be further refined into three use cases.

---

[7]http://www.novomind.de/press/press_information_2006/rel_123_en.html.

First, co-browsing can be used to advise customers during their shopping session. When visiting a web shop, a trained clerk can be called who answers questions and gives advice—like in every retail store. This kind of usage especially addresses the problems discussed in the study mentioned above. Details on how consulting in general can be accomplished with the help of co-browsing are given in Sect. 15.4.1.

Second, co-browsing can be used to transfer the idea of real-world collaborative shopping to the Web. CoCA-Browsing allows friends to meet on a specific website at a certain time, as they would do in real life. This can be an additional feature of a web shop and allows users to amble around the shop, pointing out products and maybe discussing a present for a common friend. The advantage over offline stores is that now friends do not have to be at the same place for this social event. Consequently, co-browsing combines the advantages of both the real world and the Web: shopping together—regardless of users' location.

A third possible employment of co-shopping is a mixture of the previous two use cases and is closely related to Web 2.0 applications like collaborative social networking and communities. Instead of taking along friends or relatives, one can co-browse with other present customers. Thus, co-browsing allows meeting by co-incidence between customers of a web shop, comparable to random encounters in a mall. Users can thus help each other and discuss products and thereby form a so-called "shopping community". As users already share their thoughts and knowledge in blogs or wikis, co-browsing would allow them to directly exchange their experiences on different products or to give ideas for presents on-site, which would once again increase customer loyalty.

15.4.3 Online Presentation

Online presentations are a field of application that is already covered by a multitude of products (WebEx, Adobe Acrobat Connect, etc.). Basically, these applications allow salesmen to present and promote their products over the Web. However, with existing solutions, the presentations are either image-based (which has a number of drawbacks mentioned in Sect. 15.3), or the presentation material must be prepared in a specialized format that allows for online presentations.

CoCA-Browsing also allows presentations over the Web, but avoids these disadvantages. Users don't need a high-bandwidth line to participate and because of the native support for web content, salesmen can produce their material directly for the Web and reuse it for other purposes, reducing unnecessary work.

Another employment of CoCA-Browsing within this scenario is the remote presentation and negotiation of produced work. Though basically applicable to any kind of digital work, this is especially valid for the (final) inspection of web sites produced by a third party. Client and contractor can go through the web site, point at certain parts and discuss. Because the web site is natively rendered by their browser, clients can be sure that the web site will look the same for their users.

15.4.4 Communities

Online communities are an essential part of the Web 2.0 movement. Within certain fields of interest, millions of people share their creativity, experiences and ideas. Currently, collaboration is generally asynchronous, e.g., in the form of discussion boards, mailing lists, blogs, tags and comments. Up to now, the means for synchronous web-based interaction are still limited and mostly include text chat and other proprietary communication solutions.

CoCA-Browsing, as presented in this paper, allows for much richer interaction principles available to online communities. People can actually see each other interacting with their content of interest. In a co-browsing-enriched version of social networking portals like Facebook or MySpace, members can browse collaboratively through their profiles and pictures, discuss their last holiday, exchange news via voice chat or help each other finding friends from school. Without any additional software installation required, instant synchronous collaboration can be tightly integrated with these websites. Thus, online communities become places to actually spend time together. By providing collaborative browsing, such websites can keep their users online for a longer time, thus raising advertising revenues, while being even more attractive to people.

15.5 Implementation

As a prototype implementation of the CoCaB concept, VCS (*Virtual Consulting Services*), a thin-client co-browsing application, has been developed together with Comarch.[8] In this section, we explain some of the details of VCS and the challenges that had to be dealt with during the development.

First, we explain how requested web content is pre-processed and delivered to a co-browsing group. Then we provide an insight on the implementation of the Context Modeling Component and the Adaptation Engine. After that, the configurable delivery of the client scripts and components is introduced, which enables all co-browsing activities. Finally, we describe the client-side application modules in detail and how synchronization between the clients is achieved.

15.5.1 Co-browsing Server

VCS is implemented in Java 5.0 and deployed in a J2EE container (for example, Tomcat). In order to avoid problems with firewalls and proxies, synchronization data just like regular HTTP requests is transmitted via port 80. To distinguish between both kinds of data types, requests are forwarded to different servlets.

---

[8]http://www.comarch.com.

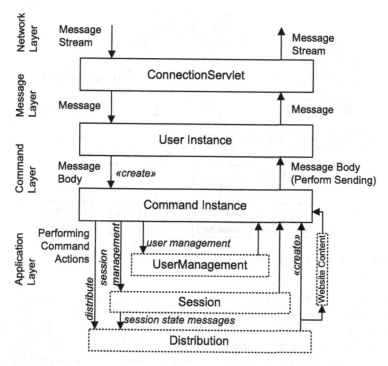

Fig. 15.11 Flow of messages in the server

The server recognizes which servlet shall be invoked by the HTTP header and identifies the client from which the message was received by the HTTP session. Further, specialized servlets exist for Ajax and for Java applet synchronization connections. Independent on the type of connection, the data transmitted (which is a stream of messages) is separated into individual messages. The message flow is shown in Fig. 15.11.

For every message, a corresponding *Command* object is instantiated, which reads the message body, parses its arguments, sets the *Origin* and finally performs message-specific *Actions* on the server if the Origin is found to have the appropriate rights. The Origin abstracts the source of a message. Thus, the source of a message is not necessarily a connected client, but can also be a server component like the Session Management or an interface to an external system (e.g., an administrative frontend).

An Action encapsulates an available feature of VCS, like `mousemove`, `enter session` or `get name for user x`. Before an Action is actually performed, the Command object verifies that the originating object has the necessary right.

The Command objects build a class hierarchy, which group and abstract common functionality. Figure 15.12 shows a small slice of this class hierarchy and examples for Origin and Action instances. This class hierarchy facilitates easy extension of co-browsing features (and thereby extensions of the text-based protocol), simply by adding new Command classes to the system. Further, this mechanism also allows

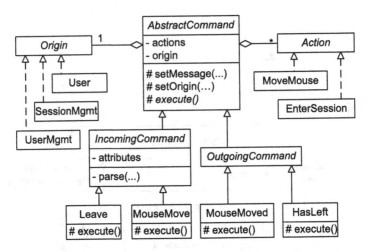

Fig. 15.12 Hierarchy of commands

to propagate a new interface to an external system by supplying the relevant Commands and defining a new type of Origin together with its execution rights. With this access control concept, the access scope and access control can be defined in great detail even for complex interfaces. Figure 15.11 shows that these Actions can currently be performed in the context of three components on the server: the User Management, a Session or the Distribution. The Distribution component sets the User as the Command's Origin, as it relays the user's messages to other participants. Note that these three components can also invoke Commands themselves.

Altogether, the use of Commands and Actions increases security when accessing VCS from external systems, further unifies the usage of the functional scope and helps keeping the system extensible.

Some Commands that trigger a message broadcast (for example, navigating to a new page), also cause these messages to be stored within the so-called *Website Content* (Fig. 15.11). This component stores the current session status, e.g., which website is currently viewed or what text was entered into form fields. It is necessary to save this information, as users who enter an existing session only receive the website—without information on filled form fields or other modifications. To synchronize them with the session's actual state, they are sent a copy of all these stored messages. Whenever a new website is requested, the previously stored messages are deleted. Still, a session recording component can be activated that stores all messages and allows users to replay a co-browsing session at a later time for evaluation or demonstration purposes.

Every client has a server-side queue that collects outgoing messages. Depending on the connection type, messages are sent in bulks when a new connection is established by the client, or sent directly over the currently open connection. If the queue builds up too much (for example, because the user has a very low bandwidth), it may drop low-priority messages like mouse moving events, which are mostly useless if they are delayed too much.

15.5.2 Content Processing and Delivery

VCS allows to co-browse both on dedicated content and on any website from the Internet. In order to enable collaboration, we need to ensure that every participant of a session sees the same content. However, this does not mean that same layout must be shown (cf. Fig. 15.10). By tracking content elements like text, paragraphs, pictures, text fields, etc., VCS can adapt the layout to a specific device and its capabilities and thus support heterogeneous devices. To achieve this, VCS processes the content in several steps. Every processing step contains its private cache and can be plugged together with other steps. Thereby, a transparent caching hierarchy is formed within a processing chain. Such a processing chain can then be used for a specific purpose, for example, to support co-browsing on new content (like Flash) or to handle known content in a different, possibly scenario-specific way.

For the basic co-browsing functionality of VCS, some default processing chains and steps are already implemented that we want to explain in more detail now. When a participant enters a session, he receives a message to request a specific web page through the VCS server.

In every processing chain, the first step is the use of the Client Library. If the resource is not found in its cache, VCS retrieves it from the Web. Thus, only the initial request in a session is relayed to the external web server. A *Client library* manages cookie handling, secured connection and other browser-related functionality required to load files from the Web.

Before being delivered to the client, the HTML code is rewritten. For this purpose, the HTML Parser[9] library is used, because it is able to parse even ill-formed HTML, which still can be found on many websites. The parser was extended in order to rewrite every link and form action to call a JavaScript method instead. Thereby, VCS can disallow certain users to navigate or perform additional checks before a form is submitted to a website. Besides the link rewriting, further modifications can be performed if needed. Images can be preloaded by the VCS server or JavaScript code incompatible with VCS can by modified. Also at this stage, the client-side co-browsing modules are embedded into the page. The result of the parsing and rewriting process is stored in a cache.

Optionally, the adaptation pipeline, as explained in Sects. 15.5.3 and 15.3.5, can be activated to adapt the content to the group and single participants. The results of this process are also stored in a cache. Figure 15.13 shows some examples of how process steps can be configured to form different processing chains.

Due to the staged caching, other participants will retrieve the same, already processed content, except for single user adaptation, which is still done individually afterwards. Therefore, the VCS server acts like a man-in-the-middle between a group of people and the Web. To avoid interference with other co-browsing sessions, the processing chains and caches are instantiated once per session. When all stages are processed, the content is finally delivered to the client.

---

[9]http://htmlparser.sourceforge.net/.

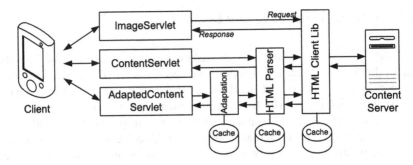

Fig. 15.13 Examples of processing chains

15.5.3 Context Modeling and Adaptation

Based on the concept explained in detail in Sect. 15.3.5, we have implemented the *Context Modeling Component* (CMC) in Java. It relies on the Jena Semantic Web Framework[10] for RDF and OWL processing tasks. To use the CMC, we have added server-side components to VCS, which act as Context Providers and Consumers. Furthermore, a DOM-based adaptation pipeline has been realized.

Figure 15.14 presents the main components of the CMC and illustrates an example workflow which is discussed in some more detail in the following. At first, a *Context Provider*, e.g., a VCS context sensor, sends new data in the form of regular RDF triples to the Context Update Service (1). Some additional information, such as a timestamp, provider id and confidence value, are transferred as well, which we will discuss later on.

The context information is forwarded to the Context Store (2), which internally manages the consistent and inferred context. The application-specific context model is based on the CoCAB Ontology presented in Sect. 15.3.5.2, which allows to model persons (users), groups, hard- and software on client devices, time, geographic information, preferences, co-browsing sessions, and much more. To ensure that the submitted context information is consistent with the internal model, it is validated by the Consistency Manager (3), which internally triggers its registered Consistency Enforcers. A consistency report is returned to the Context Store, which is added to the Context History together with the submitted context data (4). If the data is validated as consistent, the reasoning process, which is controlled by the Reasoning Manager and carried out by several registered Reasoners, is started (5). In VCS, a Reasoner based on the *GenericRuleReasoner* provided by the Jena API was implemented. It processes Jena rules which can be stored in separate files and can thus be updated and adjusted very easily. Other Reasoners, e.g., ones that also integrate the Context History, can be developed and registered with the Context Reasoner System smoothly. The knowledge inferred by the reasoning process is then again

---

[10]http://jena.sourceforge.net.

Fig. 15.14 Example workflow of the CMC

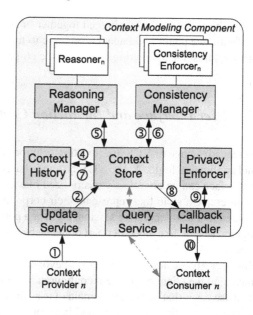

checked for consistency (6) and stored in the Context History (7). Finally, the *Call-back Handler* is informed that the context model has changed (8). If there are *Context Consumers*, which have previously registered as change listeners, they are notified of the context data changes (10), after authorization for access to this data has been granted by the *Privacy Enforcer* (10). Alternatively, consumers can query for context data via the *Query Service*. In VCS, the GACs presented in Sect. 15.3.5.3 are such consumers, as they need context data to evaluate the Adaptation Rules. GACs can alternatively request data from the *Context Update Service* directly, i.e., synchronously, with a SPARQL query [30].

To facilitate sound and useful consistency checks and reasoning, several useful mechanisms have been incorporated into the CMC. For one, each context provider is assigned a *Confidence* value (cf. [31]) representing its accuracy and reliability, which is also reflected in the Context History. Based on this value, it is possible to include the quality of context updates into consistency checks. Furthermore, the *Aging Knowledge Base* stores information about the *Variability* of contextual data. As an example, the birth date of a user is static, while his location may be highly dynamic, which means that some context information can get outdated over time and must be updated with new, even low-confidence data. A last additional parameter used in the CMC is the *Reputation* of context providers, which depends on their data quality. If a provider constantly sends inconsistent data, its Reputation decreases, ultimately resulting in lower Confidence values for context data sent by this provider. So, consistency checks and conflict detection are influenced by the age and *Variability* of context data, as well as the *Reputation* and *Confidence* of its providers.

The Adaptation Engine has been realized as a freely configurable pipeline, based on experiences from work in [19]. GACs and other XML transformation components can be configured and plugged together in an XML-based configuration file. In the future we plan to add adaptation logic to this configuration to be able to dynamically adjust the adaptation process to the co-browsing context [20].

15.5.4 User Interface and Interaction Customization

One great advantage of VCS over existing solutions like WebEx is the customizable UI and application logic. As the VCS system is based on HTML and JavaScript, the user interface can be completely customized like an HTML website. Thus, companies can create a style that represents their corporate identity. Further, when users are invited into a collaborative session, e.g., for a portfolio presentation, VCS can be configured to look like any other part of the website—the system would be smoothly integrated.

However, the customization can go beyond the user interface. The rights management and the client component configuration for user groups facilitate very fine-grained use cases that match the domain of use. Operators of VCS may even develop their own client-side components and integrate them into the system. In this manner, a completely different way of interacting with a web page can be created, e.g., for a consulting workflow, which is not limited to the interaction scope of a normal web page. The pencil tool of Sect. 15.4.1 is an example for developing such use-case-specific components—it is also implemented in the VCS system.

By combining all these abilities, the VCS system establishes a platform to create customized web-based collaboration systems.

15.5.5 Client Component Delivery

To start a web-based collaboration, a user first needs to log into VCS—just like on your average website. Afterwards, he is transferred to the waiting room. By default, this room shows all online user and all active sessions on the server. The user can then decide to join an existing session or create a new one. Finally, the VCS client components are delivered to the user and the co-browsing experience can begin. Note that for a customized VCS, there might be a different procedure, depending on the use-case or corporate identity.

15.5.5.1 Configuration of Delivered Components

The client components which shall be delivered can be configured per user group. This allows different views in specialized scenarios (cf. Sect. 15.4), e.g., for customer and consultant. By abstracting from the concrete client implementation of a component, heterogeneous devices are also taken into account.

Fig. 15.15 Overview of the configuration relations

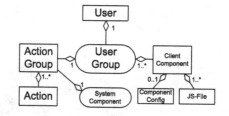

```
1   <!-- action rights for the user group customer -->
2   <entry key="customeractions">
3    mousemove,mouseover,click,kick
4   </entry>
```

Fig. 15.16 Specification of Action Group "customeractions"

```
1   <!-- client components and initial action group
2        for the user group: customer -->
3   <entry key="UserGroups.customer.components">
4    core,communication,userbar,chat
5   </entry>
6   <entry key="UserGroups.customer.initialActionGroups">
7    customeractions
8   </entry>
```

Fig. 15.17 Configuration of users, their client components and initial action group

Figure 15.15 shows how the different configuration aspects are related. Every user is assigned to a *User Group* when he registers. A User Group is characterized by a so-called *Action Group* and a number of Client Components. Action Groups, which contain the allowed Actions for a user can also be assigned to System Components in order to define their access scope. An administrative frontend can thereby be granted more privileges than a load indicator which merely displays how many users are logged in. In Fig. 15.16, a part of the Action Group configuration can be seen. In the example, the customer user may synchronize his mouse events (mousemove, click, ...) and kick other users from sessions.

Figure 15.17 shows how client components can be assigned to User Groups (e.g., core and communication components for customer users). The same configuration file also specifies which Action Groups are bound to a User Group. Here, the customer users are assigned the customeractions Action Group.

The visible outcome of the given component configuration file for a customer user is illustrated by Fig. 15.18. Typically, the four components are rendered in different frames: core frame (a), chat frame (b), content area (c) and user frame (d).

The next section offers a more detailed overview of the client-side components implemented in the VCS system and their interplay.

Fig. 15.18 Default frame set with default components: core frame (**a**), chat frame (**b**), content frame (**c**) and user frame (**d**)

15.5.5.2 Co-browsing Client

Figure 15.19 gives an overview of the module structure on the client side, which is divided into the *Connectivity*, *Management*, *Controller* and *View* Layers. The heart of the VCS client is the *Core* component (on the Management layer). It manages and initializes all other components, like the *Communication* component and the different synchronization components (Connectivity layer). Further, it keeps track of available co-browsing sessions, of participants entering or leaving and of their context data. It also keeps the state of the current session and provides such information to other components. After the Core has been loaded and started, all other client components register with it. Registration is again bound to specific message types, e.g., `mousemove`, `clicklink`.

When a message from the server arrives, it is delivered to the Core which again distributes it to the registered components (Controller layer). The Core itself can also register for certain messages. An example for such an internally handled message is the entry of a new participant into the session. This will cause the Core to update its user list and request context data about new users from the server.

The very same message is also forwarded to the *Userbar*, which is responsible for the visual representation of the user list. In turn, the Userbar adds another user entry with a picture, name and controls (like kicking him from the session or starting a call). The Userbar is one example out of a big set of supplied *GUI* components not necessarily needed for co-browsing, as they are not synchronizing browser interaction between the participants. Other examples of this kind are the *Chat* or the

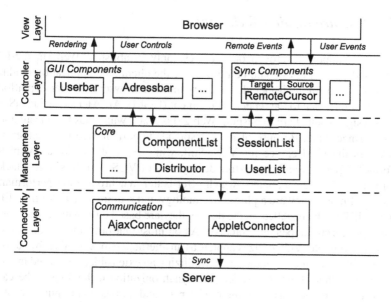

Fig. 15.19 Client-side application structure

Adressbar component. Depending on the application scenario, such components may easily be in- or excluded.

The most complex components are the ones that not only visualize remote actions, but also synchronize remotely generated document events. The mouse pointer combined with the attached picture of the other participant (called *RemoteCursor*) is the most important representative of these *Sync* components. In the case of the RemoteCursor, two actions are triggered by incoming messages. First, if the message was a "moving" message, the cursor is moved to the indicated new position. Second, local browser events are created to reflect the visible behavior. Thus, the browser (and the underlying website) are led to believe that the remote event was performed natively by the local user. This ensures that all site-specific JavaScript listeners, like rollover effects or Ajax operations, are triggered as well. The Sync component takes care that these remote events are not sent back to the server, which would cause an event loop.

Finally, there are also some components that intercept local events and send them to the server for synchronization. For example, every event triggered by the local user is received by the Source subcomponent of a Sync component (e.g., `mouse-move`, `mouseover`, `mouseclick`, `entering text`). The JavaScript events, which contain data like the event source or the mouse position, are then transformed into text-based messages, handed over to the Core and finally sent to the server by the Communication component.

15.5.6 Synchronization Techniques

In order to support heterogeneous devices, only established Web standards or widely used technologies could be utilized for the client-side application modules. JavaScript, for example, is included in every modern browser and offers a platform-independent interface to the rendered document (DOM). An extension of JavaScript that has a significant share in pushing Web 2.0 is Ajax, which has been available in browsers since 2005. Because of its widespread support, JavaScript together with Ajax offers the ideal choice for VCS. Still, while Ajax allows for a completely platform-independent and plugin-free deployment of VCS, it suffers from a lack of performance. Here, Java applets, which offer better synchronization performance, can help. Although they are a plug-in technology and require a Java Runtime Environment (JRE) to be installed on the device, they are based on a mature, widespread and also platform-independent standard. As on most platforms either Ajax or Java applets are available, VCS utilizes applets as an alternative to Ajax, thereby supporting nearly all browser configurations. By utilizing an extensible, text-based message protocol, it further allows the underlying synchronization technology to be easily exchanged at runtime, based on the preferences and software configuration of the user.

15.6 Discussion

Though CoCA-Browsing offers a plethora of new possibilities for online collaboration, it also introduces a number of new challenges that must be resolved in the future. The first and most immediate challenge concerns security in all its aspects, other challenges concern adaptation issues and dynamic web pages.

15.6.1 Security Aspects

First, because CoCAB acts as a proxy between clients and the Web, data transfer between clients and server can be intercepted, revealing visited URLs, interactions made and data entered into forms to intruders. However, this problem can easily be resolved by supporting an SSL connection between clients and the server.

Second, the rich awareness of other people that CoCA-Browsing offers, can be perceived as an intrusion into privacy. Especially if users anonymously navigate on shopping sites (as they do now), they may not want to be visible to others or even be approached. One possible solution to this problem is that, before users are made visible, they have to agree to this extended functionality. Even if they agreed, they must have the option to return to full anonymity at any time in the case that they have decided to no longer expose themselves.

Third, the synchronization of form field input may reveal sensitive data, which users may not want to share, but possibly have to enter in order to advance on a web page. This includes, for example, login data, credit card numbers, but may also affect personal data like location, name or age. We think that co-browsing in general requires a certain level of trust in other participants, especially if one is to visit personalized web sites. Still, CoCAB offers users the option to hide their form input from other participants by using the form protector (see Sect. 15.3.4). Also, password fields are protected by default. In that case, the sensitive data is not transferred at all, but only sent to the CoCAB server if the form is submitted. If the page resulting from the submit contains the protected data (e.g., for confirmation), this data is masked by the CoCAB server. However, subsequent requests do not use this functionality, thereby possibly revealing the information. Additionally, once a user has, for example, logged into his account on a web site, other participants may maliciously click links and trigger actions that the first user did not intend. This problem is alleviated in a scenario where one user has elevated rights (for instance, consultation), but not for scenarios with equal users, like co-shopping.

Fourth, operators of CoCAB can possibly read out all data that is transmitted within a session—including passwords and other private data that have been handled by the form protector. The basic question here is whether to trust the CoCAB-Server and its operator or not. As on websites where sensitive data is handled, a trust authority can be introduced to alleviate the problem. By certifying both the server code and its operator, users now must decide whether to trust the (probably known and accredited) certificate issuer.

15.6.2 Adaptation Level

We are aware of the fact that differing presentations may destroy the common ground for collaboration. Therefore we suggest that only adaptations techniques are utilized that do not change semantics of content, such as adjusting presentation or level-of-detail of information. Basically, there are two possible approaches to resolve the problem while still maintaining adapted variants for smallscreen devices.

On the one hand, a zoomable interface can be utilized to initially show the whole page resized. When a page element becomes the focus of the conversation (or someone points at it), it can be magnified, overlapping the page. While this is a suitable solution, it requires quite a bit of computing power to produce the resized page. Fortunately, a server-side resize could also eliminate that problem.

On the other hand, it is also possible to initially show only a minimum of common elements on the small device, revealing additional content as it becomes the focus of the other user. This scenario is especially applicable for on-site workers requesting some information from a manual. As they talk to the main-office supporter, more and more contents of the current page can be revealed as needed. The main disadvantage of this approach is that the owner of the smallscreen device must rely completely on the supporter, because he does not perceive the whole web page.

15.6.3 Enhanced Web Content

One big challenge for co-browsing is the advent of Ajax-enabled web sites. Because they manipulate the document and its elements at runtime, synchronization between users must be taken to a new level. An initial solution to this problem is to synchronize the document structure, which can be done by matching the DOM-trees of all participants (although this increases bandwidth need).

However, the real problem is that some of these document transformations are the direct result of user interactions while others are not: some pages periodically refresh their content or have even more intricate triggers for document changes. A final solution to this problem hasn't been found so far.

Another, quite similar challenge is the increasing use of Flash, although the problem is generic to any plugin-technology for the Web. As plugin content forms some sort of black box within the document that is not accessible via standard DOM, it is hard to synchronize user interaction done with this content. The only solution is to write special adapters that can intercept user interaction with these plugins and synchronize that as well. However, the success of such an approach is highly dependent on the quality of the interface the plugin offers to the browser. Additionally, for each type (and possibly version) of plugin content, additional adapters would need to be written, which is why this solution is not really viable.

15.7 Conclusion and Future Work

In this chapter we have described the concepts behind CoCAB, a novel approach to co-browsing, which allows a group of users to collaboratively browse arbitrary and dynamic web pages, thus enabling new forms of collaboration and consultation for the ever growing number of web applications. CoCAB acts as a mediator between users and the Web, with client-side modules running within the browser without any previous configuration or installation of software. Interactions with co-browsed content, like mouse clicks, form-filling, highlighting, etc. are synchronized within the group as well as mouse pointer positions. To address the problem of heterogeneous end user devices, we employ an adaptation mechanism that dynamically adapts the shared content to the group's and individual users' capabilities and preferences.

Most of the functionality described has been realized within VCS, a prototype that is marketed by the software company Comarch. Additionally, Comarch is working on the full implementation of more features for version 2.0 of VCS.

In the next future, we plan to add more features and domain-specific interaction techniques. Another problem we are working on is improved group awareness that will make collaborative work even more realistic. Furthermore, we want to improve the handling of concurrent interactions, such as two people filling form fields at the same time. Finally, we plan to evaluate our system regarding scalability and plan to add load balancing mechanisms to be able to cope with support scenarios on a larger scale.

As more and more applications are available online and the trend towards the social Web continues, CoCA-Browsing can be a major enabler for collaboration on the Web. By avoiding the hurdle of a huge software installation, anybody can use CoCAB, everywhere. Because it supports instant collaboration on any website, new web content is co-browsable immediately and web applications that were designed with a single user in mind can now be used cooperatively, without any changes.

Acknowledgements The VCS project was funded with means of the European Regional Development Fund 2000–2006 and with means of the Free State of Saxony. The authors especially want to thank Dr. Zoltán Fiala and the VCS team at Comarch, Dresden.

References

1. Atterer, R., Wnuk, M., Schmidt, A.: Knowing the user's every move—user activity tracking for website usability evaluation and implicit interaction. In: Proc. of the 5th Intl. World Wide Web Conference (WWW2006), Edinburgh (2006)
2. Baldauf, M., Dustar, S., Rosenberg, F.: A survey on context-aware systems. International Journal of Ad Hoc and Ubiquitous Computing 2(4), 263–277 (2007)
3. Bickmore, T.W., Girgensohn, A., Sullivan, J.W.: Web page filtering and reauthoring for mobile users. Computer Journal 42(6), 534–546 (1999)
4. Birbeck, M., Adida, B.: RDFa primer. W3C working draft, W3C. http://www.w3.org/TR/2008/WD-xhtml-rdfa-primer-20080317/ (March 2008)
5. Cabri, G., Leonardi, L., Zambonelli, F.: Supporting cooperative www browsing: A proxy-based approach. In: Proc. of the 7th Euromicro Workshop on Parallel and Distributed Processing, pp. 138–145, Madeira (1999)
6. Chen, H., Finin, T., Joshi, A.: An ontology for context-aware pervasive computing environments. In: Workshop on Ontologies and Distributed Systems (IJCAI-2003) (2003)
7. Chen, H., Perich, F., Finin, T., Joshi, A.: Soupa: Standard ontology for ubiquitous and pervasive applications. In: Intl. Conf. on Mobile and Ubiquitous Systems: Networking and Services (2004)
8. Chua, H.N., Scott, S.D., Choi, Y.W.: Framework for co-browsing on heterogeneous devices. In: AINA '06: Proc. of the 20th Intl. Conf. on Advanced Information Networking and Applications, pp. 195–199, Vienna, Austria (2006)
9. Coles, A., Deliot, E., Melamed, T., Lansard, K.: A framework for coordinated multi-modal browsing with multiple clients. In: Proc. of the 12th Intl. Conf. on World Wide Web, pp. 718–726, Budapest, Hungary (2003)
10. Cyr, D., Hassanein, K., Head, M., Ivanov, A.: The role of social presence in establishing loyalty in e-service environments. In: Interacting with Computers, vol. 19, pp. 43–56. Elsevier Science, New York (2007)
11. Dey, A.K., Abowd, G.D.: Towards a better understanding of context and context-awareness. Technical report GIT-GVU-99-22, Georgia Institute of Technology (1999)
12. Esenther, A.W.: Instant co-browsing: Lightweight real-time collaborative web browsing. In: Proc. of the 11th Intl. Word Wide Web Conf. (WWW2002) (2002)
13. Farnham, S., Zaner, M., Cheng, L.: Supporting sociability in a shared browser. In: Interact Conference (2001)
14. Fiala, Z.: Design and development of component-based adaptive web applications. PhD thesis, Technische Universität Dresden (2007)
15. Fiala, Z., Houben, G.J.: A generic transcoding tool for making web applications adaptive. In: The 17th Conf. on Advanced Information Systems Engineering (CAiSE'05), pp. 15–20 (2005)

16. Greenberg, S., Roseman, M.: Groupweb: A www browser as real time groupware. In: CHI'96: Conference Companion on Human Factors in Computing Systems, pp. 271–272. ACM, New York (1996)
17. Han, R., Perret, V., Naghshineh, M.: Websplitter: A unified xml framework for multi-device collaborative web browsing. In: Proc. of the ACM Conf. Computer Supported Cooperative Work (CSCW'00), pp. 221–230. ACM Press, Philadelphia (2000)
18. Hawkey, K., Inkpen, K.: Web browsing today: The impact of changing contexts on user activity. In: CHI '05 Extended Abstracts on Human Factors in Computing Systems, pp. 1443–1446. ACM, New York (2005)
19. Hinz, M.: Kontextsensitive Generierung adaptiver multimedialer Webanwendungen. PhD thesis, Technische Universität Dresden (2008)
20. Hinz, M., Pietschmann, S., Umbach, M., Meißner, K.: Adaptation and distribution of pipeline-based context-aware web architectures. In: Proc. of the 6th Working IEE/IFIP Conf. on Software Architecture (WICSA 2007) (2007)
21. Hoyos-Rivera, G.J., Gomes, R.L., Willrich, R., Courtiat, J.P.: Colab: A new paradigm and tool for collaboratively browsing the web. IEEE Transactions on Systems, Man, and Cybernetics 36(6), 1074–1085 (2006)
22. Hwang, Y., Seo, E., Kim, J.: Webalchemist: A structure-aware web transcoding system for mobile devices. In: Proc. of the WWW 2002 Workshop on Mobile Search, Honolulu, Hawaii (2002)
23. Jacobs, S., Gebhard, M., Kethers, S., Rzasa, W.: Filling html forms simultaneously: Coweb—architecture and functionality. In: Proc. of the 5th Intl. World Wide Web Conference on Computer Networks and ISDN Systems, pp. 1385–1395, Amsterdam, The Netherlands (1996)
24. Jensen, C., Farnham, S.D., Drucker, S.M., Kollock, P.: The effect of communication modality on cooperation in online environments. In: CHI '00: Proceedings of the SIGCHI Conference on Human Factors in Computing Systems, pp. 470–477. ACM, New York (2000)
25. Kernchen, R., Bonnefoy, D., Battestini, A., Mrohs, B., Wagner, M., Klemettinen, M.: Context-awareness in mobilife. In: Proc. of the 15th IST Mobile Summit, Mykonos, Greece (2006)
26. Khare, R.: Microformats: the next (small) thing on the semantic web. IEEE Internet Computing 10(1), 68–75 (2006)
27. Maly, K., Zubair, M., Li, L.: Cobrowser: Surfing the web using a standard browser. In: Proc. of the World Conf. on Educational Multimedia, Hypermedia and Telecommunications, pp. 1220–1225, Norfolk, VA (2001)
28. Manhart, P., Schmidt, K., Ziegler, H.: Group interaction in web-based multimedia market places. In: HICSS '98: Proceedings of the Thirty-First Annual Hawaii International Conference on System Sciences, vol. 7, p. 645. IEEE Comput. Soc., Washington (1998)
29. Marais, H., Bharat, K.: Supporting cooperative and personal surfing with a desktop assistant. In: UIST '97: Proceedings of the 10th Annual ACM Symposium on User Interface Software and Technology, pp. 129–138. ACM, New York (1997)
30. Prud'hommeaux, E., Seaborne, A.: SPARQL query language for RDF. http://www.w3.org/TR/rdf-sparql-query/ (2008)
31. Schmidt, A.: Ontology-based user context management: The challenges of imperfection and time-dependence. In: Proc. of ODBASE 2006, On the Move Federated Conferences (OTM) (2006)
32. Smith, J.R., Mohan, R., Li, C.-S.: Transcoding Internet content for heterogeneous client devices. In: Mohan, R. (ed.) Proc. of IEEE International Symposium on Circuits and Systems (ISCAS '98), vol. 3, pp. 599–602 (1998)
33. Strimpakou, M.A., Roussaki, I.G., Anagnostou, M.E.: A context ontology for pervasive service provision. In: Proc. of the 20th Intl. Conf. on Advanced Information Networking and Applications, vol. 2, pp. 775–779 (2006)

Chapter 16
NetPay Micro-Payment Protocols
for Three Networks

Xiaoling Dai and John Grundy

Abstract With the growth of information content accessible by web, peer-to-peer and mobile devices, new approaches to large volume, small value payment are needed. We describe the NetPay micro-payment protocol that we have extended from its original pay-per-click for web content to peer-to-peer networks and mobile device networks. We outline the key motivation for NetPay, the basic micro-payment protocol using e-coins and e-wallets, and our three variants of the protocol for different domains. We conclude with a discussion of our prototype implementations and evaluations of the NetPay protocol to date.

16.1 Introduction

There has been a huge growth in on-line content over the past ten years. This includes web content shared by client-server architectures e.g. newspapers, music, video, blogs, and a wide range of net communities. It also includes peer-to-peer communities to share information, music, videos, code and personal information. Mobile devices have become a common way to want to access this information.

Existing payment approaches for web-based content providers typically use macro-payment protocols i.e. credit cards or digital money. This is heavy-weight and expensive for very large numbers of very small value transactions so typically web sites utilize subscription or pay-for-volume models. These are sub-optimal for users wanting to use small fraction of the content paid for. They are also problematic if users want to use a large number of vendors (sellers) of content. Peer-to-peer networks for sharing information suffer a quite different but related problem, or lack of participation (sharing of content) by many peers. Enforcing sharing models is typically problematic and expensive and do not typically extend beyond single communities. Mobile devices used to purchase large volumes of small value content

X. Dai (✉)
The University of the South Pacific, Suva, Fiji Islands
e-mail: dai_s@usp.ac.fj

Y. Badr et al. (eds.) *Emergent Web Intelligence: Advanced Semantic Technologies,*
Advanced Information and Knowledge Processing,
DOI 10.1007/978-1-84996-077-9_16, © Springer-Verlag London Limited 2010

similar suffer problems of web-based systems, but also related connectivity and participatory issues found in peer-to-peer networks. Identity, privacy and security are problems in all domains where a level of anonymity is desired (or even required) by users but over-spending and fraud must be prevented.

We have developed NetPay, a micro-payment protocol for very large volume, small value transactions. A NetPay e-wallet and e-coins can be used for multiple vendor sites. The protocol uses one-way hashing for efficiency and it is an anonymous, off-line protocol not requiring point-of-failure and performance-reducing on-line central payment servers. We have recently extended the basic web-oriented Net-Pay protocol to the peer-to-peer and mobile commerce domains. In mobile networks NetPay must cope with the different characteristics of connectivity. In peer-to-peer networks NetPay must cope with the different dynamics of the vendor/customer (buyer/seller) relationship. We motivate the need for micro-payment systems with a concrete example in the following section, along with a survey of existing approaches to micro-payment in the web, peer-to-peer and mobile domains. We then describe each protocol in turn—the basic NetPay web-oriented protocol; the peer-to-peer content sharing protocol, and the mobile commerce-oriented protocol. We discuss advantages and disadvantages of our approaches and outline key areas for future research.

16.2 Motivation

Consider an e-greeting card site. This wants to sell e-greeting cards and related content on a per-card basis. In a traditional greeting card vendor both parties have numerous advantages: the buyer is anonymous and can use small cash transactions; the buyer pays only for what they use when they use it; and supplier is guaranteed payment (receiving cash or authorized debit or credit card payment). Disadvantages include limited volume and customer market due to physical cards, premises and payment processing. The e-greeting card company would ideally like to preserve the advantages of traditional payment approaches but with the inherent advantages of digital greeting cards and much larger potential customer base.

Traditional macro-payment systems provide disadvantages for the e-greeting card site and their customers. These include problems with having to take heavy-weight credit-card transactions, including a pay-per-transaction model, low performance due to use of a central authorization server, possible down time of this authorization server, and the overhead of large numbers of very small value transactions. Making customers use a subscription model is a disincentive for them as they may only want to produce a small number of e-greeting cards but have to pay for various services they do not require. Monthly billing of usage of the customer is risky for the e-greeting card site as the customer's credit card may have become invalid when billed. Some customers may not want to be identified by the e-greeting card provider and credit card and other e-money transactions are not anonymous like physical greeting cards.

A micro-payment approach should several potential advantages to seller and buyer. Payment may be anonymous for the buyer and large numbers of e-greetings can be bought for very small value. The buyer pays for only what they need and the seller is assured of payment with up-front fraud detection.

Consider a variation of the above with an e-greeting card provider with the sellers using mobile devices to send and receive e-greeting cards. The provider wants to provide low value, high volume content in the mobile application space—e.g. greeting "cards" via TXT, MMS or conventional web delivery, perhaps with rich content like sound, moving graphics and so on. Various approaches for payment exist from free, pay-by-advertising, to macro-payment via subscription, to debiting via the mobile network provider's billing mechanisms. All of these have disadvantages of expense and pay-for-not-using (macro-payment/subscription); inconvenience (in-situ advertising); and "clipping the ticket" additional expense (mobile provider billing system). Micro-payment offers support for very low-cost, very high-volume content (e.g. even pay per image/sound in content of e-card).

Consider a peer-to-peer network on which e-greeting cards are designed ("sold") and used ("bought") by community members, for example in the Second Life immersive reality system. In this domain a quite different dynamic exists between vendors (sellers) and customers (buyers), where ideally a community spirit would develop with mutual buying and selling of content. Unfortunately in many peer-to-peer networks a few vendors/sellers are dominating by much larger base of customers/buyers. This may work if real money is used to pay for content, but the community breaks down if too many "free-loaders" dominate. Micro-payment offers an interesting way of encouraging contribution via "token" exchange (e-coins) which may or may not be translated into real money.

Key requirements for Client–server, P2P and Mobile micro-payment systems are generally agreed to be [13, 16]:

- Security of the electronic coins ("e-coins") from both fraud and double-spending by customers
- Ideally anonymous like traditional cash—the vendor has no idea who the customer is
- Transferability:
  - Vendor-transferable e-coins allowing customers to buy coins from a broker and spend at many different e-commerce sites
  - The recipient of a coin can spend that coin with other peers without having to contact the issuer
- Off-line processing of payments i.e. no on-line bank authorization server needed by vendor or client during payment processing, and highly scalable architecture to support very large numbers of clients concurrently using a vendor site with low-impact on vendor site efficiency

Several micro-payment systems have been developed that are based on the Payword-based micro-payment protocol [18]. These systems can be classified as credit-based and debit-based. Payword [18] is an off-line credit-based system. The customer only needs to contact the broker at the beginning of each certificate lifetime in order to obtain a new-signed certificate. The system aims to minimize the number of public key operations required per payment using hash operations instead whenever possible. It is a credit-based scheme where a user's account is not debited until some time after the purchases that he or she made. This unfortunately provides more opportunities for fraud since a large number of purchases can be made against an account with insufficient funds. NMP [14] is a credit-based protocol that improves the fairness for customers from the Payword protocol. These Payword-based micro-payment systems do share a key disadvantage—they are all vendor specific. The "e-coins" (paywords) in these systems are only usable at one vendor and have no value for any other vendor. E-coupons [17] is a credit-based, off-line scheme that allows customers to pay for services from a variety of devices, not requiring users to re-register each device. It uses a delegation approach and a SPKI/SDSI multi-seed certificate [3] to ensure security of the payword chain and low-overhead hashing functions rather than public-key encryption. Unfortunately the paywords are again vendor-specific and the protocol complex to implement.

There are a number of recent Peer-to-Peer-oriented micro-payment systems such as PPay [22], WhoPay [21], and Cpay [24]. Most existing Peer-to-Peer (P2P) micro-payment technologies proposed or prototyped to date suffer from problems with communication overheads, dependence on on-line brokers, lack of scalability, and lack of coin transferability. Transferability improves anonymity and performance of the systems, but complicates the security issues. A novel concept of floating and self-managed currency is introduced by PPay [22], so that each peer's transaction does not involve any broker. The coins can float from one peer to another peer and the owner of a given coin manages the currency itself, except when it is created or cashed. WhoPay [21] is a scalable and anonymous payment system for P2P environments and inherits the basic architecture of PPay. Coins have the same life cycle as in PPay and are identified by public keys. A user purchases coins from a broker and spends them with other peers. These other peers may decide whether to spend the coin with another peer or to redeem them with the broker. Coins must be renewed periodically to retain their value. Coins are renewed or transferred through their coin owners if they are online or through the broker. CPay [24] exploits the heterogeneity of the peers. CPay is a debit based protocol. The broker is responsible for the distribution and redemption of the coins and the management of eligible peers called a Broker Assistant (BA). The Broker does not participate in any transaction, only the payer, payee and the BA is involved. The BA is the eligible peer which the payer maps to and is responsible for checking the coin and authorization of the transaction. Every peer will have a BA to check its transaction. CPay offers anonymity so that the BA peer will not know who the payee is where as in Group CPay as the number of peer escalates, the broker workload increases to overcome this, many BA peers will be responsible for one transaction.

Various micro-payment protocols that have been specifically designed for selling information goods on the Internet have been reused and further developed to support wireless communication device-based payment [1, 12, 23]. Huang and Chen [12] proposed a micro-payment system for use on mobile phones using secret-key certificates. The signature of this model is an electronic payment token which must contain a number to indicate its value and its recipient name like a cheque in the real world. Mobile-Millicent [1] protocol uses the Millicent micro-payment scheme originally developed for web-based micro-payment transactions. Mobile-Millicent is based on two "scrips" which are specific to Vendor and may be validated by a Broker namely the broker scrip and vendor scrip. Zhu [23] protocol uses payment tokens that are based on hash chain constructions. A mobile user attaches to the network through an access network operator and releases a stream of micro-payment token to pay all the vendors as he/she continues to make purchases. The connection may pass through one or more other network operators before reaching the destination vendor.

16.3 NetPay Micro-Payment Protocol for E-commerce in Client–Server Networks

We have developed a micro-payment protocol called NetPay that provides a secure, cheap, widely available, and debit-based protocol for an off-line micro-payment system in client–server networks [9]. NetPay differs from previous Payword-based protocols by using touchstones that are signed by the broker and an e-coin index signed by vendors, which are passed from vendor to vendor. The signed touchstone is used by a vendor to verify the electronic currency and the signed index is used to prevent double spending from customers and to resolve disputes between vendors. In this section, we outline the key transactions used in our NetPay protocol.

There are a number of cryptography and micro-payment terminologies used in the NetPay micro-payment protocol. A brief definition of these key terminologies are given as follows:

1. One-Way Hash Function The one-way hash function MD5 (Message Digest) used in the NetPay implementation is an algorithm that has two key properties. It seems impossible to give an example of hash function used in hash chain in a form of normal functions in mathematics. The difficulties include:
   (a) The value of a mathematical function is a real or complex number (a data value for hash function);
   (b) It is always possible to compute the set for a given y for a mathematical function h (not satisfying the two properties of the hash function).
2. Payword Chain A *payword chain* is generated by using a one way hash function. Suppose we want to generate a payword chain which contains ten *paywords* (i.e. e-coins). We need to randomly pick a payword seed $W11$ and then compute a payword chain by repeatedly hashing

   $$W10 = h(W11), \quad W9 = h(W10), \quad \ldots, \quad W1 = h(W2), \quad W0 = h(W1)$$

   where $h(.)$ is a hash function such as MD5 and $W0$ is the root for the chain. The MD5 algorithm is one of the series of messages in hash algorithms and involves appending a length field to a message and padding it up to a multiple of 512 bit blocks. This means that every payword Wi is stored as a 32 length string in a database. A payword chain is going to be used to represent a set of E-coins in the P2P-NetPay system.

3. E-coin An *e-coin* is a payword element such as $W1$ or $W10$. The value of a payword e-coin might be one cent but could be some other value.
4. E-wallet An *e-wallet* is used to store e-coins and send e-coins to a vendor paying for information goods, i.e. it shows one or more payword chains.
5. Touchstone (T) A *touchstone* is a root $W0$ and is used to verify the paywords $W1, W2, \ldots, W10$ by taking the hash of the paywords in order $W1$ first $[h(W1) = W0]$, then $W2[h(h(W1)) = W0]$, and so on. This is used to verify the e-coins are *valid* i.e. have not been forged.
6. Index (I) An *index* is used to indicate the current spent amount of each e-coin (payword) chain. For example if you have spent 2 cs $(W1, W2)$ to buy an information goods, the current index value is 3 in the previous example of a chain $W1 \ldots W10$.

16.3.1 NetPay Transactions

Suppose an e-greeting card site wants to use the NetPay micro-payment system to sell e-greeting cards on a per-card usage basis. The system involves four parties— a NetPay broker site; e-greeting card or e-music vendor sites; customer PCs; and a bank macro-payment system. Customers can be classified as registered customers and unregistered customers. Only registered customers can buy e-coins from a broker's site and use their NetPay e-wallet to click-buy an e-greeting card from an e-greeting card site. Both types of customers can search and view e-greeting cards on-line. Initially a customer accesses the broker's web site to register and acquire a number of e-coins from the broker (bought using a single macro-payment). The broker then creates an *e-wallet* that includes the e-coin ID, touchstone, and e-coins for the customer. This e-wallet may reside on the client PC (via a special application or browser cookies) or be passed server-side to vendor servers.

The customer browses the home page of the e-greeting card web site and finds a desired e-greeting card to buy. Each e-greeting card will typically have a small cost e.g. 5–20 c, and the customer would typically buy a number of these. When wishing to send the e-greeting card, the customer clicks on the send button and the vendor system debits the customer's e-coins by e.g. 10 c (by taking 1, 2 or more e-coins from their payword chain, depending on the monetary value of each, up to 10 c in value).

The e-greeting system verifies that the e-coin provided by the customer's e-wallet is valid by use of a *touchstone* obtained once only from the broker. If the payment is valid (coin is verified and sufficient credit remains), the card is sent to the receiver. The customer may browse other e-greeting cards, their coins being debited (the index of spent coins incremented) each time an e-greeting card is sent. If coins run out, the customer is directed to the broker's site to buy more. The e-greeting system keeps copies of the spent e-coins.

When the customer changes to another online vendor e.g. an e-music site (or another kind of vendor using the same e-coin broker currency), the new vendor site

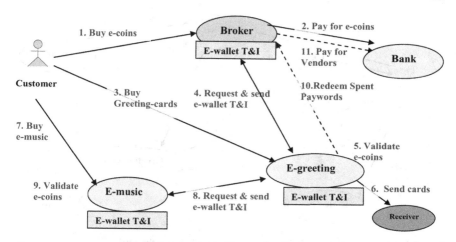

Fig. 16.1 Server-side e-wallet NetPay basic interactions between the parties

first requests the current e-coin touchstone information from e-greeting's vendor site. The e-music vendor contacts the e-greeting vendor to get the e-coin touchstone and *spent coin* index and then debits coins for further e-music.

When the e-greeting vendor system is *down*, a backup server in the system sends the e-coin ID, the touchstone, and the index to the broker. The e-music vendor could also contact the broker to get the e-coin touchstone and the *spent e-coin* index. At the end of each day, the vendors all send the spent e-coins to the broker, redeeming them for real money (done by macro-payment bank transfer from the broker to vendor accounts).

We have designed two kinds of e-wallets to manage e-coins in the NetPay system [6]. One is hosted by vendor servers and is passed from vendor to vendor as the customer moves from one site to another. The second is a client-side application resident on the client's PC. The following sub-sections briefly outline the communication architectures used to realize these two NetPay micro-payment approaches.

16.3.1.1 Server-Side E-wallet

Some people prefer to access the Internet from multiple computers (e.g. a business person who often travels around). A Server-side hosted e-wallet is suitable for these people. The server-side e-wallet is stored on the vendor server and is transferred from the broker to each vendor when required.

Initially a customer accesses the broker's web site to register and buy a number of e-coins from the broker (1) using a single macro-payment (2). The broker saves an E-wallet that includes the e-coin chain. When the customer wishes to purchase greeting cards from the e-greeting site (3), the e-greeting site sends a request to the Broker and the broker sends the customer's e-wallet and T and I to e-greeting site (4) and then the e-greeting site debits and verifies the e-coins by using T and I (5). If the payment is valid, the greeting card is sent to the destination (6). The customer

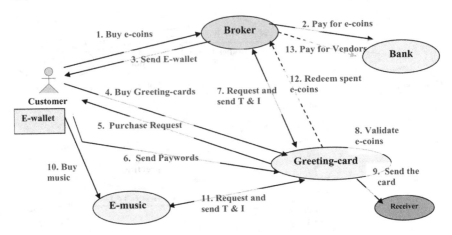

Fig. 16.2 Client-side e-wallet NetPay basic interactions between the parties

may purchase other greeting cards, their coins being debited. If coins run out, the customer is directed to the broker's site to buy more. When the customer changes to the e-music vendor site (7), the e-music site requests the e-wallet and T and I from the e-greeting site and then debits e-coins for further e-music (9). At the end of each day, the vendors send all the spent e-coins to the broker redeeming them (10) for real money (11).

In this model, each customer's e-wallet held on the server-side and passed from vendor to vendor, reducing communication overhead to the customer client PC and allowing the customer to use the e-wallet from different machines. However this approach requires the customer to log into each vendor site initially which may become annoying.

16.3.1.2 Client-Side E-wallet

Some people prefer to access the Internet using one machine (e.g. those who stay home most of the time or access sites from a single work PC only). A client-side e-wallet is more suitable for these kinds of customers. The client-side e-wallet is an application running on the client PC that holds e-coin information.

Initially a customer accesses the broker's web site to register and buy a number of e-coins from the broker (1) using a single macro-payment (1). The broker sends an *e-wallet* that includes the e-coin chain to the customer (3). When the customer wishes to purchase greeting-cards from the e-greeting vendor site (4), the e-greeting system sends a purchase request to the customer's e-wallet (5) and the e-wallet sends e-coins to the e-greeting site (6). Then the e-greeting site gets T and I from the broker (7) and verifies the e-coins (8). If the payment is valid, the e-greeting card is sent to the receiver (9). The customer may purchase other greeting-cards, their coins being debited. When the customer changes to the e-music vendor site (10), the e-music system first requests the current e-coin I and T from the e-greeting site and then debits e-coins for further e-music (11). At the end of each day, the vendors send all the spent e-coins to the broker redeeming them (12) for real money (13).

Customers can buy greeting-cards and e-music using the client-side e-wallet at different sites without the need to log in after the e-wallet application is downloaded to their PC. Their e-coins are resident on their own PC and so access to them is never lost due to network outages to one vendor. The e-coin debiting time is slower for a client-side e-wallet than the server-side e-wallet due to the extra communication between vendor application server and customer PC's e-wallet application. We have implemented a variant of this approach using browser cookies to temporarily hold part of a customer's e-wallet supporting faster repeated spends at a single vendor site.

16.3.2 NetPay Architectures

We developed a software architecture for implementing NetPay-based micro- payment systems for thin-client web applications that used hard-coded vendor facilities for micro-payment [4] and component-based NetPay vendor services, supporting much more easily and seamlessly reused vendor server-side NetPay functionality [5, 8]. This architecture is illustrated in Fig. 16.3. The vendor web sites (e-greeting or e-music) provide a web server and possibly a separate application server, depending on the web-based system architecture they use. The vendor web server pages provide content that needs to be paid for and each access to these pages require one or more e-coins from the customers' E-wallets in payment. In our architecture vendor application server accesses the Broker application server to obtain touchstone information to verify the e-coins being spent and to redeem spent e-coins. They communicate with other vendor application servers to pass on e-coin indexes and touchstones.

Vendors may use quite different architectures and implementation technology. In the example above, Vendor #1 uses a web server with Perl-implemented CGI scripts, C++-implemented application server and relational database. Vendor #2 uses a J2EE-based architecture with J2EE server providing Java Server Pages (web user interface services) and Enterprise Java Beans (application server services), along with a relational database to hold vendor data.

16.4 P2P-NetPay for Content Sharing in Peer-to-Peer Networks

A peer-to-peer architecture is a network where one peer exchanges resources with other peers as required without heavy use of a central server. A Central Indexing Server (CIS) is used to index all users who are currently online. This server does not host any content itself but provides support for peers to locate content from other peers. Queries on the index server are used to find other connected peers with content required and inform peers where to find the requested content. The peers

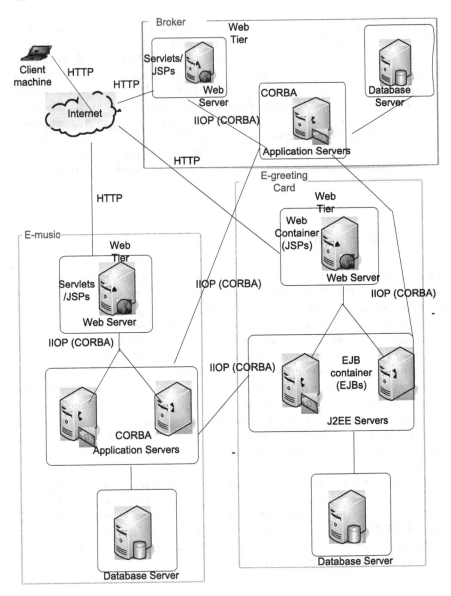

Fig. 16.3 Basic NetPay software architecture in client–server networks

will attempt to establish a connection with the computer hosting the information requested. In peer-to-peer applications, there is no any clear distinction between vendors and customers. There are simply peers which can be vendors or customers or both.

P2P applications enable users to exchange content over P2P networks. The success of these systems depend on users' willingness to share computing resources and exchange content. Napster [20] was designed to help its users to trade music files, however, P2P applications could exchange any kind of digital document. The file sharing is free by peers in most current P2P systems. Since peers do not benefit from serving files to others, many users decline to provide services to others. This emerging phenomenon of *selfish* individuals in P2P systems is known as the free-rider problem. There is a trend towards charging for every file download in order for peers make direct profit from files they upload [19]. As an alternative approach consider micro-payment coins being used as *tokens* in a P2P network. A customer (*requesting*) peer can spend tokens at a vendor (*supplying*) peer using e-coins. The P2P system broker can be used to encourage supplying as well as requesting using redeemed e-coins to track and possibly balance supplying and requesting behavior.

16.4.1 P2P-NetPay Transactions

To support this approach we introduce requesting peers (R-peers) and supplying peers (S-peers) in our protocol. Based on the client-side e-wallet NetPay protocol which is discussed in Sect. 16.3.1, we proposed an adaption to a P2P-NeyPay protocol that is suitable for P2P-based network environments [7]. P2P-NetPay protocol is an off-line system and uses touchstones that are signed by the CIS which is the broker in NetPay protocol and an e-coin index signed by supplying peers. In this section, we describe the key transactions in P2P-NetPay protocol in P2P networks. Initially an R-peer accesses the CIS's web site to register and buy a number of e-coins from the CIS (1) using a single macro-payment (2). The CIS sends an *e-wallet* that includes the e-coin chain to the R-peer (3). The R-peer searches the interesting files which are allocated on the S-peer1 with CIS and purchases files from S-peer1 (4), the S-peer1 system sends a purchase request to the R-peer (5) and the e-wallet sends e-coins and T and I to the S-peer1 system (6). Then S-peer1 verifies the e-coins (7). If the payment is valid, the R-peer downloads the files from S-peer1 (8). The R-peer may purchase other files, their coins being debited. When the R-peer changes to S-peer2, S-peer2 system debits e-coins for further music file downloading (9). At the end of each day, the peers send all the spent e-coins to the CIS redeeming them (10) for real money (11).

Good P2P community behavior can be encouraged or even enforced by the CIS. This can monitor amount of requesting vs providing and limit requests if provision insufficient. As suppliers redeem e-coins daily the CIS can limit amount of e-coins that can be purchased based on prior request/supply behavior. Real money and a real BANK may not necessarily be involved—the currency could be nominal or fictitious e.g. Second Life or other P2P network currency.

16.4.2 P2P-NetPay Architecture

We developed a software architecture for implementing P2P-NetPay micro-payment system supporting P2P-based network environments for purchasing information

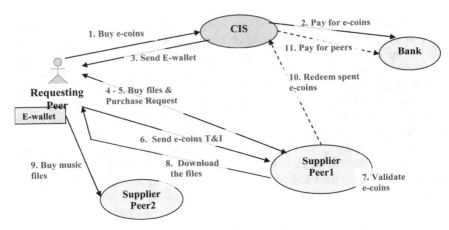

Fig. 16.4 P2P-NetPay basic interactions between the parties

goods. The transactions involve three key parties: the CIS (Broker) server, the requesting peer (R-peer) server, and the provider peer (S-peer) servers. This architecture is illustrated in Fig. 16.5.

The CIS provides a database holding all peer's information, generated coins and payments, redeemed coins and macro-payments made (buying coins and redeeming money to peers). The CIS application server provides a set of CORBA interfaces peer servers communicate with to request touchstones and redeem e-coins. We chose to provide CORBA interfaces for peers to communicate with the CIS for language and platform independence and the flexibility to add desired authentication and encryption mechanisms. The CIS web server provides a point of access for peers to buy e-coins and search for files which are allocated in other peers.

When buying e-coins the CIS's application server generates the peer's e-wallet (cached e-coin information). When purchasing information using micro-payment, the peer's server accesses e-coin information using the peer's e-wallet. The P2P-NetPay peer provides a small server and possibly a web server, depending on the peer's system architecture they use. The P2P-NetPay peer servers provide content that could be downloaded by other peers and needs to be paid for and each download to these files require one or more e-coins from the peers' e-wallets in payment.

In our architecture P2P-NetPay peer server accesses the CIS application server to obtain touchstone information to verify the e-coins being spent and to redeem spent e-coins. P2P-NetPay peer may use quite different architectures and implementation technology. P2P-NetPay peer could use a simple socket-based architecture along with a relational database to hold P2P-NetPay peer data.

16.5 Mobile-NetPay for Mobile Commerce in Wireless Networks

With the growth of mobile computing technologies, the popularity of mobile devices such as mobile phone, PDAs has increased over the past few years. A wide

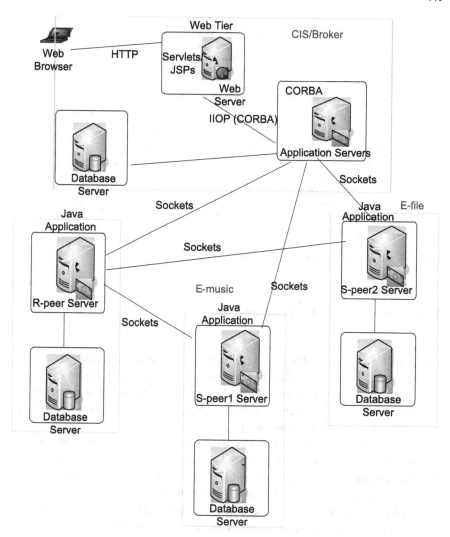

Fig. 16.5 Basic P2P-NetPay system software architecture in P2P networks

range of software applications can be deployed on these mobile terminals and can communicate with other applications or information systems through a wireless network. A mobile device user could carry out the following tasks using a mobile device: (1) purchasing images, music clips, wallpapers and ring-tones; (2) sending e-greeting cards to others; and (3) accessing various information sources for weather, shopping, tourism, etc.

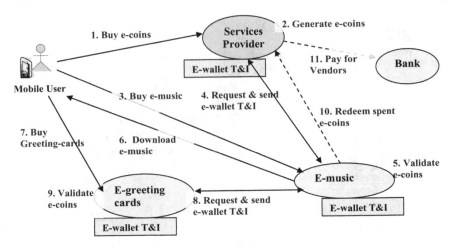

Fig. 16.6 Mobile-NetPay basic interactions between the parties

16.5.1 Mobile-NetPay Transactions

A Mobile-NetPay protocol based on the client-side e-wallet was designed for wireless network environments [10]. The problem with this approach is that mobile-users must download an e-wallet application software from a broker. This is not always suitable for mobile-phone users to buy music clips, wallpapers and ring-tones online due to the great variability of mobile devices.

Based on the server-side e-wallet NetPay, a new Mobile-NetPay protocol uses touchstones that are signed by the Service Provider (Network Operator) which could be a broker and an e-coin index signed by vendors. The e-wallet is stored on the vendor server and is transferred from the broker to each vendor when required. In this section, we describe the key transactions in the new Mobile-NetPay protocol.

Initially a mobile-user sends a request to the Service Provider (SP) and buys a number of e-coins from the SP (1). SP debits money from the mobile-user's account to pay for the e-coins and generates e-coins which are saved in an *e-wallet* (2). When the mobile-user wishes to purchase e-music from the e-music vendor site (3), the e-music site sends a request to the SP and the mobile-user's e-wallet and T and I are sent to e-music site (4). Then the e-music site debits and verifies the e-coins by using T and I (5). If the payment is valid, the mobile-user downloads the music to the mobile device (6). The mobile-user may purchase other music, their coins being debited. When the mobile-user changes to the e-greeting vendor site (7), the site first requests the e-wallet, current e-coin validating information from the e-music site (8) and then debits e-coins for further e-greeting cards (9). At the end of each day, the vendors send all the spent e-coins to the broker redeeming them (10) for real money (11).

16.5.2 Mobile-NetPay Architectures

As discussed in Sect. 16.3.2, we initially developed a software architecture for implementing NetPay-based micro-payment systems for thin-client web applications that used hard-coded and J2EE-based vendor facilities for micro-payment. We have extended this work to develop component-based Mobile-NetPay vendor services, supporting vendor server-side Mobile-NetPay functionality.

Figure 16.7 shows the architecture used in Mobile-NetPay system. There are four main parties playing the main roles Broker, e-greeting card, e-music and the mobile-users. Service provider could be a broker for debiting money from mobile-user account; generating e-coins and redeeming e-coins for vendors. Vendors have mobile-based browsing on the client side for Mobile-NetPay payments. Mobile browsing has built upon WML scripting technology and WAP technology. All the mobile browsing is done via the WAP Gateway which handles the entire mobile interface trans-coding. WAP gateway server is to convert WAP data to http compatible data.

The Vendor web server pages provide greeting-cards or e-music that needs to be paid for and each access to these pages require one or more e-coins from the mobile-users' e-wallets in payment. In our architecture Vendor Java EE application server accesses the Service Provider Java EE application server through Java RMI protocol (JRMP) to obtain touchstone information to verify the e-coins being spent and to redeem spent e-coins. They communicate with other vendor Java EE application servers to pass on e-wallets, indexes and touchstones.

Vendors use a Java EE-based architecture with Java EE Application Server providing Java Server Pages with WML (mobile-user interface services) and Enterprise Java Beans (application server services). In the application server tier, the processes can be separated on different server machines having the capabilities of multi-tasking and multi-threading for high usage performance. The Enterprise server also has the capability of multi-threading for the database connections which can run 100 users request simultaneously as configured in the system. Vendor systems could use Microsoft SQL Server 2000 database server for Enterprise Information System (EIS) tier.

16.6 Discussion

In this section, we compare the features of our P2P-NetPay and Mobile-NetPay protocols with other micro-payment protocols. We compare P2P-NetPay and Mobile-NetPay protocols' characteristics to a number of other well-known micro-payment systems and some more recent micro-payment systems. The comparison criteria we have used below are based on the key requirements identified in Sect. 16.2: an easy-to-use micro-payment system; secure electronic coins; transferable e-coins between vendors; anonymity of customer at vendors; robust, low performance impact with off-line micro-payment supported; and architecture is scalable for very large number of customers and low-value transactions.

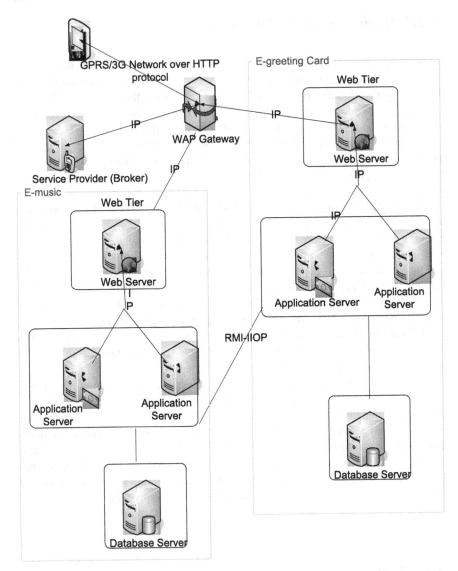

Fig. 16.7 Mobile-NetPay micro-payment architecture in mobile networks

16.6.1 P2P Micro-Payment Systems Comparison

Our comparison is for the scenario of peers downloading useful files or other content from other peers, and a Centre Index Server which includes the micro-payment brokers. Table 16.1 lists the results of our requirements satisfaction comparison for our P2P-NetPay protocol with several other micro-payment systems in the P2P domain.

Table 16.1 Comparison of P2P micro-payment methods

System property	CPay	PPay	WhoPay	TaM	P2P-NetPay
Security	**High**, detects double spending timely	**Medium**, floating coins introduces delay in fraud detection	**High**	**Medium**, the forging of tokens is still possible	**Medium+**, prevents double spending by using index
Anonymity	**High**	**Low**, Peers anonymity not supported	**High**	**Low**, Peers anonymity not supported	**High**
Transferability	**High**, the recipient of a coin can spend with other peers through BAs	**High**, the recipient of a coin can spend with other peers by using layered coins	**High**, the recipient of a coin can spend with other peers by using public key operation per purchase	**Medium**, the tokens can be spent to many P-peers with the account holders	**Medium**, an e-coin chain of R-peer can be spent at many S-peers
Low performance impact and robust	**Offline** for broker but BA peers are almost **Online**, the system contacts BA during every transaction	**Online** downtime protocol. Floating coins growing in size affects the performance which causes delay in transactions	**Online** downtime protocol, use of public key operation on every transaction	The account holders are **Online**	**Offline**, R-peers only communicate with S-peers

In the PPay downtime protocol, the broker must be on-line when the peers wish to re-assign the coins and the broker has to check when peers came back on-line. In order to avoid the above problems, a concept of *layered coins* is used in the PPay protocol. The layered coins are used to float the coins from one peer to another. Each layer represents a reassignment request and the broker and the owner of the coins can peel off all the layers to obtain all the necessary proofs. The layered coins introduce a delay to the fraud detection and the floating coins growing in size. Who-Pay presents anonymity, fairness and transferability. However it is not economical for very high-volume, low-cost transactions because it uses a heavy-weight public key encryption operation per *purchase*. CPay prevents double spending timely and it is an offline system. The performance will not be extremely high as there is involvement of the BAs in every transaction. It is also not economical since it uses heavy-weight algorithms to do consistent hashing to find the mapping BA for a peer. In Tokens as Micropayment (TaM) system [15], each token symbolizes a specific amount of money. Peers use tokens to pay for downloading files. In order to prevent double spending for each peer in the P2P system there requires a set of third peers—account holder set which keep track of the tokens issued to a peer and tokens spent by the peer. Before a service session begins, the requesting peer discloses to the provider the IDs of the tokens the requesting peer intends to spend for downloading files. The supplier peer can check if these tokens are valid. To avoid that the requesting peer double spends the tokens in a parallel transaction, account holders will mark these tokens as intended to be spent. The account holders are online. A token is not anonymous in TaM because its main purpose is to provide accountability in a P2P system.

P2P-NetPay [11] is an offline protocol with the broker only involved when purchasing and redeeming e-coins or verifying touchstone when requester first contacts a new supplier. Since only the broker knows the mapping between the pseudonyms (IDc) and the true identity of a R-peer, the protocol protects the peer's privacy. The protocol prevents peers from double spending and any internal and external adversaries from forging. Transferability is an important criterion which improves anonymity and performance of the P2P systems. The e-coin chain in P2P-NetPay protocol is transferable between S-peers to enable R-peers to spend e-coins in the same coin chain to make numbers of small payments to multiple S-peers. P2P-NetPay supports transferability between S-peers without extra actions on the part of the R-peer and the broker.

16.6.2 Mobile Micro-Payment Systems Comparison

Our comparison is for the scenario of a mobile user purchasing an on-line e-greeting card, e-greeting vendors, and micro-payment brokers which reside on the mobile Service Provider system. Table 16.2 lists the results of this requirements satisfaction comparison for our Mobile-NetPay protocol with these other payment systems.

Huang's Protocol [12] is a fully-online approach. The payment token is vendor-specific and has no value to other vendors. Mobile-Millicent protocol [1] is semi-online; mobile user has to be connected to the broker (online) in order to be able to make further purchase and payment to a new or different or next vendor. The vendor scrip is vendor-specific and has no value to other vendors though the new scrip returned to the mobile user from the first vendor after the initial purchase can be used for further transaction payments to the same vendor. Zhu's protocol [23] is an off-line system for the broker, but it is almost an on-line micro-payment system for the network operator. The network operator needs to generate a corresponding endorsement hash for every payword chain, which is sent by a mobile user. Then network operator sends the valid paywords and the corresponding endorsement paywords to the vendor in every transaction. The e-coin in the system is user and vendor specific. Extended Self-Renewal Hash Chains scheme (BSRHC) [2] is

Table 16.2 Comparison of the mobile micro-payment models

Characteristics or features	Huang's Protocol	Mobile-Millicent protocol	Zhu's Protocol	BSRHC	Mobile-NetPay
Security	**High**, MU and V cannot double spend and double deposit a valid payment token	**Medium**, double spending can be prevented by the use of Vendor-specific scrip	**High**, NO authorizes payment & generate a corresponding endorsement hash for V in every payment	**High**, according to the two important properties of Hash, the paywords will not to be forged.	**Very high**, B keeps the Seed W_{n+1} to prevent MU and V from over-spending and forging paywords.
Anonymity	**Medium**, the privacy of MU is guaranteed even if B collides with V	**Low**, B knows who and where but not what; V knows what not who	**Medium**, user releases payment token to Vendors through connection to NO	**Medium**, MU and vendor adopt anonymous methods for the transaction	**High**, user's identity is fully protected from the Vendor
Low performance impact and robust	**On-line**, the system requires MU to contact B for each payment	**Almost On-line**, MU has to be connected to the B when MU changes to new V	**Offline** for B and **On-line** for NO	**Online**, the system requires the vendor contacts broker when MU change to another vendor	**Offline**, transfer of T and I between the Vs or via NO does not involve B
Transferability	**Very low**, token withdrawn from the B is Vendor-specific	**Low**, vendor scrip is Vendor-specific and has no value to other vendor	**Medium**, generation of endorsement chain commitment for each visit	**Low**, MU and the vendor negotiate a secure one-way hash function	**High**, coins can be transferred freely between Vs for multiple purchases

an online micro-payment scheme based on SRHC and provide secure and fairness features for mobile commerce. In the protocol, the mobile user and the vendor must accomplish the identity authentication, and establish session key. The vendor requests broker to check whether mobile user's account balance exceeds price of the information services to prevent mobile user overdrawing. After authentication and verification are passed, mobile user and the vendor negotiate a secure one-way hash function for payment. Mobile user transmits the values of n hash chain nodes to the vendor as paywords. The vendor replies n units of information services. The scheme is fit for the long-term and frequent micro-transaction between mobile users and the same vendor.

Mobile-NetPay [10] is an off-line, debit-based protocol with the broker used to verify touchstones initially per vendor and to buy/redeem e-coins. The Mobile-NetPay protocol prevents mobile users from double spending using an e-coin Index and any internal and external adversaries from forging. Mobile-NetPay can easily handle multiple transactions between vendors. The paywords in Mobile-NetPay protocol are not user-specific and vendor-specific, allowing a single e-wallet to provide payment across a wide range of vendors of mobile content. Anonymity is preserved for the customer from the vendors i.e. the vendors have no way of identifying the customers spending e-coins, as in a cash-based conventional payment scenario.

16.7 Summary

We have been developing micro-payment protocols and software architectures to realize these protocols for web-based customers and vendors. These protocols can be extended to cater for peer-to-peer sharing networks and mobile e-commerce. These new domains—P2P networks and mobile e-commerce—introduce additional constraints and requirements. However the basic protocols and architectures can be reused in these application domains. Key requirements of customer anonymity to vendor; off-line (i.e. no continuous third party broker involvement) support for customer/vendor interaction; very fast and computationally feasible encryption via one-way hash algorithms; and scalable architectures for very large scale customer, vendor and very low-value transactions, can be met in these web e-commerce, P2P and mobile e-commerce domains. We are currently implementing our P2P-NetPay and Mobile-NetPay micro-payment models and validating this with on-line information vending applications (including e-greeting card, e-music and informational content sites).

References

1. Boddupalli, P., Al-Bin-Ali, F., Davies, N., Friday, A., Storz, O., Wu, M.: Payment support in ubiquitous computing environments. In: 5th IEEE Workshop on Mobile Computing Systems & Applications. Monterey, California, USA (2003)
2. Chen, L., X, Li., Shi, M.: A novel micro-payment scheme for m-commerce based on self-renewal hash chains. In: IEEE International Conference on Communications, Circuits and Systems, pp. 1343–1346 (2007)
3. Clarke, D., Elien, J.E., Ellison, C., Fredette, M., Morcos, A., Rivest, R.: Certificate chain discovery in SPKI/SDSI. Journal of Computer Security 9, 285–322 (2001)
4. Dai, X., Grundy, J.: Architecture of a micro-payment system for thin-client web applications. In: Proceedings of the 2002 International Conference on Internet Computing, pp. 444–450. CSREA Press (2002)
5. Dai, X., Grundy, J.: Architecture for a component-based, plug-in micro-payment system. In: Proceedings of the Fifth Asia Pacific Web Conference. Lecture Notes in Computer Science, vol. 2642, pp. 251–262. Springer, Berlin (2003)

6. Dai, X., Grundy, J.: Three kinds of e-wallets for a NetPay micro-payment system. In: The Fifth International Conference on Web Information Systems Engineering. Lecture Notes in Computer Science, vol. 3306, pp. 66–77. Springer, Berlin (2004)
7. Dai, X., Grundy, J.: Off-line micro-payment system for content sharing in P2P networks. In: 2nd International Conference on Distributed Computing & Internet Technology (ICDCIT 2005). Lecture Notes in Computer Science, vol. 3816, pp. 297–307. Springer, Berlin (2005)
8. Dai, X., Grundy, J.: NetPay: An off-line, decentralized micro-payment system for thin-client applications. Electronic Commerce Research and Applications **6**, 91–101 (2007)
9. Dai, X., Lo, B.: NetPay—an efficient protocol for micropayments on the WWW. In: Fifth Australian World Wide Web Conference, Australia (1999)
10. Dai, X., Ayoade, O., Grundy, J.: Off-line micro-payment protocol for multiple vendors in mobile commerce. In: The 7th International Conference on Parallel and Distributed Computing, Applications and Technologies (PDCAT'06). IEEE Comput. Soc., Los Alamitos (2006)
11. Dai, X., Chaudhary, K., Grundy, J.: Comparing and contrasting micro-payment models for content sharing in P2P networks. In: Third International IEEE Conference on Signal-Image Technologies and Internet-Based System (SITIS'07). IEEE Comput. Soc., Los Alamitos (2007)
12. Huang, Z., Chen, K.: Electronic payment in mobile environment. In: Proceedings of the 13th IEE International Workshop on database and Expert Systems Applications (DEXA '02) (2002)
13. Hwang, M.S., Lin, I.C., Li, L.H.: A simple micro-payment scheme. Journal of Systems & Software **55**, 221–229 (2001)
14. Ji, D.Y., Wang, Y.M.: A micro-payment protocol based on PayWord. Acta Electronica Sinica **30**, 301–303 (2002)
15. Liebau, N., Heckmann, O., Kovacevic, A., Mauthe, A., Steinmetz, R.: Charging in peer-to-peer systems based on a token accounting system. In: 5th International Workshop on Internet Charging and QoS Technologies. Lecture Notes in Computer Science, vol. 4033, pp. 49–60. Springer, Berlin (2006)
16. Park, D., Boyd, C., Dawson, E.: Micro-payments for wireless communications. In: 3rd International Conference on Information Security and Cryptology. Lecture Notes in Computer Science, vol. 2015, pp. 192–205. Springer, Berlin (2001)
17. Patil, V., Shyamasundar, R.K.: An efficient, secure and delegable micro-payment system. In: Proceedings of the 2004 IEEE International Conference on e-Technology, e-Commerce and e-Service, Taipei, Taiwan (2004)
18. Rivest, R., Shamir, A.: PayWord and MicroMint: Two simple micropayment schemes. In: Proceedings of 1996 International Workshop on Security Protocols. Lecture Notes in Computer Science, vol. 1189, pp. 69–87. Springer, Berlin (1997)
19. Shneidman, J., Parkes, D.: Rationality and self-interest in peer-to-peer networks. In: Proc. of 2nd International Workshop on Peer-to-Peer Systems (IPTPS '03), Berkeley, CA, USA (2003)
20. The Napster home page. http://www.napster.com/
21. Wei, K., Smith, A.J., Chen, Y.R., Vo, B.: WhoPay: A scalable and anonymous payment system for peer-to-peer environments. In: Proc. 26th IEEE Intl. Conf. on Distributed Computing Systems. IEEE Comput. Soc., Los Alamitos (2006)
22. Yang, B., Garcia-Molina, H.: PPay: Micropayments for peer-to-peer systems. In: Proc. of the 10th ACM Conference on Computer and Communication Security, pp. 300–310. ACM, New York (2003)
23. Zhu, J., Wang, N., Ma, J.: A micro-payment scheme for multiple-vendor in m-commerce. In: Proceedings of the IEEE International Conference on E-Commerce Technology for Dynamic E-Business (CEC-East'04) (2004)
24. Zou, E.J., Si, T., Huang, L., Dai, Y.: A new micro-payment protocol based on P2P networks. In: Proceedings of the 2005 IEEE International Conference on e-Business Engineering (ICEBE'05) (2005)

Chapter 17
Enforcing Honesty in Fair Exchange Protocols

Abdullah M. Alaraj and Malcolm Munro

Abstract When buying and selling digital products online both the customer and merchant need to trust each other. However, not all parties are honest and hence a class of exchange protocols has been developed that are called Optimistic Fair Exchange Protocols. This paper surveys the field of Fair Exchange Protocols and then presents a special type of protocol between a customer (C) and a merchant (M) that enforces one of them to be honest. It makes minimal use of a Trusted Third Party (TTP). The protocol has the features that it: (1) only comprises three messages to be exchanged between C and M; (2) guarantees strong fairness for both C and M; (3) allows both parties to be sure of the item that they will receive from the other party; and (4) resolves disputes automatically online.

17.1 Introduction

E-commerce provides different services such as buying, selling, transferring or exchanging products, services or information. With e-commerce, all phases of the trade cycle can be applied. These phases include the following steps. A customer searches the Internet for products or services. When the customer finds the product, they place an order to get that product. Then, the customer pays the price of the product to the merchant in order to get the ordered products from the merchant either by shipping them to the customer or simply by sending them online if they are digital products (such as a piece of music or software). Finally, the customer can get what is called after-sales services such as warranties. Figure 17.1 illustrates all these phases that occur between a customer and a merchant.

In Fig. 17.1, the main thing that the customer needs to get from the merchant is the product that they ordered (whether it is digital product, such as computer software, or physical product). Also, the main thing that the merchant needs to get

A.M. Alaraj (✉)
Department of Information Technology, College of Computer, Qassim University, Qassim,
Saudi Arabia
e-mail: arj@qu.edu.sa

Y. Badr et al. (eds.) *Emergent Web Intelligence: Advanced Semantic Technologies,*
Advanced Information and Knowledge Processing,
DOI 10.1007/978-1-84996-077-9_17, © Springer-Verlag London Limited 2010

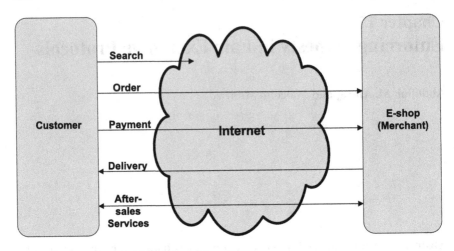

Fig. 17.1 E-commerce facilities (adopted from [40])

is the correct payment from the customer. Therefore, the customer and the merchant exchange their items which are the product (whether it is digital or not) and the payment. The exchange of items is needed to be fair. That is, by the end of the transaction, both the customer and the merchant must get each other's items or no one of them gets anything. The focus in this paper is on digital products that can be sent and received over a network.

When exchanging a payment for a digital product between a customer and a merchant, then the focus is on three processes where (1) Customer (C) sends the payment to Merchant (M), (2) M sends the digital product to C, in some order followed by (3) after-sale services if one party found a problem with the item of the other party i.e. dispute cases.

17.2 Review of Literature

The problem of fair exchange concerns with exchanging the items of parties fairly. That is, if there are two parties and each party has an item to be exchanged with the other party. The two parties do not know each other and (or) do not trust each other. Therefore, by the end of the exchange each party wants to get the item of the other party; or no one of the parties gets anything. The fair exchange protocols are designed to ensure such fairness. That is, to protect honest parties from the dishonest ones.

Fair exchange protocols appear in the context of different areas. However, the main concern for all of them is how to fairly exchange the items between the parties involved in the exchange. These contexts differ according to the items to be exchanged between parties. The following summarizes these contexts [36].

- **Certified Email:** In the certified email fair exchange protocols [1, 8, 11, 26] the items to be exchanged between parties are the email and the receipt. That is, the sender of the email wants to receive a receipt form the receiver of the email to avoid denying of receiving the email. The following presents an example protocol of a fair exchange protocol for certified email.

Nenadic et al. [24] proposed an optimistic fair certified email protocol. The protocol comprises of four messages to be exchanged between a sender and a receiver of the email. Their protocol is based on RSA [35]. The protocol starts by the sender sending their first message to the receiver. The first message includes the hash value of the email and the signature of the sender on the email. On receiving the first message, the receiver verifies it and if it is correct then they send the second message to the sender which includes their encrypted receipt of the first message. On receiving the encrypted receipt, the sender verifies it and if it is correct then they send the un-encrypted email to the receiver. When the receiver receives the email, they send the fourth message to the sender which includes the decryption key to decrypt the encrypted receipt. The TTP is contacted if one party misbehaved.

- **Certified Delivery:** The certified delivery fair exchange protocols [25] are very similar to the certified email fair exchange protocols. The difference is that the received item to be certified is not an email but any digital product or payment. The following is an example protocol for the certified delivery.

Nenadic et al. [25] proposed an optimistic fair exchange protocol that makes use of TTP in the case of disputes. Their protocol is for the exchange of digital product (that is held by a Merchant) for its receipt from a Customer when they receive the digital product i.e. the Customer will send to the Merchant a signature that represents a receipt of receiving the digital product. The protocol is called certified digital product delivery where the Merchant sends the digital product to the Customer and then the Customer sends a conformation to the Merchant sating that the digital product was received.

The exchange phase of the protocol comprises of four messages to be exchanged between the Customer and the Merchant. The Merchant starts the exchange by sending the first message to the Customer. The first message includes the encrypted digital product, the digital product's certificate and the Merchant's signature on the digital product. On receiving the first message, the Customer verifies it and if satisfied they send the second message to the Merchant. The second message includes the Customer's encrypted signature which indicates the receiving of the digital product. On receiving the second message, the Merchant verifies the correctness of the encrypted signature. If it is correct then the Merchant sends the third message to the Customer. The third message includes the decryption key used to encrypt the digital product. On receiving the third message, the Customer decrypts the digital product and sends the fourth message to the Merchant which includes the decryption key to decrypt the Customer's signature. By the end of executing the protocol, the Merchant and the Customer have fairly exchanged the digital product and the receipt (the Customer's signature). The TTP should be contacted to resolve any disputes.

- **Contract Signing:** The items to be exchanged between parties in the contract signing fair exchange protocols [7, 29, 39] are the signatures of parties on a contract. That is, if there is a contract to be signed by two parties then each party want to receive the signed contract by the other party.

As an example for the contract signing fair exchange protocols, the following protocol is presented.

Asokan et al. [7] proposed a fair contract signing protocol between two parties, let say A and B. The contract (N) to be signed is previously agreed on between the parties. The protocol comprises of four messages. Party A starts the protocol by first generating a random number a and then computing the hash value of a. Then, Party A signs both the hash value of a and the contract N i.e. Party A's signature on {N and hash value of a}. Then, Party A sends the signed message ($M1$) to Party B. On receiving $M1$, Party B verifies it and if it is correct then Party B generates a random number b and then computes the hash value of b. Then, Party B signs both $M1$ and the hash value of b; and then sends them to Party A (Party B sends to Party A the message $M2$). On receiving $M2$, Party A verifies it and if it is correct then Party A sends to Party B the random number a. On receiving a, Party B sends to Party A the random number b. By the end of executing the protocol, both Party A and Party B have a signed contract that includes ($M1$, a, $M2$, b). If anything went wrong, the TTP can be contacted to resolve any disputes.

- **Fair Purchase:** The fair purchase protocols [2–6, 12, 19, 31, 34, 41] concern with the exchange of digital products and payments. That is, one party (such as the merchant) has the digital product and the other party (such as the customer) has the payment. The fair purchase exchange protocols ensure the fairness for the two parties.

The focus in this paper is on fair exchange protocols that are for the exchange of payment and digital products. Therefore, the example protocols of this type will be presented in a separate section.

There are two types of fairness that fair exchange protocols can ensure [6] (1) strong fairness and (2) weak fairness. If there are two parties involved in the fair exchange protocol then strong and weak fairness can be defined as follows. The fair exchange protocol ensures strong fairness if that by the end of executing the fair exchange protocol the two parties will receive each other's items or none do. The fair exchange protocol ensures weak fairness if it either ensures strong fairness or provides the party (who has not received the other party's item) with a proof that the other party received their item. This proof can be used later (i.e. not within the protocol) for dispute resolutions.

The fair exchange protocols can be divided into two types according to the involvement of a Trusted Third Party (TTP). The TTP takes all or some of the following roles which ensure fairness in the exchange, acting as certificate authority that is trusted by all parties, resolving disputes and/or validating items. The first type is the protocols that do not involve the TTP and the second type is the protocols that involve the TTP. These types of fair exchange protocols will be discussed in the following sections.

Fig. 17.2 Gradual exchange protocols

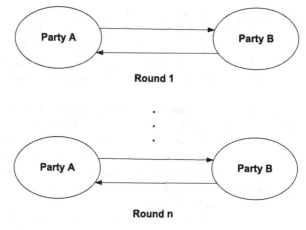

Round 1

⋮

Round n

17.2.1 Protocols that Do Not Involve a TTP

This type of protocols can be divided into gradual exchange protocols and probabilistic protocols.

The gradual exchange protocols [10, 13] are applicable to items that are easily decomposable into the same number of bits. This type of protocols is based on having a number of rounds to complete the exchange of items between the parties. In each round, each party sends a bit of its item to the other party. The number of rounds equals the number of bits by which the items is divided. The sending of these bits will continue until each party has the other party's item. Therefore, in each round each party sends a bit of its item and also receives a bit of the other party's item, see Fig. 17.2. Therefore, at any given moment the number of bits received by both parties is approximately the same [37].

One problem of this type of protocols is that many rounds are required to complete the exchange. Therefore, when the number of rounds is too large, there will be much load on the communication channel to be used for the exchange of two items between the two parties. The items to be exchanged between the two parties are assumed to have the same size [20]. Therefore, items of different sizes are not supported in this type of protocols. Another problem, as this type of protocols does not involve a TTP, it is impossible to ensure fairness without the existing of a TTP [28]. To explain the reason why this type of protocols will not ensure fairness, let us take the following scenario.

The first party (A) sends the first bit of its item to the other party (B). Then B sends its first bit to A. Then the exchange of bits will continue. If A sends its last bit to B but B disappears before it sends its last bit to A, then B will have the A's complete item but A will not have the complete item of B. So, there is a possibility that the fair exchange protocol will end in an unfair situation [28].

In the case of exchanging a payment for a digital product without any involvement of a TTP then it can be described as follows [36]. A customer sends a small amount of payment to a merchant and in turn the merchant sends a small part of the digital product to the customer. This process continues until both the customer and the merchant receive the complete items of each other i.e. the customer receives the complete digital product and the merchant receives the complete payment. There is a possibility, however, that the merchant does not send the last part of the digital product after receiving the last part of the payment. Hence, the fairness is not ensured.

This type of the exchange (i.e. exchanging small parts of payment for small parts of digital product) can be performed using the micro-payment systems [38].

Jakobsson [18] proposed a new approach for fair exchange of payment and digital product without any involvement of a TTP. The protocol is based on splitting the payment into two parts. The two parts must be combined to be consumed i.e. the first part cannot be consumed without the second part and the second part cannot be consumed without the first part.

Jakobsson's protocol starts by the customer sending the first part of the payment to the merchant. On receiving the first part, the merchant sends the digital product to the customer. On receiving the digital product the customer sends the second part of the payment to the merchant. When the merchant receives the second part of the payment they combined it with the first part to construct the whole payment. This protocol does not ensure fairness because the customer may disappear before sending the second part of the payment. That is, after the customer receives the digital product they do not send the second part of the payment. Therefore, the fairness is not ensured.

The probabilistic protocols are an improvement of the idea of the gradual exchange protocols. The same idea as the gradual secret release protocols, each party releases a bit of its item in each round. In each round, the probability of having fair exchange increases until it reaches 1 in the final round, which means the exchange is fair for both parties. Therefore, these protocols probabilistically guarantee the fairness [36]. The protocol proposed by Ben-Or et al. [9] is an example of probabilistic protocols. The same as the gradual secret release protocols, these protocols require many rounds to achieve fairness.

Although gradual exchange protocols and probabilistic protocols perform the exchange of items between parties without any involvement of TTP, it has been proven by Pagnia and Gärnter in [27] that it is not possible to ensure strong fairness without an involvement of a TTP.

17.2.2 Protocols that Involve a TTP

There are three kinds of this type of protocols according to how they use the TTP. These kinds are:

(1) protocols that are based on inline TTP,
(2) protocols that are based on online TTP, and
(3) protocols that are based on offline TTP.

The three kinds of protocols will be discussed separately in the following sections.

Fig. 17.3 Inline TTP based
fair exchange model

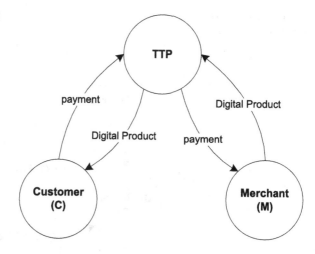

17.2.2.1 Protocols that Are Based on Inline TTP

The inline-based protocols (such as [19, 33]) use a TTP for delivering the exchanged items to the parties. That is, each party sends their item to the TTP, and then the TTP will verify the items and then will deliver them to the parties. Therefore, the TTP is always used in the protocol guaranteeing the fair exchange of items between the parties. This kind of protocols is called inline TTP based fair exchange protocols.

Although the protocols that use inline TTP ensure fairness for all parties as the TTP will deliver the items to all parties, they have some disadvantages. Firstly, protocols that use inline TTP require that the TTP be available during the execution of the protocol which will result in extra costs as the TTP is expensive to run [22]. Secondly, this kind of protocols can lead to performance problems as the TTP will be a source of bottleneck [6, 21, 34, 37]. This is because the exchange of items will be through the TTP. Thirdly, when the TTP crashes, the protocol will not be executed and the parties will not be able to receive the items that they want. Finally, the TTP will be the main target of attacks [21].

Figure 17.3 shows a model of the exchange of payment and digital product between a customer and a merchant using inline TTP.

17.2.2.2 Protocols that Are Based on Online TTP

The protocols that are based on online TTP (such as [12]) reduce the use of the TTP. In this kind of protocols, the TTP will be used during the protocol run but its use is not for delivering the parties' items. Rather, its use can be for validating an item, generating and/or storing evidence of a transaction [23].

To illustrate the use of online TTP in the fair exchange protocols, let us take the following example that uses the online TTP for validating an item. If the items to be exchanged are a payment and a digital product between a customer and a merchant; and the customer is the one who starts the exchange then after the merchant receives

Fig. 17.4 Online TTP based
fair exchange model

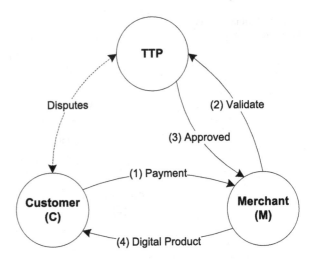

the payment from the customer then the merchant will validate it with the TTP
(a bank for example) before they send the digital product to the customer. Therefore,
the TTP must be online for the exchange to be completed.

Although this kind of protocols reduces the involvement of the TTP that is seen
in the inline TTP based fair exchange protocols, it requires the existence of the TTP
during the exchange of items. This is seen as a disadvantage because the TTP may
become a source of bottleneck.

Figure 17.4 shows a model of the exchange of payment and digital product between a customer and a merchant using online TTP.

17.2.2.3 Protocols that Are Based on Offline TTP

The protocols that are based on offline TTP (such as [3, 4, 6, 31, 34]) allow the parties to directly exchange their items without any involvement of the TTP unless one
party misbehaves. This kind of protocols is also called in the literature "Optimistic
fair exchange protocols" [6, 14, 34]. This kind of protocols will be referred hereafter
as optimistic fair exchange protocols.

To illustrate how the optimistic fair exchange protocols work, let us take the
following example. If the items to be exchanged are a payment and a digital product
between a customer and a merchant then the protocol will work as follows. The
two parties directly exchange the payment and the digital product; and if one party
misbehaves the TTP will be invoked to resolve the disputes. Figure 17.5 shows a
model of the exchange of payment and digital product between a customer and a
merchant using offline TTP (optimistic fair exchange protocols).

The optimistic fair exchange protocols reduce the problems of using inline TTP
and online TTP. This is because optimistic fair exchange protocols use the TTP very
rarely and not involve it in every exchange. Therefore, the problem of having the
TTP as a source of bottleneck that exists in the protocols that are based on both

Fig. 17.5 Offline TTP based
fair exchange model

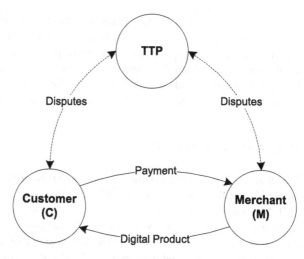

inline and online TTP is reduced. This is because optimistic fair exchange protocols reduce the use of the TTP and let the parties exchange their items directly. Another thing is that in the optimistic fair exchange protocols, the problem of having the TTP as a single point of failure is reduced as the parties will not need the TTP unless something goes wrong. Additionally, as the TTP will not be actively involved in the optimistic fair exchange protocols, the cost of running the TTP will be reduced.

17.2.3 Examples of Fair Exchange Protocols

The focus in this chapter is on fair exchange protocols that are for exchanging digital product for payment or for exchanging two documents between a customer (C) and a merchant (M). In the following, some protocols from the literature will be discussed.

17.2.3.1 Zhang et al. Protocol

Zhang et al. [41] proposed a fair exchange protocol that involves online TTP. The proposed protocol is for the exchange of payment and a product which might be a physical product. Therefore, the payment is sent online (i.e. via the protocol messages) form the customer to the merchant whereas the product is delivered to the customer using a delivery agent i.e. the delivery of the product is not using the electronic means. The protocol is based on the theory of cross validation [41].

The customer starts the protocol by requesting a product from the merchant. Then, the merchant sends the invoice to the customer. If the customer is satisfied with the invoice then they, first, send an encrypted payment to the merchant and, second, send the encrypted payment to the TTP (the bank). The merchant assumed to be able to download the encrypted payment (that was sent by the customer to the TTP) from the TTP (the bank). The merchant then compares the two encrypted payments. If they are compared then the merchant is sure that the encrypted payment is correct. After verifying the encrypted payment, the merchant sends the product to the delivery agent. Then the customer collects the product from the delivery agent. When the customer finds that the product is the same as they expected, they send the decryption key to the merchant who will then decrypt the encrypted payment.

17.2.3.2 Ray et al. Protocol

Ray et al. [34] proposed an optimistic fair exchange protocol. The protocol is based on the idea of the theory of cross validation. The cross validation theory states that [32] "*if a message is encrypted with the product key of two compatible keys and another message is encrypted with either of the two compatible keys and the two encrypted messages compare, then the two original un-encrypted messages must also compare if a message is encrypted with the product key of two compatible keys and another message is encrypted with either of the two compatible keys and the two encrypted messages compare, then the two original un-encrypted messages must also compare*". Therefore, by using the cross validation theory the customer will be able to validate the encrypted digital product to be received from the merchant without decrypting it.

Some steps take place before the protocol starts. A merchant (M) needs to register with a trusted third party (TTP). The TTP generates the key pair K_{M1} and K_{M1}^{-1}. The TTP then provides M with K_{M1} and keeps K_{M1}^{-1} with itself. A customer (C) needs to have an account in a bank. The bank generates the key pairs K_{C1} and K_{C1}^{-1}. The bank then provides C with K_{C1} and keeps K_{C1}^{-1} with itself. The merchant needs to send the digital product, its description and its price to the TTP. The TTP encrypts the digital product using the key K_{M1} and then advertises it on its website i.e. the TTP's website. The customer visits the website and downloads the encrypted digital product from the TTP to be used for validating the digital product that they will receive from the merchant. If the customer is interested in the digital product then they can contact the merchant and starts the protocol as follows.

The actual interaction between the customer and the merchant in the Ray et al. protocol [34] consists of four messages. The four messages can be summarized as follows.

The customer (C) sends to the merchant (M) the first message. The first message includes (1) the purchase order and (2) the payment that is encrypted with the product key of $K_{C1} \times K_{C2}$. On receiving the first message, M verifies it and if it is correct then M sends the second message to C. The second message includes the digital product that is encrypted with the product key of $(K_{M1} \times K_{M2})$. On receiving the second message, C compares the encrypted digital product that was received from the TTP with the encrypted digital product that is included in the second message. If the two are compared then C can be sure that the un-encrypted digital products will be the compared as well (in here the cross validation theory is applied). Therefore, if the two encrypted digital products are compared and C is still interested in the exchange then C sends the third message to M which includes the decryption key for the encrypted payment. Finally, M sends the fourth message to C which includes the decryption key of the encrypted digital product. If there is any dispute, C can contact the TTP.

As can be seen in the Ray et al. protocol, the TTP will have a copy of all digital products that M wants to sell. Therefore, this will result in extra storage in the TTP side as well as extra security assurance. Another problem with this protocol is that the customer needs to download the digital product twice (one from the TTP before the exchange and then from the merchant). Therefore, the twice download of the digital product will be a communication overhead.

17.2.3.3 Asokan et al. Protocol

Asokan et al. [6] proposed an optimistic fair exchange protocol i.e. the TTP will only be involved in the case of disputes. If the parties interested in the exchange want to exchange a payment and a digital product, the protocol comprises of four messages which can be explained as follows.

A merchant (M) and a customer (C) promise each other to exchange their items (i.e. the payment and the digital product). The agreement between C and M is represented in messages 1 and 2. That is, C sends to M the amount of payment that they are willing to pay; and then M will send to C the description of the digital product. Then, C sends the payment to M in message 3. On receiving message 3, M sends the digital product to C in message 4.

If C found that the digital product is not the same as described in the agreement, then C contacts the TTP. The TTP verifies C's request, if it is valid then the TTP cancels the payment. If the TTP could not cancel the payment then the TTP can provide affidavit proof to be used in the court to resolve the disputes.

As can be seen in the Asokan et al. protocol, it seems that this protocol is not the best solution for fairly exchanging digital product and payment because there is a possibility that the TTP could not cancel the payment in case of dispute which will result in not resolving disputes automatically. Imagining that the customer and the merchant are located in different parts of the world and the TTP cannot resolve the dispute automatically; then, if something goes wrong i.e. the digital product was not the same as expected, then the customer needs to travel to the country of the merchant in order to go to courts. Therefore, the protocol used for fair exchange should ensure fairness for all parties and in the case of dispute, it should provide online and automated dispute resolution as the parties might be located in different parts of the world.

17.2.3.4 Zhang et al. Protocol

Zhang et al. [42] (will be called hereafter Zhang protocol) describe an optimistic fair exchange protocol for exchanging two valuable documents (the two documents can be a payment and digital product) between two parties (the two parties can be a Customer and a Merchant).

The exchange of items in Zhang's protocol comprises of four messages to be exchanged between party A and party B. Party A starts the exchange by sending the first message to party B. The first message includes the encrypted document and the encrypted key that decrypts the decrypted document. On receiving the first message, party B verifies it and if satisfied then they send the second message to party A. The second message includes the encrypted document and the encrypted key that decrypts it. On receiving the second message, party A verifies it and if satisfied then they send the decryption key to party B in the third message. When party B receives the decryption key, they use it to decrypt the encrypted document that was received in the first message. Then party B sends to party A the fourth message which includes the decryption key. Finally, when party A receives the decryption key, they use it to decrypt the encrypted document that was received in the second message. If there is any dispute, the TTP will be contacted to resolve it.

17.2.3.5 Devane et al. Protocol

Devane et al. [12] proposed an e-commerce protocol for the purchase of digital products over the Internet. The protocol ensures fair exchange of a digital product for a payment between a merchant and a customer. However, the protocol involves an online TTP which is a bank in which both a customer and a merchant have accounts. The exchange phase of Devane's protocol comprises of seven messages to be exchanged between customer, merchant, and the bank.

In Devane et al. protocol [12], the customer initiates the protocol by sending the first message that includes a signed purchase request by the customer. On receiving the first message, the merchant verifies it and if satisfied sends the second message to the customer. The second message includes a signed invoice in addition to the encrypted digital product. On receiving the second message, the customer verifies it and checks the signed invoice. If the customer is satisfied then they send the third message to the merchant. The third message includes a signed payment. On receiving the third message, the merchant verifies it and if satisfied then they send the fourth message to the bank. The fourth message includes the decryption key for the digital product and the message three that was received from the customer and singed by the merchant (i.e. the merchant signs the signed payment by the customer and sends it to the bank along with other things). On receiving the fourth message, the bank verifies it. If the message four is verified correctly then the bank sends the fifth message to the merchant. The fifth message includes the bank's signature of the signed payment and the decryption key. On receiving the fifth message, the merchant forwards it to the customer. On receiving the sixth message, the customer gets the decryption key and decrypts the encrypted digital product that was received in message two. If the customer found that the decrypted digital product is the one they specified in message one then the customer sends message seven to the bank. Message seven includes customer's acknowledgement about the digital product. On receiving the seventh message, the bank transfers the payment from the customer's account to the merchant's account.

Devane et al. [12] have not discussed what to send to the TTP (the bank) in case a party has a dispute. Rather they claimed that their protocol is designed in a way that resolves all disputes. Therefore, the messages to be executed in the case of dispute have not been discussed.

17.2.4 Discussions

All optimistic fair exchange protocols specified in the literature [6, 14, 19, 25, 31, 34] exchange items in two phases: exchange of the encrypted items; and then the exchange of keys to decrypt the encrypted items. Therefore, the number of messages needed in the exchange phase of these protocols is four or five messages. As a consequence in order to reduce the communication load a way is needed to reduce the number of messages in the protocol. In some protocols [34] the TTP is used to hold the item of one party (the digital product) and this in itself can be seen as a load on the TTP. A further issue is that in some protocols [6, 14] the parties check the items that they want after receiving them, which can mean that they receive incorrect items. Therefore, a way is needed to give the parties a conformation that they will receive the items that they want before the exchange of items takes place. One solution is to use certificates that allow one party to be sure that they will receive the correct item. Finally, the dispute resolution should be part of the protocol so that all disputes can be resolved automatically even if one party disappears or misbehaves.

Alaraj and Munro [2–5] originated a new idea in which once the parties (C and M) have agreed to exchange their items (payment for digital product) then one of them will be enforced to be trustworthy (the other party can verify whether the party is trustworthy or not) and the other party will be enforced to be honest. By applying this idea the number of messages can be reduced in an optimistic fair exchange protocol by one and hence the protocol will be more efficient.

Alaraj and Munro [4] described a protocol for exchanging digital products and payments. Their protocol consists of three messages to be exchanged between the customer (C) and the merchant (M). M starts the exchange by sending an encrypted digital product and its certificate to C. On receiving M's item, C verifies it and if satisfied, C sends to M a payment that is encrypted using a key that M already has. Finally, the decryption key is sent to C by M when M is satisfied with the payment. This protocol enforces the customer to be honest.

Alaraj and Munro [3] described another protocol but the merchant is the one who is enforced to be honest. In this paper, a modified and extended version of the protocol in [3] will be presented and evaluated.

17.3 Enforcing Merchant Honesty (EMH) Protocol

17.3.1 Notations

This section defines the notation used in describing the protocol:

- EMH protocol: Enforcing Merchant Honesty Protocol which is the protocol presented in this paper
- C: Customer
- M: Merchant
- TTP: Trusted Third Party which is a party neither M nor C that is trusted by all parties. The TTP is assumed not collude with any other party
- D: Digital product
- P: payment
- CA: Certificate Authority
- CB: the customer's bank. While the CB can also be considered as a TTP, or the role can be taken on by the TTP, they are considered different here to separate out their different roles
- $desc$: description of digital product that C wants from M
- $h(X)$: a strong-collision-resistant one-way hash function, such as SHA-1 [15]
- $pkx = (ex, nx)$: RSA Public Key of the party x, where nx is a public RSA modulus and ex is a public exponent
- $skx = (dx, nx)$: RSA Private Key of the party x, where nx is a public RSA modulus and dx is a private exponent
- kx: a symmetric key generated by x
- P-$Cert$: payment's Certificate that is issued by the CB. The contents of P-$Cert$ are:
  - $amount$: the amount of payment
  - $payee$: the name of the party who will receive the payment
  - hP: hash value of payment
  - heP: hash value of encrypted payment with kc
  - $heKc$: hash value of encrypted kc with $pkct$
  - $Sig.CB$: CB's signature on P-$Cert$
- DG-$Cert$: Digital product certificate that is issued by CA. DG-$Cert$ includes the following:
  - Price: price of D
  - d: Description of D, the description may be the ID of the digital product
  - hDG: hash value of D
  - $Sig.CA$: CA's signature on DG-$Cert$
- $C.ct$: the certificate for the shared public key between C and the TTP; $C.ct$ is issued by the TTP. A standard X.509 certificate is used to implement $C.ct$ [30]
- $enc.pkx(Y)$: an RSA [35] encryption of Y using the public key $pkx(ex, nx)$ i.e. $enc.pkx(Y) = Y^{ex} \bmod nx = Z$
- $enc.skx(Z)$: an RSA decryption [35] of Z using the private key $skx(dx, nx)$ i.e. $enc.skx(Z) = Z^{dx} \bmod nx = Y$

- *enc.kx(Y)*: encryption of *Y* using a symmetric key *kx* (*kx* can be used for decrypting *enc.kx(Y)*)
- *Sig.x(A)*: the RSA signature [35] of party *x* on *A* i.e. encrypting the hash value of *A* using the private key *skx(dx, nx)* as follows: $Sig.x(A) = (h(A))^{dx} \bmod nx$
- *A → B*: *X*: *A* sends message *X* to *B*

17.3.2 Protocol Description

The purpose of this protocol is for exchanging a digital product *D* for a payment. It is assumed that the payment is in the form of a payment order that is issued by the customer's bank and it specifies the amount of payment to be paid, the payee and the payer. Double spending of the same payment is also assumed to be detected and therefore will be eliminated. It is also assumed that The communication channel between TTP and C is resilient as is also the communication channel between TTP and M i.e. all sent messages will be received by their intended recipients. C and M will agree on the TTP to be used in both the pre-exchange phase (by C) and the dispute resolution (by M) before they start the exchange.

The trustworthiness of C is governed by two factors; the payment certificate (*P-Cert*) issued by CB; and the public key certificate (*C.ct*) issued by TTP. Thus, the payment that will be sent by C is certified by CB; and the public key to be used by C to encrypt the key that encrypts the payment is certified by TTP.

The enforcement of M to be honest is governed by letting M encrypt the digital product using a key that is sent to M by C. This is to let C be able to decrypt the digital product without assistance from M. Hence, M will send a correct encrypted digital product as C will be able to decrypt it as soon they receive it.

In essence this protocol is like C saying to M: this is the encrypted payment; and I am a trustworthy as these certificates (*P-Cert* and *C.ct*) show BUT be honest with me by sending the correct digital product in order to receive the decryption key for the payment. By this means C is trustworthy by having the correct certificates from the CB and the TTP, and also M is enforced to be honest.

The protocol is in two phases: the pre-exchange and the exchange phases.

17.3.3 Pre-exchange Phase

In the pre-exchange phase (Fig. 17.6), C needs to get the certificate *C.ct* of the shared public key from the TTP to be used to encrypt the key that is used to encrypt payment. Therefore, C needs to request the shared public key certificate from the TTP and then the TTP will send it (that is in messages PE-M1a and PE-M1b of Fig. 17.6). C also needs to get the payment and its certificate *P-Cert* from the CB (that is in messages PE-M2a and PE-M2b of Fig. 17.6). The *P-Cert* is unique for each transaction (completed exchange) because the payment can only be used once.

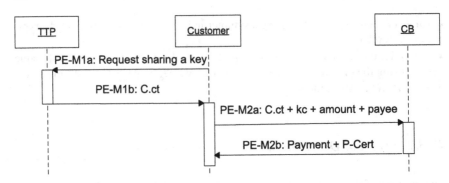

Fig. 17.6 The pre-exchange phase

M also needs to get a special version of digital product certificate *DG-Cert* from CA. This *DG-Cert* is assumed to be publicly available e.g. for example in M's website. Therefore, C can get it easily to help them in specifying what they want from M in the exchange phase that will be discussed later. The *DG-Cert* is unique for each digital product and it is issued once and can be used as many times as possible for the certified digital product. The content of this *DG-Cert* is shown in the notation section.

In this protocol C and TTP share a public key. The keys of the parties are as follows:

- Each party x ($x \in$ C, M, TTP and CB) has its own public (pkx) and private (skx) keys
  - The CB's public key is denoted as $pkcb = (ecb, ncb)$ and its corresponding private key is denoted as $skcb = (dcb, ncb)$
  - The TTP's public key is denoted as $pkt = (et, nt)$ and its corresponding private key is denoted as $skt = (dt, nt)$
  - C's public key is denoted as $pkc = (ec, nc)$ and its corresponding private key is denoted as $skc = (dc, nc)$
  - M's public key is denoted as $pkm = (em, nm)$ and its corresponding private key is denoted as $skm = (dm, nm)$
- The shared public key between C and TTP is denoted as $pkct = (ect, nct)$ and its corresponding private key is denoted as $skct = (dct, nct)$

17.3.4 The Exchange Phase

It is assumed that the exchange phase will take place after C finds the wanted digital product (D) with M either in M's website or through search engines, and that C and M agree on the digital product and negotiated the price. Hence this phase is about the actual exchange of payment and digital product D.

There are only three messages to be exchanged between M and C in the exchange phase (Fig. 17.7).

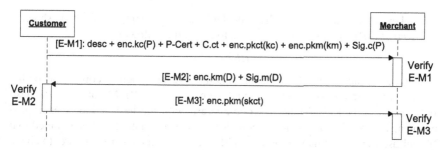

Fig. 17.7 The exchange phase

These three messages are as follows:

[E-M1]   C → M: $desc + enc.kc(P) + P\text{-}Cert + C.ct + enc.pkct(kc)$
$+ enc.pkm(km) + Sig.c(P)$

C sends message E-M1 to M which contains the following:

- *desc*: specifies what C wants from M. *desc* includes two fields, they are
  - description of *D* that C wants. The description can be the digital product ID number
  - *hDG*: hash value of *D*. *C* can get it from *DG-Cert* that is assumed to be publicly available

  Note that, *desc* is signed by C but for simplicity C's signature is omitted
- *enc.kc(P)*: the payment that is encrypted with the key *kc* that is generated by C
- *P-Cert*: the payment certificate that is issued by CB
- *C.ct*: the shared public key certificate that is issued by TTP
- *enc.pkct(kc)*: the key *kc*, that is used to encrypt the payment, encrypted using the shared public key *pkct* that is certified in *C.ct*
- *enc.pkm(km)*: a key *km* that will be used by M to encrypt the digital product. *km* is encrypted using the public key of M *pkm*. The reason for encrypting *km* using *pkm* is to prevent any other party from gaining *km* as it will be used to encrypt the digital product by M
- *Sig.c(P)*: C's signature on the payment. This signature can serve as non-repudiation of origin which allows M to be sure that the payment is sent by C. As explained in the notations section, C's signature on payment is the encryption of the hash value of payment using C's private key *skc*

[E-M2]   M → C: $enc.km(D) + Sig.m(D)$

On receiving message E-M1 from C, M checks the correctness of *enc.kc(P)*, *enc.pkct(kc)*, *P-Cert* and *C.ct*. The correctness of *P-Cert* can be checked by verifying CB's signature on *P-Cert*. Also the correctness of *C.ct* can be checked by verifying TTP's signature on *C.ct*.

To check the correctness of payment (*P*), M needs to check two things which are the payment itself and the encrypted payment with *Kc* i.e. *enc.kc(P)*. Firstly, to check the correctness of *P*, M needs to get the hash value of payment (*HP*) by decrypting *Sig.c(P)* contained in message E-M1 using C's public key *pkc* (the public keys of all parties are publicly available) and then compare it with hash value of *payment* (*hP*) contained in *P-Cert* i.e. to check the following:

$$HP? = hP$$

If they are the same then M can be sure that the actual payment is correct. Secondly, to check the correctness of the encrypted payment *enc.kc(P)*, M computes the hash value of *enc.kc(P)* (*HeP*) and then compare it with the hash value of encrypted payment with *kc* i.e. *heP* which is contained in *P-Cert* (note that it is assumed that M will use the same function used by CB to compute the hash value) i.e. to check the following:

$$HeP? = heP$$

If they are the same then M can be sure that C encrypted the payment using *kc* and not another key.

M also needs to check the correctness of *kc* which is used to encrypt *payment*. To do so, M computed the hash value of *enc.pkct(kc)* (*HeKc*) and then compare it with *heKc* that is included in *P-Cert*, so M will check the flowing:

$$HeKc? = heKc$$

If they are compared then M can be sure that the encrypted key is *kc* and not another key. The point here is to make sure that C is honest by sending the key used to encrypt the payment.

Therefore, if all comparisons are correct then, at this point, M will have the following fact. The encrypted payment is correct (i.e. it is the one described in *P-Cert*) and it is indeed encrypted with *kc*. In addition, the key encrypted using the shared public key *pkct* is indeed *kc* and not another key. The shared public key *pkct* used to encrypt *kc* is certified by TTP. Therefore, once M got the private key of the shared public key then C will be able to get the payment (by first decrypting *enc.pkct(kc)* to get *kc* and then decrypting *enc.kc(P)* using *kc*).

Now, it is M's choice to complete the exchange or abort the protocol. If M wants to exchange *D* with the payment then M sends the following (note that M must be sure that the encrypted payment matches their requirements as explained earlier, otherwise M will be at risk if they send message E-M2 to C as C already has the decryption key for *D*. Also, M must send *D* that matches C's requirement i.e. that matches *desc* included in E-M1):

- *enc.km(D)*: M first needs to get *km* by decrypting *enc.pkm(km)* included in E-M1 using their private key skm as *km* encrypted using M's public key. Once M got *km* then they encrypt *D* using the key *km*
- *Sig.m(D)*: M's signature on *D*. This signature can serve as non-repudiation of receipt which allows C to be sure that M has received the encrypted payment

Note that if M decides to abort the transaction after receiving message E-M1 and before sending message E-M2 to C then neither M nor C lose anything. But once M sends a correct message in E-M2 to C then the transaction must be completed and the protocol will guarantee that the exchange of *D* and payment will be fair.

$$[\text{E-M3}] \quad C \rightarrow M: enc.pkm(skct)$$

On receiving message E-M2, C decrypts D using the key km (km is originated by C and sent to M in E-M1 to allow M encrypts D using it) and then checks whether it is correct or not. If M encrypted D using different key then C ignores the transaction and aborts the protocol. If however D is correct then C sends the decryption key $skct$ (it is encrypted using M's public key to prevent any other party from gaining $skct$) to M to be able to decrypt kc and then decrypt the payment.

It is clear that if D is incorrect then C will not send $skct$ to M because it is M's responsibility to send the correct D to be able to receive the decryption key in message E-M3. Using this way this protocol enforces M to be honest and hence sends the correct D to C. If M sends incorrect D, then C can ask M to re-send the correct D to be able to receive the decryption key, but it depends on C if they want to do so.

17.3.5 After Exchange (Dispute Resolution)

It is likely that there will be disputes when buying and selling products because some customers may find that the product they have bought from a merchant is not the same as they wanted or the product has some problems. The same notion applies to the buying and selling of digital products online.

There are many forms of disputes. For example, a customer complains that they did not get the right product or a merchant complains that they did not get the right payment. Disputes can be resolved formally in courts of law. There are however some alternatives for resolving disputes without going to a court. They are called Alternative Dispute Resolution (ADR). Arbitration and mediation are examples of ADR.

In e-commerce the need to resolve disputes online is vital because customers and merchants might be located in different parts of the world. When the dispute resolution is done online, it is called Online Dispute Resolution (ODR). Many techniques are available for ODR. Some of the techniques will be discussed including those by [17] and [16]:

- **Arbitration**: it means having a neutral third party who collects information from the two parties who have a dispute. Then the third party makes a decision that is intended to be binding
- **Evaluation**: it is the same as arbitration but the decision made by the neutral third party is a recommendation rather than binding
- **Mediation**: it means to have a third party who helps the two parties to reach an agreement. So, it is not the same as arbitration that lets the third party make the decision
- **Automated negotiation**: it is used to resolve disputes that are related to monetary amounts. It is based on having blind bids, in which the parties enter their suggestions to resolve the dispute. Each party does not know what the other party has offered. Finally, a computer program proposes a solution when the offers of the parties are sufficiently close

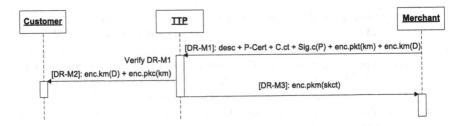

Fig. 17.8 The dispute resolution

- **Mock Trial**: it is based on having a jury of peers who volunteer for making a decision on a case of dispute using web-based platform. The decision made by the jury is not binding
- **Complaint Assistance**: it is a tool that helps the person who writes a dispute. Some tools have interactive forms that the user needs to complete. This kind of tools provides advice, similar cases that have been assisted by the tool
- **Credit Card Charge Back**: This technique allows credit card issuers to act as a third party between a customer and a merchant. So, the credit card issuer will study the dispute and then if the customer dispute is accepted, it will give the customer's money back

With regard to the EMH protocol, the way in which the dispute is resolved is using a similar technique used in arbitration but the TTP does not need to collect the information (evidences) from both parties. Rather, the TTP will receive the information from the party who has a dispute and then the TTP will make the resolution to both parties.

All disputes in the EMH protocol, if any, will come from M because C will not have to raise disputes as they receive the encrypted D and decrypt it using the key km that they know of before they send the decryption key to M. Therefore, the weakest link in this exchange is M as they have to send the correct D in order to receive the decryption key for the encrypted payment that they have received in message E-M1.

Therefore, if M has a dispute, then the following three messages are executed (Fig. 17.8):

$$[DR\text{-}M1] \quad M \rightarrow TTP: desc + P\text{-}Cert + C.ct + Sig.c(P)$$
$$+ enc.pkt(km) + enc.km(D)$$

In case M has a dispute, they need to send to TTP the following:

$$desc + P\text{-}Cert + C.ct + Sig.c(P) + enc.pkt(km) + enc.km(D)$$

$$[DR\text{-}M2] \quad TTP \rightarrow C: enc.km(D) + enc.pkc(km)$$

On receiving message DR-M1 above, TTP, firstly, checks the correctness of $P\text{-}Cert$ and $C.ct$ by checking their signatures. In addition, TTP verifies C's signature on $desc$. Then, TTP decrypts $enc.pkt(km)$ using their private key skt to get km then uses km to decrypt D.

If all these are correct then TTP computes the hash value of D then compare it with hDG included in $desc$. This comparison makes TTP be sure that C ordered this D and not another D. TTP will also compare the hash value included in $sig.c(P)$ with the hash value of payment included in $P\text{-}Cert$. If TTP found the comparisons are correct then TTP forwards the D (that is encrypted using km) and the key km to decrypt D (km is sent to C encrypted using C's public key pkc to prevent any other party from gaining km) to C.

There are many reasons for forwarding D and km to C. They are as follows:

- M may have sent to C incorrect D in message E-M2 (in the exchange phase)
- M may have not sent D at all; i.e. M contacted TTP before sending E-M2 to C
- M may have encrypted D in E-M2 using different km; therefore, TTP forwards the key km that decrypts D

Otherwise, if TTP found that the two hashes do not math then TTP sends an abort message to M. So, if the DR-M1 is incorrect then TTP will not contact C at all.

$$[\text{DR-M3}] \quad \text{TTP} \rightarrow \text{M: } enc.pkm(skct)$$

or

$$\text{TTP} \rightarrow \text{M: aborts}$$

The same as message DR-M2 above, if TTP found that the hash value of D matches hDG included in $desc$ then TTP sends to M the decryption key $skct$ that is encrypted using M's public key pkm. Otherwise, if the two hashes do not match then TTP sends an abort message to M.

It is clear that if either M has not sent the correct D to C in E-M2, M has not sent D at all or M encrypted D in E-M2 using different km then M will not get an advantage over C because TTP will check D and see whether it meets what C wants. If the hash value of D matches hDG then TTP will send the decryption key $skct$ to M and also TTP will forward the encrypted D and its decryption key km to C and this is to ensure fairness in all cases. Therefore, the fairness is guaranteed for both M and C. However, if D is incorrect (e.g. the hash value of D does not match hDG) then TTP will reject M's request for the dispute.

As can be seen in the dispute resolution phase, TTP does not need to have both C and M to be involved in order for the dispute to be resolved; rather only the disputant (M in this protocol) and TTP will be involved. That is, TTP does not need to contact C to verify whether or not they have received the correct D; rather TTP asks M to provide all needed information (that is in DR-M1) and will be able to make the resolution. C will only be contacted by TTP if the dispute has a resolution. Therefore, this will reduce the number of messages needed to resolve dispute and as a result will reduce the load on the communication channels.

17.4 Disputes Analysis

In the EMH protocol, after receiving the message E-M1 from C then the exchange between C and M is for the digital product (by M) and the decryption key for the

Table 17.1 All disputes possibilities for EMH

	C	M	Result
	Receive digital product	Receive decryption key	
1	✓	✓	No dispute
2	X	✓	Not applicable in EMH protocol
3	✓	X	M makes dispute
4	X	X	No dispute/Not applicable in EMH protocol/M's fault

encrypted payment (by C). This is because C sends encrypted payment to M and then M will verify it and if satisfied then the exchange of the digital product (by M) and the decryption key (by C) will take place. The order of the exchange of the digital product and the decryption key in the EMH protocol is as follows. C will receive a correct digital product before M receives the decryption key. So, to study all the possibilities for the EMH protocol, Table 17.1 is presented.

In Table 17.1, (X) means either the party (C or M) has not received the item (decryption key or digital product) at all or they received incorrect item; whereas (✓) means the correct item is received. The dispute in here will be made to a TTP for resolution. Note that the resolution for dispute is not specified as we are talking the exchange and resolution in general.

Table 17.1 shows all possible cases for disputes in the EMH protocol. The following discusses these cases.

- In case 1, both C and M receive the correct item (i.e. C received the correct digital product and M received the correct decryption key) from each other. Hence, there is no disputes
- In case 2, C has either received incorrect digital product or not received the digital product at all, and M received the correct decryption key. This case is not applicable in the EMH protocol because M has to send a correct digital product to be able to receive the correct decryption key
- In case 3, C received a correct digital product, and M either received incorrect decryption key or has not received the decryption key at all. In this case M will make a dispute to TTP
- In case 4, there are four possibilities which are:
  - Both C and M have not received anything from each other. So, no dispute will be made as both of them have not revealed their items. This represents the case where M received E-M1 and did not send E-M2 to C
  - Both C and M have received incorrect items from each other. That is, C received incorrect digital product and M received incorrect decryption key. This case is not applicable in the EMH protocol because M has to send a correct digital product to be able to receive the correct decryption key. So, if C found that the digital product is incorrect then C will not send the decryption key at all i.e. neither correct decryption key nor incorrect decryption key

- C received incorrect digital product and M has not received the decryption key at all. This case is normal to occur because if the digital product is incorrect then C will not send the decryption key to M. That is, M has to send a correct digital product to be able to receive the correct decryption key from C. Therefore, if this case occurs then for M to raise a dispute to the TTP, M needs to send to the TTP a correct digital product and other things (see message DR-M1 of the dispute resolution phase of the EMH protocol). If M sends the correct digital product to the TTP then the TTP will make a resolution to both C and M. That is, C will received two digital products (the incorrect digital product from M, and the correct digital product from TTP) and this is the penalty that M pays for being dishonest. However, if the TTP found that the digital product is incorrect then M's dispute will be rejected. Note that the incorrect digital product that C may have received from M means either a digital product that is not valid (not working software for example) or a digital product that is not the one C wants (C wants a piece of music for artist X and receive a piece of music for artist Y)
- C has not received the digital product at all and M received incorrect decryption key. This case is not applicable in the EMH protocol because M has to send a correct digital product to be able to receive the correct decryption key. So, if C has not received the correct digital product then C will not send the decryption key at all i.e. neither correct decryption key nor incorrect decryption key

It is clear that the design of the EMH protocol reduces the possibilities for having disputes. Additionally, in the EMH protocol only M will raise disputes as C will not send the decryption key unless the correct digital product is received from M. Hence, the EMH protocol enforces M to be honest. As a result, the possibilities for disputes are reduced by preventing them.

In addition to the previous cases, the following cases (scenarios) are studied:

- M disputes to TTP that they have received incorrect payment: this is not possible because *P-Cert* guarantees that the payment is correct; and if M found that *payment* is incorrect or not the same as they requested then they should have not sent the digital product to C. So, it is M's fault if they send the digital product to C if they have a doubt about the correctness of the payment. But once M sends the digital product to C then this means that they are satisfied with the payment. Therefore, this dispute will not happen because M knows the rules of the protocol which allow M to check the payment before they send the digital product to C; and as a result M will not put themselves at risk
- It is clear that C will not raise a dispute because C will receive the digital product before they send the decryption key to M. However, the following cases are studied:
  - C claims that they have received incorrect digital product from M: this will not happen because M knows that if they send incorrect digital product then they will not receive the decryption key. Again, the idea of this protocol is to have one trustworthy party and enforce the other party to be honest if they are willing to exchange their item. Therefore, if C received incorrect digital product then they will not send the decryption key to M

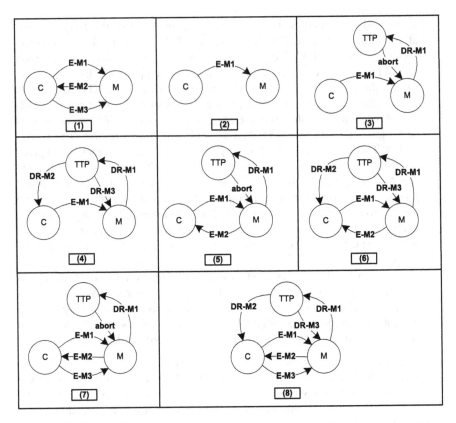

Fig. 17.9 EMH protocol scenarios

- C claims that they have not received the decryption key to decrypt digital product: this is not applicable in this protocol because digital product is encrypted with *km* that is sent by C; and hence C is able to decrypt the digital product as soon as they get it

17.5 All Possible Cases (Scenarios) of Executing EMH Protocol

There are different scenarios for executing the EMH protocol by C and M. These scenarios include:

- having both C and M are behaving honestly
- C is behaving dishonestly and M is behaving honestly
- M is behaving dishonestly and C is behaving honestly
- having both C and M are behaving dishonestly

The scenarios are, as can be seen in Fig. 17.9 (the numbers here refer to the numbers in Fig. 17.9):

1. C and M are honest which results in normal execution. That is, C sends a correct E-M1, M sends a correct E-M2, and C sends a correct E-M3

2. After receiving E-M1, M quits the protocol because either E-M1 is incorrect or M is no longer interested in the exchange

3. After receiving E-M1, M contacts the TTP before sending E-M2 to C. However, the TTP found that DR-M1 is incorrect and the TTP sends an abort message. In this scenario M tries to cheat but they gained nothing

4. Similar to scenario 3 but here, the TTP finds that DR-M1 is correct. Therefore, the TTP will make it fair for both C and M by sending the resolution to C in DR-M2 and also by sending the resolution to M in DR-M3. In this scenario M tries to cheat but the TTP makes it fair for both C and M

5. After M received E-M1 from C they found it to be correct and M sends E-M2 to C. M waited to receive E-M3 from C but nothing is forthcoming. M contacts the TTP for resolution. The TTP finds that DR-M1 is incorrect and hence sends an abort message to M. Note, there are two possibilities why C did not send E-M3 to M: because C found that E-M2 is incorrect or because C is dishonest. If it is the former then it is M's fault in sending an incorrect message to C. While, if it is the later then M needs to send the correct DR-M1 to the TTP to be able to receive a resolution

6. Similar to scenario 5 but here the DR-M1 that M sent to TTP is correct. The TTP can resolve the problem by sending DR-M2 to C and DRM3 to M. Again, the reason for C not sending E-M3 to M is either because E-M2 is incorrect or because C is dishonest. If it is the former then for M to receive the DR-M3 then M has to send the correct DR-M1 to the TTP. When TTP receives the correct DR-M1 then the TTP will make it fair for both C and M. While if C did not send E-M3 to M because C is dishonest, then M has to send the correct DR-M1 to the TTP for the dispute to be resolved

7. After M received E-M1 from C, it finds that E-M1 is correct and hence M sends E-M2 to C. Then, C finds that E-M2 is correct and so sends E-M3 to M. After receiving E-M3 M contacts the TTP for resolution. However, the TTP found that DR-M1 is incorrect. The TTP sends an abort message to M. There are two possibilities why M contacted the TTP. The first one is because E-M3 is incorrect, and the second is because E-M3 is correct but M wants to see what they can receive from the TTP and thus trying to get an advantage over C. In both cases, M has to send correct DR-M1 to receive a resolution

8. Similar to scenario 7 but here the DR-M1 that M sends to the TTP is correct. Therefore, the TTP resolves it by sending DR-M2 to C and DR-M3 to M

17.6 Comparisons

In this section the EMH protocol is compared to protocols in the literature that have the same characteristics. That is, the EMH protocol will be compared to fair exchange protocols that are based on public-key cryptography [15] and for exchanging digital products and payments. Therefore, the EMH protocol will be compared against Ray et al. protocol [34] (denoted as Ray protocol), Zhang et al. protocol [42] (denoted as Zha protocol), Devane et al. protocol [12] (denoted as Devane protocol), Alaraj and Munro protocol [4] (denoted as ECH protocol), and Alaraj and Munro protocol [5] (denoted as ECMH protocol).

The comparisons will be made on different criteria, (1) the number of messages in both the exchange and dispute resolution phases, (2) the type of TTP, (3) whether or not the TTP needs to hold a copy of an item to be exchanged, (4) whether or not all parties (M and C) will be involved to enable the TTP to resolve any disputes, and (5) number of modular exponentiations in both the exchange and dispute resolution phases. The modular exponentiations are considered to be the most expensive operations [25].

The Ray et al. protocol [34] did not give detail for the dispute resolution phase so the number of messages in this phase and the number of modular exponentiations had to be calculated manually. In addition, the number of modular exponentiations for Zha's protocol [42] has also been calculated manually. With regard to Devane et al. protocol [12], the number of modular exponentiations has been calculated manually; and the authors of [12] did not give details on messages to be sent in case of dispute. Hence, the number of modular exponentiations in the dispute phase of [12] is not clear.

The EMH protocol and the ECH protocol [4] have the same number of messages in both the exchange phase and dispute resolution phase. The two protocols have also the same number of modular exponentiations in both the exchange phase and the dispute resolution phase. The reason for this similarity is that both protocols are designed using the same concept which is enforcing a party to be honest. In the EMH protocol the merchant in the one who is enforced to be honest whereas in the ECH protocol [4] the customer is the one who is enforced to be honest.

As can be seen in Table 17.2, the EMH protocol presented in this paper and the ECH protocol [4] have the lowest number of messages needed to be exchanged between C and M. Ray's protocol lets the TTP hold M's item before the exchange between C and M takes place. Therefore, this requires more storage and security assurance to be added to the TTP's jobs. Additionally, this may compromise the confidentiality of the items to be exchanged.

Ray's protocol requires both parties (C and M) to be contacted by the TTP in case one party raises a dispute; whereas in the EMH protocol, ECH protocol, ECMH protocol and Zha's protocol only the disputant and the TTP will be involved. Involving both parties in dispute resolution would require more messages to be sent and hence more load on the communication channels.

The EMH protocol and the ECH protocol [4] have the lowest number of modular exponentiations needed to generate and verify messages in the exchange phase. While in the dispute resolution phase the number of modular exponentiations is roughly the same. However, most of modular exponentiations in the EMH protocol are for adding more security assurances such as encrypting the content of messages to prevent any other party (not those involved in the protocol) from gaining any useful information. That is, 4 out of 11 modular exponentiations in the exchange phase and 6 out of 7 modular exponentiations in the dispute resolution phase are for

Table 17.2 Protocols comparisons

	Ray protocol [34]	Zha protocol [42]	Devane protocol [12]	ECH protocol [4]	ECMH protocol [5]	EMH protocol
# messages (exchange phase)	4	4	7	3	4	3
# messages (dispute resolution)	3 to 5	3	Not specified	3	3	3
TTP type	Off-line	Off-line	On-line	Off-line	Off-line	Off-line
TTP hold item	Yes	No	No	No	No	No
Both parties are involved in dispute resolution	Yes	No	Not specified	No	No	No
# modular exponentiations (exchange phase)	27	20	28	11	14	11
# modular exponentiations (dispute resolution phase)	5 to 6	6	Not specified	7	9	7

adding such security assurances. This means that if there is the assumption that the channels are secured then the number of modular exponentiations are 7 and 1 for the exchange phase and dispute resolution phase, respectively.

It is clear from the comparison presented in Table 17.2 how the idea of enforcing honesty in fair exchange protocol reduces both the number of messages and the number of modular exponentiations.

17.7 Conclusion

This paper has reviewed fair exchange protocols that can be used by a Customer (C) for buying digital products from a Merchant (M). A new type of protocol has been developed which encourages one party to be trustworthy and enforces the other to be honest. A fair exchange protocol that enforces the Merchant to be honest is described and evaluated. The protocol comprises of only three messages to be exchanged between C and M which is the lowest number of messages to be exchanged between two parties in fair exchange protocols in the literature. The protocol uses certificates that are issued by trusted parties such as the TTP and the CB. These certificates are *P-Cert* which allows M to check the correctness of *payment*; and *C.ct* which allows M to check the origin of the key used to encrypt the key that encrypts the *payment*. The only way in which C might misbehave after receiving the digital product D from M is by sending incorrect decryption key or by not sending it at all. This can be resolved automatically by the TTP. The protocol guarantees strong fairness for both C and M.

References

1. Abadi, M., Glew, N., Horne, B., Pinkas, B.: Certified email with a light on-line trusted third party: Design and implementation. In: Proceedings of the 11th International World Wide Web Conference (WWW'02), USA, pp. 387–395. ACM, New York (2002)

2. Alaraj, A., Munro, M.: An e-commerce fair exchange protocol for exchanging digital products and payments. In: Proceedings of the IEEE/ACM ICDIM'2007, France, pp. 248–253 (2007)

3. Alaraj, A., Munro, M.: An efficient fair exchange protocol that enforces the merchant to be honest. In: Proceedings of the IEEE International Conference on Collaborative Computing: Networking, Applications and Worksharing 2007, CollaborateCom 2007, USA, pp. 196–202 (2007)

4. Alaraj, A., Munro, M.: An e-commerce fair exchange protocol that enforces the customer to be honest. International Journal of Product Lifecycle Management 3(2/3), 114–131 (2008)

5. Alaraj, A., Munro, M.: An efficient e-commerce fair exchange protocol that encourages customer and merchant to be honest. In: Proceedings of the 27th International Conference on Computer Safety, Reliability and Security (SafeComp 2008), UK. Lecture Notes in Computer Science, vol. 5219, pp. 193–206. Springer, Berlin (2008)

6. Asokan, N., Schunter, M., Waidner, M.: Optimistic protocols for fair exchange. In: Proceedings of the 4th ACM Conference on Computer and Communication Security, Switzerland, pp. 8–17 (1997)

7. Asokan, N., Shoup, V., Waidner, M.: Asynchronous protocols for optimistic fair exchange. In: Proceedings of the IEEE Symposium on Research in Security and Privacy, pp. 86–99 (1998)

8. Ateniese, G., de Medeiros, B., Goodrich Tricert, M.: Distributed certified e-mail schemes. In: Proceedings of the ISOC 2000 Network and Distributed System Security Symposium, USA (2000)

9. Ben-Or, M., Goldreich, O., Micali, S., Rivest, R.: A fair protocol for signing contracts. IEEE Transactions on Information Theory 36(1), 40–46 (1990)

10. Blum, M.: How to exchange (secret) keys. ACM Transactions on Computer Systems 1(2), 175–193 (1983)

11. Deng, R., Gong, L., Lazar, A., Wang, W.: Practical protocols for certified electronic mail. Journal of Network and Systems Management 4(3), 279–297 (1996)

12. Devane, S., Chatterjee, M., Phatak, D.: Secure e-commerce protocol for purchase of e-goods—using smart card. In: Proceedings of the 3rd IEEE International Symposium on Information Assurance and Security, IAS 2007, UK, pp. 9–14 (2007)

13. Even, S., Goldreich, O., Lempel, A.: A randomized protocol for signing contracts. Communications of the ACM 28(6), 637–647 (1985)

14. Ezhilchelvan, P., Shrivastava, S.: A family of trusted third party based fair-exchange protocols. IEEE Transactions on Dependable and Secure Computing 2(4), 273–286 (2005)

15. Ferguson, N, Schneier, B: Practical Cryptography. Wiley, Indianapolis (2003)

16. Galitsky, B., Kovalerchuk, B.: Analyzing attitude in customer emails: A tool for complaint assessment. In: Proceedings of the SIGIR 2006 Workshop on Directions in Computational Analysis of Stylistics in Text Retrieval, USA, pp. 17–36 (2006)

17. Hörnle, J.: Online dispute resolution in business to consumer e-commerce transactions. Journal of Information, Law and Technology 2002(2) (2002)

18. Jakobsson, M.: Ripping coins for a fair exchange. In: Lecture Notes in Computer Science, vol. 921, pp. 220–230. Springer, Berlin (1995)

19. Ketchpel, S: Transaction protection for information buyers and sellers. In: Proceedings of the Dartmouth Institute for Advanced Graduate Studies, DAGS'95: Electronic Publishing and the Information Superhighway, USA (1995)

20. Kremer, S., Markowitch, O., Zhou, J.: An intensive survey of fair non-repudiation protocols. Computer Communications 25(17), 1606–1621 (2002)

21. Liu, P., Ning, P., Jajodia, S.: Avoiding loss of fairness owing to process crashes in fair data exchange protocols. In: Proceedings of the International Conference on Dependable Systems and Network, pp. 631–640 (2000)

22. Micali, S.: Simple and fast optimistic protocols for fair electronic exchange. In: Annual ACM Symposium on Principles of Distributed Computing, PODC 2003, pp. 12–19. ACM, New York (2003)

23. Nenadic, A.: A security solution for fair exchange and non-repudiation in e-commerce. PhD Thesis, University of Manchester, UK (2005)

24. Nenadic, A., Zhang, N., Barton, S.: Fair certified email delivery. In: 2004 ACM Symposium on Applied Computing, SAC '04, Cyprus (2004)

25. Nenadic, A., Zhang, N., Cheetham, B., Goble, C.: RSA-based certified delivery of e-goods using verifiable and recoverable signature encryption. Journal of Universal Computer Science 11(1), 175–192 (2005)

26. Nenadic, A., Zhang, N., Shi, Q.: RSA-based verifiable and recoverable encryption of signatures and its application in certified e-mail delivery. Journal of Computer Security 13(5), 757–777 (2005)

27. Pagnia, H., Gärtner, F.: On the impossibility of fair exchange without a trusted third party. Technical Report TUD-BS-1999-02, University of Darmstadt, Germany (1999)

28. Pagnia, H., Vogt, H., Gärtner, F.: Fair exchange. The Computer Journal 46(1) (2003)

29. Park, J., Chong, E., Siegel, H.: Constructing fair exchange protocols for e-commerce via distributed computation of RSA signatures. In: Proceedings of the 22nd Annual Symposium on Principles of Distributed Computing. USA, pp. 172–181 (2003)

30. Public-Key Infrastructure (X.509), The PKIX working group. http://www.ietf.org/html. charters/pkix-charter.html. Accessed on 08-06-07

31. Ray, I., Ray, I.: An optimistic fair exchange e-commerce protocol with automated dispute resolution. In: Proceedings of 1st Electronic Commerce and Web Technologies Conference EC-Web 2000. Lecture Notes in Computer Science, vol. 1875, pp. 84–93. Springer, Berlin (2000)

32. Ray, I., Zhang, H.: Experiences in developing a secure and optimistic fair-exchange e-commerce protocol using common off-the-shelf components. Journal of Electronic Commerce Research and Application 7(2), 247–259 (2008)

33. Ray, I., Ray, I., Narasimhamurthi, N.: A fair-exchange e-commerce protocol with automated dispute resolution. In: Proceedings of the 14th Annual IFIP WG 11.3 Working Conference on Database Security, The Netherlands, pp. 27–38 (2000)

34. Ray, I., Ray, I., Narasimhamurthy, N.: An anonymous failure resilient fair-exchange e-commerce protocol. Decision Support Systems 39(3), 267–292 (2005)

35. Rivest, R., Shamir, A., Adleman, L.: A method for obtaining digital signatures and public-key cryptosystems. Communications of the ACM 21(2), 120–126 (1978)

36. Schunter, M.: Optimistic fair exchange. PhD Thesis, University of the Saarland, Germany (2000)

37. Shmatikov, V., Mitchell, J.: Analysis of a fair exchange protocol. In: Proceedings of the 1999 FLoC Workshop on Formal Methods and Security Protocols, Italy (1999)

38. Song, W., Kou, W., Tan, C.: An investigation on multiple e-payment and micro-payment. In: Proceedings of the International Conference on Electronic Commerce, pp. 216–223 (2002)

39. Wang, G.: An abuse-free fair contract signing protocol based on the RSA signature. In: Proceedings of the 14th International conference on World Wide Web, WWW-2005, pp. 412–421 (2005)

40. Whiteley, D.: E-Commerce: Strategy, Technologies and Applications. McGraw-Hill, London (2000)

41. Zhang, Q., Markantonakis, K., Mayes, K.: A practical fair exchange e-payment protocol for anonymous purchase and physical delivery. In: Proceedings of the 4th ACS/IEEE International Conference on Computer Systems and Applications, AICCSA-06, UAE, pp. 851–858 (2006)

42. Zhang, N., Shi, Q., Merabti, M., Askwith, R.: Practical and efficient fair document exchange over networks. Journal of Network and Computer Applications 29(1), 46–61 (2006)

Index

Y. Badr et al. (eds.) *Emergent Web Intelligence: Advanced Semantic Technologies,*
Advanced Information and Knowledge Processing,
DOI 10.1007/978-1-84996-077-9, © Springer-Verlag London Limited 2010